FINANCIAL ACCOUNTING

Expanding Horizons

FINANCIAL ACCOUNTING

Expanding Horizons

Joel H. Amernic
Faculty of Management
University of Toronto

McGraw-Hill Ryerson

Toronto • Montreal • New York • Auckland • Bogotá • Caracas • Lisbon
London • Madrid • Mexico • Milan • New Delhi • San Juan • Singapore • Sydney • Tokyo

McGraw-Hill
Ryerson Limited
A Subsidiary of The ***McGraw-Hill*** *Companies*

Financial Accounting: Expanding Horizons

ISBN: 0-07-551653-5

1 2 3 4 5 6 7 8 9 10 BG 7 6 5 4 3 2 1 0 9 8

Printed and bound in Canada

Sponsoring Editor: Sarah Kimball/Lisa Feil
Senior Associate Editor: Susan Calvert
Developmental Editor: Lenore Gray Spence
Production Editor: Matthew Kudelka
Production Co-ordinator: Nicla Dattolico
Cover/Interior Design: VISU*TronX*
Typesetter: VISU*TronX:* Susan Calverley
Printer: Best Book Manufacturers

Canadian Cataloguing in Publication Data
Amernic, Joel H. (Joel Henry), 1946–
Financial accounting: expanding horizons

1st ed.
Includes index.
ISBN 0-07-551653-5

1. Accounting. I. Title.
HF5635.A43 1997 657'.044 C97-930616-7

To Lilly, for everything, always

About the Author

Joel Amernic is Professor of Accounting at the University of Toronto's Faculty of Management and is cross-appointed to the Centre for Industrial Relations. Honours include the Canadian Academic Accounting Association's Outstanding Educator Award, an FCA from the accounting profession, and several teaching awards. He is the author of numerous refereed scholarly and practitioner articles in accounting and other management disciplines, and has served on several editorial boards and as editor of the Education Department of *CA Magazine*. Amernic and his co-authors were recipients of the Walter J. Macdonald award for their work on professional needs, attitudes, and characteristics of Canadian professional accountants. Recent publications include articles in *Accounting Education: An International Journal, Issues in Accounting Education, Critical Perspectives on Accounting,* and *Journal of Collective Negotiations in the Public Sector.*

Contents

Chapter 3 TRANSACTIONS, EVENTS, AND FINANCIAL ACCOUNTING: AN INTRODUCTION TO DOUBLE-ENTRY BOOKKEEPING

Chapter 4 A CONCEPTUAL FRAMEWORK FOR FINANCIAL ACCOUNTING

Chapter 5 Making Revenue Accounting and Expense Accounting Decisions in Different Situations

Chapter 6 ACCOUNTABILITY: AN INTRODUCTION TO FINANCIAL REPORTING AND AUDITING

Chapter 7 ACCOUNTING INFORMATION ABOUT CASH AND CASH FLOWS

Chapter 8 User Orientation: Analytical Uses of Financial Accounting Information

Chapter 9 PUSHING THE BOUNDARIES OF ACCOUNTING

Chapter 10 The Accounting Entity and Substance over Form: Debt, Equity, and Intercorporate Investments

Chapter 11 Accounting and Change: Past, Present, and Future

Preface

Rapid-fire change is all around us as we head for the year 2000. Individuals, organizations, and entire societies have had to develop strategies for adapting to a vast range of changes, of which the following are only a small sample: social upheaval in Eastern Europe and elsewhere; new global and regional trade alliances such as the North American Free Trade Agreement; the emergence of vigorous global competition; and the uncertain impact of technology both on work and on how we live our daily lives.

New companies and industries are emerging, while familiar ones are being altered beyond recognition, or disappearing altogether. The very nature of work is evolving quickly, so that yesterday's specific skills and abilities may be a poor fit for today's and certainly tomorrow's requirements. Flexibility and understanding, continuous learning, and a tolerance for uncertainty, ambiguity, and change are becoming vital for a full and productive life.

How can a textbook about accounting help students acquire these qualities? An answer to this question is suggested by the following comments:

1. Accounting, as a professional discipline, is deeply implicated in many aspects of the changes mentioned above. Managers and politicians rely partly on accounting information and systems when they make or justify decisions about expanding production, cutting back jobs, restructuring organizations, providing subsidies, and so on. So understanding accounting can help both those making such decisions and those affected by them.

2. This understanding of accounting should, however, be anchored in reality. Accounting teaching materials, such as this textbook, can make a substantive contribution by offering a wide variety of realistic, and real, case situations in which accounting is important. It's only when a discipline makes a difference that most people are willing to become engaged at more than just a superficial level.

3. The need for flexibility and understanding, and for the ability to tolerate uncertainty and change, strongly suggests that a discipline—especially an applied, practical discipline such as accounting—should be introduced in such a way that both its historical importance and its international diversity are not only acknowledged, but seen as central.

4. If students are to begin to understand accounting, the technical features of the discipline must be part of the introductory curriculum. But the judgmental and analytical essence of accounting must be given a preeminent role. Accounting cannot really be understood by any person in any meaningful sense of the word unless that person is provided with an opportunity to develop these two personal qualities: tolerance of uncertainty and change, and flexibility. Thus, learning and teaching materials for accounting, including most especially introductory textbooks, should include a wide variety of unstructured (case) situations, so that students will have a fair chance of enhancing their cognitive abilities to the utmost.

This textbook is based on the idea that an introduction to accounting should be designed with the above four guidelines in mind.

Accounting education, like many other things in our lives, is undergoing significant change, and the change is in a direction that is largely consistent with these guidelines. For example, an important body established to stimulate reform in accounting education, the Accounting Education Change Commission, believes that students completing their first course in accounting should:

- *Have a broad view of accounting's role in satisfying society's need for information and its function in business, in government, in other organizations, and in public accounting ... Students should gain ... an appreciation of the role of auditing in enhancing the credibility of publicly reported information.*
- *Understand the basic features of accounting and reporting by organizations.*
- *Understand fundamental accounting concepts ... and the ethics of internal and external reporting.*
- *Understand that some accounting systems are more effective than others in given circumstances ...*
- *Possess enhanced analytical skills and the ability to confront unstructured problems ...*
- *Gain an appreciation that accounting as a discipline is the focus of constructive debate and intensive rethinking caused by economic and technological change ...*[1]

I hope you will find this book both interesting and challenging. You are beginning to study accounting just as all this change is reaching its full bloom. At the same time, though, all of us should keep in mind that accounting's double-entry model has been around for at least 500 years, and that some form of accounting can be traced back to ancient Sumerian society circa 8000 B.C. I hope your tolerance for ambiguity is beginning to kick in!

---

[1] Accounting Education Change Commission, *Position Statement No. 2: The First Course in Accounting,* June 1992. Published in *Issues in Accounting Education*, Vol. 7, no. 2, Fall 1992, pp. 249–251.

Acknowledgements

Many people at the University of Toronto were instrumental in the development of this text. Wendy Rotenberg and Len Brooks supported the reform of our introductory course, which served as the motivation for beginning the project. Irene Wiecek and Ramy Elitzur, each of whom I've had the great pleasure of engaging in a "dialogue about teaching accounting" for many years, undoubtedly stimulated many of my better ideas. Connie Reed, my cohort in teaching introductory financial accounting, was a dedicated and creative colleague, and Catherine Seguin provided useful insights. Students in introductory courses at the undergraduate and graduate levels in the Faculty of Management offered valuable feedback, as did students at the Centre for Industrial Relations.

The following reviewers provided many helpful comments and suggestions: Jeff Archambault, *Emporia State University*; George Baxter, *University of Saskatchewan*; Don Brown, *Brock University*; Joan Conrod, *Dalhousie University*; Craig Emby, *Simon Fraser University*; Ray F. Carroll, *Dalhousie University*; Duncan Green, *University of Calgary*; Charlotte Heywood, *Wilfrid Laurier University*; Elizabeth Hicks, *Mount Saint Vincent University*; Al Hunter, *University of Lethbridge*; Darlene Kelly, *University of Ottawa*; Margaret Kelly, *University of Manitoba*; Valorie Leonard, *Laurentian University*; Don Lockwood, *University of British Columbia*; John Morelli, *Seneca College*; and Richard Pedlar, *Wilfrid Laurier University*.

Kelly Smyth of McGraw-Hill Ryerson, who initially broached the idea of an introductory financial accounting textbook, helped guide the project through the crucial stage up to a first draft. Dennis Bockus provided very useful advice during this phase. Sarah Kimball, who took over as sponsoring editor from Kelly in mid-1995, played a key role in shaping a book from a rather overgrown manuscript. Developmental editor Lenore Gray Spence contributed in a very professional way to the successful completion of the project. The production team of Lisa Feil, sponsoring editor; Susan Calvert, senior associate editor; and Matthew Kudelka, production editor; provided helpful comments and suggestions throughout the editing and typesetting stages.

During the three-plus years that this book was being written, my family provided the emotional sustenance and encouragement that only those who are closest can offer. Lilly, my wife and best friend, and my daughter Heidi and son David, help me understand the importance of an open and constructively critical mind.

CHAPTER 1 *one*

Accounting: An Overview

Learning OBJECTIVES

After you have read, thought about, and discussed this chapter, and completed a selection from the end-of-chapter material, you will have made significant progress in achieving the following learning objectives:

- Be able to give examples of how accounting affects many aspects of our lives.
- List and briefly describe the many subdisciplines of accounting.
- Be aware of recent research that suggests the historical importance of accounting.
- Explain what the following financial statements are: balance sheet, income statement, retained earnings statement, cash flow statement.
- Be able to compute simple accounting ratios, such as the current ratio, the quick ratio, and the gross profit ratio, based upon accounting information.
- Be aware that management is responsible for making decisions about accounting, including how much detail to disclose in financial statements that outsiders will read.
- Be aware that financial accounting involves estimates and judgments.
- Be able to identify the basic accounting equation, and explain how it may be used to account for simple transactions and other business events.
- Be able to prepare simple balance sheets, income statements, retained earnings statements, and cash flow statements using the basic accounting equation.

Language was invented by accountants.

Cuyler Young, former director of the Royal Ontario Museum[1]

Recent archaeological research offers revolutionary insight about the precursor of abstract counting and pictographic as well as ideographic writing. This precursor was a data processing system in which simple (and later complex) clay tokens of various shapes [represented] assets and economic transactions ... The economic-philosophic implications of this discovery are important. First, it suggests that accounting preceded abstract counting as well as writing ..."

Richard Mattessich, University of British Columbia[2]

INTRODUCTION

This chapter introduces accounting as a field of study that is both interesting and important. After describing how accounting affects our everyday life and the behaviour and beliefs of the people and organizations we deal with, this chapter sets out the various areas within accounting. After that, one of the important outputs of accounting, the set of financial statements, is introduced through two examples. The first example adopts the perspective of an *outsider* who wishes to learn about an Ottawa-based software company, Corel Corporation, and provides an overview of four key financial statements: the balance sheet, the income statement, the retained earnings statement, and the cash flow statement. The second example takes the perspective of an *insider* of a business: specifically, that of an entrepreneur starting up a small publishing company to target the adult recreational hockey market. This example introduces the basic accounting equation, and describes how it may be used to account for the activities of a simple organization. The chapter ends with an article that explains, in a little more detail than the two opening quotations, the apparently crucial role that accounting played in the development of civilization.

Accounting: A Preliminary Definition

A popular Canadian dictionary defined "accounting" in the following way:

> *The bookkeeping methods involved in making a financial record of business transactions and in the preparation of statements concerning the assets, liabilities, and operating results of a business.*[3]

Accountants would not accept this as a very good definition. It ignores the scope and depth of accounting. It also mentions nothing of the historical

[1] This comment was made by Mr. Young in the *Toronto Star*, Tuesday, May 14, 1991, page A20, as he was describing his archaeological research into ancient Sumerian society.

[2] See R. Mattessich, "Prehistoric Accounting and the Problem of Representation: On Recent Archaeological Evidence of the Middle East from 8000 B.C. to 3000 B.C.," *The Accounting Historians Journal*, Vol. 14, no. 2, Fall 1987, pp. 71–91.

[3] *The Houghton Mifflin Canadian Dictionary of the English Language*, Markham, ON: Houghton Mifflin Canada.

importance of accounting, which is suggested by this chapter's opening quotations. In fact, the "bookkeeping methods" that are the focus of the definition are a relatively small part of accounting. Accounting as a discipline is much richer, more interesting, and more socially pervasive than the definition suggests. Unfortunately, for many people this dictionary stereotype is what comes to mind when they hear the word "accounting." One of the main objectives of this book is to convince you that accounting is much more important, and thus worthy of your attention, both as the subject of this introductory text and perhaps, later, as a career. We'll hold off suggesting better definitions of accounting until Chapter 2; first, we want to describe accounting and some of its roles.

Just How Pervasive Is Accounting?

Accounting information is used in a wide variety of situations to help people do many things: make decisions, discharge their accountability to others, exert control over other people, plan, justify actions, and so forth. A "laundry list" of some of these situations suggests just how widespread accounting is in our lives:

- Accounting information is often used by governments to monitor and control businesses. For example, every year the huge electric utility Ontario Hydro must submit comprehensive reports to the Ontario Energy Board, an agency of the Ontario government. Accounting statements, which the board examines in great detail at public hearings, are an important part of these reports.
- Each year, the Parliament of Canada receives a document called the Report of the Auditor General of Canada to the House of Commons. The Auditor General is a senior official whose job is to provide independent information to Parliament about the financial activities of the various federal government departments and agencies. He or she acts as a watchdog to see just how wisely our tax dollars are being spent. Much of this information is expressed in the form of accounting statements and concepts. The Auditor General (AG, for short) in recent years has been dissatisfied with a number of aspects of government accounting; for example, the AG once wrote:

  In my judgment, the government's financial statements are incomplete. They include government activities of departments, but they do not include government activities of Crown corporations. The government is bigger, and its activities more diverse, than the statements now reveal.

  The AG was concerned about the fact that companies owned by the government ("Crown corporations"), such as Canada Mortgage and Housing Corporation, were not included in the financial statements of Canada, but were accounted for as separate entities. This meant that Members of Parliament and other users of the Government of Canada's financial statements apparently didn't have the full picture; as a result, the quality of the decisions they made regarding these companies was perhaps not quite as good as it could have been.
- Managers of organizations often rely on accounting information in making decisions ranging from whether to acquire a new machine, to how much to charge for a new product. For example, Canadian companies that

relocate their manufacturing operations to Mexico under the North American Free Trade Act (NAFTA) may point out that they do so because manufacturing costs are much lower in Mexico (mainly due to lower labour costs). The province of Alberta cut health care and other public services, apparently in order to reduce costs. As we shall see, "cost" is a complex accounting concept and one that must be used carefully. In fact, there are many terms in accounting that are identical to commonly used words and phrases, but that don't mean the same thing as in everyday English.

- Managers need to control the activities of their organizations. This is true whether the enterprise is a small corner store or a large multinational with manufacturing and sales operations in a number of countries. Managers use accounting information and processes to exercise this control. For example, the chemical manufacturer Polysar Corporation has its headquarters in Sarnia, Ontario, and has production facilities both in Canada and abroad. Central management in Sarnia controls its production units partly through a requirement that each unit prepare financial statements and submit them to head office on a monthly basis. These financial statements are then examined by the head office managers, who then presumably take action if costs are too high or profits too low.
- When individuals or organizations enter into a contractual relationship, key parts of the contract are often based on accounting concepts and information. For example, McDonald's has a contract with Toronto's SkyDome which specifies that the rent it pays the SkyDome is to equal 38% of the total sales revenue (an accounting number) from its SkyDome fast food outlets.
- Many companies that are set up under the federal Canada Business Corporations Act, or the corresponding provincial acts, or similar laws in other countries, are required to discharge their accountability to the public and to their shareholders partly by preparing and distributing financial accounting statements. When financial statements are prepared under these laws, it is usually required that an independent auditor examine the statements and their backup documentation before they are distributed to shareholders.
- Accounting statements are often used to help make a variety of decisions about an organization. For example, financial statements have been important in negotiations between unions and management. As an illustration, accounting information was one of the key points of contention in the collective bargaining negotiations between the major-league baseball owners and the players' union. Both sides hired accounting experts to analyse the baseball teams' financial statements, in order to find out how much of a pay increase the teams could afford.
- Accounting information systems are central to the everyday administration of an organization. For example, it is through such systems that an employee's paycheque is completed and distributed. The various important pieces of information that are needed to prepare the cheque (such as rate of pay, amount of work performed, income tax to be deducted, and provincial hospitalization premiums and pension deductions to be held back) are stored in the organization's accounting information system.

This relatively short list suggests that accounting information and accounting systems are common throughout our economy and society. In a wide variety of ways, our personal lives are influenced almost every day by accounting. When the Calgary Flames hockey team sets the ticket prices for its home games, the decision is probably made at least partly on the basis of projections of future revenues and expenses, both of which are accounting concepts. When a hospital decides to close some of its beds, the decision is often based in part on an assessment of "cost," which is an accounting concept. When a food manufacturer discontinues a brand of biscuits that you especially liked, you can be fairly sure that the manager responsible for the decision estimated that the company's profits would increase if that particular product were dropped — and profit is, of course, an important accounting concept.

Clearly, accounting information exerts considerable influence on society — on individuals, organizations, and governments. It seems reasonable to suggest that a well-informed citizen should have at least a general appreciation of accounting and its various roles in society, as well as a basic understanding of some of the more important concepts and technical aspects of the discipline. We hope this book will provide you with all of the above.

The Areas of Accounting

Accounting is a broad professional discipline, and is made up of several different but related subdisciplines or areas:

- financial accounting and reporting
- operational accounting
- management and cost accounting
- accounting information systems
- management control
- regulatory accounting
- taxation
- auditing
- not-for-profit and governmental accounting
- international accounting

Financial accounting and reporting deals mainly with the decisions and processes involved in the preparation of financial statements. Often these statements are intended for users *outside* the organization. Example: the financial statements in the annual reports that Canadian companies send to their shareholders. Excerpts from a recent annual report compiled by Corel Corporation of Ottawa — which designs and produces computer graphics software such as CorelDRAW and WordPerfect — are reproduced in Appendix A of Chapter 6.

Operational accounting is the area of accounting dealing with the day-to-day financial administration of an organization. For example, ensuring that a company's suppliers get paid on time, and that the services or products for which they are being paid were in fact ordered and received by the company, is the responsibility of the operational accounting system.

Management and cost accounting focuses on providing information to an organization's managers so that they are able to run the organization effectively and efficiently. An example of management and cost accounting information is the estimated cost of a proposed new labour contract that an organization is negotiating with a union. Management must have such information in order to assess whether the company can afford to agree to the contract.

Accounting information systems are concerned with the design, implementation, and maintenance of the technical aspects of accounting systems. Traditionally, introductory courses in accounting focused almost entirely on this aspect of accounting; this partly explains the stereotype mentioned at the start of the chapter. Accounting information systems (the term is often abbreviated to AIS) have become largely computer-based over the past several years, even for very small organizations, since the cost of hardware has declined tremendously and all kinds of user-friendly software is available.

Management control uses accounting-based systems and processes, such as setting and reviewing budgets, to provide incentives for managers and other employees to make decisions and take actions that will further the interests of the organization. For example, in a car dealership both the new car sales manager and the used car sales manager might be held accountable for reaching sales targets each year. If they meet or exceed their sales targets they may receive a bonus; if they fall short perhaps they will be penalized.

Regulatory accounting deals with the accounting requirements that many organizations *must* follow. Often those organizations are subject to the regulatory control of a government agency. For example, telephone rates in parts of Canada are regulated by government agencies, and telephone companies such as Bell Canada and BC Tel must submit financial statements to these agencies. Often, the financial statements must be prepared according to rules set by the agencies.

Taxation, as a specialized branch of the accounting discipline, deals with ensuring that individuals and organizations have complied with all tax laws that apply to them (the Income Tax Act, goods and services tax rules, and so on), and that they have planned their affairs so as to minimize their tax burden in a legal and ethical manner.

Auditing professionals attempt to ensure that organizations have complied with the rules of preparing financial statements, usually under a legal requirement. The auditor's detailed assessment results in an audit opinion stating whether the organization's financial statements have complied with accepted accounting principles. The audit opinion is a professional opinion, and external users of financial statements rely upon it. Recently, auditing has begun to be recognized as valuable in other areas of business; for example, some companies are participating in environmental audits in order to assure their stakeholders that there is little likelihood they are violating pollution abatement and other similar requirements.

Not-for-profit and governmental accounting is a specialized branch of accounting that deals with the design and operation of accounting systems for charities, social service agencies, various levels of government (such as countries, provinces, and municipalities), and other nonbusiness organizations.

International accounting includes all the areas of accounting mentioned above, but deals with them in an international setting. In addition, international accounting deals with the special problems of designing, implementing, and operating accounting systems for multinational organizations (that is, organizations operating in several countries). An example of an interesting problem in international accounting has to do with choosing the currency in which accounting records are to be kept: if a company produces and sells its products in four or five countries, in which country's money should the accounting records be kept?

As the above list shows, there is a lot to accounting, and a wide variety of different accounting fields or areas. Although each of these areas is somewhat specialized and unique, there is a fair bit of overlap among them. This book introduces financial accounting to you; however, since many financial accounting concepts apply in other accounting areas, and are also affected by these other accounting areas, we will provide you with at least some sense of the field as a whole.

Financial Statements: The Output of Accounting

While a study of accounting can begin in several ways, the approach we have chosen for this book is to start with the "big picture" — that is, with the financial statements that are the output of the financial accounting process. The ways these statements are prepared will be discussed later, along with the significance of many of the details in them; at this point we present some overall relationships so that the term "financial statements" will be more concrete for you. Financial statements will be introduced in two phases: First, we will examine the financial statements of Corel Corporation, the Ottawa software company we mentioned earlier. Second, we will provide additional insight into financial statements by building them up from the business activities of a hypothetical company established and run by a single entrepreneur (On Ice Incorporated).

Financial statements can vary in a number of ways. For example, we wouldn't expect the financial statements of a charity to resemble those of a giant retailer such as Sears Canada. There are, however, some broad similarities, so ideas that are learned in one situation may be useful in other situations, as long as we have the common sense to expect that different situations will result in differences in accounting.

Corel Corporation: A Canadian High-Tech Business and Its Financial Statements

Corel Corporation was established in 1985 by Michael Cowpland, who has a PhD in engineering from Carleton University in Ottawa. Along with several other products, the company develops, markets, and supports a full-featured graphics software package for the Microsoft Windows operating environment, intended for both general business users and graphics professionals. This package — CorelDRAW — integrates in a single package all the graphics functions: illustration, charting, photo editing, painting, and presentation. Corel's customers include individuals and small organizations, as well as many major companies such as IBM, General Electric, Bell Canada, and General Motors. Our focus will be on Corel's financial statements from the early 1990s, which are simple enough to illustrate the points we wish to make in this chapter, but still capture the company's interesting accounting practices.

The company's management was very optimistic about the future of CorelDRAW and its other, newer software products, but cautioned that Corel, like most businesses, faced certain risks. In Corel's case, management identified the following as especially important:

- In the early 1990s, 87% of Corel's total sales revenue came from one product, CorelDRAW. As management put it, "A decline in demand for this product as a result of competition, technological change or other factors would have a material adverse effect on the Company's result of operations."
- The market is very competitive and changes quickly. Corel's strategy of bundling several modules in its CorelDRAW product may encourage other companies to do the same, and to attempt to undercut Corel on price. Since user upgrades and competitors' upgrades are priced much lower than the full-priced CorelDRAW, as the

percentage of user and competitors' upgrades increases, the average unit price of the company's products may decline.

- The industry is one of rapid technological change and frequent new product introductions. Research and development is therefore crucial.
- The transition from older versions of a product (such as, for example, CorelDRAW 3.0) to newer versions (such as CorelDRAW 4.0) must be managed in such a way that customers are not disrupted or in any way upset.
- Other possible risk factors include the dependence of the company's major product on the Windows interface, the general impact of the recession of the 1990s, the need to manage the rapid growth of the company (total sales revenue had increased from just $223,000 in 1987 to over $52 million by 1991), the company's dependence on independent distributors, and its dependence on a few key personnel.

As of August 1992, Corel had 252 full-time employees, of whom 82 worked in research and development, 117 in marketing and administration, and 53 in customer support. The company's employees are not members of a union. The company leases about 6,000 square metres of office space in Ottawa. According to the company's management:

The principal materials and components used in the Company's products include computer media (diskettes, CD-ROM's or tapes), user manuals and videotapes. Manufacturing involves the duplication of computer media, user manuals and videotapes, assembly of components, spot testing of the product and final packaging ... The Company's products are generally shipped as orders are received and, accordingly, the Company has historically operated with little backlog.

We will highlight some features of four financial statements prepared by Corel Corporation: the balance sheet, the income statement, the statement of retained earnings, and the statement of cash flows.

Corel's balance sheet

This financial statement is shown in Exhibit 1–1. The balance sheet presents information about an organization's resources (the things it uses in its business, or its assets), and about the sources of the money it used to acquire these resources. These sources are usually of two types: liabilities, and shareholders' equity. *Liabilities* refers to money (or its equivalent) provided by the organization's suppliers, employees, and so on — in general terms, by individuals and other organizations that do not own Corel. *Shareholders' equity* refers to sources of money provided by the owners of Corel.

Notice that Corel's balance sheet is dated November 30. A balance sheet presents information about assets, liabilities, and shareholders' equity *at a specific point in time*. It represents the quantity (as measured in money) of assets, the quantity of liabilities, and the quantity of shareholders' equity; and a quantity only has meaning as of a particular point in time. Balance sheet information is also provided by Corel's management for the preceding year, as at November 30, 1990. Such comparative accounting information may be useful in spotting trends and dramatic changes that need explaining.

From Exhibit 1–1, Corel's total assets as at November 30, 1991, were $59,358,000. This also happened to be the total reported by Corel for "Liabilities and Shareholders' Equity." This equality is no coincidence, since the total of all money available from all sources is necessarily equal to the total of all uses to which that money has been put. This equality is often referred

EXHIBIT 1–1
COREL CORPORATION*
Balance Sheet

(in thousands of Canadian dollars)	As at November 30	
	1990	1991
ASSETS		
Current assets:		
Cash and short-term investments	$21,720	$25,919
Accounts receivable	11,573	18,300
Inventory	5,830	6,675
Prepaid expenses	79	712
	39,202	51,606
Capital assets:		
Furniture, equipment, and leasehold improvements	2,656	7,752
	$41,858	$59,358
LIABILITIES AND SHAREHOLDERS' EQUITY		
Current liabilities:		
Accounts payable and accrued liabilities	$ 4,150	$ 5,140
Income taxes payable	3,135	3,022
Deferred income taxes	443	1,102
Deferred revenue	250	325
	7,978	9,589
Shareholders' equity:		
Share capital	26,760	31,292
Contributed surplus	470	470
Retained earnings	6,650	18,007
	33,880	49,769
	$41,858	$59,358

*The financial statements have been simplified for ease of exposition. All excerpts from Corel's 1993 Annual Report are reprinted with permission from Corel Corporation.

to as the *basic* (or *fundamental*) *accounting equation.*

The "Assets" section of Corel's balance sheet shows some of the specific assets making up Corel's business that have been accounted for. Corel has $25,919,000 of an asset called "Cash and short-term investments." This represents assets, including cash, that the company has on deposit in banks; miscellaneous or petty cash its managers and other employees have on hand and are responsible for; and financial investments that can readily be turned into cash.

The second asset in Corel's balance sheet is "Accounts receivable," which represents the amount of money Corel's customers owed to Corel on November 30, 1991. Notice that this amount has gone up from $11,573,000 as at November 31, 1990, to $18,300,000—an increase of 58.1%. That is:

$$\frac{18{,}300{,}000 - 11{,}573{,}000}{11{,}573{,}000} = 58.1\%$$

It is hard to say whether this increase is good or bad: perhaps Corel this year is selling to more customers who are poorer credit risks, and the increase is the result of a greater number of uncollected bills. If so, perhaps Corel's management should carefully examine the dollar amount it recorded for its accounts receivable — perhaps these are not worth $18,300,000. On the other hand, perhaps the increase is due to a corresponding increase in sales to good, creditworthy customers. We'll check on this later, when we examine Corel's income statement.

The third asset in Corel's balance sheet is "Inventory." This asset category represents things that Corel intends to sell as part of its everyday operating activities: computer diskettes, CD-ROMs, user manuals, packaging, and so on that will be used to produce the final shrink-wrapped boxes of CorelDRAW and other products. Recall that Corel's management mentioned that it generally shipped orders as received; this means that we shouldn't expect an excessive amount of inventory. In fact, the $6,675,000 in inventory as at November 30, 1991, represents 11.2% of the total assets of $59,358,000; the year before, inventory of $5,830,000 was 13.9% of total assets at that time. Notice that inventory went up from $5,830,000 to $6,675,000, an increase of 14.5%.

A fourth asset category, "Prepaid expenses," represents certain things that Corel has paid for in advance but has not yet made use of. A common example is the premium on an insurance plan. If Corel had paid two year's worth of premiums in advance, the portion of the prepayment that represented the remaining as-yet-unused coverage would be accounted for as an asset in this category.

The first four asset categories in Corel's balance sheet are grouped together as current assets, which — according to accounting convention — are assets that management expects to turn into cash or otherwise use within a time period that is the greater of the following:

- one year, or
- one operating cycle of the business, if the operating cycle is longer than one year.

An operating cycle for a business like Corel's is the total time interval between the acquisition of inventory and the receipt of cash from customers; this would be considerably less than one year for Corel. Thus, Corel's current assets would include those assets expected to be turned into cash in less than one year.

This "one year" convention for deciding whether an asset belongs in the current asset category seems rather arbitrary, and it is. However, grouping all current assets together provides information to the reader of the balance sheet about the approximate amount of cash that the business expects to generate in the short run. In Corel's case, current assets increased from $39,202,000 to $51,606,000, that is, by almost $12.5 million — a hefty increase for a company with only about $59 million in total assets. Does this mean that Corel will have more ready cash to pay off its upcoming obligations (an ability that both managers and accountants call "liquidity")? Perhaps. But what if those accounts receivable are really not worth $18,300,000? One rough way to determine whether Corel's liquidity has increased is to compare the ratio of current assets to current liabilities as at the end of 1990, with the same as at the end of 1991 (this ratio is called the *current ratio*). Even though we haven't yet discussed current liabilities, you've probably already guessed that they represent amounts that Corel must pay out in short order, usually within one year. The ratios are shown in the table at the bottom of this page.

	Current Assets ($000s)	Current Liabilities ($000s)	Ratios
November 30, 1990	$39,202	$7,978	4.9
November 30, 1991	$51,606	$9,589	5.4

Clearly, the ratio has increased significantly over the year, indicating that each current liability dollar is covered by an increasing number of current asset dollars. But such an increase should be interpreted only with caution as an increase in Corel's liquidity. Users of balance sheet information often compute the ratio in a modified way, without including inventories or prepaid assets in the current asset total. Such a modification of the current ratio is called the *quick ratio*; for Corel it works out to be 4.2 as at November 30, 1990, and 4.6 as at November 30, 1991.

Why do you think that inventory is excluded from the calculation of the quick ratio for a business such as Corel's? The reason is that it is "farther" from being cash than accounts receivable (and, of course, cash itself). Inventory has to be finished (if it is not yet in final form), marketed, and shipped, and then the customer has to accept it.

Suppose you are interested in estimating the liquidity for a fresh fruit and vegetable business. How might you treat inventory? Since fresh fruits and vegetables are sold out (or, as accountants and businesspeople would say, "turn over") almost daily, a produce business has no "distance from cash" problems of the kind faced by a company like Corel. Therefore, its inventory could very well be included when liquidity is estimated.

Corel's remaining assets fall outside the current asset category, and thus are expected to affect Corel over a considerable period of time. "Capital assets" is a major category of assets on Corel's balance sheet, with $7,752,000 as at November 30, 1991, and $2,656,000 as at November 30, 1990. Accountants have developed the following definition of capital assets:

Capital assets, comprising property, plant and equipment and intangible properties, are identifiable assets that meet all of the following criteria:
(a) are held for use in the production or supply of goods and services, for rental to others, for administrative purposes or for the development, construction, maintenance or repair of other capital assets;
(b) have been acquired, constructed or developed with the intention of being used on a continuing basis; and
(c) are not intended for sale in the ordinary course of business.[4]

In a footnote to its balance sheet, Corel disclosed seven types of capital assets. Footnotes are an integral part of financial statements; they contain important details that expand on the information provided in the financial statements themselves. Corel's management may have felt that in placing the following details about its capital assets in a footnote, it simplified its balance sheet without neglecting to provide crucial information. Corel's footnote on capital assets is shown in the table below.

	Net Book Value (000s)	
	Nov. 30, 1991	Nov. 30, 1990
Furniture and office equipment	$2,238	$1,351
Trade show booth	185	—
Computer equipment	2,522	1
Production equipment	138	113
Research and development equipment	1,421	1,148
Clipart libraries and licences	1,075	—
Leasehold improvements	173	43
	$7,752	$2,656
Cost	$10,226	$3,758
Accumulated depreciation	2,474	1,102
Net book value	$7,752	$2,656

The $7,752,000 for 1991 represents the "net book value" of all of Corel's capital assets as of the date of the balance sheet, November 30, 1991. Net book value is the difference between the cost of the capital assets and the total depreciation that has accumulated for the individual capital assets since they were acquired by the company. The cost of a given capital asset is the sum of all the monies expended to acquire that asset and to ensure that it is ready to operate. For example, suppose that included in Corel's "Furniture and office equipment" capital asset category was a microcomputer that Corel used to keep track of the hours worked by its employees. Not only would the actual price Corel paid for the computer be included in the computer's cost, but also all taxes and shipping costs.

"Accumulated depreciation" refers to the total depreciation that has been recorded on a particular capital asset since the date it was acquired. Accountants record depreciation as a way of measuring — very approximately — the cost of using up a capital asset. Usually, a portion of the cost of the capital asset is accounted for as an expense each year that the asset is in use, and this current year's portion is included in the income statement as an expense.

When "Accumulated depreciation" is deducted from the capital asset's "Cost," the result is called "Net book value" (NBV) by accountants. NBV refers to the

[4] The source of this definition is section 3060 of the *CICA Handbook*, published by the Canadian Institute of Chartered Accountants. We'll have more to say about the *Handbook* later on.

portion of the cost of capital assets that is not yet depreciated. The ratio of NBV to the cost of the various fixed assets provides a rough estimate of the proportion of the assets' service life that remains. For Corel, this calculation cannot be made for each of the seven capital asset categories individually, since information on both cost and accumulated depreciation has been provided only for capital assets as a group. However, keeping in mind that we are aggregating a variety of different types of capital assets, this ratio has changed as follows over the year:

First, we collect the available information on the cost and accumulated depreciation of Corel's capital assets —

	November 30			
	1991		1990	
	(all amounts in $000s)			
	Cost	NBV	Cost	NBV
Corel's capital assets	10,226	7,752	3,758	2,656

Then we compute the ratio of NBV divided by cost for the capital assets —

	1991	1989
NBV/Cost	0.76	0.71

Thus, Corel's capital assets have, on average, about 76% of their service lives left as at November 31, 1991, assuming that the accounting numbers are reasonably accurate reflections of the underlying phenomena they represent. (This assumption is probably very weakly based in the case of the calculation that we have just made for Corel, since we were forced to use the aggregate capital asset information on cost and accumulated depreciation.)

Of the seven categories of capital assets in the footnote to Corel's balance sheet, the first five represent actual, physical assets; the final two, "Clipart libraries and licences" and "Leasehold improvements," are intangible capital assets. Such assets lack physical substance but nevertheless are valuable to the company.

Notice that Corel's accounting for its capital assets is based on a particular measure: actual cost — specifically, the actual cost of acquiring the capital assets and getting them ready for use. Published financial statements almost invariably base capital asset accounting on actual cost, rather than on other possible measures such as estimated selling price or "replacement cost" (which is an estimate of what it would cost to replace the capital assets at the date the balance sheet is prepared). The pros and cons of such measurement choices have important implications for the usefulness of accounting reports, and we will explore them throughout this book. For now, though, keep in mind that there is no *obvious* reason why actual cost should dominate financial accounting, as it now seems to do.

Recall that at the beginning of this chapter we noted that "cost" is a complex accounting term that must be used carefully. One reason is that there are many different types of cost concepts in accounting. The one we have been discussing in connection with Corel's capital assets may be more precisely described as "actual, historical, total (or full) cost." "Actual" because the cost represents the number of dollars paid out by cheque for the particular assets making up the various categories of capital assets. "Historical" because the cost represents the dollars paid at past points in time when the asset was acquired. "Total" because the cost includes all the dollars paid out to get the various capital assets up and running (that is, it includes freight charges, GST payments, and so on).

The "Liabilities and Shareholders' Equity" portion of Corel's balance sheet begins with a listing of four current liability categories that Corel's management has decided to account for. "Accounts payable" represents monies owed to suppliers of, for example, computer diskettes, who have issued invoices to

Corel. "Accrued liabilities" (which Corel has grouped with "Accounts payable" for the purpose of preparing the published balance sheet) refers to amounts owed to suppliers who have not issued formal invoices, but whose services or products Corel has already used (for example, Corel might estimate the amount it owes for electricity). "Income taxes payable" is self-explanatory; notice that it has stayed at about the same level as the previous year.

"Deferred income taxes" is an item which, frankly, is difficult even for accountants and managers to interpret. It is really not a liability, nor is it strictly speaking part of shareholders' equity. Rather, it represents an accounting category that arises because of the interaction of two areas of accounting that were introduced earlier — financial accounting and taxation. The estimate of income tax expense that financial accountants record on an income statement is based on financial accounting measurement rules, which often differ from the *actual* amount of income taxes that a company must pay based on the Income Tax Act. The difference between the two numbers is referred to as "Deferred income taxes." We will explore the significance of this in Chapter 5.

"Deferred revenue" refers to the current liability created when a company receives payment from the customer *before* it provides the particular product or service. Perhaps Corel has accepted the $325,000 accounted for in this category from customers who want to be the first to be sent upcoming versions of CorelDRAW.

The "Shareholders' equity" section of Corel's balance sheet contains information about the ownership structure of the company. From other parts of Corel's financial statements not described here, we know there are 11,318,000 common shares of Corel; each share represents evidence of ownership in the corporation.[5] Michael Cowpland owns 3,678,399 of these common shares, or 32.5% of the total outstanding common shares as of November 30, 1991. Corel is permitted to issue an unlimited number of common shares in order to raise the ownership resources it may need. The dollar amount of the common shares equals the amount of money that the company received when the shares were first issued to the shareholders. This dollar amount is often referred to as the "capital" of the company. The next accounting item, "Contributed surplus," refers to gifts and similar contributions that the company has received. The final account on Corel's balance sheet, "Retained earnings," represents the cumulative sum of net income that Corel has earned since it was established, that has not as yet been paid out as dividends to Corel's owners (that is, the common shareholders).

Balance sheets may be represented in the form of an equation, as follows:

Assets = Liabilities + Shareholders' (or owners') Equity

This equation is the basic accounting equation.

Corel's statement of income

This financial statement (see Exhibit 1–2) summarizes Corel's operating and other income-generating activities for the year. In practice, this statement has also been called the earnings statement, the statement of profit and loss, and similar. (Learn to tolerate some variation in accounting terminology. More on this later!)

The first item in Corel's income statement is "Sales," which increased from $29,230,000 in 1990 to $52,242,000 in 1991, an increase of 78.7%. These numbers refer to the total dollar value of CorelDRAW and other software products that Corel sold during each of these two years. An important point to note about income statements is that they summa-

[5] A corporation is an organization that is set up under the rules of a law. For example, many corporations in Canada are set up under the rules of the Canada Business Corporations Act. We will describe this and other ways of setting up organizations in Chapter 2.

EXHIBIT 1–2
COREL CORPORATION
Statement of Income

(in thousands of Canadian dollars)	Year ended November 30 1990	1991
Sales	$29,230	$52,242
Costs of sales	6,015	7,735
Gross profit	23,215	44,507
Expenses:		
Marketing and administration	11,363	21,128
Research and development	2,171	4,400
Depreciation and amortization	484	1,371
	14,018	26,899
Income from continuing operations	9,197	17,608
Interest and dividend income	2,675	2,609
Income from continuing operations before income taxes	11,872	20,217
Income taxes:		
Current	4,478	7,798
Deferred	323	362
	4,801	8,160
Net income from continuing operations	7,071	12,057
Income (loss) from discontinued operations, net of income taxes	(81)	(700)
Net income	$ 6,990	$11,357

rize activities over a period of time; thus, they can be prepared for a year, or a month, or whatever time interval seems appropriate in the circumstances. However, for formal, audited income statements that companies send to their shareholders, the period of time chosen is almost always one year.

Turning back to Corel's sales numbers: sometimes it is easy for accountants to determine when to record a sale, and sometimes it is not. In Corel's case, should a sale be recorded:

(a) when Corel's software designers think up a new product or an improvement in an existing software product such as CorelDRAW? (certainly not; this is way too early, and there are too many risky steps still ahead)

(b) when all the design bugs have been worked out of the product, and user manuals have been written and tested for usability? (still way too early; how do we know if anyone will actually buy the product?)

Accounting and Business Decision A

(a suggested answer is provided at the end of the chapter)

Suppose you were the top executive of a company that operated a large chain of retail clothing stores across Canada (something like Mark's Work Wearhouse, which operates about 150 stores across the country and has its head office in Calgary). How would you benefit from requiring store managers to prepare income statements for their individual stores, for you to examine at head office? How often would you want income statements from each store? Does requiring frequent income statements involve costs as well as benefits?

(c) when the new software product is produced in quantity, with eye-catching carton logos and so on? (no one's purchased anything yet)

(d) after the customer places an order — say, when a software retailer orders 200 copies of the software product — but before the order has been shipped? (still premature to account for this as a sale)

(e) when the diskettes or CD-ROMs are transferred to a freight carrier? (getting close at this point; most companies choose this as the point at which a sale is accounted for, although circumstances vary)

(f) when the customer receives the diskettes or CD-ROM?

(g) when the customer learns how to use the new software product?

(h) when Corel receives its money from the customer? or

(i) at some other point in time?

For a business such as Corel's, point (e) will probably be chosen, because by then Corel has fulfilled its obligation to the customer; also, at that point Corel's accountants can estimate with a high level of confidence the total amount of cash that ultimately will be received by Corel. This estimate will include a deduction from the total, gross sales number to allow for any returns of the product by customers. If a particular software product is extremely complex, or unproven under the customer's normal operating conditions, or otherwise risky, it would be prudent for a company like Corel to delay its accounting for a sale until perhaps point (g). Again, different situations require different accounting approaches to ensure that the resulting information is as fair as possible.

We can combine information from Corel's balance sheet and income statement to gain a bit more insight into Corel's activities in 1991. If, for example, we divide the accounts receivable numbers for 1991 and 1990 by the corresponding years' sales numbers, we obtain the ratios provided in the table below.

	($000s) 1991	1990
Accounts receivable	$18,300	$11,573
Sales	$52,242	$29,230
Ratio		
(= Accounts receivable/Sales)	0.35	0.40

Recall the questions that were raised when we were examining accounts receivable in the discussion of Corel's balance sheet. At that time, we computed that Corel's receivables had increased by 58.1% over the year, and we wondered whether that was "good" or "bad." From the income statement, we can compute that Corel's sales have increased by 78.7%, so accounts receivable have increased at a slower rate than sales. Also, the ratio of accounts receivable to sales has *decreased*, from 0.40 to 0.35, or by about 12.5%; thus, in spite of the very significant increase in accounts receivable, it appears that Corel is managing this asset category well, since on a relative basis it has decreased.

The next line item on Corel's income statement is "Cost of sales," which has risen from $6,015,000 in 1990 to $7,735,000 in 1991, an increase of 28.6%. Cost of sales represents the dollar amount of the cost (historic, actual, total) of Corel's inventory that was sold over the year. Here, think of the sales amount on the income statement as representing an output price, and the cost-of-sales amount as representing an input price. This ratio —

$$\frac{\text{Cost of sales}}{\text{Sales}}$$

may provide information about how much a company marks up its inventory to establish its selling price. A related ratio —

$$\frac{\text{Sales} - \text{Cost of sales}}{\text{Sales}}$$

called the "gross profit ratio," indicates how much of each sales dollar is "gross profit," which is available to cover other expenses and (hopefully!) provide some overall profit for the shareholders of the company. For Corel, this ratio has changed as follows:

	($000s)	
	1991	1990
$\frac{\text{Sales} - \text{Cost of sales}}{\text{Sales}}$	$\frac{52,242 - 7,735}{52,242}$	$\frac{29,230 - 6,015}{29,230}$
	= 0.85	= 0.79

The gross profit ratio for Corel has improved by (0.85 – 0.79)/0.79, or 7.6%, over the year, suggesting that Corel is producing its software more efficiently this year. This is probably good news for those who are interested in Corel (unless Corel's competitors have improved their efficiency even more).

	Years ended December 31 (thousands of Canadian dollars)	
	1994	1993
Revenue	$613,560	$414,938
Costs and expenses		
Operating costs other than those shown below	303,686	207,463
Depreciation and amortization	55,167	41,981
Research and development	2,153	2,227
Selling, distribution, and administrative	69,031	58,528
Provincial mining and other taxes	45,383	24,963
	475,420	335,162
Operating income	138,140	79,776
Interest expense	5,291	12,185
Income before income taxes	132,849	67,591
Income taxes	4,887	4,890
Net income	$127,962	$62,701

Sometimes companies do not disclose cost of sales by itself, but group it with other items, thus making analysis of financial statements difficult for an outside user. For example, the Saskatoon-based Potash Corporation of Saskatchewan (PCS), which mines and sells the important plant nutrient potash, published the income statements (as adapted) shown at the bottom of this page.

As may be seen, there is no separately disclosed "cost of sales." It has been grouped together with other expenses in the category that PCS management terms "operating costs other than those shown below."

In its published income statement, PCS has aggregated, or combined, several expense items. Its activities would have been easier to understand if the expenses had been reported in disaggregated form. If PCS's managers are using income statements to help them run the company (that is, if they are using income statements as management accounting information), we can be virtually certain that they are using disaggregated versions; after all, they would want as much detail as is necessary to run the business effectively. One piece of information that they would surely include as a separate item in the management accounting version of their income statement is cost of sales. The management at PCS appears to believe that this information should be kept confidential, and left out of the published "financial accounting" version of PCS's income statement. In contrast, Corel has disclosed its cost of sales number. Why might this be so?

Deciding how much detail to provide in financial statements, and how much information to disclose in general, is an important management decision. PCS may not want its customers in the potash industry to know its gross profit, in case they then attempt to bargain down its prices on potash. However, readers of PCS's income statement (such as financial analysts and shareholders) may react negatively to such limited disclosure because it does not provide all the information they need to understand PCS's operations. Now, back to Corel.

Corel's "Marketing and administration" expense category has gone from $11,363,000 in 1990, to $21,128,000 in 1991, an increase of 86%. However, as a percentage of the sales in each year, the change was as follows:

	($000s) 1991	1990
Marketing and administration / Sales	21,128 / 52,242	11,363 / 29,230
	= 40.4%	= 38.9%

The relative increase was slight, suggesting that the marketing and administration activities in the business were roughly as efficient at the current year's (1991) much higher level of sales activity as they were last year. Even so, Corel's management would probably want to investigate even the relatively small increase in the ratio. Note how much of Corel's total activity involves marketing and administration (40.4% of each sales dollar in 1991). This reflects the crucial importance of advertising, sales, and distribution in the segment of the software industry that Corel operates in.

"Research and development" expense (R&D) increased from $2,171,000 in 1990 to $4,400,000 in 1991, an increase of 102.7%. As a percentage of sales in the respective years, R&D was 7.4% in 1990, and 8.4% in 1991 — an increase, but still surprisingly small for a company whose management has made the following public assertion about the importance of R&D:

The software industry is characterized by frequent changes in technology and user preferences. Accordingly, the Company must be able to provide new software products and modify existing products on a timely and continuing basis to be competitive. To accomplish this objective, the Company employs a strategy of both internally developing software and, where appropriate, acquiring technology that will, in most cases, be enhanced by the Company ... The Company is committed to devoting significant resources to research and development activities ...

Canadian accounting principles require that companies disclose R&D separately. This provides crucial information to those who use the financial statements of R&D-sensitive companies like Corel. Note that in spite of the obvious importance of R&D to Corel's success, marketing and administration (40.4% of sales) was over five times as "important" as R&D (8.4% of sales) in 1991.

The next expense line item on Corel's income statement is "Depreciation and amortization," which was $484,000 in 1990, and $1,371,000 in 1991. This doesn't represent any cash costs to Corel in either 1990 or 1991; rather, it is merely an allocation of the original cost of Corel's various capital assets over the years during which those assets are expected to provide services to the company. To illustrate, suppose a company (Algor Ltd.) purchases a delivery truck for $15,000 (including GST, the truck dealer's freight, and so on), and the truck is expected to provide delivery services for five years before being scrapped. Assume also that Algor pays cash, by issuing a cheque, on the day the truck is picked up. One of Algor's costs of doing business for each of the next five years will be depreciation on the truck; accountants will account for this depreciation by creating a depreciation expense on Algor's income statement, and by increasing accumulated depreciation on Algor's balance sheet (the mechanics of doing this will be explained later in this chapter, in the On Ice case). Since the truck is expected to provide delivery services to Algor for five years, a depreciation expense of $3,000 per year might be charged. Notice that the only cash flow occurred way back when Algor purchased the truck; the annual depreciation expense is simply a way of accounting for each year's depreciation cost.

By the way, the terms "depreciation" and "amortization" both refer to this same process of accounting for the cost of the benefits provided by a capital asset. *Depreciation* is used when tangible capital assets are being accounted for, and *amortization* when intangible capital assets are being accounting for.

The sum of "Marketing and administration," "Research and development," and "Depreciation and amortization" was $26,899,000 in 1991. This amount is deducted from the 1991 gross profit of $44,507,000 to give the line item "Income from continuing operations," which was $17,608,000 in 1991 ($9,197,000 in 1990). A more precise title for this line item would be "Income from continuing operations before the deduction of income taxes" (don't forget the caution to be aware of some looseness in accounting terms). This number represents the accounting measure of before-tax profits from the ongoing regular business activities of the company, not including any results from businesses that the company may have shut down during the year. It has increased by an impressive 91.5% over the year; even Corel's sales number did not increase this much. As a percentage of sales, income from continuing operations was 33.7% in 1991, and 31.5% in 1990, indicating an improvement of about 7.0%. We saw earlier that the gross profit ratio increased by 7.6% over the year, so it seems that the entire relative improvement in income from continuing operations resulted from increased efficiency and product cost control, as suggested by the increase in the gross profit ratio.

Next, Corel accounts for its "Interest and dividend income," which was slightly down, from $2,675,000 in 1990 to $2,609,000 in 1991. The short-term investments that Corel grouped along with cash in the current assets section of its balance sheet must have provided the source of this "non-operating" income. Notice that Corel does not show any interest expense. It probably has incurred such expense — at least, it is likely that it would have had to pay interest charges on its accounts payable liability from the balance sheet. Perhaps the line item "Interest and dividend income" is really the *net* balance of such income.

The next item, "Income from continuing operations before income taxes," might better be labelled "Income before income taxes" (after all, Corel included non-operating interest and dividend income in this subtotal!). Let's consider the "Income taxes" totals of $8,160,000 for 1991, and $4,801,000 for 1990. Governments levy income taxes on corporations in Canada, just as they do on individuals, and the $8,160,000 represents Corel's accountant's estimate of 1991's income tax expense. However, recall that financial accounting measures of income taxes follow the rules of financial accounting, while the actual amount that Corel must pay is established by applying the rules of the Income Tax Act. In fact, Corel must actually pay the government $362,000 *less* than the tax expense of $8,160,000 that its management recorded on the income statement. For now, just think of this rather confusing situation as representing what happens when two accounting systems — financial accounting on the one hand, and the government's income tax accounting rules on the other — brush against each other. The explanation for all this must wait until Chapter 5.

Finally, we arrive at the income statement's bottom line, "Net income," which went from $6,990,000 in 1990 to $11,357,000 in 1991, an increase which (as we saw above) seems largely due to improvements in the gross profit ratio.

Corel's statement of retained earnings

This statement, shown in Exhibit 1–3, serves as a link between the balance sheet and the income statement. A simple equation that summarizes this statement is as follows:

$$RE_e = RE_s + NI_y - DIV_y$$

where

RE_e is retained earnings at the end of the year (or other accounting period)

RE_s is retained earnings at the start of the year

NI_y is net income (or net earnings, or profit, etc.) for the year

DIV_y is Dividends for the year

EXHIBIT 1–3
COREL CORPORATION
Statement of Retained Earnings (deficit)

(in thousands of Canadian dollars)	Year Ended November 30	
	1990	1991
Retained earnings (deficit) at beginning of period	$ (340)	$ 6,650
Net income	6,990	11,357
	6,650	18,007
Deduct: dividends	0	0
Retained earnings at end of period	$6,650	$18,007

Dividends are (usually) cash payments by a company to its shareholders, and represent a return on their investment in the company. Accountants do not account for dividends as an expense on the income statement, but rather as a *distribution* of a portion of net income; this means that dividends declared or paid out[6] by a company do not appear as an expense on the company's income statement. While this treatment follows the law (for example, the Income Tax Act does not permit corporations to deduct dividends on their corporate income tax returns), it ignores the costs companies incur in using the financial resources provided by shareholders. This raises a question: Since the cost of interest on loans is treated as an expense, why not dividends also? In Corel's case, no dividends have been declared or paid. This reflects Corel's policy concerning dividends, as set out in the following announcement by Corel's management in October 1992.

The Company has neither declared nor paid dividends on Common Shares and does not anticipate paying any dividends in the foreseeable future, but intends to retain earnings for reinvestment to finance the growth of its business.

Corel's statement of changes in financial position

The last of the four most common financial statements is more accurately known as the cash flow statement. Corel's is shown in Exhibit 1–4. The main purpose of this financial statement is to summarize the important actual flows of cash that occurred over the accounting period, which is one year in this case. Companies usually separate their cash flows into three categories:

- Cash flows that arose from everyday operating activities, such as (in Corel's case) buying computer diskettes, paying programmers, and so on. Corel generated $4,701,000 in actual cash from its operating activities in 1990, and $6,834,000 in 1991. The details of how this category of cash flows is dealt with in Corel's statement of changes in financial position (SCFP) will be briefly explained later on.
- Cash flows that arose from activities related to investing in and disposing of capital assets.
- Cash flows related to financing activities, such as paying out dividends (which Corel doesn't do) and raising money by issuing new common shares to either existing or new owners (which, as may be seen from the

[6] Before a dividend is paid out in cash (by issuing cheques), the most senior management group of a company — the board of directors — must formally vote or *declare* that the dividends are to be paid.

EXHIBIT 1–4
COREL CORPORATION
Statement of Changes in Financial Position

	Year ended November 30 1990	1991
	(in thousands of Cdn$)	
CASH* PROVIDED BY (USED FOR):		
Operations:		
Net income from continuing operations	$ 7,071	$12,057
Items that do not involve cash:		
Depreciation and amortization	484	1,371
Deferred income taxes	323	362
(Increase) decrease in accounts receivable	(4,421)	(6,727)
(Increase) decrease in inventory	(2,859)	(845)
(Increase) decrease in other current assets	(49)	(633)
Increase (decrease) in accounts payable and accrued liabilities	2,234	990
Increase (decrease) in income taxes payable	2,138	(113)
Increase (decrease) in other current liabilities	(220)	372
Cash provided by (used for) operations	4,701	6,834
Income (loss) from discontinued operations	(81)	(700)
Financing:		
Issue of share capital	201	4,532
Investments:		
Purchase of capital assets	(1,937)	(6,467)
Summary:		
Increase (decrease) in cash	2,884	4,199
Cash at beginning of period	18,836	21,720
Cash at end of period	$21,720	$25,919

* Cash is defined as cash and short-term investments.

cash flow statement, Corel did in both 1990 and 1991).

This three-way classification often provides useful information, because the timing, magnitude, and behaviour of cash flows in the three categories can be expected to vary with the type of company and how well it is doing. For example, a fashion retail company that has recently been established and that has great prospects might reasonably be expected to have a small, perhaps even negative cash flow from operations, as it purchases increasing amounts of inventory, extends credit to customers, and so on. One might expect its cash flow from investment to be *very* negative as it acquires retail display furniture, computers for administration, delivery trucks, and the like. At the same time, its financing cash flows would be very positive, as investors rush in to invest their money in an attractive, growing company. We will have a lot more to say about cash flow financial statements in this book, especially in Chapter 7.

If you haven't already noticed, the "Operations" section of Corel's cash flow statement seems rather strange. While the investing and financing sections of the cash flow statement are relatively straightforward, and just list the actual cash inflows and cash outflows, the section for operating activities begins with Corel's net income number. It then adjusts this number to squeeze out all the non–cash flow information in order to arrive at a "pure" cash flow number. For example, recall that the income statement expense of $1,371,000 for depreciation and amortization didn't represent any cash outflow at all in 1991, even though Corel's management accounted for it — legitimately — as an expense on the income statement. Since it didn't use up any cash, it's added back to the net income number as we head toward the operating cash flow number. The same explanation holds for all the other adjustments in the operations section of the cash flow statement — in fact, this section of the statement is simply a reconciliation between the net income number and the "cash provided by operating activities" number. Why do accountants present published cash flow statements in this confusing way? It's hard to be really sure about this, but many accountants suggest that it's important to show how the cash flow statement is linked to the income statement, and what makes up the difference between net income and cash flow from operations.

Different Organizations, Different Characteristics, Different Financial Accounting

Corel designs and produces state-of-the-art specialized software products; Potash Corporation of Saskatchewan (the potash company we briefly mentioned earlier) extracts a natural resource from the earth and markets it. Each company needs certain types of capital assets to operate in the way it does. PCS generates its sales by acquiring sites rich in potash, investing large amounts of money in building facilities to mine the potash, and arranging for transportation of the product to customers. Its financial statements, and the various types of accounting decisions that PCS's managers and accountants must make, reflect the nature of the organization. We wouldn't expect different types of organizations to provide the same details in their financial statements. For another example, a professional services organization such as a public accounting firm has very little inventory (probably some supplies, but nothing that it sells), and generates its "sales" by providing its clients with accounting, auditing, and related services. In fact, the term "sales" seems inappropriate for the activities of such an organization, so the more general term "revenues" is used. When would an organization like this one record revenue? The decision-making process here is far different than for a company like Corel or one like PCS, because there is no obvious sales event, such as the customer physically receiving a shipment of shrink-wrapped software, or receiving a container shipload of potash.

At this point, we turn away from a real, operating Canadian company, Corel Corporation, to look at a simple, one-person organization. Since our goal in this is to see how financial accounting information is "built up," we will use a hypothetical and relatively straightforward example. Here, we are shifting from the perspective of an *outsider* looking in on a company through its financial statements, to that of an *insider* who has access to the transactions and other events which affect the company day to day, and which are the raw materials for the financial statements that will eventually be prepared.

Building Up Financial Statements From Transactions and Other Events

In order to account for the transactions that an organization enters into, we need to formalize our examination of some basic financial accounting ideas. Let's start with the fundamental relationship between assets on the one hand, and liabilities and shareholders' equity on the other.

The basic accounting equation can be represented in symbols:

Uses of financing (assets) = Sources of financing (liabilities and shareholders' equity)

or, $A = L + SE$ [equation 1]

where A stands for assets, L stands for liabilities, and SE stands for shareholders' equity (sometimes referred to as owners' equity).

Subdividing these broad categories, we can express the fundamental accounting identity in this way:

$$CA + LTA = CL + LTL + CAP + RE$$ [equation 2]

where CA and CL refer to current assets and current liabilities, respectively, LTA and LTL refer to long-term assets and long-term liabilities, CAP refers to owners' capital invested in the organization (such as common shares), and RE refers to retained earnings. The relationship in equation 2 holds at a point in time; thus, it can be rewritten using the subscript "t," as follows:

$$CA_t + LTA_t = CL_t + LTL_t + CAP_t + RE_t \quad \text{[equation 3]}$$

If we use the subscript "s" to signify the *start* of an accounting period, and the point in time t is any time *after* s, then the following time line represents the situation:

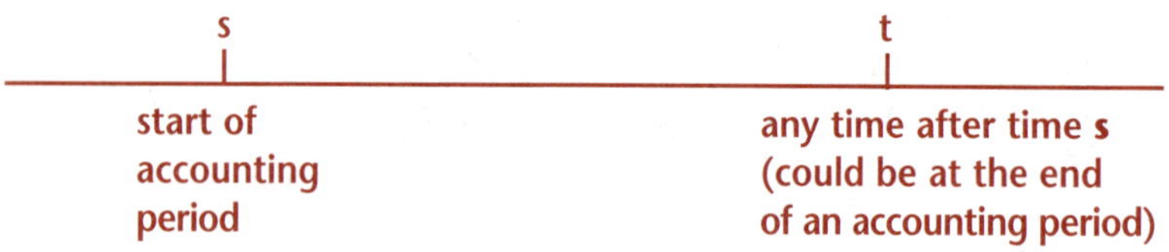

Thus, we can rewrite equation 3 to explicitly set out the current period's activities, as follows:

$$CA_t + LTA_t = CL_t + LTL_t + CAP_t + RE_s + [R_p - E_p] - D_p \quad \text{[equation 4]}$$

where R_p is the current period's revenues (up to time t); E_p is the current period's expenses (up to time t), and D_p is the current period's dividends that have been declared (up to time t). Note that we have substituted the last four terms in equation 4 for the end-of-period retained earnings, RE_t, of equation 3. **The expression in equation 4 can be used to convert any transaction that the organization enters into, or any other accountable event (such as the recording of depreciation), into financial accounting information. The expression is therefore a framework by which financial accounting views an organization.**

Let's look at how equation 4 can be used to collect accounting information about a simple organization, and then prepare the four financial statements for the organization: a balance sheet, an income statement, a statement of retained earnings, and a cash flow statement. On Ice Incorporated (OI for short) was established in August 1993 by Devo Green, a Vancouver writer, and will publish *On Ice*, a magazine intended for recreational hockey players. The events that occurred during the first two months of the company's existence are summarized as follows:

1. On August 5, 1993, Devo Green was told by his lawyer that OI's process of incorporation was now complete; Devo withdrew \$10,000 of his \$11,000 life savings from his personal savings account at the local bank, and redeposited the money in an account in the company's name. On the way home from the bank, he stopped at his lawyer's office and picked up a certificate that stated he was the owner of 10,000 shares of stock in OI.

2. The lawyer's bill arrived on August 9. It included \$350 for professional services, and \$225 that the lawyer had paid out to the provincial government so that Devo could incorporate OI.

3. On August 10, Devo flew to Winnipeg to interview a retired hockey star for the lead article of the first issue of *On Ice*. The plane tickets, hotel, and taxi fare cost \$530, paid in cash.

4. Back in Vancouver on August 15, Devo was thrilled to learn that a major manufacturer of hockey sticks had purchased advertising space in the magazine's first issue. The agreed-upon amount was \$1,300; half of this was to be paid at the end of August, the other half when *On Ice* was published on September 9 or 10.

5. Devo felt so good about his first ad sale that he marched right out the same day and purchased a new computer system from Super Computers Limited, for his business. The total cost, including all taxes, was \$3,590. The computer retailer's payment terms are "2/10, net 30," which means that if Devo pays the bill within ten days of making the purchase, he gets a 2% discount off the purchase price. He must, however, pay within 30 days.

6. On August 16, Devo issued a cheque for $1,000, payable to Kim Mulroney, a well-known hockey writer who had just dropped off a story on NHL old-timers hockey for *On Ice*.

7. Devo paid his August rent, a total of $1,500, on the 16th. Since the entire downstairs of the house he rented was now used for his OI business, he prepared a cheque payable to his landlord for $750 out of the OI bank account, and gave the landlord the other $750 in cash, which he had withdrawn from his personal account.

8. Four days later, the largest regional hockey rink ordered ad space for $1,950, to be paid for in 30 days. Devo was ecstatic, and felt sure that his new business had a great future.

9. Also on August 20, he purchased $295 in office supplies from a local retailer, who agreed to let OI pay in two months, "once it got its feet off the ground."

10. On August 23, Devo paid a local sportswriter $925 for an interesting story that would fit right in with the theme of the first issue.

11. All the copy and ads were set for the first issue. Devo did the magazine layouts himself on his new computer, using a really user-friendly desktop publishing package. He arranged to have 6,000 copies of the first issue printed by September 7. The printer agreed that the total cost would be $10,000. On August 25, Devo gave the printer a cheque representing a down payment of $5,000, with the remaining $5,000 payable on September 5, two days before Devo was to pick up the magazines.

12. On August 27, Devo issued a cheque for $1,000 payable to Super Computers Limited. Even though he intended to arrange a bank loan shortly, he felt that he had to watch OI's cash flow, and he decided that he couldn't pay off Super's bill all at once.

13. On August 30, the assistant manager of the bank approved a $9,000 loan to OI. The loan was a "demand loan," which meant that the bank could demand payment in full at any time. The assistant manager assured Devo that "as long as OI continued to sell ad space and put out such a relevant magazine, the bank would not require repayment." Devo had discussed OI's financial results thus far and its plans for the coming year with the assistant manager, who told Devo that the bank would require a complete set of financial statements every three months, beginning on September 30. The terms of the loan required that "interest of 1% of the outstanding balance is due and payable on the first day of every month, beginning October 1st, 1993. The principal amount of the loan (i.e., the $9,000) is due 'on demand', but no later than August 30, 1994."

14. At 10 a.m. on the morning of September 3, a major skate manufacturer, to whom Devo had been trying to sell ad space since early August, ordered a three-page layout in the first issue, for an agreed-upon price of $4,000. Devo was absolutely thrilled, and hurried over to the manufacturer's office to pick up a cheque for the initial payment of $1,000. He spent the rest of the day in front of his computer redoing the first issue's layout, since he well knew that this particular ad absolutely had to go in the first issue of the magazine. By 4 p.m., he had everything set up, and hurried with his diskette over to the printers. He was slightly deflated to learn that the printer required an additional $1,500 for the changes, which Devo agreed to pay, along with the remaining $5,000, on September 5.

15. Devo personally delivered the cheque for $6,500 to the printer on September 5.

16. On September 7, Devo drove his van over to the printer's and picked up 6,000 copies of *On Ice*.

17. On September 10, he issued cheques totalling $1,295, representing various costs incurred in connection with distributing the magazine, to hockey rinks throughout the Greater Vancouver region. At each rink, the magazine would be placed on racks beside the snack bar. The selling price would be $3 a copy; the rink owner would keep $1, and $2 would be remitted to OI one week after the end of each month. All the rink owners agreed that they would telephone Devo between 5 p.m. and 7 p.m. on September 30 to let him know how many magazines had been sold. They also agreed to send along Devo's cash from the magazine sales by October 30.

18. The stick manufacturer's cheque arrived on September 15. Devo was slightly irritated that the cheque was for only $300.

19. On September 16, OI issued a cheque for $750 representing its portion of the September rent.

20. The afternoon mail on September 20 included a bill from the telephone company for $125 for OI's business line, which Devo had had installed on August 9.

21. That same day, Devo issued an OI cheque for $1,000 to himself for his salary for August and September.

22. He knew that he would have to provide the bank with financial statements in just a few days. How could he account for depreciation on his computer, which the owner of Super said would last for "at least two years"?

23. He also was unsure about how he should account for the interest on the bank loan, which was due on October 1, one day *after* the financial statements had to be prepared.

24. As he sat at his desk on September 30, thinking about the financial statements that he had to prepare, he took a small break and determined that only about $50 worth of his supplies were left. "Better get some more soon," he said to himself.

25. Between 5 p.m. and 7 p.m. on September 30, Devo received telephone calls from 30 rink owners, informing him that all of the 6,000 magazines had been sold.

26. He sat with a big grin on his face when he realized that all of the first issue had been sold out.

27. The corporate income tax rate for OI is 20% of the company's net income before income taxes.

The spreadsheet provided in Exhibit 1–5 shows how equation 4 (modified to show only a single column for retained earnings) can be used to collect accounting information for OI. The retained earnings column can be used to construct an income statement (keep in mind, however, that since OI is a new company, there is no beginning retained earnings). Also, the cash column can be used to construct a cash flow statement running from the date the business was started up to September 30, the date as of which the bank requires an accounting. The final sums in each column can be used to prepare a balance sheet as of September 30, 1993. All the financial statements are shown in Exhibit 1–6.

Some comments on the accounting decisions made on the spreadsheet in Exhibit 1–5 follow:

- The accounting is being done on September 30, or soon after. Devo Green (or Devo's accountant) knows that the first issue of the magazine

EXHIBIT 1–5
SPREADSHEET ACCOUNTING FOR ON ICE'S ACTIVITIES USING EQUATION 4

		ASSETS								=	Liabilities and Shareholders' Equity						Comments on the Retained Earnings Impact
DATE (D/M/Y)	EVENT	Cash	Accounts receivable	Inventory	Organization costs	Office supplies	Prepaid printing costs	Capital asset	Accumulated depreciation	=	Accounts payable	Interest payable	Income Tax payable	Loan payable	Common stock	Retained earnings	
5/8/93	1. 'On Ice' Incorporated	10,000								=					10,000		
9/8/93	2. Lawyer's bill and fees				575					=	575						
10/8/93	3. Interview in Winnipeg	-530								=						-530	an expense
15/8/93	4. Ad sold to stick mfg		1,300							=						1,300	a revenue
11/8/93	5. Buy computer (2/10N30)							3,590		=	3,590						
16/8/93	6. Pay writer	-1,000								=						-1,000	an expense
16/8/93	7. Aug rent (1/2 for 'On ice')	-750								=						-750	an expense
20/8/93	8. Ad sold to rink		1,950							=						1,950	a revenue
20/8/93	9. Purch. office supplies					295				=	295						
23/8/93	10. Pay writer	-925								=						-925	an expense
25/8/93	11. Down pay't to printer	-5,000					5,000			=							
27/8/93	12. Pay $1,000 on computer	-1,000								=	-1,000						
30/8/93	13. Arrange loan @ 1%PM	9,000								=				9,000			
3/9/93	14. Ad sold to skate mfg	1,000	3,000							=						4,000	a revenue
5/9/93	15. Pay off printer	-6,500					6,500			=							
7/9/93	16. Magazines picked up			11,500			-11,500			=							
10/9/93	17. Distribute magazines	-1,295								=						-1,295	an expense
15/9/93	18. Collect part of #4	300	-300							=							
16/9/93	19. Sept rent	-750								=						-750	an expense
20/9/93	20. Business phone calls									=	125					-125	an expense
20/9/93	21. Devos's salary	-1,000								=						-1,000	an expense
30/9/93	22. Depreciation								-225	=						-225	an expense
30/9/93	23. Accrue interest									=		90				-90	an expense
30/9/93	24. Only $50 off./sup. left					-245				=						-245	an expense
30/9/93	25. Record revenue		12,000							=						12,000	a revenue
30/9/93	26. Record cost of printing			-11,500						=						-11,500	an expense
30/9/93	27. Income taxes									=			163			-163	an expense
	Totals	1,550	17,950	0	575	50	0	3590	-225	=	3,585	90	183	9,000	10,000	652	

EXHIBIT 1-6
ON ICE INCORPORATED'S FINANCIAL STATEMENTS

(A) Balance sheet

On Ice Incorporated
Balance Sheet
As at September 30, 1993

ASSETS	
Cash	$ 1,550
Accounts receivable	17,950
Office supplies	50
CURRENT ASSETS	19,550
Organization costs	575
Capital asset, at cost	3,590
Less accumulated depreciation	(225)
	$23,490
LIABILITIES AND SHAREHOLDERS' EQUITY	
Accounts payable	$ 3,585
Income tax payable	163
Interest payable	90
Bank loan	9,000
CURRENT LIABILITIES	12,838
Common stock	10,000
Retained earnings	652
SHAREHOLDERS' EQUITY	10,652
	$23,490

(B) Income statement

On Ice Incorporated
Income Statement
For the period August 5 to September 30, 1993

REVENUES	
Sale of magazines	$12,000
Sale of advertising	7,250
	19,250
EXPENSES	
Cost of magazines sold	11,500
Writing fees	1,925
Rent	1,500
Distribution expenses	1,295
Salary	1,000
Telephone	125
Depreciation	225
Travel	530
Interest	90
Supplies	245
	18,435
Net income before income taxes	815
Income taxes	163
Net income	$ 652

(C) Retained earnings statement

On Ice Incorporated
Retained Earnings Statement
For the period August 5 to September 30, 1993

Retained earnings, August 8, 1993	—
Add: net income for the period	652
	652
Deduct: dividends declared for the period	—
Retained earnings, September 30, 1993	$ 652

(D) Cash flow statement

On Ice Incorporated
Cash Flow Statement
For the period August 5 to September 30, 1993

OPERATING ACTIVITIES	
Sale of advertisements	$ 1,300
Travel	(530)
Writers' fees	(1,925)
Printing costs	(11,500)
Distribution costs	(1,295)
Rent	(1,500)
Salary	(1,000)
Net cash (outflows) due to operating activities	(16,450)
INVESTING ACTIVITIES	
Purchase computer	(1,000)
FINANCING ACTIVITIES	
Issue common shares	10,000
Bank loan	9,000
	19,000
TOTAL CASH FLOW	$ 1,550

was successfully produced, and sold out. Thus, a lot of uncertainty is eliminated by that date, and the accounting can proceed with considerably fewer estimates than would otherwise have been the case.

- Devo Green still had some money in his personal bank account. We ignored it, on the grounds that OI and Devo are separate entities, and we were doing the accounting strictly for OI.
- Notice that each row's accounting maintains the balance sheet's balance.

Let's go over some of the spreadsheet items in detail:

- Item 1: On Ice is established. Devo's company, On Ice, now has its first asset, $10,000 in cash, so the asset "Cash" is increased by that amount. Shareholders' equity (in this case, common shares) has also increased by $10,000, representing Devo's ownership interest in OI. If we had stopped right at this point to prepare a balance sheet, it would have looked like this:

On Ice Incorporated
Balance Sheet
As at August 5, 1993

Assets		Liabilities and Shareholders' Equity	
Cash	$10,000	Common stock	$10,000

- Item 2: The $575 creates a future benefit (that is, the state of being incorporated), so OI has an asset equal to this amount. We accounted for it as an asset called "Organization cost." It is an intangible asset with (hopefully) long-term benefits. More conservative (or perhaps, prudent) accountants would classify it as an expense, on the grounds that estimating its future benefit is impossible. Note that the event also increases OI's accounts payable.
- Item 3: This reduces cash and also creates an expense, which reduces retained earnings.
- Item 4: This represents money owed to OI, so it increases accounts receivable. It also represents the first bit of revenue for OI (we know this for sure by the time we do the accounting on September 30 or later), so it has the effect of increasing retained earnings. If we were preparing a set of financial statements right on August 15, we would list the $1,300 as an "unearned revenue" among the current liabilities on OI's balance sheet. However, we know that by the time OI's balance sheet *is* prepared (September 30), OI will have published its first issue of *On Ice* with the ad in it, and will therefore have earned its money. Similar reasoning holds for items 8 and 14.
- Item 20: Even though OI didn't pay out any cash, it did use the services of the telephone company for August and September, so we record the expense of $125 as a reduction of retained earnings (and also, of course, record the $125 that OI owes as a liability).
- Item 22: The $3,590 cost of the computer is spread over the two years apparently suggested by the computer retailer. This works out to about $150 per month, or $225 for the month-and-a-half that OI used the computer.
- Item 23: The $9,000 loan has been outstanding for one month, so OI owes the bank 1% of $9,000, or $90. The $90 also represents the cost of interest for the accounting period, and so is an expense on OI's income statement (and thus also reduces retained earnings). Note that as of the date of the financial statements (September 30), OI hasn't paid the bank any cash in respect to the interest, but its cost and the associated liability are still accounted for. Balance sheets and income statements account for more than just cash flows!

- Item 24: Since there is only $50 of supplies left, OI must have used up $245 worth. This $245 now represents an expense, since it has no more future benefits associated with it (an expired asset becomes an expense).
- Item 25: This records OI's revenue for the magazine sales. "Accounts receivable," which is of course an asset, is increased by $12,000 (the asset "cash" is not increased; recall that the rink owners don't have to send the money to Devo until October 30). As well, retained earnings is increased by $12,000, since this is a revenue item.
- Item 26: OI doesn't have the magazines anymore — they were sold to generate the $12,000 in revenue that we accounted for just above. So their cost (actual, historic, total) must be removed from the balance sheet's "Inventory" category (after all, we shouldn't account for what's no longer there!) and charged off as an expense, specifically as "Cost of magazines sold."
- Item 27: From OI's income statement in Exhibit 1–6, we see that "Net income before income taxes" is $815. Since income tax is computed at 20% of this amount (we are assuming that there is no difference between financial accounting and income tax rules for this example; this is not in fact true, but we don't want to complicate the example unnecessarily), income tax expense is $163.

Accounting and Business Decision B

Suppose you were OI's banker, and received the set of four financial statements in Exhibit 1–6 in mid-October of 1993. What questions would you ask Devo Green?

On Ice and Corel: A Comparison

A useful exercise is to compare the perspectives we adopted in the above two examples. When we examined Corel Corporation's four financial statements, we were on the outside looking in. The window through which we were able to observe a little of what had happened to Corel was the set of financial statements that its management had prepared for outsiders to use. Even though we were able to gain a fair bit of insight into the company — at least to the extent that we began to understand which questions to ask and how accounting information was interrelated with other business information — much of the detail was missing and unavailable to us.

In the On Ice example we had access to the everyday transactions of the company, and we built up the financial statements from this "insider" information. These two perspectives — user/outsider and preparer/insider — provide us with an understanding of some of the possible tensions in accounting. As outside users, we wanted as much information as possible about Corel — about its business, its accounting details, and so forth — and Corel's management had to continually assess whether to provide us with everything or hold some things back. The same holds for the On Ice situation: Devo Green certainly wants to provide the accounting information the bank requires (after all, that's a condition of the loan agreement, and is therefore surely necessary to help Devo maintain good relations with the bank), but he would probably be loathe to provide absolutely everything.

Final Comment

The various types of accounting (financial, managerial and cost, tax, regulatory, and so on) affect our lives in a surprisingly large number of ways. In this chapter we have suggested the importance of accounting, and illustrated four key accounting statements. Perhaps an appropriate way to end this first chapter is to suggest that accounting can help bring about massive social and economic change. Consider the Peoples' Republic of China (the PRC), which, in spite of the continuing ideological struggles between conservatives and reformers, is still determined to move at least partly toward a market-based economy.

As the PRC encourages entrepreneurs to develop new businesses, and to form partnerships with foreign companies, it is facing a tremendous need for accounting and auditing education, for the development of ways to perform financial accounting, for the development of accounting techniques to regulate organizations, and so on. In a very real sense, the lack of an existing developed discipline and profession of accounting in the PRC is acting as a significant hindrance to that nation's shift toward a market economy. The investment required in accounting education is enormous, of course, but perhaps there is an equally important issue: Should a country such as the PRC adopt, in an uncritical manner, the features of accounting already present in developed market economies such as Canada and the United States? Or should it instead develop principles more appropriate to its own culture and national goals?

Accounting, Organizations, and Society

Each chapter in this text will end with an example of how accounting affects how we live and think about our world. The following article, which appeared in the *Toronto Star* (January 9, 1994, E9), links us back to the two quotations that opened this chapter.

Was Civilization Built on Clay Balls?

by Boyce Rensberger

Generations of archeologists digging in humanity's earliest settlements ignored the unspectacular little artefacts of clay that turned up in so many Mesopotamian excavations.

If they wrote about them at all, they called the thumb-sized balls, cones, disks and other shapes "enigmatic objects" or guessed they were merely children's toys.

Since the 1970s, however, University of Texas specialist Denise Schmandt-Besserat, a professor of Middle Eastern studies, has been building a strong case that the objects are fundamental clues to nothing less than one of the more important advances in human intellectual evolution.

The hardened bits of clay, she has shown, reveal how the ancient Sumerians developed the world's first writing. They also strongly challenge the longstanding belief that Sumerian cuneiform, as the most advanced form of the writing is called, evolved from "picture writing" — the use of little drawings, or pictographs, of real objects to stand for words.

More than that, according to Schmandt-Besserat's newest discoveries, clay tokens, as she calls them, also tell how the Sumerians developed the concept of abstract numbers.

In fact, her evidence suggests that the need to count led to the ability to write, and that literacy and its mathematical equivalent, numeracy, rose in tandem, together transforming the nature of civilization.

The French American scholar's discoveries have won high praise in a field noted for discord.

"Every so often, a field of study is revolutionized by a single discovery or a unique hypothesis," William Hallo, a Yale University expert on the ancient Middle East, wrote of the new findings in a foreword to Schmandt-Besserat's monograph, *Before Writing*, published earlier this year. Her research, Hallo said, "promises to play such a role in our understanding of the emergence of civilization."

The origin of writing had long been a puzzle. The oldest known examples have been found in digs at Uruk (the Biblical Erech), one of the major cities of Sumer, the world's first civilization.

The Sumerian culture arose in the fertile Tigris and Euphrates river valleys of what is now Iraq, a region called Mesopotamia, about 6,400 years ago.

Sumerian writing emerged about three centuries later. About the same time, the ancient Egyptians developed their hieroglyphic writing. In later centuries, writing also arose — probably independently — in China and among the Maya of Central America.

At one time, some scholars supposed writing was the invention of individual geniuses who simply thought it up. More recently, it has been seen as the result of a gradual process. Until Schmandt-Besserat's research, however, the nature of that process had been elusive.

"My work on the clay tokens suggests that these were the early form of the activity that would become writing," Schmandt-Besserat said. She has discerned the roots of writing twice as far into the past as had been supposed — to a time about 10,000 years ago, when agriculture was just beginning to replace hunting and gathering.

The tokens first came to light in archeological digs into strata of that antiquity in what is now Iran. The origin of token-making — bits of clay formed by hand into balls, balls flattened into disks, oblongs, cylinders, cones, cubes and tetrahedrons — it turned out, predated the manufacture of pottery.

Tokens were, in fact, the first clay objects hardened by fire. About 10,000 of the objects have been found in more than 100 archeological sites.

Schmandt-Besserat said major clues to their meaning came from two scholarly predecessors. In a 1966 paper, Pierre Amiet, a specialist in Middle Eastern antiquities at the Louvre in Paris, suggested that the tokens were counters, pieces used to represent specific commodities.

He cited an earlier discovery by Leo Oppenheim of the University of Chicago. This was a hollow clay ball found in the 1920s at a site near ancient Babylon that was occupied long after the invention of writing. The outside had a cuneiform inscription that read: "Counters representing small cattle: 21 ewes that lamb, 6 female lambs ... " and so on until 49 animals were described. When workers broke open the ball, out tumbled 49 bits of fired clay.

Oppenheim speculated that the

objects were part of an accounting system by which the local bureaucracy kept records.

On reading Amiet's paper, Schmandt-Besserat said, "Two pieces of the puzzle snapped together for me." She immediately saw a link to the many tokens from sites occupied thousands of years before writing began. They too might have been part of a preliterate accounting system.

Schmandt-Besserat's subsequent research has shown that before the advent of writing, hollow clay balls were used as "bills of lading" to accompany shipments of goods. When a shipper delivered a cargo of jars of oil, for example, he would surrender the clay ball to the recipient, who could break it open and confirm that the correct quantities had arrived.

In later years, the Texas scholar said, Sumerian accountants thought of a simple way to verify the contents of a ball without destroying it. They would press each token against the outer surface of the ball before it hardened, then put them through a hole and seal the ball.

Soon after, the accountants realized that once they made the impressions, there was no need for the tokens. The shape of the token, showing in the hardened clay, carried the meaning.

Indeed, Schmandt-Besserat has found that the shapes correspond closely to the first kind of Sumerian writing, which has been called pictography but, as she stresses, is not very pictographic. The symbols are incised in wet clay with stylus, but only a few of the symbols are pictorial; most are abstract shapes and correspond to the shapes left by tokens pressed in wet clay.

At least as important, she found the switch to "pictographic" writing came at the same time as another key intellectual advance. When tokens were used, each stood for one unit of a commodity. To indicate, say 10 jars of oil, 10 "jar-of-oil" tokens would be put inside the clay ball. When writing appeared, the same meaning was conveyed by one "jar of oil" pictograph plus a new kind of symbol that meant "10."

"We knew there was something that had to come before writing," Schmandt-Besserat said. "Nobody in archeology had asked what came before arithmetic. Mathematicians had predicted that something concrete had to come before abstract numbers. The tokens were the concrete numbers. When writing begins, mathematics begins."

She said it looks as if the same intellectual leap of symbolizing that led to incising the token shapes also led to thinking of numbers as something apart from what is being counted.

A century after "pictographic" writing began, the curving symbols were converted to the more angular form created by square-cornered styluses being pressed into clay. The result was the cuneiform (from the Latin for "wedge-shaped") writing that quickly swept the ancient Middle East.

CHAPTER SUMMARY

In this first chapter, examples were provided of the many ways in which accounting affects our everyday life. The importance of accounting was shown to reach all the way back into prehistory. The many subdisciplines that accounting has evolved into were also described.

Four important financial statements — the balance sheet, the income statement, the retained earnings statement, and the cash flow statement — were explained, and their preparation was illustrated using a spreadsheet based upon the basic accounting equation.

Suggested Answers to Accounting and Business Decisions

Decision A

Top management probably doesn't want to get too involved in the day-to-day operations of the stores, unless something undesirable is happening at a particular location. The fact that a large number of stores is involved would prevent such involvement; also, top management is usually interested in setting overall strategy for the organization, not in operating individual stores. By requiring each retail store to submit income statements, top management is able to monitor sales, cost of goods sold, other key expenses (such as local TV advertising expense), and important ratios such as the gross profit ratio, and perhaps compare all of these to the numbers for all the other stores. The managers at the retail store level are held accountable for achieving profit and other targets, and are controlled by top management in part through the system of submitting income statements to head office. The use of store income statements to control store managers has these benefits, among others:

- Head office is able to monitor and control many individual stores, by holding the managers of the stores accountable for achieving profit and related targets, and by noting unusual trends in, for example, certain key expense categories.
- Individual store managers have well-defined profit and related targets; a manager whose store meets the targets receives an appropriate reward (a bonus, perhaps). Deciding just what to include in the store income statements may be a challenge; if the statements are poorly designed, the store managers may be encouraged to make poor decisions, or may perhaps become frustrated.

How often would top management want the store managers to submit income statements? Anything more frequent than monthly might result in information overload at the top management level, and too short a leash on the store managers. Also, as the time period covered by an income statement gets shorter and shorter (that is, as the frequency of submitting the reports increases), more and more estimates are required in determining revenues and the various expenses; as a result, disputes may arise between top management and the store managers about the quality of the various numbers on the income statement.

Decision B

The banker is in the business of making loans — that's one of the important financial services that the bank sells. The interest the bank receives helps cover its expenses and perhaps contributes toward a profit as well. The bank decided to make a relatively small loan for $9,000 to Devo's company, and is charging interest of 1% per month — that is, $[(1.01)^{12} - 1]$, or 12.68% on an annual basis. By the standards of late 1993, that's a fairly high interest rate, so the bank must view On Ice as a fairly risky loan customer. This is not surprising, since On Ice is a new company with no track record.

The bank wants to know how secure its loan is, and therefore wants to monitor the quality of the business decisions Devo is making. Notice that the bank didn't require that Devo provide personal guarantees by, say, pledging his personal assets as collateral for the loan (he doesn't appear to have much in the way of personal assets anyway). Also, On Ice itself doesn't have a lot in the way of tangible assets that the bank could have used as collateral. It seems that the bank was interested in helping a small business that had some potential. This could be part of a larger bank program to provide initial financing for entrepreneurs starting up risky but promising small businesses. So the future profitability of On Ice is crucial to the bank.

The banker might ask the following questions, among others, on receiving the four financial statements:

- *Balance sheet.* How collectible is the $17,950 in accounts receivable? Can On Ice speed up the cash receipts from the rink owners? Was it necessary to purchase the computer? (Perhaps Devo could have saved cash by renting it.) Accounts payable of $3,585 are classified as current liabilities; is it possible to spread out the required payments without incurring any penalties, since On Ice's cash balance is quite low? Is it possible to interest anyone else in investing in On Ice's common stock, in order to provide more cash for the business during the crucial start-up phase?
- *Income statement.* Is the advertising space priced right? Are the magazines priced right? Is the one dollar that rink owners keep for each magazine sold too generous? Would they do it (as enthusiastically) for less, at least for a while? Are expenses such as printing, writers' fees, travel, and so forth being watched carefully? For example, is it possible to negotiate a longer-term contract with the printer at a lower price? Is the $1,000 salary that Devo took really a fair measure of the services Devo provided? In other words, would a fair measure of the entrepreneur's salary have resulted in a loss?
- *Statement of cash flows.* Although net income was slightly positive at $652, operating cash flow was very negative at minus $16,450. How many issues of the magazine will it take for operating cash flow to turn positive?

KEY TERMS

Accounting is what this book is all about, and we haven't as yet provided a workable definition! This we promised to do in Chapter 2. For now, please think of accounting as including all the areas or subdisciplines that were described in the chapter. So if someone asks you, at this point in your reading of this text, "what's accounting?" you can say:

Well, financial accounting is that part of accounting that deals with the preparation and dissemination of financial statements to people outside of the organization that's being accounted for, and management accounting focuses on the provision of information to managers, such as information about the cost of a company's product, which will help the managers run the company better than they otherwise could, and ...

Accounts payable is the total of monies owed to a company's suppliers.

Accounts receivable is the total of monies that a company's customers owe the company.

Accrued liabilities are the amounts a company owes to suppliers who have not as yet issued formal invoices (or other notification that they are owed money), but whose services or products have already been used or acquired by the company.

Accumulated depreciation is the cumulative total to date of all the depreciation expense recorded on capital assets of the organization, from the date that the capital assets were acquired and put in use.

The ***Auditor General*** is a senior official appointed by the federal government whose job it is to provide independent information to Parliament about the financial activities of the various government departments and agencies. Most governments (provincial, foreign, and so on) appoint a similar official.

Assets are the resources of an organization, the things it uses in its business. A more formal, accounting-based definition of this important term will be provided in Chapter 4, when we discuss some theory about accounting.

The ***balance sheet*** is the financial statement that records assets, liabilities, and shareholders's (or owners') equity. It presents information about an organization's resources and about the sources of money that organization used to acquire those resources. The balance sheet is a formal financial statement that organizes information in ways established by accountants over the years. For example, current assets (see below) are shown first on Canadian balance sheets.

The ***basic accounting equation*** is represented by —

Assets = Liabilities + Shareholders' (or owners') Equity

It may be broken down into specific individual components, as was done with the On Ice example, to help in accounting for various transactions and other business events. Note that the term "owners' equity" is more general than "shareholders' equity," since the latter refers only to companies that have issued share capital (say, common shares), while the former also includes companies that have no share capital, such as sole proprietorships and partnerships (which we'll describe in Chapter 2).

Capital assets are defined by accountants as follows:

Capital assets, comprising property, plant and equipment and intangible properties, are identifiable assets that meet all of the following criteria:

(a) are held for use in the production or supply of goods and services, for rental to others, for administrative purposes or for the development, construction, maintenance or repair of other capital assets;

(b) have been acquired, constructed or developed with the intention of being used on a continuing basis; and

(c) are not intended for sale in the ordinary course of business.[7]

Cash includes money that a company has deposited in banks or other financial institutions (such as trust companies), miscellaneous or petty cash on hand, and cheques from customers and others that are not as yet deposited.

Cash flow is the actual change, or flow, of cash that occurred over an accounting period for an organization. Cash flow is usually quite different from income (also called net income, or net earnings, or similar).

Common shares are individual evidence of ownership in a corporation. A corporation may have any number of common shares.

Cost is a term with many meanings. The Canadian Institute of Chartered Accountants, in *Terminology for Accountants*, defined it in the following way: "The amount, measured in money, of the expenditure to obtain goods or services." The *Houghton Mifflin Canadian Dictionary* defines "cost" as

> *1. An amount paid or required in payment for a purchase. 2. A loss or penalty ...*

Both of these definitions are very general and too broad to be that helpful in specific situations, but they do emphasize that "cost" refers to an outflow of resources. It's advisable to always qualify this term with adjectives that help managers, accountants, or others understand as precisely as possible which cost concept is being used in the particular circumstances. For example, throughout this text we will use the terms "actual cost," "historic cost," "replacement cost," and so on.

Cost of sales, when unmodified by an adjective, represents the actual, historic, total cost of a company's inventory that was sold during an accounting period.

Current assets are assets that management expects to turn into cash or otherwise use within a time period that is the greater of the following two time intervals:

- one year, or
- one operating cycle of the business, if the operating cycle is longer than one year.

Current liabilities are liabilities that are expected to be paid or otherwise disposed of within one year, or one operating cycle of the business (if longer than one year).

Deferred revenue refers to the current liability created when a company receives payment from a

[7] *CICA Handbook*, section 3060. We'll have more to say about the *Handbook* later on.

customer before it provides that customer with the particular product or service.

Depreciation was referred to in the chapter as an allocation of a capital asset's original (historic) cost over the accounting periods during which the business is expected to benefit from the use of that asset. This is the most common accounting definition of the term. The *Houghton Mifflin Canadian Dictionary* provides the following definition:

> **1.** *A decrease or loss in value because of wear, age, or other cause.* **2.** Accounting. *An allowance made for this loss.*

This dictionary definition is quite useful, since it distinguishes the everyday definition from the one accountants use.

Dividends are payments or distributions by a company to its shareholders. They do not appear as expenses on a company's income statement because accountants consider them to be a *distribution* of net income, rather than a *determinant* of net income.

Expense is a cost that helped an organization generate its revenue in a particular year or other accounting period. It is not necessarily equal to cash payments. A more precise definition is provided in Chapter 4.

Footnotes are an integral part of financial statements; they provide important details about the information appearing on the balance sheet, the income statement, the cash flow statement, and the retained earnings statement.

Income — also called net income, net earnings, earnings, profit, or net profit — is the excess of revenues over expenses for an accounting period. If revenues are less than expenses for the period, the organization is said to have incurred a loss.

Intangible assets are capital assets that lack physical substance but that are valuable to the company.

Inventory represents assets that an organization intends to sell as part of its everyday operating activities.

Liabilities are amounts of money owed to an organization's suppliers, employees, and all others supplying resources to the organization. A more formal definition will be introduced in Chapter 4.

Liquidity refers to an organization's ability to pay off its upcoming obligations.

Net book value refers to the amount derived by subtracting the accumulated depreciation of a capital asset (or group of capital assets) from the cost of that asset (or group of capital assets).

The operating cycle is the interval of time between the acquisition of inventory and the receipt of cash from the customers who purchase the products made from the inventory. Some organizations will have a very short operating cycle (for example, a fresh-produce vendor may have an operating cycle of one day or less); others will have a very long one (for example, a whisky distiller's operating cycle may be several years).

Prepaid expenses represent the actual, historic cost of current intangible assets that an organization has paid for but has not yet made use of, such as insurance premiums. Notice that even though the word "expense" appears as part of this term, the term itself refers to assets.

Replacement cost is a hypothetical number that represents an estimate of what it would cost to replace assets such as inventory or capital assets, as of a particular date (usually a particular balance sheet date).

Retained earnings is the cumulative net income that a company has recorded over the years since its inception, less the cumulative dividends that it has declared over the same time interval.

Revenue refers to the money amounts accounted for as sales of inventory, proceeds from services, and so on, in an accounting period. Revenues do not necessarily equal cash received. Revenue is a more general term than sales. A more formal definition is provided in Chapter 4.

Sales refers to the total proceeds (amounts receivable and received) from the selling of products or services during an accounting period.

Shareholders' equity is defined in *Terminology for Accountants* as "the interest of the shareholders in the net assets of a limited company." This definition refers to a slightly rearranged basic accounting equation:

Shareholders' equity = Assets – Liabilities

Short-term investments are the financial investments a company makes that can readily be turned into cash. More commonly called "marketable securities," they include investments in the common shares of large companies, such as Molson's, NOVA Corporation, and so on, which management intends to hold for relatively short periods of time, and which are easily sold.

FACT AND DESCRIPTION QUESTIONS

1. List and describe ten uses of accounting information, including at least five not mentioned in the chapter.
2. List and describe the subdisciplines of accounting.
3. Why is the preliminary definition of accounting given in the chapter unsatisfactory?
4. List and describe five different types of accounting assets.
5. List and describe five different types of accounting liabilities.
6. List and describe five different types of expenses for each of the following: a computer software developer; a printing company; an oil exploration company; a firm of architects; a telephone company providing both local and long-distance service; an automobile manufacturer.
7. Describe how each of the organizations in question 6 generates its revenues.
8. What is the current ratio? What might it be used for? Identify its strengths and weaknesses.
9. What is the quick ratio? What might it be used for?
10. What is the gross profit ratio? What might it be used for?

Questions for Analysis and Discussion

11. The owner of a chain of 20 retail computer stores located in larger towns and cities across Canada needs a variety of different types of information to run the business. Major business activities include deciding which makes of computers to carry, negotiating prices and purchasing computers from manufacturers, marketing and sales (which requires a very knowledgeable sales staff), and following up customer complaints. Sales are made on a "cash only" basis. Suggest, with reasons, the types of information the owner might require.
12. Nova Scotia Power Inc. generates, transmits, and distributes electricity in Nova Scotia. Its total revenues for the year ended December 31, 1994, were $715.6 million, compared with $709.1 million the previous year. The company's comparative balance sheets for the years ended December 31, 1994 and 1993, are provided here. Notice that like other utility companies engaged in the same activities, its balance sheet lists capital assets before current assets, and shareholders' equity before liabilities.

Required:

(a) Based on the information provided, list as many facts as you can about Nova Scotia Power Inc.

(b) What questions might your list in question (a) lead to?

Nova Scotia Power Inc.
Balance Sheet
As at December 31, 1994 and 1993 (as adapted)

millions of dollars	***1994***	*1993*
Assets		
Property, plant and equipment	**$2,255.2**	$1,807.1
Construction work in progress	**20.4**	456.9
	2,275.6	*2,264.0*
Current assets		
Cash	**0.1**	2.3
Accounts receivable	**78.9**	70.3
Unbilled revenue	**53.4**	50.4
Federal taxes receivable	**5.0**	28.2
Inventory	**74.9**	81.1
Prepaid expenses	**0.6**	1.9
	212.9	*234.2*
Deferred charges	**272.1**	180.8
	$2,760.6	*$2,679.0*
Shareholders' Equity and Liabilities		
Shareholders' equity		
Common		
Shares	**$ 653.4**	$ 650.7
Retained earnings	**152.2**	123.0
	805.6	*773.7*
Preferred shares	**200.0**	200.0
	1,005.6	*973.7*
Long-term debt	**1,101.2**	1,299.7
Current liabilities		
Debt due within one year	**511.3**	264.8
Accounts payable and accrued charges	**96.6**	88.7
Dividends payable	**3.0**	2.9
Income taxes payable	**4.7**	8.9
Accrued interest on long-term debt	**38.2**	40.3
	653.8	*405.6*
	$2,760.6	*$2,679.0*

13. Intrawest Corporation is a Vancouver-based resort company that is a leading developer of four-season destination mountain resorts. Its comparative balance sheets as at September 30, 1994 and 1993, are shown below.

Required:
Based on the information provided, critically assess Intrawest's activities for 1994.

Intrawest Corporation
Consolidated Balance Sheets
(as adapted)

As at September 30, 1994 and 1993	1994	1993
	(in thousands of dollars)	
Assets		
Cash and short-term deposits	$ 50,372	$ 61,886
Ski and resort operations	168,212	136,651
Properties	325,037	371,726
Amounts receivable	71,117	36,099
Other assets	14,264	8,330
	$629,002	$614,692
Liabilities		
Bank and other indebtedness	$300,629	$346,316
Amounts payable	47,695	34,277
Deferred revenue	8,609	5,025
Non-controlling interest in subsidiaries	6,530	12,594
	363,463	398,212
Shareholders' Equity		
Capital stock	195,973	158,374
Retained earnings	67,176	55,608
Foreign currency translation adjustment	2,390	2,498
	265,539	216,480
	$629,002	$614,692

With permission of Intrawest Corporation.

14. Financial statements from the early 1990s for T.C.C. Beverages Ltd., which uses the trade name "Coca-Cola Beverages" and is the largest bottler of soft drinks in Canada, are presented below. Based upon your examination of the statements, how well did Coca-Cola Beverages do?

T.C.C. Beverages Ltd.
Consolidated Statements of Income

Years Ended December 31

(THOUSANDS)	1991	1990
Net operating revenues	$1,012,024	$1,005,646
Cost of sales	538,717	556,379
Gross profit	473,307	449,267
Selling, administrative and general expenses	410,777	376,154
Operating income	62,530	73,113
Net interest expense	45,002	42,126
Amortization of goodwill and other intangibles	6,039	5,823
Other deductions	809	674
Income before income taxes	10,680	24,490
Income taxes	5,380	11,275
NET INCOME FOR THE YEAR	$ 5,300	$ 13,215
Preferred share dividends	4,938	4,938
Net income available to common shareholders	$ 362	$ 8,277
Earnings per common share	$ .01	$ .21

T.T.C. Beverages Ltd.
Consolidated Statements of Retained Earnings

Years Ended December 31

(THOUSANDS)	1991	1990
Balance at beginning of year	$ 37,288	$ 31,011
Net income for the year	5,300	13,215
Dividends - common shares	(2,001)	(2,000)
- preferred shares	(4,938)	(4,938)
Balance at end of year	$ 35,649	$ 37,288

T.T.C. Beverages
Consolidated Balance Sheets

December 31, (THOUSANDS)	1991	1990
ASSETS		
CURRENT ASSETS		
Cash	$ 6,318	$ 8,000
Trade accounts receivable	116,812	94,870
Inventories	60,371	56,409
Prepaid expenses and other assets	26,595	25,836
	210,096	185,115
PROPERTY, PLANT AND EQUIPMENT		
Land	28,238	27,425
Buildings and improvements	112,129	98,793
Machinery and equipment	412,650	381,929
Containers	59,605	57,821
	612,622	565,968
Less accumulated depreciation	(209,261)	(177,681)
	403,361	388,287
DEFERRED PENSION SURPLUS	6,080	2,453
GOODWILL AND OTHER INTANGIBLES	227,595	208,757
	$ 847,132	$ 784,612
LIABILITIES AND SHAREHOLDERS' EQUITY		
CURRENT LIABILITIES		
Accounts payable and accrued expenses	$ 126,324	$ 82,646
Due to related companies	1,466	7,662
Loans and notes payable	1,104	2,378
Taxes payable	9,737	6,988
Current portion of long-term debt	8,579	9,437
	147,210	109,111
LONG-TERM DEBT	336,362	299,941
DEFERRED INCOME TAXES	47,223	58,286
SHAREHOLDERS' EQUITY		
Share capital	280,688	279,986
Retained earnings	35,649	37,288
	316,337	317,274
	$ 847,132	$ 784,612

15. Comparative balance sheets for a hypothetical Australian company are presented below.

(a) Identify the differences between these balance sheets and "typical" Canadian company balance sheets.

(b) Do the Australian balance sheets follow the basic accounting equation?

(c) Is the company profitable?

Australian Metal Fabricators Pty.
Balance Sheets
As at December 31, 1994 and 1993
(in Australian $000,000s)

	1994	1993
Shareholders' equity		
Common shares	11.0	11.0
Retained earnings	35.6	31.3
Total	46.6	42.3
Represented by:		
Assets		
Current:		
Cash	1.6	0.8
Accounts receivable (net)	26.0	20.0
Inventory	34.0	33.6
Noncurrent:		
Property, plant, and equipment (net)	36.7	33.9
Investment in Newcastle Products Ltd	2.0	2.0
Intangible:		
Goodwill	2.0	3.0
	102.3	93.3
Less:		
Liabilities		
Current:		
Bank overdraft	7.7	5.0
Accounts payable	16.0	14.0
Income taxes payable	6.0	6.0
Current portion of long-term debt	2.0	2.0
Noncurrent:		
Long-term debt	14.0	16.0
Deferred Credits:		
Deferred income taxes	10.0	8.0
	55.7	51.0
Equals		
Net Assets	46.6	42.3

16. Micor Limited (ML) is a small Canadian company that manufactures inexpensive but good-quality furniture, mainly for the residential market. The company has established a niche in the Canadian domestic market by designing and developing modular furniture that enables consumers to enlarge tables, wall units, and so on, as the need arises. Recently, ML and Wuhan Industries of China have signed an agreement to form a company in which each will be a 50% partner. The new company is to be known as Micor Wuhan Furniture Industries, and will manufacture and distribute furniture (based on ML's unique designs) in the emerging Chinese urban market.

    Each partner will contribute cash to the new venture. ML designers and production engineers will be in charge of manufacturing for the first five years; managers from Wuhan Industries will be in charge of marketing and sales, and also have overall responsibility for Micor Wuhan Furniture Industries. The Canadian government has loaned the new venture a considerable amount of money.

    Assume that the agreement between the two partners specifies that each partner is to receive 50% of the new venture's net income each year. Identify the decisions that the partners will have to make about how net income is to be computed.

17. Explain what information is provided in each of the four financial statements published by Corel Corporation (see pages 9, 14, 19 and 20).

18. Comparative balance sheets for Pilot Insurance Company are presented below. Pilot is in the automotive and property insurance business.
    (a) Explain each item on the company's balance sheet.
    (b) Do you agree that the nature of items on a balance sheet, as well as their relative proportions, depends on the nature of the particular business? Explain.
    (c) Is Pilot doing well, based on the information provided here?

Pilot Insurance Company
Condensed Statement of Financial Position
December 31
($000s)

	1991	1990
ASSETS		
Cash	70	12,642
Investments (market value, 1991: $526,529; 1990: $466,166)	484,462	440,364
Net premiums in course of collection	57,172	50,844
Deferred policy acquisition expenses	32,981	31,074
Other assets	66,926	56,261
Total assets	641,611	591,185
LIABILITIES AND SHAREHOLDERS' EQUITY		
Provision for unpaid claims	287,402	266,320
Unearned premiums	159,766	153,665
Other liabilities	9,692	8,787
Total liabilities	456,860	428,772
Shareholders' equity	184,751	162,413
Total liabilities and shareholders' equity	641,611	591,185

19. This discussion question draws on the information about Devo Green and his company OI (provided on pages 22–29) of this chapter. Suppose you were the assistant manager at Devo's bank, and had just today (October 10, 1993) received the set of financial statements provided in Exhibit 1–6. What action would you take in connection with the demand loan you had made to OI? How would you justify your actions? Assume that you, as the officer of the bank branch who is responsible for approving or rejecting loan applications and deciding whether existing demand loans should be called in, are evaluated every six months by your superiors based on the "profits" you helped generate.

20. Prepare a brief summary of the article "Was Civilization Built on Clay Balls?" Explain why the Sumerians needed a system of accounting. Why is the research described in the article important to the accounting discipline?

TECHNICAL QUESTIONS

21. (a) Set up a spreadsheet similar to the one in Exhibit 1–5, either manually or using a spreadsheet program. Collect accounting information for the following business events for Spur Limited, a small business set up by Orin Hatch to sharpen knives.

    - Orin, a 20-year-old university student, deposited $1,000 in a newly opened bank account of Spur Limited, his new business venture, on May 1, 1996. He intended to purchase a used, wheel-mounted, manual knife-sharpening machine, and to make the rounds of the residential district where he lived, ringing a bell to gain the attention of homeowners.
    - May 2: Orin purchased the machine for $450 in cash, including sales tax of $35. He made repairs to the machine; parts and lubricants cost $50, which he paid for in cash, and he only needed to use about half of them.
    - May 3: His first day on the job, he received $120 for sharpening about 60 knives. He spent $5 on lunch.
    - May 4: The day started off well, with $85 taken before 11 a.m., but when he ran into an ice-cream shop (he just intended to slip in for a single-scoop vanilla), a car attempting to parallel park creamed the knife-sharpening machine, which he had left by the curb. After muttering something about "what the heck was that thing doing there, anyway," the driver gave Orin $100 "for his trouble," and drove off. Orin sat down on the curb and ate his ice cream (which had cost him $2, for two scoops), and marvelled at his good fortune. He had made a total of $183 today, and it wasn't even noon yet!
    - May 5: He spent all day repairing the machine, using the remaining parts that were left over from May 2.
    - May 6: Rained all day. He went to a movie, spending $10 on a ticket and snacks.
    - May 7: A great day, nice and sunny. Just the kind of day on which people would want their knives sharpened. He made $157, and didn't even have time for lunch!
    - May 8: With business booming, he hired Tom Montana, a 16-year-old acquaintance, as an assistant. Tom would be paid 20% of all the money he made sharpening knives, in cash at the end of each day. On this day, Orin spent all of his time lining up customers for next week, and Tom did $120 in business.

That evening, the two had an argument. Orin paid Tom $24, and told him to "@!??&##."

- May 9: Orin did $210 in business — a red-letter day!

(b) Assume that the knife-sharpening machine will last for 20 weeks, then be scrapped. Account for the impact of depreciation for the first week of Orin's business venture in your spreadsheet.
(c) Prepare an income statement and cash flow statement for the nine days ended May 9, 1996, and a balance sheet as of that same day.

22. Using equation 4 on page 22, show how the following business events are accounted for (each business event relates to a separate business):

Example: Jones Inc. purchases a used car for $1,500, paying $900 in cash and promising to pay the remainder in 60 days. The impact on equation 4 is:

CA_t	$+ LTA_t$	=	CL_t	$+ LTL_t$	$+ CAP_t$	$+ RE_s$	$+ R_p$	$- E_p$	$- D_p$
cash, -900	car, +1500		A/P, +600						

(a) Receives $2,500 on account, for a sale made last month.
(b) Issues a cheque for $75,000 to pay off a bank loan.
(c) Sells merchandise for $32,000 on credit; the merchandise had cost $20,000.
(d) Issues common shares for $10,500,000.
(e) Replaces a long-term loan payable of $15,000,000 with common shares of the same amount.
(f) Records the $1,000 interest on a bank loan, even though it's not due until tomorrow.
(g) Gives employees merchandise that had cost $20,000, in lieu of this month's wages.
(h) Purchases a new delivery truck for $20,000, paid in cash.
(i) Receives a cheque for $200,000, which represents a bank loan that has just been approved.
(j) Pays $23,500 for common shares of Apex Limited; two months later, learns that Apex Limited has gone out of business, and that there is no chance of recovering anything.
(k) Discovers oil on company-owned land; a geologist is paid a $9,000 fee (in cash) for her report that the oil, at current market prices, is worth $25,000,000 or so.

23. Since $RE_e = RE_s + R_p - E_p - D_p$, derive the missing quantity in the following independent situations:

(a) Retained earnings increased by $4,500,000 over the accounting period, and net income was $6,000,000. Derive dividends for the period.
(b) In the first year of a company's existence, expenses exceeded revenues by $100,000, and no dividends were declared. Common shares were issued for $2,000,000. Compute closing retained earnings.
(c) "Break even" is when revenues equal expenses for a company. For a break-even company, what is the maximum dividend if opening retained earnings are $350,000, and retained earnings must never go below that amount?
(d) In its first year of operations, Peabody Inc.'s net income was $500,000. Its net income increased by 30% for the next nine years (that is, the third year's net income was $1.3^2 \times 500{,}000$, or $845,000). The company's policy is to pay out dividends equal to 50% of its net income each year. If there are 100,000 common

shares outstanding, compute the per share dividend for each of the first ten years of the company's existence. Compute the earnings per share for each year, as well.

24. Prepare a balance sheet and an income statement for Fisher Limited, using the following information, for the year ended January 31, 1997. Begin by indicating which of the items belong on the balance sheet and which belong on the income statement.

Advertising expense	$420,000
Cash	135,000
Prepaid insurance	72,500
Revenues	5,575,000
Retained earnings, 31/01/97	?
Retained earnings, 31/01/96	1,910,000
Accumulated depreciation	997,500
Accounts payable	610,200
Accounts receivable	825,000
Loan payable	1,900,000
Common shares	125,000
Cost of sales	2,090,000
Dividends	?
Salaries expense	1,629,000
Salaries payable	100,900
Machinery	1,400,000
Building	2,000,900
Land	575,000
Prepaid office supplies	19,500
Inventory	890,000
Interest payable	35,500
Interest expense	190,000
Deferred revenue	210,000
Income tax expense	95,250
Income tax payable	100,000
Administration expense	565,000
Research expense	300,500
Depreciation expense	190,000

25. **"On Ice" Revisited.** This question continues the On Ice story that was introduced in the chapter. Recall that Devo Green had prepared financial statements for the period ended September 30, 1993. Three more months have now passed; please account for the following events that occurred in October, November, and December 1993 by setting up a spreadsheet similar to the one in the chapter. Of course, as of October 1, 1993, there will be opening balances in the categories on OI's balance sheet.

Then, using the data in your completed spreadsheet, prepare the four financial statements for OI for the three months ended December 31, 1993. Assume that you are doing the accounting in early 1994.

(a) October 1 to 4, 1993: An elated but exhausted Devo Green celebrated the sell-out of the first issue of On Ice by taking four days off and renting a cabin in a remote area of Vancouver Island. Total cost of the trip was $635, including just $15 for meals (Devo was an avid angler, and caught most of his meals).

(b) Back in Vancouver on October 5, Devo was relieved that all of the rink owners, except one, had remitted their cheques by mail for the first issue of the magazine. The cheques totalled $10,850. The one "deadbeat" would declare bankruptcy on November 5, still owing Devo $1,150.

(c) Devo decided to have 10,000 copies printed for the magazine's second issue.

On October 15, he negotiated the following arrangements with the printer:

- A $5,000 deposit would be required on October 15.
- Final copy would be provided to the printer no later than November 20; a final payment of $8,000 was due on that date.
- The $13,000 total included all sales taxes.
- The magazines were to be picked up by Devo on November 25.

Everything unfolded as planned, except that when Devo picked the magazines up on November 25, he dropped a bundle of 50 in the mud, which rendered them unsaleable.

(d) Devo made the following payments during the October to December period:

- October 5: paid lawyer $575.
- October 8: paid $500 on computer.
- Paid rent of $1,500 on the sixteenth of each of the three months.
- October 17, November 1, and December 1: paid loan interest on each of these dates.
- October 20, November 1, and December 1: paid telephone bills of $125 on each of these dates.
- October 20, November 20, and December 20: issued salary cheques to himself, for $1,000 on each of the first two days, and for $1,500 on the third day.
- December 20: issued five cheques totalling $3,500 to five writers who had prepared material for OI; actually, six writers had written articles for the second issue of OI, but the sixth writer's article was rescheduled for issue #3 (to be published in February), and she agreed not to demand payment until then.

(e) Devo received the following cheques:

- October 12: $1,200 from *Maclean's*, for an article Devo wrote in August 1993.
- October 15: $2,000 from the major manufacturer of hockey sticks that had purchased ad space in the first issue; the same company took ad space in the second issue as well.
- October 16: $1,950 from the regional hockey rink for ad space in the first issue of OI.
- October 20: $3,000 from the major skate manufacturer, for an ad that appeared in issue #1. The skate manufacturer also ordered an ad to be run in the second issue, for $3,500.
- November 15: five cheques, totalling $7,000, for the total agreed-upon price for five ads to be run in the second issue. The ads were placed by area sports stores and restaurants.
- December 20: a $1,000 cheque from a financial consultant who wanted to place an ad in issue #2.

(f) Devo's banker agreed to an arrangement by which OI would have automatic approval to borrow money in order to maintain a minimum cash balance of $1,000. This arrangement is to be reviewed every six months.
(g) The magazine was published and distributed according to plan. Between 5 p.m. and 7 p.m. on December 31, 1993, all the rink owners telephoned Devo to report on magazine sales. Devo summarized the results of these calls as follows:

	Number	Dollar Value
Magazines available for sale	9,950	$19,900
Magazines reported sold	9,100	18,200
Magazines reported stolen*	100	200
	9,200	18,400
Unsold magazines	750	$ 1,500

* Apparently, two bundles were stolen at one location.

CASE

Family Shoes

This case focuses on how accounting information, in the form of a balance sheet and income statement, may be used by an individual to help make an important personal decision, as long as the information is used *in context*. The individual's objectives and constraints are central in the case. Cash flow information, as derived from the income statement and balance sheet, is a key element in the analysis.

Mitch was the regional sales manager for a plastics fabricating company, ECH Ltd., that specialized in manufacturing and distributing coffee cups, plates, and similar products. At the time of this case (1994), Mitch was in his early thirties, was married to Susie, had two young children, and had been with ECH for about four years. Early one morning in March, Mitch called on his friend Bob, who had a small accounting practice. Their conversation was as follows:

BOB Hi Mitch, how's the family? What brings you out of bed so early on a Sunday?

MITCH Bob, listen, I really appreciate your seeing me so early. It's about a deal that Sandy Proper and I are thinking of going into. You know that I've always wanted my own business. Well, Sandy's father is going to sell his shoe store, and I figure that since I had three or four years selling shoes before I got married, maybe this store could be what I'm looking for.

BOB Where does Sandy fit in?

MITCH Well, Sandy and I would go in as partners. Sandy would keep his job, and work in the store one or two days a week and I would run the store along with the full-time person there now and draw a salary. We'd split any profit left over at the end of the year. Sandy's father doesn't draw any salary from the business now.

BOB So you would each put up half the investment?

MITCH That's right. Sandy's father doesn't want anything for the name, just the stock — you know, the shoe inventory, and some office and display furniture. About 41,000 to 42,000 dollars all together.

BOB Sounds interesting. Is the location OK?

MITCH Oh yeah. Floor space is about 90 square metres, and it's right at

Burton and Main. He's been at that location for years, and he's got another year to run on his seven-year lease. The stock's fine, too — Sandy's father let me look it over last week. Here's the financial statements for the store, Bob [see exhibit]. What do you think? Frankly, I'm tired of working for somebody else. Here I am, thirty-three years old, earning about 25,000 dollars a year in commissions after expenses, and what have Susie and I got? She has to work part-time to help pay the rent, *and* take care of the kids! I want a situation I can control, to try to get ahead of the game for once!

Required:

Adopt the role of Bob. How would you advise Mitch? (Note: In Canada, the net income of unincorporated businesses is not subject to income taxes; that is why no income tax expense appears on Family Shoes' income statement. The Income Tax Act requires that the owners of such businesses add their share of the net income to their personal income for tax purposes, whether or not they have actually withdrawn the funds.)

EXHIBIT
FINANCIAL STATEMENTS OF FAMILY SHOES
Balance Sheets

	January 31	
	1994	1993
Current assets:		
Cash on hand and in bank	$ 2,195	$ 3,220
Inventory, lower of cost or net realizable value	38,790	44,310
	40,985	47,530
Capital assets, at cost:		
Furniture, fixtures, and office equipment	4,290	4,290
Accumulated depreciation	(3,975)	(3,760)
	315	530
	$41,300	$48,060
Current liabilities:		
Accounts payable and accrued charges	$ 4,310	$ 2,175
Note payable	—	2,175
Proprietor's equity:		
Capital, S.O. Proper	36,990	43,710
	$41,300	$48,060

INCOME STATEMENTS

	Year Ended January 31	
	1994	1993
Sales (net of returns)	$152,890	$137,235
Cost of sales:		
Opening inventory	44,310	40,705
Purchases	75,420	74,809
Closing inventory	(38,790)	(44,310)
	80,940	71,204
Gross margin	71,950	66,031
Wages	21,260	19,741
Payroll costs	2,109	1,910
Accounting	200	175
Express and cartage	1,400	1,247
Advertising and display	2,775	2,310
Depreciation	215	215
Travel	525	390
Credit card discounts	790	645
Lighting	1,042	977
Telephone and fax	1,910	1,670
Wrapping and packaging	2,470	2,095
Rent	3,600	3,600
	38,296	34,975
Net income	33,654	31,056
Capital, February 1	43,710	43,210
	77,364	74,266
Drawings	(40,374)	(30,556)
Capital, January 31	$36,990	$43,710

CHAPTER 2 *two*

Why Accounting Is Important: Some Basic Ideas About Accounting

Learning OBJECTIVES

After you have read, thought about, and discussed this chapter, and completed a selection from the end-of-chapter material, you will have made significant progress in achieving the following learning objectives:

- Be able to define accounting in three ways, with the different definitions emphasizing different aspects of accounting.
- Explain the importance of accountability, and how it involves accounting.
- Describe how the accounting entity is chosen in different situations, and the importance of making careful choices.
- List and describe the different legal forms of business organization, such as proprietorships, partnerships, and corporations.
- Explain the significance of the user orientation in accounting, and list a variety of potential users of accounting information.
- Be able to explain the concept of substance over form, and apply it in a variety of accounting situations.
- Describe the net present value criterion, and be able to perform simple net present value calculations.
- Explain the significance of classification in accounting.
- Explain why a concern for ethical behaviour should be a pervasive aspect of decision-making in accounting.
- Understand that accountability, the concept of the accounting entity, the user orientation, substance over form, the net present value criterion, classification, and ethics are impor-

tant concepts not only for financial accounting, but in other subdisciplines of accounting as well.

- Be able to describe the general structure of the Canadian accounting profession, the three groups that make up the accounting profession in Canada, and the evolution of the accounting stereotype.

A decade ago, studies ... generally offered a conventional portrait of the accountant's personality that conformed with the historical stereotype ... conservative, conscientious, ... practical thinkers, ... [they] prefer to work with clear and well-defined instructions. Recent studies, however, are discovering that accountants and auditors have much stronger personalities ... For starters, accountants tend to be more assertive, independent-minded, unconventional, cheerful, enthusiastic, rebellious, experimenting, liberal, self-sufficient ... These findings contrast sharply with the conventional personality reported [for accountants] just ten years earlier.

Ronald A. Davidson, Simon Fraser University[1]

Grayson was a long stooped yellow-faced man with high shoulders, bristly eyebrows and almost no chin. The upper part of his face meant business. The lower part was just saying goodbye. He wore bifocals ... He was a CPA and looked it every inch. He even had ink on his fingers and there were four pencils in the pocket of his open vest.

Raymond Chandler[2]

INTRODUCTION

The purpose of this chapter is to further develop your understanding of accounting, its context, and those who are involved in its practice. We begin this chapter by refining the definition of accounting. We then introduce seven sets of ideas that are central to most areas of accounting, but especially to financial accounting. A demonstration case, "Gord and James," is presented that ties together the concepts introduced in the chapter. The chapter concludes with a description of the various professions that practise accounting; here we also consider some aspects of the "accounting stereotype" alluded to in this chapter's opening quotations.

---

[1] Davidson, "Straw Accountants — New research suggests that CAs no longer fit their traditional stereotype," *CAmagazine*, September 1991, pp. 43–47.

[2] Raymond Chandler, *The Lady in the Lake* (New York: Pocket Books, 1966), p. 118.

Accounting Definitions Revisited

The definition of accounting that began Chapter 1 was very narrow, and failed to capture the importance and pervasiveness of accounting suggested by that chapter's examples and discussion. A very succinct definition that highlights some the essential characteristics of accounting was published back in 1966 by the American Accounting Association (AAA), an organization whose membership consists mainly of accounting educators. It says that accounting is

the process of identifying, measuring, and communicating economic information to permit informed judgments and decisions by users of the information.[3]

Let's briefly examine the key parts of this definition: It begins by calling accounting a "process"; this word emphasizes that things like financial statements (which are the outputs of the process) are the result of a whole series of steps. The AAA definition labels these steps "identifying," "measuring," and "communicating" something called "economic information."

"Identifying" suggests that accounting systems must have some rules for deciding what types of information to include and what types to exclude. Financial accounting, management accounting, tax accounting, and other accounting subdisciplines have developed such rules — for example, all accounting disciplines admit economic information resulting from transactions between an organization and other organizations. The accounting for On Ice Incorporated in Chapter 1 was based almost entirely on information from transactions. However, other economic information was also included, such as information about depreciation. Accounting for depreciation in the On Ice case was triggered not by transactions but rather by the passage of time — as the months went by, Devo Green had to account for the cost of using the computer in his business.

"Measuring" requires that accountants assign labels (or words having an agreed-upon meaning) to the numbers. Measuring systems may be of four broad types: nominal, ordinal, interval, and ratio. A *nominal* measuring system simply assigns labels to different categories of things, in order to highlight important differences between the members of each category for some specific purpose. For example, our society usually distinguishes "adult" from "child" when it comes to important activities requiring experience, such as driving a car. In accounting, we saw an example of a nominal measuring system in Chapter 1, when current assets were distinguished from noncurrent assets. Recall that accountants believe that such a distinction provides useful information to users of financial statements.

Ordinal measurements involve the assignment of (usually) numbers to things, to signify some sort of hierarchy. For example, standing in downtown Winnipeg is a lot colder when it's -30°C than when it's +20°C. Here we use temperature to signify a hierarchy of coldness or warmness. Recall from Chapter 1 that the current assets in Corel Corporation's balance sheet were listed in order of apparent liquidity — an example of an ordinal measurement.

Interval measures are like those on a metre-stick: the interval between (say) the 10 cm mark and the 19 cm mark is the same as the one between the (say) 21 cm and 30 cm marks. In other words, an interval of 9 cm means the same thing wherever you measure it on the scale. The metre stick also is a *ratio* measuring

[3] American Accounting Association, *A Statement of Basic Accounting Theory* (Evanston, Illinois, 1966), p. 1.

scale, because the ratio of (say) 20 cm to 10 cm is 2 to 1; there are twice as many 1 cm segments in 20 cm as there are in 10 cm. In accounting, if Company A has $75,000 in cash on hand and Company B has $150,000, we may assert that Company B has twice as much cash as A. We have to be careful when we treat the numbers that accounting systems assign to things like assets, liabilities, and so on as interval or ratio measures: sometimes they are (as in the case of the cash in the example above for companies A and B), but sometimes they aren't. More on this later in the book.

"Communicating" involves ensuring that the identified and measured information is transmitted clearly and effectively to those who wish to use it. Accountants have developed financial statements as one of the means of communication. But it is important to note that means of communicating are dynamic, and change must be expected. Computing technology costs less each year, so it is quite possible that very soon, those who wish information about an organization will be able to bypass the periodic financial statements entirely, and extract the information they want from a corporate database that is accessible to the public. In the On Ice example in Chapter 1, Devo Green could have permitted the banker to tap into his spreadsheet at any time as events were unfolding (this assumes that Devo accounted for events on a daily basis). For now, however, we can be certain that the four financial statements that were introduced in Chapter 1 will continue to be an important part of financial accounting.[4]

"To permit informed judgments and decisions by the users of the information" is the last part of the AAA definition of accounting. This phrase emphasizes that accounting information is intended to help people make better judgments and decisions, so ideally, the information should be tailored to the types of decisions that must be made. This doesn't always happen, for reasons that we will discuss in detail later on. Keep in mind that the ability to control the flow of information, and to decide on the types of accounting rules to be used, confers great power on decision makers. There may be a host of competing pressures relating to how information is to be prepared, how it is to be disclosed, and who should see it.

Accounting and Business Decision A

Here's another definition of accounting. This one was prepared by the CICA,[5] an important professional accounting group:

> *The process of classifying and recording transactions of an individual or organization, in terms of money or some other unit of measurement, in the books of account, and of summarizing, reporting and interpreting the results thereof.*

Compare and contrast this definition with the AAA definition. Which one, in your opinion, is better? Why? Both definitions stress aspects of accounting. The AAA definition is broader, and emphasizes that accounting is an information system. The CICA definition emphasizes the more technical aspects of accounting. Perhaps the two perspectives complement each other.

[4] Indeed, even if society decides on a widespread conversion to a database approach to financial reporting, many people argue that there will still be a demand for measures such as "income" and "cash flow," and for many other accounting-based numbers.

[5] CICA, *Terminology for Accountants*, 4th Edition, 1992, p. 3.

Seven Key Sets of Ideas for Accounting

We now introduce seven very important ideas that are common to most areas of the accounting discipline. One of the goals of this book is to show how accounting can be seen as consisting of the several subdisciplines that were mentioned in Chapter 1. To this end, it will be helpful to focus on some basic ideas that are found in most of these areas.

1. Accountability in Organizations and Society

The root of the word *accounting* is, of course, the word *account*, and both are related to the word *accountability*. All three are based on the notion of one party, the *accountor*, "giving an account" of something to another party, the *accountee*. Indeed, the importance of the word *account* to the field of accounting is even clearer when we note that much of the raw information used to prepare financial statements is stored (usually in a computer) in categories ("capital assets," "inventory," and so on) that are themselves called *accounts*.

Accounting information is often used to give an account of the actions of one individual to another, and to discharge any obligations of accountability between the two. Thus, *accountability* is a central idea in the discipline of accounting. Two accounting professors, Joni Young and Orace Johnson, describe the idea as follows:[6]

> *What is accountability? Accountability, as defined here, denotes the responsibility of one party ... to undertake only specific, allowable acts on behalf of another party ... The parties can be individuals, small groups, political coalitions, business firms, government departments, etc. Implicit in the notion of accountability are two elements — accountable* for *specific, allowable actions; and accountable* to *a specific party.*

How might accounting information be involved in accountability, in a practical sense? The answer is that accountants help individuals and organizations discharge their accountability by providing specific types of information and also by helping to specify the approach that should be used in preparing the information. For example, a sales manager may require subordinates to submit reports at the end of each month, indicating whether they have achieved their sales targets for their various product lines. The sales targets and the reports represent a type of budgetary control — the subordinates are held accountable for achieving the targets. The sales manager relies on the company's accountants to develop procedures for designing the reports. The accountants establish rules, which are used to indicate when a sale may be counted in the monthly report: Should it be when a customer makes an order? When the product is put on the transport company's delivery truck? When the product is received by the customer? When the customer remits payment? When the warranty period expires?

Taxpayers discharge their accountability to Revenue Canada by accurately completing and submitting an income tax return. Companies discharge their accountability to their shareholders in part by providing them with audited financial statements that comply with "generally accepted accounting principles" — GAAP for short.

[6] Young and Johnson, "On the Logical Foundation for Self-Regulation: Rules, Corporations and Financial Accounting," *Research in Accounting Regulation*, Vol. 3, 1989, pp. 133–151.

Accountability is a central feature of our society. We demand it from politicians, governments, businesses, charities, teachers, subordinates, superiors, partners, and many other institutions and individuals. And, of course, almost everyone demands some form of accountability from us. One of the three major Canadian professional accounting organizations, the Society of Management Accountants of Canada (SMAC), felt that accountability was such an important concept that it published a special "Statement on Accountability." The statement had some interesting things to say about the accountability of managers, and how accounting could help provide information about the extent to which managers were discharging that accountability. Some excerpts:

Management is responsible for effectively managing resources to ensure both the short and long term viability of the enterprise.

Management accountability is the obligation of management to answer for the discharge of that responsibility.

Management can fulfill that obligation by providing relevant information on performance to meet the requirements of managers, the board, stakeholders, governing bodies, and the public, as required by law, agreement, custom, and evolving expectations ... Profitability is only one attribute that is used to evaluate the success of an enterprise. Stakeholders need management assertions on other attributes such as strategic direction, market ... The Society expects its members to meet the challenge of providing the information that management needs to respond to the increasing pressures for accountability.[7]

The SMAC suggests that accounting information is one of the important types of information that managers need to discharge their accountability to others. We saw this in the On Ice example in Chapter 1: Devo Green agreed to provide the bank with the financial statements of OI every three months. From Chapter 1 also, Corel Corporation's accountability to its shareholders was partly discharged through the set of financial statements it sent to them. Whether financial statements (or indeed any accounting information) are really an effective means of complying with legal, contractual, or customary accountability requirements depends to a large extent on how easily the recipients can use the information provided in them. It also depends on the ethical integrity of the managers and others involved in producing the information. We will see this in the Gord and James case at the end of this chapter.

2. The Focus of Accounting: The Accounting Entity

Another important idea is the concept of the "accounting entity." The entity is the focus of the accounting; it is the individual, group, or organization that is being accounted for. For example, the organization known as the Toronto Maple Leafs might qualify as an accounting entity, for which financial statements would therefore be prepared. The idea seems simple enough, but is somewhat subtle. In the case of the Maple Leafs, the corporation that owns the hockey team also owns Maple Leaf Gardens, a valuable building and land in downtown Toronto. Should the accounting entity be defined as the entire corporation, with its two types of businesses (hockey operations and real estate operations)? Or should each business be considered a separate accounting entity? For some purposes, such questions are resolved by the requirements of particular laws; for other purposes, it is basically a matter of what makes the most sense for the user.

[7] The Society of Management Accountants of Canada, *Statement on Accountability*, Hamilton, Ontario, 1988.

The laws governing corporations in Canada specify that the legal corporation and its subsidiaries (that is, the other corporations it owns) must be accounted for as a single, large accounting entity for the purposes of preparing whatever financial statements the federal and provincial companies acts require. (GAAP also requires this approach.) Therefore, when preparing financial statements to discharge its accountability under the provincial Corporation Act, Maple Leaf Gardens' top management *must* base its definition of the accounting entity on its total corporate activities — the team *and* the real estate operation. The rationale for this approach is that even though there may be many corporations involved, they all operate under a single, unified leadership, and thus they do not act independently of one another. The Income Tax Act, on the other hand, requires each individual corporation within a multicorporate group to file its own, separate corporate tax return. So, for a given organization, the accounting entity for income tax purposes may be different from the accounting entity for financial accounting purposes.

Top management at the Gardens is naturally interested in the risks, results of operations, and financial position of each of its businesses separately, since hockey and real estate, as businesses, have quite different characteristics (the Maple Leafs always fill the arena, win or lose; but the commercial real estate market in Toronto in the early 1990s was not doing well). It follows that for internal, or management accounting, purposes, top management may define *two* accounting entities, and collect information on each separately. In this way, the same organization can be divided into different accounting entities for different purposes.

This example suggests that the concept of the accounting entity must be approached with some care. In situations where laws specify the entity to be used, management and other users of accounting information have relatively little discretion in defining the accounting entity. In other situations, management must carefully designate which accounting entities they believe will enable them to run the business effectively.

Just what an accounting entity should include is subject to dispute. And these disputes arise in the not-for-profit sector of the economy as well as in the for-profit sector. Recall from Chapter 1 that the Auditor General felt that the accounting entity representing the federal government should include Crown corporations; the people responsible for the design of the government's financial statements apparently did not agree. The AG's contention was that when the federal government excluded Crown corporations such as Petro-Canada from its financial statements, taxpayers and other users of those statements were misled about the scope of the government's activities. While a disagreement of this kind may seem at first rather abstract, remember that the consequences to Canadian taxpayers and others may be quite important: a poorly defined accounting entity can lead to poor decisions by users of the accounting information, such as Members of Parliament. An example, on a more human scale, of the importance of carefully defining the accounting entity involved the Tarascan Indians of Mexico.[8] A social anthropologist lived for a time among the Tarascans in order to observe their economic behaviour, and noticed that even though they were excellent entrepreneurs in other respects, many of them switched from apparently profitable businesses to businesses that had very poor prospects, and quickly thereafter went bankrupt. The anthropologist attributed this curious behaviour to the fact that the Tarascan

[8] James M. Acheson, "Accounting Concepts and Economic Opportunities in a Tarascan Village: Emic and Etic Views," *Human Organization*, vol. 31, no. 1, pp. 83–91, 1972.

entrepreneurs were unable to evaluate the potential profitability of a business in a fair manner, because of the way the business's financial statements were prepared. A basic problem, he concluded, lay in the fact that the current owners of the business were preparing financial statements based on a concept of an accounting entity that combined the personal and family activities of the owner with that of the business. Since most businesses were small and family-run, the work provided "free" by the owner, his wife, and his children was not accounted for. Such businesses appeared much more profitable than would have been the case *had the accounting entity been redefined to focus only on the business operation*. In other words, if the business had had to pay the prevailing local wage rates, the so-called profits would have disappeared. By viewing a business separately on its own account, and estimating what its profits would have been had it had to pay for its labour, the Tarascan entrepreneurs might have made better decisions for themselves, and possibly better decisions for their entire community.

The Tarascans operate small businesses. Many small businesses are not set up under legislation (that is, they are not incorporated under companies acts), but instead are operated as either proprietorships or partnerships. Maple Leaf Gardens, on the other hand, is a corporation.

A *proprietorship* is a business that is owned (and often managed) by a single individual who has provided the financial resources; Devo Green from the Chapter 1 example could have set up OI as a proprietorship. From the law's perspective, such a business is not distinguished from the other activities of the owner. For example, if the business is behind in paying its bills, the creditors have the right to lodge a legal action against the owner's nonbusiness assets. The owner thus has unlimited liability for the business's debts. The owner and the business are one *legal* entity. Whether or not they are one accounting entity depends on the situation and on the owner's (and other information users') needs.

If, for example, a business owner wished to borrow money to finance an expansion of her business, she would prepare accounting information to present to the bank that was based upon the *business* as the accounting entity. In this way, the loan officer at the bank could estimate the soundness of the business venture itself. The owner's equity section for a proprietorship differs from that for a corporation. Recall from Chapter 1 that OI's owner's equity section looked like this:

Owner's Equity	
Common stock	$10,000
Retained earnings	652
	$10,652

If OI had been a proprietorship, it would have looked like this:

Devo Green, capital	$10,652

One reason for the difference in the accounting is that the corporation, under law, has to be careful not to let its total owner's equity go below the original amount invested in the business — $10,000 in OI's case. This requirement prevents dividends from being paid out of the invested capital.

Alternatively, if the owner wished to determine what her personal balance sheet was like (perhaps for a marriage contract), she would view all her personal assets and liabilities, plus the business's assets and liabilities, as making up one accounting entity.

A *partnership*, like a proprietorship, is also not incorporated, but since misunderstandings or disputes can develop, the owner–partners should really formalize their relationship by having a lawyer assist them in preparing a legal contract, called a partnership agreement. Such an agreement usually specifies the duties of each partner in the business, how the net income of the business is to be divided among the partners, and what will happen if one or more partners wish to leave the business. For situations where disputes among partners arise and there is no partnership agreement (a situation that prudent partners would have avoided), there are partnership acts that set out some general legal principles, such as how the assets of a partnership are to be divided if the business is to be dissolved.

If Devo Green's OI were a partnership — consisting, say, of Devo and his friend Jim Blue — the owners' equity section of the balance sheet would look like this, if they each contributed one-half of the original $10,000 and shared equally in the net income:

Partners' Equity	
Devo Green	$ 5,326
Jim Blue	5,326
	$10,652

A *corporation*, unlike a proprietorship or a partnership, is a distinct legal entity that exists until it is dissolved by law. A corporation has a legal existence of its own, separate from its owners, and can own property, owe debts, and be sued or sue other parties. Organizations that operate as corporations usually have a word such as "Incorporated," "Corporation," "Limited," or abbreviations for those terms as part of their formal name. People obtain ownership in a corporation by acquiring *shares* of the corporation. Devo Green acquired 10,000 shares of OI by investing $10,000 in the company. The per share price was $1. If Devo subsequently sold 1,000 of his shares to someone else — say, for $3.00 each — the balance sheet of OI would not be affected, since the transaction would have been between Devo as an accounting entity and the other person as an accounting entity, and OI would not have been involved.

Refer back to Corel's balance sheet on page 9 in Chapter 1. Notice that on page 13 the shares are referred to as "common shares." Owners of common shares can vote (in proportion to the number of shares they hold) on important events that affect the corporation — for example, to elect members of the most senior management group in the corporation, the board of directors. Common share owners are often called the "residual owners": they enjoy the prospect of watching their shares increase in value; however, when the corporation is in serious financial trouble they are the last ones to get their money out (and as sometimes happens, they may get just pennies on the dollar). In addition, common shareholders have no guarantee of receiving a dividend. Many corporations have other categories of share capital. These other categories are often referred to as "preferred shares." Holders of preferred shares have different rights than the common shareholders. Typically, they have a right to receive a dividend before common shareholders do; but typically as well, they do not have the right to vote at shareholder meetings.

Deciding whether to set up a corporation or to operate a small business as a proprietorship or a partnership involves considering various trade-offs. Some of the advantages and disadvantages of each legal form of business organization are set out in Exhibit 2–1.

EXHIBIT 2–1
SOME ADVANTAGES AND DISADVANTAGES OF CHOOSING VARIOUS BUSINESS FORMS

Form of Business Organization	Advantages	Disadvantages
Proprietorship	Low start-up costs Owner in control Minimal regulations	Unlimited personal liability May be hard to raise money All responsibilities fall on single owner's shoulders Business may terminate when owner leaves
Partnership	Low start-up costs More owners means more money to invest in business More ideas and energy than a single owner Minimal regulations	Unlimited liability Are partners suitable? Business still has no continuous legal life Need a contract to resolve potential conflicts
Corporation	Limited legal liability Ownership is transferable (shares may be sold) Continuous existence	Many legal regulations Legal and accounting costs High degree of regulation

Accounting and Business Decision B

In early 1994, two lifelong friends named Leanne and Margo decided to purchase a lovely old brick house in Cape Breton, with the intent of establishing a bed-and-breakfast operation. Help them decide on the legal form of business that would be best for them. Also, suggest what information they would need to run the business, and whether financial statements might be useful to them.

3. The User Orientation of Accounting

The accountability concept suggests that accounting information should be designed with the needs of the *user* (that is, the party to whom one is accountable) firmly in mind. The AAA definition of accounting analysed at the start of this chapter said that accounting is intended "to permit informed judgments and decisions by users of the information." This seemingly straightforward idea is actually fairly new to accounting, partly because at one time other considerations were often presumed to be more important. For instance, many accountants believe that more objective (but less user-relevant) information should be included in accounting statements, as opposed to less objective (but more user-relevant) information. An example of this phenomenon is that in financial statements prepared in accordance with GAAP, tangible capital assets such as buildings and machinery are accounted for based upon their original cost to the company (the asset's "historic cost"), rather than on the basis of their current value. Specifically, the *CICA Handbook*, which contains much of GAAP in Canada, says in section 3060 that "a capital asset should be recorded at cost," by which is meant the asset's historic, actual cost.

Current value information is probably more useful to shareholders and other users of the company's financial statements. After all, current value may be a quite accurate representation of what the building or machine would cost to replace at the present time, while the historic cost may be many years out of date. The historic cost is, however, more objective, in the sense that an actual, real transaction occurred (albeit perhaps some time ago) when the item was acquired, and therefore evidence in the form of invoices and cancelled cheques exists to objectively verify the event and the resulting historic cost. The current value number is more hypothetical, since it represents a transaction that has *not* happened. Thus, it is less objective. Some critics argue that the present practice suits auditors (who really do need to have considerable objective evidence) more than it suits the users of the accounting statements, who are left with old, irrelevant information. However, this criticism ignores the value of objective information from the user's perspective.

Even though many areas in accounting still emphasize objectivity over relevance, there has been considerable movement toward adopting more user-oriented practices, and providing users with information more relevant to their decision-making needs. This trend is most apparent in those areas of accounting that are not governed by laws or by the threat of lawsuits. In preparing accounting information for use by internal management, for example, current value may be used because it is more relevant for management decisions. However, a company's tax returns cannot account for the company's capital assets using current values, because the regulations to the Income Tax Act specify that historic cost must be used. Governments prefer to base their tax assessments on objectively verifiable accounting information.

The idea that accounting should provide users with information relevant to their decision-making needs becomes somewhat complicated in the case of financial accounting. There are different types of users, and they may have conflicting ideas of what they want from financial accounting information. Users of financial accounting information in any given situation could potentially include the groups discussed below.

Owners

Owners may be proprietors or partners of small businesses, or partners in relatively large businesses (such as accounting practices or law firms), or shareholders in corporations. Companies, pension funds, and other organizations may also own corporate shares. All these types of owners need information on the performance of the business in which they have an ownership interest. Often in the case of corporations and large partnerships, the owners are not the same people as the managers, and will want to know whether the resources they have invested are being used properly. Examples of information that may be desired by owners include trends in net income, cash flows, important ratios, and so forth. The sources from which owners could obtain such information would include the following:

- Financial statements.
- Detailed information behind the statements, if available.
- Direct observation of business activities (especially for small proprietorships).

Potential owners

Accounting information may provide useful insights for people considering buying a business or common or other shares in a corporation. This requires, of course, that the accounting information (usually in the form of financial statements) be prepared in a reasonable manner. Recall the Tarascans: for them, the accounting entity was not defined appropriately; as a result, potential owners were misled into investing in poor business ventures.

Sources of information for investment decisions include the following:

- Financial statements.
- Advice from advisers, such as financial information intermediaries (see below).

Creditors

Creditors lend money to an organization. Usually, the loans are for a specified period of time (the "term") and are governed by a contractual arrangement. Creditors receive interest payments as well as the return of the amount they loaned (the principal). The principal may be returned either at the end of the term or bit by bit over the term. Creditors are interested in the safety of their loan (which, from their perspective, is an investment), and therefore are interested in the security (or collateral) the borrowing company offers. Collateral represents evidence that the borrower can indeed meet the periodic interest payments (which may be every month) and repay the principal. It may consist of the borrowing company's assets, such as land or inventory, information about which appears on the balance sheet. In the event that the borrower defaults on the loan (that is, fails to pay), the collateral may be seized by the creditor.

Information sources for creditors include the following:

- Balance sheets, including details of the assets used for collateral.
- Cash flow statements and forecasts.
- Income statements.

Suppliers

The suppliers of goods or services to an organization often have a considerable interest in its operations. Suppliers are concerned with the continuity of the relationship as well as with receiving the agreed-upon prices for the goods and services they have supplied. For many companies, suppliers are also the main creditors.

Employees

Employees who work for an organization are interested in receiving their fair share of the resources of the organization and in ensuring that they have secure and continuous employment. In the 1990s, full-time, long-term jobs are less plentiful than they were in the four previous decades. As a result, many people who would have earlier been employees in organizations now find themselves in the role of short- or long-term contract suppliers. In such a role, they will have perhaps an even greater interest in the financial viability of the organization, especially when it comes to being assured that the terms of their contract will be fulfilled; therefore, they will be vitally interested in the financial statements of their employer organization. Also, if the employees belong to a pension plan sponsored by the employer, the financial statements of the pension plan will be of great interest.

Unions

By law, if unions represent some or all of the employees of a company, the company must negotiate the terms and conditions of employment with the union. In other words, the union is the legal representative of the employees in all employment-related matters. Therefore, unions are interested in the ability of the employing organization to pay a wage or salary increase, the company's continuing viability, and the details of the costs of various benefits, such as pension plans and health care. One complication for unions as users of accounting information is that published financial accounting statements are almost always prepared for the accounting entity as a whole, while often unions are interested in bargaining with the part of the overall organization that employs the specific people they represent (the "bargaining unit"). The following sources of company information are important to unions:

- The company's financial statements.
- Details behind the financial statements.
- Financial forecasts about the company's income, financial position (as revealed in forecasted balance sheets), and cash flows.

Customers

Customers may be individuals, businesses, municipalities, charities, or similar. They are interested in receiving the agreed-upon quantity and quality of goods or services at an agreed-upon fair price. They are also interested in the ability of the selling organization to fulfil any warranty agreements and service contracts, and to continue to serve as a responsive source of supply. Accounting information about the supplier may be important in providing insight into some of these issues. For example, the most recent financial statements of a tire supplier could provide information on its profitability and financial position; thus, a taxi company (the customer) could gain some assurance that the seller has the potential of continuing in business and honouring the prepaid service contract on the tires.

Competitors

An organization's competitors usually have a keen interest in how well an organization is performing, and financial statements may provide part of the information they need. One technique that many companies employ is called "benchmarking." In this approach, a competitor is identified who is an acknowledged leader in the industry. Key performance indicators are computed from the leader's financial statements. These performance indicators are then compared with the same indicators for the company, and strategies are developed to close the gap. For example, suppose that "our" company is a manufacturer of mouse devices for PCs, and that our top competitor's ratio of cost of sales to sales is 30%, while our own ratio is 40%. Clearly, we must explore why this leading company is able to charge more than us, or produce a product for less.

Management

Management is interested in all variety of accounting information about the organization. Managers also have a key role in preparing the accounting information that is seen by others. Even though financial accounting is intended primarily for users outside the organization, managers within the organization are very interested in how the results of their efforts and decisions are portrayed (that is, accounted for). In corporations in which management and ownership are separated (for example, in corporations whose common shares are actively traded and widely held on an organized stock exchange), managers want to demonstrate to shareholders that they have performed well in administering the resources of the company, and the financial statements are one means of addressing that accountability. Bonuses may be awarded to managers if the company, or a part of the company under their control, achieves targets expressed in accounting terms, such as "a 10% increase in sales." Management looks to the following sources for such information:

- Financial statements and their supporting details.
- Forecasted financial statements.

Tax authorities

Revenue Canada and other tax authorities, such as provincial governments, are interested in the performance of organizations subject to tax. Corporations are generally required to pay an income tax in Canada; thus, measurement of corporate income for tax purposes is an important management activity. Although most of the transactions that a corporation is involved in are accounted for in the same way for financial accounting and tax accounting purposes, there are many differences between the two systems. We will describe some of these differences later in this book. Sources of information for tax authorities include the following:

- Financial statements prepared according to financial accounting standards.
- Financial statements prepared according to tax rules.

Financial information intermediaries and advisers

Financial analysts, stockbrokers, and other intermediaries are in the business of interpreting how well businesses are performing. Thus, they are avid consumers of financial accounting information. Users of accounting information who are less expert in interpreting financial statements — such as many shareholders — may rely on the advice of these professionals, whose sources for financial information include the following:

- Financial statements.
- Information about the company's competitors and industry.

Other organizations, and the public at large

Many other individuals and organizations, and the public at large, qualify as users of accounting information. You have now joined that group!

Other government entities

Government departments, such as those concerned with the development of economic policy, also require information about corporate performance. The government may wish to help areas of the country that are economically depressed and have high unemployment rates. Also, to ensure a productive and internationally competitive economy, the government may wish to support the efficient segments of the corporate sector, while at the same time identifying those businesses which should be phased out. Financial accounting provides some of this information, and so the financial statements of businesses and other types of organizations are important sources for various government entities.

The potential user groups described above are summarized in Exhibit 2–2.

Conflicting goals

The above users of an entity's accounting information often have diverse and conflicting sets of objectives. Owners of a corporation are usually interested in higher profits and higher dividends, while employees may want higher salaries or wages. But the higher the salaries or wages paid to the employees, the lower will be the corporation's profits, and the less will be available for dividends. The government wants each corporation to pay its "fair" share of taxes, but it is in the interest of management and shareholders to legally and ethically arrange their affairs so that corporate taxes are minimized. Customers wish to pay low prices, while at the same time ensuring that they receive the required quality of goods or services, and the organization that is providing those products or services is pulling to some extent in the other direction. Unions may wish to know about the detailed cost of specific benefits such as the employee pension plan, in order to determine whether sufficient corporate resources are available for a wage hike, but management may resist such disclosure.

All the user groups are potentially stakeholders in an organization. That is, they have — to varying degrees — a stake in how successful the organization

EXHIBIT 2–2
SOME USER GROUPS AND THEIR INFORMATION NEEDS

Users	Examples of Use of Information	Examples of Types of Information About the Organization	Sources of Information
Owners	To evaluate the use of invested resources; to make decisions about the business operations; to make a decision to sell or hold investments.	Trends in net income and in the expense and revenue components of net income; cash flows; financial ratios.	Financial statements; detailed internal accounting reports and documents; direct observation, where possible.
Potential owners	To make a decision to invest or not to invest in a particular business.	General financial health of the business; potential for growth; potential for dividends.	Financial statements prepared according to GAAP; advice from financial intermediaries.
Creditors	To decide if money should be lent to an organization.	Ability of the potential borrower to repay principal and interest; general financial health of the borrower; existence and value of collateral.	Balance sheets and supporting details about assets, and details of existing loans and other obligations; cash flow statements; income statements.
Suppliers	To decide to supply a potential customer with goods and/or services.	Ability of the customer to pay on time; ability of the customer to engage in repeat business; general financial health of the customer.	Financial statements.
Employees	To decide to work for an employer (for potential employees), or to continue to work for an existing employer; to monitor any pension plans the employee belongs to.	Ability of the employer to fulfil the employment relationship, promote employees through growth and expansion; ability of the pension plan (if any) to meet pension promises made to the employees.	Financial statements.
Unions	To help unions negotiate terms and conditions of employment for the employees that the union represents. For example, to help the union determine the amount of a wage increase to demand, or the amount of a wage decrease (called a wage concession) to agree to if the employer is in financial difficulty.	General financial health of the employing organization; ability of the organization to pay various levels of wage increases and still remain healthy.	Financial statements and forecasted financial statements; specific financial information for individual bargaining units, if made available by management.

Users	Examples of Use of Information	Examples of Types of Information About the Organization	Sources of Information
Customers	To decide whether to purchase goods and/or services from the organization.	General financial health of the potential supplier. Does the supplier have the ability to deliver the specified goods and/or services at the required time, in the required location, of the required quality, and for the agreed-upon price? Can the supplier fulfil any required post-delivery obligations, such as warranties?	Financial statements.
Competitors	To identify potential competitive threats; to benchmark versus the best-performing competitors.	How well is the organization doing overall? What segments of the business are profitable? What types of assets and liabilities does the organization have?	Financial statements, and financial ratios derived from the financial statements.
Management	To inform outside users, including shareholders and potential shareholders, about the company's results; to set performance targets for other members of management; to evaluate the performance of the organization.	What information should/must be disclosed, and how should/must it be accounted for? What performance targets, such as a 10% increase in net income from one year to the next, should be required?	Financial statements and financial ratios derived from the financial statements.
Tax authorities	To decide if taxable entities, such as corporations and individuals, prepared income tax and other tax returns accurately, and on a timely basis. To decide if the proper amount of tax was paid.	What sources of taxable revenues does a taxpaying accounting entity have? What sources of tax deductions are there?	Financial statements prepared according to GAAP; tax returns.
Financial information intermediaries	To assist other users, perhaps not as expert, in using accounting information to make decisions about an accounting entity.	Has a company performed beyond the average in its industry for the past few years, with performance measured by indicators such as increase in net income, ratio of net income to shareholders' equity, and so on?	Financial statements; other information about the company.

Users	Examples of Use of Information	Examples of Types of Information About the Organization	Sources of Information
Other organizations, and the public at large, and other government entities	Which companies in which industries are performing well, and which may need assistance such as low-interest government-guaranteed loans in order to become satisfactory performers? Which companies are earning excessive profits, and appear to be unfairly exploiting consumers?	Trends in net income; cash flows; revenues.	Financial statements.

is, how it affects its physical environment, how it ensures that all its employees are treated equitably, and so on. Although all stakeholders likely have an interest in ensuring the long-run survival and well-being of an organization, they are to varying degrees in competition with one another. Furthermore, it may be that anything one group gains, another group may lose to some extent.

Because their objectives differ, each group may be interested in different kinds of information, although there will usually be some information that all will find useful. It is the differences that put some stress on the accountant's role, and this makes it important that the judgments made in producing accounting information be made with care. For example, the managers of a corporation in financial difficulty may prefer not to disclose the extent of the problem for fear that shareholders will sell their shares and potential shareholders will be reluctant to buy shares. These actions may result in the share price being pushed down to levels that may encourage another company to take over the corporation by acquiring its shares cheaply. Management's greatest fear in a situation like this may be the possibility that the new owners will fire them.

Such information conflicts are a result of the fact that different user groups often require different kinds of information about the accounting entity. For example, creditors are interested in monitoring the amount of wealth available to ensure that the loans they have made to the company are properly secured (that is, that the assets of the company can be sold to generate sufficient cash to pay off the loans), while shareholders may be less concerned with the immediate cash value of parts of the company than with the company's earning power as a total entity.

These information conflicts are exacerbated on occasion because GAAP and our legal system create a bias toward providing information to certain groups of users. For example, shareholders have traditionally been favoured over other groups such as unions. This lack of even-handedness in the regulatory system is counterbalanced in the case of those users that have the power to demand information from an accounting entity (for example, Devo Green's bank), but many users don't have such power and are left out in the cold.

An interesting example of this took place during the collective bargaining negotiations between professors (the union) and administration (management) at a Canadian university. The professors' bargaining representatives requested specific accounting information in addition to that included in the university's financial statements, in order to bargain more effectively, but the administration refused the request. The union obviously lacked the power to demand the information, and there was no law requiring that such information be provided. Along with other factors, this conflict over accounting information led to a breakdown in negotiations.[9]

4.Substance over Form

"If it walks like a duck, quacks like a duck, and looks like a duck, call it a duck." This seemingly silly little piece of advice underlies an important idea in accounting. Accountants are supposed to be continually on the alert to account for the substance of an event, and not just its form. For example, suppose that in the On Ice example in Chapter 1, the skate manufacturer that had purchased advertising for $4,000, and that owed On Ice $3,000 at the end of September 1993, was unable to pay its bills. Perhaps, like many businesses during the recession of the early 1990s, it just didn't have enough cash, and little likelihood of being able to pay anything for several years. From the perspective of On Ice, the $3,000 in accounts receivable no longer represents $3,000, and should be reduced, perhaps down to zero. Even though the $3,000 still has the legal form of a receivable from the skate manufacturer, the substance of the situation is rather different, and accountants would argue that accounting for the substance would provide the more meaningful information. After all, why account for money that you no longer expect to get? In terms of equation 4 from Chapter 1, the current asset "Accounts receivable" would be reduced, and an expense called "Bad debt expense" would be increased.

Deciding just what the substance of a situation is may not always be that easy. Even in the above case of the $3,000 account receivable, it may be that On Ice will receive part of the money, so only a portion of the $3,000 should be "written off." Judging how much of the $3,000 to keep on the books as an asset may be difficult. Try and decide what the substance is for the following events. As well, indicate the degree to which making your judgment is hard or easy (suggested answers follow):

A. Company A acquires a machine for an agreed-upon price of $25,000. The machine is delivered to the company on September 1, 1993, and is put into use the next day. Because ready cash was not available, the company acquired the machine under a conditional sales contract arrangement, under which the company promised to pay $1,000 per month plus interest beginning September 30, 1993. The word "conditional" in the phrase "conditional sales contract" means that the legal title to the machine remains with the company selling the machine (Company B) until the last payment is made by Company A, which will be September 30, 1995. Should Company A account for the machine as an asset starting September 1, 1993? Explain.

B. Company C assembles and sells PCs from a small location in downtown Edmonton, just across from the municipal airport. Its location enabled Company C to fulfil effectively the computing needs of several small businesses in the area, including a number of aviation supply companies. Because direct jet flights have been instituted between the municipal airport (which is near the centre of Edmonton) and Vancouver, several adjacent businesses have moved away, citing noise pollution. Company C's customer base has therefore eroded, and while its management still expects to be able to sell 486- and Pentium-based computers, it now has several outdated 386-based boards, which cost company C $15,200. It expects to sell these boards only slowly, if at all. Should the 386-based inventory still

[9] J.H. Amernic, "The Roles of Accounting in Collective Bargaining," *Accounting, Organizations and Society*, Vol. 10, no. 2, 1985, pp. 227–253.

be accounted for as an asset, or should it be written off as an expense?

C. Company D is in the funeral business. Up until now it has sold funerals (the service, the casket, and so on) only on an "as needed" basis; that is, when an individual died, the relatives or friends made the purchase. Company D's management has decided that it will attempt to sell some of its funerals in advance. The arrangement will work as follows: An individual will sign a contract for funeral services to be provided sometime in the future, when needed, and pay the company an agreed-upon amount. What is the substance of these advance arrangements? Are they "sales"?

D. Ms. X owns 100% of the common shares in two small corporations, E and F. Company E is very active in small-project commercial construction, but needs a bank loan. Company F is inactive. Ms. X wishes to apply for a bank loan for E, but E's income statement shows virtually no profits for the most recent year. Someone has suggested to Ms. X that she have F sign a contract with E: F will arrange for the construction of a small building, under very profitable terms for E. The total contract amount will then be accounted for by company E as an account receivable. Has a real transaction occurred?

A suggested approach to dealing with these four events follows:

Event	Form	Substance	Hard/Easy?
(a)	A does not own the asset as of 1/09/93.	A controls the asset, and will probably make the future payments. Thus, account for it as an asset on A's balance sheet.	Easy
(b)	The 386 chips still physically exist; C owns them and spent $15,200 on them.	The 386 chips have little potential to generate future benefits for C; they should be written down to what we may reasonably expect to get for them.	In between
(c)	Company D has the cash.	D has not yet provided the services or related assets. Wait until the services and assets are provided, then a "sale" is recorded. Thus, account for the cash as a liability ("unearned revenue") when it is received.	Hard
(d)	A contract has been signed between two companies.	The contract is a sham designed just to create the impression of profits. There was no negotiation between truly independent parties operating "at arm's length."	Easy

5. The Net Present Value Criterion in Accounting

The adoption of a user orientation in accounting has resulted in the widespread acceptance of a general decision criterion in accounting and related disciplines. This is the "net present value" criterion, and it is an example of a normative decision rule. A normative rule is a rule that people say you should follow in order to achieve some apparently desirable goal. For example, in the field of public health, some health economists suggest that increasing taxes on cigarettes will discourage people from smoking. The fact that increased taxes also provide incentives for cigarette smuggling, which in turn results in increased smoking, shows how careful we must be when we suggest a normative decision rule.

The net present value criterion in accounting is based on the following assumptions:

A. People should prefer more money than less.

B. People do not like to invest their money in risky situations.

C. People prefer money sooner rather than later.

Before we explain what we mean by the net present value criterion, a simple example will clarify some of the issues involved. Suppose Ms. X is offered the following two financial gifts, of which she may choose only one:

I. $1,000 today.

II. $1,000 one year from now.

Based upon assumption C, Ms. X would choose option I, and take the money today. If she receives the $1,000 today, she can invest it in (for example) a bank deposit and earn about 8%[10] over the year. Thus, she will have $1,080 at the end of the year; she would have had only $1,000 if she had accepted alternative II. To compare the two alternatives at the present point in time (Ms. X's "today"), we can compute the net present value (NPV) of each gift. The NPV for each gift is the hypothetical cash amount to be received today, that Ms. X would feel is equivalent in monetary terms. It can be computed as follows:

Option I Receive $1,000 today	**Option II** Receive $1,000 one year from today
$1,000	$1,000/1.08 = $ 925.93

Let's clarify how the NPV for Option II was derived. Ms. X is to receive $1,000 one year from today. If $925.93 were deposited in the bank at 8% interest, it would grow to 925.93 [1 + .08], or $1,000.00.[11] Conversely, the NPV of the $1,000 that is to be received one year hence is 1,000.00/(1.08), or $925.93.

The NPV of the $1,000 gift to be received today is $1,000. The NPV of the $1,000 gift to be received one year from today is the present value of the $1,000, or $925.93. Since the NPV of alternative I is greater than that of alternative II by $74.07, Ms. X chooses I. Of course, only the $1,000 of alternative I actually exists today. The $925.93 of alternative II is a hypothetical amount that is thought to be the economic equivalent today of the $1,000 to be received one year from now. Also, alternative II entails some risk to Ms. X, since she must wait to receive it (perhaps the bank will fail, and there will be no deposit insurance).

A slight change in the example will introduce a little more realism. Suppose Ms. X will be required to pay for each

[10] Interest rates change all the time. The 8% was chosen just for illustrative purposes.

[11] Actually, 925.93 [1 + .08] equals $1,000.0044; we ignore the rounding error of 44/100 of a penny.

gift; alternative I will cost her $1,150, payable two years from today, and alternative II will cost her $900, payable today. The expected cash flows for the two alternatives, and the timing of these expected cash flows, is as follows:

	Today	One year	Two years
Alternative I	**+$1,000**		**–$1,150**
Alternative II	**–$900**	**+$1,000**	

If the only interest rate in the economy in which Ms. X lives is 8%, then the NPVs of the two alternatives may be computed as follows:

	Alternative I	**Alternative II**
NPV	+1,000	–900
	$-1,150/(1.08)^2$	+1,000/1.08
	= $14.06	= $25.93

Alternative II now beats alternative I by $11.87. However, if the interest rate rises to 10%, then I's NPV is $49.59, while II's NPV is $9.09 — a difference of $40.50 in I's favour. So, it seems that a number of factors determine NPV:

- The magnitude of expected cash flows.
- The timing of expected cash flows (that is, when they occur).
- The magnitude of the interest rates used.

The user orientation and the NPV criterion go hand in hand. In management accounting, for example, a company that is contemplating a proposal that involves investing in a new production process might make forecasts of the cost of the machinery and other resources required (all of which are negative cash flows), and of the expected positive cash flows to be generated by sales of the product produced. The NPV of the proposal would then be computed, using an interest rate that represents the rate the company's shareholders and other providers of financial resources could earn on projects of similar risk. If the NPV is greater than zero, then — at least according to this user-oriented criterion — the proposed project should go ahead.

The NPV criterion can be more formally defined as follows: if the NPV of a project (examples: investing in new machinery, setting up a training program for employees, purchasing a sports team) is greater than zero, the project is acceptable.

In practice, the processes of estimating the costs involved, forecasting expected cash flows, and determining the appropriate interest rate to use are all quite complex. Income tax effects tend to make the entire process even more challenging, and we have ignored taxes in our examples. It is also important to keep in mind that the NPV criterion, which focuses on shareholders and other providers of a company's financial resources as the ultimate "users" whose NPV is to be maximized, is really just a common assumption made when choosing among alternative courses of action.

In financial accounting, the NPV criterion offers an alternative to historical cost when it comes to measuring various assets and liabilities. Some accountants and managers suggest that assets should be accounted for equal to the present value of the estimated future cash inflows they will generate, while liabilities should be measured equal to the present value of the estimated future cash outflows that they will require to be made. This suggestion seems more feasible for some assets and liabilities than for others — a matter to be discussed in more detail later in the book.

6. Classification in Accounting

When the AAA definition of accounting was discussed at the start of this chapter, one of the types of measures that was described was the nominal measuring scale. Making measurements according to this scale involves classifying items according to characteristics that are meaningful. The accounting example we used at the time related to classifying assets on the balance sheet as either current on noncurrent. In fact, a significant part of accounting involves classifying items into categories that users of the resulting information may find useful.

Let's take a look at some classification decisions that accountants make:

Classifying items on the balance sheet

Not only are asset classifications important: other balance sheet classifications are as well. Suppose that Company A has borrowed money from Company B, and B wishes, naturally, to attempt to ensure that A will be able to pay the money back according to the contractual arrangements between the two. As part of the loan contract, A agrees that its current ratio (which is, recall, the ratio of current assets divided by current liabilities) will not go below 2:1. Company A has $900,000 in current assets, as of today, and $430,000 in current liabilities; thus, the ratio is 2.09:1. However, $50,000 in loans payable to another company (Company C) are due in five months. The $50,000 has been classified by A's accountant as a long-term liability, on the grounds that when it comes due for repayment, Company A will borrow another $50,000 to replace it. How reasonable is it to classify the $50,000 as a long-term liability and thus keep it out of the current liability category?

If the $50,000 is reclassified as a current liability, the ratio declines to 900,000/480,000, or 1.88, which is below the amount specified in the loan contract. This could trigger a demand for repayment or, at the very least, a costly requirement to renegotiate the terms of the loan. Usually, liabilities that come due within one year are classified as current liabilities. Here, however, it seems that management intends to replace the $50,000 with another loan; it appears to really be (that is, in "substance") a long-term liability. If a definite arrangement to refinance the $50,000 has been made, classifying it as a long-term liability is reasonable.

Classifying amounts as assets or expenses

Company D just spent $350,000 on an advertising campaign. Should the entire amount be classified as an expense? As an asset? Partly as an expense and partly as an asset? What criteria do you think are important to this classification decision? In the On Ice case in Chapter 1, we saw that assets that had served their purpose and helped generate benefits for the company were reclassified into the expense category. Magazine inventory became the expense "Cost of magazines sold" after the magazines were sold, office supplies became expenses as they were used up, and the cost of capital assets such as OI's computer slowly became depreciation expense over time. It seems apparent that for the magazine inventory and the office supplies, the classification as between asset and expense depends to an extent upon whether the items are still physically under the control of the company. Other classifications between asset and expense, such as that for depreciation, are much more difficult. This is the case with the $350,000 spent on the advertising campaign. Because of the high level of uncertainty about future benefits, it would probably be expensed as soon as it was incurred.

Classifying cash flows into three mutually exclusive categories

Recall from Chapter 1 that one of the financial statements we prepared for On Ice was a statement of cash flows. One feature of this accounting statement is that it classifies all of an accounting entity's cash flows into one of three categories: operating, investing, and financing. This three-way classification system is intended to provide useful information to users of the financial statements, since each category of cash flows is expected to behave differently (examples: operating cash flows are recurring, while investing cash flows are not; investing cash flows are expected to be negative for a growing company, while financing cash flows are expected to be positive).

7. Ethics, Accounting, and Accountants

So far in this chapter, we have described six ideas that are basic to a wide variety of accounting areas: accountability, the accounting entity, the notion of user orientation, substance over form, the NPV criterion, and the importance of classification in accounting. A seventh idea, that ethical conduct should be an embedded part of every accountant's professional behaviour, is fundamental to the disciplines of accounting — so basic that until recently discussing it was considered almost redundant. However, because of the increasing complexity of society, and some recent and well publicized business failures that were attributed at least partly to accounting and auditing, many leaders in the profession now recognize that ethics deserves a key place in all accounting education.

An "ethic" may be defined as a "principle of right or good conduct".[12] Being sensitive to the ethical implications of issues is an important step on the way to developing responsible and mature decision-making, in accounting, in other areas of business, and in life in general. This is not a textbook on ethics, but we do have a duty to begin sensitizing people who are starting the study of accounting to the fact that ethical dilemmas are a fact of every practitioner's life.

Professor Stephen Loeb has suggested the following list of goals for education in accounting ethics:

1. *Relate accounting education to moral issues.*
2. *Recognize issues in accounting that have ethical implications.*
3. *Develop "a sense of moral obligation" or responsibility.*
4. *Develop the abilities to deal with moral conflicts or dilemmas.*
5. *Learn to deal with the uncertainties of the accounting profession.*
6. *"Set the stage" for a change in ethical behavior.*
7. *Appreciate and understand the history and composition of all aspects of accounting ethics and their relationship to the general field of ethics.*[13]

Developing into an "ethical professional person" is a lifelong process of *becoming*. Ethical issues are part of daily business and personal life, and we may be so used to our everyday ways of doing things that important ethical issues are not obvious to us. Or there may be overriding social and personal pressures on us that obscure more fundamental ethical considerations, as the Gord and James case presented after this section illustrates.

	Unethical person	**Ethical person**
Unaware of ethical implications	A1	A3
Aware of ethical implications	A2	A4

Consider the matrix on the left.

In cell A1, the person has little in the way of personal ethics and is also blithely unaware of the ethical implica-

[12] *Houghton Mifflin Canadian Dictionary* (Markham, Ont.: Houghton Mifflin Canada), page 450.
[13] Stephen E. Loeb, "Teaching Students Accounting Ethics: Some Crucial Issues," *Issues in Accounting Education*, Vol. 3, no. 2, Fall 1988, pp. 316–329.

tions of his or her behaviour. In cell A2, the individual is overwhelmingly self-centred and unethical, but understands the ethical implications of such behaviour. In cell A3, the person's ethics are intrinsically high but he or she may make decisions that have deleterious ethical consequences out of lack of awareness of the implications of those decisions. Cell A4 is the "ideal" — the person is ethical, and also sophisticated and aware enough to understand and analyse personal and business situations, and to thus make the "right" decision.

The role of education in the context of this matrix may be as follows: Demonstrating the ethical implications of various business, accounting, and personal situations to someone in cell A1 might help shift that person into cell A2. In cell A2, sufficient tension may be created between that individual's new-found understanding and his or her personal ethics, that some shift toward cell A4 is possible. A person beginning in cell A3, by gaining experience in identifying and analysing ethical situations, will likely move into (or at least toward) cell A4. Thus, the role of education is to help people become aware of the ethical implications of the disciplines they are studying or practising, and that is the goal we adopt in this book. There are, however, some important complications.

One complication has to do with this question: Are ethics absolute or situational? For example, in some societies bribery is a common way of getting things done. Salaries for bureaucrats may be so low that a bribe is expected when, say, a company applies for a licence to import equipment. Is bribery acceptable in this situation? In order to fully consider this question, we need more details. Who benefits and who gets hurt by the bribe? Does the bribe contribute to corrupt behaviour in other, related situations? What is the nature of the company's activities? Is the equipment that will be imported life-saving medical equipment? Is it cigarette-making equipment?

It's easy to see that ethics is not simple. Let's turn to the Gord and James demonstration case, in which ethical considerations are central, but which also illustrates various aspects of the basic ideas about accounting that were introduced in this chapter.

The Gord and James Case

In June 1993, Gord and James joined Algor Limited (AL), a medium-sized manufacturer of various types of extruded plastic pipe. Gord, an engineer by training, was hired as AL's director of new product development. James, an accounting graduate, was the company's new chief accountant, reporting to the vice president of information systems. The two men hit it off right from the start, and they and their families developed a close friendship.

It is now about two years after the two friends joined the company. AL's profits as reported on its income statement have declined to a slight loss for the year just past, because of intense competition by new, innovative competitors in the plastic pipe market. Gord's department is under pressure from top management to develop and introduce into the marketplace plastic pipe that will quickly make a profit and restore the company's market share to previous levels. Key members of top management have made vague comments to the business and financial press that "a return to profitability is imminent." AL's common shares are traded on a national stock exchange.

Just yesterday, Gord met with James over lunch to discuss informally a new product concept, labelled "Project X" by Gord, that would in Gord's words "really bowl top management over." Gord mentioned to James that an investment of $1.5 million was required, to be spent on or about August 1, 1995, and that the project had a "very positive net present value, based upon my forecast of the expected cash flows, which I consider to be reasonable." Gord then gave James the net present value analysis shown in Exhibit 2–3.

EXHIBIT 2–3
NEW INVESTMENT PROPOSAL
Net Present Value Analysis

Date: June 15, 1995 Director's Approval: Gord . . .
Project name: "Project X" Chief accountant's approval:
Prepared by: Gord . . .

Estimated total cash investment, on or about August 1, 1995	–$1,500,000
Future expected cash flows:	
FYE* July 31, 1996	
Cash inflows (from new product sales)	+$350,000
Cash outflows (raw material, labour, and other costs)	–$200,000
FYE July 31, 1997	
Cash inflows	+$600,000
Cash outflows	–$300,000
FYE July 31, 1998 to 2003, each year,	
Cash inflows	+$800,000
Cash outflows	–$400,000
FYE July 31, 2004	
Cash inflows	+$600,000
Cash outflows	–$300,000

Project to be scrapped on July 31, 2005, at a net cash outflow for the year of $25,000.

Assuming that all cash flows, except for the initial investment of $1.5 million, take place on July 31, the NPV at 16% is +$20,822.

* FYE = for year ended

The Algor Limited project approval system

When a proposal to invest more than $50,000 is made by a manager at the director level at AL, the proposal is first subjected to a net present value analysis. If the NPV is greater than zero, using an interest rate of 16%, the project is submitted to top management for final approval. Only rarely is such approval denied: for example, if there are severe resource shortages in the company. According to AL's Procedures Manual, before the NPV analysis is submitted to top management, it must be "verified" by AL's chief accountant in an "independent test for accuracy and reliability."

The lunch meeting between the two friends ended with James telling Gord that he would look over the NPV analysis that afternoon. After picking up the check, Gord responded by saying, "I really need this project, James. If I don't produce something right away, something that looks like it's going to prove top management's predictions about the turnaround are right, I think they're going to fire me."

Later that afternoon, James reviewed Gord's analysis. It seemed that all the arithmetic in the NPV calculation was correct, and that the forecasts for the cash inflows and cash outflows for the years 1996 to 2004 were reasonable. However, James felt uncomfortable with the forecast for 2005; it seemed that the estimated cost of scrapping the project at the end of its expected useful life was rather low. James felt that a cost in the $110,000 to $120,000 range was probably more realistic, based on his past experience with similar projects. At a net cash outflow of $120,000 for the year 2005, the NPV sank to -$715, according to James's calculations.

When James phoned Gord with his concerns, Gord said, "Look, James, how can you know what's going to happen ten years from now? By then, both of us will probably be long gone from the company. Besides, it's a good project —

we both know that. I just want to help the numbers show how good the project is to top management. And don't forget that the year after next, the company's income statement will show that companywide profits will be boosted by about \$150,000[14] if we launch the project. That can't hurt our bonuses, you know."

James hung up the receiver, feeling a little ill. Was it because of the quiche he had eaten at lunch?

Required:

(Note: This case is to be answered assuming that taxes do not exist, in order to simplify matters at this stage in the book.)

1. How is financial accounting affected by this situation?
2. How is management accounting affected by this situation?
3. Verify Gord's and James's calculations.
4. Who are the stakeholders in this situation? In other words, what individuals and groups of individuals are potentially affected — positively or negatively — by this situation? Provide justifications for your selections.
5. To whom is Gord accountable? To whom is James accountable? Are there any other accountability relationships involved in this case?
6. Both AL and Project X are accounting entities. Why is this so? Who are the users of AL's financial accounting statements?
7. Project X as an accounting entity doesn't have a balance sheet and income statement — at least, not according to the management accounting system for AL. Describe the accounting information that is prepared at AL in order to control the approval for a proposed project such as Project X.
8. Do you think AL's management should, in some fashion, keep track of what happens to projects after they have been approved? Can you suggest a way for them to do so?
9. What is the relationship between AL's financial statements and Project X?
10. What are the ethical issues involved?
11. In your opinion, what should James do? Why?
12. Optional: Using an spreadsheet program such as Lotus, Quattro Pro, or Excel, prepare a model of the NPV calculation. How sensitive is the NPV to changes in the final year's cash flow estimation? To changes in the interest rate?

The Gord and James case may seem a bit farfetched, but the ethical dilemmas faced by James (and by Gord!) are not so unusual. Accountants deal with accountability, with information (which is often a powerful resource), and with issues affecting other people's economic well-being; therefore, they are constantly dealing with issues of ethics. As different accounting situations are described throughout this book, you should be on the lookout for possible ethical dilem-

[14] The expected incremental impact on AL's income statement for 1997:

1997 cash inflows		\$600,000
1997 cash outflows	(300,000)	
Depreciation on the new equipment (\$1,500,000/10 years)	(150,000)	(450,000)
Expected increase in net income		\$150,000

mas. Here are some preliminary ideas for the questions relating to the case:

Question 1: AL's financial statements will, according to the information in footnote 14, show an increased net income of $150,000 for the year 1997 if the project is undertaken. Since managers at AL receive a bonus based on financial accounting income, this increased income will lead directly to a benefit for both Gord and James. However, information from the company's management accounting system suggests, as James has shown, that the NPV of the project is negative, so it's unattractive on the basis of the NPV criterion. Gord's unethical biasing of the estimated future cash flow in 2005 would lead to acceptance of a project that should not be accepted. The resulting financial statements for the company may well be "correct" in the sense that they account for the transactions that Algor has undertaken, but they will be accounting for a "fraudulent" decision.

Question 2: AL's management accounting system has checks and balances built in to ensure that the estimates of a new project's cash flows are as reasonable as possible, given the goals of the company. If the two managers collude to subvert the system, the company will invest in a project that is unacceptable on the basis of the NPV criterion.

Question 3: Gord's calculations were as shown in the table below. He assumed that all the cash flows will occur at year end each year. This assumption is reasonable most of the time.

James's calculations were identical except for the July 31, 2005, cash flow, which he assumed was –$120,000. The present value of this cash flow is $[-120{,}000/(1.16)^{10}]$, which is –$27,202. If this amount is substituted for the –$5,667 in the table, the net present value for Project X becomes –$715.

Point in Time	Net Cash Flows at That Point	Present Value (as at August 1, 1995)
August 1, 1995	–1,500,000	$-1{,}500{,}000/(1.16)^0 = -1{,}500{,}000$
July 31, 1996	+350,000-200,000 = +150,000	$+150{,}000/(1.16)^1 = +129{,}310$
July 31, 1997	+600,000-300,000 = +300,000	$+300{,}000/(1.16)^2 = +222{,}949$
July 31, 1998	+800,000-400,000 = +400,000	$+400{,}000/(1.16)^3 = +256{,}263$
July 31, 1999	+800,000-400,000 = +400,000	$+400{,}000/(1.16)^4 = +220{,}916$
July 31, 2000	+800,000-400,000 = +400,000	$+400{,}000/(1.16)^5 = +190{,}445$
July 31, 2001	+800,000-400,000 = +400,000	$+400{,}000/(1.16)^6 = +164{,}177$
July 31, 2002	+800,000-400,000 = +400,000	$+400{,}000/(1.16)^7 = +141{,}532$
July 31, 2003	+800,000-400,000 = +400,000	$+400{,}000/(1.16)^8 = +122{,}010$
July 31, 2004	+600,000-300,000 = +300,000	$+300{,}000/(1.16)^9 = +78{,}885$
July 31, 2005	–25,000	$-25{,}000/(1.16)^{10} = -5{,}667$
NET PRESENT VALUE (equals the sum of all the present values) = +20,820		

Question 4: Stakeholders include Gord, James, their families, AL management (other than Gord and James), AL shareholders, AL employees, and others. A justification for including members of AL management (other than Gord and James) is that these managers are responsible for making prudent decisions, and depend upon the integrity of the information they receive. AL managers have

chosen to evaluate proposed projects using the NPV criterion, and have set up a system in which the chief accountant has a key role in validating the information. If the system is misused, the company and the managers' jobs are threatened. Can you suggest justifications for including as stakeholders Gord, James, the shareholders, and the others?

Identifying the stakeholders in a situation is often an important step in assessing the ethical implications of an accounting or business decision. Sometimes, identifying stakeholders is relatively straightforward; at other times it is not so easy.

Question 5: Accountability and ethics are two basic accounting ideas and are closely related. James is accountable to his superior, the vice president of information systems. He is also accountable to AL management in general, to the board of directors, and to the shareholders. In addition, since it is likely that James is a professional accountant, he is accountable to his profession. An argument can also be made that he is accountable to his family. Thus, accountability relationships may be legal, formal (as with a subordinate to a superior), or even relatively informal. To whom is Gord accountable? Explain.

Question 6: AL is an accounting entity since various groups are interested in its performance as a business. Its common shares are traded on a national stock exchange, so actual and potential shareholders, as well as securities regulators, are concerned about monitoring the company. Project X is also an accounting entity, since AL's management is responsible for selecting acceptable projects and monitoring their actual performance against expectations. Possible users of AL's financial accounting statements include current and potential shareholders, regulators (such as officials of the stock exchange and provincial securities regulators), AL's management, competitors, and Revenue Canada.

Question 7: AL's management accounting system is designed so that projects having an expected cost of greater than $50,000 are required to have a net present value greater than zero when a 16% interest rate is used. Such a decision criterion is fairly common in profit-seeking organizations. In order for such a system to function, the interest rate, the magnitude of the expected cash flows, and the timing of the expected cash flows, must all be estimated as forthrightly as possible. In AL's case, the interest rate is a given, so our focus must be on the cash flows. It is Gord's apparently intentional misestimation of the cash flow forecasted for 2005 that is at issue.

Question 8: Exerting some control over decisions before they are made is important, but so is following up to see how well the project is actually doing, and to judge the accuracy of the original forecasts and decision. Perhaps an income statement that will keep track of actual sales and costs related to the project would be worthwhile — in other words, an income statement for the project.

Question 9: If the project is approved, future revenues and expenses of AL as a whole will be affected, since approval will have been granted for the company to enter into a series of transactions that it would not have otherwise engaged in. For example, Gord estimates that AL's net income the year after next will increase by $150,000. Also, since it appears that AL's management has a bonus system tied into financial accounting net income, Gord's and James's personal remuneration will increase. All this from a project that James has significant concerns about!

Question 10: Some ethical issues (there may be lots of others):

- Effectiveness of the management accounting system.
- Chief accountant's integrity.
- Chief accountant's loyalty to a friend.
- Top management's right to know about an intended breach in the management accounting system.
- Shareholders' interests.

- Chief accountant's obligation to be a "whistle blower."
- Chief accountant's obligation to the company and its shareholders, and to his profession.
- Fairness of project approval system (that is, does it discourage managers from submitting "good" projects?)
- Fairness of a bonus system based on financial accounting numbers.
- Gord's obligations to his family and career.
- Gord's obligation to a colleague — that is, is he applying "unfair" pressure because they have a personal relationship?).

Question 11. What should James do? This one's up to you.

Question 12. The optional question. This question requires a sensitivity analysis of the NPV — that is, investigating just how the NPV changes for given changes in key variables such as (in this case) the interest rate and the cash outflow in 2005.

Some Comments on the Gord and James Case

Unstructured learning materials and accounting education

Back in the preface to this book, it was suggested that you should be exposed to a wide variety of accounting teaching and learning materials. Some material should be highly directed and structured (that is, very specific), while other material should be much less directed, and unstructured. Exposure to and practice with many different types of questions and case materials is important for helping you develop judgment.

It's often useful to think about learning materials as having three dimensions. The first dimension is the *complexity* of the information given; in the shorter technical questions at the end of each chapter, the information provided is usually quite straightforward, although there can be a lot of it. On the other hand, there is a fair bit of complexity in the Gord and James case, and it's necessary to sort out those things which may be relevant from those which clearly are not. The scenario contains a wealth of information about accounting systems, the business, interpersonal relationships, and so on.

A second dimension is the *level of technical knowledge and sophistication expected.* Some very short, highly technical questions in accounting, taxation, and information systems may require a considerable amount of knowledge about accounting principles, tax legislation, computer software applications, and so on, while other short technical questions may only require entry-level technical knowledge. Obviously, the shorter technical questions in the first few chapters of this book require entry-level knowledge.

The third dimension is the *degree to which the "required" is directed.* This third dimension is extremely important; it takes considerable practice to be able to skilfully interpret the "required" of a case, so we'll spend the next several paragraphs discussing this dimension.

The degree to which the "required" is more directed or less directed

Reread the 12-part "required" in the Gord and James case. Now, let's substitute the following "required" for the original 12-part one:

Required:
What should be done?

By simply asking "What should be done?" we are placing an enormous burden on the student. This question is many times more challenging than the original 12-part "required"; the original was much more directive, and provided the student with a framework of attack. When we ask "What should be done?" we are leaving students to their own devices: they are forced to develop their own structure; and the structure so developed must be custom-tailored to the situation, or it won't be credible, and the student's analysis will be seriously inadequate.

A place to begin providing structure in this case might be by first adopting a perspective, or role. Perhaps many roles will be needed to satisfactorily deal with the profound question of "What should be done?"

Now, let's change the "required" again:

Required:

1. Verify Gord's and James' calculations.
2. Using spreadsheet software, such as Lotus 1,2,3 or Quattro Pro, prepare a model of the NPV calculation. How sensitive is the NPV to changes in the final year's cash flow estimation? To changes in the interest rate?

This "required" forces the student to ignore most of the uncertainty, potential for conflict, and overall richness and realism of the scenario. This "required" is very specific and highly directed.

Let's examine one last potential "required" for the Gord and James case:

Required:

1. Who are the stakeholders in this situation? What are the ethical principles and issues involved?
2. In your opinion, what should James do? Explain.

This "required" results in a considerably less demanding case than the "What should be done?" version. Because it is much more directive, less of a burden is placed on the student's shoulders.

Be careful how you interpret the "required" in a question or case.

Too often, people who have studied hard and learned a lot about accounting or business subjects prepare poor responses to cases or questions because they neglected to take care in interpreting the "required." It is sometimes very tempting to focus on a familiar word or phrase and more or less ignore the substance of what is being asked. This is merely a caution for you to read the "required" carefully, pause for a second to decide whether the "required" is highly directed or less directed, and then judge just what is being asked of you.

The Profession of Accounting: Three Professional Groups

Medicine, fire prevention, art, and many other aspects of life and society are important — probably much more important in most people's eyes than accounting. After all, when a building is burning, the most important person to have around is a professional firefighter. And relative to the life-saving skills of doctors and nurses, the things accountants do often seem rather trivial and mundane. Accounting simply seems part of the woodwork, something innocuous. But it is *because* it first appears so mundane and innocuous that informed citizens must have some understanding of accounting.

Perhaps a well-designed management control system in a hospital could improve the delivery of medicine. Perhaps a comprehensive analysis of the costs of alternative firefighting equipment might enable a municipality to have first-class firefighting services while still having sufficient resources for other important civic purposes. Perhaps informative financial statements prepared by the management of a not-for-profit art gallery would encourage potential donors to provide resources so that the gallery would be able to subsidize promising young Canadian artists. Accounting information, as pointed out in this and the previous chapter, has an impact on our daily lives in a wide variety of contexts.

Who are the people who perform the important but relatively unknown functions of accounting? In this section, we describe the three major professional accounting groups in Canada, whose members are largely responsible for designing, implementing, and operating accounting systems.

The groups are the chartered accountants (CAs), the certified general accountants (CGAs), and the certified management accountants (CMAs). Each of these professional groups is organized both provincially and nationally. The provincial branches focus on education, professional regulation (which includes lobbying provincial governments on behalf of their members), the development of codes of professional ethics, and similar activities. The national branches focus on conducting research, developing national policies, and co-ordinating interprovincial activities such as the setting of national examinations. The national body of CAs, the Canadian Institute of Chartered Accountants (CICA), has led the way in establishing professional accounting standards in Canada. For example, over the past half-century the CICA through various committees (such as its Accounting Standards Board) has been instrumental in codifying generally accepted accounting principles (GAAP) and generally accepted auditing standards (GAAS). Through its Public Sector Accounting and Auditing Committee (PSAAC), the CICA has also established standards for various levels of governments and other public sector accounting entities.

The CMAs, through the Society of Management Accountants of Canada (SMAC), have made their mark mainly in the area of management accounting. SMAC publishes research studies and guidelines on various areas of management accounting practice; for example, a recent guideline dealt with the design of management compensation plans.

The CGAs, through the Certified General Accountants Association of Canada (CGAAC), also have an active research program, and have been very innovative in recent years in developing materials for accounting education. All three national groups publish professional journals directed mainly to their own members (*CAmagazine*, *CMA Magazine*, and *CGA Magazine* respectively). Both nationally and provincially, the three Canadian accounting groups co-operate in some activities and compete in others.

One way to classify accountants is by whether they are public practitioners. Accountants in public practice provide professional services to clients and receive a fee in return. They may operate as sole practitioners, in small partnerships, in larger regional partnerships, or as part of large national or international firms of professional accountants. Public practitioners may be engaged in any or all of the following:

- Providing a wide variety of accounting services to clients, including designing accounting systems, preparing accounting statements, and offering advice on accounting matters.
- Providing management advisory services (management consulting) in a wide range of areas, including the design of computer-based information systems, executive recruiting, and so on.
- Offering tax advice and tax return preparation.
- Auditing, which is an independent examination of accounting reports. Public accountants gather evidence so that they can form an opinion as to whether accounting reports comply with certain established standards, such as GAAP. Independent examinations, called "reviews," are also performed by public practitioners.

Reviews are much less intensive than audits and do not provide the same level of assurance to users of the accounting information. Audits are required by law in a wide variety of situations, such as for Canadian companies that issue shares and other financial instruments to the public. Also, provincial hospitals acts require that hospitals be audited annually, and federal election legislation requires that candidates' election contributions and expenditures be audited. These are only a few of the many situations where audits are required by law. However, there is increasing pressure to reduce the extent of legally required audits. For example, in 1994 Parliament passed legislation exempting wholly owned Canadian subsidiaries of foreign-owned companies from the audit requirement.

Although in general anyone may offer accounting, tax, and management advisory services to the public, various regulations are in force across Canada as to who may perform an audit with a view to rendering an opinion on financial statements. The jurisdictions have the following rules:[15]

- Yukon and Northwest Territories: No restrictions.
- British Columbia: Organizations established under the Company and Society acts must be audited by CAs, CGAs, or persons licensed by the Auditor Certification Board. Private companies (that is, companies whose shares do not trade on public stock exchanges such as the Vancouver Stock Exchange), and societies not registered under the above acts, are not restricted as to who may conduct an audit.
- Alberta: By law, only CMAs, CGAs, or CAs can provide audit or review services.
- Saskatchewan: At present, anyone may perform audits. The three national accounting professional bodies are lobbying the provincial government to adopt legislation to restrict the practice of auditing to their members.
- Manitoba: There are no restrictions on public practice. However, the provincial CA institute is attempting to persuade the other two accounting groups to join it in lobbying the provincial government to introduce a system for licensing public accountants.
- Ontario: Audits may be performed only by public accountants licensed by the provincial government's Public Accountancy Council. For all practical purposes, individuals must have a CA designation to be so licensed. There is a history in Ontario of significant acrimony between the CAs and the CGAs over public practice rights — especially those rights other than the right to perform an audit.
- Quebec: With some exceptions, only CAs may perform audits. CMAs and CGAs may audit unions, municipalities, and small businesses, and may provide some commentaries on financial statements.
- New Brunswick: CAs and CGAs are licensed to perform audits required under various laws.
- Nova Scotia: Only licensed public accountants may perform audits.
- Newfoundland and Prince Edward Island: Audits must be performed by CAs, although a recent court challenge to the Public Accounting and Auditing Act of P.E.I. may change this situation.

CAs, CGAs, and CMAs may perform their professional duties *other than* as public practitioners — that is, as employ-

[15] This section is based on material published in *CMA Magazine*, December/January 1993.

ees of organizations such as governments, industrial companies, financial institutions, and so on. Most professional accountants in Canada are not in public practice, and have roles such as that of James in the Gord and James case.

An interesting issue for accountants who are not in public practice relates to the question of "dual allegiance." For instance, if a professional accountant employed by a company is faced with subtle pressure from superiors to choose less-than-optimum accounting principles in order to ensure the survival of the company, which should take precedence — the accountant's duty to the employer, or the accountant's duty to the profession, including its code of ethics? The economic and social pressures in a situation such as this are not trivial; even so, duty to the profession must win out if the accountant's personal integrity and the well-being of the accounting profession are both to be maintained. Clearly, there's a lot to accounting, and practising accountants face a wide variety of challenges.

The two quotations that began this chapter offer some insight into the stereotype that society has had of accountants over the years. The perception exemplified in Raymond Chandler's image of the CPA (certified public accountant — the American analogue to the CA) seems to be changing, albeit very slowly. Ron Davidson's research suggests that modern professional accountants are far more interesting — and more human! The stereotype lives on, however, as evidenced by Gary Larson's cartoon from his series "The Far Side," which used to appear in many newspapers in North America. The cartoon, titled "Punk Accountants," showed three people (two men and a woman) in an elevator. Two pens pierced the nose of one of the men, and a pencil pierced his ear. The other man wore a calculator on his pierced ear, and had the tattoo "Add, Subtract, and Die" on his forearm.

Why do you think accountants were such a good choice for Larson's cartoon? Would it have been as effective if he had drawn "punk doctors" or "punk lawyers"? What is it about our stereotype of accountants that makes Larson's image so funny? The humour seems to lie in the sharp discrepancy between the nonconformist behaviour of people whom we believe are really members of the punk culture, and that of the two accountants, whom Larson portrays to look like punks, which we "know" they could never be. If accountants have such a grey, conventional stereotype, then perhaps what they do (that is, accounting) has a similar stereotype. What do you think? Is this dangerous?

Accounting, Organizations, and Society

In the following article,[16] two topics are discussed: how to define the accounting entity, and how to establish who the users are of the entity's financial statements. The entity under discussion is a sovereign state; the authors are the top accountants in the governments of Canada and the United States.

[16] *Accounting Horizons*, March 1987, pp. 17–24. Kenneth M. Dye was the Auditor General of Canada and Charles A. Bowsher was the Comptroller General of the United States at the time this article was published.

Financial Statements for a Sovereign State: The Federal Government Reporting Study

by Kenneth M. Dye and Charles A. Bowsher

Editor's Note: When Kenneth M. Dye, the Auditor General of Canada, issued a qualified audit opinion on his country's financial statements, he raised a series of questions to which authoritative answers did not exist. How should a sovereign nation report its financial position and results of operations? By what standards should the fairness of presentation of such reporting be judged? Who cared, anyway? Did anyone want or use that kind of information for any serious purpose? If so, how?

Seeking answers, Mr. Dye consulted with knowledgeable acquaintances, including Charles A. Bowsher, Comptroller General of the United States. In the United States, the General Accounting Office, headed by the Comptroller General, has the legal responsibility to promulgate federal government accounting standards. Out of their conversations came an extended research study, some interesting answers to these questions, an experimental set of financial statements for each government, and a number of unresolved issues.

... Specifically, the Canadian Group was to begin by having expert representatives of each identified user group explain their activities and needs. This information was later used to develop an illustrative Annual Financial Report. Members of the U.S. Group were to draw on the literature and their own expertise to develop an illustrative Annual Financial Report for subsequent discussion with users.

Jointly, the Core Group identified experts in both countries to serve on an International Advisory Group (IAG) for the study. These 22 advisers included senior government officials, recognized authorities in accounting and auditing, representatives of standard-setting groups, and professional accountants practicing in the public sector.

The User Groups

Based on the literature, discussions with advisers, and the experience of its members, the Core Group agreed to organize the study around six user groups. These groups were:

1. legislators;
2. citizens, the media, policy analysts, special interest groups, and other levels of government;
3. government planners and managers;
4. economists;
5. corporate users; and
6. lenders, security dealers, and their advisers.

In Phase II, the Canadian experts consulted 89 users across the six user groups, and an additional 50 citizens in five focus group discussions, and prepared reports on the findings for each user group. The U.S. Group and its advisers developed a first draft illustrative U.S. Annual Financial Report, based on their experience during the past several years with the Treasury prototype consolidated financial statements. The illustration also reflected the preliminary Canadian Phase II findings as well as a set of assumptions that had survived internal debate and challenge.

In Phase III, structure was added to allow Canadian and U.S. interview teams to test the Phase II findings and ensure that all respondents were expressing their opinions and preferences with respect to identified issues. This structure was achieved in two ways:

- Sixteen major questions were identified from the findings of the Phase II interviews. These were focused on information that could be presented in a summary-level Annual Financial Report.
- The Canadian group drafted an illustrative Annual Financial Report designed to satisfy as many as possible of the information needs identified in Phase II.

At the Phase II interviews, all respondents were asked to express an opinion on the potential usefulness of an Annual Financial Report such as was illustrated and to react to the questions on the other 15 issues. In all, 131 users were consulted in Canada and 125 in the U.S. across the six user groups during Phase III ...

Interrelationships Among the User Groups

An early finding of the study was that user groups varied greatly in their ability to describe their information needs clearly and to relate specific information needs to their specific activities. They also differed in how they obtained financial information about the federal government. Some user groups seldom used federal government financial reports directly, relying instead on other users to process the information for them. To get a better understanding of the differences and relationships among user groups, the central Core Group integrated the findings from all six studies into a model of user activities and information flows. The model ... organizes the six user groups, by the nature of their activities, into three sets, each set represented by two overlapping circles.

1. and 3. Legislators and Government Planners and Managers.
Users in this set have responsibility, directly or indirectly, for the flow of financial information to other users. They also have responsibility for the real effects — the impact of government activities on people and organizations in society — to which the financial information relates.

2. and 5. Citizens and Corporate Users.
These are the beneficiaries of federal government operations. Through taxes, they also pay the bills. Other levels of government are not shown on the model. Some are similar to corporations in their use of information; others do extensive economic analysis and have information needs similar to those in the next set of users.

4. and 6. Media and Analysts.
Users in this set are concerned with analyzing and disseminating information. Analysts include social policy analysts, economic analysts, and the financial market analysts in the lenders' group.

At the top of the model, the main flow of financial and operating information is shown as going direct from government to the media and analysts. It must be remembered, however, that the reported financial information reflects government activities that have a real impact on citizens and corporations. In various ways, information about these real effects reaches media and analysts. The latter combine the financial and other information in reports and commentaries that are read by citizens and corporate users, legislators and government planners, and managers.

Citizens and corporate users, for the most part, do not read the financial reports of the federal government. They have neither the time nor the expertise to analyze such information in terms of its significance in their planning, investing, financing, lending, borrowing, spending, and saving activities. They look to analysts in the media, financial institutions, policy institutes, etc., to do such analysis for them.

Canadian legislators, although they are direct users of federal government reports in many of their legislative activities, also rely heavily on the media and outside analysts for reports on the social and economic effects of government activities. They often have difficulty getting access to the federal government's own studies of this type, and suffer the same constraints of too little time and a lack of expert knowledge as do the citizens and corporate users. They also point out that, in addition to being a source of information, many reports of the media, analysts, and special interest groups demand a political response.

Legislators in the U.S. often turn to professional staff to interpret and analyze financial data in areas of special interest to a member, but they also rely heavily on the media and outside analysts for interpretation of data outside their own areas of specialization.

Key Role of Analysts and the Media
In considering the study's findings on the information needs of the different user groups, it is important to keep in mind the role played by the media and analysts. They are the most direct users of federal government financial reports, the major source of information about the government for citizens and corporations, and an important source of information for legislators. Federal government financial reports will serve the needs of legislators, citizens, and corporations well only if the needs of the media and analysts are adequately met. By the same token, the media and analysts are the users best able to define clearly the nature of the financial information about government that they need and the characteristics that such information should have to suit their needs best.

Information Needs of Analysts and Media
The financial information needs of the media and analysts are as

diverse as the many different kinds of reports and analyses they prepare. Nevertheless, there are several characteristics that are common to their information needs. A fundamental concern of these groups is to obtain a clear understanding of government finances and activities at the summary level as an overview and lead-in to detailed analysis. Accordingly, they need financial information organized in successive levels of detail, starting with a succinct overall picture of federal government finances, what it owns and what it owes, where its revenue comes from, and how it is spent.

The very diversity of the financial information needs of these direct users requires that financial reports be organized to provide maximum flexibility in the use of the information presented. Summary information should be referenced to supporting detailed information that should be coherent and consistent with aggregate information. Where possible, detailed information should be cross-classified and referenced to other sources of related or more detailed information. A further requirement is that information should be presented objectively, without bias; estimated or projected information should be accompanied by a clear description of the assumptions and methods used in calculating it.

Most analytical work involves investigating relationships between financial information and other economic and social information. It is important to these users, therefore, that financial information on government activities be classified and presented in such a way that it can be related to observed or predicted social and economic effects of the activities.

For analysis of social impact, program efficiency, and long-term economic effects, information is needed to show both the acquisition and consumption of resources in the periods that they are acquired and consumed. The cost of long-lived physical assets would be allocated (as depreciation) over the periods in which they provide benefits. For short- and medium-term analyses of financial market and other economic effects, information is needed on the aggregate cash flows arising from operations and from acquiring and disposing of long-lived physical assets, acquiring and holding investments, and incurring and discharging liabilities.

Analysts often wish to examine trends in reported financial information and compare the trends with related non-financial information or with the performance of other governments. Therefore, they need accounting policies and classifications that remain relatively consistent from period to period. To the extent possible, they need reported information that covers consecutive periods of at least ten years, in both current and constant dollars. Where accounting changes are made to improve the relevance or reliability of reported information, they need amounts reported for prior periods to be adjusted accordingly.

Much of the analysis carried out by these groups of direct users depends for its rigor on the comparability of forecast financial information with actual financial information, or on the comparability of federal government financial information with financial information on other sectors of the economy, other levels of government, or foreign governments. Therefore they need financial information in government budgets, estimates, and historical accounts all prepared in accordance with the same accounting policies and classified in the same manner. To the extent possible, they need accounting policies for the federal government that will provide comparability with other sectors of the economy and other governments, both domestic and foreign. Analysts must have a clear understanding of the exact nature of the information they are using to ensure that they are using it meaningfully. To this end, they need a full description of the accounting policies followed in the preparation of financial information and of the nature and effect of changes in the accounting policies from those followed in the prior period.

Analysts and members of the media study and report on the size and growth of the federal government and on the scope and influence of its activities. They stressed that, to ensure a complete picture, they need a summary financial report that encompasses all activities of the government, including those of its various agencies and government-owned corporations. They find that the abundance of detailed financial data published by the government does not give them a succinct, comprehensive, and understandable overall picture. Similarly, the report should provide information on activities that do not necessarily require an outlay of funds, such as tax expenditures, insurance programs, and loan guarantees.

A particular concern of members of the media is that financial information be presented in ways that they can readily communicate to their readers, listeners, or viewers. For this purpose, they need graphic displays of the relative magnitude of various activities such as spending, taxation, and borrowing, and their trends over time. This together with per capita and percentage of Gross National Product displays, helps overcome the communication barrier imposed by large numbers. They also need graphic displays of changes over time in economic indicators that can serve as overall measures of performance or help to explain period-to-period variations in reported financial information.

Importance of a Summary Annual Financial Report

The need for a concise summary Annual Financial Report was expressed by virtually all users in all user groups. Users believe that such a report would bring together in an easily read and understood format a consistent set of basic data about the federal government to:

- give an overview of the financial position and operating results of the entire government;
- provide a common framework to enhance users' understanding of government operations;
- provide an common data base for analysis and for developing and debating policy decisions;
- provide an historical perspective from which to consider future budget and spending proposals;
- assist users in demanding an accountability for actual results by comparison with earlier projections or budgets;
- provide a key to matters of interest about which users may want further, more detailed information;
- facilitate the communication of information on government to others (for example, by legislators to their constituents or by media representatives to their audiences); and
- save users the time otherwise needed to search through voluminous reports for desired information about the government and to work out the required reconciliations.

Most users wanted physical assets included in reported assets and allocated to expense as they are sold or consumed. Users need this information to get:

- a complete picture of financial position, including all the resources available to government;
- an accurate picture of the size of government;
- a complete measure of the annual cost of government services;
- a measure of cost that is useful for analysis of trends and for comparison with measures of output or benefit;
- an indication of future replacement needs; and
- a measure of annual deficit that reflects the consumption of resources to finance current operations.

Inclusion of All Government Activities

The U.S. findings disclosed no significant divergence in users' needs respecting inclusion of all government activities in the reporting entity. Most users studied in the U.S. wanted all government activities consolidated regardless of the nature of the activities or the organizational form in which they are carried out. The same agreement does not hold for Canada. Many users in Canada believe that full consolidation is necessary to disclose fully the financial position and borrowing requirements of the government, to assess the socio-economic impact of government activities, and to assess the size and growth of government. Many others, however, saw a fundamental distinction between the commercial and non-commercial operations of government and wanted two separate consolidations — a basic consolidation of "governmental-type" activities that excludes commercial activities carried out by government-owned business enterprises, and a separate consolidation of those government-owned business enterprises.

Liabilities for Pension Plans and Social Programs

With few exceptions, users wanted the federal government's financial statements to include the full actuarially-calculated liability for employee pension plans. Almost all users were in agreement that future-oriented information on social programs should also be included in the summary financial statements. This could take the form of an actuarial projection of future benefit payments and future contributions, or the actuarial liability represented by the summation of the present values of the streams of future benefit payments less contributions. Disagreement existed among users as to whether this information should be included in the body of the financial statements, thus affecting performance data, or only in footnotes ...

Conclusion

If we had entertained any idea that the variety of ways in which information can be presented in financial reports was an esoteric matter of interest only to accountants and of no great relevance to those who actually make financial decisions, we should have been disabused of that erroneous notion by the results of this study. The governments of Canada and the United States are continually involved in financial transactions and commitments amounting to billions of dollars that affect every segment of the nation's economy. Massive federal programs encompass housing, health, education, income security, and defense. Finding the money to pay for these programs has an enormous impact on financial markets.

The people needing information about these activities include those who have primary responsibility for making and implementing government policies — the legislators and government managers — and those external to the government who are concerned with or affected by its policies — citizens, corporations, lenders, analysts, and the media. The understanding of government activities by any of these groups is significantly affected by the form and content of the government's financial reports.

Many unanswered questions still remain ...

Our common interest is in the development of consistent accounting and reporting standards that are based on users' needs for financial information. Well-thought-out standards on this basis will have immense value in improving the relevance, comparability, and credibility of financial reporting by governments at all levels in Canada and the United States, and possibly in other nations throughout the world ...

CHAPTER SUMMARY

In the first two chapters, you have been introduced to definitions that emphasize different aspects of accounting. Chapter 2 has also described seven key ideas that are important for all accounting subdisciplines: accountability, accounting entity, user orientation, substance over form, net present value, classification, and ethical behaviour.

The Gord and James case illustrated several of these key ideas. The discussion that followed it emphasized the importance of interpreting the "required" of a question or case. The chapter concluded with a description of the Canadian accounting profession.

Suggested Answers to Accounting and Business Decisions

Decision A

Both definitions stress important aspects of accounting: the AAA definition is broader, and emphasizes that accounting is an information system that has the requirement to identify, measure, and communicate information to users so as to satisfy their information needs. For its part, the CICA definition emphasizes the more technical aspects of accounting, focusing on the detailed steps in a process. Perhaps both perspectives are necessary complements to each other. Like most definitions, these enlighten us yet also limit our perspective. As you gain more experience with accounting, you'll likely conclude that it has both technical and nontechnical aspects. A good example of this "split personality" of accounting is found in the Gord and James case: here, the technical side of accounting is represented by the NPV calculations, by the ways new projects affect income statements (through depreciation and so on), and by the procedures managers must follow to get new projects approved. The nontechnical (or behavioural, or social) side of accounting is represented by the effect that the project approvals system has on managers' behaviour, integrity, and interpersonal relations.

Decision B

Leanne and Margo need help in the following areas: (1) deciding on the legal form of their business; (2) deciding what information they would need to run the business; and (3) deciding whether financial statements would be useful to them.

(1) We don't know much about Leanne and Margo (Are they in their 20s? Their 60s? Are they retired? Are they well off?), so let's assume they're both about 50 years old, have recently taken early retirement from their employer (an all-too-common phenomenon in the 1990s), and have just enough money to put a decent amount down on the "lovely old brick house." We'll also assume that the house will be their only residence.

Their bed-and-breakfast operation will start off as a small business, so the costs of incorporation probably will outweigh any benefits. They seem to have some resources to pay for their day-to-day operations (remember that we assumed they took early retirement; they probably have pensions of some sort), but they may still want a bank loan or line of credit. Being incorporated won't be of much help here, since the banker will most likely require personal guarantees anyway. So, operating as a partnership seems the better option. This means that they must draft, with the help of legal advisers, a partnership contract; otherwise, we can just about guarantee that eventually they will be at each others' throats. Better to plan ahead regarding questions such as, "How should profits be split?" "How should they be computed?" "Who is responsible for what?" "What happens when one of the partners wants out?" and so on.

(2) Information needs: Leanne and Margo will need to keep track of room bookings, cash receipts, cash payments, supplies (soap, linen, food, and the like), taxes such as the GST, guest telephone calls, and so forth. They also will need to determine what portion of general household expenses, such as property taxes, cable TV, and interest on the mortgage, are business and what portion are personal. In effect, they need to decide on the "boundaries" of their business entity. Keeping track of various categories of expenses and payments will probably be very important to them, since they will then be able to exercise a bit of control over at least some expense categories. It also may help them in setting the room rates, although competitors' prices may be the real determining factor.

The information on expenses as well as the information on actual booking revenues would probably be kept by month. There is a lot of other information that they might find useful — competitors' rates and room quality, booking forecasts, and so on. It is imperative to know about the business before considering in depth what information will be needed.

(3) Will financial statements be useful to the partners? Most of the accounting and other information suggested in (2) is *not* formal financial statement information. The detailed accounting records the two friends keep will be mainly for their own use, as part of a management accounting and operational accounting system. However, detailed cash-flow financial statements (and detailed cash-flow forecasted financial statements to compare the actual statements with) will be very useful. Keeping control over cash flows will be one of their most critical activities. Also, preparing an income statement every quarter-year, and certainly annually, will probably be important, since they are going to share profits. Deciding *before the fact* how profits, or net income, is to be computed is crucial. Perhaps they will want to use GAAP or an agreed-upon variant. They may decide to have the statements audited, just so that business won't interfere with friendship.

KEY TERMS

Accountability is the responsibility of one party to take only specific, allowable acts on behalf of another party, and to keep that other party fully informed. The obligation arising under an accountability relationship may be discharged by the provision of information, such as financial statements.

Accounting was defined in one way in Chapter 1, and in two additional (and better) ways in Chapter 2. There have been many other definitions over time and in various countries. The 1966 American Accounting Association definition that was described at the start of the chapter is one that focuses on a user orientation and is also general enough to be adaptable to changes in how accounting information is handled by technology:

... the process of identifying, measuring, and communicating economic information to permit informed judgments and decisions by users of the information.

Accounting entity is the focus of an accounting — the individual, group, organization, part of an organization, or group of organizations that is being accounted for. The CICA in *Terminology for Accountants* provides the following definition: "One or more accounting units that are treated as one for purposes of financial reporting."

Certified general accountants are members of one of the major professional accounting groups in Canada, the Certified General Accountants Association.

Chartered accountants are members of one of the major professional accounting groups in Canada, the Institutes (in Quebec, the *ordre*) of Chartered Accountants.

Certified management accountants are members of one of the major professional accounting groups in Canada, the Society of Management Accountants.

Classification in accounting refers to classifying items into categories that users of the resulting accounting information may find useful. Say, for example, that a capital asset cost $100,000 and is expected to provide ten years of service to an accounting entity that has total assets of $250,000. If the $100,000 is classified as an expense as soon as it is expended, the resulting balance sheet and income statement may not provide useful measures of financial position and results of operations, respectively. Preferably, the $100,000 should be classified as a capital asset on the balance sheet, and its cost depreciated over the ten years.

A ***corporation*** is a distinct legal entity that exists until it is dissolved by law. It has a legal existence of its own, separate from its owners, and can own property, owe debts, be sued, and sue other parties.

Ethics refers to the study of right or good conduct. To ensure that our society operates fairly and in a caring manner, ethical conduct should be an embedded part of behaviour. And in order to increase the likelihood that it is, accountants must make themselves aware of the ethical implications of accounting and business decisions and behaviour. Sometimes it will be relatively easy to identify the ethical implications of a situation; other times, it may not be so easy. Even when the ethical implications have been identified, it may be virtually impossible to make a choice that will be regarded as "ethical" by everyone.

Interval measures are like the measures on a metre-stick or ruler. A given interval of a certain number of centimetres means the same thing wherever you measure it on the scale.

Net present value (NPV) of a project or other accounting entity is a hypothetical amount of money that is derived by computing the present value of expected future cash inflows of the project or other accounting entity, and subtracting the present value of expected future cash outflows of the project or other accounting entity.

Net present value criterion is a criterion for accepting or rejecting a project (for example, purchasing a new manufacturing facility, introducing a new product); it must almost always be considered along with other information about the project. The NPV criterion is widely, although not universally, accepted by businesspeople, government decision-makers, and others. It is an estimate that involves forecasting the amounts and timing of future cash flows, and choosing discount (or interest) rates.

Nominal measures are labels assigned to different categories of things, in order to highlight important differences for some specific purpose. In accounting, we distinguish between "liabilities" and "owners' equity," since they represent the two broad categories of the sources of an accounting entity's resources. As another example, "current liabilities" are distinguished from "noncurrent (or long-term) liabilities," since predicting when the accounting entity may have to pay out cash is of crucial importance to various users.

Ordinal measures involve the assignment of numbers to things, to signify a hierarchy. Current assets on a company's balance sheet are usually listed in order of declining liquidity.

A ***partnership*** is an arrangement among two or more people, or groups of people, to conduct business or other economic or social activity on (usually) an ongoing basis. A partnership is not a legal entity; however, the partners usually have negotiated a partnership agreement, which is a written legal contract that specifies their duties and rights.

Present value is a hypothetical amount derived by computing what cash amount would be equivalent *today* to one or more cash flows expected to be received or paid at specific points in the future.

A ***proprietorship***, also called a sole proprietorship, refers to a business owned, and usually operated, by a single individual. It is not a legal entity, and so from the law's perspective such a business is indistinguishable from the other activities of the owner.

Ratio measures refer to measures in which the ratio of two numbers can be meaningfully interpreted. For example, if Company A has cash of $10,000, and Company B has cash of $5,000, then it is meaningful to say that Company A has twice as much cash as Company B. Company A has twice as many units of cash, and thus may have twice as much buying power.

Substance over form means that the essence, or substance, of a business event should determine how the event is accounted for.

User orientation refers to an approach to developing accounting standards and rules, and preparing accounting information, that focuses on providing users with accounting information that is relevant to their needs. This seems like a reasonable approach to take, but often it is not possible, for reasons such as the following:

- Users may not really know what they need.
- It may be very costly to provide all users, or even the more influential ones, with what they need or want.
- Some information desired by users may be dangerously unreliable.
- Some information desired by users may, in the opinion of management, have the potential to damage the accounting entity in various ways, such as by providing competitors with key information.

Users are the various categories of people who need accounting and other financial information about an accounting entity. Users may include actual and potential owners, managers, creditors, employees, unions, and so on. Not every conceivable category of people is always a user of accounting information about a particular accounting entity. For example, the tax authorities are not a user of accounting information prepared by an accounting entity that is not taxable, such as a government agency.

FACT AND DESCRIPTION QUESTIONS

1. Are accounting items on the asset side of the balance sheet nominal, ordinal, interval, or ratio measures?
2. Partnerships and proprietorships are not legal entities, but may be accounting entities. How is this possible?
3. A corporation that is a legal entity may consist of several accounting entities. Conversely, several corporations may make up a single accounting entity. How is this possible?
4. Different users of accounting information may have different information needs. How might accounting information satisfy these diverse needs?
5. Explain how different users may have conflicts over the desirability of disclosing particular information.
6. Describe five instances in which classification is important in accounting.
7. Explain the significance of the net present value criterion. Suggest another, competing criterion.
8. "An understanding of the ethical implications of business and accounting decisions is important." Explain.
9. Describe the three major professional accounting groups in Canada. How are they similar? How do they differ?
10. Explain the relationship between accounting and accountability.

Questions for Analysis and Discussion

11. In the following article, forensic accountant Michael Beber argues that numbers, including accounting numbers, should always be challenged for their integrity.

Accountants Should Look Past Raw Numbers to Accurately Gauge Prospects for Profitability

by Michael Beber

Numbers never lie, goes the old saying, That may be true. But numbers alone rarely tell the whole story. As the following case history illustrates, the accurate assessment of financial information usually requires a process far more complex than simply providing calculations and projections.

In 1987, following a long, bitter court battle with a business conglomerate, George Koharski was awarded ownership of a 40-acre lakefront property.

Koharski successfully claimed title based on his great uncle's will, which had been missing for more than 20 years, before it was discovered in 1980 in an old photograph album.

Soon after the will surfaced, Koharski launched a suit against the conglomerate, Carbeth Industries Inc., which claimed ownership of the property. Carbeth was operating the property as a public beach while waiting for zoning changes.

The court ordered Carbeth to compensate Koharski for lost income dating back to 1977, the year in which Koharski would have assumed control of the land under the terms of the will.

Koharski's accountants presented Carbeth with a $3.05-million claim, including interest. According to their report, if Koharski possessed the land, he would have earned that amount from two main sources:

- $2.1 million in profits from a waterslide and amusement park that he could have operated on the site and
- $950,000 in parking revenues.

"We consider our findings to be a conservative estimate of the income Mr. Koharski could have generated during the period in question," the report concluded.

"Carbeth did not exploit the revenue potential of the property to the extent that a successful businessman like Mr. Koharski would have," it added.

It was true that Carbeth had not yet developed the property as a revenue-generating business. The land was, however, purchased with the intention of building luxurious waterfront condominiums. But those plans stalled after local residents opposed the zoning changes.

That process dragged on at a snail's pace for more than a decade, during which time Carbeth opened the beachfront to the public and derived its income solely from daily parking rates.

Carbeth considered Koharski's claim to be excessive and retained forensic accountants to assess his report.

The primary issue the forensic accountants addressed was the claim for future profits from the hypothetical waterslide and amusement park.

While Koharski's accountants produced extensive calculations of revenues and profits from various rides and confection stands, it did not question the economic viability of the project.

Rather, it automatically assumed the park would have existed if Koharski had wanted, an incorrect assumption.

Although Koharski was an experienced and successful entrepreneur, it was apparent from financial statements that he lacked the capital necessary to purchase the equipment required. Interviews with experts also raised the possibility he may not qualify for insurance coverage.

"With litigation settlements skyrocketing," an insurance expert said, "we're very reluctant to issue policies to someone with no experience in such a high-risk business. But if we did, I guarantee the cost would hardly make it worthwhile."

These findings placed his financial projections in serious doubt.

In addition, Carbeth's forensic accountants discovered the type of operation described in Koharski's report was far from a sure thing.

It found that similar ventures experienced serious financial problems during the 1980s. More significantly, an amusement park less than 30 miles from Koharski's property, which offered almost identical services to those he proposed, had—after several years of financial losses—gone bankrupt in 1986.

An interview with the trustee revealed that an "insufficient local population base" was a major reason for the park's demise. The trustee also indicated it had been unable to sell the park because it could not provide a guarantee that new owners would obtain liability insurance.

Following an interview with the forensic accountants, the former owner said if he was asked in court for his opinion on Koharski's chances for success in the same market, he would estimate it to be "uncertain at best."

Carbeth's forensic accountants then turned their attention to Koharski's projected parking revenues. They accepted that Koharski would have been able to generate higher returns than Carbeth, but they disagreed with the amount.

Carbeth earned $175,000 from parking during the period in question. However, it had not increased its rates consistent with inflation, nor were they at the highest level the market could bear.

Koharski's figure of $950,000 for parking revenues was based on assumptions that Carbeth's experts questioned.

One was the average annual visitor total. Koharski's accountants selected visitor totals from a 1982 research report to represent an average year. But a study of weather conditions for the area showed that 1982 was one of the hottest and sunniest years of the century. In other years, weather conditions were much poorer and visitor totals were lower.

The Koharski report also projected increased revenues from a larger parking lot that would have been constructed to accommodate the increased number of visitors attracted to the site because of the amusement park. Since the nearby park had gone bankrupt due to dwindling attendance figures, Carbeth's forensic accountants said that supposition was highly unlikely.

In their final report, Carbeth's forensic accountants pegged Koharski's lost income between $550,000-$620,000, based entirely on parking revenues. In their opinion, the issue of profits from the amusement park was too remote to warrant consideration.

Koharski's lawyers agreed. A few days before the matter was scheduled for trial, an out-of-court settlement was reached for $575,000.

Numbers—especially large and significant ones in impressive-looking reports—can dazzle and intimidate. But they should never be accepted without first examining the assumptions and information upon which they are based. Failure to do so will inevitably cost you the kind of numbers that deplete your bottom line.

The Bottom Line, *May 1993, p. 18. With permission of Michael Beber and* Bottom Line.

(a) How reliable, in your opinion, are numbers such as net income, total assets, and other accounting numbers? How reliable are they in the case of Devo Green's On Ice? in the case of Corel Corporation?

(b) Comment on Michael Beber's opinions.

12. Users of accounting information often demand more and more information — complete disclosure is their byword. Is such a policy always in the best interests of users of financial accounting information?

13. Assume that it is the year 2000, and the Futures Committee of the national body for setting accounting standards is meeting to discuss a proposal by one of its members. The proposal relates to the potential use of databases in financial reporting, and focuses on the economic and social desirability of such an approach. A database approach to financial reporting would involve the computer-based capture, storage, and distribution of data on individual economic "events"; the individual users of this data would make their own decisions as to how the data are to be aggregated and values assigned. A major benefit claimed for this approach is that the "arbitrary" valuations and aggregations currently made by accountants would be done away with, and this would minimize information loss. Many argue, further, that the current distinction between insiders/preparers and outsiders/users would all but disappear. Key excerpts from a discussion paper distributed before the meeting are reproduced in the exhibit to this case on page 95.

A move toward database corporate financial reporting would obviously have profound effects on the corporate reporting system as we now know it. The committee wishes to explore the possible ramifications of such a move on all those who could be affected, and has engaged an independent consultant to evaluate the concept, given the perspectives offered in the discussion paper.

Required:

Adopt the role of the independent consultant, and prepare an appropriate report for the committee's use.

EXHIBIT

I. Technology

a. Inexpensive mass storage devices capable of securely storing data about events and software capable of efficient management and retrieval of this data is available.
b. Database disclosure would require the ability to securely transmit large volumes of data reliably, cheaply, and quickly from the company's database to users. Such technology is available.
c. Limitations of user data processing are being overcome; further, intermediaries specializing in the extraction, aggregation, valuation, and interpretation of database events will probably arise.

CONCLUSION: Technological constraints to a database approach to financial reporting are probably not serious.

II. Economic and Social Feasibility (It should be noted that "assessing the economic feasibility of database disclosure is certainly much more complex than assessing its technical feasibility."*)

d. There would be no need for the standard-setting committee to resolve controversies over issues involving when to record revenues, the need to account for depreciation, classification, etc. Thus, the direct and indirect costs of standard-setting would radically decrease, as would the costs of corporate compliance and user education.
e. Users could monitor important transactions and other events in 'real-time', and not have to wait for traditional financial accounting reports.
f. Unions and employees could benefit by having access to labour-related information in the database.
g. There will be need for data standardization, in terms of transaction codes, record structures, etc. The accounting standard-setting committee could be involved here, as would government.
h. The ongoing costs of continuously updating and maintaining such a system might be significant. An industry offering such services might be expected to arise, thus resulting in reduced costs, including possible economies of scale.

* B.E. Cushing, "On the Feasibility and the Consequences of a Database Approach to Corporate Financial Reporting," *Journal of Information Systems*, Spring 1989, Vol. 3, no. 2, pp. 29–52.

14. A professional accountant wrote the following in *CAmagazine:*[17]

> *Laws have been enacted to govern the emission of harmful substances, production and handling of dangerous goods, storage and ultimate disposal of or dispersal of toxic substances ... Tough new legislation and regulations will naturally bring new (and greater) risks, demands and costs to business. Already, government agencies can:*
>
> - *Force management to prepare environmental assessments and impact studies before allowing project development work to commence.*
> - *Require extensive testing, control or containment of emissions that are caused by production activities.*
> - *Specify packaging, handling, shipment and storage procedures; and require closure plans and financial assurance that such plans will be carried out in accordance with approved guidelines.*
>
> *These complications must be managed by corporate directors and officers, but they are borne either directly or indirectly by stakeholders, a word that encompasses shareholders, lenders, employees, customers, suppliers and governments, among others.*
>
> *Each stakeholder has a vested interest in both the enterprise's financial health and its effect on the land we use, the air we breathe and the water we drink. Obviously, information about an enterprise's impact on the environment and the resulting or potential cost of its activities must be communicated to them.*
>
> *But not all stakeholders are created equal. Some are able to influence management and consequently receive special information about environmental matters. Lenders, for example, often demand and receive special reports designed to provide specific information about environmental impact, risks and costs. Government prerogatives enable them to dictate the form and content of environmental reports. Similarly, influential shareholders, unions, customers and suppliers can often obtain information designed for their special needs. The privileged relationship between a limited number of stakeholders and management facilitates communication and satisfies certain information needs. Others, including minority shareholders, do not have direct access to or influence over management and, therefore, may lack important decision-making information — information that should be provided by general-purpose financial statements.*
>
> *A search of the Canadian Financial Database, which contains the annual reports from 1983 to 1989 of more than 500 public Canadian companies, revealed that very few described how they accounted for environmental costs ... This indicates either that environmental costs ... are, for the great majority of companies, immaterial or that there has been a reluctance to communicate the necessary information. Given the significance of the issues ... it seems unlikely that environmental matters really have been immaterial ... Rather, it seems a breakdown in communication has occurred between financial statement preparers and stakeholders about environmental risks and costs.*

Required:

(a) Are stakeholders users?

(b) Do you agree that "not all stakeholders are created equal"? Does this also apply to financial statement users?

[17] Anthony Hawkshaw, "Status Quo Vadis — Few companies describe how they account for environmental costs even though existing standards allow for such disclosure", *CAmagazine*, March 1991, pp. 22–26. Reprinted with permission from *CAmagazine*, published by the Canadian Institute of Chartered Accountants, Toronto, Canada.

(c) Suppose you are the CEO of a mining company that has just, by accident, dumped toxic liquids in a nearby river. What personal, organizational, and societal considerations may be important as you develop a policy to disclose and account?

15. In the following article, a Vancouver-based environmentalist brings the issue of accountability down to a very personal level. After reading the article, answer these questions:

    (a) How can accounting, including its various subdisciplines, contribute to Suzuki's notion of accountability?
    (b) Does "too much" accountability act as a deterrent?

If Nobody Is Accountable, Fairness Is Unteachable

by David Suzuki

When I was a boy, my parents banged home the message that growing up meant taking responsibility. And, they taught me, once a responsibility is accepted or assigned, if I did my best, I would be rewarded with appreciation.

But there was a catch. I also carried the burden of accountability for what I did. Fibbing or evading would only gain temporary relief and I would have to face up to it in the end.

As a father, I find myself parroting my parents' messages to my children. But these days it's hard to be credible because my daughters can see all around them in the real world that responsibility, accountability and honesty are readily evaded without paying the consequences. And as my daughter Severn asks: "How can we be any different from adults when you are our role models? You teach us how to behave by what you do."

Children are concerned about what they know is the destruction of their future and some feel strongly enough to be arrested for protesting. Yet they see people who are lionized for being successful while evading accountability for the ecological impact of their activities.

Youth know industry executives don't go to jail for promulgating policies that destroy the ozone layer, release radioactive tailings into water or permanently destroy old growth forests. So where is the fairness and accountability?

I was taught in school that we have the best political system in the world.

In a democracy, we elect people to represent and lead us into the future. The general public pays for government programs knowing that we are their beneficiaries.

Politicians deserve recognition when they do well. But they seem to want it both ways, bearing no accountability for poor decisions. In the election, they have again pushed the environment aside as a marginal issue. But who will be hold accountable when the price of today's failure to act becomes apparent? Mulroney is no longer accountable for what his two governments failed to do.

What of the environment ministers appointed since 1988, when Mulroney announced the environment was one of his major priorities? Lucien Bouchard quickly jettisoned his concern over global warming for the cause of Quebec independence. Robert de Cotret brought in an inadequate Green Plan very late, was shuffled out of the portfolio and has now retired. Jean Charest defended the Green Plan while his government gutted it in the name of fiscal responsibility and now has gone on to bigger political pastures.

Bouchard told me in 1989 that "global warming endangers the very survival of our species," yet he could not cancel Hibernia and other oil megaprojects because it was a commitment made by the last government. "We cannot annihilate the past," he told me.

And now Prime Minister Kim Campbell, having served faithfully in the past cabinet, boldly states that history and the past do not count in this election. New faces, new positions and new rhetoric now obliterate the past and with it, any accountability.

In 1987, the United Nations Commission on Environment and Development under Gro Harlem

Brundtland published *Our Common Future*, a report documenting the perilous state of the Earth and the need to act quickly and profoundly to get off our destructive path. Mulroney and the premiers endorsed the Brundtland Report and pledged themselves to implementing its recommendations. Less than a year later, it was clear there was no follow-through. Who can we hold accountable?

In June, 1992, over 100 world leaders and representatives of 180 countries gathered at Rio de Janeiro for the Earth Summit. Again we heard the warnings of deep ecological crisis as politicians paraded before the cameras pledging their commitments. Yet even Maurice Strong, the secretary-general of the Earth Summit and an inveterate optimist, has had to admit that there has been a terrible backsliding on the commitments made at Rio. Isn't there anyone we can blame?

I fear for my children, who are confused by the contradictions between my old-fashioned lessons about responsibility, honesty and accountability and what they see going on.

I'm afraid they find much to prove me wrong.

16. The following article describes how a Canadian company — CT Financial Services Inc. (owner of Canada Trust, the country's largest trust company) — implements the concept of accountability using the annual report as a communication instrument. As the article points out, such an emphasis on accountability seems consistent with the views put forward by the eminent management theorist Peter Drucker. After reading the article, answer these questions:
    (a) Should companies hold themselves publicly accountable for achieving quantitative targets, as CT Financial Services does? What are the advantages and drawbacks?
    (b) Are there qualitative goals that companies should be held publicly accountable for achieving?
    (c) The company's CEO "sees the annual report card as a useful instrument for measuring progress and setting goals." Who controls the content of this "report card"?

Perspective: Report Card

by David Olive

Any government, whether that of a company or a nation, degenerates into mediocrity and malperformance if it is not clearly accountable to someone for results.

–Peter Drucker, management guru, in his just-published The Post-Capitalist Society

Would-be masters of management strategy can learn a great deal from studying the track record of CT Financial Services Inc., holding company of Canada Trust, the biggest trust company in the nation. Check out the last 10 years' worth of CT annual reports and see for yourself how, with single-minded purpose, CT has stolen a march on the banks. It now ranks fourth against the Big Six banks in residential mortgage market share, fifth in total personal deposits, and fifth in mutual fund assets. Its profits in 1992 are down a modest 21% from the 1989 peak of $246 million. Elsewhere in the industry profits have been pretty much wiped out and many weak institutions (First City Trust and Central Guaranty Trust, for instance) have disappeared. Unlike most of the banks, the cautious Canada Trust was not seduced during the boom times to lend to blue-chip borrowers on an unsecured basis: it will likely recoup 90% or so of its loans to troubled developers Olympia & York, Bramalea and Lehndorrf, while its peers can expect to recover 25 cents or less on the dollar from many of their unsecured loans.

Canada Trust has thrived by sticking to one business: retail banking. Some 95% of its deposits come from individual Canadians, and not from the wholesale money markets, where funds are more costly to raise and in severe cases cannot be raised at all (explaining the sudden 1986 collapse of Continental Bank of Canada). Understanding that customer and employee satisfaction are strongly linked, CT conducts elaborate surveys of clients, complete with an incentive reward program for branch teams where customer service levels exceed those of CT's major competitors; and regular Employee Opinion Surveys, which reveal areas of dissatisfaction requiring attention. Not surprisingly, absenteeism and turnover rates at CT are lower than at rival firms. Flextime and Work Choice programs are in place to enable working parents to tailor their working hours to the demands of raising a family.

By now CEOs at CT's rivals will be objecting, correctly, that they, too, have pursued similar innovations, if not with quite the same speed, enthusiasm or consistent commitment to keeping employees and everyone else with a stake in the enterprise up to date on the firm's mission and its progress in achieving it.

But the most appealing aspect of CT's open corporate culture isn't the internal cheerleading over past triumphs, but the candid appraisal of shortcomings. My favourite part of the Canada Trust annual report sets out "Performance against Objectives" and CT's objectives for next year. This is where CT's employees, shareholders, creditors, suppliers and customers can learn in clear language exactly what CT's management is trying to accomplish with the resources at its disposal, and where it has exceeded or fallen short of goals.

Politicians, who we are to believe are ever less accountable, have a tough time of it compared to the coterie of top managers and directors who oversee our major corporations. Routinely re-elected to their stations of power by shareholders deprived of revelatory information, the stewards of Corporate Canada are most reluctant to account for their behaviour. Every year at about this time, the mails are clogged with overdesigned annual reports drafted by generously compensated spin doctors who torture the language with new variations on "it has been a challenging year" (profits have evaporated, we don't know why, and we don't know what to do about it) and the more ominous "results were disappointing" (insolvency beckons).

Canada Trust has been publishing frank report cards of its activities for more than a decade, in good years and bad. Last year was not so good:

"OBJECTIVE ONE: *Return on Equity*
Achieve after-tax return of 15% on common shareholders' averaged equity—fully diluted.
PERFORMANCE: 10.22%

"OBJECTIVE THREE: *Operating Expense Control*
Contain operating expenses to less than 2.2% of averaged corporate assets.
PERFORMANCE: 2.31%

"OBJECTIVE FOUR: *Canadian Deposit Growth*
Increase market share of Canadian demand deposits by achieving 105% of the growth rate of similar chartered bank deposits.
PERFORMANCE: Canadian demand deposits declined 8%. Similar chartered bank deposits declined 6%."

To the seasoned CT observer, these are disturbing developments, graphically described. The company isn't as profitable as its management and directors think it should and can be; it hasn't been controlling its costs very well; and CT's long-standing mission to steal market share from the banks appears to have stalled. Naturally this raises questions, to which even the casual observer can find answers elsewhere in the report. In the accompanying Simplified Financial Statements, for instance, we learn that corporate assets were $44.3 billion last year, up only 5%, and total investment income was down 10%. Yet salary costs soared, up 12%. Further investigation, with the assistance of the Ten Year Record, shows that salary expenses have increased an average of 14.1% in each of the past five years, well above the inflation rate. Question: Why are salary costs — the firm's biggest non-interest cost—outpacing asset and profit growth year after year?

A quick survey of management's goals for 1993 raises more questions: Why has CT lowered the bar on its return-on-equity goal, aiming for only a 12% after-tax rate of return? Similarly, why is it now striving for the more modest goal of growing its market share at 102% of the rate of other banks—down from 110% back in 1991? And what about the missing goals? Mutual funds targets, a feature of previous reports, apparently aren't a priority in 1993. With the funds market so hot, shouldn't they be?

To be this well equipped to pose tough questions without the benefit of completing the Canadian Securities Course or being a veteran interpreter of corporate obscurantism is a tribute to former CEO Merv Lahn, a rare business leader who enjoyed being personally accountable. Like his predecessor Lahn, CEO Peter Maurice sees the annual report card as a useful instrument for measuring progress and setting goals.

Drucker predicts a day when restless pension funds and other institutional investors will no longer simply sell, or "walk away from," managerial mediocrity and malperformance. "The holdings of large pension funds — even of medium-sized ones — are so big that they simply cannot be sold. The only market for them is other pension funds. Pension funds, in other words, can neither manage a business nor walk away from it. *They have to make sure that the business is being managed.*" (Drucker's italics).

Drucker believes that the push to make managers accountable will manifest itself in the form of a "'business audit.' It will track the performance of a company and its management against a strategic plan and specific objectives. This will then show, over a period of a few years, whether a business is performing well or not."

As the pioneer of the "management by objectives" (MBO) concept, Drucker would be pleased to know that at least one of North America's major financial institutions has taken his MBO idea to its logical conclusion — CT's annual business audits. In the long sad tradition of adopting only the best foreign ideas, it's likely that other Canadian corporations won't embrace CT's commitment to brave self-appraisal until Drucker can be lured north to claim spiritual paternity for Canada Trust's most worthy innovation.

Report on Business Magazine, *May 1993, pp. 19–20. Reprinted with permission from* The Globe and Mail.

17. In the following article the author, an accountant, expresses concern about whether accountants in public practice are dealing appropriately with the moral foundation on which they, their partners, and others in their firm operate. Discuss.

Many Accountants Confront Moral Dilemmas in Real-Life Game of "Truth or Consequences"

by Morden Shapiro

Professional accountants often grapple with moral dilemmas:

- Jim has just "sold" a long-time client on having quarterly financial statements, even though Jim knows that because of external forces these quarterly statements will not impact on the operations of the business. Should he have told the client the truth?
- Barbara has allegedly resisted bringing a new person into one of her client accounts because the client will not put up with a new face.

  In fact, Barbara is considering leaving her firm and doesn't want to risk losing control over the client.

  Should she tell her partners the truth?
- Don, an audit partner, feels uneasy about the results of an audit test.

He has decided, for reasons of fees and time pressures, to live with his discomfort and release the audit report.

Should Don have communicated the truth to either his partners or the readers of these financial statements?

How are we to regard these decisions to withhold information?

Is the withholding of information equivalent to lying? Is the behaviour wrong? And in what circumstances might these decisions have been justified?

Are there different grades of truth or untruth? If so, who defines the scale?

Easy definitions of truth don't abound. Truth is often equated with the facts. And accountants have long been portrayed as public keepers of facts. Accountants' communications have long been characterized as reflecting the truth.

The accounting profession has some rarely discussed problems:

- How are its members trained to identify the truth?
- How are its members supposed to assess the inherent truthfulness of a situation, a fact or a representation?

This is not to refer to the shortcomings of the traditional double entry accounting model.

Any such model requires that judgments about truthfulness be made within the constructs of that model.

For example, do the undepreciated dollars of a capital asset reflect a truth?

Are the unearned dollars of a long-term contract the true balance to be earned?

Contemporary issues of truthfulness for members of the accounting and other professions go beyond a principal product such as financial statements.

They extend to the realms of practice management, marketing, employer-employee, partner-partner and partner-client relationships.

The pressures of today's economic environment (fee constraints, aggressive and constant competition), the open season on actions against professionals (both lawsuits and professional misconduct allegations) and the growing burden of being an employer (employee settlements, improper dismissal actions, etc.) all impact directly on "truth decisions."

In many cases, the truth can hurt one's self interest or the interest of their firm. For example:

- If Jim tells his client that there really is no value to be had from quarterly financial statements, then Jim may be at risk in terms of keeping his staff fully employed;
- If Barbara tells her partners that she's thinking of leaving, then they may become more proactive in loosening her grip on those clients with whom she deals exclusively;
- If Don withholds the financial statements pending additional audit work to satisfy his discomfort then he may lose money by the time the final fee has been determined.

Most people, when exploring truth models try to develop universal rules with which to classify situations and so fit truth decisions into simply stated decision boxes.

Such efforts are usually unsuccessful.

Consider the problems encountered when you try to apply universal judgments to our scenarios:

- How many professionals can say with virtually no discomfort that everything they do for a client is of value?
- How many partners can say with absolute confidence that they have never made decisions or taken actions that were designed (in the final analysis) to protect their own position *vis-à-vis* profit share, client control, *et cetera* and for which they offered some explanation that masked or denied their self-interest?
- How many accountants can say they never released a financial statement over which they had professional concerns (as to accuracy, fullness of disclosure, etc.) that had not been addressed?

We all live side by side on this thorny ledge. Sometimes we create safe havens with well-constructed rationalizations or poorly-designed risk analyses.

It's unlikely that most people are consciously untruthful. But the discomfort, the hesitation and the resulting anxiety from the situation itself is nevertheless real.

This column is not about being pure or saintly. It is about learning to identify and address truth decisions.

This becomes even more critical when you're in partnership with others who are making their own truthfulness decisions based on a belief system of which you are not aware.

It can be frightening to realize that your future may be bound with someone else's perception of the truth while you never have an opportunity to input your own beliefs.

Many profession practices could benefit from an in-depth review of the truth systems being practised in the name of the firm.

Even though partnership agreements often refer to moral and professional behaviour of the highest order, rarely are the details addressed or defined.

These considerations apply not only to partners but to all who make decisions for the firm.

When did you last provide your staff with guidance about how to make moral choices on behalf of your firm?

These questions are not easy. There are no simple answers. In fact there may be no answers for some situations.

But unless you try to come to grips with the moral foundation on which you expect to have your dilemmas addressed, then you are as likely to be unhappy as you are to be content with decisions that are made.

One thing is for sure, if you don't address the moral foundation on which people in your firm are operating then you are completely justified in feeling scared about what decisions might be made.

Early attention to such matters is prudent because for many firms the fuzziness around such belief systems is an uncontrolled time bomb.

The Bottom Line, *May 1993, p. 16. Morden S. Shapiro, B. Com., FCA, CMC, CFE, is a Toronto-based consultant to accountants and accounting firms.*

18. In this chapter's "Accounting, Organizations, and Society" section, Kenneth Dye and Charles Bowsher expressed concern that the financial statements for an entire country be "based on users' needs for financial information."
    (a) Do you agree with the particular list of users they have developed for the accounting entity about which they are concerned?
    (b) Do you agree that financial accounting information should be developed based upon "users' needs"?
    (c) How should the accounting entity, in the case of a sovereign state, be defined?

CASE

The Red Bearded Baron

This case[18] focuses on the process of developing accounting information to assist an "owner/manager" in evaluating the performance of two subordinates. Financial accounting information in the form of financial statements is an important output, so financial accounting is often used in a management accounting context.

In addition to being aware that different types of organizations have different types and relative magnitudes of items in their financial statements and may have different accounting decisions to make, it is important for you to be flexible in regarding accounting's areas as being "distinct" from one another. In fact, there is a view among some educators that it is artificial to separate some of the areas. For example, two American accounting professors, Bruce Baldwin and Robert Ingram, offer the view that teaching financial accounting and management and cost accounting as separate areas is ill-conceived. They make this point as follows:

Rather than teaching internal and external information dissemination as if they spring from separable processes, accounting at the elementary level should be taught as an integrated process related to information needs of those who make decisions about organizations ... It should be taught that financial accounting is the basis for many management decisions as managers make

[18] From W.T. Andrews, "Another Improbable Occurrence," Academic Notes, *The Accounting Review*, April 1974, pp. 369–370. Adapted.

use of detailed information available from the accounting information system. This information is then also reported to external parties on a highly aggregated basis.[19]

The case runs as follows:

Once upon a time many, many years ago, there lived a feudal landlord in a small province of Central Europe. The landlord, called the Red Bearded Baron, lived in a castle high on a hill, and this benevolent fellow was responsible for the well-being of many peasants who occupied the lands surrounding his castle. Each spring, as the snow began to melt, the Baron would decide how to provide for all his serf-dependents during the coming year.

One spring, the Baron was thinking about the wheat crop of the coming growing season. "I believe that 30 acres of my land, being worth five bushels of wheat per acre, will produce enough wheat for next winter," he mused, "but who should do the farming? I believe I'll give Ivan and Igor the task of growing wheat." Whereupon Ivan and Igor, two gentry noted for their hard work, were summoned for an audience with the Baron.

"Ivan, you will farm on the 20 acre plot of land and Igor will farm the 10 acre plot," the Baron began. "I will give Ivan 20 bushels of wheat for seed and 20 pounds of fertilizer which itself could fetch 2 bushels of wheat in the market. Igor will get 10 bushels of wheat for seed and 10 pounds of fertilizer. I will give each of you an ox to pull a plow but you will have to make arrangements with Feyador the Plowmaker for a plow. The oxen, incidentally, are only three years old and have never been used for farming, so they should have a good 10 years of farming ahead of them. Take good care of them, because an ox is worth 40 bushels of wheat. Come back next fall and return the oxen and plows along with your harvest."

Ivan and Igor bowed low and withdrew from the Great Hall, taking with them the things provided by the Baron.

The summer came and went, and after the harvest Ivan and Igor returned to the Great Hall to give an accounting to their master for the things given to them in the spring. Ivan, poring 223 bushels of wheat onto the floor, said, "My Lord, I present you with a slightly used ox, a plow, broken beyond repair, and 223 bushels of wheat. I, unfortunately, owe Feyador the Plowmaker three bushels of wheat for the plow I got from him last spring. And, as you might expect, I used all the fertilizer and seed you gave me last spring. You will also remember, my Lord, that you took 20 bushels of my harvest for your own personal use."

Igor, who had been given 10 acres of land on which to farm for the season, spoke next. "Here, my Lord, is a partially used-up ox, the plow for which I gave Feyador the Plowmaker three bushels of wheat from my harvest, and 105 bushels of wheat. I, too, used up all my seed and fertilizer last spring. Also, my Lord, you took 30 bushels of wheat several days ago for your own table. I believe the plow is good for two more seasons."

"Knaves, you did well," said the Baron. Blessed with this benediction and not wishing to press their luck further, the two serfs beat a hasty departure.

After Ivan and Igor had taken their leave, the Baron, watching the two hungry oxen slowly eating the wheat piled on the floor, began to contemplate what had happened. "Yes," he thought, "they did well, but I wonder which one did better?"

[19] Bruce A. Baldwin and Robert W. Ingram, "Rethinking the Objectives and Content of Elementary Accounting," *Journal of Accounting Education*, Vol. 9, pp. 1–14, 1991. Reprinted with permission from Elsevier Science Ltd., Oxford, England.

Required:

Adopt the role of an adviser to the Red Bearded Baron. He has asked — no, ordered — you to prepare one or more reports showing "which one did better." You have decided to approach this assignment by first answering the following questions:

(a) For measurement purposes, what standard unit of measure should be chosen?
(b) Determine the accounting entity or entities. What are the accountability relationships? Who is (are) the user(s) of the accounting information? For what period of time is the accounting being performed?
(c) What criteria should be used in deciding "which one did better"?

You then decide to set up a spreadsheet, much like the one set up in Chapter 1 for On Ice Inc., to see if you can account for what went on. You then complete your reports and rush back to the Baron with your results.

CASE

Trader Armlock Limited

Jane Armlock was for a long time a salesperson in the retail appliance and furniture industry. After thinking about it for a year or so, she decided to go into the retail appliance sales business for herself, and arranged to incorporate a company called "Trader Armlock Limited" (TAL). Average monthly sales for the type and size of store that Jane opened were in the $40,000 to $45,000 range. The information that follows summarizes TAL's first three months of operations.

January 1, 1995: Jane Armlock incorporates TAL. Total capital stock of $45,000 is issued to Jane, who has withdrawn over half of her life savings from the bank. Incorporation costs are $1,000, paid in cash.

January 1, 1995: TAL purchases a small store for $110,000. The down payment is $25,000, and the remainder is financed by a short-term mortgage at 12%. Interest is payable monthly, and $20,000 of the principal is due at the end of every three months, with the first payment to fall on April 1, 1995. The purchase price of $110,000 represents $80,000 for the building and $30,000 for the land.

January 5, 1995: TAL purchases $8,000 of store equipment and $3,000 of office supplies; terms are "due in 30 days."

January 7, 1995: Jane convinces her old boss's suppliers to ship her $15,000 of appliances and furniture on 30-day credit terms.

Jane has two salespeople working for her on a straight commission basis of 10% of retail sales. During January 1995, TAL sells merchandise whose cost is $11,000, for $16,000. Half the sales are for cash, and the other half are for extended credit terms. On January 30, 1995, TAL sells the receivables to a finance company for 80% of their face value (Jane plans to do this every month). On January 31, the following monthly bills are paid. See the table on the left.

Interest on mortgage ($85,000 × 12% per year × 1/12 year)	$ 850
Salespeople — commissions (10% × $16,000)	1,600
Telephone and fax	100
Heat, water and power	200
Real estate taxes	400
Manager's salary (Jane acted as manager)	1,000

During February, TAL orders and receives an additional $35,000 of merchandise. Retail sales (50% for cash) are $40,000 for merchandise that cost $32,000. At the end of February, Jane discovers that henceforth all of her suppliers will require a 50% down payment on any purchases, with the balance due in 30 days. To encourage her customers to pay cash, Jane decides to offer a 5% discount for cash (of course, TAL's salespeople will still receive their 10% commission on the gross retail price), beginning March 1, 1995. During March, TAL orders and receives $34,000 of merchandise. Retail sales (70% for cash) are $43,000 (at gross retail) for merchandise that had cost $36,000.

TAL made all the appropriate payments at the end of February and March.

Required:

(a) Using the basic accounting equation, prepare a spreadsheet accounting for events involving TAL for the three months ended March 31, 1995.

(b) Prepare an income statement for each of January, February, and March 1995. What important accounting decisions did you make?

(c) Compute TAL's gross margin as a percent of sales for each of the three months. Gross margin as a percent of sales in the industry is about 25%.

(d) Calculate cash flow from operations for each of January, February, and March.

(e) Identify the major business (as distinct from accounting) decisions that Ms Armlock should be concerned with by the end of March.

(f) Advise Ms. Armlock.

CHAPTER 3 three

Transactions, Events, and Financial Accounting: An Introduction to Double-Entry Bookkeeping

Learning OBJECTIVES

After you have read, thought about, and discussed this chapter, and completed a selection from the end-of-chapter material, you will have made significant progress in achieving the following learning objectives:

- Be able to identify and give examples of transactions.
- Be able to distinguish transactions from other events.
- Explain the differences between double-entry accounting and single-entry accounting.
- Know and be able to apply the rules for debits and credits in accounting for transactions and other business events.
- Be able to prepare journal entries for a variety of transactions.
- Describe and explain the significance of the accounting cycle.
- Explain why adjustments are necessary, and describe the five categories of adjustments.
- Be able to prepare a variety of adjusting journal entries.
- Be able to prepare closing journal entries.
- Be able to use journal entries and T-accounts both to analyse accounting information and in the accounting cycle.
- Be familiar with the historical and present-day importance of double-entry accounting.

> *The success of the personal computer industry, and Microsoft, is based on the spreadsheet. And the spreadsheet is a direct evolution of the double-entry system published by Luca Pacioli.*
>
> Francis J. Gaudette, Microsoft Corporation[1]

INTRODUCTION

One of the many current debates in accounting education revolves around this issue: Should educational materials focus on the mechanics of preparing accounting information, or on the development of judgment and analytical skills? While the debate is couched in "either/or" language, it is reasonable to suggest that both aspects of accounting are important for an understanding of the roles of accounting in organizations and in society. Therefore, this chapter will emphasize some of the technical aspects of accounting, but will also show how these technical features are of use not only to accountants, but also to managers and to outside users of accounting information.

Transactions and Other Events

Every time you make a deposit or a withdrawal at your bank or trust company, you are engaging in a transaction. The money amounts that the bank inscribes in your bankbook are a record of the transaction. An accounting entity is likely to perform many transactions with other accounting entities in its environment as time goes by. These transactions may be relatively simple (as when a church purchases some art supplies for a daycare program it operates on behalf of the children of its congregation, paying cash), or highly complex (as when the parent company of a major league baseball team signs a star player to a multiyear contract, agreeing to pay a signing bonus, along with a series of payments over several future years, as well as bonuses based on the player's future performance).

Usually, but not always, it is quite easy to tell whether a transaction has occurred. For example, suppose Company A owns 40% of the common shares of Company B, and B borrows $1 million from a bank. A guarantees the bank that if B is unable to repay the loan, A will do so. Has A entered into a transaction? A has made a promise to do something (repay B's loan), but *only if* something else happens (B cannot to do so). A transaction involving Company A hasn't yet occurred, but it may occur in the future. Accountants classify such events as *contingencies*. The *CICA Handbook* defines "contingency" as follows:

A contingency is defined as an existing condition or situation involving uncertainty as to possible gain or loss to an enterprise that will ultimately be resolved when one or more future events occur or

---

[1] Mr. Gaudette, Microsoft's chief financial officer, made this remark during an interview for *"Luca Pacioli: Unsung Hero of the Renaissance,"* William L. Weiss, David E. Tinius, and Chauncey Burke, producers (Cincinnati: South-Western, 1990, videocassette, 30 minutes).

fail to occur. Resolution of the uncertainty may confirm the acquisition of an asset or the reduction of a liability or the loss or impairment of an asset or the incurrence of a liability.[2]

So a contingency is a transaction that hasn't yet happened and that may not happen at all. Accountants prefer to disclose contingencies in the footnotes rather than the body of the financial statements.

Transactions are important in accounting because they provide a significant amount of the raw information that accounting deals with. They are just as important as the seven key sets of ideas for accounting that were introduced in Chapter 2. In fact, transactions are so important that we'll spend some time describing some of their characteristics in detail. In doing so, we will focus on two important features of a transaction:

- Did the transaction *actually* happen, or is it *hypothetical*?
- Are we talking about the *past*, the *present*, or the *future*?

Actual transactions that have occurred in the past

This category includes all the transactions the accounting entity has engaged in up to the present time. The record of these transactions is an important part of the history of the company, and represents the database from which the financial accountant prepares its income statement, balance sheet, and cash flow statement. Events #1 and #12 in the On Ice example in Chapter 1 were obvious actual transactions. Recall that in event #1, Devo Green invested $10,000 in On Ice Incorporated; this was a transaction between two accounting entities — On Ice Incorporated and Devo Green. In event #12, Devo, acting on behalf of On Ice, issued a cheque for $1,000 to Super Computers Limited; this was a transaction between On Ice and Super.

Hypothetical transactions that could have occurred in the past

This category includes all the transactions that the accounting entity *did not* participate in, up to the present moment. Out of the countless number of such transactions, only a small subset would be of interest to the users of accounting information. The shareholders of a company that specializes in the design and installation of electronic data interchange (EDI) systems would not be interested in the fact that the company failed to purchase an abandoned gold mine last year, since the gold-mining business is so remote from the company's operations. However, the shareholders *would* be interested if the company's management did not make their corporate income tax payments on time or did not purchase computer software that was crucial to the continued success of the company. Thus, a few transactions among the virtually infinite number that could have occurred may provide relevant information. They would represent opportunities not taken, or perhaps dangers not avoided.

Transactions actually being undertaken by the accounting entity at the present time

Transactions such as this are undoubtedly relevant to users of accounting information. These are transactions-in-progress — that is, transactions that have begun but have not yet been completed. With this category of transactions, estimates and judgments must be made in order for an accounting to take place. Sometimes the estimates and judgments are fairly straightforward, and sometimes they are quite difficult to make. Suppose that a company has contracts with commissioned salespeople, who are to receive

[2] *CICA Handbook*, "Contingencies," 3290.02.

10% of their monthly sales as a commission. Sales for any given month are estimates until the product has been received by all the customers, and the customers are satisfied with and have paid for the product. Much of this activity occurs after the month that the salesperson is to receive the commission; the company's commission expense on its month-end income statement, and the corresponding commission payable in the current liability section of its balance sheet, must be based on estimates and judgments, because the transactions are incomplete. All accounts receivable and accounts payable amounts on the balance sheet are estimates based on incomplete transactions. Most often, reasonable estimates can be made (as in the commission example); however, some transactions will be so far from completion at the present time that preparing financial statements such as balance sheets will require considerable effort and ingenuity.

All possible transactions that the accounting entity could at present be a party to but is not

This category contains a subset of transactions of interest to shareholders, managers, and other users. For example, information about the current replacement cost of inventory would be important to the management of a furniture retailer when it comes to deciding whether to restock a particular product line. The current replacement cost of the inventory represents the total cost that would have to be incurred to replace the inventory "today." Under GAAP, hypothetical financial information is sometimes required to be reported for outside users of financial accounting statements. For example, the aggregate market value of financial securities (such as investments in other companies' common shares) held as current assets by the accounting entity is reported, in addition to the actual historic cost of the securities.

Planned future transactions

This category consists of transactions that the accounting entity's management fully intends to undertake; such transactions are planned, future transactions. Information based on such transactions is crucial to managers as they prepare budgets for the coming year or for other planning periods; it is central to the management accounting process. And outside users of financial statements, such as actual and potential shareholders, will be vitally interested in the major transactions that the accounting entity plans to undertake. For example, a movie production company might disclose its plans to purchase a chain of video retail outlets. Disclosing the details of planned future transactions isn't always a straightforward process, however, since plans don't always unfold as management intends; also, there may be plans that management doesn't wish to disclose because competitors might take advantage of the information.

Hypothetical future transactions

This category can be viewed as including possible transactions that perhaps could (or should) be converted into planned future transactions (for example, if management decides that diversifying is a strategically sound idea), as well as transactions that must be avoided at all costs (perhaps a significant product liability lawsuit). Contingencies, such as Company A's guarantee to pay off Company B's loan (discussed above), can also be placed in this category.

The matrix at the top of the next page summarizes the above discussion and classifies transactions according to whether they are actual or hypothetical events, and also according to the time in which they take place or do not take place (past, present, future):

	Past	Present	Future
Actual transactions	**Cell A1** Actual transactions that have occurred in the past	**Cell A3** Transactions actually undertaken by the accounting entity at the present time	**Cell A5** Planned future transactions
Hypothetical transactions	**Cell A2** Hypothetical transactions that could have occurred in the past	**Cell A4** All possible transactions that the accounting entity could at present be a party to but is not	**Cell A6** Hypothetical future transactions

Transactions are important in many of the subdisciplines of accounting. For example, Exhibit 3–1 indicates, for four subdisciplines of accounting, which of the six transaction types introduced above are relevant.

EXHIBIT 3–1
RELEVANCE OF TRANSACTION TYPES FOR ACCOUNTING SUBDISCIPLINES

	Transaction Type					
Accounting Subdiscipline	A1 (past, actual)	A2 (past, hypothetical)	A3 (present, actual)	A4 (present, hypothetical)	A5 (future, planned)	A6 (future, hypothetical)
Financial accounting	●	❍	●	●	●	●
Operational accounting	❍	❍	●	❍	❍	❍
Management accounting	●	●	●	●	●	●
Taxation (income tax)	●	❍	●	❍	●	❍

● = relevant
❍ = not relevant

Accounting and Business Decision A

Try to justify the ●'s and ❍'s in the cells in Exhibit 3–1.

Exhibit 3–1 indicates that past, completed, actual transactions are important to financial accounting, management accounting, and taxation accounting. Financial accounting reports to users about the results of past transactions (among other things); management accounting uses information about past transactions to assess whether good decisions were made by managers and how profitable various activities and products were; and taxation accounting determines how much income tax the company should pay (assuming, for simplicity, that there were no incomplete transactions). We are really talking here about the same set of transactions — all three of these accounting subdisciplines would use the same set of transactions in cell A1. Thus, all three subdisciplines could be served by storing the transactions in a single database. However, each of the subdisciplines would treat the transaction information differently.

Up to this point we have used the term "transaction" without defining it. Since it is such an important concept in accounting, we had better provide a definition. The organization that sets accounting standards in the United States — the Financial Accounting Standards Board (FASB) — defined "transaction" in the following way, as a subcategory of an "event":[3]

An event is a happening of consequence to an entity. It may be an internal event that occurs within an entity, such as using raw materials or equipment in production, or it may be an external event that involves interaction between an entity and its environment, such as a transaction with another entity, a change in price of a good or service that an entity buys or sells, a flood or earthquake, or an improvement in technology by a competitor ... Many events are combinations. For example, acquiring services of employees or others involves exchange transactions, which are external events; using those services, often simultaneously with their acquisition, is part of production, which involves a series of internal events ... An event may be initiated by an entity, such as a purchase of merchandise or use of a building, or it may be partly or wholly beyond the control of an entity and its management, such as an interest rate change, an act of vandalism or theft, or the imposition of taxes ... A transaction is a particular kind of external event, namely, an external event involving transfer of something of value (future economic benefit) between two (or more) entities.

FASB's description of a transaction specifies that transactions are a subset of "external events." Of the 27 events recorded in the accounting records of On Ice Incorporated in Chapter 1, #22 (depreciation) is an internal event (financial accounting accounts for depreciation, even though it is not a transaction). Thus, transaction-based information is not the only information captured in accounting systems.

[3] FASB, "Statement of Financial Accounting Concepts No. 3 — Elements of Financial Statements of Business Enterprises," December 1980, pp. 37–38.

Debits, Credits, and Transactions, and Other Accountable Events

The On Ice example illustrated how transactions and other accountable events affected the A = L + SE accounting model and, ultimately, wound up in an income statement, balance sheet, and cash flow statement. Systems of accounting based on A = L + SE are said to be based on double-entry accounting, since each event is accounted for in two ways (for example, event #1 increased On Ice's cash and also increased common stock). Systems of accounting that just keep track of one aspect of a transaction are referred to as single-entry. Since a single-entry accounting system doesn't bother to analyse transactions or other accountable business events using A = L + SE, it captures far less information than would a double-entry system. Double-entry forces the accountant and manager to think about the impact of a transaction or other event on assets, liabilities, and shareholders' equity. For instance, referring to the On Ice example, in a single-entry system transaction #13 would just be listed as an increase in cash. In a double-entry system, for the purpose of restoring balance to the A = L + SE equation, a decision would have to be made to do one of the following *in addition to* increasing cash:

- Decrease another asset.
- Increase a liability.
- Increase shareholders' (owners') equity.

In the On Ice case, we implemented double-entry using an expanded version of A = L + SE. The version of double-entry accounting found most often in practice is based on the technical tools accountants use called "accounts," "debits," "credits," and "journal entries." To see just what these are and how they fit together, we need some terminology:

Account

An account is a record of a specific category of asset, liability, revenue, expense, or shareholders' equity. For example, "Cash" is an account. An account is a means of collecting information about a particular type of asset, or liability, or the like. It keeps track of increases, decreases, and balances over time. It is important to bear in mind that a record of something merely *represents* that thing; it is not the thing itself. That being said, having an accurate record of something, such as a company's business transactions, does much to reassure those to whom one is accountable that "everything is all right."

When designing accounts, accountants and managers must consider certain things:

- The amount of detail. For example, should there be just one account for "Cash" for the entire organization? In an organization with more than one location, there could be a separate cash account for each location; in such a system, each location's manager would be held responsible and therefore accountable for the cash under his or her control. This is a design consideration for management accounting; when financial statements for external users were prepared, all the individual cash accounts would be pulled together. In the On Ice example, Devo Green needed only a single account for each of cash, inventory, the capital asset, and so on.
- Different types of assets, and different types of liabilities, and so on, may require different accounts. Devo Green didn't just dump all of On Ice's assets into one large "Assets" account; rather, he decided that separate

accounts were needed for accounts receivable, inventory, capital assets, and so on. He made this accounting design decision presumably because the information needed to manage and evaluate the different asset categories was somewhat different for each category. For example, tangible capital assets have a long life and depreciate over many accounting periods, while accounts receivable are often current assets that require careful monitoring in order to ensure that amounts owed to the accounting entity are collected.

Asset accounts:	101	Cash
	102	Accounts receivable
	103	Office supplies
	104	Organization costs
	105	Capital asset
	106	Accumulated depreciation[4]
Liability accounts:	201	Accounts payable
	202	Income tax payable
	203	Interest payable
Shareholders' equity accounts:	301	Common stock
	302	Retained earnings
Revenue accounts:	401	Sales of magazines
	402	Sales of advertising
Expense accounts:	501	Cost of magazines sold
	502	Writing fees
	503	Rent
	504	Distribution expenses
	505	Salary
	506	Telephone
	507	Depreciation
	508	Travel
	509	Interest
	510	Supplies
	511	Income taxes

In explanations of the concept of an account, the following schematic is often used:

Debits	**Credits**

In this schematic, called a "T-account" because of its obvious resemblance to the letter T, the left is the "debit" side and the right is the "credit" side. As used in modern accounting, the words *debit* and *credit* are merely labels: debit refers to money amounts recorded in the left side of a T-account, and credit refers to money amounts recorded in the right side. However, these words have a historical significance, which is explained in the "Accounting, Organizations, and Society" article at the end of this chapter.

Chart of accounts

A chart of accounts is a comprehensive listing of all the titles of all the accounts used by an organization. As an example, on the left of this page we show the chart of accounts used by On Ice Incorporated. Note that a code number has been assigned to each account.

Even a small business like On Ice has quite a few accounts. Typically, sequential account numbers are assigned to broad categories and subcategories of accounts. A chart of accounts provides an important system of reference for accountants and others working with an organization's accounting system. Deciding to create a new account is usually an important decision in accounting system design.

The number and type of accounts an organization has depends on the degree of detail desired and the characteristics of the organization. A small business such as On Ice will have relatively few

[4] An account such "Accumulated depreciation," which appears on the asset side of the balance sheet but has a credit balance, is called a "contra account."

accounts; an organization the size of Corel Corporation may have hundreds; larger organizations may have thousands. An accounting system can provide very detailed information (for example, a department store may account for each customer's sales separately), or it can maintain information in a more aggregated form (for example, just one sales account for all customers). Similarly, asset accounts can group together various kinds of assets, or separate accounts can be established to monitor changes in each individual class of assets. The number of accounts that an organization has is based on a tradeoff between the benefits to be derived from the information and the cost of preparing it. The more information available, the more thoroughly it can be analysed, but the greater the cost of keeping track. Deciding on the number and type of general ledger accounts to be established in an accounting system is an important process.

We will now describe the rules for using the debit and credit terminology. These rules are arbitrary, but they do result in a systematic approach to accounting for transactions and other events.

Debit

The word *debit* in accounting means "increase" when we are dealing with assets, expenses, or dividends; it means "decrease" when we are dealing with liabilities, revenues, and capital stock.

Credit

The word *credit* in accounting means "decrease" when we are dealing with assets, expenses, or dividends, and "increase" when we are dealing with liabilities, revenues, and capital stock.

To illustrate, suppose Company A began the month of January 1995 with $4,550 in cash, received a payment of $2,000 on January 10, and paid out $3,000 on January 30 in order to buy office furniture for cash. A cash asset account recording this information would look like the first table on the left.

Cash			
Opening balance 01/01/95	4,550.00		
Payment received 10/01/95	2000.00	3,000.00	Payment 30/01/95
Closing balance	3,550.00		

Accounts Payable			
01/10/95		27,055.00	Opening balance
Payment 10/10/95	17,000.00		
Payment 25/10/95	10,055.00		
		32,750.00	20/10/95
		32,750.00	Closing balance

The opening balance in the cash account at the start of January is a debit of $4,550. The payment of $2,000 received on January 10 is a debit, while on the other hand the payment made on January 30 is a credit to the cash account. The month-end January 31 closing balance is a debit of $3,550.

As a further illustration, suppose that Company B owed $27,055 to its suppliers at the start of October 1995, issued a cheque for $17,000 on October 10, issued another cheque for $10,055 on October 25 (both cheques were to its suppliers), and received merchandise costing $32,750 on October 20. See the bottom table on the left.

Since accounts payable is a liability account, both the opening balance and all the increases during the month are recorded on the credit side. The payments, which reduce the liability, are recorded on the debit side.

The information recorded in the T-accounts deals with only parts of transactions. To record entire transactions, accountants use journal entries. A journal entry is a record, using the terminology of debits and credits, of a transaction or other accountable event. If the payment of $2,000 received above on January 10, 1995, was to pay off an amount previously recorded as an account receivable (perhaps we sold something last month on credit), then the journal entry to record this transaction in Company A's accounting system would be —

January 10, 1995				
Dr	Cash		2,000.00	
Cr		Accounts receivable		2,000.00

(Notice that debit is abbreviated "Dr" and credit "Cr," and that the credit side of a journal entry is indented relative to the debit side).

The $3,000 payment of January 30 would be recorded in the following way:

January 30, 1995				
Dr	Capital asset (office furniture)		3,000.00	
Cr		Cash		3,000.00

In practice, journal entries are recorded in a company's journal, which is simply a chronological listing of the journal entries. Each journal entry should contain a brief explanation outlining the reasons for the entry and how the amounts were determined. The journal is often referred to as a *book of original entry*; this simply indicates that it is the first place in an accounting system in which the information is captured. The use of the word "book" harks back to the time when journals were almost always actual, physical books; today, of course, journal information and entries are most commonly entered and stored on computer.

Accounting and Business Decision B

Prepare journal entries for the October 1995 transactions that affected the accounts payable account for Company B, above.

What Do Actual Accounts Look Like?

The T-account we introduced earlier is merely a schematic representation of an individual account. During the Renaissance, actual accounts were often written in an elaborate and fanciful style. Commercial activities were less socially acceptable at that time, and merchants strived to prove their honesty and fairness through the care they took with their accounting. By the late nineteenth and early twentieth centuries, however, accounts were kept on plain cardboard and typically looked like this:

Date	Explanation	Reference	Debit	Credit	Balance

Today, most accounting systems are computerized, and accounts are usually stored on a hard drive. Our schematic representation of accounts by means of the T-account captures the essential information stored in such a system.

Why Debits Equal Credits

The debit and credit rules introduced earlier, in combination with the basic accounting equation A = L + SE, result in the following key characteristic of an entity's accounting system: at any point in time, the grand sum of all net *debit* money amounts for all accounts should be equal to the grand sum of all net *credit* money amounts. In other words, in a double-entry accounting system total debits should equal total credits at every point in time. Let's see why this is so.

Let A be the total dollar amounts assigned to assets, L be the total dollar amounts assigned to liabilities, and SE be the resulting shareholders' equity. Since

$$A = L + SE$$

it follows that

$$SE = A - L \qquad \text{[Equation 1]}$$

Equation 1 holds at every point in time; this is the same as saying that it holds both before and after a particular transaction has been accounted for. We will use the Greek letter Δ (delta) to represent the change in each of A, L, and SE resulting from recording a transaction or other accountable event (such as the recording of depreciation).

Therefore, it must be true that

$$\Delta SE = \Delta A - \Delta L \qquad \text{[Equation 2]}$$

For each of A, L, and SE, a change must equal the net of increases less decreases. When we use the subscript "i" to stand for increases, and the subscript "d" to stand for decreases, equation 2 becomes

$$(SE_i - SE_d) = (A_i - A_d) - (L_i - L_d) \qquad \text{[Equation 3]}$$

On rearranging equation 3, we get:

$$A_i + L_d + SE_d = A_d + L_i + SE_i \qquad \text{[Equation 4]}$$

If we label all items on the left side of equation 4 "debits," and all items on the right side "credits," then

Debits = Credits[5]

[5] The presentation showing that debits equal credits is based on Stanley Martens, "Why Debits Equal Credits," *Accounting Instructors' Report*, Vol. XI, no. 1, Spring 1992, pp. 3–4.

This equality of debits and credits for an entity's accounting system provides a convenient means of control. We will illustrate how this control works and its significance later in this chapter. Now we will redo double-entry accounting for the On Ice example from Chapter 1, this time using debits, credits, and journal entries.

On Ice Revisited

First, we will record all 27 of the accountable events that we originally recorded in Exhibit 1–5, but this time in journal entry form. Exhibit 3–2 shows the journal for On Ice for the period August 5, 1993, to September 30, 1993. Please ignore journal entry #28 for now; it will be explained a little later. Notice that each of the 27 journal entries follows the rules for debits and credits (debit means an increase in assets, and so on), and that the sum of the debit amounts equals the sum of the credit money amounts for each journal entry, even for "compound" journal entries such as #14. Most of the journal entries in Exhibit 3–2 account for transactions between On Ice and other entities. The transactions include both transactions involving cash (for example, #'s 1 and 3), and transactions not involving cash (for example, #'s 4, 5, and 8), since, as we know, financial accounting accounts for more than just cash transactions. There are events accounted for in Exhibit 3–2 which are not easily classified as transactions, but which it seems necessary to account for in order to provide a fair picture of what happened to On Ice. Specifically, these are events 22, 23, 24, and 27.

Adjusting entries

Event #22 accounts for the depreciation of On Ice's depreciable capital asset. It records the expense (that is, one of the costs of operating On Ice for the period August 5, 1993, to September 30, 1993, is the cost of using its depreciable capital assets over that period, and this cost is depreciation); it also records the decrease in the net book value of the capital asset (by way of the accumulated depreciation account). There was no explicit transaction on September 30, 1993, to provide a signal that such an event should be recorded; there was only the rationale that depreciation is one of the costs of doing business, and thus should be accounted for. Accountants call the depreciation journal entry an adjustment (or an adjusting journal entry). Adjusting entries account, for example, for the conversions of assets to expenses (say, the using up of a little bit of the depreciable capital asset) that have taken place during the period but that have not been part of any explicit transaction.

Event #23 is another adjusting entry. On Ice has benefited from the cash that was provided by the bank loan, so it seems reasonable to account for the cost of the loan — that is, the interest expense — and to record the associated liability. There has been no explicit transaction; rather, there is just the commonsense notion that costs incurred should be accounted for, even though the interest payment has not yet actually been made.

Accounting and Business Decision C

Events #24 and #27 may be regarded as adjusting entries as well. Why?

EXHIBIT 3–2
JOURNAL ENTRIES FOR ON ICE
As Recorded in On Ice's General Journal

Date	Event	Description	Account	Debit	Credit
5/08/93	#1	Issue common stock	Cash	10,000	
			Common stock		10,000
9/08/93	#2	Lawyer's bill and fees	Organization costs	575	
			Accounts payable		575
10/08/93	#3	Interview in Winnipeg	Travel expense	530	
			Cash		530
11/08/93	#4	Ad sold to stick manufacturer	Accounts receivable	1,300	
			Sales — advertising		1,300
11/08/93	#5	Buy computer	Capital asset	3,590	
			Accounts payable		3,590
16/08/93	#6	Pay writer	Writing fees expense	1,000	
			Cash		1,000
16/08/93	#7	Pay August rent	Rent expense	750	
			Cash		750
20/08/93	#8	Ad sold to rink	Accounts receivable	1,950	
			Sales — advertising		1,950
20/08/93	#9	Purchase office supplies	Office supplies	295	
			Accounts payable		295
23/08/93	#10	Pay writer	Writing fees expense	925	
			Cash		925
25/08/93	#11	Down payment to printer	Prepaid printing costs	5,000	
			Cash		5,000
27/08/93	#12	Pay $1,000 on computer	Accounts payable	1,000	
			Cash		1,000
30/08/93	#13	Arrange loan @1% per month	Cash	9,000	
			Loan payable		9,000
3/09/93	#14	Ad sold to skate manufacturer	Cash	1,000	
			Accounts receivable	3,000	
			Sales — advertising		4,000

Date	Event	Description	Account	Debit	Credit
5/09/93	#15	Pay off printer	Prepaid printing costs	6,500	
			Cash		6,500
7/09/93	#16	Magazines picked up	Inventory	11,500	
			Prepaid printing costs		11,500
10/09/93	#17	Distribute magazines	Distribution expenses	1,295	
			Cash		1,295
15/09/93	#18	Collect part of #4	Cash	300	
			Accounts receivable		300
16/09/93	#19	September rent	Rent expense	750	
			Cash		750
18/09/93	#20	Business phone calls	Telephone expense	125	
			Accounts payable		125
20/09/93	#21	Devo's salary	Salary expense	1,000	
			Cash		1,000
30/09/93	#22	Record depreciation	Depreciation expense	225	
			Accumulated depreciation		225
30/09/93	#23	Record interest	Interest expense	90	
			Interest payable		90
30/09/93	#24	Record supplies used	Supplies expense	245	
			Office supplies		245
30/09/93	#25	Record magazine sales	Accounts receivable	12,000	
			Sales — magazines		12,000
30/09/93	#26	Record cost of magazines sold	Cost of magazines sold	11,500	
			Inventory		11,500
30/09/93	#27	Record income taxes	Income tax expense	163	
			Income tax payable		163
30/09/93	#28	Record closing entry	Sales — magazines	12,000	
			Sales — advertising	7,250	
			Cost of magazines sold		11,500
			Writing fees expense		1,925
			Rent expense		1,500
			Distribution expense		1,295
			Salary expense		1,000
			Telephone expense		125
			Depreciation expense		225
			Travel expense		530

Date	Event	Description	Account	Debit	Credit
			Interest expense		90
			Supplies expense		245
			Income tax expense		163
			Retained earnings		652

The general ledger

Next, the information recorded in the 27 journal entries is transferred to the *accounts* (see Exhibit 3–3; the T-accounts we're using are a little fancier than the "plain vanilla" one we introduced above. And keep ignoring journal entry #28). The collection of accounts for all assets, liabilities, revenues, expenses, common stock, and so on is called the general ledger. The words "debit" and "credit" are included in the cash account merely to remind you that the left side of a T-account is called the debit side, and the right side the credit side. The debits and credits from the 27 transactions and other accountable events are coded with their respective event numbers in the various accounts, to maintain a "trail" of information. In practice, the accounts could be kept in alphabetical order, or grouped as they appear on the balance sheet (for example, all current assets together, and so on).

EXHIBIT 3–3
GENERAL LEDGER FOR ON ICE INCORPORATED
September 30, 1993

CASH

Date	Event	Dr	Cr	Balance
5/08/93				0
5/08/93	#1	10,000		10,000
10/08/93	#3		530	
16/08/93	#6		1,000	
16/08/93	#7		750	
23/08/93	#10		925	
25/08/93	#11		5,000	
27/08/93	#12		1,000	
30/08/93	#13	9,000		
3/09/93	#14	1,000		
5/09/93	#15		6,500	
10/09/93	#17		1,295	
15/09/93	#18	300		
16/09/93	#19		750	
20/09/93	#21		1,000	
30/09/93				1,550 Dr

ACCOUNTS RECEIVABLE

Date	Event	Dr	Cr	Balance
5/08/93				0
11/08/93	#4	1,300		
20/08/93	#8	1,950		
3/09/93	#14	3,000		
15/09/93	#18		300	
30/09/93	#25	12,000		
30/09/93				17,950 Dr

INVENTORY

Date	Event	Dr	Cr	Balance
5/08/93				0
7/09/93	#16	11,500		
30/09/93	#26		11,500	
30/09/93				0

ORGANIZATION COSTS

Date	Event	Dr	Cr	Balance
5/08/93				0
9/08/93	#2	575		
30/09/93				575 Dr

OFFICE SUPPLIES

Date	Event	Dr	Cr	Balance
5/08/93				0
20/08/93	#9	295		
30/09/93	#24		245	
30/09/93				50 Dr

PREPAID PRINTING COSTS

Date	Event	Dr	Cr	Balance
5/08/93				0
25/08/93	#11	5,000		
5/09/93	#15	6,500		
7/09/93	#16		11,500	
30/09/93				0

CAPITAL ASSETS

Date	Event	Dr	Cr	Balance
5/08/93				0
11/08/93	#5	3,590		
30/09/93				3,590 Dr

ACCUMULATED DEPRECIATION

Date	Event	Dr	Cr	Balance
5/08/93				0
30/09/93	#22		225	
30/09/93				225 Cr

ACCOUNTS PAYABLE

Date	Event	Dr	Cr	Balance
5/08/93				0
9/08/93	#2		575	
11/08/93	#5		3,590	
20/08/93	#9		295	
27/08/93	#12	1,000		
18/09/93	#20		125	
30/09/93				3,585 Cr

INTEREST PAYABLE

Date	Event	Dr	Cr	Balance
5/08/93				0
30/09/93	#23		90	
30/09/93				90 Cr

INCOME TAX PAYABLE

Date	Event	Dr	Cr	Balance
5/08/93				0
30/09/93	#27		163	
30/09/93				163 Cr

LOAN PAYABLE

Date	Event	Dr	Cr	Balance
5/08/93				0
30/08/93	#13		9,000	
30/09/93				9,000 Cr

COMMON STOCK

Date	Event	Dr	Cr	Balance
5/08/93				0
5/08/93	#1		10,000	
30/09/93				10,000 Cr

RETAINED EARNINGS

Date	Event	Dr	Cr	Balance
5/08/93				0
30/09/93	#28		652	
30/09/93				652 Cr

SALES — MAGAZINES

Date	Event	Dr	Cr	Balance
30/09/93	#25		12,000	
30/09/93	#28	12,000		

SALES — ADVERTISING

Date	Event	Dr	Cr	Balance
11/08/93	#4		1,300	
20/08/93	#8		1,950	
3/09/93	#14		4,000	
30/09/93	#28	7,250		

COST OF MAGAZINES SOLD

Date	Event	Dr	Cr	Balance
30/09/93	#26	11,500		
30/09/93	#28		11,500	

WRITING FEES EXPENSE

Date	Event	Dr	Cr	Balance
16/08/93	#6	1,000		
23/08/93	#10	925		
30/09/93	#28		1,925	

RENT EXPENSE

Date	Event	Dr	Cr	Balance
16/08/93	#7	750		
16/09/93	#19	750		
30/09/93	#28		1,500	

DISTRIBUTION EXPENSE

Date	Event	Dr	Cr	Balance
10/09/93	#17	1,295		
30/09/93	#28		1,295	

SALARY EXPENSE

Date	Event	Dr	Cr	Balance
20/09/93	#21	1,000		
30/09/93	#28		1,000	

TELEPHONE EXPENSE

Date	Event	Dr	Cr	Balance
18/09/93	#20	125		
30/09/93	#28		125	

DEPRECIATION EXPENSE

Date	Event	Dr	Cr	Balance
30/09/93	#22	225		
30/09/93	#28		225	

TRAVEL EXPENSE

Date	Event	Dr	Cr	Balance
10/08/93	#3	530		
30/09/93	#28		530	

INTEREST EXPENSE

Date	Event	Dr	Cr	Balance
30/09/93	#23	90		
30/09/93	#28		90	

SUPPLIES EXPENSE

Date	Event	Dr	Cr	Balance
30/09/93	#24	245		
30/09/93	#28		245	

INCOME TAX EXPENSE

Date	Event	Dr	Cr	Balance
30/09/93	#27	163		
30/09/93	#28		163	

General ledger trial balance

The next step is to compute the net sum for each account and prepare a general ledger trial balance, as in Exhibit 3–4. This helps the accountant verify that the grand sum of debit amounts computed over all the accounts equals the grand sum of credit amounts computed over all the accounts. This equality must exist if the claim that all events were recorded properly is to be supported (recall the comment earlier in the chapter about the equality of debits and credits being an important control feature). By itself, however, such equality is not sufficient to prove that the accounting is correct, since even apparently nonsensical journal entries, such as the following one, will maintain the equality:

Dr		Inventory	XXX	
	Cr	Accumulated depreciation		XXX

EXHIBIT 3–4
GENERAL LEDGER TRIAL BALANCE FOR ON ICE INCORPORATED
September 30, 1993 (after adjustments)
(only accounts with nonzero balances are shown)

Account	Dr	Cr
Cash	1,550	
Accounts receivable	17,950	
Organization costs	575	
Office supplies	50	
Capital asset	3,590	
Accumulated depreciation		225
Accounts payable		3,585
Interest payable		90
Income tax payable		163
Loan payable		9,000
Common stock		10,000
Sales — magazines		12,000
Sales — advertising		7,250
Cost of magazines sold	11,500	
Writing fees expense	1,925	
Rent expense	1,500	
Distribution expenses	1,295	
Salary expense	1,000	
Telephone expense	125	
Depreciation expense	225	
Travel expense	530	
Interest expense	90	
Supplies expense	245	
Income tax expense	163	
TOTALS	**42,313**	**42,313**

Closing entries

One final journal entry must be recorded in the general journal in Exhibit 3–2, as follows:

30/9/93 Event 28	Dr Sales — magazines	12,000	
	Dr Sales — advertising	7,250	
	Cr Cost of magazines sold		11,500
	Cr Writing fees expense		1,925
	Cr Rent expense		1,500
	Cr Distribution expense		1,295
	Cr Salary expense		1,000
	Cr Telephone expense		125
	Cr Depreciation expense		225
	Cr Travel expense		530
	Cr Interest expense		90
	Cr Supplies expense		245
	Cr Income tax expense		163
	Cr Retained earnings		652

Such a journal entry is called a "closing" entry, since it closes out all the revenue and expense accounts for the accounting period that has just been completed, transfers their overall grand net balance (which in this case is a net income of $652) to retained earnings, and leaves the revenue and expense accounts with zero balances so that they can be used to record revenues and expenses for the next accounting period.

Recall from Chapter 1:

$$RE_e = RE_s + NI_y - DIV_y$$

That is, retained earnings at the end of an accounting period is equal to retained earnings at the beginning, plus net income created during the period, less any dividends for the period. In On Ice's case this is:

$$652 = 0 + 652 - 0$$

Thus, the closing entry is just a way of calculating end-of-period retained earnings.

All of the accounts whose balances are transferred to retained earnings are called "nominal" or "temporary" accounts. These nominal accounts are the revenue and expense accounts, and they need to be zeroed out at the end of each accounting period so that they will be ready to record the next period's income-generating activities. The balance sheet accounts, which represent the ongoing, cumulative history of the accounting entity, are called "real" or "permanent" accounts.

In summary, transactions and other events provide important information about an accounting entity, and the accounting model based upon the A = L + SE relationship provides a way of accounting for the "dual aspect" of each transaction or other event. Further, techniques based on debits, credits, journal entries, accounts, and the general ledger trial balance provide a way of keeping organized track of large numbers of such transactions and other events. Also, income statements, balance sheets, and cash flow statements can be prepared from databases pulled directly from the A = L + SE model (as in the spreadsheet in Exhibit 1–5 in Chapter 1); or from the trial balance in Exhibit 3–4 (for the income statement and balance sheet) and the cash account in Exhibit 3–3 (for the cash flow statement).

The concept of transactions and other events is, as we mentioned earlier, one of the basic ideas in accounting. The double-entry system of accounting for these transactions and other events has proven over the past five centuries to be a valuable way of "doing accounting."

Accounting and Business Decision D

Cash flowing into and out of the accounting entity On Ice for the period August 5, 1993, to September 30, 1993, is presented in the "Cash" general ledger account, which is represented in T-account form in Exhibit 3–3. Code each debit and credit as (O) operating, (I) investing, or (F) financing, and prepare a cash flow statement for On Ice.

What Happens When the Volume of Transactions and Other Accountable Events Increases?

The On Ice example included just 27 accountable events (28 if the closing entry is included). Since even small businesses may have hundreds of transactions and adjustments to record in any given accounting period, methods for handling large volumes of information were established during the pre-computer era. Basically, specialized books of original entry were developed in addition to the general journal. These specialized books of original entry handled high-volume transactions (such as the large number of sales and purchases that a company might make); the general journal was reserved for adjustments and other (usually low-volume) accounting events.

For example, a sales journal may be used to record all of a company's sales transactions. Its design might be like the table shown below.

The October totals from the sales journal thus provide information for the accountant to debit the cash general ledger account for $7,285.90, to debit the accounts receivable general ledger account for $35,975.15, and to credit the sales general ledger account for $43,261.05.

Depending on the situation, a company might have a Purchases Journal, a Cash Disbursements Journal, a Payroll Journal, and so on.

EXAMPLE COMPANY — SALES JOURNAL

Date	Customer	Invoice #	Cash	Accounts Receivable
1/10/95	Peach Co.	651	275.50	
2/10/95	McGraw Ltd.	652		3,500.75
2/10/95	See Inc.	653		1,235.00
.	.	.	.	.
.	.	.	.	.
.	.	.	.	.
31/10/95	Monitor Ltd.	795		1,257.90
31/10/95	McGraw Ltd.	796	957.25	
OCTOBER TOTALS			7,285.90	35,975.15

Adjusting Entries Again

While we were discussing On Ice's double-entry accounting earlier in this chapter, we described adjusting entries as necessary to account for the conversion of assets into expenses, and other events which have taken place during the accounting period but which have not been part of an explicit transaction. We'll now delve more deeply into the concept of an adjusting entry.

Such accounting entries are recorded at the end of an accounting period, after a general ledger trial balance for all the transactions has been prepared. Here are some examples of adjusting entries: accounting for the second year of a prepaid three-year insurance policy (the transaction occurred last year, but the second year's insurance cost is an expense of the second year); the recognition of interest receivable when the cash will not be received until some future accounting period; and the recording of property taxes that will not be paid until some future time (the transaction will occur in the future, but an accountable event — the cost of the benefits of conducting a business in the municipality — should be recorded).

Adjusting entries may be classified into five categories, which relate to the following five general situations:

1. The accounting entity has earned revenues that are measurable, but the revenues have not yet been billed or collected.
2. Revenues have been collected in advance of being earned (the opposite of 1).
3. Expenses have been incurred, but not yet paid. An example would be the interest expense for On Ice's bank loan.
4. Money or other resources have been paid out (such an outflow of resources is called an expenditure), but the accounting entity has not yet received the benefit of the expenditure.
5. Part of the cost of an asset has been allocated to expense in an accounting period. Examples of such costs include depreciation expense and amortization expense.

Next, each of these situations is described further:

1. *The accounting entity has earned revenues that are measurable, but the revenues have not yet been billed or collected.* Company A loaned $100,000 to Company B on November 1, 1993, receiving a one-year, 6% note with interest payable at the end of the year (that is, October 30, 1994). Company A has a January 31 year end, so on that date the following adjusting entry must be recorded in A's accounting records. See the upper journal entry on the left.

Dr Accrued interest receivable (a current asset account)	1,512.33	
Cr Interest revenue		1,512.33

$100,000 × 0.06 × (92/365) = $1512.33. There are 92 days from November 1 to January 31.

When Company A receives the total payment of principal plus one year's interest on October 30, 1994, the accounting should be like the journal entry on the lower left.

Dr Cash	106,000.00	
Cr Accrued interest receivable		1,512.33
Cr Loan receivable		100,000.00
Cr Interest revenue		4,487.67

This second entry is not an adjusting entry, since it is recorded in response to a transaction.

The upshot of all this is that Company A records $1,512.33 in interest revenue for the fiscal year ended January 31, 1994, and $4,487.67 in interest revenue for the fiscal year ended January 31, 1995. The act of recording the revenue of $1,512.33 and its associated receivable in the year ended January 31, 1994, is called accruing the revenue. The receivable is called an *accrued* interest receivable since it is not yet legally due, but it has been earned.

2. *Revenues have been collected in advance of being earned.* Suppose a landlord collected $12,000 from a tenant on December 1, 1993, for rent from December 1, 1993, through to May 31, 1994. The landlord has a December 31 fiscal year end. The tenant has prepaid the rent but has not yet enjoyed the benefit of the service, so the landlord has not yet earned a portion of the rent revenue. The adjusting entry in this situation will depend upon how the landlord accounts for the collection of the $12,000 — that is, the original transaction. In practice, either of two alternative journal entries can be used to account for the original transaction (that is, the receipt of the $12,000 cash).

   (a) Suppose the $12,000 transaction was initially credited to a liability account, which makes sense, since by accepting the money the landlord has become obligated to provide future benefits to the tenant:

December 1, 1993		
Dr Cash	12,000	
Cr Unearned revenue		12,000

Then, the adjusting journal entry would be:

December 31, 1993		
Dr Unearned revenue	2,000	
Cr Rent revenue		2,000

Here the $2,000 represents one month's rental revenue out of the six months' total. The account "Unearned revenue" is a current liability account on the balance sheet, while "Rent revenue" is a revenue account on the income statement.

   (b) If the transaction represented by the collection of the cash had initially been credited to a revenue account, the original treatment would have been as follows:

December 1, 1993		
Dr Cash	12,000	
Cr Rent revenue		12,000

and the adjusting journal entry would have been:

December 31, 1993		
Dr Rent revenue	10,000	
Cr Unearned revenue		10,000

This adjustment records the fact that five-sixths of the rental revenue has not been earned as at December 31, 1993.

3. *Expenses have been incurred, but not yet paid.* Event #23 for On Ice represents this type of adjusting entry. The event in On Ice is the accounting for the interest cost of a loan from the point of view of a borrower. Another example would be when a company has a $100,000 weekly payroll, and employees are paid each Friday but the current accounting period ends on Wednesday (say the company has a calendar fiscal year, and December 31 falls on a Wednesday this year). The following adjusting entry records the expenses and liabilities of the company with respect to employee costs:

December 31, 1993		
Dr Salaries expense	60,000	
Cr Accrued salaries payable		60,000
3/5 of $100,000, assuming a five-day week.		

The accountant is said to have accrued the expense and its associated liability.

4. *Money or other resources have been paid out, but the accounting entity has not yet received the benefit of the expenditure.* Suppose a company with a fiscal year end equal to the calendar year paid the $48,000 premium on a fire insurance policy on January 1, 1995. Insurance coverage began on that day and will extend for a three-year period ending on December 31, 1997. The accounting period under consideration is the fiscal year ended December 31, 1995. As for example 2, the adjusting entry required depends on how the initial transaction (that is, the payment of the $48,000) is accounted for.

   (a) If the payment was originally debited[6] to an asset account, the transaction would have been accounted for as follows:

January 1, 1995		
Dr Unexpired insurance	48,000	
Cr Cash		48,000

(The account "Unexpired insurance" is an asset account on the balance sheet, and it is usually classified as a current asset, even though strictly speaking only a portion of it is current. The account title "Prepaid insurance" is also often used.)

The required adjusting entry on December 31, 1995 would then have been as follows:

December 31, 1995		
Dr Insurance expense	16,000	
Cr Unexpired insurance		16,000

(Where $16,000 represents the cost of one-third of the three-year insurance premium.)

   (b) If the original transaction had been charged to the expense account, as follows:

January 1, 1995		
Dr Insurance expense	48,000	
Cr Cash		48,000

then the required adjusting journal entry would have been this:

December 31, 1995		
Dr Unexpired insurance insurance	32,000	
Cr Insurance expense		32,000

(The $32,000 represents the two-thirds of the insurance premium that will be a cost of doing business, or an expense, in the future.)

5. *Part of the cost of an asset has been allocated to expense in an accounting period.* Event #22 for On Ice — the depreciation journal entry — is an example of this type of adjusting entry.

The above five types of entries *adjust* a company's accounting records from a pure transactions-based accounting system, to one based on two important ideas: that revenue-type events should affect income only when the revenues are earned and measurable; and that expense-type events should affect income only when the accounting entity has benefited from the expense.

[6] Accountants often say "charged to" instead of "debited to." This is an example of accounting/business jargon.

Inclusiveness of a Financial Accounting System

Under GAAP, financial accounting accounts for both the cash and noncash transactions of an accounting entity, as well as the five types of events that are classified as "adjustments." The dividing line between events that are accounted for and those that are not is continually changing, so it is useful to learn a bit about the inclusiveness of a financial accounting system with respect to the types of events that are accounted for. The table on the next page distinguishes four different financial accounting systems in terms of what the systems include. System 1 accounts for cash transactions only. Since it is usually easy to determine whether cash has been received or paid out, this system is very objective. There is still some uncertainty, however, since there is some risk associated with uncashed cheques that the organization has received.

System 2 includes all the cash transactions of system 1, and also all the noncash transactions that the accounting entity has entered into. Selling a product on credit, purchasing furniture on credit, and accepting a gift of a capital asset from a shareholder are all examples of noncash transactions that would not have been accounted for under system 1, but that *are* accounted for under system 2. The range of information accounted for is thus broader, and so is the necessity to exercise judgment.

System 3 includes all that system 2 includes, plus the five types of adjustments described earlier. This is the system that GAAP follows. The range of information is much greater than for system 2 (since it includes numerous nontransaction events, such as accounting for depreciation); the need for making estimates is also much greater. Thus, the potential for bias in financial accounting becomes greater as we move from system 2 to system 3. Deciding on a reasonable depreciation expense, and estimating accruals for receivables or payables, and judging the amount by which a capital asset should be written down if management feels that its value has sunk permanently below net book value, are all examples of financial accounting decisions that could lead to bias, or to disputes between management and the company's auditors. Occasionally, companies in trouble that have just had new management installed will decide to record adjustments writing off all sorts of assets, on the theory that since this is a bad year anyway, they may as well get rid of as many assets of depressed value as possible. This has the important side-benefit of automatically improving reported income for future years, since asset amounts for depreciation and so on will be a lot lower after such a "big bath." Even in years in which a "big bath" is not taken, some managers may be tempted to artificially "smooth" income by choosing adjustment amounts with a view to manipulating income rather than fairly recording the impact of nontransaction events on the organization. For these reasons, it makes sense to monitor carefully the adjustments that an organization records, to test them for credibility.

System 4 includes everything in system 3, plus events in addition to those accounted for through the five adjustment categories. Here are some examples of these additional events, which GAAP does not now normally account for:

- A competitor improves its technology.
- The replacement cost of the company's raw material increases.
- A civil war ends in a foreign country.

Inclusiveness of Financial Accounting System for an Accounting Entity		Comments
System 1.	Include just cash transactions	Very objective; very narrow set of information
System 2.	Include cash transactions **plus** noncash transactions	
System 3.	Include cash transactions **plus** noncash transactions **plus** adjustments to account for certain events	
System 4.	Include cash transactions **plus** noncash transactions **plus** adjustments to account for certain events **plus** other events affecting the accounting entity	Very subjective; very broad set of information

The boundaries between transaction events and nontransaction events are continually changing in accounting. In other words, how accountants allocate events between these two categories has been and still is subject to change. For example, up until 15 or so years ago, at the point in time when an organization entered into a long-term rental agreement (also called a lease agreement) that extended over substantially the entire expected useful life of the asset being rented, accountants felt that no transaction had occurred. But by the late 1970s, accountants had decided that an organization entering into such a contractual arrangement was in about the same position economically as a company that had borrowed money to buy the asset: both companies had control of the asset for approximately its entire expected service life, and both companies had obligated themselves to make future payments. In 1978 GAAP in Canada was changed so that companies entering into long-term lease agreements (that is, capital lease agreements) had to debit a capital asset account, and also credit a liability account called something such as "Obligations under lease." The amount of the debit and credit was set equal to (usually) the present value of the future payments established by the lease. This is an example of a formerly unaccounted for business event becoming an accountable business transaction.

A current example of a nonaccountable business event slowly moving in the direction of becoming an accountable event is the environmental liability. As society becomes more conscious of the causes and consequences of environmental degradation by pollution, the need for corporate accountability increases. Social expectations change, and this results in new laws and accountability. A polluter who 20 years ago would have ignored the costs of pollution entirely, or at most disclosed its possible existence as a contingency in a financial statement footnote, may now be required to formally account for such costs and the associated liability by means of a journal entry.

Accounting Cycle

The process of recording transactions, preparing a general ledger trial balance, recording any necessary adjustments, preparing another, post-adjustment general ledger trial balance, and finally preparing financial statements, is called the accounting cycle. The appendix to this chapter (p. 164) summarizes the cycle.

Further Important Uses of Journal Entries and T-Accounts

We have seen how journal entries are an important part of the accounting cycle. The journal entry is the first place in which transaction or other information is captured by the accounting system. Also, we saw how the account — represented schematically by the T-account — was used to collect information about various assets, liabilities, and so on. Apart from their role in this accounting record-keeping process, journal entries and T-accounts have other important uses from the perspective of managers and outside users of financial accounting information.

Using journal entries in "what if" analysis

Managers and others are often interested in predicting what will happen in the future. Questions such as these —

- "What will happen to our company's balance sheet and income sheet if a particular transaction is undertaken?"
- "What will be the impact on our financial statements if we choose one accounting method rather than another?"

may be answered by designing the hypothetical journal entry that would result if the particular transaction was undertaken, or if the particular accounting choice was followed. Let's see how this would work in a simple situation, using the following hypothetical data:

Grover Limited (GL) is a (hypothetical) company established in 1995. It provides other companies with advice on the optimum layout of their offices or manufacturing facilities. At present, GL management records revenues only *after* a consulting job has been completed; based on this accounting method, $500,000 in revenues was recorded in 1995. GL management wishes to assess the effect of recording revenue on *all* jobs, even those which are still in process at the end of the accounting period. If this accounting method had been followed, revenues of $800,000 would have been recorded in 1995.

If GL has a corporate income tax rate of 40% and financial accounting and income taxation follow the same rules, then the journal entry under the second alternative would be —

Dr Accounts receivable	800,000	
Cr Sales		800,000
Dr Income tax expense	320,000	
Cr Income tax liability		320,000

Alternatively, if the method GL uses now is followed:

Dr Accounts receivable	500,000	
Cr Sales		500,000
Dr Income tax expense	200,000	
Cr Income tax liability		200,000

Thus, the overall effects of switching are as seen in the chart on the left.

Account	Status Quo Dr	Status Quo Cr	New Accounting Method Dr	New Accounting Method Cr	Impact of Change
Accounts receivable	500,000		800,000		300,000 Dr
Sales		500,000		800,000	300,000 Cr
Income tax expense	200,000		320,000		120,000 Dr
Income tax liability		200,000		320,000	120,000 Cr

This method of analysing accounting changes will become very valuable as we deal with more complex transactions later on.

EXHIBIT 3-5
EXCERPTS FROM UNITED GRAIN GROWERS LIMITED'S 1992 ANNUAL REPORT*

Earnings
For the Year Ended July 31, 1992

	1992	1991
Sales and other operating revenue (note 1)	$1,034,268,000	$1,138,074,000
Cost of sales	886,402,000	989,469,000
Operating, general and administrative expenses (note 3)	134,651,000	135,639,000
	1,021,053,000	1,125,108,000
Earnings from continuing operations before provision for income taxes	13,215,000	12,966,000
Provision for income taxes (note 4)	5,964,000	6,581,000
Earnings from continuing operations	7,251,000	6,385,000
Loss on disposition of United Oilseed Products Inc., a discontinued operation	—	3,591,000
Net earnings	$ 7,251,000	$ 2,794,000

Financial Position
As at July 31, 1992

	1992	1991
ASSETS		
Current Assets		
Cash	$ 10,086,000	$ 8,157,000
Deposits — The Canadian Wheat Board	7,611,000	11,079,000
Accounts receivable and accruals	88,909,000	82,793,000
Inventories (note 5)	94,562,000	175,433,000
Prepaid expenses	3,771,000	3,674,000
	204,939,000	281,136,000
Deferred Charges (note 6)	8,147,000	6,473,000
Investments (note 7)	6,509,000	6,521,000
Properties (note 8)	129,532,000	135,299,000
	$ 349,127,000	$ 429,429,000

(continued...)

Use of T-accounts to reconstruct business events: An outsider's perspective

When we were illustrating the double-entry accounting system for On Ice, we transferred debits and credits to the appropriate general ledger accounts, which were represented schematically by the T-account. Outside users of financial accounting information do not of course usually have access to the detailed accounting records, and must rely upon the heavily condensed information in the published financial statements. They may be able to use T-accounts to gain more insight into what the organization did during the accounting period. For analysts, T-accounts can be an extremely useful tool for understanding the flow of accounting information in published financial statements; they can also help accountants and accounting students resolve accounting questions.

The T-account's role in these endeavours is based on two identities. The first relates to asset, expense, and dividend accounts, and the second to liability, capital, and revenue accounts.

For every T-account representing an asset, expense, or dividend —

Opening balance + All incoming debits – All outgoing credits = Closing balance

For every T-account representing a liability, capital, or revenue (and for accounts such as accumulated depreciation, which have "credit" balances even though they are on the asset side of the balance sheet) —

Opening Balance + All incoming credits – All outgoing debits = Closing balance

For both of these equations, if all items but one are missing, the missing item may be derived since all the other items are known. Let's see how this works using the published income statement and balance sheet from the 1992 annual report of Winnipeg-based United Grain Growers Limited, (see Exhibit 3–5; the company abbreviates its name as UGG).

(continued...)

LIABILITIES AND SHAREHOLDERS' EQUITY		
Current Liabilities		
Bank and other loans (note 9)	$ 86,454,000	$140,144,000
Unpresented grain and other cheques	21,069,000	46,902,000
Accounts payable and accruals	34,602,000	36,104,000
Share dividends payable	1,203,000	1,203,000
Long-term debt due within one year	8,255,000	7,116,000
	151,583,000	231,469,000
Long-term Debt (note 10)	51,293,000	58,419,000
Deferred Income Taxes	50,882,000	50,192,000
Commitments (note 11)		
SHAREHOLDERS' EQUITY		
Share Capital (note 12)	24,434,000	24,443,000
Retained Earnings	70,935,000	64,906,000
	95,369,000	89,349,000
	$349,127,000	$429,429,000

*Footnotes not included.

Assume that we, as external analysts, wished to estimate the total of all additions to UGG's grain inventory during the fiscal year ended July 31, 1992. We can use the above asset T-account equation to help analyse the inventory account (to the nearest $000). See the chart below.

Using the equation for asset T-accounts, we have:

94,562 = 175,433 + All incoming debits - 886,402

Therefore, all incoming debits must have totalled $805,531,000, which is the total additions to UGG's grain inventory for 1992. By comparing this number with its counterparts in the recent past — say, 1991 and 1990 — we may be able to glean some information about grain salability.

INVENTORY			
Opening Balance, August 1, 1991	175,433		
All incoming debits	(unknown)		
		All outgoing credits (which must be the cost of sales)	886,402
Closing balance, July 31, 1992	94,562		

Accounting, Organizations, and Society

The quotation that began this chapter was selected to suggest that double-entry accounting has both present-day and historical significance. Double-entry accounting has been around a long time, at least since (according to some accounting and business research) the early Middle Ages. As we saw in Chapter 1, some forms of accounting have been part of human civilization for many thousands of years.

Business and accounting historians have provided contradictory evidence and theories about how double-entry accounting influenced the rise of business and capitalism. For example, R.A. Bryer of the Warwick Business School, University of Warwick, England, provides evidence that double-entry accounting, which permits businesspeople to calculate the effect of every transaction on the rate of return on capital (that is, profit divided by opening capital), was adopted only when merchants and other entrepreneurs began to pool their capital and thus needed a convenient, reliable method for making such calculations.[7] Bryer writes that double-entry accounting "emerged, simultaneously and apparently independently, in several northern Italian cities at the high-point of the 'commercial revolution' of 1250 to 1350, where it quickly became the ... dominant method" (p. 114).

In an interesting article, James A. Aho attempts to argue that double-entry accounting became important to medieval European business not so much for its usefulness in providing information for decision-making or control purposes; rather, "its purpose was largely rhetorical — that is, to justify an activity about which there existed in medieval Christian Europe a considerable suspicion: namely, commerce itself."[8] Aho is using the term "rhetoric" not in its modern, pejorative sense of excessive style without much substance, but rather in its older sense, which is concerned with the way arguments are conducted in an attempt to persuade someone.

Historical research suggests that double-entry accounting was important in facilitating business and commercial activities at the beginning of the Renaissance and thereafter. When we combine this with the views of managers such as Microsoft Corporation's Gaudette (quoted at the beginning of this chapter), we can begin to appreciate the social and economic significance of double-entry accounting and the information revolutions that it spawned. It seems only just, then, that books on accounting devote at least a few lines to the Renaissance figure who is credited with codifying and popularizing the essential features of double-entry accounting. That figure was a Renaissance scholar named Luca Pacioli. He was an Italian who was interested mainly in mathematics, who collaborated with such notables as Leonardo da Vinci, and whose major work, *Summa de Arithmetica Geometria Proportioni et Proportionalita*, (called the *Summa* for short, and published over 500 years ago, in 1494) contained a section devoted to double-entry accounting that has had a lasting influence on accounting and consequently on business practices worldwide. The *Summa* was felt to be so important in its time that it was one of the first books to be printed on the newly invented printing press. Following is an all-too-brief chronology of Pacioli's life. Many of the facts are in dispute among scholars; however, the general elements, including the importance of the *Summa*, are well accepted.[9]

- Luca Pacioli, the child of a lower-middle-class family, was born between 1445 and 1450 in Borgo San Sepolcro, southeast of Florence. (The town is also the birthplace of the great Renaissance artist Piero della Francesca, 1416–92.)
- Pacioli studied at the local monastery, where one of his teachers in mathematics was Piero della Francesco, who recognized the boy's talent in mathematics and recommended him to the eminent Renaissance scholar Leon Battista degli Alberti (1404–72), who in turn arranged for a private teaching position for Pacioli in Venice (beginning about 1464).
- Pacioli remained in Venice for about six years, teaching mathematics to the sons of Ser Antonio de Rompiasi, a wealthy merchant, and generally assisting de Rompiasi (a duty that apparently required Pacioli to accompany the merchant's trading ships).

[7] Bryer, "Double-Entry Bookkeeping and the Birth of Capitalism: Accounting for the Commercial Revolution in Medieval Northern Italy," *Critical Perspectives on Accounting*, Vol. 4, 1993, pp. 113–140.
[8] Aho, "Rhetoric and the Invention of Double Entry Bookkeeping," *Rhetorica*, Vol. 3, no. 1 (Winter 1985), pp. 21–43. The quote is from p. 22.
[9] The source for the chronology is Osuma Kojima and Tsuneo Nakano, "Luca Pacioli and His Treatise on Bookkeeping," *The Annals of the School of Business Administration*, Kobe University, no. 36, 1992, pp. 29–42.

- During his years in Venice, Pacioli apparently developed his knowledge of business and the importance of accounting.
- About 1470, Pacioli moved to Rome, where he lived with Alberti. A year later Alberti died, and Pacioli became a Franciscan monk.
- In 1475, he began to teach mathematics at the University of Perugia.
- He travelled extensively in Italy, lecturing on mathematics at universities in Florence, Rome, Naples, and elsewhere.
- Pacioli worked on his *Summa* from about 1486 to about 1494, making extensive use of the library assembled by the Duke of Urbino — one of the few great book collections of the time.
- In 1494, Pacioli's *Summa* was published (in Italian, rather than in Latin as was the custom of the time; thus, it was more accessible to a wider audience than most books of that era). His reputation grew among the élite of Italy (such as the Duke of Milan) and the élite of the Renaissance (such as Leonardo da Vinci). Its publication was probably arranged with at least some help from the powerful Bishop of Urbino.
- Pacioli continued to lecture on mathematics and to contribute to monastic life, and died sometime in 1517.

To complete our introductory examination of double-entry accounting, we end this chapter with an article that describes how a liberal arts undergraduate student began a study of accounting:

Where's the "R" in Debit?

by W. Richard Sherman

Abstract: *The common abbreviation for the accounting term "debit" is a puzzling one—"Dr." Today, particularly with our depersonalized treatment of the accounting or bookkeeping "debit," there is no obvious clue as to why there is an "r" in "debit" at all. An investigation of the history and evolution of the "debit" in bookkeeping reveals the reason for the abbreviation—a reason almost totally lost without historical perspective. Whereas the accounting "debit" is now viewed as a "technical" term, devoid of any value considerations, referring simply to the left side of a journal entry or ledger account, this was not always the case. Originally, "debits" did have a "bad" side. They were used to record the debts of the merchant or businessman.* Debits *were* debtors. *And the abbreviation for "debtor" is "Dr."*

As a liberal arts undergraduate, I spent part of the summer of my sophomore year enrolled in an introductory accounting course at the University of Pennsylvania's highly regarded Wharton School. At an accelerated pace, meeting three hours a day, four days a week, we flew through ledger accounts, journal entries, financial statement preparation — and accounting struck a chord in me. I found its symmetry satisfying. It appealed to my sense of order by its ability to organize and summarize diverse and seemingly chaotic transactions. Even journal ent made sense to me almost from start. Debit Accounts Receiva credit Sales Revenue; debit Ca credit Accounts Receivable; de Accounts Payable, credit Ca and so on. I genuinely enjo this introduction to account EXCEPT for one thing — whe the "r" in debit?

One of the first obstacles learning (or teaching, as I disc ered later) the basics of account is the need to dispel the notion "bad" debits or "good" cred Students come to accounting h ing already acquired (or suffer experience with bank stateme and credit card receipts and ot everyday exposure to the ter "debit" and "credit." Quite naturally, they assume that the same characteristics which debits and credits possess in those limited situations will apply in all accounting transactions — *viz.* credits are "good" because they add to one's account or worth (*e.g.* the bank "credits" one's account for a deposit or an individual is given "credit" for his accomplishments), debits are "bad" because they are "charges against" or diminish one's account or value. It is no small task to overcome the years of common-sense experience to the point of accepting that there are no value judgments which can be associated with the accounting "debit" and "credit." They simply mean "left" and "right." No more, no less.

After overcoming this first obstacle, I found the use of debits and credits to be nothing less than perfectly reasonable and logical. But I was still troubled by the abbreviations for these two basic bookeeping terms. On the surface it was easy enough—"DR" for debit, "CR" for credit. But wait a minute. Even as a sophomore liberal arts student, I could see how we get the "CR"; but show me an "r" in debit! Why isn't it "De"? or "Db"? I'd even settle for "Dt." Why "Dr"?

This anomaly bothered me enough that I began asking a few accountants, both practitioners and academics, to explain it. Though my research for the "r" in debit was by no means systematic, neither were the explanations I received. These varied widely in intellectual and aesthetic appeal. Perhaps the worst was the totally predictable — "because that's the way it's always been done." Not only was this unsatisfactory because it left unanswered the question — WHY has it always been done that way, but it isn't even accurate. At various times, in various texts, debit has been abbreviated as "Dr," "Deb," "Debr," "Debtr," and even as the "Dt" which I was willing to accept as justifiable [Dafforne, 1636; Hayes, 1741; also see excerpts cited in Yamey, Edey & Thomson, 1963]. So the search continued.

One of my favorite theories was that the abbreviation for debit was indeed the entirely logical "De." At least it was originally "De"; but due to some sloppy handwriting, the "De" was mistaken for a "Dr." The result was that an unclear manuscript begot a printer's error in a published treatise. Debit, as abbreviated as "Dr," was thus memorialized and, what is worse, became accepted as correct. As absurd and outlandish as this theory might seem, it would not be the first time one author's mistake was perpetuated in another's work. As Professor Yamey notes in his essay on the development of bookkeeping, "demonstrable errors were sometimes transmitted from one author to another" [Yamey, 1980, p. 81]. Thus, sloppy handwriting may have been the culprit behind the "r" in debit. Too whimsical to be true? Unfortunately yes — but it makes a good story.

Maybe it has something to do with the Italians. After all, the invention and use of double-entry bookkeeping, with its diabolical system of debits and credits, is commonly linked to the development and growth of the great merchant cities of Italy — Genoa, Florence, and Venice [Yamey, 1980, p. 88; Peragallo, 1938, p. 2]. Modern Italian does indeed provide a likely explanation for the abbreviation "Dr" — the Italian word for the accounting term "debit" is *dare*. Finally, I had accounted (no pun intended) for both the "D" and the "r" in "debit." It was easy enough. I had just been looking in the wrong language. *Dare* seems to be the answer to my sophomoric question. There's only one slight problem. If the abbreviation "Dr" is from the Italian word for debit, then where's the "Cr" in *avere*? (*Avere* is the Italian word for the bookkeeping "credit.") If it was troublesome enough to find an "r" in debit, what will it take to get the "Cr" out of *avere*? Perhaps I had better look elsewhere for the "r" in debit.

Modern Italian seemed a good starting point. Maybe the problem is that it is TOO modern. Lurking a few steps back in time is the reputed "father" of double-entry bookkeeping — the Franciscan monk Luca Pacioli. His *Summa de Arithmetica Geometria et Proportionalita*, printed in Venice in 1494, provides an interesting historical perspective on the development of accounting. Pacioli took no credit (again no pun intended) for inventing the system of bookkeeping he described in his treatise. Instead, he sought merely to present the system already in use in Venice at the end of the 15th Century [Brown & Johnston 1963, p. 4]. This system bears remarkable similarities to the bookkeeping methods we use today — even to the point of having developed fairly stylized journal and ledger entries. Today we have an established format for our journal entries, *viz.* first debit the appropriate account(s), then indent and credit the other appropriate account(s). For example, to journalize the collection of an open account the entry would be:

Cash	XX	
Accounts Receivable		XX.

Anyone familiar with modern bookkeeping can identify which accounts are being debited or credited by simply noting the order and position in which the account appears on the page of the journal. Pacioli's *Summa* reveals a similarly stylized entry. Though in full paragraph form, the recording of a transaction follows a set pattern with the account being debited always being preceded by the Italian preposition *Per* and the account credited being preceded by another preposition — *A*, thereby revealing, at a glance, the accounts affected by a particular transaction.

Per and *A*? If there's a "Dr" or a "Cr" in the Pacioli debit and credit, I am certainly not able to find it. But this is trying to be a bit too literal, trying to pluck abbreviations directly out of what Professor Littleton calls "technical" terms [Littleton 1933, p. 157]. These "technical" terms — debit & credit, *dare* & *avere*, *Per* & *A* — have all acquired meanings in an accounting or bookkeeping sense quite apart from any other meanings which they may have in other contexts. As noted before in regards to the non-judgmental nature of "debit" and "credit," in an accounting sense, these terms have taken on a simple "technical" meaning of "left" and "right." But initially at least, these terms had other non-accounting, non-technical meanings. These other meanings may well shed some light on the rather peculiar abbreviations we use today.

The modern Italian *dare* and *avere* are derived from the Latin *debent dare* and *debent habere* and are the equivalents of the English verbs "to give" and "to have." A similar, though somewhat condensed meaning can be given to the Pacioli prepositions *Per* and *A*. These can be literally translated as "for" and "to." Finally, the English "debit" and "credit" can be traced to the old Italian words *debito* and *credito*, which translate as "oweth" and "trusts," respectively [Jackson, 1956, p. 296; Baladouni, 1984, p. 108]. Combining these terms into one thought, one could say that the *dare/Per/debit* entry refers to a person who *owes* something and is obligated *to give* to another person *for* goods or services which that other person has provided. The *avere/A/credit* entry represents the other side of the transaction — *i.e.* the person to whom an obligation is owed, who has a right *to have* something paid or returned *to* him by the "debitor" inasmuch as he has en*trust*ed this other person with his goods or services. In short, these "technical" terms were originally used to summarize and record personal debt relationships among merchants — they recorded debtor-creditor transactions.

Debtor and *creditor*? At last — the "Dr" and the "Cr"! These simple abbreviations are for the English translation of Italian terms denoting the parties to a debt relationship. Can it really be so easy? Does it really explain the "r" in debit? After all, "debits" are used in all kinds of transactions which have nothing to do with debts or liabilities to creditors. In fact, if "Dr" is short for "debtor," then we are thrown back into the old problem of "good" credits and "bad" debits because certainly the "debtor" status is unfavorable and the position of the "creditor" is preferred and superior. So value judgments do apply to the accounting "debit" and "credit." Right?

Wrong. Though it is true that ledger accounts and journal entries were originally developed to note debt relationships among merchants, their use was expanded to cover an increasing number of business dealings. A fiction was created whereby accounts totally unrelated to the original debtor-creditor status became "personified" and treated, for bookkeeping purposes at least, as either a debtor (debit) or creditor (credit) [Littleton, 1933, p. 49]. As one writer notes, "it became the practice to extend the meanings of the term 'debit' and 'credit' beyond their original personal connotation and apply them to inanimate objects and abstract conceptions..." [Jackson, 1956, p. 295]. In the process, "debit" and "credit" lost their original characteristics of being "good" or "bad"; and also lost was the rather obvious source of the "r" in debit.

A look at the complete titles of early English treatises on the "Italian" system of double-entry bookkeeping confirms the origin of the "Dr" abbreviation. The first known English text, printed as early as 1543 and reprinted by Mellis in 1588, bore the descriptive title —

> Here ensueth a profitable treatyce called the instrument or boke to learne to knowe the good order of the kepyn of the famouse reconying, called in latyn Dare et Habere, and in Englyshe *Debitor* and *Creditor*.

A similarly long and descriptive title was given to Richard Dafforne's master-work, published in London in 1636, as —

> The Merchants' Mirrour: or, Directions for the Perfect ordering and keeping of his Accounts, Framed by way of *Debitor* and *Creditor*, after the (so-tearmed) Italian manner: containing 250 rare Questions with their Answers.

The use of the terms "debitor" (or "debtor") and "creditor" in describing the proper methods for the recording of transactions and the keeping of books is indeed the rule rather than the exception in these early works. In fact, it was not until quite recently that the use of the mere technical terms "debit" and "credit" became the vogue [Jackson, 1956, p. 312]. Contrast the rule of double-entry as enunciated by Mellis in 1588 with the explanation offered by a modern accounting text.

> Know yee for certaine that for euery one parcell that is sette in your Journall ought to bee made two parcels in your Leager, that one in *Debitor*, and that other in *Creditor*, aforesaide for each of them ought to be one parcell by himselfe in the Leager [Mellis, 1958].
>
> The double entry rule states that when recording each transaction, the total amount of the *debit* entries must be equal to the total amount of the *credit* entries for that transaction. Thus for each recorded transaction there must be at least one *debit* entry and one *credit* entry (although there could be more entries of each type), and the total amounts must be equal [Nikolai & Bazley, 1983, p. 40].

As Littleton concludes, this modern presentation of the bookkeeping "procedure now leads one to think of *debit-entries* waiting to be posted, not *debts* or *debitors*; that is, to think of 'accounting units' to be transferred or tabulated and not of personified obligations" [Littleton, 1933, p. 233]. It is small wonder that the accountants I had asked knew nothing of the "r" in debit. They had been taught an abstraction, just as we now teach an abstraction, which is unrelated to the very real and personal dealings for which "debits" and "credits" were used in helping merchants remember who owed whom what. As Professor Baladouni concluded in an article which recently appeared in this journal, "the modern meaning of debit and credit cannot in any way be related to the original words [Baladouni, 1984, p. 108]. And without the knowledge of the use of the original words, the "r" in debit cannot be found.

Now the mystery is solved — "Dr" is an abbreviation for "debtor"; "Cr" is short for "creditor." But when were these abbreviations first used? Certainly by the 18th century, writers on the methods of bookkeeping were using "Dr" and "Cr" extensively [Yamey, Edey & Thomspon, 1963]. Littleton has traced the use of "Dr" back to 1690 in Stephen Monteage's *Debtor and Creditor Made Easie* [Littleton, 1933, p. 232]. However, there are even earlier uses of the dreaded "Dr." The 1690 treatise cited by Littleton was the third edition of Monteage's work. Both the first (1675) and second (1682) editions use this abbreviation, first in describing the proper keeping of the "Country Gentleman's" accounts, and then throughout the remainder of the text.

Dafforne's *Merchants' Mirrour*, cited earlier, appeared in editions dated 1635, 1636, 1651, 1660, and 1684. The "Dr" abbreviation appeared in the 1636 and later editions, along with other abbreviations — "Debtr," "Dtr," and "Debr," and may well have been used in the 1635 edition, though I have not been able to find a copy of this earliest printing. (The 1635 and 1636 editions appear to have been the same in every way except for the year in which they were printed and are, therefore, usually cited as the same First Edition of Dafforne's work.)

An even earlier treatise, Handson's *Analysis or Resolution of Merchant Accompts*, contains the abbreviation in both its third (1633) and fourth (1669) editions. The first and second editions may well also use the "Dr," thereby moving the first appearance of this abbreviation back to an even earlier period, but, as with Dafforne's earliest printing, I have not been able to locate copies of these editions of Handson's work.

In sum, even if the "Dr" makes little sense today as an appropriate abbreviation for "debit," it does have quite a long history behind its use. Where's the "r" in "debit"? Today it's in convention; but the basis of this convention lies in the history and evolution of accounting and the need of businessmen to remember who owed whom.

References

Baladouni, Vahé, "Etymological Observations on Some Accounting Terms". The *Accounting Historians Journal*, Vol. 11, No. 2, (Fall, 1984), pp. 101-9.

Brown, R. Gene and Kenneth S. Johnston, *Pacioli on Accounting*. New York: McGraw-Hill, 1963.

Dafforne, Richard, *The Merchants' Mirrour*. London: R. Young, 1636; 2nd Ed., London: Nicolas Bourne, 1651.

Handson, Ralph, *Analysis or Resolution of Marchant Accompts*. 3rd Ed:, London: Nicholas Bourne, 1633; 4th Ed., London: Robert Horne, 1669.

Hayes, Richard, *The Gentleman's Complete Bookkeeper*. London: John Noon, 1741.

Jackson, J.G.C., "The History of Methods of Exposition of Double-Entry Book-keeping in England." *Studies in the History of Accounting*, A. C. Littleton and Basil S. Yamey (eds.). Homewood, Ill.: Richard D. Irwin, 1956, pp. 288-312.

Littleton, A. C. *Accounting Evolution to 1900*. New York: American Institute, 1933.

Mellis, John, *A Briefe instruction and Maner How to Keepe Bookes of Accompts . . .* London: John Windet, 1588. [Attributed to Hugh Oldcastle's *Profitable Treatyce* with an original edition appearing in 1543.]

Monteage, Stephen, *Debtor and Creditor Made Easie*. London: Billingsley, 1675; 2nd Ed., London: John Briscoe, 1682.

Nikolai, Loren A. and John D. Baxley, *Financial Accounting*. Boston: Kent, 1983.

Peragallo, Edward, *Origin and Evolution of Double Entry Bookkeeping*. New York: American Institute, 1938.

Yamey, Basil S. "Early Views on the Origins and Development of Book-keeping and Accounting." *Accounting and Business Research*. Vol. 10, No. 37A (Special Issue, 1980), pp. 81-92.

Yamey, Basil S., H. C. Edey, and Hugh W. Thomson, eds. *Accounting in England and Scotland: 1543-1800*. London: Sweet & Maxwell, 1963.

The Accounting Historians Journal, *Vol. 13, no. 2, Fall 1986.*

CHAPTER SUMMARY

After first describing transactions and events, and showing how transactions are important raw material for accounting, the chapter explained how double-entry bookkeeping, using debits, credits, journal entries, and so on, is used to collect accounting information and prepare financial statements over the accounting cycle. The need for the five types of adjusting entries was illustrated, and four accounting systems, differentiated by the inclusiveness of their information, were described. The chapter finished with a discussion of uses of journal entries and T-accounts in addition to their usefulness in the accounting cycle. The "Accounting, Organizations, and Society" section of the chapter provided some information about the historical importance and evolution of double-entry accounting.

Suggested Answers to Accounting and Business Decisions

Decision A

Please refer to the discussion in the chapter. Some additional comments follow:

The entries in the cells in Exhibit 3–1 indicate that different accounting subdisciplines may often, but not always, use common transaction information. For example, the four subdisciplines listed in the exhibit all make use of present, actual transaction information, as follows:

- Financial accounting reports on incomplete transactions in order to measure income and financial position as completely as possible.
- Operational accounting is responsible for ensuring that incomplete transactions that the accounting entity has entered into are completed as efficiently and effectively as possible, so transaction information about unpaid bills, payroll, and so forth is important to this subdiscipline.
- Management accounting is concerned with current, incomplete transaction information; the point here is to ensure that management's objectives are being achieved.
- Taxation is concerned with how current, incomplete transactions affect the tax burden of the company. Tax rules often permit taxpayers to defer paying income tax until cash has been received.

Decision B

October 10, 1995		
Dr Accounts payable	17,000	
Cr Cash		17,000

October 20, 1995		
Dr Inventory	32,750	
Cr Accounts payable		32,750

October 25, 1995		
Dr Accounts payable	10,055	
Cr Cash		10,055

Decision C

Journal entry #24 adjusts the current asset account "Office supplies" to its appropriate end-of-period amount. The original transaction in which the supplies were purchased triggered journal entry #9. Since that time, Devo Green has been slowly using up the supplies while conducting the business.

Journal entry #27 accounts for the fact that by generating a positive net income, On Ice has also created an obligation to pay taxes. They are not yet legally due, but they must be accounted for so that we may obtain as complete a picture as possible of On Ice's income activities for the accounting period ended September 30, 1993, and of the financial position on that date.

Decision D

The individual cash flows are classified in Exhibit 1–6, part D.

KEY TERMS

Account A formal record of a specific category of asset, liability, revenue, expense, or shareholders' (or owners') equity, in which the effects of transactions or other accountable events (such as adjustments) are measured in terms of money. Compare this with a general dictionary definition:

1a. A narrative or record of events. b. A written or oral explanation, as of blame or cause.[10]

So, as used in accounting, the word "account" refers to a record of *financial* events.

Accounting cycle The recurring process of opening the books of account, recording transactions and other accountable events during an accounting period (by means of journal entries and their effects on general ledger accounts), preparing a general ledger trial balance, recording any necessary adjustments, preparing financial statements, and closing the books of account.

Adjusting entry A journal entry recorded at the end of an accounting period, after all transactions have been recorded. It is the means by which a revenue earned or expense incurred by the accounting entity (such revenue or expense not being part of an explicit transaction) is accounted for. Adjusting entries fall into five categories, as explained in the chapter. Such entries convert what is largely transactions-based accounting information into accounting information based on the accrual system, which (as is shown in the chapter) is much more comprehensive.

Chart of accounts A comprehensive listing of all the titles of all the accounts used by an organization. Individual accounts in the listing may have been assigned unique code numbers.

Closing entry The final (usually) journal entry recorded for an accounting period, after all the transactions and adjustments have been accounted for. This entry closes out all the revenue and expense accounts (called "nominal" or "temporary" accounts) in the general ledger to zero, so that they are ready for use to measure the revenues and expenses of the next accounting period. The net balance of all the revenues and expenses is transferred to the retained earnings general ledger account, so that the closing entry balances.

Contingency An existing condition or situation involving uncertainty as to possible gain or loss that will ultimately be resolved when one or more future events occur or fail to occur.

Contra account A general ledger account that offsets another general ledger account. For example, "Accumulated depreciation" is a contra account.

Credit Means "decrease" when referring to assets, expenses, or dividends, and means "increase" when referring to liabilities, revenues, and capital stock and other subdivisions of owners' equity. *Terminology for Accountants* provides the following definitions:

- as a noun: "1. The ability to buy or borrow in consideration of a promise to pay at a later date. 2. An entry recording the creation of or addition to a liability, owners' equity or revenue, or the reduction or elimination of an asset or expense."
- as a verb: "To record a credit entry in books of account."

Debit Means "increase" when referring to assets, expenses, or dividends, and means "decrease" when referring to liabilities, revenues, and capital stock and other subdivisions of owners' equity. *Terminology for Accountants*, 4th Edition (p. 69), provides the following definitions:

- as a noun: "An entry recording the acquisition of, or addition to, an asset, the incurring of an expense, or the reduction or elimination of a liability, owners' equity or revenue."
- as a verb: "To record a debit entry in books of account."

Event A happening of consequence to an accounting entity. Events may be internal or external to an accounting entity; transactions are a subcategory of external events.

[10] *Houghton Mifflin Canadian Dictionary.*

Expenditure An outflow of resources, such as money or other assets, from an accounting entity, or the incurrence of a liability by an accounting entity. Expenditures must be carefully distinguished from expenses. For instance, the payment of $100,000 in cash to acquire a capital asset such as a computer system is an expenditure. The depreciation of the capital asset over accounting periods in the future is an expense.

General ledger Accounting entities may have several different types of ledgers. The general ledger is the collection of all the accounts of an accounting entity — all the asset, liability, revenue, expense, and owners' equity accounts. A **subsidiary ledger** is a ledger in which individual accounts all of the same type are kept. For example, an accounting entity may keep its customers' accounts receivable in separate subsidiary ledgers (also called sub-ledgers); the total money amount of the sub-ledger balances would equal the balance in the general ledger account "Accounts receivable." Such a general ledger account, for which individual details are stored in sub-ledgers, is called a control account.

General ledger trial balance A listing of the net balances (either debit or credit) in all general ledger accounts. The general ledger trial balance must balance; that is, the sum of all debits must equal to sum of all credits. *Terminology for Accountants*, 4th Edition (p. 217), provides the following definition of "trial balance":

> *A list of all account balances in a ledger, usually showing the account numbers or names, prepared to ascertain whether the ledger is in balance and, in the case of the general ledger, used as the starting point in the process of preparing financial statements.*

Journal entry A record, using the terminology of debits and credits, of a transaction or other accountable event. Journal entries are recorded in an accounting entity's **journal**, which is a chronological listing of the journal entries. Very small organizations with few transactions and other accountable events may just use a general journal; organizations with larger volumes of transactions may require specialized journals, such as sales journals.

Spreadsheet A rectangular grid arranged in columns and rows on which information is entered and stored.

T-account A schematic representation of a general ledger account, based upon the capital letter T, with the account title above the horizontal line, and with debits shown to the left of the vertical line, and credits to the right.

Transaction An external event involving the transfer of something of value between two or more accounting entities.

FACT AND DESCRIPTION QUESTIONS

1. Why are adjusting entries needed to convert transactions-based financial accounting information to more comprehensive accounting information?
2. Distinguish between transactions and events. Are all transactions events? Are all events transactions?
3. List five categories of adjustments, and provide one example for each category.
4. What is the accounting cycle?
5. Why should the money sum of debits always equal the money sum of credits for each journal entry?
6. Why should the money sum of debits always equal the money sum of credits for all accounts in the general ledger considered together?
7. Is it true that journal entries are used both in the process of financial accounting record-keeping, and in "what if" analyses? Distinguish between the two uses.

8. How might a T-account be used to reconstruct business events entered into by an accounting entity? In what way is this use of the T-account different from its use to represent a general ledger account?

9. Why is the title "double-entry accounting" appropriate for the accounting system that is in widespread use today?

10. Distinguish between the following pairs of terms:
    (a) debit versus credit
    (b) adjusting entry versus closing entry
    (c) transaction versus contingency
    (d) financial statement versus trial balance

Questions for Analysis and Discussion

11. Belverd E. Needles, Jr., an accounting professor, wrote the following about the curriculum of introductory accounting courses:[11]

> *One frequent suggestion for change in the principles course impacts its structure and content: "less emphasis on debits and credits and double-entry accounting." Some authorities even suggest removing these topics from the principles course because they are inappropriate for the business majors who make up the majority of its enrollees. Further, those authorities suggest that an emphasis on double-entry accounting discourages students from majoring in accounting.*
>
> *This is, of course, a controversial proposal; it often results in heated debates that confuse the issues. The inclusion of double-entry accounting in the principles course requires careful consideration because the course is so important to the business curriculum and so fundamental for upper-level accounting courses such as intermediate accounting... Three aspects of double-entry accounting are often confused when people debate this issue: (1) the system of journals and ledgers in which transactions are recorded and accumulated in order to prepare financial statements; (2) the use of debits and credits to describe the ways in which transactions are recorded; and (3) the analysis of the effects that transactions have on economic entities.*
>
> *It is my impression that when some authorities label accounting as boring and tedious, they are referring to the first aspect of accounting, the procedures of recordkeeping. These bookkeeping procedures, which can be time consuming and repetitious, are more relevant to accounting majors than to those in other majors and can affect the popularity of accounting courses. In much the same way that a person does not need to know how to write a computer program to use computer software effectively, some feel that students need not know bookkeeping procedures in order to use accounting information effectively.*
>
> *Although it is an integral part of bookkeeping systems, the second aspect of double-entry accounting, the use of debits and credits, does not necessarily mean a strong emphasis on bookkeeping. The terms "debit" and "credit" can be used effectively to describe the effects of transactions on financial position, operations, and cash flows without reference to recording and posting. However, they may give an archaic quality to an accounting course that leads students to feel that accounting is stuffy and irrele-*

[11] "Change in Accounting Education: The Place of Double-Entry Accounting," *Accounting Instructors' Report*, Vol. XI., no. 1, pp. 1–2.

vant. In other words, the terms "debit" and "credit" may symbolize to some all that is unpopular about accounting.

The third aspect of double-entry accounting is its use in analyzing the effects of business transactions on economic entities. This powerful analytical tool can serve every business student well, regardless of major. Every economic entity engages in a set of transactions that uniquely defines it. A credit sale has important differences in effect from a cash sale. The implications for an entity are different for a sale of services versus a sale of merchandise or a sale of manufactured product. Financing via short-term instruments versus long-term debt or capital stock affects the financial structure, operations, and cash flows of the entity. A manager's ability to understand the effects of transactions in which the entity engages is critical to its future success. Double-entry accounting is a very efficient way of describing the effects of all these transactions and their importance to the entity's future.

Required:

What are your views?

12. (a) What are some important design considerations when choosing a chart of accounts?

    (b) Design a chart of accounts for each of the following businesses:
    - A corner convenience store.
    - A computer retailer with five locations in five cities.
    - A professional accounting firm.
    - A small town.
    - An independent minor-league baseball team.
    - A farm that keeps milk cows.

13. The balance sheet and income statement for RON Ltd. at the end of its first year of operations are presented below. Reconstruct, as best as you can, the journal entries accounting for the activities of RON for the year. In addition, prepare a "Cash" T-account and a cash flow statement.

RON Ltd.
Balance Sheet
December 31, 1995

Assets		
Cash		$ 10,000
Accounts receivable		35,000
Inventory		75,000
Prepaid insurance expense		5,000
		125,000
Equipment	110,000	
Building	200,000	
	310,000	
Accumulated depreciation	(25,000)	285,000
		$410,000

Liabilities	
Accounts payable	$ 30,000
Wages payable	10,000
Income tax payable	20,000
	60,000
Mortgage payable	100,000
	160,000
Shareholders' equity	
Common shares	200,000
Retained earnings	50,000
	250,000
	$410,000

RON Ltd.
Income Statement
Year Ended December 31, 1995

Sales	$445,000	
Cost of sales	210,000	
		235,000
Expenses:		
Wages	54,000	
Depreciation	25,000	
Insurance	6,000	
	85,000	
Interest on mortgage	10,000	
		95,000
Net income before taxes		140,000
Income tax expense		60,000
Net income		$ 80,000

14. Provide an example of a transaction or other accountable event for each of the following descriptions:
    (a) Increase expense and increase liability.
    (b) Increase liability and increase asset.
    (c) Increase revenue and increase asset.
    (d) Increase expense and decrease asset.
    (e) Decrease an asset other than cash and increase cash.
    (f) Increase liability and decrease retained earnings.

15. (a) Back in Chapter 1, the various business events of On Ice Incorporated were recorded on a worksheet, line by line. This worksheet was a computer spreadsheet, which was constructed using the software product Excel 3.1 for Windows. Using any computer spreadsheet you have available (Lotus 1,2,3, Quattro Pro, Excel, or similar), construct your own version of On Ice's accounting event database. Be sure to include the events that occurred during the period October 1, 1993, to December 31, 1993, as described in question 1–25 from Chapter 1.
    (b) Some observers of the business scene have suggested that such a database is all that is needed in financial accounting, and that financial statements are unnecessary and even misleading. Such a "database approach" to financial accounting would permit outside users to tap into a company's event database via a personal computer. What are your views on this?

16. Explain how accrual accounting provides more information than pure transactions-based accounting, and how pure transactions-based accounting provides more information than a pure cash-based system. Is "more" necessarily "better"?

17. Re-do question 1–25, "On Ice Revisited," using journal entries, ledger accounts, and trial balances.

18. To do the following, you must refer to the chapter appendix on pages 164–171.
    (a) In Chimo Ltd.'s preadjustment trial balance, the sum of all debit money amounts equals $371,000, as does the sum of all credit money amounts. Why is this equality a *necessary*, but *insufficient*, condition for proving that the accounting has been done properly up to the point of the preadjustment trial balance in the accounting cycle?
    (b) Why do many accounts ("Cost of goods sold," "Unearned interest income," "Accrued interest receivable," and so on) have no balances in the preadjustment trial balance?
    (c) In the accounts that have nonzero balances in the preadjustment trial balance, what type of information has been collected—transactions-based or some other type?
    (d) Explain why none of the adjusting journal entries affect "Cash."
    (e) The spreadsheet's four leftmost columns are headed "Income Statement" (for two of the columns) and "Balance Sheet" (for the two final columns). Are these the actual financial statements, or trial balance representations of the information?
    (f) Prepare an income statement and a balance sheet for Chimo for the year ended December 31, 1995.

19. Design, as best as you are able, journal entries for the following, and explain your choices.
    (a) Chair Limited has $10,000,000 of bonds payable on its balance sheet. The company persuaded the holders of the bonds to exchange them for common shares.
    (b) Winston's Inc.'s warehouse, located on the Cree River, was destroyed during a severe winter gale. The warehouse had cost $7.2 million, and was fully depreciated. The company's insurance coverage on the warehouse was $1.0 million. A representative of the insurance company has assured Winston's management that it will collect in full.
    (c) Mr. Filo Green donated $1,000,000 in cash to Seymour Ltd. because he was impressed with the company's employment equity practices. Prepare a

journal entry from the company's perspective.

(d) Instead of declaring a cash dividend, the board of directors of Grimaldi Limited declared a dividend such that each holder of one of the company's common shares received a pen set manufactured by the company. The cost of manufacturing the pen set was $1.00, and it was normally sold for $5.00. Grimaldi has 100,000 common shares issued and outstanding. Prepare entries for both declaration and payment.

(e) The local baseball team paid a new rookie a signing bonus of $100,000.

20. Briefly summarize the important points made by W. Richard Sherman in his article (refer to this chapter's "Accounting, Organizations, and Society" section). Can you offer any ideas as to why the debit and credit terminology still exists? Are the conclusions by Bryer and Aho credible, concerning the importance of double-entry accounting?

SHORTER TECHNICAL QUESTIONS

21. Identify the accountable business events in the following list, being sure to indicate the accounting entity or entities involved. Which events are transactions?

(a) Miles Obregon purchased 1,000 common shares in Four Seasons Limited, an operator of hotels whose common shares trade on the stock exchange, for $10.00 per share, plus $40 in fees to the broker. Everything was paid in cash.

(b) The Four Seasons common shares declined in price on the stock exchange to $9 per share. Miles Obregon was very upset.

(c) The University of Alberta hired a new professor to teach accounting.

(d) Mr. Lean purchased a new suit from The Bay, paying $214 in cash. The price included $14 GST.

(e) Bigelow Limited permits the holders of its notes payable to swap them for common shares in the company. On January 31, 1995, holders of $100,000 of notes payable swapped those notes for common shares.

(f) The board of directors of Simon Inc. declared a $1 million dividend on common shares on December 31, 1995, the company's year end. The dividend was paid in late January 1996.

(g) Malcolm Ltd. guaranteed in writing that if Juniper Inc., Malcolm's subsidiary, could not pay off a $5 million loan, Malcolm would do so.

(h) Miles Loomis, a local Vancouver basketball player, made an oral agreement to sign with the Grizzlies, with the details to be worked out later.

(i) Oldis Inc., a small new-car dealer, awarded its top salesperson a $5,000 bonus in December 1995, to be paid in January 1996.

(j) Mitchell Ltd. owned land near Burnaby, B.C., and Sookum Inc. owned land near Calgary, Alberta. Top management of the two companies signed an agreement to swap their parcels of land, effective January 1, 1996.

22. Design adjusting entries for the following independent situations. Assume that the organizations all have December 31 year ends:

(a) RSP Ltd. received a cheque for $1,000 from one of its customers on December 20, 1995. RSP had agreed to rent office furniture to the customer for the month of January 1996, and had given the customer "a great deal," since the customer paid in December.

(b) CBF Inc. purchased a delivery van for $11,000 on June 1, 1995. The van is expected to have a 50-month service life, and no net scrap value.

(c) VOL Ltd. purchased $3,200 of envelopes, letter-quality stationery, computer diskettes, and other office supplies on November 30, 1995, debiting "Office supplies expense." On January 10, 1996, VOL's accountant found the following note in her pocket, just as she was about to prepare the financial statements for the year ended December 31, 1995: "Inventory of office supplies, December 31, 1995, is $2,900."

(d) When Agisto Inc.'s accountant sat down to prepare the company's financial statements for the year ended December 31, 1995, he realized that a turbine acquired early in the year, which had an expected service life of ten years and then would probably be scrapped, had been recorded as follows:

Dr Repairs expense	17,500	
Cr Cash		17,500

(e) Pen Limited issued a cheque for $5,300 on March 5, 1995, recording the transaction as follows:

Dr Insurance expense	5,300	
Cr Cash		5,300

The property insurance policy runs for two years, beginning April 1.

23. Prepare journal entries to record the business events in the following list. Each part is independent.

(a) Lunenberg Inc. pays a bill totalling $15,000 that it owed to its supplier of raw materials.

(b) Ziploc Ltd. borrowed $150,000 from one of its shareholders on December 1, 1995. The company agreed to pay the loan back on January 1, 1997, including all the interest. Ziploc has a December 31 year end. The loan carries an interest rate of 1% per month.

(c) Jack Abbott, an engineer, provided $2,000 of professional services to a large corporate client. GST is 7%. The services were provided during February 1996. The client had agreed to pay Jack $500 on January 10, and the remainder (including GST on the total $2,000) on June 30, 1996. Everything occurred as expected. Jack Abbott's professional year end is January 31.

(d) The balance in Allcott Inc.'s allowance for doubtful accounts was $235,710 as of December 31, just before the company's accountant recorded the year-end adjusting entries. The balance that management decided should be in the account, based on an analysis of accounts receivable, was $310,000.

24. Perfect Sorters Limited (PSL) is a new small business begun on May 1, 1995, by Pat Cordero. The company is in the business of sorting various types of scrap glass, plastic, paper, and metal. It is hired by manufacturing companies and other organizations to perform this service prior to recycling, and receives a fee based on the weight of material sorted. For PSL, prepare all necessary journal entries and trial balances, and an income statement, for the period ended May 31, 1995, based on the following information (assume there are no taxes):

- May 1, 1995: Pat deposited $20,000 in a bank account in the name of PSL. All the company's common shares were issued to her. She paid $400 in legal and related fees to incorporate PSL; these incorporation costs were considered an expense.
- May 2, 1995: Pat presented a business plan to the bank, and the bank loaned PSL $10,000, which was immediately deposited in PSL's bank account. Interest on the loan was 1% per month or part thereof, and was payable two weeks after the month end. The loan was short-term.
- May 4, 1995: PSL signed a contract to provide sorting services to a local high school, and received a $100 deposit.
- May 6, 1995: PSL signed a contract to provide sorting services to a local manufacturer, and received a $500 deposit.
- May 10, 1995: Pat hired Joe Cart at a total salary of $1,500 per month, beginning May 15.
- May 11, 1995: Pat spent all day sorting scrap plastic, glass, and paper at the local high school, and presented an invoice to the principal for $150 (less, of course, the $100 deposit) at the end of the day.
- May 15, 1995: Pat purchased a used dump truck for $5,000, paying cash, to use in hauling sorted scrap. The expected useful life of the truck is 50 months, after which time it will probably be worth nothing. Joe went with Pat to look over the truck. "Looks OK to me," Joe said.
- May 16 to May 19, 1995: Pat and Joe spent four days sorting and hauling scrap at the local metal foundry, at the end of which time Pat submitted an invoice for $2,000.
- May 22 to May 31, 1995: Pat and Joe spent their time trying to generate new business. Pat spent $300 on gas and oil for the truck during May.
- June 1 to June 14, 1995: Pat and Joe spent two weeks repainting the truck. The paint cost $200.
- June 15, 1995: PSL issued a cheque to Joe for $1,000, for his May 15 to June 15 salary. "Where's the other $500!?" screamed Joe.

25. Paper Limited manufactures and sells all varieties of paper products. The general ledger trial balance, pre- and post-adjustments, as at December 31, 1995 (the end of the new company's first accounting period), is as follows (all amounts in thousands of Canadian dollars; credits are shown in brackets):

Account	Pre-adjustments	Post-adjustments
Cash	$1,000	$1,000
Accounts receivable	2,000	2,000
Inventory	3,000	3,000
Prepaid insurance	100	75
Capital assets	4,500	4,500
Accumulated depreciation	0	(450)
Accounts payable	(1,500)	(1,500)
Salaries payable	(750)	(750)
Bonuses & commissions payable	0	(300)
Accrued interest payable	0	(400)
Income taxes payable	(700)	(700)
Loan payable (long-term)	(5,000)	(5,000)
Common shares	(2,050)	(2,050)
Retained earnings	0	0
Sales	(7,500)	(7,500)
Cost of sales	3,000	3,000
Salaries, bonuses, and commission expense	2,100	2,400
Depreciation expense	0	450
Research expense	200	200
Administration expense	1,500	1,525
Interest expense	100	500

(a) Reproduce all the adjusting entries that Paper Limited's accountant recorded.
(b) What is the dollar amount of "Retained earnings" on Paper Limited's balance sheet as of December 31, 1995?

Multiple CHOICE QUESTIONS

Questions 26 and 27 are based on the following information:

	Sept. 30 1992	**Sept. 30** 1993
Prepaid insurance	$14,238	$10,987
Interest payable	9,734	7,199
Payments during the year:		
Insurance		$12,550
Interest		$11,667

26. Insurance expense for the year ended September 30, 1993, is:

(a) $15,801
(b) $12,675
(c) $12,550
(d) $ 9,299
(e) None of the above

27. Interest expense for the year ended September 30, 1993, is:

(a) $14,202
(b) $21,401
(c) $ 9,132
(d) $ 5,266
(e) None of the above

28. If a hospital purchased a plot of land in 1990 at a cost of $100,000, and at the end of 1996 the land's market value was estimated to be $200,000, the land would be reported on the hospital's December 31, 1996, balance sheet at:

(a) $200,000
(b) $100,000 less applicable depreciation
(c) Something between $100,000 and $200,000
(d) $100,000 less estimated residual value
(e) None of the above

29. The role of the financial accountant is to:

(a) Identify the economic activities of an entity that are to be recorded
(b) Measure the economic activities of the entity
(c) Communicate recorded information to external users
(d) All of the above
(e) None of the above

30. The following information is available at the end of BJ Welding Limited's first year in business:

Cash on hand at the start of the year	$ 1,200
Collections of cash from customers	60,650
Payments to suppliers	59,210
Accounts receivable, ending balance	6,920
Accounts payable, ending balance	8,440
Ending inventory, at cost	2,170
Depreciation expense	860
Dividends declared during the year	1,000

The balance in the "Cash" balance sheet account at the end of the year is:

(a) $ (240)
(b) $1,440
(c) $1,200
(d) $2,640
(e) None of the above

31. Accounting information, many people claim, must be prepared so that it is useful to external decision-makers. External decision-makers do not have access to the detailed accounting records of an organization; most often,

they rely on a standard set of published financial statements. Because of this, there are certain rules that accountants must follow when preparing financial statements for external users. One such rule is that assets must be recorded at "historic cost." The reason for this rule is that:

(a) Historic cost is more relevant than market value
(b) Historic cost is less reliable (objective)
(c) Historic cost is not well understood by users
(d) Market values are often difficult to estimate with acceptable reliability
(e) Both(b) and (c) above

32. Some business entities are separate legal entities, while others are only separate accounting entities. Which of the following statements is *not* true?

(a) A separate accounting entity may not be legally separate from its owners; a separate legal entity is legally separate from its owners.
(b) A separate legal entity files its own tax returns (that is, management files the tax return).
(c) A separate legal entity is responsible for its own debts.
(d) A separate accounting entity has its own set of accounting records.
(e) All of the above are false.

33. Determining income is one of the most important tasks in accounting. The way accountants measure income is quite different from the methods that most economists would use. Financial accounting reports are usually based upon accrual accounting, which requires that judgments and estimates be made in determining income. Consequently, there may be opportunities for the management of some organizations to engage in biasing income and other financial statement items. Such manipulation is often called "income smoothing."

(a) The so-called "big bath" is an example of income smoothing, especially by companies that only use cash flow accounting.
(b) Management may prefer to engage in income smoothing in order to make it appear that the company has more risk.
(c) Suppose a company that operates a hotel in downtown Toronto, and has a December 31 year end, receives $40,000 in cash in December 1993 from another company whose management wishes to hold a convention in the hotel in February 1994. If the hotel company records the $40,000 as revenue in 1994, it is engaged in income smoothing.
(d) Accrual accounting attempts to measure the impact of economic events on the company, not necessarily the change in cash. Realistically, such measures may be far from perfect.
(e) Strict adherence to single-entry accounting would prevent income smoothing.

34. Which of the following statements is true?

(a) It is undeniable that the Spanish monk, Friar Pacioli, invented double-entry accounting.
(b) Double-entry accounting arose during the Middle Ages and flowered during the Renaissance. It is rarely used today because of the introduction of computer-based accounting.

(c) Double-entry accounting implies a duality — every accountable event is recorded in the accounting system twice, by means of two separate, self-balancing journal entries.
(d) If an organization borrowed money from a bank, double-entry accounting would treat the addition to the amount of cash as a resource. The source would be represented by the obligation or liability to repay the bank.
(e) The concept of stewardship is quite a recent one, and was unknown until the modern era of stock markets.

35. Which of the following statements is true?

(a) "Substance over form" provides guidance for accountants in deciding how to account for those events whose "form" differs from their "substance." Therefore, a lease contract that covers almost the whole life of the machinery or other item in question usually results in an asset (with a corresponding liability) being recorded on the balance sheet of the lessee (the user of the machinery), even though the lessee does not own the item. It might also be argued that the idea of an accounting entity not necessarily being identical to a legal entity is another illustration of "substance over form."
(b) The account "Accumulated depreciation" appears on what is conventionally the asset side of the balance sheet. It is used to collect the cumulative amount of depreciation with respect to depreciable assets, and usually has a debit balance.
(c) Double-entry accounting requires that only actual cash transactions be utilized in calculating net present value.
(d) Since they are employees of the accounting entity, external auditors cannot serve as independent accountants of the accounting entity.
(e) If an accounting entity's balance sheet includes the account "Accounts receivable," this signifies that accrual accounting is not being used.

36. Which of the following statements is true?

(a) An income statement is like a photograph of a business at an instant in time.
(b) Historic cost information and current value information represent the same concept.
(c) Users of an entity's accounting information never have diverse and conflicting sets of objectives. This supports the use of cash flow statements.
(d) If the following entry was recorded by the accountant for a business, the balance sheet would not balance:

Dr Accounts receivable	10,000	
Cr Accounts payable		10,000

(e) A proprietorship, a partnership, and a corporation may each be an accounting entity. In fact, two or more corporations could conceivably represent a single accounting entity.

37. Which of the following statements is true?

(a) Current liabilities, noncurrent liabilities, and owners' equity are major categories into which all assets may be classified; also, classification is one of the seven important ideas underlying all of accounting.
(b) With the widespread use of computers, many more companies than before are using the single-entry accounting method. If ABC Company's

beginning inventory was $200,000, its purchases for the accounting period were $600,000, and its ending inventory was $300,000, then its cost of sales must have been $1,100,000.
(c) The balance sheet reports what the organization's position is at a point in time. It shows the assets that management has chosen to acquire for the organization, and also how management has decided to finance those assets. Income measurement, it must be admitted, is a process that involves judgment.
(d) Financial accounting deals with unequivocal facts; judgment is unnecessary.
(e) Companies often write inventories up to market when market value exceeds cost.

38. Please refer to the following five statements:

Statement 1: "Depreciation expense represents a cash flow *out of* the accounting entity."

Statement 2: "Suppose a depreciable asset (a truck) costs $44,000; it is estimated that the truck will provide services for 180,000 km and have a residual value of $4,000, so only $44,000 less $4,000, or $40,000, should be depreciated over the life of the truck. The second year that the truck is in service it is driven 15,000 km. Thus, depreciation recorded for that year is $3,333."

Statement 3: "Wages earned but not yet paid to employees are recorded by an accounting entity as assets."

Statement 4: "An 'account' is a money record of accounting events collected together to summarize the impact of cash inflows and/or cash outflows on debited credits. Its use is consistent with double-entry accounting."

Statement 5: "Indianapolis Jones decided to establish an ocean touring business called 'Adventure for Sale Limited' (ASL). To this end, he transferred the ownership of the boat he had purchased the year before (for his own personal use, at a cost of $35,000) to ASL. He recorded the following as the first item in the accounting records of the new company:

Dr Boat	35,000	
Cr Capital stock		35,000

Mr. Jones's accountant insisted that the $35,000 be removed from both sides of this entry, and replaced by what she estimated the market value of the boat to be — that is, $20,000."

(a) All five statements are valid.
(b) Statements 2 and 4 are valid.
(c) Statement 5 reflects an inappropriate action on the part of the accountant, since the cost of the boat to Mr. Jones, as an accounting entity, was $35,000.
(d) All five statements are incorrect.
(e) Statements 2 and 5 are reasonable.

39. A reasonable description of an accrued revenue is:

(a) A revenue that has been received but is not yet earned.

(b) A revenue that has not been earned during an accounting period but has been recorded in advance.
(c) A revenue that has been earned during an accounting period but has not been received.
(d) A revenue that has not been earned, received, or recorded.
(e) A revenue that has been both earned and received.

40. Which of the following is true?

(a) Financial accounting is oriented toward helping managers and others inside an enterprise.
(b) Accrual accounting is not permitted for financial accounting purposes.
(c) Assets are expenses that have been used up.
(d) Auditors prepare financial statements, while managers are responsible for verifying them.
(e) Every manager should understand how accounting is measuring his or her performance.

41. Balint Company sells magazine subscriptions for one-year, two-year, or three-year periods. Cash receipts from subscribers are credited to the account "Magazine subscriptions collected in advance." This account had a balance of $1,700,000 at December 31, 1995. Information for the year ended December 31, 1996, is as follows:

Cash received from magazine subscribers	$2,100,000
Magazine subscription revenues for 1996	1,500,000

What amount should the company report on its December 31, 1996, balance sheet for "Magazine subscriptions collected in advance"?

(a) $2,300,000
(b) $1,900,000
(c) $2,100,000
(d) $1,400,000
(e) None of the above

42. Which of the following is true?

(a) Accounting involves just numbers representing money.
(b) As organizations grow in sophistication, they move from accrual to cash-flow accounting reports.
(c) Long-term assets are always recorded on balance sheets at their market value.
(d) A = L + SE is consistent with the double-entry concept.
(e) "Income" is just another word for "cash flow."

43. Under a certain company's accounting system, all insurance premiums paid are debited to an account called "Prepaid insurance." The following information is available from the company's records for the year ended December 31, 1992:

Prepaid insurance as at 12/31/91	$150,000
Debits to insurance expense for 1992	625,000
Prepaid insurance as at 12/31/92	175,000

What was the total amount of insurance premiums paid by the company in 1992?

(a) $475,000
(b) $600,000
(c) $625,000
(d) $650,000
(e) None of the above

44. In an effort to increase sales, Nick Razor Blade Company (referred to as "Nick" in the remainder of this question) inaugurated a sales promotion campaign on June 30, 1992, whereby Nick placed a coupon in each package of razor blades sold, the coupons being redeemable for a "free" gift. Each gift cost Nick $0.50, and 5 coupons had to be submitted by a customer for him to receive the gift. Nick estimated that only 60% of the coupons issued would be redeemed. For the six months ended December 31, 1992, the following information is available:

Packages of razor blades sold	Gifts purchased by Nick	Coupons redeemed
800,000	60,000	200,000

What is the estimated liability for free gift claims outstanding as at December 31, 1992?

(a) $28,000
(b) $20,000
(c) $36,000
(d) $48,000
(e) None of the above

CASE

Scaramouche Dental Products Limited

Part A: The Set-up

Jack Scaramouche graduated in 1990 from a community college course as a denturist, and quickly developed a superb reputation among dentists and their patients in his hometown of Halifax. Denturists construct bridgework and other dental appliances for dentists, using artificial teeth made of plastics or ceramic composites.

By 1996, Jack was looking for business opportunities to, as he put it, "expand my creative horizons." By chance, while on a holiday trip to a South American country late that year, he met Ms. Aria Del Rio, marketing representative for South American Dentalwork Producers (henceforth, SADP), a company that manufactured artificial teeth. Aria showed Jack a sample of SADP's products and mentioned their prices, which were about one-third of Canadian prices owing to extremely low labour costs. Jack immediately realized that the combination of high quality and low price might be just the opportunity he was looking for, and he readily accepted Aria's invitation to visit SADP's head office and manufacturing facilities in a nearby city.

As a result of the visit to SADP, the following took place:

- Jack learned that the better-quality ceramic composite teeth were priced at the equivalent of $3.00, and the lower-quality plastic teeth were priced at the equivalent of $0.90. Jack invoiced dentists back in Canada at $15.00 and $7.00 per tooth, respectively.

- Jack decided that he wanted to establish himself as the exclusive Canadian distributor for SADP artificial teeth to denturists. SADP's managers (who had coincidentally been thinking about expanding into Canada soon) agreed to a three-year exclusive contract, provided that Jack established a company that would purchase at least $50,000 of product over each of the three years.
- At the end of the initial three-year period, Jack would have the option to renew the arrangement at prices to be negotiated.
- Before Jack agreed to the arrangement, he took a sample of SADP's teeth back to his lab in Halifax, and satisfied himself as to the product's superior quality "under actual preparation and use conditions." He decided that the teeth could be sold at a 100% markup over his cost of $3.00 and $0.90 for the two product lines.

Jack then immediately incorporated Scaramouche Dental Products Limited (henceforth, SDPL) under Nova Scotia legislation, invested his savings and the proceeds from mortgaging his house in SDPL voting stock, and placed his first order for SADP artificial teeth, all as follows:

Date	Events
November 20, 1996	SDPL incorporated; legal fees and disbursements totalled $1,500.
November 21, 1996	Jack withdrew $35,000 from his personal bank account, and finalized arrangements for a mortgage loan of $70,000 on his house (the house had cost $120,000 in 1992, but a qualified real estate appraiser estimated its value in November 1996 at about $140,000). The total of $105,000 was deposited in a bank account in the name of SDPL (with Jack as the sole signing officer) in exchange for 1,000 shares representing 100% of the common shares of the company.
November 25, 1996	Jack signed an agreement with SADP's representative at a meeting in Miami. The contract gave SDPL exclusive rights to purchase, market, and distribute SADP artificial teeth in Canada for an initial period of three years from the date of signing, subject to minimum annual purchases of $50,000. Each order would have to be prepaid, and SDPL would be responsible for all shipping and insurance costs. Total cost of airline tickets and hotel (including food of $410) was $3,050. Jack had brought his wife along "for a quick trip to the Sunshine State in the middle of a cold Canadian winter." The hotel had cost $200 Canadian per day, for six days; Jack had signed the agreement with SADP on the first day, but — "Since we're already here, why not stay a while and soak up the sun?"
December 1, 1996	Back in Halifax, Jack signed over a small, old frame building to SDPL. The building, which was suitable for an office (although several kilometres out of town), had cost Jack $175,000 in 1993. It had an existing mortgage for $80,000 at 1% per month, and was estimated to have a market value of

	$130,000 in late November 1996, with a remaining useful life of about 20 years, after which its value would probably be zero. The building contained furniture and fixtures suitable for SDPL's operations. The furniture and fixtures had been purchased by Jack in 1993 for $10,000. Their accumulated depreciation totalled $2,000 as of December 2, 1996, when Jack signed them over to SDPL. Jack believed they were worth about $5,000, and would last another ten years, at which time they would be scrapped. Jack also purchased a Pentium PC, monitor, fax machine, and printer for his new business, for which he paid $4,500 in cash. He also purchased three laptops for $10,500 (payable in 30 days). Computers usually last about three years, after which time they are scrapped or donated to a local school or charity.
December 3, 1996	Jack faxed an order down to SADP for merchandise totalling $37,440; by return fax, SADP confirmed the order (which was for 300 complete sets of 32 teeth for each of the high-quality product and low-quality product, at $3.00 and $0.90, respectively), and guaranteed shipment within one week. Dental products are not subject to any duties, taxes, or other similar charges.
December 4, 1996	Jack interviewed three candidates for the three sales positions he believed he must fill: one to visit denturists in Western Canada, one for Ontario, and one for Quebec. He intended to cover the Maritimes and Newfoundland himself ("I know practically every denturist on the East Coast," he told each of the candidates). He hired two of the candidates — the ones who had at least some minimal experience in the dental equipment supply field. The two were Tom for Western Canada, and Nancy for Ontario. He intended to fill the Quebec position later, "with someone with a bilingual background." Both Tom and Nancy would begin calling on denturists in their respective regions in early January. Each would receive a commission equal to 10% of sales. The commissions would be paid in the month following the month in which the sales were made.
December 5, 1996	Jack arranged for a $100,000 line of credit with his banker, on the understanding that use of the line would cost 1% per month.

The sales call

Jack instructed Tom and Nancy to "cold call" on denturists, and to leave a free sample of both product lines along with price details and a testimonial prepared by Jack about the quality of the artificial teeth. The samples consisted of two sets of five artificial teeth, for both the higher-quality ceramic composite and the lower-quality plastic. No more than one week later, a follow-up phone call would be made, to arrange a meeting. "I'm convinced these things will sell themselves," Jack told Tom and Nancy at a pre-Christmas dinner meeting (total cost, $105). "Qualitywise, they're indistinguishable from anything the Europeans make and they beat the price to heck!"

If, as expected, the denturist agreed to use SPDL's artificial teeth, a consignment agreement would then be signed. A small, attractive cabinet containing the teeth would be left with the denturist, who would then use the artificial teeth to fill orders for bridgework, and so on. About once every month, the SDPL sales representative would call on the denturist, physically inspect the cabinet's contents to determine how many teeth of each type (molars, incisors, and so on), shade, size, and quality (ceramic composite or plastic) had been used, prepare an invoice to leave with the denturist, and send one copy of the invoice (via modem installed in the laptop computer) back to the office in Halifax. The invoice sent by modem would serve two functions: (1) to initiate the recording of an account receivable and sale; and (2) to initiate a customer sales order to replenish the denturist's cabinet and update SPDL's inventory records. Other software, stored on each laptop's hard drive, would maintain a running record of the specific type, shade, and quality ordered by each customer, primarily for marketing purposes. Orders were to be sent by overnight courier with a 9 a.m. delivery guarantee, since the last thing Jack wanted was a disgruntled denturist/customer who couldn't meet a dental order because of a shortage of artifical teeth ("Quality and service . . . that'll be our motto!" said Jack).

End of December 1996

Everything was set for operations to begin after New Year's. On December 19, Jack gave Tom and Nancy each a cheque for $3,500, "to cover travel expenses for January, as well as a $2,000 advance against their first commission cheque," which wouldn't be issued until sometime in February.

The first order from SADP was received on December 20. As agreed, SDPL paid for the freight charge and in-transit insurance, totalling $1,500. On December 23, Jack purchased 200 small cabinets (each of which included trays capable of storing 60 complete sets of artificial teeth), at $90 each, payable in 30 days. Office supplies costing $2,100 had been ordered, received, and paid for in late November. Only $100 worth of these were used in 1996.

Required for Part A:

Prepare all journal entries up to and including December 31, 1996 (the end of SDPL's first accounting period), as well as trial balances and financial statements for the period ended December 31, 1996. Assume no income taxes for 1996.

Part B: SDPL Begins Operations

The following events happened to SPDL and Jack in 1997:

- January 10–20: Tom flew out to Vancouver and called on potential customers in the Greater Vancouver area, spending $700 of his expense money on airline tickets (including $200 for freight charges on the 30 small cabinets he took along), $1,100 on hotels, and $410 on meals. He also purchased a portable phone for his wife out of his advance against his commission, distributed 25 sets of free samples, and signed up ten customers. He left each customer one of the small cabinets containing 40 complete sets of 32 high-quality teeth, plus 20 complete sets of 32 lower-quality plastic teeth. The sets were of a variety of shades and sizes.
- January 10: Nancy flew out to Toronto, landing at Pearson International Airport at 8 p.m. after enjoying a delicious in-flight dinner. Unfortunately, she became violently ill while waiting for her luggage and cabinets (food poisoning is suspected), and was rushed by ambulance to a local hospital ("Not life-threatening," said the emergency room doctor, "but we're going to have to keep you here for a couple of weeks."). Nancy, an American who had moved to Halifax in 1994, had

no health or hospital insurance of any kind. Jack agreed over the phone (at 2 a.m., Halifax time) to cover all her medical bills ("It's the right thing to do ... after all, she was on company business."). Her Halifax–Toronto flight cost $500, which she paid for by personal credit card.

- January 11–15: Jack called on potential customers in Moncton, Bathurst, Edmundston, and Fredericton. He spent $400 on a rental car (including gas), and $600 on hotels and food. Jack had called on 15 potential customers in total, and left a sample with each one. None ever placed any orders.
- January 16–20: Jack spent some time visiting friends in the Miramichi. On arriving back in Halifax on January 20, he was elated to receive a fax from Tom with the details about the 10 customers.
- January 21: Nancy got out of hospital early.
- January 21–31: Nancy "cold called" 40 potential customers in the Greater Toronto area, and was able to leave 15 samples (the other 25 denturists were either too busy to see her, or were happy with the product they were using). She followed up with each of the 15 a few days after leaving the samples, but was able to sign up only five, since her shipment of small cabinets had disappeared while she was in hospital, and Jack could only courier five to her in time. Nancy spent $1,100 on hotels and $700 on meals (including $150 entertaining one of the denturists). She paid for everything by means of her personal credit card.
- January 30: Jack received invoices in his Halifax office in respect of Nancy's medical and hospital charges, totalling $3,175.
- January 21–February 5: Tom rented a car in Vancouver, called on denturists in Victoria, then proceeded up the B.C. coast. He signed up a total of 15 new customers (he had left samples with 20). After arriving back in Vancouver, he flew on to Calgary (ticket, paid by cheque, was $200), where he rented another car. In Calgary and Lethbridge, he signed up six customers, having left samples with 10. He spent $970 on car rentals, $800 on hotels, and $700 on food. On January 22, he faxed Jack an urgent request for more expense money, and Jack sent Tom a new SDPL company credit card by overnight courier (cost of courier: $35).
- February 6–10: Tom flew back to Vancouver to see how his original 10 customers were doing. (Jack was furious when he learned about this, since Tom was to have gone to Edmonton, then on to Winnipeg, before heading back to Vancouver. "What a waste of travel money!" fumed Jack.) One of the 10 had decided to opt out of the agreement, and returned the small cabinet. Two high-quality complete sets of teeth were missing because (as the denturist put it), "They're crap... I tried them on two orders and they fell apart like chalk!" Tom left, small cabinet in hand, noticing the two complete sets in a jar behind a vase on the window sill opposite the denturist's desk. The good news was that the other nine customers were delighted with the product, and placed replacement orders for a total of 100 complete high-quality sets and 100 complete lower-quality sets (cost of total order: $12,480), which Tom immediately faxed to Halifax.
- Unfortunately, Jack was in Saint John, visiting his aunt, and didn't arrive back in the office until February 11, at which time he couriered the orders to Vancouver (courier charges: $959). He then placed an order with SADP for 300 complete ceramic composite sets and 1,000 complete plastic sets, which was received one week later (freight: $1,900; insurance: $990). Not

wanting to be caught away from the office again when orders arrived, he hired an "order clerk/office manager" to begin work immediately, on February 12, at $500 per week.

During the remainder of 1997, Tom left samples with 525 denturists, and signed up 115, who then ordered a total of 2,550 complete high-quality sets (of which 200 were sold in December) and 3,100 complete low-quality sets (of which 190 were sold in December). Nancy, who quit in August after a disagreement with Jack about the commission percentage, left samples with 411 denturists, and signed up 85, who then ordered a total of 3,200 complete high-quality sets and 1,900 complete low-quality sets. Jack wasn't able to make any further calls in 1997 other than those described above, since he fired the "order clerk/office manager" after just two weeks, and stayed in the Halifax office throughout the year ensuring that Tom's and Nancy's customers' orders were promptly filled, placing orders with SADP, and dealing with the bank. He was so busy that he wasn't able to hire a sales representative to replace himself in the Atlantic provinces, or one for Quebec. Tom spent a total of $17,515 on travel and meals over the year, and Nancy spent $22,600.

In addition to orders placed with SADP mentioned above, SPDL ordered and received a further 6,750 complete ceramic composite sets and 6,000 complete plastic sets during 1997. SADP's management, impressed with the volume of business they were doing with SDPL, agreed to pay for all freight and insurance. Denturists who had ordered a total of 150 ceramic composite sets and 200 plastic sets went bankrupt and were unable to pay SDPL. All the office supplies that remained from the November 1996 purchase were used up in 1997; $3,010 in additional supplies were received and paid for in 1997, of which $1,500 remained on hand at year end. Insurance coverage (fire and theft, liability) for two years was purchased effective February 1, 1997, for $4,800.

Any remaining commissions owing for 1997 sales were paid by a cheque dated December 31, 1997. In addition, Jack paid himself a salary of $80,000 in 1997.

Required for Part B:

Prepare all journal entries up to and including December 31, 1997 (the end of SDPL's first complete accounting period), as well as trial balances and financial statements for the period ended December 31, 1997. Assume an income tax rate of 30% in 1997, applied to net income before taxes, as derived according to financial accounting. Also, assume that income taxes are due and payable one month after the end of the year to which they relate.

Appendix
Adjusting Entries and Spreadsheets

The spreadsheet, or worksheet, is a useful tool that accountants use to systematically keep track of large amounts of information. The development of electronic spreadsheets has made this tool even more flexible and easier to use. In this Appendix we show how a spreadsheet can be used as part of the accounting cycle we described in the chapter — specifically, to handle adjustments. This is only one of the many ways that spreadsheets can be used in accounting.

The accounting cycle

The cycle followed by the financial accounting recording process may be summarized as consisting of seven stages:

1. Transactions between the accounting entity and other accounting entities take place during the accounting period.
2. These transactions are recorded as journal entries, using the convention of debits and credits. For high-volume transactions, specialized books of original entry (such as the Sales Journal) can also be used.
3. The money amounts from the journal entries are transferred to the appropriate accounts in the accounting entity's general ledger (accountants call this process "posting").
4. After the accounting period ends, a preadjustment general ledger trial balance is prepared in order to ensure that the sum of all the debits equals the sum of all the credits. At this stage in the accounting cycle, it is important to ensure that all transactions have been accounted for.
5. The accountant then designs and prepares the adjusting entries, in order to convert the transactions-based information to a more complete accounting measurement system.
6. A post-adjustment general ledger trial balance is then prepared.
7. Financial statements are prepared and disseminated to users. Up until very recently, financial statements were almost always distributed in hard copy (paper), by surface mail. But as of 1996, most large and many medium-sized companies are providing Internet access to their financial statements.

Steps 4, 5, and 6 involve the spreadsheet.

Adjusting entries and the spreadsheet

The example that follows shows how a spreadsheet is used to prepare a pre-adjustment general ledger trial balance, to keep track of all the adjusting entries, and finally to prepare the post-adjustment general ledger trial balance. The spreadsheet is shown in Exhibit 3A. The first column lists all the accounts in the company's general ledger. The second column is reserved for the account's code number; accounts that appear on the balance sheet have a "B" at the end of their code number, while accounts that appear on the income statement have an "N." The two columns under the heading "Trial balance," labelled "Dr" and "Cr," contain the net balances for each account after all the transactions that occurred during the accounting period have been accounted for. Thus, at this point "Cash" has a balance of $20,000 and "Salaries expense" has a balance of $22,000. Notice that this preadjustment general ledger trial balance has total debits and total credits equal to $371,000; this is a necessary but insufficient condition to prove that the accounting has been done properly thus far.

Notice that a number of accounts ("Cost of goods sold," "Unearned interest income," and so on) have zero balances at this stage. This is so because — given the particular way this company does its accounting — these accounts do not collect any transactions information. It's only after adjustments are recorded that they have a balance. This is the case for our example company; it is not true in general (different companies will design different accounting systems, but the final numbers should be unaffected).

The next three columns in the spreadsheet contain information about the end-of-period adjustments. The column headed by the "#" symbol contains code numbers for the various adjusting entries; the next two columns contain the particular debit and credit amounts needed for the adjustments. The information in these columns will, of course, be transferred to the various general ledger accounts affected by the adjustments. Notice that the sum of all debit adjustment money amounts and the sum of all credit adjustment money amounts are both equal to $178,300. This is, of course, no coincidence.

The final four columns of the spreadsheet contain the balances for the various income statement and balance sheet accounts, after the adjustments. The "Retained earnings" account still has its opening balance of $12,500 because the net income of $25,600 hasn't yet been transferred in by means of the closing journal entry, which is:

Dr Sales	206,000	
Dr Interest income	300	
Dr Rent income	500	
Cr Sales returns and allowances		2,000
Cr Sales discounts		4,000
Cr Advertising expense		800
Cr Delivery expense		300
Cr Miscellaneous expense		200
Cr Rent expense		500
Cr Repairs expense		300
Cr Salaries expense		22,500
Cr Supplies expense		500
Cr Tax expense		1,300
Cr Utilities expense		1,200
Cr Interest expense		1,900
Cr Cost of goods sold		137,000
Cr Insurance expense		700
Cr Bad debt expense		1,000
Cr Depreciation expense — Del. equipment		1,000
Cr Depreciation expense — Equipment		4,000
Cr Depreciation expense — Bldg.		2,000
Cr Retained earnings		25,600

But we are getting a bit ahead of ourselves. Let's go back to see how the adjusting entries are derived.

Chimo Ltd. is a hypothetical company that is in the retail clothing business. It has one location, plus a small satellite location in a local mall, and has been in business for a number of years. The following adjustments are required to convert Chimo's transactions-based accounting information into accounting that is more consistent with GAAP:

#1. At the end of 1995, a physical count of Chimo's inventory indicated that $25,000 of inventory was on hand.

#2. Chimo sold $4,000 worth of 1920s costumes to a local theatre group. Unfortunately, the group had a bit of trouble paying on time, and agreed to convert Chimo's account receivable to a note receivable. During December 1995, the theatre group sent Chimo a cheque for $500, representing what the theatre group's manager called "evidence of our good faith — interest in advance." Chimo's accountant determined that $100 of the payment was really interest for the year ended December 31, 1995, and that only $400 was a prepayment.

#3. Interest that Chimo has earned, but has not yet received, on a second loan is $200.

#4. Chimo Ltd. is subject to income taxes. Thus far, $1,000 has been paid of the $1,300 total income taxes that Chimo's accountant estimates will be owed to the government.

#5. The store manager reported that office supplies costing $100 were on hand at December 31, 1995.

#6. Salaries remaining unpaid at the year end amounted to $500. The first payday after the year end was January 15, 1996, so $500 of salaries for work performed in the last week of 1995 had not been paid by year end.

#7. Prepaid rent (on Chimo's satellite location) was $400 at year end.

#8. During the year, Chimo rented out part of its satellite location to a charity. The charity paid $600 for six months beginning on August 1, 1995.

#9. Chimo issued a cheque for $400 to Chiquita Inc. on December 31, 1995. The cheque was for January 1996's interest on the money that Chimo had borrowed from Chiquita. The loan has been paid off except for a final payment of $10,000, due on December 1, 1996.

#10. There is still a $30,000 mortgage on Chimo's building. Chimo's accountant issued a cheque for the December 1995 interest payment of $800 on January 2, 1996.

#11. At December 31, 1995, unexpired insurance premiums on Chimo's building amount to $500. Chimo has no other insurance coverage.

#12. Half of Chimo's sales are for cash. Years ago Igor Chimo, the founder, established a policy of "no credit cards," since he disliked paying the 3% discount. However, Chimo does have its own company credit card, which carries no interest charges. A bad debt allowance equal to 0.6% of net sales is considered adequate by Chimo's accountant. This allowance — called an "allowance for doubtful accounts" — is a deduction from accounts receivable on the balance sheet.

#13. Depreciation expense on the second-hand delivery van is $1,000.

#14. Depreciation expense on the other equipment is $4,000.

#15. Depreciation expense on the building is $2,000.

The journal entries to record the above adjustments are as follows:

#1. Chimo Ltd. is in the business of buying and selling. It accounts for its purchases of clothes by debiting "Purchases" and crediting either "Cash" or "Accounts payable." "Purchases" is debited with the total invoice amount of the various purchases that Chimo made throughout the year. However, Chimo's suppliers often give the company discounts ($3,000 in 1995; see account 423N), and Chimo occasionally returns merchandise that it finds to be unsuitable ($1,000 in 1995; see account 422N). Further, Chimo considers that the cost of transportation it must pay on some of its merchandise is part of the cost of the merchandise (this is a common way of accounting for such a cost). In 1995, this amounted to $2,000. The total merchandise inventory available for sale in 1995 was, therefore:

Opening inventory	$ 30,000
Add:	
Purchases	134,000
Transportation–in	2,000
Deduct:	
Purchase returns and allowances	(1,000)
Purchase discounts	(3,000)
Total cost of merchandise available for sale in 1995	$162,000

The cost of the merchandise inventory that must have been sold during 1995 is determined by Chimo's accountant as follows:

Total cost of merchandise available for sale in 1995	$162,000
Deduct:	
Actual inventory on hand at the end of 1995	25,000
Therefore, cost of goods sold must be	$137,000

To adjust "Purchases," "Purchase returns and allowances," "Purchase discounts," "Transportation–in," "Inventory," and "Cost of goods sold" all to their appropriate year-end balances, the following adjusting journal entry is needed:

Dr Inventory	25,000	
Dr Purchase returns and allowances	1,000	
Dr Purchase discounts	3,000	
Dr Cost of goods sold	137,000	
Cr Inventory		30,000
Cr Purchases		134,000
Cr Transportation–in		2,000

This adjusting journal entry is coded as #1 in the spreadsheet. Where does this adjustment best fit in the set of five categories of adjustments described in the chapter? In category 5.

#2. The preadjustment trial balance contains interest income of $500; therefore, when the $500 was received, the transaction was accounted for as follows:

Dr Cash	500	
Cr Interest income		500

But we know that $400 of this is a prepayment, so an adjusting entry is required to adjust the accounts:

Dr Interest income	400	
Cr Unearned interest income		400

#3. The adjusting entry for the estimated interest income is:

Dr Accrued interest receivable	200	
Cr Interest income		200

The word "accrued" indicates that although the interest is not yet legally due and receivable, Chimo has earned the income and thus it should be recorded. The cash inflow in this case will be received after the income is recorded, probably next period.

#4. The adjusting entry is:

Dr Tax Expense	300	
Cr Accrued tax payable		300

Here, the word "accrued" indicates an estimated liability that, although not legally due, should be accounted for in order to record Chimo's financial position and results of operations as completely as possible.

#5. Supplies expense is listed as $600 on the preadjustment trial balance, and no "Supplies" asset account is shown. Therefore, Chimo's accountant must have accounted for the purchase of supplies (a transaction) as follows:

Dr Supplies expense	600	
Cr Cash or accounts payable		600

But we know that supplies costing $100 are still on hand as at the end of the accounting period, so the accountant must record the following adjusting journal entry:

Dr Supplies	100	
Cr Supplies expense		100

#6. The adjusting journal entry is:

Dr Salaries expense	500	
Cr Accrued salaries payable		500

Again, even though the salaries are not payable until January 15 of the next accounting period, the $500 represents the cost of work that benefited 1995.

#7. This one is similar to #5:

Dr Prepaid rent	400	
Cr Rent expense		400

#8. Only $100 of the "Unearned rental income" is still unearned by the end of 1995, so the remaining $500 should be transferred to "Rental income" (an income statement account) by means of the following adjusting entry:

	Dr	Cr
Dr Unearned rental income	500	
Cr Rental income		500

#9.

	Dr	Cr
Dr Prepaid interest	400	
Cr Interest expense		400

#10.

	Dr	Cr
Dr Interest expense	800	
Cr Accrued interest payable		800

#11. The current asset account "Prepaid insurance" is seen to have a balance of $1,200 in the preadjustment trial balance, but we know that only $500 of coverage remains as at December 31, 1995:

	Dr	Cr
Dr Insurance expense	700	
Cr Prepaid insurance		700

#12. Net sales are $206,000, less the total of $6,000 in the accounts "Sales returns and allowances" and "Sales discounts." The balance in "Allowance for doubtful accounts" is equal to 0.6% times the $200,000, or $1,200. Since there is only $200 in this account in the preadjustment trial balance, a further $1,000 must be added, as follows:

	Dr	Cr
Dr Bad debt expense	1,000	
Cr Allowance for doubtful accounts		1,000

#13.

	Dr	Cr
Dr Depreciation expense — delivery equipment	1,000	
Cr Accumulated depreciation — delivery equipment		1,000

#14.

	Dr	Cr
Dr Depreciation expense — equipment	4,000	
Cr Accumulated depreciation — equipment		4,000

#15.

	Dr	Cr
Dr Depreciation expense — building	2,000	
Cr Accumulated depreciation — building		2,000

PROBLEM FOR SELF-STUDY

Prepare an income statement and a balance sheet for Chimo Ltd. for the year ended December 31, 1995.

EXHIBIT 3A

CHIMO LTD		WORKSHEET FOR THE YEAR ENDED DECEMBER 31/95								
	Account	Pre-adjustment trial balance			Adjustments		Income Statement		Balance Sheet	
Account	Code	Dr	Cr	#	Dr	Cr	Dr	Cr	Dr	Cr
Cash	101B	20,000							20,000	
Accounts receivable	102B	10,000							10,000	
Allowance for doubtful accounts	103B		200	12		1,000				1,200
Notes receivable	104B	6,000							6,000	
Inventory	105B	30,000		1	25,000	30,000			25,000	
Prepaid insurance	106B	1,200		11		700			500	
Land	121B	7,000							7,000	
Building	122B	80,000							80,000	
Accum. Dep.- Building	123B		7,200	15		2,000				9,200
Equipment	124B	40,000							40,000	
Accum. Dep.- Equipment	125B		4,000	14		4,000				8,000
Delivery equipment	126B	6,000							6,000	
Accum. Dep.- Delivery equipment	127B		1,000	13		1,000				2,000
Accounts payable	201B		5,000							5,000
Notes payable	202B		10,000							10,000
Unearned rental income	203B		600	8	500					100
Mortgage payable	221B		30,000							30,000
Capital stock	301B		90,000							90,000
Retained earnings	302B		12,500							12,500
Sales	401N		206,000					206,000		
Sales returns and allowances	402N	2,000					2,000			
Sales discounts	403N	4,000					4,000			
Purchases	421N	134,000		1		134,000				
Purchase returns and allowances	422N		1,000	1	1,000					
Purchase discounts	423N		3,000	1	3,000		0			
Transportation-in	424N	2,000		1		2,000	0			
Advertising expense	431N	800					800			
Delivery expense	432N	300					300			
Miscellaneous expense	433N	200					200			
Rent expense	434N	900		7		400	500			
Repairs expense	435N	300					300			
Salaries expense	436N	22,000		6	500		22,500			

Account	Account Code	Pre-adjustment trial balance Dr	Pre-adjustment trial balance Cr	#	Adjustments Dr	Adjustments Cr	Income Statement Dr	Income Statement Cr	Balance Sheet Dr	Balance Sheet Cr
Supplies expense	437N	600		5		100	500			
Tax expense	438N	1,000		4	300		1,300			
Utilities expense	439N	1,200					1,200			
Interest income	440N		500	2	400			300		
				3		200				
Interest expense	441N	1,500		10	800		1,900			
				9		400				
TOTALS		**371,000**	**371,000**							
Cost of goods sold	411N			1	137,000		137,000			
Unearned interest income	404B			2		400				400
Accrued interest receivable	107B			3	200				200	
Accrues taxes payable	204B			4		300				300
Supplies	108B			5	100				100	
Accrued salaries payable	205B			6		500				500
Prepaid rent	108B			7	400				400	
Rent income	405N			8		500		500		
Prepaid interest	109B			9	400				400	
Accrued interest payable	206B			10		800				800
Insurance expense	421N			11	700		700			
Bad debt expense	422N			12	1,000		1,000			
Depreciation expense- Del. eqmt.	423N			13	1,000		1,000			
Depreciation expense- Equipmt.	424N			14	4,000		4,000			
Depreciation expense- Bldg.	425N			15	2,000		2,000			
TOTALS					**178,300**	**178300**	**181,200**	**206,800**	**195,600**	**170,000**
Net income	450N						25,600			25,600
GRAND TOTALS							**206,800**		**195,600**	**195,600**

CHAPTER 4 four

A Conceptual Framework for Financial Accounting

Learning OBJECTIVES

After you have read, thought about, and discussed this chapter, and completed a selection from the end-of-chapter material, you will have made significant progress in achieving the following learning objectives:

- Explain what a conceptual framework for financial accounting is, and how such a framework may be used.
- Describe the following parts of a conceptual framework for financial accounting: objectives, users, elements, qualitative characteristics, recognition and measurement criteria, and pervasive constraints.
- Describe the characteristics of professional judgment in financial reporting, and explain the importance of such judgment.
- Identify the differences between the accrual accounting model based upon the realization and matching principles, and the cash-flow accounting model.
- Describe the efficient markets hypothesis criterion and the economic consequences criterion, and explain how they affect accounting decisions.
- Be aware of the differences in point of view between those who believe that accounting can be neutral and portray an underlying reality, and those who believe that such neutrality is impossible.

> *The company's chief accountant [was] bent over his books... making correct entries of perfectly correct transactions; and fifty feet below the doorstep I could see the still treetops of the grove of death.*
>
> Joseph Conrad, *Heart of Darkness*[1]

INTRODUCTION

In this chapter we examine the conceptual framework for financial accounting. This framework is intended to help those who set new accounting standards, or new GAAP, and also to provide guidance to accountants and managers in making accounting decisions in those many situations where there is no specific GAAP or in which existing GAAP is vague. The goal at all times is to develop as faithful, comprehensive, and realistic a picture of an organization as possible, so that users of the accounting information will be well served.

This goal of providing a realistic and honest picture of what is going on seems to be at variance with the image of accounting suggested by this chapter's opening quotation, which is from Conrad's *Heart of Darkness*. There, the accounting record takes no account of the "grove of death" just fifty feet away. In Conrad's novella, the activities of a late-nineteenth-century European ivory-trading company are creating chaos, death, and despair in the African jungle; yet that company's accounting system only accounts for the wealth in ivory extracted from the country, along with the expenses of running the whole affair. Perhaps the directors of the company back in Europe got the accounting they really wanted.

Theory and the Subdisciplines of Accounting

Exhibit 4–1 reviews the subdisciplines of accounting that were introduced in Chapter 1, this time in the form of a matrix. The horizontal headings indicate three broad categories of accounting entities for which the subdisciplines down the vertical axis are relevant. This presentation emphasizes that — for example — financial accounting and reporting is important not only for profit-seeking entities in Canada, but also for not-for-profit entities (such as charities) and for governments, and for all these types of entities outside of Canada as well. The blank cell reminds us that not-for-profit and government entities are not subject to income taxes. The exhibit suggests that financial accounting and reporting is somewhat different for each of the three categories, but that these differences shouldn't be taken to an extreme. Indeed, in Canada and elsewhere attempts are currently being made to merge accounting for not-for-profit

[1] Conrad's famous novella was first published in 1902.

EXHIBIT 4–1
THE SUBDISCIPLINES OF ACCOUNTING REVISITED

	Profit-Seeking entities	Not-for-Profit and Government Entities	International Accounting
Financial accounting and reporting	X	X	X
Operational accounting	X	X	X
Management and cost accounting	X	X	X
Accounting information systems	X	X	X
Management control	X	X	X
Regulatory accounting	X	X	X
Taxation	X		X
Auditing	X	X	X

"X" indicates that the subdiscipline of accounting is relevant for the particular type of accounting entity.

and profit-seeking entities; significant attempts are also being made to reduce international accounting differences, especially between countries that are major trading partners.

The matrix also suggests, however, that accounting may be subject to different influences in profit-seeking Canadian organizations, not-for-profit organizations, and organizations operating in an international environment. As an example, recall from Chapter 2 that the net present value criterion is important in both financial and managerial accounting. In managerial accounting, it is used extensively as the basis for choosing among alternatives, as the Gord and James case in that chapter demonstrated. In financial accounting, it serves as a basis for assigning measures to certain assets and liabilities. However, in countries in which commercial activities are regulated by Islamic thought, the concept of "interest," and thus present value, is unacceptable; as a result, the difference between Islamic and non-Islamic accounting in this area is quite considerable. Another example: in France, financial accounting principles are part of formal laws, but in Canada and the United States they are not.

A considerable body of concepts, theory, and practice has built up over the years that applies to all the cells in Exhibit 4–1 (except for the blank cell, of course). We saw in Chapters 2 and 3 that many accounting concepts are important to most accounting areas; these concepts include the following: accountability, accounting entity, user orientation, substance over form, net present value criterion, classification, ethics, and transaction. In this chapter, we focus more specifically on particular theoretical concepts that have been developed for the subdiscipline of financial accounting and reporting.

A Theoretical Framework for Financial Accounting

Theories can help us understand how concepts and facts fit together, so that more sense can be made out of those aspects of the world which we are studying. Each of the many areas of accounting has a number of theories associated with it. Some of these theories are rather elaborate and some are quite simple. In this section we introduce and describe a theoretical framework for financial accounting. This framework sets out what the objectives of financial accounting *should* be, what sorts of qualities financial accounting information *should* have, the general rules governing how financial accounting statements *should* be constructed, and other similar matters. Note that we used the word "should" several times in the previous sentence; theories that focus on how things *should* be done are called *normative* theories, and are distinguished from theories that attempt to explain and understand what is going on (which are called descriptive theories). Actually, the theoretical framework for financial accounting that we are about to outline, and that is known as financial accounting's "conceptual framework," has both normative and descriptive aspects. It provides an overview that is very helpful in learning about financial accounting.

What Is a Conceptual Framework for Financial Accounting?

Before describing the conceptual framework for financial accounting that is predominant in Canada, the United States, and many other countries, we'll briefly explain what we mean by the term. That is, just what is a conceptual framework, and what is it supposed to be used for? The Financial Accounting Standards Board (FASB, the organization that sets GAAP in the United States, and that has strongly influenced accounting thought elsewhere) wrote that an accounting conceptual framework is:

> *a constitution ... a coherent system of interrelated objectives and fundamentals that can lead to consistent standards and that prescribes the nature, function, and limits of financial accounting and financial statements. The objectives identify the goals and purposes of accounting. The fundamentals are the underlying concepts of accounting, concepts that guide the selection of events, and the means of summarizing and communicating them to interested parties. Concepts of that type are fundamental in the sense that other concepts flow from them and repeated reference to them will be necessary in establishing, interpreting, and applying accounting and reporting standards.*[2]

Conceivably, there can be a variety of accounting constitutions or conceptual frameworks. For example, one type might define accounting's objectives quite narrowly (for instance, "to provide information about operating cash flows"), while another might favour broad objectives (for instance, "to provide information about profitability and efficiency"). Similarly, one type might define the elements of financial statements very precisely, while another might not. Further, differences concerning important matters, such as deciding who the users of financial statements are, might distinguish one conceptual framework for financial accounting and reporting from another.

The parts of financial accounting's currently accepted conceptual framework are listed in Exhibit 4–2, and described in Exhibits 4–3 to 4–7. This framework is "user-oriented," in the sense that its ultimate purpose is to ensure that users' information needs relating to an organization are satisfied.

[2] FASB, *Scope and Implications of the Conceptual Framework Project*, December 2, 1976.

EXHIBIT 4–2
OVERVIEW OF FINANCIAL ACCOUNTING'S USER-ORIENTED CONCEPTUAL FRAMEWORK

Part of the Conceptual Framework	Comments
1. The overall **objectives** of financial accounting information, including financial statements, are chosen.	Agreeing on the objectives and developing the framework took many years. There was widespread consultation, especially in the United States. See Exhibit 4-3 for the objectives and users selected in the Canadian version of the conceptual framework. Those who developed the Canadian conceptual framework were members of committees of the Canadian Institute of Chartered Accountants. CMAs, CGAs, CAs, and many others participated in this process.
2. The **users** of financial accounting information, including financial statements, are selected by those who develop the framework.	
3. The **elements** of financial accounting are defined.	General financial statement categories such as "assets," "liabilities," "equity," "revenues," "expenses," and so on are what the conceptual framework is referring to when it uses the term "elements." See Exhibit 4–4 for a summary of the elements defined in the Canadian conceptual framework.
4. The desirable **qualitative characteristics** that accounting information should have are identified.	Four of the broad desirable qualitative characteristics of financial accounting information are "understandability," "relevance," "reliability," and "comparability." It's reasonable to expect accounting information to fulfil some sorts of quality criteria; after all, in everyday conversation we tend to devalue rumour since it doesn't have many desirable qualitative characteristics. Refer to Exhibit 4–5 for a summary of desirable qualitative characteristics of financial accounting information.
5. The **recognition and measurement criteria** for financial accounting are set out.	This part of the conceptual framework provides criteria for helping accountants and managers decide when an element is to be recorded in the accounts (recognition), and in what amount (measurement). Exhibit 4–6 summarizes the Canadian choices in this area. The second half of this chapter provides a more detailed discussion of some of the issues in this area.
6. **Pervasive constraints** affecting management's decisions about financial accounting are part of the conceptual framework.	The "benefit versus cost" constraint and "materiality" are described in Exhibit 4–7.

Objectives of Financial Statements

The first and most crucial task in developing a conceptual framework for financial accounting is to agree on objectives. Exhibit 4–3 gives the text of the objectives as set out in the *CICA Handbook*. Notice that the CICA has decided to provide objectives not for financial accounting or reporting, but rather for financial statements — a more restricted information set. Also notice the assertion (in paragraphs 1000.09 and 1000.10) about owners and similar groups being segregated from management. This fundamental assumption about the separation of management from ownership is what has created the need for concepts and rules to fulfil accountability through the preparation and dissemination of financial statements.

Notice also that paragraph 1000.15 specifies certain groups as the users of financial statements, and states the objectives of financial statements in terms of the information needs of those groups. This suggests that the needs of other potential users of financial accounting information (including financial statements) may not receive adequate attention. For example, when a union goes seeking relevant financial information about an employer for the purpose of determining how much of a wage increase the employer may be able to afford, usually it is frustrated by financial statements. This is partly because the statements are prepared for the employer accounting entity as a whole, and not for the particular bargaining units that the union is representing in its wage negotiations with the company.

Notice also that matters relating to the objectives of financial statements for not-for-profit (or nonprofit) entities, and to the users of such accounting information, are also dealt with in section 1000. This illustrates the accounting profession's ongoing attempts to establish as much common ground as possible between profit-seeking and not-for-profit entities.

EXHIBIT 4–3
OBJECTIVES AND USERS OF FINANCIAL STATEMENTS AS SET OUT IN SECTION 1000 OF THE *CICA HANDBOOK*

[It is helpful to be exposed to the original literature in a discipline. With this in mind, we provide here the paragraphs of section 1000 of the *CICA Handbook* that set out the CICA's view of what the objectives of financial statements should be, and who the users should be.]

1000.09 Ownership of profit oriented enterprises is often segregated from management, creating a need for external communication of economic information about the entity to investors. For the purposes of this Section, investors include present and potential debt and equity investors and their advisers. Creditors and others who do not have internal access to entity information also need external reports to obtain the information they require. In the case of financial institutions, investors, creditors and others include depositors and policyholders.

1000.10 Members of and contributors to non-profit organizations are also often segregated from management creating a similar need for external communication of economic information about the entity to members and contributors. As is the case with profit oriented enterprises, creditors and others who do not have internal access to entity information also need external reports to obtain the information they require.

1000.11 It is not practicable to expect financial statements to satisfy the many and varied information needs of all external users of information about an entity. Consequently, the objective of financial statements for profit oriented enterprises focuses primarily on information needs of investors and creditors and, for non-profit organizations, focuses primarily on information needs of members, contributors and creditors. Financial statements prepared to satisfy these needs are often used by others who need external reporting of information about an entity.

1000.12 Investors and creditors of profit oriented enterprises are interested, for the purpose of making resource allocation decisions, in predicting the ability of the entity to earn income and generate cash flows in the future to meet its obligations and to generate a return on investment.

1000.13 Members, contributors and creditors of non-profit organizations are interested, for the purpose of making resource allocation decisions, in the entity's cost of service and in predicting the ability of the entity to generate cash flows in the future to meet its obligations and achieve its objectives.

1000.14 Investors, members and contributors also require information about how the management of an entity has discharged its stewardship responsibility to those that have provided resources to the entity. Information regarding discharge of the stewardship responsibilities is especially important in the non-profit sector where resources are often contributed for specific purposes and management is accountable for the appropriate utilization of such resources.

Objective

1000.15 The objective of financial statements is to communicate information that is useful to investors, members, contributors, creditors and other users ("users") in making their resource allocation decisions and/or assessing management stewardship. Consequently, financial statements provide information about:

(a) an entity's economic resources, obligations and equity/net assets;
(b) changes in an entity's economic resources, obligations and equity/net assets; and
(c) the economic performance of the entity.

Elements of Financial Statements

The elements of financial statements — those general categories of items that make up financial statements — are defined in Exhibit 4–4. As with definitions in most aspects of life, the ones in Exhibit 4–4 must be used with care. As we explore various aspects of accounting, you will find that although these definitions are often useful, at times they are too limiting and at other times not limiting enough. Even so, learning and understanding these definitions is a good, practical starting point in many accounting decision situations. Although simply applying a definition may not lead to a completely satisfactory solution, it will often provide an interesting perspective.

For example, the definition of "asset" permits an accounting entity to include as assets equipment and buildings which are not legally owned by the entity, but which are controlled by the entity and from which the entity is expected to derive future economic benefits. This definition, while it is consistent with the notion of "substance over form" that was introduced in Chapter 2, requires a careful exercise of judgment on the part of managers, accountants, auditors, and users. Ensuring that an asset has the following attributes (see Exhibit 4–4), even though the entity may not have legal ownership of the economic resource in question, is crucial:

- The economic resource is *controlled* by the entity.
- Such control is a result of *past* transactions or events.
- *Future* economic benefits flow to the entity.

An example of a situation in which the above definition supports classifying a non-owned economic resource as an asset relates to capital leases. Suppose that QUE Company signs a rental agreement for a new delivery truck for a four-year period, with monthly rental payments of $300 beginning one month from the date the contract is signed. QUE will have sole use of the truck for the four years, is responsible for all maintenance and repairs, and must pay a very significant financial penalty if it decides to break the agreement. The truck is expected to have a four-year useful life; at the end of this time it will probably be scrapped. Rental, or lease, agreements that cover more or less the entire expected life of an economic resource, and that can only be broken under heavy penalty, are called capital leases in the *CICA Handbook* (section 3065). Such agreements transfer most of the risks and rewards of ownership to the user of the resource (QUE Company, in this case), or lessee. Since the definition of an asset given in section 1000 of the *CICA Handbook* seems to be fulfilled, the resource must be accounted for as an asset on QUE's books. Thus, on the day the agreement (called a lease agreement) is signed, QUE will record the following journal entry:

Dr Leased asset — delivery truck	XX	
Cr Lease obligation		XX

The asset "Leased asset — delivery truck" is classified as a capital asset, and depreciated like all depreciable capital assets; while the liability "Lease obligation" is classified as a long-term liability (except when payments are due within the next year, in which circumstances a portion must be classified as current). The amount XX is computed as follows: The present value of $300 per month for four years, or 48 months, beginning one month hence, is computed. This present value depends on the interest rate chosen. Considerations relating to choosing the rate are beyond the scope of this text. However suppose in this case that the interest rate is one percent per month. The present value will be as shown in the following equation:

$$\frac{300}{(1.01)^1} + \frac{300}{(1.01)^2} + \frac{300}{(1.01)^3} + \cdots\cdots + \frac{300}{(1.01)^{47}} + \frac{300}{(1.01)^{48}} = \$11{,}392.19$$

Accounting and Business Decision A

Use the definition of "liability" in Exhibit 4–4 to justify that \$11,392.19 should be included among QUE Company's liabilities on the balance sheet as a result of the lease agreement.

What journal entry would QUE's accountant prepare to record the first month's payment?

EXHIBIT 4–4
ELEMENTS OF FINANCIAL STATEMENTS: SECTION 1000'S VERSION

Element	**"Official" CICA Definition**	**Comments**
Assets	"... economic resources controlled by an entity as a result of past transactions or events and from which future economic benefits may be obtained."	An entity doesn't have to be the legal owner of an economic resource in order for the resource to qualify as an asset of the entity.
Liabilities	"... obligations of an entity arising from past transactions or events, the settlement of which may result in the transfer or use of assets, the provision of services or other yielding of economic benefits in the future."	Obligations don't have to be legally enforceable in order to qualify as liabilities.
Equity	"... the ownership interest in the assets of a profit-oriented enterprise after deducting its liabilities."	This is just another way of asserting that equity equals the residual of assets less liabilities.
Revenues	"... increases in economic resources, either by way of inflows or the enhancements of assets or reductions of liabilities, resulting from the ordinary activities of an entity. Revenues of entities normally arise from the sale of goods, the rendering of services or the use by others of entity resources yielding rent, interest, royalties or dividends. In addition, many non-profit organizations receive a significant proportion of their revenues from donations, government grants and other contributions."	
Expenses	"... decreases in economic resources, either by way of outflows or reductions of assets or incurrences of liabilities, resulting from an entity's ordinary revenue generating or service delivery activities."	
Gains	"... increases in equity ... from peripheral or incidental transactions and events affecting an entity ..."	
Losses	"... decreases in equity ... from peripheral or incidental transactions and events affecting an entity ..."	

Desirable Qualitative Characteristics That Financial Accounting Information Should Have

This part of a financial accounting conceptual framework consists of what accountants believe are the desirable qualitative characteristics that financial accounting information should have. This is an inherently normative part of financial accounting's conceptual framework. It provides a set of criteria against which to assess accounting information. If the information does not meet the standards to an acceptable degree, then it should not be included as part of the financial statements. Determining just what an acceptable degree is in particular circumstances requires experience.

Since the conceptual framework has adopted a user-oriented perspective, the most fundamental qualitative characteristic of accounting information is that it must be useful for the decision(s) of the users. The essential idea behind decision usefulness is quite straightforward, and may be illustrated by drawing upon the net present value criterion that we described in Chapter 2. Recall the example that involved Ms. X having to choose between two alternatives: pay $1,150 two years from today in order to receive $1,000 in cash today, or pay $900 today in order to receive $1,000 one year from now. We showed that if the interest rate is 8%, and if Ms. X believes in the NPV criterion, then the second alternative is preferable (that is, it has the larger NPV). So, if a specific decision model can be chosen (in this case, the decision model that says "choose the alternative with the higher NPV if the interest rate is 8%"), the information useful to the decision can be determined (in this case, the future expected cash flows of the two alternatives). Other information about the two alternatives may have been available, but may well have been not at all useful. For example, perhaps five years ago Ms. X could have paid just $850 in order to receive $1,000 in one year; however, the $850 is not very relevant to Ms. X's current decision situation. So here we have a situation in which a historic cost number (the $850) is not relevant, but the current and future numbers are. However, if Ms. X wishes to assess how effective her decision-making ability has been in the past, then perhaps the historic number is useful.

The idea behind decision usefulness is easy to understand. However, because we live in a world in which decision models are rarely as neatly specified as was the case for Ms. X, implementing decision usefulness requires that we assess several aspects of the qualitative characteristics of accounting information. The qualitative characteristics described in Exhibit 4–5 are, by and large, just common sense. One important thing to keep in mind is that perhaps none of these qualitative characteristics can ever be completely fulfilled in a given situation. This has led the CICA to conclude (s. 1000.24):

> *In practice, a trade-off between qualitative characteristics is often necessary, particularly between relevance and reliability. For example, there is often a trade-off between the timeliness of producing financial statements and the reliability of the information reported in the statements. Generally, the aim is to achieve an appropriate balance among the characteristics in order to meet the objective of financial statements. The relative importance of the characteristics in different cases is a matter of professional judgment.*

EXHIBIT 4–5
DESIRABLE QUALITATIVE CHARACTERISTICS OF FINANCIAL STATEMENT INFORMATION: SECTION 1000's VERSION

Principal Qualitative Characteristic	Components of the Principal Characteristic	"Official" Definition
Understandability		"For the information provided in financial statements to be useful, it must be capable of being understood by users. Users are assumed to have a reasonable understanding of business and economic activities and accounting, together with a willingness to study the material with reasonable diligence."
Relevance		"For the information provided in financial statements to be useful, it must be relevant to the decisions made by users."
	Predictive and feedback value	"Information that helps users to predict an entity's future income and cash flows has predictive value ... Information that confirms or corrects previous predictions has feedback value."
	Timeliness	"For information to be useful for decision making, it must be received by the decision maker before it loses its capacity to influence decisions."
Reliability		"For the information provided in financial statements to be useful, it must be reliable [which means] it is in agreement with the actual underlying transactions and events, the agreement is capable of independent verification and the information is reasonably free from error and bias."
	Representational faithfulness	"... transactions and events are accounted for and presented in a manner that conveys their substance rather than necessarily their legal or other form."
	Verifiability	"The financial statement representation of a transaction or event is verifiable if knowledgeable and independent observers would concur that it is in agreement with the underlying transaction or event with a reasonable degree of precision."
	Neutrality	"Information is neutral when it is free from bias that would lead users towards making decisions that are influenced by the way the information is measured or presented. Bias in measurement occurs when a measure tends to consistently overstate or understate the items being measured. In the selection of accounting principles, bias may occur when the selection is made with the interests of particular users or with particular economic or political objectives in mind."
	Conservatism	"Use of conservatism in making judgments under conditions of uncertainty affects the neutrality of financial statements in an acceptable manner. When uncertainty exists, estimates of a conservative nature attempt to ensure that assets, revenues and gains are not overstated and, conversely, that liabilities, expenses and losses are not understated. However, conservatism does not encompass the deliberate understatement of assets, revenues and gains or the deliberate overstatement of liabilities, expenses and losses."
Comparability		"Comparability is a characteristic of the relationship between two pieces of information ... It enables users to identify similarities in and differences between the information provided by two sets of financial statements. Comparability is important when comparing the financial statements of two different entities and when comparing the financial statements of the same entity over two periods or at two different points in time. "Comparability in the financial statements of an entity is enhanced when the same accounting policies are used consistently from period to period. Consistency helps prevent misconceptions that might result from the application of different accounting policies in different periods. When a change in accounting policy is deemed to be appropriate, disclosure of the effects of the change may be necessary to maintain comparability."

Accounting and Business Decision B

"'Representational faithfulness' and 'substance over form' are essentially the same idea, and an important aspect of 'reliability.' However, there are many situations in which it is difficult to identify the substance in order that the resulting financial accounting will be representationally faithful. Examples include:

— capital lease arrangements;

— paying a signing bonus to an established major league baseball star; and

— accounting for depreciation expense."

Do you agree with this statement?

Recognition and Measurement Criteria for Financial Accounting

This part of a financial accounting conceptual framework deals with concepts related to recognition and measurement (see Exhibit 4–6). "Recognition" is a technical accounting term that refers to the process of including something in the financial statements of an accounting entity. As an illustration, a transaction between the accounting entity and another independent party serves as a trigger for recognizing changes in the financial statements. Other events besides transactions may act as recognition triggers, and deciding whether a bona fide transaction has occurred may at times be difficult. For example, when the accounting entity and the other party are related by common ownership, transactions involving the transfer of assets may be suspect. Clearly from this, issues in financial accounting relating to recognition are very important and at times complex. Because we will spend considerable time on these issues in the chapters that follow, we won't delve too deeply into this topic at this time. However, in the second part of this chapter, two aspects of recognition will be dealt with at length. These two aspects are *revenue realization*, which focuses on the way accounting admits information about revenues into financial statements; and *expense matching*, which describes how financial accounting makes decisions about recording expenses.

"Measurement," according to the *CICA Handbook*, 1000.53, "is the process of determining the amount at which an item is recognized in the financial statements." The *Handbook* goes on to describe current accounting practice as "primarily using the historical cost basis of measurement whereby transactions and events are recognized in financial statements at the amount of cash or cash equivalents paid or received or the fair value ascribed to them when they took place." Like recognition, measurement is an important, pervasive, and complex topic; we will discuss it in greater detail as we go through the book, and just mention it here.

EXHIBIT 4–6
RECOGNITION AND MEASUREMENT CRITERIA FOR FINANCIAL ACCOUNTING

What the *CICA Handbook* Says
[author's commentary in square brackets]

Recognition Criteria

1000.41 Recognition is the process of including an item in the financial statements of an entity [including] a narrative description of the item (e.g. "inventory", "sales", or "donations") in a statement ..."

[Just including an item in footnotes is not recognition: footnotes are intended to provide further information about items already recognized in financial statements, or information that does not meet the criteria for recognition.]

1000.44 The recognition criteria are as follows:
(a) the item has an appropriate basis of measurement and a reasonable estimate can be made of the amount involved; and
(b) for items involving obtaining or giving up future economic benefits, it is probable that such benefits will be obtained or given up.

[Items may meet the definition of a financial statement element (see Exhibit 4–4), but fail to meet the recognition criteria; in that case, information about them should be disclosed in footnotes.]

1000.47 Revenues are generally recognized when performance is achieved and reasonable assurance regarding measurement and collectibility of the consideration exists ...

1000.51 Expenses of profit oriented enterprises that are linked to revenue in a cause and effect relationship are normally matched with revenue in the accounting period in which the revenue is recognized.

[Determining whether revenues and expenses should be recognized is so important in financial accounting that the entire second half of this chapter is devoted to this topic.]

Measurement

"Measurement," according to *CICA* 1000.53, "is the process of determining the amount at which an item is recognized in the financial statements."

[The *CICA Handbook* goes on to describe current accounting practice as "primarily using the historical cost basis of measurement whereby transactions and events are recognized in financial statements at the amount of cash or cash equivalents paid or received or the fair value ascribed to them when they took place." Like recognition, the topic of measurement is so important and pervasive in accounting in general and in financial accounting in particular, that much of this book is devoted to it.]

Constraints on Financial Accounting Information

The conceptual framework ideas outlined in the *CICA Handbook* contain two other useful concepts: benefit versus cost constraint, and materiality. These ideas are described in Exhibit 4–7. The benefit versus cost constraint encourages accountants and managers to bear in mind that providing information is costly, and that the costs are not only of the easily measured variety. It also reminds those involved in accounting that different parties may bear different costs. For example, if shareholders are not provided with information about the decline in value of a company's major asset, they may suffer significant losses as a result of not selling their shares in a timely fashion.

The materiality constraint has both a quantitative and a qualitative dimension.

The Canadian accounting theorist and practitioner Ross Skinner has observed:

The concept of materiality in accounting is firmly based on the orientation of financial statements to user needs. That is to say, there will be a failure in communication if the statements contain a material error, misrepresentation, or omission ... The accepted concept of materiality is that some information or some aspect of statement preparation is material if its omission or misrepresentation could affect a decision by a reasonably intelligent reader of the financial statements. Although logical, this concept presents considerable difficulty in implementation. Since information that might affect one reader's decision could leave another completely unmoved, what financial statement reader are we talking about? ... Unfortunately, we do not have very concrete evidence explaining how people make investment or credit decisions. Thus, how can we know what they would consider material?

... research suggests that (1) there can be considerable dispersion in opinions held by various observers as to what is or is not material, (2) enough consensus exists that some guidance can be given in broad quantitative terms, and (3) there are some factors ... that can only be expressed in qualitative terms.[3]

The most commonly used reference against which to assess the quantitative aspect of materiality is net income. Thus, if not following GAAP in a certain situation results in an "error" of just a percent or two in net income, the error is said to be immaterial. An example might be if $10,000 in capital assets were expensed instead of being recorded as long-term assets in a company that has $100,000,000 in net income. Keeping track of the assets, including accounting for depreciation, might be viewed as costing more than the effort is worth. But what if income fell to just $20,000 the next year? Would the expensing of $10,000 in capital assets then be considered material? Surely, the relative impact on net income would be much greater than in the previous year. Thus, we can see that setting quantitative measures of what is material is not particularly easy.

The need to be aware of the qualitative dimension of materiality further complicates the situation. Some transactions or other business events seem to be material in spite of their tiny size. Say, for example, that the president of a billion-dollar (by assets) company stole $100 from the company's petty cash. Such an action would be material, and users of the company's financial statements would have an unequivocal right to know about it, even though in dollar terms it is trivial.

EXHIBIT 4–7
PERVASIVE CONSTRAINTS

Benefit versus cost constraint

1000.16 The benefits expected to arise from providing information in financial statements should exceed the cost of doing so ... the benefits and costs may accrue to different parties and ... the evaluation of the nature and amount of benefits and costs is substantially a judgment process.

Materiality

1000.17 Users are interested in information that may affect their decision making. Materiality is the term used to describe the significance of financial statement information to decision makers. An item of information, or an aggregate of items, is material if it is probable that its omission or misstatement would influence or change a decision. Materiality is a matter of professional judgment in the particular circumstances.

Other Important Financial Accounting Concepts

Financial statements are prepared under the assumption that the entity being accounted for is a **going concern**. If this going concern assumption were not fol-

[3] Ross M. Skinner, *Accounting Standards in Evolution*, Holt, Rinehart and Winston of Canada, Toronto, 1987, pp. 422–423.

lowed, then the assets and liabilities on the accounting entity's balance sheet would be accounted for at their liquidation values—that is, the amounts that the assets, including capital assets such as machinery and buildings, could be sold for in the near future, and the amounts that would be required to pay off the liabilities in the near future. These amounts are usually very different from the amounts recorded under the assumption of a going concern. For example, suppose a software developer has accounted for expenditures incurred in the improvements of computer programs that it markets as an intangible capital asset. This asset is included on the balance sheet since it is expected, under an assumption that the software developer is a going concern, that its incurrence will generate future revenues. However, if the company is about to go bankrupt and thus the going concern assumption can no longer be supported, this intangible capital asset may have to be written off if it has no current market value.

Some accountants suggest that the going concern assumption can be used to support the continued use of historic cost for items such as tangible capital assets, but this ignores the superiority of current values for most decision purposes.

The **money unit** assumption in accounting has two aspects. First, it has been used to support the idea that financial accounting deals mainly in quantitative measures based on money units such as the Canadian dollar. In other words, accounting — as the "language of business" — ignores nonqualitative information. Although it is undeniable that money amounts are attached to accounting elements such as assets, liabilities, revenues, expenses, and so on, it is also undeniable that these elements have important qualitative attributes as well. For example, when we classify an item as a current asset rather than a noncurrent asset, we are describing an important qualitative feature of the asset. Indeed, categorizing a current asset as cash rather than as inventory provides further important qualitative information. So financial accounting information is a mix of both money unit quantitative information, and qualitative information. Therefore, this first aspect of the money unit assumption is too limiting, and doesn't accord with the vast increase in financial accounting disclosure in footnotes and elsewhere in the financial statements.

The second aspect of the money unit assumption involves the obviously unrealistic assumption that the money unit used in financial accounting — say, the Canadian dollar — is stable over time. By making this assumption, accountants ignore the impact of inflation on financial statements, and thus managers and other users of financial statements receive biased information as input into their decisions. Of course the value of the Canadian dollar has changed over time; general inflation and the changes in the prices of specific products in the marketplace are evidence of this. One of the most insidious impacts of this assumption of money unit stability is that the asset side of an accounting entity's balance sheet is usually composed of asset amounts that are incommensurable — that is, are not strictly speaking able to be added together since it would be like adding apples and oranges. For example, suppose a company purchased a hectare of land in 1940 for $1,000, and a second hectare of land adjacent to the first in 1997 for $100,000. The balance sheet category for "Land" shows a cost of $101,000, which is true if all we are interested in is the arithmetic sum of the two transactions, but false if we require the cost of the two parcels of land to be measured in dollars of equivalent purchasing power; the 1940 dollar could buy a lot more than the 1997!

The **periodicity assumption**, often called the time period assumption, is the basis for preparing **periodic** financial statements. For example, annual reports, quarterly reports, and monthly reports are in common use in financial accounting. With advances in technology, there is a move to shorter and shorter reporting time periods, with some thought of a future with continuous reporting. As the reporting period gets shorter, however, accounting decisions such as those relating to accruals and depreciation may be more difficult to make since less time has passed and less information is available. With annual reports, managers have the luxury of being held accountable over a time interval in which the positive (as well as negative!) results of many of their decisions may come to fruition. But as the accountability interval shortens to zero with continuous reporting, managers can be expected to make decisions that favour projects with very short payoffs, and perhaps ignore longer-term projects that won't show results until well into the future.

Financial Accounting's Conceptual Framework and Generally Accepted Accounting Principles

The aspects of a conceptual framework described in this chapter provide a way of thinking about financial accounting. However, the existing set of detailed financial accounting rules, which are collectively termed generally accepted accounting principles, or GAAP, were developed without the benefit of a coherent conceptual framework. Much of GAAP was either codified as part of the *CICA Handbook* or became accepted practice before the conceptual framework was developed and published. Indeed, even principles that have been developed since the publication of the conceptual framework have at times ignored the framework. This is because accounting principles are often as much a product of political processes and compromise as they are of "rational" thinking.

A good example of the chasm between a specific GAAP and the ideas in the conceptual framework is the accounting treatment of the costs related to research. The *CICA Handbook* sets out GAAP for research costs in section 3450, in which it defines research as "planned investigation undertaken with the hope of gaining new scientific or technical knowledge and understanding. Such investigation may or may not be directed towards a specific practical aim or application" (paragraph 3450.02). According to paragraph 3450.16, the GAAP for research is as follows: "Research costs should be charged as an expense of the period in which they are incurred." In other words, under Canadian GAAP, if a company expends $1,000,000 on research in 1995, the following journal entry must be recorded:

Dr Research expense	1,000,000	
Cr Cash (or other assets)		1,000,000

However, it may be that such research expenditures qualify as an intangible asset, under the definition of assets in the conceptual framework. This may be so especially in situations where a well-established company has carried on a long-standing program of research involving a portfolio, or set, of research projects. Yet the GAAP rule would prevent the asset classification.

Judgment, the Conceptual Framework, and Accounting Decisions

In the above exhibits, the word "judgment" was used several times in the description of a conceptual framework. In everyday life, some people think that just because judgment is required in making a decision, "anything goes." Nothing could be further from the truth, especially in a discipline like accounting. Michael Gibbins of the University of Alberta and Alistair Mason of the professional accounting firm Deloitte and Touche, in a research study published by the CICA, offer the following working definition of professional judgment in financial reporting:

Professional judgement in financial reporting" is judgement exercised with due care, objectivity and integrity within the framework provided by accounting and other applicable standards, by experienced and knowledgeable people on accounting and financial reporting issues arising in the preparation and issuance of financial statements, annual reports, prospectuses, and similar documents.[4]

Exhibit 4–8 sets out various attributes of professional judgment in financial reporting. As you read the exhibit, consider the implications of each attribute for the decision-making process that you must go through as you make financial reporting decisions. Many of the attributes may at first seem abstract; however, as you gain experience in dealing with financial reporting situations, the concrete importance of the attributes will become increasingly apparent to you.

EXHIBIT 4–8
ATTRIBUTES OF PROFESSIONAL JUDGMENT IN FINANCIAL REPORTING*

(a) A meaningful choice must exist — a problem or issue must be identified that has reasonably plausible alternative resolutions.

(b) The choice must have nontrivial consequences to affected parties.

(c) The choice must be carried out under a condition of uncertainty.

(d) A depth of knowledge of the subject is required — superficial attempts at exercising professional judgment are at the very least incomplete, and may be harmful to clients, specific third parties, the public interest, the reputation of the professional, and the reputation of the profession.

(e) Experience is an important element in exercising professional judgment in financial reporting, which enables those making such judgments to be sensitive to subtle differences in situations.

(f) Due care, objectivity, and integrity are essential.

(g) Professional judgment must not be exercised in a social vacuum. Gibbins and Mason (p. 130) write: "Professional judgement in financial reporting is exercised within an environment that provides motivations, constraints, costs, benefits, risks, and other (often changing) factors important to the way the professional judgement process works and to the position of the person(s) exercising such judgement." Some factors that may be important here are:

- deadlines
- costs of obtaining information
- impact on career and reputation

[4] M. Gibbons and A.K. Mason, *Professional Judgment in Financial Reporting*, CICA: Toronto, 1988, p. 6.

(h) Professional judgment must usually involve a number of information-processing activities:

- collection of information
- evaluation of information
- problem definition
- analysis of alternatives
- assessment of likely consequences
- documentation
- justification of recommendations
- acceptance of personal responsibility

Memory, learning, cognitive, and other human mental processes are important aspects of these information-processing activities.

(i) Exercising professional judgment in financial reporting is often a group process involving consultation among colleagues.

(j) Professional judgment in financial reporting is exercised within a framework of accounting standards, where they exist. However, there are no promulgated standards for many situations, and even where there are, they usually require interpretation.

(k) Professional judgment can only be said to exist when the person exercising such judgement takes some responsibility for the consequences.

* Based on Gibbons and Mason, *Professional Judgment in Financial Reporting.*

The Accrual Model, the Cash Flow Model, and Financial Accounting's Conceptual Framework: "Realization" for Revenues and "Matching" for Expenses

Definition of income

Income is a basic indicator of economic well-being for profit-seeking accounting entities, and one that the accountant attempts to measure and communicate. Income can be seen as a measure of the amount by which wealth increases or decreases in a certain period of time — for instance, one year. Income thus describes the time-related change in economic well-being of an accounting entity. The accountant measures income as the difference between revenues (that is, the inflows of resources to a business earned in the normal course of operations) and expenses (that is, the outflows of resources used up in the process of generating revenues). More conceptually, economic income can be regarded as the amount of resources that can be consumed or disposed of and still leave the organization as well off at the end of the time period as it was at the beginning.[5] This general definition suggests that income is the change in an organization's economic "well-offness" over a period. As we saw in Chapter 3, under accrual accounting the focus is on the transactions and events that caused this change in well-offness, and not on the actual cash flows that happened to occur in a particular accounting period.

The problem of measuring income

In order to measure income under accrual accounting, the accountant requires rules or guidelines regarding when and how to recognize, classify, and measure revenues and expenses so that the resulting records will yield a meaningful picture of economic activity. On the surface, this may seem to be a fairly straightforward procedure; yet as we have seen, even the simplest economic transactions can be interpreted in several different ways, producing different measures of income.

[5] J.R. Hicks, *Value and Capital*, 2nd Ed. (Oxford: Clarendon Press, 1946), p. 172.

To illustrate some of the choices the accountant must make in applying the conceptual framework concepts of "recognition" and "matching" to income measurement, let's take as an example a very common business transaction. Suppose you take an article of clothing to a neighbourhood dry cleaner to be cleaned. You give the garment to the clerk, who in exchange gives you a ticket with a promise date and the amount due for the cleaning. The cleaner then takes the garment into the back of the store and puts it on a stack of clothing awaiting cleaning. Sometime later, the garment is cleaned, pressed, packaged, and put on a rack. You return to the store and present your claim check, and the dry cleaner gives you the garment. You then say you can't pay for the cleaning right away but will come back tomorrow with the cash. Although you have been doing business with the cleaner for a long time and she trusts you, she asks you to sign a written promise to pay (which she will keep as security), and you do so. The next day you return and retrieve your promissory note by paying her the cash owed. When you return home and inspect the garment, you find that it still has a spot that was not removed. You return the garment to the clerk, who takes it into the back, removes the spot, and then returns it to you. She asks if you are now satisfied and you say you are. She goes back to her operations, and you take your garment home.

When should the revenue from this transaction be recognized by the dry cleaner and recorded in the books? Should it be entered into the accounts when the garment is initially dropped off for cleaning, when the dry cleaner performs her service by cleaning it, when you pick it up, when you pay cash for it, or when you finally accept it as being satisfactory?

The accountant faces a similar problem in deciding when to recognize expense. To perform her cleaning services, the dry cleaner must have labour, equipment, and supplies on hand. When should the costs of these items be recognized and recorded as expenses? Expense may be regarded as the using up of resources for the purpose of generating revenue. But do assets such as the dry cleaner's equipment and supplies become expenses before revenue is recognized? Or must revenue be recognized before expenses can be recognized? When do dry-cleaning chemicals become expenses? Is it when they are purchased, or when they are paid for in cash, or when they are used in the process of cleaning a garment, or when the cleaning charge for the garment has finally been paid? By choosing a particular point in time at which to recognize revenue and expense, the accountant is affecting the amount of income that is measured for a time period. If the accountant changes the point at which revenue and expense are recognized, the amount of income measured will be different even though exactly the same business transactions have occurred.

In this part of the chapter, we are going to examine two financial accounting systems that are in wide use: the accrual model and the cash flow model. The main difference between these two ways of doing financial accounting lies in the stimulus they use for recording financial information. The cash flow model quite simply records the cash transactions between the accounting entity and other entities; all other events that might affect the well-being of the entity are not recorded. Say, for example, that a computer company's inventory of PCs is sold on credit. The cash flow model would ignore this transaction since no cash has changed hands; however, the accrual model would record the sale and the accompanying account receivable, since the sales transaction itself was the trigger.

Similarly, if a manufacturing company purchased a machine several years ago, the cash flow model would not perform any accounting for the machine in the current period (since there are no current-period cash flows relating to the machine's acquisition); however, the accrual model would account for the machine's depreciation by recording a journal entry having the following form:

Dr Depreciation expense	XXX	
Cr Accumulated depreciation		XXX

Notice that neither the debit side nor the credit side of this journal entry affects "Cash."

The two models capture very different aspects of what has happened to an accounting entity, and both aspects may be useful for the insight they provide about the accounting entity. In this part of the chapter we explain some important aspects of the accrual model, and then use a demonstration example to compare the accrual and cash-basis models. The accrual model of financial accounting is the model that results when revenues are accounted for using the concept of realization, and when expenses are accounted for using the concept of matching, as described below.

The above discussion should make it clear that in order to measure the income earned by a business, the accountant needs certain rules that can be applied consistently to help decide when to recognize and record revenues and expenses. Several of these rules make up the accounting measurement model called accrual accounting.

Accrual Accounting

Accrual accounting differs significantly from the simple measurement of the flow of cash into and out of a business. It might seem that the most straightforward way to measure income would be simply to record the cash inflows and outflows during the accounting period. The information conveyed by this method, however, is limited and sometimes misleading, and does not necessarily produce the most useful indication of an organization's progress. Cash accounting shows only when expenditures have been made and when revenues have been received. It does not necessarily reflect the actual time at which the firm receives the *benefit* from a revenue, nor can it always show the *relationship* between revenues and the expenses that were incurred to generate those revenues. Accountants, therefore, prefer to recognize and measure revenues and expenses not by the flow of cash, but in terms of the flow of some economic value into and out of the firm. The separation of receipts and payments from acquisition and use — that is, the measurement of this economic value flow — is the essence of accrual accounting.

Realization

Accrual accounting attempts to measure the economic effects of the activities that have taken place in a given period of time, as opposed to focusing solely on when cash changes hands. In accrual accounting, revenue is recognized and recorded not necessarily when cash is received or paid, but when the transaction has proceeded to some point at which it can be logically expected to be carried through to completion. This point is called the "realization point." In other words, revenue is realized when the economic value is assumed to flow out of the firm to the customer, whether or not cash has actually been received from the customer. Realization is one of the key measurement rules of accrual accounting. In the dry cleaner example, revenue would be recognized when the cleaned garment was first returned to its owner, because that is the point at which the service is assumed to be completed or "realized" in accounting terminology. Of course, the choice of realization point will depend on the nature of the industry and even on the nature of the individual business. The choice of an appropriate realization point at which to recognize revenue is one of the critical decisions an accountant must make in designing an accounting system.

Matching

Accountants measure income as revenues less expenses. Hence, to measure income, the accountant must not only determine when revenue has been earned but also which expenses have been incurred to generate that revenue. Accrual accounting measures expenses in much the same way it measures revenue. An asset becomes an expense when economic value is assumed to have flowed out of the accounting entity, and it is accounted for as an expense at that point, regardless of when the cash outlay for the asset was actually made. The principle used to relate expenses to the revenues that those expenses have helped earn is called "matching." Matching is simply a measurement principle that involves tracing and linking expenses to the revenues they have generated, and ensuring that those revenues and their matched expenses are both recorded as income statement items in the same accounting period. Under the accrual accounting model, the measure of income is the residual obtained by subtracting matched expenses from revenues.

The CICA's conceptual framework section supports the dominant role of accrual accounting. Paragraph 1000.46 states:

Items recognized in financial statements are accounted for in accordance with the accrual basis of accounting. The accrual basis of accounting recognizes the effect of transactions and events in the period in which the transactions and events occur, regardless of whether there has been a receipt or payment of cash or its equivalent. Accrual accounting encompasses deferrals that occur when a cash receipt or payment occurs prior to the criteria for recognition of revenue or expense being satisfied.

This doesn't prevent cash flow information from being prepared and presented: it just stresses the additional information content of accrual information.

These two decision rules — recognizing revenue only at the realization point, and recognizing expenses and computing income through matching — are two of the basic principles of the accrual accounting model.

An example of alternative measurement rules

To demonstrate the alternative decision rules open to the accountant and the information provided by accrual accounting, let's consider a simple example. The events to be considered are as follows:

January 1: A firm (the Tamarack Company, or TTC) rented a building for two months, paying $400 cash in advance.

January 3: TTC purchased two units of product for $250 each, paying cash for one and charging the second to its account.

January 20: TTC sold the two units for $500 each, receiving cash immediately for one and a promissory note for the other.

What is the income of this business for the month of January?

Exhibit 4–9 provides eight different income statements, each of which measures a different version of the change in economic well-being of TTC as a result of the events described above. Each income statement uses different rules for revenue and expense recognition. But which of these statements best reflects financial reality?

Revenue

The revenue figure of $1,000 in income statements 1 to 4 is derived by counting the revenue from the sale of the two units of inventory regardless of whether cash has already been received for them. The revenue figure of $500 in statements 5 to 8 counts only the actual cash received for the one unit and not the amount promised for the other.

Cost of sales

The $500 amount in income statements 1, 2, 5, and 6 reflects the cost of both units sold, regardless of whether they have been paid for. The $250 cost of sales in statements 3, 4, 7, and 8 counts as an expense only the cost of units that have already been paid for.

Rent expense

Statements 2, 4, 6, and 8 classify the total cash payment for rent made on January 1 as expense. The rent expense of $200 in statements 1, 3, 5, and 7, on the other hand, indicates that although $400 was expended for the right to use the facility for two months, only one month has passed. Therefore, since only half of the rental payment has been used in generating revenue, only half should be shown as an expense. (If we had also prepared a balance sheet, the other half would be accounted for as the asset "Prepaid rent.")

These eight different income statements are the result of combining several alternative measurement rules: recognizing revenue when the sale is made or only when cash is received; recognizing the cost of sales expense when goods are paid for or when they are sold; and recognizing rent expense when the cash is expended (paid out) or when the time period that the rental payment covers has expired.6 The statements show a $950 variation in income, from a high of +$550 in income statement 3, to a low of -$400 in income statement 6. If the accountant's goal is to measure income as the change in well-offness over the accounting period of January, then he or she must decide which of these statements best reflects the amount of resources the accounting entity could consume or dispose of (say, by paying out a dividend) and still be as well off at the end of the period as it was at the beginning.

EXHIBIT 4–9
A VARIETY OF INCOME STATEMENTS

Income Statement Number (all amounts in dollars)

	1	2	3	4	5	6	7	8
Revenue	1,000	1,000	1,000	1,000	500	500	500	500
Cost of sales	500	500	250	250	500	500	250	250
Rent expense	200	400	200	400	200	400	200	400
	700	900	450	650	700	900	450	650
Income	300	100	550	350	(200)	(400)	50	(150)

[6] Since three items are being measured — revenues, cost of sales, and rent expense — and each has two possible ways of being measured, there are 2^3 or eight possible income statements. You can see that as accounting choices increase, the number of possible "bottom lines" proliferates!

Recognizing and Measuring Revenues: Realization

Income statements 5 to 8 of Exhibit 4–9 show revenue to be only $500 — the cash received for one unit of the two that were sold. No indication in the revenue number is assigned to the fact that the second item has been sold but not yet paid for. This is a conservative measure of the change in economic well-being. But on the other hand, since the goods sold but not yet paid for at the time of sale may never be paid for, to show revenue from this transaction might be overly optimistic.

When there is a delay between a sale and the receipt of cash, should revenue be recognized when the article is sold or only when it is paid for? When is the economic well-being of the accounting entity changed — when the sale is made or when cash is received? Under accrual accounting, decisions regarding when to count revenue are based on whether the following criteria have been satisfied:

- The accounting entity has fulfilled its side of the bargain by providing essentially all the goods or services promised.
- There are relatively few costs that the accounting entity must still incur in order to complete the bargain.
- There is little uncertainty about both the *amount* of revenue to be received and the *timing* of its receipt.

These criteria are referred to as "revenue recognition criteria."

Deciding when to account for revenues requires professional judgment on the part of managers and accountants: in many situations the revenue recognition decision is fairly straightforward; in other situations it is not. In the above example $1,000 would probably be recognized as revenue in January, since in most such commercial retail transactions the revenue recognition criteria are fulfilled at the point of sale. However, if other factors cause any of the criteria to be less than fulfilled, revenue recognition will be delayed under the accrual model until the criteria are complied with. As an illustration, suppose that TTC had guaranteed the performance of the product that it sold, and that the product was a high-tech electronics component with about a 25% chance of failing. In such a situation the company has not provided all the services promised at the point of sale, and still may incur substantial warranty costs; thus, revenue recognition should be delayed until some time after the point of sale — that is, until the uncertainty surrounding fulfilment of these criteria has been resolved. This point may be even after TTC has received cash! For most retail transactions, however, the $1,000 would be recorded as revenue in January.

Accounting and Business Decision C

Suppose that on January 1, 1995, you send a cheque for $104 to Mercury Publishers for a one-year subscription to a weekly magazine. The publisher receives your cheque on January 3, deposits it in the company's bank account on the same day, and begins sending you the magazines on January 5. When should Mercury count the $104 as revenue, assuming it uses accrual accounting? Mercury has a fiscal year that ends on January 31.

Recognizing and Measuring Expenses: Matching

Deciding when revenue should be recognized is only half the income measurement problem. Since income is the net of revenues less expenses, the accountant must decide at what point in time to recognize expenses on the income statement.

Consider income statement 2 in Exhibit 4–9. If the $400 expended on January 1 for rent is counted as the rent expense, an income figure of $100 is produced. According to the definition of income we introduced earlier, this figure should indicate the amount that the accounting entity could consume or dispose of and still be as well off at the end of January as it was at the beginning. But this income figure could be misleading because, in addition to the $100 increment over the period, TTC also has the right to use the facility for a second month. This right to use the facility for an additional month is part of the "well-offness" of TTC. Under the accrual model the *matching* concept helps the accountant determine what portion of the total of $400 is to be accounted for as an expense in any given accounting period. The matching principle would seem to support a rent expense of just $200 in January.

An asset becomes an expense when it is consumed for the purpose of generating revenue. Thus, when the two units of TTC's product are sold in January and the realization criteria guide the accountant to record the $1,000 as revenue, the total cost of the two units — that is, $500 — is said to be *matched* against the revenue it helped generate. Thus, it becomes an expense of the same accounting period in which the revenue is recognized. Under the accrual accounting model, expense recognition through matching is therefore contingent upon revenue recognition. When part of an asset is used up in generating revenue, only the dollars representing the part used are matched to the revenue they helped generate. Note again that it is not the expenditure of cash itself that signals the recognition of an expense under the accrual model: that is done by first applying the revenue recognition criteria and then by matching expenses to the revenue thus determined.

In Exhibit 4–9, statements 1 through 4 show $1,000 in revenue; thus, revenue for both units has been recognized in January. Consequently, the "Cost of sales" expense to be matched against this revenue must be $500, and "Rent expense" must be $200, reflecting the using up of only one-half the total available rental resource. Accordingly, only income statement 1 among the first four statements is based on accrual accounting. If, however, after the revenue recognition criteria have been applied, only $500 in revenue is recognized in January (suppose, for example, that the uncertainties surrounding the measurement of revenue measurement are great, and are only resolved when actual cash is received), then only statement 7 is an accrual-based statement. It should be stressed that most typically, the entire $1,000 would be recognized, and thus statement 1 would be the only accrual income statement.

Accrual Versus Cash Accounting Models

Cash-basis and accrual-basis accounting systems use different rules to trigger recognition of revenue and expense items, and therefore yield different measures of income. Cash accounting recognizes revenues and expenses at the point in time when cash is received or cash disbursements are made. In fact, a cash accounting system is often called a "receipts and expenditures" system, and the terms "revenue," "expense," and "income" are reserved solely for accrual systems (although many people sometimes loosely use these terms when referring to cash inflows and outflows; this is why it makes good sense to be sure that you know exactly what accounting model people have in mind, whatever jargon they use).

The only completely cash-based income statement in Exhibit 4–9 is statement 8, which shows an income of negative $150. No attempt at applying either the revenue recognition criteria or the matching concept has been made in the accounting model of statement 8. In a cash-based accounting model, the -$150 in statement 8 is called "net operating cash flow." If we assume that accrual revenue in Exhibit 4–9 is measured by the $1,000 amount, then statements 2, 3, 4, 5, 6, and 7 are mixtures of accrual and cash accounting.

Which income statement in exhibit 4–9 is correct?

The answer to this question depends on the circumstances. If the users and preparers of accounting reports decide that accrual accounting is the system that should be used, because it provides a reasonable measure of the achievements of the accounting entity, then statement 1 is the one to choose. If the users and preparers wish to keep track of cash flows (in order to see if a bank loan is necessary, for instance), then model 8 is the appropriate one. In Canada and many other countries, audited financial statements issued by companies to external users must comply with accrual accounting; thus, in such situations, income statement 1 is compulsory. But cash flow information is also usually required as well.

Accounting and Business Decision D

Why do you think the financial statements issued with an audit opinion must be prepared under accrual accounting? What are the benefits and costs of such a general requirement to the various groups affected by financial statements?

For situations where accrual accounting is not compulsory, deciding which system to use (accrual, or cash basis, or one of the other "mixed" systems in Exhibit 4–9) is a matter of assessing the benefits and costs relating to the use of particular systems in the situation at hand. For example, suppose you are the chief financial officer (CFO) of a company that has ten separate and highly distinct divisions. You are faced with the problem of designing an accounting system suitable for evaluating the performance of each of the ten divisions; you must also determine bonuses for the divisional general managers. To these ends, you decide that each division will prepare an income statement. What rules should you require the income statements to follow? Should accrual accounting be used for such internal management purposes? (You know that it has to be used for the audited financial statements that are to be sent to your company's shareholders.) Should the cash model be used, or one of the mixed models? It depends on the benefits and costs. An example of determining such benefits and costs is set out in the case situation that follows.

DEMONSTRATION CASE

Varity Corporation

Varity Corporation is a large multinational industrial management company with three main lines of business: automotive components, farm machinery, and diesel engines. Corporatewide revenues for fiscal 1991 were $3.2 billion. Now headquartered in the United States, Varity was a Canadian-based company until the early 1990s, and one of the most important companies in Canadian business history. Back in the latter part of the 1960s, when Varity was known as Massey-Ferguson, the company was mainly a manufacturer of agricultural equipment. It distributed its tractors, combine harvesters, and other products for its North American sales region by means of a huge network of independent dealers. When the company shipped, say, a tractor to one of its dealers, it recorded revenue both for its external, audited financial statements, and for the internal management-accounting system that it used to evaluate and reward its managers. The accounting entry was of the following general format:

Dr Accounts receivable	XXX	
Cr Revenue		XXX

In the late 1960s, farm incomes were low and dealer inventories had built up to very high levels. In 1970 the company's top management decided to stop accounting for shipments to dealers as sales for internal or management accounting purposes, and to switch to a system that recorded revenue only when the dealer sold to the farmer. This was done to encourage the company's operating managers to focus their selling efforts on the real customer — the farmer (that is, rather than the dealer). The new revenue-accounting system for management accounting was a success, since inventory in dealers' hands decreased significantly.

In 1973, Varity adopted the same revenue-recognition system for its external financial accounting statements, since it wanted its internal management-accounting system to be consistent with its reports to outsiders. However, in 1979 the company switched back to its previous method of recognizing revenue for external reporting because — according to management — the company's major competitors had not adopted the new method.

Notice that legal ownership of the farm machinery was not the determining factor in 1973, when the company made its switch to the new method for financial accounting purposes, since the dealers were the legal owners once they received the machinery. Management presumably applied the revenue recognition criteria introduced in this chapter, and decided that waiting until the dealer shipped to the farmer was a better recognition point. However, the company found it difficult to rationalize the switch back in 1979.

Extensions of the Users' Needs Criterion: Efficient Markets and Economic Consequences

A fundamental question in accounting is this: "Which accounting system provides the best accounting information for the user, whatever the context (financial accounting, management accounting, tax accounting), keeping cost considerations in mind, of course?" This users' needs criterion is extremely important in accounting, and is an integral part of the conceptual framework described in this chapter. Other, related criteria for making accounting decisions have been suggested in the literature, however, and have been considered as well from time to time by those who set accounting standards. Two of these criteria are the efficient markets criterion and the economic consequences criterion.

The Efficient Markets Criterion

In the 1960s and early 1970s, considerable empirical and theoretical work was carried out at universities on the subject of the "efficiency" of well-organized markets for financial securities (for example, common shares), such as the stock exchanges in Montreal, Vancouver, Toronto, and Calgary. However, most of the research was performed on the New York Stock Exchange. Accounting researchers then applied the concept of financial-security market efficiency to numerous accounting issues, and an impressive literature built up over the years. The importance of the resulting efficient market hypothesis (EMH) to accounting decision-making is still unclear, however, because of conceptual and methodological problems in EMH research.

The notion behind EMH is explained succinctly in a now-classic article by William Beaver:[7] "A market is said to be efficient if security prices act *as if* they 'fully reflect' publicly available information, including financial statement data. In other words, in an efficient market the investor is playing a 'fair game' with respect to published information." So, the price for a share of common stock, as set in the stock market at any point in time, depends on all the information that is publicly available that could affect the price. If the common shares are those of a gold-mining company and the global demand for gold goes up, the gold-mining company's common share price will probably go up, all other things being equal. If the company's geologists discover that the company's main source of gold ore contains less precious metal per ton than previously thought, the common share price will decline after this news is announced.

EMH implies the following:

- That published information, such as financial statements, cannot be used to earn better-than-average returns, since the information seems to be already reflected in the stock's price.
- That prices of securities, such as common shares on a well-organized, competitive stock market, react quickly and in an unbiased manner to a variety of factors and events, including financial statement data (which may get into the market by leaks).
- That the stock market acts as if it uses a broad set of data to price securities, not just accounting numbers. Thus, changes to alternative accounting

[7] W.H. Beaver, "What Should Be the FASB's Objectives?" *Journal of Accountancy*, August 1973.

methods (with full disclosure) do not affect the market.

In stock markets such as the Toronto Stock Exchange and the Vancouver Stock Exchange, many people are continuously competing for an edge over everyone else. This means that when some new information about a company is released, it is quickly reflected in the price of the company's shares trading on the stock market.

After describing the EMH, Beaver went on to outline what he believed were its implications for accounting decision-making:

- Many financial accounting and reporting issues do not warrant an expenditure of decision-making resources, since the alternatives involved cost the firm the same to report, and since statement users incur little cost in converting from one method to their preferred method. According to this view, a company's accountants could, say, expense the cost of depreciable tangible capital assets, rather than depreciate the cost over the expected service life of the asset, and provide users with enough information to make their own depreciation calculations. Beaver suggested that companies should use one accounting method, with sufficient footnote disclosure to permit adjustment to the other method(s), and let the market interpret the data when pricing the company's securities.
- He suggested that the efficient market criterion also means that the "role of financial statement data is essentially a pre-emptive one — that is, to prevent abnormal returns accruing to individuals by trading upon inside information." He suggested that this leads to a disclosure policy based upon the notion that, if there are no additional costs of disclosure to the firm, there is *prima facie* evidence that the item in question should be disclosed. Presumably, "no additional cost" also includes *indirect* cost, such as loss of market if sensitive information is disclosed.
- Setters of accounting standards and other decision-makers — such as corporate managers, who decide on their company's financial accounting policies — should reconsider their concern for the "naïve" investor who, acting as a price-taker in an efficient, competitive stock market, faces a "fair game": the going price of the shares impounds — that is, already reflects — all publicly available information. Beaver suggested that "naïve" investors in an efficient market can only be harmed because of *inadequate* disclosure by the company, or by incurring transactions and other costs in a belief that they can "beat the market" by using financial accounting data. He argued that this also implies that accounting decision-makers should "not attempt to reduce the complex events of multi-million dollar corporations to the level of understanding of the naïve ... investor," and should not choose accounting methods that, for example, arbitrarily smooth income, since "the market can decide for itself how it wishes to interpret a given piece of information."
- Accountants must realize that consumers of information about companies have other information sources, in addition to financial statement data. Thus, setters of accounting standards and other decision-makers should attempt to minimize the total cost of providing information about the firm. If a given type of information can be provided via the financial accounting system at less cost than an alternative source, Beaver suggested that the accounting system should provide it in that manner.

The potential implications of the EMH for accounting decision-making are significant, and shift the focus of financial accounting away from worrying about how to best measure assets, liabilities, revenues, and expenses, and toward questions of disclosure. In other words, the debates about which revenue recognition or expense measurement approaches are best for a certain user's needs become very secondary, since the disclosure of important facts is really the key.

It is important, however, to consider some possible misinterpretations of the EMH for accounting decision-making, along with some possible shortcomings of the concept, and of the research upon which its accounting implications rest. Following are some possible misinterpretations:

- *Common shares and other securities are priced "correctly" on the stock exchange — that is, they reflect the intrinsic value of the firm — and thus financial accounting is irrelevant.* As Beaver pointed out, "merely because the market is efficient with respect to published data does not imply that market prices are also efficient with respect to non-published information. Disclosure is a substantive issue." The British accounting academic Whittington makes this point even more forcefully when he writes that "efficiency" in the context of efficient-markets theory "means that the market discounts information quickly, even instantaneously. It does *not* mean that the result of this process is a set of share prices which reflect the intrinsic worth of shares."[8] So the role of deciding which information to disclose still exists for financial accounting, even if we accept the EMH as being relevant.

- *Simply find and use the accounting method that correlates best with security prices.* This misinterpretation ignores such issues as the relative cost of reported versus nonreported methods. That is, suppose a nonreported accounting method is more highly associated with security prices than a currently reported method; it does not follow from this that the nonreported method should be adopted, since its cost may exceed the cost of the reported method.

Another misinterpretation concerns the fact that the users of financial accounting information are many and have varied information needs. We saw in Chapters 2 and 3 that there are numerous users of financial accounting information. Since the EMH is concerned mainly with users who buy, sell, and hold shares in an efficient securities market, it focuses — as far as accounting decision-making is concerned — on investors and creditors. Ignored are other users, such as employees, investors, and creditors of firms whose securities are *not* traded in an efficient market.

Apart from these serious potential misinterpretations, EMH research has also been criticized by academics, mainly on methodological grounds. Even so, the EMH concept has significant implications both for setters of accounting standards and for other accounting decision-makers, since it serves as a general reminder that disclosure is extremely important and should not be treated trivially.[9] For example, for the purpose of promoting stock market efficiency, securities regulators across Canada require companies that issue securities to the public to disclose information concerning the company immediately, whether the information is "good news" or "bad news."

[8] G. Whittington, "Beware Efficient Markets Theory," *The Accountants' Magazine*, April 1979.

[9] Accounting researchers and others interested in understanding the characteristics and implications of efficient securities markets distinguish between various types of market efficiency. The type that is of concern to accountants is "semi-strong efficiency," the characteristics of which are described in the chapter's text. Other types of market efficiency, such as "strong-form efficiency," in which share prices are assumed to impound *all* information (both public and private), are not descriptive of how actual securities markets work, and do not have implications for accounting decision-making.

The Economic Consequences Criterion

Under the "economic consequences" approach to accounting decision-making, the focus shifts to the impact an accounting choice can be expected to have on the welfare of the users and other stakeholders of the accounting entity. An example: The CICA's standard-setting committee suggested that Canadian companies account for research expenditures as expenses instead of as intangible capital assets to be amortized. Accountants, managers, and others who were concerned about the economic consequences of such an accounting rule then pointed out that this would result in a decline in reported accounting income for smaller, growth-oriented, research-based companies; banks and other financial institutions might then reduce or cut off such companies' access to loans. The argument was that suppliers of capital to this sector of the industry would perceive higher risks because of the lower net income, and thus charge higher interest or be unwilling to provide firms with any financing at all. Thus, there would be a decrease in research efforts and competition would decline. Such arguments were not successful, however; the CICA did indeed adopt GAAP requiring that companies expense research expenditures in the accounting period that those expenditures were incurred. Note that someone who believed in the efficient markets criterion would think that this debate was a waste of time, as long as research costs were fully disclosed in the footnotes to the financial statements.

A variation of the economic consequences approach to accounting decision-making focuses exclusively on the effect of financial accounting reports on the *sender* of the reports — that is, on management. Accounting researchers Prakash and Rappaport[10] suggested that when managers are faced with financial accounting alternatives that result in different pictures of the firm's performance, they can (a) modify the description of the performance either by selecting one of the alternative accounting methods or by altering disclosure, (that is, omitting important information), or (b) modify their *real* management decisions (that is, make different operating, investing, and/or financing decisions than they otherwise would have), possibly adversely with respect to the company's interests, so that reported results are what management feels outsiders want to see, or (c) modify their objectives. This phenomenon — that of accounting reports affecting the *sender* in addition to the receiver, or traditional user — is termed by Prakash and Rappaport "information inductance."

In the late 1970s, when the economic consequences criterion began to receive considerable attention in the financial accounting and business press, Stephen Zeff stressed the significance of the change in orientation away from traditional accounting decision-making approaches (which are based on the ideas in the conceptual framework described earlier in this chapter) toward the "economic consequences" approach:[11]

> *The economic consequences argument represents a veritable revolution in accounting thought. Until recently, accounting policy-making was either assumed to be neutral in its effect or, if not neutral, it was not held out to the public for being responsible for those effects. Today, these assumptions are being severely questioned, and the subject of social and economic consequences has become* the *central contemporary issue in accounting.*

[10] P. Prakash and A. Rappaport, "Information Inductance and Its Significance for Accounting," *Accounting, Organizations and Society*, Vol. 2, no. 1, 1977, pp. 29–38.
[11] S.A. Zeff, "The Rise of 'Economic Consequences'," *Journal of Accountancy*, December 1978, pp. 56–63. Reprinted with permission from the American Institute of Certified Public Accountants, Inc.

Unfortunately, identifying which economic consequences are important enough to consider is a rather perplexing problem. Some groups may prefer certain types of economic consequences to be considered; other groups may object and prefer other types of consequences.

Not all writers feel comfortable with the idea that accounting decision-makers should employ the "economic consequences" approach. For example, David Solomons (whose ideas are described in the "Accounting, Organizations, and Society" section of this chapter) believes that financial accounting information must have a high degree of "neutrality" and thus "representational accuracy." Financial accounting alternatives, according to Solomons, cannot be neutral, and therefore cannot be reliable, if they are selected "for the purpose of producing some chosen effect on human behavior." Solomons draws an analogy between his desired approach to accounting and the discipline of cartography, pointing out that people "do not judge a map by the behavioral effect it produces. The distribution of natural wealth or rainfall shown on the map may lead to population shifts or changes in industrial location, which the government may like or dislike. That should be of no concern to the cartographer. We judge his map by how well it represents the facts. People can then react to it as they will."[12]

This concept of "representational accuracy" and "neutrality" is not new in the accounting literature. For example, often the accountant is viewed as a sort of trained observer, or reporter. There is, thus, an apparent conflict between the "economic consequences" approach to accounting decision-making and the traditional "economic reality" approach, which focuses on neutrality and on reporting "what is." The conflict appears to have two extremes:

- A "pure" economic consequences approach asserts that accounting decisions are to be made on the basis of what effect accounting decision-makers feel the resulting reports should have on the behaviour of various user groups. An example of this would be the government mandating particular financial accounting standards in order to *influence* (not to measure the *results* of) economic decisions: this almost happened in Canada in the early 1980s and in fact happened in the United States in 1971. While we won't go into the technical details of either of these situations, suffice to say that both resulted in severe stress on the credibility of financial accounting.[13] The reason is that the approach turns financial accounting upside down, and a desired economic consequence rather than the goal of fairly measuring income becomes the stimulus for accounting decisions.
- A pure "neutrality" approach attempts to measure and report the "economic reality" of the situation. Deciding what the important aspects of economic reality are for the various user groups is often a frustrating exercise for accounting decision-makers.

A compromise position between these extremes was taken by the 1980 CICA research study *Corporate Reporting: Its Future Evolution*, by Edward Stamp, which urged setters of accounting standards to adopt "neutrality" or "freedom from bias" as a primary criterion. At the same time, however, "standard setters will be wise to make an assessment of the likely economic consequences of a

[12] D. Solomons, "The Politicization of Accounting," *Journal of Accountancy*, December 1978, pp. 65–72. Reprinted with permission from the American Institute of Certified Public Accountants, Inc.

[13] For a lively description of the Canadian example, see "Government Intervention — The PIP Grant Accounting Controversy," by Robert H. Crandall of Queen's University, in *Cost and Management*, September–October 1983. This is the official journal of the Society of Management Accountants of Canada; it now goes by the name *CMA Magazine*.

proposed standard if they are to avoid creating unnecessary trouble for themselves and for the community after the standard is issued" [pp. 60–61].

Accounting, Organizations, and Society

The quotation that opened this chapter suggested that accounting can sometimes, in certain circumstances, ignore the obvious and portray a result that is the exact opposite of what the qualitative characteristic "representational faithfulness" requires. Such accounting also does not achieve the qualitative characteristic of "neutrality," since the resulting information is biased — in the case of Conrad's *Heart of Darkness*, apparently tragically so.

Some observers of accounting practice doubt that financial accounting can ever be neutral and representationally faithful; others believe that it is possible to set accounting standards and affect accounting practice so that these desirable qualitative characteristics are achieved to a reasonable degree. The article excerpts that follow have been pulled from a debate between advocates of these two positions: David Solomons of the Wharton School, University of Pennsylvania, who argues that accounting can and must be neutral, is originally from the United Kingdom and has held many prestigious positions of academic and professional leadership in accounting; Tony Tinker, who argues that accounting cannot be neutral and representationally faithful, is well known for his leadership of the "radical" accounting view. He teaches at Baruch College, City University of New York, and also originally comes from the United Kingdom. The debate was prompted by Tinker's publication of *Paper Prophets: A Social Critique of Accounting*.

Accounting and Social Change: A Neutralist View*

by David Solomons

Abstract

This paper takes the position that the task of accountants is to provide information as free from bias as possible that will be useful to decision makers (possibly including accountants themselves) who may be concerned with social and economic issues. Though accountants may sometimes fail to achieve the faithful representation of economic phenomena, that should be their goal. In developing this argument, the paper criticizes Radical Accounting, as represented by Tony Tinker's Paper Prophets, *and others who assert that accounting policies should be chosen for their supposedly desirable economic consequences rather than for their capacity to depict relevant phenomena faithfully. Like journalists, accountants should report the news, not make it. Neutrality in accounting may not always be easy to secure, but without it the credibility of accounting is endangered ...*

With social change in the broadest sense accounting has little to do. One of the most significant social changes that has occurred in this century is the dramatic improvement in the position of women. Like most social changes, this one has been accompanied by economic changes, such as changes in the pattern of consumption and the distribution of income. Another great social change during the last fifty years is the disappearance of colonialism. That too has brought economic changes in its wake. To suggest any direct connection between those broad develop-

The following excerpt, Tony Tinker's response, and Solomons's rejoinder all are found in Accounting, Organizations and Society, *Vol. 16, no. 3, pp. 287–312, 1991. Reprinted with permission from Elsevier Science Ltd., Oxford, England.*

ments and accounting would be farfetched indeed.

But on a smaller stage, accounting does have a part to play. It has been asserted, for example, that an accounting standard that requires research and development expenditures to be written off as incurred, in spite of the probable future benefits that are expected to flow from it, depresses the earnings of small immature high technology companies and thereby discourages technological innovation. Without regard, for the moment, to the truth or falsity of that assertion, it exemplifies the part that accounting may play in encouraging or inhibiting social and economic change.

The question to be addressed here is this. Should accountants see themselves and their discipline as agents to promote (or sometimes to retard) social and economic change? Or should they see themselves as providers of unbiased information, to facilitate social and economic activity by others? By "others" I mean, of course, to include accountants themselves in their capacity as citizens, not as accountants.

A Radical View of Accounting

I want to leave no doubt as to where I stand on this issue. I believe that accountants are like journalists. They should report the news, not make it. This is the view that I shall explore more fully in what follows. But in case it is thought that the opposite view is merely a straw man, I propose to bring into court an outspoken proponent of that other view, and, so far as possible I shall allow him to speak for himself. I am refering to Dr. Tony Tinker, of Baruch College, CUNY. His views are set out at length in a book published in 1985, entitled *Paper Prophets: A Social Critique of Accounting*. Tinker and others who think like him use the term "radical accounting" as a label for their views, and it will be convenient if I follow their example . . .

A Plea for Neutrality

If accounting is to retain any credibility — and without credibility it is worthless — its guiding light must be neutrality in financial reporting. The FASB has defined neutrality as the "absence in reported information of bias intended to attain a predetermined result or to induce a particular mode of behavior." This is a guidepost that all standard setting bodies should follow, and the FASB's record in this respect has been good. Dennis Beresford, the chairman of the Board, reaffirmed the importance that the Board attaches to this concept in an address on 1 November, 1988 to a gathering of financial executives. "Neutrality," he said, "is written into our Mission Statement as a primary consideration. And the neutrality concept dominates every Board meeting discussion, every informal conversation, and every memorandum that is written at the FASB."

In a May 1986 address by Arthur Wyatt, then a member of the FASB, there is a clear recognition that neutrality is not always easy to achieve.

The Board believes that its conclusions should be as neutral as they can be when considering the various competing interests within our society ... Being neutral in this activity does not mean being unaware of potential consequences, but it does mean focusing on the accounting and economic issues and submerging other biases that might influence the conclusions reached ... As private sector standard setters ... our mission is to establish and improve standards of financial accounting and reporting so that decision makers have available credible, concise and understandable financial information. That mission precludes placing any particular interest above the interests of the many who rely on financial information ...

I draw attention to Wyatt's recognition that neutrality means "submerging other biases that might influence the conclusions reached." Radicals like Tinker question whether reported information can ever be neutral, because the preparer will always have some biases that will creep in. The bias may be due to a desire to avoid taxation, or to increase managerial bonuses, or to keep reported profits down to avoid public censure for overcharging, or, for those who see accounting as an instrument of the class struggle, to benefit capital at the expense of labor. It is perhaps true that perfect neutrality of information can never be achieved. But it would be as foolish to stop *seeking* it on that account as it would be to stop trying to reduce air and water pollution because completely pure air and pure water can never be attained, or to stop seeking fair-minded judges on the ground that no human being is entirely free from bias, or (to return to an analogy that I use earlier) to stop esteeming journalists who know the difference between reporting and editorializing. We know how much credibility newspapers have in totalitarian countries. If those responsible for regulating accounting ever abandon neutrality as a guiding light, accounting will have lost all value as a provider of useful information. It would then be no more than an exercise in futility.

The Accountant as Partisan

by Tony Tinker

David Solomons is an evangelist, not a positivist. He does not say that accounting *is* neutral; only that it should be. We might agree on this point, provided his "neutrality" was tempered and informed by a notion of social justice that acknowledged the diversity of conflicting social interests invested in accounting situations, and that accounting inevitably takes sides in such conflicts. A candid admission by David Solomons of accounting's partisanship in social conflicts would then open up for investigation how we might make the accountant's choice of sides a deliberate and systematic one: a choice that is socially reflective and critically self-conscious.

Unfortunately, Solomons never undertakes this kind of analysis. Instead, he relies on spurious analogies about cartography ... and journalism in an attempt to legitimatize the neutrality of the FASB and the status quo. Below I question the validity of these analogies and the fallacious notion of financial cartography that springs from them.

Remembering Jim Jones, and Jim and Tammy Bakker, we must be mindful that evangelists have a checkered history. In David Solomons' case, I will argue that his failure to appreciate the radical accounting literature leaves him closer to Canute than to Moses in his call to reverse the tide of radical accounting thought.

The Assumptions of Financial Cartography

The essence of Solomons' financial cartography is that accounting should confine itself to accurately measuring and reporting the monetary values associated with market transactions ... Financial symbols are the ultimate data for Solomons because, for him, they "faithfully represent" economic reality. Accordingly, he opposes those who question the integrity of financial symbols by trespassing beyond the market realm to their political and social underpinnings. These are areas in which, he argues, accountants have "no special expertise"...

Solomons believes that economic reality exists, independent of our apprehension of it, and that this is the ultimate touchstone of truthfulness and accuracy for accounting symbols ... While bias, distortion and "noise" may interfere in short term reporting, economic reality eventually prevails in business performance and survival. Thus, for Solomons, accounting *should* report on this underlying economic reality ...

Consider the commonsense examples Solomons offers to bolster his case for financial cartography: journalism, map-making, and telephone communications. Does the telephone really, "convey one party's thoughts to the other"? ... Surely, the telephone doesn't convey "thoughts" but what people say. Thoughts and words may be made to differ, intentionally or otherwise. Even if words are like those of Lavinia in Shakespeare's *Titus Andronicus* — "the pure engine of thought" — there is no guarantee that they will conform to "what is understood." The telephone is selective, and inevitably reflects intended and unintended biases ...

Do we really, "judge a map by how well it represents the facts ... not ... by the behavioral effects it produces"? ... Color and size "distortions" to the Manhattan and London subway maps actually facilitate "the behavioral effect of" reaching a destination. Moreover, maps have frequently been political tools in struggles to secure behavioral compliance. European colonial powers "enlarged" their own vicinities and diminished those of others. These "errors" have prompted a flurry of "corrections" in recent years. Maps are never mere miniatures of the original; they are shaped by jingoistic, political, recreational, religious, economic, technical, and otherwise. As the semanticist Alfred Korzybski noted, "The map is not the territory" ...

Consider an Australasian map of the world that "inverts" centuries of Eurocentric cartography. Eurocentrics will no doubt argue that this inversion is inconsequential, provided the globe is eventually restored to its "normal" position ...

Solomons' Political Lacunae

David Solomons does not say that journalists actually "do" report the news, only that "they should." Similarly, he recognizes that bad cartography does occur, and that "the need to be selective ... does not normally (although it could) rob the map of its neutrality" ... Further, he catalogues a range of real and potential violations of Representational Faithfulness in accounting: ... proposals to exclude leases from balance sheets ...; the amortization of actuarial pension fund gains and losses; the FASB's adherence to historical cost rather than current cost accounting — something he regards as "the primary threat to the credibility of accounting standard setting" ...

How does Solomons account for the variegations in interpretation of Representational Faithfulness in accounting, journalism, and cartography? In the main, he doesn't. He gives scant attention to analyzing transgressions. Like Edmund Burke, he seems resigned to the presence of a "swinish multitude," but refuses to dignify its presence with any systematic theoretical interrogation.

Research that investigates accounting errors and distortions by exploring their political and social structural underpinnings is curtly dismissed by Solomons. He rejects the ... notion that regulatory bodies, such as the FASB, are captive of the industry they purport to regulate ...

Representational Faithfulness can only be justified by a process of infinite regression to ever-higher criteria for validation. In this sense, it has no final authority and is based on an arbitrary assumption ...

But what meta-meta-criterion legitimates the meta-criterion of usefulness; especially one that doesn't entertain conflicts between classes of people about "usefulness"? Even if we were to answer this question satisfactorily, it only invites another about what criterion to employ at the next higher level, and the next, *ad infinitum*. This is infinite regress; Solomons' criterion of Representational Faithfulness is ultimately founded on an unexamined (arbitrary) premise ...

[David Solomons's Rejoinder]

... At the end of this debate, we are as far apart as ever. Tinker and I simply have different notions of what accounting is about. I think its function is to convey unbiased information on which users can base their own decisions. I acknowledged in my paper that, accountants being human, the avoidance of all bias may not always be achieved; but that should be the aim ...

Representational faithfulness is at the root of our differences. I think it is central to accounting's mission. Tinker simply dismisses it: "... the search for Representational Faithfulness is futile because there is nothing to seek!" He then states: "Ironically, Solomons himself provides one of the most convincing cases against representational faithfulness and confirming the arbitrariness of accounting signs, in his advocacy of current cost over historical cost accounting. Historical cost is clearly a more accurate record of 'what actually happened'." If there is indeed "nothing to seek," we are really in bad shape, unless we are all willing to become solipsists, and dismiss the external world as fantasy. If signs are "arbitrary" and are "independent" of what is being signified, then we are all beating the air, *including the philosopher who makes such a statement, for his signs are also independent of the reality that he is vainly trying to depict.*

As for historical cost accounting, it does indeed give an accurate record of *some* of the things that happened in the past, but it fails to record other relevant events (e.g. relative value changes, price level changes) that may supervene between the date of a transaction and the accounting date. It therefore does not result in faithful representation ...

It is unnecessary for Tinker to assert that accounting measures are "socially constructed ..." Of course they are. That is why it is important to make them, to the best of our ability, representationally faithful. The same is true of other socially important measures such as the census, price indices, measures of GNP, or statistics of road deaths following a change in the speed limit. It is irresponsible to argue that these should *seek* to do anything but represent what they purport to represent ...

CHAPTER SUMMARY

Chapter 4 first described a conceptual framework for financial accounting that included objectives, users, elements, qualitative characteristics, recognition and measurement criteria, and pervasive constraints. The importance of professional judgment in making accounting decisions, including applying a conceptual framework, was explained, and the attributes of such judgment were listed.

The accrual accounting model, based upon realization and matching, was then described and compared with the cash-basis accounting model. Neither model (nor any variations) was claimed to be "correct," since user needs and other constraints were important factors. Next, the efficient markets hypothesis and the economic consequences criterion were explained, along with their implications for financial accounting. The EMH suggests that for accounting entities whose common shares trade on well-established stock exchanges, deciding what information to disclose and how to disclose it are the main issues in financial accounting. The economic consequences criterion reminds those who set accounting standards and make accounting choices that the welfare of users and other stakeholders in the accounting entity cannot be ignored. The chapter text material finished with a "debate" between two accounting professors over whether neutrality was an achievable goal in accounting.

Suggested Answers to Accounting and Business Decisions

Decision A

The definition of a liability in Exhibit 4–4, which comes from the *CICA Handbook's* section 1000, is: "obligations of an entity arising from past transactions or events, the settlement of which may result in the transfer or use of assets, the provision of services or other yielding of economic benefits in the future." QUE Company is an accounting entity, and it has signed a contract (the lease agreement) that — although it may not be a past transaction as the term transaction is described in Chapter 3 — is surely a past event. To settle this obligation, QUE will have to make monthly payments of $300 in the future (for four years) — payments that seem virtually unavoidable because of the significant penalty. This obligation appears to qualify under the definition of a liability, and should appear as such on QUE's balance sheet.

The journal entry to record the first month's rent is:

Dr Interest expense (an income statement account)	113.92	
Dr Lease obligation (a balance sheet account)	186.08	
Cr Cash		300.00

The $113.92 is computed by multiplying the liability of $11,392.19 by 1%, since QUE has in effect borrowed to acquire the delivery truck.

Decision B

Capital lease arrangements

In Accounting and Business Decision A and the example situation on which it was based, it was argued that QUE should account for the delivery truck lease arrangement as the creation of an asset and liability. Deciding that the "substance" of the arrangement resulted in an asset and a liability required an assessment as to whether the definitions of asset and liability were fulfilled. We decided that they were, since the lease was for the entire expected life of the delivery truck and could not be broken without severe penalty. But what if a lease agreement is only for part, say 60%, of the expected useful life of a machine? And what constitutes a "severe penalty"? Quite possibly, particular lease arrangements could be written so as to make identifying the substance quite a challenge.

Paying a signing bonus to an established major league baseball star

Suppose the bonus was for $1 million — should it be accounted for as an asset or as an expense of the baseball team? Is the substance of the transaction such that an asset is created? Or do we have an expense to be recorded on the income statement of the current accounting period? Applying the definitions of "asset" and "expense" from Exhibit 4–4 would require a detailed assessment of the facts of the particular bonus situation. For example, if the established star was young, healthy, and at the beginning of what was expected to be a very successful career of, say, ten years or so, then accounting for the payment as an asset might be justified. In such a case, amortizing the payment by annual amortization expense journal entries would also be required.

Suppose next that the established star was in the twilight of a great career, and that the team purchased the contract and paid the signing bonus just for a short-term box office boost to take advantage of the great player's name one last time (as happened to Babe Ruth). In this case, accounting for the signing bonus as an expense would seem more reasonable. Many accountants would also argue that expense treatment makes more sense even in the case of the young star, given the uncertainties of professional sport and the human condition (just look at what happened to Mario Lemieux and Bobby Orr). This is where the aspect of reliability called "conservatism" (see Exhibit 4–5) comes into play.

Accounting for depreciation expense

We saw in the On Ice example in Chapter 1, and in other examples, that depreciation accounting under historic cost is fairly arbitrary, and subject to the numerous uncertainties that face much of financial accounting. Just how do we know what a capital asset's expected service life is? Companies and industry associations have considerable data on the physical deterioration of various classes of machinery, equipment, and buildings, but accelerated obsolescence resulting from economic factors often means that capital assets are disposed of even though they still are physically sound. It is true, then, that depreciation accounting offers a challenge to accountants. This does not mean that it should be ignored; it does mean, however, that users should be especially vigilant when it comes to interpreting the significance of somewhat "fuzzy" accounting numbers such as depreciation expense.

Decision C

If the accrual accounting model is to be followed, we must decide when the revenue criteria are fulfilled. A possible analysis of this specific situation might run as follows: When the magazine publisher receives your money, it has not yet been earned because no magazines have been mailed to you. Mercury Publishers earns the $104 at the rate of $2 per week, by sending out weekly editions of the magazine. In accounting for the revenue in this situation, only $2 per week should be recognized; the remaining portion of the cash already received by Mercury at any point in time is in a very real sense a liability owed to the subscriber (you!) by the magazine publisher, pending satisfaction of the obligation under the subscription agreement. Mercury would account for these events under the accrual model as follows:

January 3, 1995 — Mercury receives your cheque:

Dr Cash	104	
Cr Unearned subscription revenue (a current liability on the balance sheet)		104

The account "Unearned subscription revenue" complies with the definition of a liability in Exhibit 4–4.

January 5, 1995 — Mercury mails out the first magazine:

Dr Unearned subscription revenue	2	
Cr Revenue		2

This first $2 no longer qualifies as a liability, and now qualifies as a revenue.

Of course, Mercury would probably have thousands of subscribers, and would design journal entries to account for all the cash and revenues together instead of for each subscriber individually. Note that the matching concept would require Mercury to estimate and account for the expense of possible returned magazines.

Decision D

Financial statements issued with an audit opinion must be prepared under accrual accounting because accrual accounting is much more comprehensive than cash-basis accounting. A more complete picture of financial position and results of operations is obtained when receivables and payables are accounted for. An audit opinion — which reports on financial position and results of operations — is more consistent with accrual accounting than with cash basis accounting. Of course, other types of audit opinions may require that auditors report on cash flows, or other accounting bases. In such cases, these other approaches to accounting would be preferable.

Assessing the benefits and costs to the various groups affected by financial statements of having a general requirement that the accrual model be followed, is quite a challenge.

Benefits include the following:

- To shareholders of companies in which ownership and management are separated: receive a more holistic, complete picture of assets and liabilities entrusted to management; are better able to hold management accountable for the effective management of these accounting elements; receive a more comprehensive income measure.
- To managers: have an incentive to effectively manage not only cash flows, but also other economic flows, since they are held accountable for accrued assets and liabilities, and all items under the accrual model.

Costs include the following:

- To shareholders: the cost of auditing is probably higher than for a pure, cash-basis accounting system.
- The resulting accounting reports require more expertise, and costly advice.

KEY TERMS

Accrual accounting is a financial accounting system that records revenues when they have been earned and expenses when they have been incurred. Criteria for helping managers and accountants judge when revenues and expenses should be recorded are provided, in general terms, by the revenue recognition and matching criteria (see glossary entries for these terms, below). The CICA's *Terminology for Accountants* provides the following definition:

The method of recording transactions by which revenues and expenses are reflected in the determination of results for the period in which they are considered to have been earned and incurred, respectively, whether or not such transactions have been settled finally by the receipt or payment of cash or its equivalent.

The same source defines the term **accrue** as (p. 5):

To record a claim by or against another party that has increased with the passage of time or the receipt or rendering of services (e.g., interest, taxes, royalties, wages) but is not yet enforceable at the time of recording.

So accrual accounting is far different from the cash accounting model (also called the cash basis of accounting and the cash flow basis of accounting; see glossary entry, below).

Assets are economic resources controlled by an entity as a result of past transactions or events and from which future economic benefits may be obtained.

Benefit versus cost constraint alerts managers and accountants to the requirement that benefits expected to arise from providing information in financial statements should exceed the cost of doing so. The determination of which parties enjoy which benefits and which parties incur which costs is substantially a judgment process.

Cash accounting model (also called cash basis of accounting, cash flow accounting) records only cash receipts (that is, inflows of cash) and disbursements (that is, outlays of cash); it does not account for revenues and expenses, as these two terms are defined in accrual accounting.

Comparability is a characteristic of the relationship between two pieces of information. It enables users to identify similarities in and differences between the information provided by two sets of financial statements. Comparability is important when comparing the financial statements of two different entities and when comparing the financial statements of the same entity over two periods or at two different points in time. Comparability in the financial statements of an entity is enhanced when the same accounting policies are used consistently from period to period. Consistency helps prevent misconceptions that may result from the application of different accounting policies in different periods. When a change in accounting policy is deemed to be appropriate, disclosure of the effects of the change may be necessary in order to maintain comparability.

Conceptual framework in accounting refers to a system consisting of objectives, users, elements, qualitative characteristics, recognition and measurement criteria, and pervasive constraints. The Financial Accounting Standards Board (the FASB, the organization that sets GAAP in the United States, and that also has strongly influenced accounting thought elsewhere) wrote that an accounting conceptual framework is:

a constitution ... a coherent system of interrelated objectives and fundamentals that can lead to consistent standards and that prescribes the nature, function, and limits of financial accounting and financial statements. The objectives identify the goals and purposes of accounting. The fundamentals are the underlying concepts of accounting, concepts that guide the selection of events, and the means of summarizing and communicating them to interested parties. Concepts of that type are fundamental in the sense that other concepts flow from them and repeated reference to them will be necessary in establishing, interpreting, and applying accounting and reporting standards.[14]

[14] FASB, *Scope and Implications of the Conceptual Framework Project*, December 2, 1976.

Conservatism. When uncertainty exists, estimates of a conservative nature attempt to ensure that assets, revenues, and gains are not overstated and, conversely, that liabilities, expenses, and losses are not understated. However, conservatism does not encompass the deliberate understatement of assets, revenues, and gains or the deliberate overstatement of liabilities, expenses, and losses.

Descriptive theories attempt to help us *explain* and *understand* what is going on in human affairs and nature.

Economic consequences. Under the economic consequences approach to accounting decision-making, the focus shifts to the impact an accounting choice can be expected to have on the welfare of the users and other stakeholders of the accounting entity.

Efficient markets hypothesis refers to a set of ideas that are based on the role of accounting and other information in setting prices in stock exchanges and similar markets. If the prices, on average, of the shares that are traded in such markets quickly impound all publicly available information, including information in financial statements, then disclosure may become more important than measurement in making financial accounting decisions.

Elements are general categories of items that make up financial statements. They include the following categories: assets, liabilities, equity, revenues, expenses, gains, and losses.

Equity is the ownership interest in the assets of a profit-oriented enterprise after its liabilities are deducted. More generally, it is the "residual interest in assets after deducting related liabilities" (*Terminology for Accountants*). The term "equity" is used in several ways in accounting and business; this is only one of its meanings.

Expenses are decreases in economic resources, through outflows, or reductions of assets, or incurrences of liabilities, resulting from an entity's ordinary revenue-generating or service-delivery activities.

Feedback value. Information that confirms or corrects previous predictions has feedback value.

Gains are increases in equity from peripheral or incidental transactions and events affecting an entity.

Going concern assumption is the view that an accounting entity will continue in operation in the foreseeable future.

Liabilities are obligations of an entity arising from past transactions or events, the settlement of which may result in the transfer or use of assets, the provision of services, or other yielding of economic benefits in the future.

Losses are decreases in equity from peripheral or incidental transactions and events affecting an entity.

Matching is a measurement principle that involves tracing and linking expenses to the revenues that the expenses have helped to generate, and ensuring that those revenues and their matched expenses are both recorded as income statement items in the same accounting period. The residual obtained by subtracting matched expenses from revenues is the measure of income under the accrual accounting model.

Materiality constraint. Users are interested in information that may affect their decision making. Materiality is the term used to describe the significance of financial statement information to decision makers. An item of information, or an aggregate of items, is material if it is probable that its omission or misstatement would influence or change a decision. Materiality is a matter of professional judgment in the particular circumstances. In *Terminology for Accountants*, the term is defined as follows:

> *The quality of being important. As a general rule, in the context of financial reporting, materiality may be judged in relation to the reasonable prospect of an item or aggregate of items being significant to users in making decisions.*

Measurement criteria, according to CICA 1000.53, relate to "the process of determining the amount at which an item is recognized in the financial statements." The *CICA Handbook* goes on to describe current accounting practice as "primarily using the historical cost basis of measurement whereby transactions and events are recognized in financial statements at the amount of cash or cash equivalents paid or received or the fair value ascribed to them when they took place."

Money unit assumption refers to the view that financial accounting deals mainly in quantitative measures based upon money, and that the money unit used is stable.

Neutrality. Information is neutral when it is free from bias that would lead users toward making decisions that are influenced by the way the information is measured or presented. Bias in measurement occurs when a measure tends to consistently overstate or understate the items being measured. In the selection of accounting principles, bias may occur when the selection is made with the interests of particular users or with particular economic or political objectives in mind.

Normative theories are theories that attempt to tell us how things *should* be done, while descriptive theories attempt to help us *explain* and *understand* what is going on in human affairs and nature. The conceptual framework for financial accounting is mainly a normative theory.

Periodicity assumption refers to the preparation of financial statements at periodic intervals over the life of an accounting entity.

Predictive value. Information that helps users predict an entity's future income and cash flows has predictive value.

Professional judgment in making accounting decisions requires that due care, objectivity, and integrity be brought to bear within the framework provided by accounting and other applicable standards (such as laws), by experienced and knowledgeable people. Although the important attributes of such judgment may be listed (see Exhibit 4–8), acquiring the ability to exercise such judgment is a long-term developmental process.

Qualitative characteristics, in accounting, are those parts of a financial accounting conceptual framework that consist of what accountants believe are the desirable features that financial accounting information should have. This is an inherently normative part of financial accounting's conceptual framework. It provides a set of criteria against which to assess accounting information. If the information does not meet the standards to an acceptable degree, then it should not be included as part of the financial statements. Determining just what an acceptable degree is in particular circumstances requires experience in applying judgment.

Realization. In accrual accounting, revenue is recognized and recorded not necessarily when cash is received or paid, but when the transaction has proceeded to some point at which it can be logically expected to be carried through to completion. This point is called the realization point. In other words, revenue is realized when the economic value is assumed to flow out of the firm to the customer, regardless of whether cash has actually been received from the customer. Realization is one of the key measurement rules of accrual accounting. In the dry cleaner example, revenue would be recognized when the cleaned garment was first returned to its owner, because that is the point at which the service is assumed to be completed or "realized" in accounting terminology. Of course, the choice of realization point will depend on the nature of the industry, and even on the nature of the individual business. Choosing an appropriate realization point at which to recognize revenue is one of the critical decisions an accountant must make in designing an accounting system.

Relevance. For the information provided in financial statements to be useful, it must be relevant to the decisions made by users.

Reliability means that the information provided in financial statements is in agreement with the actual underlying transactions and events, the agreement is capable of independent verification, and the information is reasonably free from error and bias.

Representational faithfulness means that transactions and events are accounted for and presented in a manner that conveys their substance rather than necessarily their legal or other form.

Revenue recognition criteria. Under accrual accounting, decisions on when to count revenue focus on whether the following criteria have been satisfied:

- The accounting entity has fulfilled its side of the bargain by providing essentially all the goods or services promised.
- There are relatively few costs that the accounting entity must still incur in order to complete the bargain.
- There is little uncertainty about both the *amount* of revenue to be received and the *timing* of its receipt.

The criteria for recognizing revenue are an important subset of the more general criteria for recognizing assets and liabilities in financial statements. See Exhibit 4–6.

Revenues are increases in economic resources through inflows, or enhancements of assets, or reductions of liabilities, resulting from the ordinary activities of an entity. Revenues of entities normally arise from the sale of goods, the rendering of services, or the use by others of entity resources (yielding rent, interest, royalties, or dividends). Many nonprofit organizations receive a significant proportion of their revenues from donations, government grants, and other contributions. Notice that under this definition, an accounting entity does not require a cash inflow in order to record revenue.

Timeliness requires that accounting information be received by the decision maker before that information loses its capacity to influence decisions.

Understandability. For the information provided in financial statements to be useful, users must be able to understand it. Users are assumed to have a reasonable understanding of business and economic activities and accounting, together with a willingness to study the material with reasonable diligence.

Verifiability. The financial statement representation of a transaction or event is verifiable if knowledgeable and independent observers would concur that it is in agreement with the underlying transaction or event with a reasonable degree of precision.

FACT AND DESCRIPTION QUESTIONS

1. List and describe the parts of a conceptual framework for financial accounting.
2. Are the objectives set out in the CICA's version of a conceptual framework unique? Explain.
3. Why would the segregation of ownership from management create "a need for external communication of economic information about the entity to investors," as section 1000 of the *CICA Handbook* suggests (see Exhibit 4–3)?
4. In the On Ice example in Chapter 1, Devo Green was owner *and* manager. Are accounting principles and a conceptual framework needed in such a situation?
5. Why does section 1000 of the *CICA Handbook* focus on the information needs of investors and creditors (see Exhibit 4–3)?
6. Do you agree with *CICA* 1000.12? With *CICA* 1000.13? Refer to Exhibit 4–3.
7. How is a gain different from a revenue? How is a loss different from an expense?
8. The desirable qualitative characteristics set out in Exhibit 4–5 are part of the conceptual framework for financial accounting. In your opinion, would some or all of these characteristics also be desirable for management accounting? for taxation?
9. Conservatism has often been used to justify the deliberate understatement of assets or overstatement of liabilities. It has been alleged that such an accounting policy might overstate earnings in the future. Is this possible? Does this mean that conservatism is a poor concept?
10. Does the notion of consistency suggest that an accounting entity should never change its accounting policies?
11. "'Materiality' means that just about anything can be justified in financial accounting, and often has been." Do you agree?

12. Is there a gap between financial accounting's conceptual framework and GAAP? If there is, why does it exist?

13. Why is professional judgment necessary in financial reporting?

14. List the attributes of professional judgment in financial reporting. Describe why each is important.

15. What does the term "income" mean?

16. Which model, accrual or cash flow, provides financial statements that are:
    (a) more useful? (Be sure to specify to whom.)
    (b) more objective?
    (c) easier to understand?
    (d) more comprehensive?
    (e) less costly?

17. Why is it potentially useful to classify cash flows into different categories, such as "operating," "investing," and "financing"? What aspects of financial accounting's conceptual framework would support such a three-way classification?

18. (a) Describe the efficient markets hypothesis in your own words, and explain its possible importance in financial accounting.
    (b) Suppose the president of a gold-mining company issues a press release that states: "Substantial deposit of high-quality ore discovered on company's property." The company's common shares trade on a major stock exchange. Predict what will happen to the price of the common shares just after the news release, and explain why you expect this will happen.
    (c) Suppose the president issues the same press release as in (b); however, the day before, the president had been charged with fraud. Predict what will happen to the share price just after the press release.
    (d) Accrual accounting is required under GAAP. Would it be required if the EMH were the only criterion for setting accounting standards?

19. (a) Describe the economic consequences criterion in your own words, and explain its possible importance in financial accounting.
    (b) Suppose you were the CEO of a small pharmaceutical company that was established three years ago. The company has a staff of exceptionally creative researchers, whom you feel are almost certain to make some discoveries in the next year or two that will have a major impact on the treatment of disease. In order to bring these discoveries all the way to the commercial stage, your company needs to raise about $10 million in new capital. Revenues this past year have been $3.2 million, while expenses have been $3.1 million.

    Let's assume that the Accounting Standards Board, the committee that has the responsibility and authority to set accounting standards in Canada, proposes to issue a new accounting standard that will require all expenditures on research to be accounted for as expenses in the accounting period in which they were incurred. If this proposed accounting standard had been in effect in the past year, your company's expenses would have been $6.3 million. Explain how you would use the economic consequences criterion to argue against the proposed accounting standard.

Questions for Analysis and Discussion

20. Published annual reports of Canadian companies include both accrual-model income statements and cash flow statements? Why?

21. Suppose you are a researcher employed by a Canadian labour union, and have been given the job of assessing how large a wage increase a company whose

employees your union represents can afford to offer for the coming year. Would financial statements be of use to you? Explain.

22. A well-established construction company signs an agreement to build a head office building for a major Canadian resource company. It is expected that construction will take three years. No significant problems are anticipated, since the design is fairly standard. The CEO of the construction company wants to record one-third of the total contract price of $21 million as revenue each year, on the grounds that about one-third of the construction effort and accomplishment is expected to take place each year. As the company's auditor, what would your reaction be?

23. Beverley A. Brennan is the vice-president, finance and administration, of PhilomBios, a small, Saskatoon-based biotech company. In the June 1992 issue of *CAmagazine*, she argued that GAAP does a disservice to small, knowledge-based firms such as hers, since it prevents the recognition of the "invisible capital" in such companies.[15] This disservice, she alleged, has important implications for our national prosperity and quality of life, since it may affect the competitiveness of Canadian companies. She added:

> *The accounting profession should examine whether our financial statements are in fact relevant and reliable ... We need to assess the balance between relevant and reliable, and, for knowledge-based companies, we need to consider the implications of getting the balance wrong. Finally, we should ask ourselves whether our standards create a negative bias for the knowledge-based company as compared to the traditional manufacturer or resource company.*
>
> *The major, long-term assets of a resource-based company are its reserves of the resource, its building, equipment and manufacturing processes, and its marketing network. For an innovative company in its early years, the major long-term assets are highly educated employees, technology under development, manufacturing arrangements and marketing and distribution systems. Based on current accounting practices, a comparison of two such companies' financial statements would probably show the resource-based company had the greater value ...*
>
> *Conventional financial statements reveal little of the value built through product development and say nothing of a company's ability to market its products successfully. Financial statements do not recognize as assets the knowledge and skill level of the employees, training, technological development, technology licensing agreements or marketing and distribution agreements. All of these, however, are valuable to the company and necessary for its future success — they are its "invisible capital."*
>
> *Accountants recognize the future value of the development work of resource companies by recognizing the costs of providing resources. By not recognizing the invisible capital of knowledge-based companies, CAs hobble them in their quest for capital. Investors, financial analysts and governments look at financial statements as the basic information needed to assess whether companies can be expected to achieve returns. When financial statements do not recognize invisible capital, investment in traditional industries appears more attractive than investment in innovative, knowledge-based companies. That is the wrong signal to give if we want to build a competitive country.*
>
> *Why don't we recognize invisible capital? Our myopia seems to have at least three causes: accounting standards that have been developed to focus on traditional indus-*

[15] Beverley A. Brennan, "Mind Over Matter: How Current Accounting Practices Hobble Innovative Companies," *CAmagazine*, June 1992, pp. 21–24. Reprinted with permission from *CAmagazine*, published by the Canadian Institute of Chartered Accountants, Toronto, Canada.

tries, concern about third-party liability, and the view that, if there is a measurement problem, then no measurement is preferable to risking a mistake in measurement. That approach gives more importance to conservatism than to relevance, even though the Handbook *presents relevance as more important ...*

The flaws in our present financial reporting system that hobble innovative companies in their quest for capital can be summarized as follows:

- *No recognition of the value of research and development.*
- *The appearance that companies that do not perform research and development have greater value over the short term.*
- *Recognition only of tangible and purchased intangible assets, which implies that "invisible capital" has no value.*
- *No recognition of licensing agreements and strategic alliances.*

A complete revamping of financial statements, so that they reflect the growing knowledge base of companies, might well be necessary. A more realistic, practical approach is called for in the short term. It would be possible to provide on the balance sheet a reference to an accompanying schedule that would give details on the amounts spent on research and development for products not yet on the market, when the products are expected, their market potential, and the amount spent on licensing agreements and strategic alliances.

There is also a case to be developed for the recognition in financial statements of the value of trained and motivated employees and the investments in marketing and distribution networks. These are extremely important elements of a company's "invisible capital." We need to investigate methods of recognizing these assets.

Required:

(a) Summarize how Beverley Brennan believes existing GAAP adversely affects smaller, innovative, knowledge-based companies.

(b) Does the conceptual framework support such a bias?

(c) If she is to be believed, it would seem that the picture portrayed by accounting has enormous consequences. Is this confounding the reality with a mere representation of that reality?

(d) Can the article be interpreted as self-serving?

24. J. Alex Milburn, a partner with the Canadian branch of the accounting firm Ernst and Young, and chair of the CICA's Accounting Standards Board in 1994–1995, wrote that:

It's no secret that financial accounting is under stress. One only has to look at daily newspapers to see reports of alleged accounting failures. Our traditional historical-based model is creaking, if not cracking, under the pressure of coping with highly complex transactions and economic conditions within a volatile global marketplace. It is well recognized that historical-cost accounting loses relevance under inflationary conditions. This can be a serious problem, but in addition, new issues are challenging traditional accounting principles. We are confronted with the need to find acceptable methods of recognition and measurement for modern financial instruments, as well as approaches for determining accrued expenses and liabilities for environmental reclamation, pension and other post-employment benefits. These require the use of advanced estimation and measurement approaches that have not been part of the everyday accountant's experience or training, and their application within generally accepted accounting principles is often unclear.

Add to this the fact that capital is more mobile — that it can be moved quickly across borders in response to perceived changes in costs, risks and income-generating potential. Expectations are rising as sophisticated investors and other external users look for accounting information that will be truly useful in evaluating these risks, costs and income potential.

These challenges are leading some thoughtful accountants to go back to the conceptual foundations upon which accounting measurement and recognition principles have been based. In their view, the profession is not going to resolve the complex issues currently confronting it to the satisfaction of an increasingly sophisticated and demanding public without an improved conceptual framework ... [Existing] conceptual frameworks have been incomplete, and only of limited value in the development of accounting standards.[16]

Required:

Conceptual frameworks for financial accounting were the major topic of this chapter. The Canadian version, especially, was described in some detail. Do you agree with Milburn's comments? Explain.

25. (a) Summarize, to the best of your ability, the arguments of David Solomons and Tony Tinker (refer to this chapter's "Accounting, Organizations, and Society" section). Solomons was a major participant in writing the FASB's version of the conceptual framework.
    (b) Is it possible that "neutrality" and "representational faithfulness" are unachievable for accounting? Discuss.

CASE

Melody Music Inc.

Melody Music Inc. (MMI) is a recording and distribution company that was established ten years ago to capitalize on the emergent interest among music connoisseurs in the high-quality sound that compact discs (CDs) provide. MMI produces only top-of-the-line CDs featuring new orchestral arrangements of classics. These are recorded on top-grade CD blanks and marketed only through well-established prestige music retailers.

MMI is owned by the Melody family, with the shares distributed as follows (no family members are currently active in the business):

Family member	Common shares[a] owned	Preferred shares[b] owned
Joachim Melody (founder; 60 years old)	2,500	4,000
Minnie Melody (estranged spouse of the founder; 50 years old)	1,500	1,000
Seymour Melody (son; 30 years old)	1,500	3,000
Suite Melody-Jones (daughter; 32 years old)	1,500	3,000
Harmon E. Melody (brother of Joachim; 58 years old)	1,500	3,000
N. "Les" Melody (cousin of Joachim)	1,500	500

[a] The common shares have full voting rights, except that according to a shareholder agreement and the bylaws of the corporation, any disposal of shares totalling more than 10% of the total common shares outstanding must be approved by holders of more than 50% of the common and preferred shares, with each class of shares considered separately. No dividends on common shares have ever been declared.

[b] The preferred shares have no voting rights, except as noted in the first footnote, but are cumulative as to a $10.00 per share annual dividend.

[16] J. Alex Milburn, "Building a Better Conceptual Framework," *CAmagazine*, December 1991, pp. 43–48. Reprinted with permission from *CAmagazine*, published by the Canadian Institute of Chartered Accountants, Toronto, Canada.

Joachim Melody stopped being active in the business late last year. Before he retired, he arranged for the board of directors to appoint Ms. T.O. Endeff as president and CEO. Endeff has all creative and financial responsibility for MMI, and reports directly to the board (which consists of all the members of the Melody family listed above). Her background as a successful concert pianist, and later as an orchestra's business manager, made her ideal for the position.

The music arranging, production, and distribution process

After Endeff identifies a "classic" composer whose work would fit in with MMI's strategic market niche, she engages legal counsel to ascertain the status of the rights to the music. Some of the music is in the public domain, but most of what MMI records is not, and royalty and other fees must be paid to the rights holders. Since much of the music was written decades (and more) ago, legal searches typically take from two to four months.

It is only after the legal status has been clarified that Endeff proceeds with further arrangements. She hires a producer — usually a veteran of the live orchestra industry — and together they block out the recording approach to the music, called a "series." These planning sessions take about three months and involve considerable scoring and rearranging of the original creative work. Invariably, because of the technical complexity of most pieces, consultation with other creative outsiders is required.

Once the score has been drafted to Endeff's satisfaction, she — in consultation with the producer — hires a conductor and makes arrangements for studio space. An MMI wholly owned subsidiary, Bang-Bang Sound Ltd., owns a recording studio, which is leased out to a variety of independent recording companies. The studio is in heavy demand because of the high quality of its recording equipment and the expertise of its technicians. Endeff has the authority to "bump" the independent companies but is reluctant to do so, since she wishes to maintain their good will. About half of MMI's consolidated revenues of $25,000,000 come from Bang-Bang, with the other half coming from its CD production and distribution business.

The conductor is given responsibility for organizing an orchestra, and hires the appropriate musicians through the union local. Many musicians have worked on a number of "classic" pieces for MMI over the years. Since the union has a standard scale, Endeff can estimate the "Musicians' salary and related costs" line item in the series budget fairly precisely, although sometimes, with a particularly challenging piece, rehearsals take longer. Typically, about 30 musicians are hired for each series, with rehearsals lasting two to three weeks. Rehearsals take place in a rented hall, since Bang-Bang's studio is usually rented. After the level of quality has been reached that Endeff, the producer, and the conductor require, the entire group moves over to the studio as it becomes available. A final one-day rehearsal takes place in the studio. Recording then takes place over five or six days.

The high-quality "master" is then mixed and edited by Bang-Bang's technicians, under the supervision of Endeff and the producer. This detailed, careful process takes seven or eight weeks. The CDs themselves are then "pressed" at facilities at Bang-Bang. The resulting inventory is stored in MMI's climate-controlled warehouse, ready for distribution to independent retailers.

At about the time that Endeff and the producer complete their planning sessions, MMI arranges for the writing and layout of promotional materials. Within three or four weeks a "retailer promo release" is sent to retailers, to inform them about the upcoming series. As well, advertisements are placed in selected publications and on cable TV specialty-music channels, offering the series directly to consumers under one of two options:

- The "prepaid" option, under which all the CDs in a series (typically, a series has five or six CDs, sent at the rate of one every two months) are paid for before the first one is shipped.
- The "pay-as-you-go" option, under which consumers "subscribe" to a series and pay only for the CDs they have received. Payment must be made within a month of receiving a CD, and subscribers may cancel at any time.

Under both the prepaid and pay-as-you-go options, direct mail consumers receive the first CD "free." About one-third of MMI's series sales are to direct mail consumers; the other two-thirds of sales are through independent retailers. However, these proportions can vary considerably for any given series. Twenty to thirty percent of "prepaid" customers cancel before the series is over, and most of these ask for a refund, which MMI willingly sends them. No attempt is made to recover CDs already shipped. Only about one-third of all pay-as-you-go subscribers stay for a complete series.

CDs are shipped to retailers in boxed sets of complete series (consisting of the entire set of five or six CDs), on terms that are usually based upon a requirement that the retailer submit payment to MMI within 60 days. Merchandise has a shelf life of one year (or more in the case of some "all-time favourite" series).

The meeting

On January 15, 1995, all members of the board except N. "Les" Melody met with Endeff. The subject of the meeting was Joachim Melody's stated desire to raise capital for expansion of Bang-Bang's studio facilities, and also to convert about half of his holdings into more liquid assets. To this end, he wished to sell 1,250 of his common shares to Big Sound Ltd., a major recording company. However, he felt obliged to offer his shares first to the other members of his family — "except that !?*! Minnie!"

Required:

Until recently, MMI's accounting policies and systems had been set up strictly to comply with income tax and GST requirements. However, since consolidated revenues had tripled over the past year, and since both the CD and the studio rental businesses had "grown like topsy" (for example, currently 25 CD series were on the market, and another 10 were at various stages of production), a more substantive assessment of the type of accounting system needed was becoming crucial. As a consultant hired by Endeff, prepare a report detailing the accounting policies and procedures that should be followed.

Cott Corporation

In the annual report for the fiscal year ended January 29, 1994, the chairman and CEO of Cott Corporation wrote the following:[17]

Your Company was challenged in the media on certain of its accounting policies, despite the fact that our policies are fully within both Canadian and U.S.A. Generally Accepted Accounting Principles and most appropriately reflect the nature of our business. A report was recently written by Dr. Roman L. Weil, the Sigmund E. Edelstone Professor of Accounting at the Graduate School of Business of the University of Chicago. He has consulted to many major corporations and is considered a leading expert on financial accounting standards, policies and instruments. In his summary of findings he states:

[17] Cott Corporation, Annual Report, 1994.

"Based on my review and analysis of Cott's business and accounting methods, I find allegations of improper accounting and mismanagement directed at the Company are, without exception, unfounded, unfair and uninformed.

"Cott's accounting methods fully comply with Generally Accepted Accounting Principles (GAAP) in the U.S. Moreover, they are appropriate to the nature of the Company's business and consistent with a policy of complete and timely disclosure."

"Despite the rough ride we received at the hands of certain reporters, we are committed to the idea of open, responsive and forthright relationships with the media and with the investing public for whom they write ..."

The company

Cott Corporation (henceforth Cott), incorporated in 1955, is a leading supplier of retailer-branded private-label beverages (such as *President's Choice*) and also branded soft drinks. It provides its retail clients, among whom are Loblaws, Wal-Mart, A&P, and Safeway, with customized soft drink concentrates, flavours, and formulas, and with packaging and design services. Along with a variety of other beverage products, Cott produces, packages, and distributes a large selection of bottled and canned carbonated beverages under private label for over 70 major retail and mass merchandise chains in Canada and the United States, as well as overseas. It also is the licensed bottler and distributor for *RC Cola* and *Diet Rite* in Ontario, the Atlantic provinces, and most of Quebec. Cott's common shares are listed on the Toronto and Montreal stock exchanges and are quoted through the NASDAQ National Market System in the United States.

Cott operates research, manufacturing, marketing, and customer service facilities in Canada, the United States, South Africa, Australia, the United Kingdom, and continental Europe. In the fiscal year ended January 29, 1994, Cott had sales of $665,370,000 (a 16-fold increase since 1990), year-end assets of $404,449,000, and approximately 1,350 employees. Selected recent financial results obtained from the 1994 Annual Report are as shown in the table below.

Financial Results (in $000s)	**1994**	**1993**	**% Change**
Sales	665,370	331,551	101
Net income	35,376	12,796	176
Operating cash flow	56,911	19,787	188
Capital expenditures	34,305	17,837	92
Cash & short-term deposits	79,436	7,894	906
Capital assets	76,291	48,178	58
Long-term debt	16,776	24,112	(30)
Shareholders' equity	283,684	75,915	274

Excerpts from the footnotes of the audited 1994 financial statements provide the following information:

From footnote #1, "Accounting Policies":

Deferred development and prepaid contract costs
Costs incurred in the development of new packaging are deferred and amortized against income on a straight-line basis over their estimated useful lives of three years.

Prepaid contract costs are amortized against sales over the term of the related contracts.

From footnote #7, "Other Assets," see the table below:

(in thousands of Canadian dollars)	**Jan. 29, 1994**	**Jan. 30, 1993**
Prepaid contract costs, net of accumulated amortization of $5,736,000 (Jan. 30, 1993 – $1,303,000)	$19,909	$4,626
Deferred development costs, net of accumulated amortization of $2,674,000 (Jan. 30, 1993 – $787,000)	7,452	3,114

Accounting Controversies

In a review of Cott's accounting policies,[18] Weil noted that critics have alleged that:

- Management employs misleading, "go-go" accounting to minimize (and hide) expenses and inflate earnings to create the illusion of profitable growth.
- Management manipulates Cott's balance sheet to sustain an unreasonable market valuation through the inclusion of artificial, even worthless, assets.
- Management has failed to disclose a growing cash crisis which, if not addressed, will result in insolvency.
- Management enriches insiders at the expense of other shareholders through sweetheart deals and incentive programs that encourage accounting irregularities.

Weil concluded his review of Cott's accounting policies by writing:

Based upon my review and analysis of Cott's business and accounting methods, I find allegations of improper accounting and mismanagement directed at the Company are, without exception, unfounded, unfair and uninformed ... Cott's accounting methods fully comply with generally accepted accounting principles ... they are appropriate to the nature of the Company's business ...

The accounting controversies to which Weil and the chairman and CEO of Cott referred involved, among other items, the accounting policies that Cott had chosen for the costs of new customer acquisitions. These costs included deferred development costs and prepaid contract costs.

[18] Roman L. Weil, *Analyzing the Issues: A Report on the Accounting Methods of the Cott Corporation*, May 25, 1994. Reprinted with permission from Roman L. Weil, Sigmund E. Edelstone Professor of Accounting, Graduate School of Business, University of Chicago.

Deferred development costs

Cott described these costs, in its Annual Information Form with the securities commission, as follows:

Whenever the Company reaches agreement with a new customer who is prepared to launch their own label of soft drinks, the Company will request that the retailer permit it to develop the conceptual design and graphics of the label for the new product. In most cases, the conceptual design of the label is carried throughout all products in the retailer's store brand program. The Company recognizes that for the program to succeed the product must have a "look and feel" which appeals to the retailer's customer, and therefore dedicates considerable resources to this activity. The Company believes that without exceptional shelf presence the program is unlikely to be successful and the Company is therefore reasonably certain that this expenditure will result in future revenues. As such the Company matches the cost of the label development to the future revenues by capitalizing the direct costs of development and amortizing them against income over their estimated useful life of three years.

Once a unique labelling "look and feel" has been accepted by Cott's customer, the packaging and labels for the individual flavours and beverages offered by that particular customer must comply with the chosen "look." One particular flavour in one type of packaging is referred to as a "stockkeeping unit," or "SKU"; thus, Cott may develop anywhere from 20 to 60 SKUs for any given customer, with all the particular customer's SKUs being required to be consistent with the chosen "look." In the year ended January 29, 1994, Cott developed more than 1,000 new "looks" for its 31 new customers.

In contrast, Cott's national brand competitors, such as Coca-Cola, create just one "look" for a single brand, which they sell to all their customers. Professor Weil notes:

For each new customer, Cott incurs the following development costs for each SKU:

- *The cost surrounding the registration of trade names (e.g., legal searches, registrations). This cost is so small that Cott expenses it.*
- *The cost of designing the label. Cott partly expenses and partly capitalizes this cost. Cott capitalizes the direct labor of its employees or its subsidiary's employees as shown on the employees' time cards and the amounts paid to non-employees, such as for photographs or materials, directly related to the project. Cott expenses the overhead costs associated with the cost of employees.*
- *The cost to take the design to engraving (i.e., so that labels and cans may be printed). Cott capitalizes the cost of this work, all of which involves payment for goods and services to outsiders or non-employees ...*

Recall that assets can be physical or intangible. Cott believes the unique label/design/name or look *developed by Cott is an asset, albeit an intangible one. Thus, the development costs lead to an asset (the* look*) whose benefits lead to the revenues provided by the sale of soft drinks.*

Weil concluded his discussion of Cott's deferred development costs by observing:

The uncertainty surrounding Cott's recovery of its investment in development costs is no greater than the uncertainty of recovery of the equipment in Cott's test kitchens — physical assets no one questions ... In summary, I find that Cott's deferred development costs do embody a future benefit that will contribute directly to Cott's cash flows. These future benefits satisfy the additional requirements of an accounting asset: Cott controls them, has access to them, and acquired them in transactions with outsiders. Thus, Cott appropriately capitalizes deferred development costs as an asset.

Prepaid contract costs

In Cott's Annual Information Form, these costs were described in the following manner:

The Company has relatively few customers when compared to the customer base of its national brand competitors. The risk that the Company will lose any single customer can be reduced by signing customers to long-term contracts. With certain of its customers the Company is able to obtain a long-term contract only with the payment of an up-front fixed amount of money or the provision of free services. In most cases the retailer will use these funds or services to launch the new retail branded program, thereby providing the Company with additional incentive to pay the up-front amounts. It is the Company's business strategy to encourage retail customers to sign long-term contracts as it provides the Company with more certainty as to the longevity of its relationship with its retail customers and the future income stream. The contracts entered into generally provide: (i) that the Company will be the exclusive supplier of premium retailer branded soft drinks; (ii) for minimum annual volume targets to be purchased from the Company; and (iii) that minimum shelf space is allocated to the Company's products for the duration of the agreement. Because these amounts are paid with the objective of realizing a revenue stream over a period of more than one year the Company elects to capitalize these amounts as Prepaid Contract Costs and amortizes them over the term of the related contracts, the majority of which are for terms of three to five years.

With regard to both deferred development and prepaid contract costs, the Company periodically re-examines its ability to defer these costs with reference to the anticipated profit to be derived from the related customer. Should the Company determine that any of the capitalized costs are not recoverable, they are immediately written off.

Retailers and the companies that supply them with private-label products (such as Cott) have typically had very short-term contractual relationships, such as month-to-month, and usually no longer than one year. The actual products are usually commodities, so that any supplier can fulfil any retailer's needs. Cott wished to alter this relationship by focusing on quality private-label product development and customer awareness of premium private labels. Thus, Cott focused on signing longer-term exclusive-supply contracts, of three to five-year duration with its retailer customers. Such longer-term contracts, with their attendant dependable customer base, enabled Cott to enjoy a more predictable revenue stream, and an overall reduction in uncertainty, and to plan for more rational expansion of its physical capacity.

Some of Cott's retailers, however, insist on advance payments in connection with the start-up costs they will incur as part of these longer-term contracts. Cott's management observes that these costs will be recovered through higher invoice charges for products purchased by the retailer over the contract. Weil, in his review of Cott's accounting policies, concluded:

Cott's choice in accounting for prepaid contract costs as assets is appropriate ... Cott makes cash advances for marketing and promotion to some retailers with whom it signs long-term contracts. These contracts contain provisions for Cott to be the retailer's exclusive supplier of private label products and establish volume targets for the retailer. With such retailers, Cott sets price terms within its contracts, with the retailer's knowledge, to recover the cash advance over the life of the agreement. The future benefit is the future cash collection from the retailer ... Cott correctly capitalizes prepaid contract costs as an asset ... Moreover, under the matching principle, Cott should amortize these costs against the higher revenues that Cott will receive over the course of the contract ... Management reports that it has never failed to recover the amounts capitalized for prepaid contract costs.

Required:

(a) Suggest reasons why Cott Corporation's top management might be concerned about the media's and others' challenges to certain of the company's accounting policies.

(b) Estimate Cott's net income for the year ended January 29, 1994, if development and prepaid contract costs had not been deferred and amortized, but rather had been expensed as incurred. Assume a corporate income tax rate of 40%.

(c) Evaluate, based on the information provided, Cott's accounting policies with respect to deferred development costs and prepaid contract costs.

CASE

Chicoutimi Limited

Chicoutimi Limited, a designer and producer of women's high-fashion apparel, was established 15 years ago by Ms. Sabo Lee. She was the sole shareholder and had never needed to borrow money from the bank for the business. Until now, that is. The recession that ended in the early 1990s hadn't ended for Chicoutimi by early 1995: sales were down as long-time customers switched to more affordable and fashion-insensitive garments, and several of Chicoutimi's competitors had gone bankrupt. It was only because of Lee's tenacity and ability that the company had survived.

Lee has asked you to prepare an income statement and balance sheet for the company's fiscal year ending January 31, 1995. She wishes to take it to the bank for her meeting with the loan officer. The balance sheet for the year ended January 31, 1994, is as in the chart to the left.

ASSETS	
Cash	$ 3,010
Accounts receivable	35,790
Inventory — finished goods	24,800
Inventory — cloth and other raw materials	42,150
Sewing machines, office equipment, and van	65,900
Trademarks	125,000
	$296,650
LIABILITIES	
Accounts payable	$ 41,500
Income taxes payable	15,700
Loan payable — S. Lee	100,000
Common stock	100,000
Retained earnings	39,450
	$296,650

The receivables are from retailers and individual retail customers who have made purchases over the past 18 months. Lee kept excellent track of how much she was owed, and dealt with only "the finest people," whom she was certain would eventually be able to pay her what they owed. This, even though certain customers, owing her $12,500 as of January 31, 1994, had declared bankruptcy.

Finished goods inventory consisted of high-fashion Fall and Winter season dresses and outerwear that either hadn't sold or had not been picked up by the purchaser because of the recession (this represented 40% of the total); and also of merchandise for the Spring 1994 season (this was 60% of the total, and had sold out by late March 1995, although at deeply discounted prices). Lee had never had to discount her merchandise before, and was shocked that the discounted prices averaged about 10% below cost. She had become accustomed to marking up her merchandise by 100% over cost, and had never experienced any resistance to this practice in the past.

The inventory of cloth and other raw materials was accounted for at its cost.

The sewing machines had been purchased three years earlier for $35,000. Trade publications indicated that they had an expected service life of five years, with no net salvage value. There was also other equipment, which had cost $10,900 on February 1, 1993. This consisted of exercise equipment that Lee had purchased for her use at home. On January 30, 1994, the company had purchased a van for $20,000, to be used for business purposes. Similar vans, you discover, have an expected service life of three years, with a net salvage value equal to about 20% of their original cost.

Lee was exceptionally proud of her designs; after all, before the recession Chicoutimi had been "making money hand over fist." Her designer labels were a mark of class and taste among her clientele. In order to reflect this in the financial statements, Lee had told Sigmot Thurd, her dressmaker and part-time bookkeeper, to record the following journal entry on February 1, 1993:

Dr Trademarks	125,000	
Cr Gain		125,000

When you asked Lee how she arrived at the $125,000 figure, she said that Alhambra Fashions Inc., a major player in the industry with 1993 revenues of over $35 million, had offered her that much for her shares in Chicoutimi, exclusive of any receivables, inventory, or tangible capital assets. She provides you with a letter from Alhambra's CEO that sets out the details of what seems to have been a *bona fide* offer.

The accounts payable of $41,500 were all due to Chicoutimi's suppliers and employees. Suppliers were owed $35,500, as follows:

For purchases less than 120 days before year end	$10,000
For purchases made 120 days or more before year end	25,500

The $25,500 was from one major supplier, who had insisted that Lee, as Chicoutimi's CEO, sign a promissory note for the amount due.

The remainder of the $41,500 was owed to employees for pre-Christmas overtime in November and December 1993. This amount was regarded as a bonus by Lee, and was to be paid out sometime in early 1994.

The income taxes payable of $15,700 related to a reassessment of Chicoutimi by Revenue Canada for the 1989 fiscal year. When she received the reassessment on July 2, 1993, Lee told Sigmot to record the following journal entry:

Dr Income tax expense	15,700	
Cr Income taxes payable		15,700

The loan of $100,000 was made to Chicoutimi by Lee on August 1, 1993. Lee had taken a mortgage on her house at 10%.

The following information is available to you about the fiscal year that just ended on January 31, 1995:

- Total wages and salaries paid to employees was $172,000. This included $15,000 for the week ended Friday, February 2, 1994. There was no pre-Christmas overtime in calendar year 1994.
- January 31, 1995, was also a Friday, and the employees receive their cheques on Fridays. Chicoutimi's accounting system is such that the general ledger account for cash is credited when a cheque is disbursed.

- Sales were $235,000, not counting returns of $16,500. Chicoutimi had received payments of $23,290 from customers who had made purchases during the previous fiscal year. As of January 31, 1995, accounts receivable totalled $74,950. You analysed the age of the receivables and came up with the following results:

More than 365 days old	$12,500
Between 365 and 180 days old	32,000
Between 180 and 90 days old	24,200
Less than 90 days old	6,250
	$74,950

From an industry trade association, you learn that on average, 75% of receivables between 365 and 180 days old are paid, 90% of those between 180 and 90 days old are eventually paid, and virtually 100% (specifically, 98%) of those less than 90 days old are paid.

- No finished goods were on hand on January 31, 1995. Cloth and other raw materials that cost $31,450 were on hand, however, even though the $42,150 of such inventory that was on hand at the start of the year had all been used up, and Chicoutimi's general ledger showed that the purchases account had been debited for a total of $194,500 during the year. Lee paid suppliers $75,000 on account for this year's purchases. The $10,000 owing on last year's purchases had also been paid.

- One irate retailer had returned $15,000 of outerwear (at Chicoutimi's selling prices) on January 20, 1995, because (at least according to Lee) the "creature has no taste for fashion!" When you telephoned the retailer, he said that while he could appreciate zebra-striped top-of-the-line women's ski jackets, he had ordered down-filled parkas, and had a purchase order to prove it. Lee was adamant that "a sale is a sale ... besides, it cost us $12,000 to make those things... it was a verbal order ... I'll never take one from a new customer again!"

- Special dyes and other chemicals costing $7,500 had been purchased this year, and used as part of what Lee called Chicoutimi's "forefront research" on customized designer materials. "No one else does this ... this is real innovation, customizing the texture and colour of cloth to each customer's preferences ..." Sigmot Thurd, who had graduated in chemistry from a prestigious university before switching careers, was Chicoutimi's part-time researcher. Sigmot was told by Lee to record the research activity by debiting a new general ledger account, to be called "Research asset." The $17,500 represented the $7,500 in chemicals, $2,000 for the portion of Sigmot's time spent on the project, and $8,000 in consulting fees charged by a professional engineer who was an expert in the chemistry of dyes.

- A longtime individual retail customer, Annie Orfan, had sued Chicoutimi for $100,000 in March 1994, claiming that the material used in a custom-made dress had caused her to turn ill. Lee mentioned to you that she now realized that the dye Sigmot Thurd had used to prepare a special "experimental and unique" cloth was probably the culprit. "Thank goodness only one dress was made before we tossed that bolt out. But I tell you, I'm going to have my lawyer work as hard as she can to keep any settlement down in the $10,000 to $15,000 range ... I'll be damned if I'm going to put Orfan's kids through university!"

Required:

(a) Should you follow GAAP in preparing the financial statements? Explain. If not, what other basis of accounting should you follow?

(b) For this part, assume that GAAP should be used. Reconstruct Chicoutimi's January 31, 1994, balance sheet. Explain every change that you make using the conceptual framework described in the chapter, or other authority such as GAAP.

(c) Prepare journal entries accounting for the events of the fiscal year ended January 31, 1995. Explain the decisions you made for each entry.

(d) Prepare an income statement and a balance sheet for the year ended January 31, 1995.

(e) Prepare, as best you can, a cash flow statement (you may want to refer back to the On Ice example in Chapter 1). How much of a bank loan, if any, do you believe Chicoutimi needs?

(f) Do you think the bank will give Chicoutimi the loan?

CHAPTER 5 five

Making Revenue Accounting and Expense Accounting Decisions in Different Situations

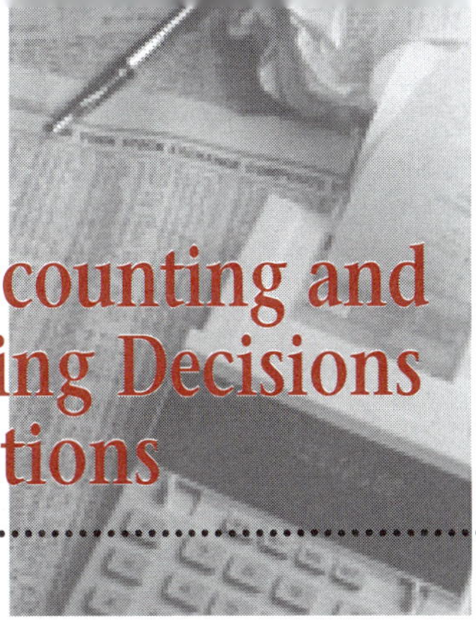

Learning OBJECTIVES

After you have read, thought about, and discussed this chapter, and completed a selection from the end-of-chapter material, you will have made significant progress in achieving the following learning objectives:

- Explain at what point revenue is recorded in a variety of industries such as construction, real estate, and banking, the different methods of measuring revenue, and the reasons for the various methods.
- Be able to prepare journal entries for the percentage of completion and completed contract methods of revenue recognition.
- Explain how expenses are recorded in a variety of different industries and situations, and the reasons for such methods.
- Describe various depreciation methods, be able to compute depreciation expense using the methods, and explain the effect of each method on the income statement and balance sheet.
- Describe how financial accounting and income tax accounting interact in accounting for income tax expense.
- List the differences between inventory valuation methods, identify when each method would be the most appropriate, and explain the effect of each method on the income statement and balance sheet.

CBC Salvo Blasts CTV's 'Gutter Accounting' — Public network rejects allegations of CTV report, which says sport is a multimillion-dollar loser.

Christopher Harris, *The Globe and Mail*, July 20, 1994, C8

A report commissioned by [the CTV Television Network] charges that "CBC sports is estimated to be 'losing' $60-70 million per year, thus requiring direct taxpayer subsidization and impairing CBC's ability to deliver on the key programming priorities that a publicly funded broadcaster should be addressing."

The report attempts to demonstrate that, because of the way CBC allocates overhead and other non-production expenses, the real cost of sports is hidden. That, if CBC did its books the way CTV says it should, attributing a percentage of every paper clip used in the president's office to sports, what looks like a moneymaker would turn out to be a loser. A big loser.

Naturally, uninformed readers of the report would conclude that CBC should get out of sports because it's sucking taxpayer dollars out of The Nature of Things. *You can bet that many CBC critics will take the report at face value, neither questioning its assumptions nor its assertions. That's happened already.*

Smart play on the part of CTV.

Too bad it fumbled.

For one thing ... the consultants which prepared the report ... relied exclusively on CBC financial documents available to the public — annual reports, CRTC applications, that kind of thing.

But let me tell you, while getting an MBA — which included suffering through endless seminars trying to piece together the financial statements of a company that's destroyed by fire leaving only an invoice, a bank statement, a ledger page and a few bills — I learned a few tricks of accounting. And try as I could, I couldn't come up with the same calculations that [they] did, no matter how mighty my calculator.

Antonia Zerbisias, media reporter, "CTV Fumbles on Its End Run Around CBC Sports," *Toronto Star*, July 15, 1994, A21[1]

INTRODUCTION

As discussed in Chapter 4, GAAP sets out standards for measuring and reporting on revenues, expenses, assets, and liabilities. If there are no restrictions on a situation in which financial accounting information is prepared (for example, if there is no need to comply with GAAP, or another legislated or agreed-upon system of accounting), then accounting choices may be made so that the resulting accounting information is custom tailored for a specific purpose.

An example of accounting not constrained by GAAP being used to fulfil corporate objectives is described briefly in the quotes that open this chapter. This is an illustration of accounting being used in an adversarial manner. CTV commissioned a report to examine the profitability of competitor CBC's sports broadcasting, and then leaked the report to the media. The two national networks, one shareholder-

[1] Reprinted with permission of the Toronto Star Syndicate.

owned (CTV) and the other owned by the government of Canada (CBC), were fierce competitors when it came to TV sports programming, and CBC had recently beat out CTV in bidding for Canadian broadcast rights to the 1996 Olympics held in Atlanta, Georgia. Antonia Zerbisias, in her quote, cautions those who read the CTV report to question assumptions and assertions made about the revenues and expenses used to construct the alleged CBC sports income statement. This is good advice, which all preparers and users of all accounting information should make a point of remembering.

Another conclusion that you should have come to by now is that even *within* GAAP, managers and accountants have considerable choice. Establishing what to disclose in financial statements and footnotes, how to disclose it, how to recognize revenues and expenses, and so on, all involves making decisions. Even within the confines of the historic cost, transactions-based accounting model, many choices are available. For example, the TTC illustration in Chapter 4 resulted in eight different income numbers. Of course GAAP, including the contents of the *CICA Handbook*, and the conceptual framework we described in Chapter 4 provide guidance and constrain decisions; even so, considerable emphasis must be placed on high-quality, ethical professional judgment when those decisions are made.

In this chapter we consider a variety of revenue accounting and expense accounting decision situations, some of which are controversial and open to debate. The decisions we look at fall within GAAP, and are worthy of examination because they illustrate the point that an important factor influencing accounting decisions is the nature of the industry or organization for which the accounting is being done. To a significant degree, accounting decisions must be custom-tailored to the situation at hand. The method of recognizing revenue for a company that operates a fresh fruit stand makes little sense for a company that manufactures Great Lakes freighters that take two or more years to build.

Some Examples of Revenue Accounting Decisions

The general criteria for revenue recognition under GAAP were provided in Chapter 4, along with some examples. Recall that these criteria were as follows:

- The accounting entity has fulfilled its side of the bargain by providing essentially all the goods or services promised.
- There are relatively few costs that the accounting entity must still incur in order to complete the bargain.
- There is little uncertainty about both the *amount* of revenue to be received and the *timing* of its receipt.

These are general criteria for helping managers and accountants decide when to record revenue. These criteria must, however, be applied in specific business situations, and since different types of businesses generate revenues in different ways, it's important to *understand* how businesses operate so that the criteria can be applied effectively. For the ice cream vendor working the holiday crowds on July 1, the revenue recognition decision is straightforward: when an ice cream cone is sold for cash, the criteria for revenue recognition have been fulfilled:

- The accounting entity, the ice cream vendor, has fulfilled its side of the bargain by providing the ice cream cone to the customer.
- There are no costs that the accounting entity must still incur in order to complete the bargain.
- There is no uncertainty about both the *amount* of revenue to be received and the *timing* of its receipt.

However, even for businesses as simple as Devo Green's On Ice Incorporated (from Chapter 1), revenue recognition may be relatively complicated. (For example, should revenue be recorded when an advertisement is ordered, or when it is designed, or when the magazine containing the ad is sold?) So our intention in this part of the chapter is to provide you with a bit of "experience" in applying these general revenue-recognition criteria in a sample of businesses. We'll describe how revenue is accounted for in three industries important to the Canadian economy: construction (and similar long-term production industries), real estate, and banking.

Construction and Similar Long-Term Production Industries

Banister Inc. is a Canadian construction company whose common stock is listed on the Alberta Stock Exchange, the Montreal Stock Exchange, the Toronto Stock Exchange, and the American Stock Exchange. In 1993 the company recorded \$182 million in revenues from pipeline construction, \$71 million in revenues from underground work (installation and repair of natural gas mains, telephone, cable, and electrical utilities, and so on), and \$216 million in revenues from civil, industrial, and building construction. Many of the construction projects undertaken by Banister last for a number of accounting periods; for example, Banister's construction work at the new University of Northern British Columbia will take several years. In the "Summary of Significant Accounting Policies" in its 1993 Annual Report, Banister described its accounting policy for these long-term contracts as follows:[2]

Revenue and income from long-term construction contracts ... are determined on the percentage of completion method ... Provision is made for all anticipated losses as soon as they become evident. Claims for additional contract compensation are not recognized until resolved.

Deferred contract costs and unbilled revenue represent costs incurred and revenue earned in excess of amounts billed on uncompleted contracts. Unearned revenue and contract advances represent the excess of amounts billed over costs incurred and revenue earned on uncompleted contracts and payments received from clients in advance of the performance of the work. Provisions for anticipated losses on uncompleted contracts are deducted from related deferred contract costs with any excess being included in unearned revenue ...

Organizations like Banister that earn their revenues (and incur the costs of earning those revenues) over many accounting periods, use either the percentage of completion revenue recognition method or the completed contract method. Under the percentage of completion method, revenues and gross profit for a company's construction project are recognized each period, based upon the amount of progress made on the project, even though the project has not yet been completed and the asset under construction (say, a building) has not yet been legally transferred to the purchaser. Under the completed contract method, revenues and gross profit are recognized only when the project is com-

[2] Reproduced with the kind permission of Banister Foundation Inc.

plete. The two methods are not alternatives under GAAP, but apply to different circumstances. The *CICA Handbook* offers the following guidance in section 3400:

***.13** Revenue from service transactions and long-term contracts is usually recognized as the service or contract activity is performed, using either the percentage of completion method or the completed contract method.*

***.14** The percentage of completion method is used when performance consists of the execution of more than one act, and revenue would be recognized proportionately by reference to the performance of each act. Revenue recognized under this method would be determined on a rational and consistent basis such as the basis of sales value, associated costs, extent of progress, or number of acts ...*

***.15** The completed contract method would only be appropriate when performance consists of the execution of a single act or when the enterprise cannot reasonably estimate the extent of progress toward completion.*

So Banister's accounting policy seems consistent with the *CICA Handbook*. Let's see how the accounting mechanics of these revenue recognition methods work.

Suppose that Banister signs a contract in which it agrees to construct a bridge for $10,000,000, beginning on April 1, 19X1. The contract specifies that the bridge is to be completed and legal title handed over to Banister's customer on March 31, 19X3. Banister's engineers and accountants estimate that the bridge will cost $9,000,000 to complete. Banister has a December 31 fiscal year end. Suppose that the percentage of completion revenue recognition method will be used and that as of December 31, 19X1, the following information about the bridge construction project has been collected by Banister's accountants:

Costs incurred to date	$ 750,000
Estimated costs to complete	8,250,000
Estimated total project costs	$9,000,000
Progress billings	$ 700,000
Cash collected	$ 600,000

"Progress billings" refers to the total invoices that Banister has submitted to its customer during the accounting period.

The percentage of the project that has been completed could be determined in a number of ways. For example, a joint engineering team representing Banister and its customer could inspect the project in progress and estimate what percentage of the total work effort has been completed. Alternatively, other measures of progress, such as labour hours worked in 19X1 as a percentage of estimated total project labour hours, could be applied. The following formula is often used to measure the percentage of completion of a long-term construction project based on the percentage of costs incurred:

$$\frac{\textbf{Costs incurred up to end of current accounting period}}{\textbf{Estimate of total expected project costs}}$$

For our example, in 19X1 this formula gives 750,000/9,000,000, or 8.333%. Thus, using the percentage of completion method, Banister's 19X1 income statement would include 8.333% of the project's total estimated gross profit of $1,000,000 (= $10,000,000 agreed-upon contract price less the $9,000,000 estimated total costs), or $83,333 in profits. A complete set of journal entries for 19X1 would be:

1. Accounting for construction costs incurred (where the "B" represents a balance sheet account, and the "I" represents an income statement account):

Dr Construction in progress (B)	750,000	
Cr Various (B) accounts, such as Cash, Accounts payable, etc.		750,000

2. To account for the progress billings:

Dr Accounts receivable (B)	700,000	
Cr Billings on construction in progress (B)		700,000

3. To account for the cash received from the customer:

Dr Cash (B)	600,000	
Cr Accounts receivable (B)		600,000

4. To account for the recognition of revenues and the associated gross profits using the percentage of completion method:

Dr Construction in progress (B)	83,333	
Dr Cost of construction (I)	750,000	
Cr Revenue from long-term construction contracts (I)		833,333

If Banister had no other projects in 19X1, the impact of the above on its income statement and balance sheet for the year ended December 31, 19X1, would be as follows:

Income statement excerpt, year ended December 31, 19X1:

Revenue from long-term construction contracts	$833,333
Cost of construction	750,000
Gross profit	$ 83,333

Balance sheet excerpt, as at December 31, 19X1:

Current assets:		
Accounts receivable		$100,000
Inventories:		
Construction in progress	$833,333	
Less: Billings	700,000	
Cost and recognized profit in excess of billings		133,333

The current asset "Cost and recognized profit in excess of billings" of $133,333 represents the $83,333 in gross profit that the company has accounted for under the percentage of completion method, plus the $50,000 excess of $750,000 in actual construction costs incurred in 19X1 over the $700,000 amount billed to the customer. Setting up the accounts this way on the balance sheet accomplishes the following objectives:

- It avoids double-counting, since the billings of $700,000 had already been debited to accounts receivable.
- It helps keep track of the remaining investment in construction in progress, which at the end of fiscal 19X1 is $833,333.

If billings had exceeded construction in progress, the excess in this case would have been reported on Banister's balance sheet as the current liability "Billings in excess of costs and recognized profit."

Under the completed contract method, Banister would have reported the total project revenue and gross profit only in 19X3; nothing would have been reported on 19X1's income statement. All the above journal entries that affected only balance sheet accounts, however, would still have been recorded (that is, entries 1, 2, and 3).

Accounting and Business Decision A

Suppose that Banister's experience with the bridge contract in 19X2 and 19X3 is as follows:

	19X2	19X3
Costs incurred to date	$5,500,000	$9,100,000
Estimated costs to complete	3,600,000	—
Progress billings during the year	4,000,000	5,300,000
Cash collected during the year	3,500,000	5,900,000

Prepare all journal entries under both methods — percentage of completion and completed contract — for both 19X2 and 19X3.

Real Estate

Bramalea Limited was a major North American public corporation and was involved in the development, ownership, and management of real estate. The company leased office, retail, industrial, residential, and hotel properties; it also designed, built, and marketed homes ranging from the affordable to the luxury in Ontario and California. The following information appeared in Bramalea's "Summary of Significant Accounting Policies" in its 1991 Annual Report:

RECOGNITION OF EARNINGS

Rental operations

Revenues and earnings from rental properties are recorded from the time a break-even point in cash flow after debt service is achieved, limited to a reasonable period after substantial completion. Prior to this time, the properties are classified as rental properties under development and the net operating results from such properties are applied to reduce other capitalized costs.

The Company, as lessor, has retained substantially all the risks and benefits of ownership of its rental properties and therefore accounts for leases as operating leases. Rental revenues are recognized over the term of the individual leases as they are earned. When applicable, rental revenues include percentage rents and recoveries of operating expenses together with property, capital and large corporation taxes.

Real estate sales

Revenues and earnings from the sale of land and other properties are recorded when the collection of the sale proceeds is reasonably assured and all other significant conditions of the sale are met.

The sale of a single home or townhouse is recorded when title to the completed house is conveyed to the purchaser.

The sale of a condominium housing unit is recorded when the purchaser pays the amount due on closing, becomes entitled to occupancy and undertakes, if applicable, to assume a mortgage for the balance of the purchase price.

Notice the practical accounting decisions that Bramalea's management must make with respect to choosing the point in the revenue-generating process at which revenue is to be accounted for. The company custom tailors its choices to each of its "product lines." For rental properties — that is, building properties that Bramalea has built and the ownership of which it has retained — the company begins crediting a revenue account on its income statement only when "a break-even point in cash flow after debt service is achieved." Bramalea purchases raw land, negotiates with zoning authorities, designs and constructs the building, rents out the suites in the building, and provides ongoing services to the tenants. Each of these phases may take several months or years, and choosing a point at which to begin counting revenue is somewhat arbitrary. Each rental building has been financed with debt, and both interest and principal payments must be made on the debt. As well, each rental building incurs operating costs, such as repairs and maintenance. Bramalea waits until the rental payments from the building's tenants (that is, the cash inflows) just equal the sum of all these cash outflows before it begins recording the following journal entry:

Dr Cash (B)	XX	
Cr Rental revenue (I)		XX

Another possible point at which a company engaged in renting could begin accounting for rental payments as revenue could be when a certain number of suites, say 50%, have been rented out. The issue here is deciding on a point that is a reasonable representation of the time when the rental property can be regarded as operational.

Bramalea says that for its real estate sales, it records revenues according to this general criterion: "when the collection of the sale proceeds is reasonably assured and all other significant conditions of the sale are met." It then specifies more precisely when this general criterion is met for its two real estate sales product lines: single homes and townhouses, and condominium housing units.

Accounting and Business Decision B

(a) List the various ways that Bramalea Limited generates revenues.

(b) For each of Bramalea's revenue activities, explain in detail and in your own words the company's accounting policy. Are the various policies in accordance with GAAP?

Banking

Banks and similar financial institutions generate their revenues in a variety of ways, and this leads to a variety of accounting policies for revenue recognition. For example, the Bank of Montreal disclosed information on its revenue accounting policies in the footnotes to its 1993 Annual Report's audited financial statement (see Exhibit 5–1). Notice the numerous references to management's judgment and expectations. There is an enormous burden on management to ensure that the particular revenue accounting policies chosen for the particular revenue-generating activities are consistent, in the Bank of Montreal's case, with GAAP and thus with the requirements described in Chapter 4.

One of the basic decisions the bank's management must make relates to whether the loans it has made are performing or nonperforming — that is, whether the borrower is fulfilling the terms and conditions of the loan agreement (by making interest and principal payments on time, for example), or not. This dichotomous decision is another example of the concept of classification, which is pervasive in accounting, and to which you were introduced in Chapter 2.

Bank of Montreal calls nonperforming loans "non-accrual." Non-accrual loans and performing loans are accounted for in very different ways, as the audited footnote in Exhibit 5–1 explains: "Interest income is recorded on an accrual basis except on loans classified as non-accrual." Accrual accounting means that, in the case of a bank's loan to a borrower, interest revenue is recorded as time goes by (that is, as the bank earns the revenue). An example is provided in Exhibit 5–2.

EXHIBIT 5–1
BANK OF MONTREAL'S REVENUE RECOGNITION POLICIES

SECURITIES

Securities comprise investment, trading and loan substitute securities.

Investment securities are securities where the bank's original intention is to hold to maturity or until market conditions render alternative investments more attractive. Equity securities are carried at cost and debt securities at amortized cost. Gains and losses on disposal of these securities and write-downs to reflect declines in value which are considered to be other than temporary are recorded as a credit or charge to interest, dividend and fee income from securities in the year in which they occur.

Trading securities are securities purchased for resale over a short period of time. Such securities are carried at market value. Adjustments to market value and gains and losses on the sale of trading securities are recorded in interest, dividend and fee income from securities in the year in which they occur. Obligations related to securities sold but not yet purchased are recorded in other liabilities.

Loan substitute securities are customer financings structured as after-tax investments to provide the borrower with an interest rate advantage over what would otherwise be applicable on a conventional loan. Such securities are accorded the accounting treatment applicable to loans.

LOANS

Loans are stated net of any unearned income, unamortized discounts and allowance for credit losses.

Interest income is recorded on an accrual basis except for loans classified as non-accrual.

Loan syndication fees are recorded in other income upon completion of the syndication arrangement. Loan origination, restructuring and renegotiation fees are recognized in interest income over the expected term of the loan. Commitment fees are accorded the same treatment if it is considered likely that the commitment will be exercised. Otherwise such fees are recognized in other income over the term of the commitment period. Deferred loan fees are recorded in other liabilities.

The accounting treatment for non-accrual loans is as follows:

Consumer instalment and credit card loans	**Sovereign risk loans***	**Residential and non-residential mortgages, other personal loans and loans to business and governments**
Accounting for interest on non-accrual loans		
Classification as non-accrual		
Consumer loans are classified as non-accrual when payments of interest or principal are contractually past due 90 days. Credit card loans are classified as non-accrual and written off when payments of interest or principal are contractually past due 180 days.	Loans are classified as non-accrual when: 1. in the opinion of management there is reasonable doubt as to the ultimate collectibility of principal or interest, or 2. payment of interest or principal is contractually past due 90 days unless in the opinion of management there is no significant doubt as to the ultimate collectibility of interest and principal, or 3. payment of interest or principal is contractually past due 180 days, or 4. in the opinion of management it is considered prudent or desirable to cease accruing interest, irrespective of the status of interest or principal payments.	Loans are classified as non-accrual when: 1. in the opinion of management there is reasonable doubt as to the ultimate collectibility of principal or interest, or 2. payment of interest or principal is contractually past due 90 days unless the loan is both well secured and in the process of collection, or 3. payment of interest or principal is contractually past due 180 days, or 4. in the opinion of management it is considered prudent or desirable to cease accruing interest, irrespective of the status of interest or principal payments.

Interest

When a loan is classified as non-accrual, all accrued and unpaid interest is reversed and charged against interest income in the period in which the loan is classified as non-accrual. Interest is not capitalized if a loan is non-accrual nor is it capitalized to prevent classification of a loan as non-accrual.

Application of subsequent payments

Subsequent payments are applied first to interest, then to principal, unless directed otherwise by the borrower.	Subsequent payments are applied first to interest, then to principal, unless directed otherwise by the borrower.	Subsequent payments are recorded in interest income after any prior write-off has been recovered and if management has determined that a specific provision is not required, otherwise they are recorded as a reduction of principal.

Source: 1993 financial statements. Published with permission of Bank of Montreal.

* These are loans made to a sovereign, or independent, state.

EXHIBIT 5–2
EXAMPLE OF ACCRUAL REVENUE ACCOUNTING FOR A BANK LOAN

Suppose that Bank A loaned $100,000 to Disk Ltd. on January 15, 1995. The terms of the loan are that Disk Ltd. must pay interest at an annual rate of 10% on the fifteenth of each month, and repay the $100,000 principal on January 15, 1996. The bank has an October 31 year end.

An annual interest rate of 10% is approximately 10%/12 for an "average" month, so we will use 10/12% as the monthly rate to compute the monthly interest of 10/12% x $100,000, or $833.33.

On February 15, 1995, and for each month in the bank's current fiscal year up to October 15, 1995, the bank will receive a cash payment of $833.33, and account for it according to the following journal entry:

	Dr	Cr
Dr Cash (B)	833.33	
Cr Interest revenue (I)		833.33

However, since the bank's year end is October 31, it must account for the fact that it has earned interest revenue from the 15th of that month to the 31st, even though no cash has been received. So, an accrual adjusting journal entry is put through the general journal on October 31, 1995, to account for the half-month's interest revenue (that is, half of $833.33) that the bank has earned but has not yet received:

	Dr	Cr
Dr Interest receivable (B)	416.67	
Cr Interest revenue (I)		416.67

But we musn't forget that the cash payment of $833.33 will be received by the bank on November 15, 1995. Since we don't wish to double-count, we must reverse the $416.47 debit to interest receivable on that date:

	Dr	Cr
Dr Cash (B)	833.33	
Cr Interest receivable (B)		416.67
Cr Interest revenue (I)		416.66

In 1985 two banks in Western Canada, the Canadian Commercial Bank and the Canadian Northlands Bank, went out of business. The customer base for these banks was mainly in Western Canada. The recession of the early 1980s, which collapsed property values, hit these banks hard when many of their loan customers found it difficult to pay interest or repay principal. These failures were a shock to the Canadian banking system, in which similar bank failures are rare (the last had occurred in 1923). The government established a Royal Commission to investigate the matter. The commission reported[3] that among many business practice, governance, and accounting problems the Canadian Commercial Bank had had, bank management had made inappropriate accounting decisions related to revenue. Since at least 1983, customers had not been repaying loans on time, and the percentage of such loans out of the total loans receivable of the bank was rising. The commission report observed:

Faced with this rise in bad loans in 1983 through 1985, CCB had a difficult choice to make. If it called the loan and disposed of the security posted by the borrower in the Alberta and British Columbia economies then existing, the bank would take large losses. The evidence is that the losses would have exceeded the bank's capital. The bank would be insolvent by any definition. On the other hand, the bank could revise the terms of the loans in a number of ways in cooperation with the borrower. The primary object of the workouts (as such arrangements were known) in the circumstances of CCB was not to insure the survival of the borrower but, of necessity, the survival of the lender, the bank itself. Survival of the lender meant in short the avoidance of capital loss which would follow the realization of the security. The survival of CCB therefore required that the problem loans in the bank be maintained at a classification above the level where a loss provision must be taken according to CCB's own rules, and income recognition cease ...

The report suggested that CCB management kept on accruing interest revenue even though there was considerable evidence that the loans should have been classified as (to use Bank of Montreal's jargon) "non-accrual."

Thus far, we've examined some of the revenue accounting decisions of three types of businesses that are among the most important to the Canadian economy: construction, real estate, and banking. One conclusion we can make is that the general revenue-accounting principles set out in the *CICA Handbook* in sections 3400 and 1000, and discussed in Chapter 4, must be custom tailored to the particular circumstances that revenue-generating organizations face. No hard-and-fast specific rule governing all revenue recognition situations is possible; indeed, such a rule would lead to highly misleading accounting results.

Accounting and Business Decision C

Organizations in different industries generate revenue in a wide variety of ways. For the following organizations, suggest (with reasons) revenue accounting policies:

[3] *Report of the Inquiry into the Collapse of the CCB and Northland Bank*, August 1986, Minister of Supply and Services, Government of Canada, 1986.

Organization's Industry	The Ways It Generates Revenue
Franchising (as the franchisor).*	• Franchisor requires a franchise fee from each new franchisee; the fee may be paid up front, or spread over some future time interval. • Franchisor may sell assets (for example, a sign) and services (for example, staff training) to the franchisee before the franchisee opens for business. • Franchisor may provide ongoing assets (for example, "special sauce" for a fast-food outlet) and services (for example, quality control, advertising, bookkeeping) to the franchisee.
Newspaper	• Newspapers are sold through "street sales" via independent vendors; through home delivery by subscription, and also on a "weekly pay" basis. • Advertising is sold on both a prepaid and a non-prepaid basis.
University	• Students pay a fee (nonrefundable after a certain portion of the course has passed) for degree and nondegree programs. The fee covers about one-sixth of the estimated cost of delivering such programs; the provincial government pays the university the other five-sixths, subject to a verification of student enrolment. • The university operates food services, parking facilities, a bookstore, and a publishing house.

* A wide variety of products and services, ranging from all varieties of fast foods through to hotel and dry cleaning services, are marketed via franchise operations, in which the franchisor provides independent businesspersons (the franchisees) with advertising, business expertise, products, and so on.

Some Examples of Expense Accounting Decisions

The general criteria for expense accounting under GAAP were provided in Chapter 4, along with some examples. Recall that "matching" was a key concept. In this part of the chapter we will describe how expenses are accounted for in a variety of situations.

Canadian Resource Companies: Full Cost Versus Successful Efforts

Barrington Petroleum Ltd., a company with headquarters in Calgary, is involved in the exploration and development of natural gas and oil, mainly in Alberta. Barrington's accounting policy footnote, included in the company's 1991 audited financial statements, was as follows:

1. SIGNIFICANT ACCOUNTING POLICIES
Petroleum and natural gas operations
The Company follows the full cost method of accounting whereby all costs relating to the exploration for and development of petroleum and natural gas reserves are capitalized. Such costs include land acquisition costs, geological and geophysical expenses, engineering fees, related direct administrative expenses and costs of drilling both productive and non-productive wells, including production equipment. Also capitalized are identifiable carrying charges on undeveloped properties. Proceeds received from disposal of property interests are credited against accumulated costs except when the disposition results in a significant change in the depletion rate in which case a gain or loss on disposal is recognized.

The carrying value of the Company's petroleum and natural gas property and equipment is compared annually to an estimate of future cash flow from the production of proven reserves, less future removal, restoration and capital costs as well as general and administrative expenses, financing costs and income taxes based on year end prices and costs. Should this comparison indicate an excess carrying value, a write-off would be recorded. No such write-off was required in 1991 or 1990.

Estimates are made of the future removal and site restoration costs relating to the Company's petroleum and natural gas properties at the end of their economic life, based on year end values net of expected recoveries, in accordance with current legislative requirements and industry practice. The Company has reviewed these requirements and determined that salvage and residual values exceed the abandonment liability. Accordingly no provision has been recorded at this time.

The costs related to petroleum and natural gas properties are depleted on the unit-of-production method based on the estimated proven reserves as determined by independent consultants, before deduction of royalties and after conversion to units of common measure based on relative energy content.

Before explaining some of the other technical accounting terms in this footnote, such as "proven reserves" and "depleted," we'll focus on the method Barrington uses to account for its exploration and development costs. Barrington tells us it uses the "full cost" method of accounting for such costs. The two methods in common use are the full cost method and the "successful efforts" method. We'll abbreviate them to FC and SE respectively. To see how they work, let's assume that a petroleum company spends $1 million on exploration in each of five drilling sites in 1995, and that it discovers oil on two of the sites. The other three sites are "dry holes." The two productive sites are expected to produce a total of 10,000,000 barrels of oil, 1,000,000 of which are produced and sold for $19 each in the current year (1995). The FC versus the SE results for 1995 are shown on the next page, assuming (for simplicity) no other taxes or expenses:

	Full Cost	Successful Efforts
Revenue (1,000,000 bbls @ $19)	$19,000,000	$19,000,000
Expenses		
Dry hole costs (3 dry holes @ $1 million each)	not applicable	3,000,000
Depletion		
• FC (($5 million/10 million bbl) × 1 million bbl raised and sold in 1995)	500,000	
• SE ($2 million/10 million bbl × 1 million bbl raised and sold in 1995)		200,000
Total expenses	500,000	3,200,000
Net income	$18,500,000	$15,800,000

The two methods of accounting for exploration and development costs may result in, as we can see, significant differences in reported net income for such companies. Generally speaking, smaller resource companies that concentrate on the exploration and development phases of the business might be expected to prefer the FC method, since dry hole costs are deferred and spread over future years. In contrast, the SE method expenses dry hole costs immediately in the accounting period in which management decides that the exploration site is nonproductive.

The Barrington footnote said that the costs related to the company's petroleum and natural gas properties were "depleted on the unit-of-production method." "Depletion" is defined in the CICA's *Terminology for Accountants* as "a charge in an accounting period to reflect that portion of the cost or other recorded value of wasting assets consumed or removed in that period." In other words, depletion is the natural resource analogue of depreciation. For a description of the unit-of-production method, refer to the section "Depreciation Accounting: Multiperiod Expense Decisions" presented later in this chapter.

The Barrington footnote also referred to "estimated proven reserves." *Terminology for Accountants* defines this term, along with related terms, in the following way:

In the extractive industries, [reserves are] unexploited minerals or hydrocarbons underground within the boundaries of the organization's property.

possible reserves
Estimates of quantities of minerals or hydrocarbons that are based largely on broad knowledge of geological characteristics of the area and for which there are few, if any, samples or measurements.

probable reserves
Quantities of minerals or hydrocarbons adjacent to proved reserves that may be expected to exist based on the results of scientific measurement, sampling and extrapolation.

proved reserves
proven reserves
Quantities of minerals or hydrocarbons having commercial value, scientifically estimated by measurement and sampling, that can be extracted and processed within the general limits of existing technology and regulations.

Resource companies such as Barrington typically disclose their proven and probable reserves. For example, Chauvco Resources Ltd., another Calgary-based Canadian oil and gas company, disclosed the following in its 1992 Annual Report:

Working interest reserves

	1992	1991	% Change	1990
Crude oil and [natural gas liquids] — Mbbls				
Proven	39,039	33,087	+18	21,672
Probable	13,439	9,708	+38	8,082
	52,478	42,795	+23	29,754
Natural gas — Bcf				
Proven	320.4	99.5	+222	96.9
Probable	146.2	14.3	+923	12.7
	466.6	113.8	+310	109.6

In the above table, Mbbls means "thousands of barrels" and "Bcf" means "billions of cubic feet."

Accounting for Future Removal and Site Restoration Costs

Back in Chapter 2, we described accountability as one of the basic ideas in accounting. As individuals, governments, and society in general become more aware of their responsibilities to minimize environmental damage, levels of accountability increase. Industrial companies are beginning to account for the costs and liabilities of the pollution they create, natural resource companies are beginning to account for the costs of restoring the sites they exploit, and so on. And GAAP standards are evolving to reflect these changes, albeit too slowly in the eyes of some.

For example, in the early 1990s the following paragraphs were added to the *CICA Handbook* section "Capital Assets":

.39 When reasonably determinable, provisions should be made for future removal and site restoration costs, net of expected recoveries, in a rational and systematic manner by charges to income.

.40 Future removal and site restoration costs include costs, net of expected recoveries, for dismantling and abandoning a property. Provisions are needed to accrue the liability for future removal and site restoration costs, when the likelihood of their occurrence is established as a result of environmental law, contract, or because the enterprise has established a policy to restore a site, and when such costs can be reasonably determined ...

.41 When future removal and site restoration costs cannot be reasonably determined, a contingent liability may exist ...

Thus, under Canadian GAAP, resource companies such as mines, logging companies, and oil and gas exploration and development companies, are now held accountable for measuring and reporting future removal and site restoration costs. This is an application of the concepts of a liability and of expense matching, as discussed in Chapter 4. In other words, restoring the environment to as close to its original state as possible is now regarded as just another cost of doing business for these companies, and such a cost is to be estimated and recorded as an expense in the accounting period in which the mining or other resource extraction activity took place and the company's revenues were earned. It doesn't matter that the actual cash payments for site restoration may not occur for many years, until the mine (say) is shut down. The costs accrue as the mining or other revenue-generating activity takes place.

Disclosing these costs and liabilities, however, is left to management's discretion, as suggested in section 3060.63 of the *CICA Handbook*:

Additional desirable disclosures include: (a) the accumulated provision for future removal and site restoration costs and the major assumptions used and the basis for determining the provision; and (b) the amount of the future removal and site restoration costs charged to income for the period.

Note that GAAP permits these disclosures to be voluntary. Exhibits 5–3 shows how Cathedral Gold Corporation, a small mining company headquartered in Vancouver, made such expense-related disclosures for its mine site restoration costs.

EXHIBIT 5–3
EXCERPTS FROM CATHEDRAL GOLD MINE CORPORATION'S 1992 AUDITED FINANCIAL STATEMENTS

On the balance sheet, as a long-term liability:

	1992	1991
Future Site Restoration Costs	$44,127	$21,046

In its consolidated statements of cash flows, the company disclosed "future site restoration costs" of $21,046 and $23,081 in 1991 and 1992, respectively, as one of the items reconciling between net income and cash provided by operating activities. [In other words, these amounts were not expended in cash; they were accrued.]

In the "Significant Accounting Policies" note:

"Future Site Restoration Costs

The estimated costs for restoration of producing resource properties are accrued and charged to operations over commercial production using a rate based upon total estimated site restoration costs and recoverable reserves. The estimated costs for restoration of non-producing resources are accrued as liabilities when the costs of site clean-up and restoration are probable and the costs can be reasonably estimated. Actual site restoration costs will be deducted from the accrual."

The journal entry that Cathedral recorded to account for its estimate of future site restoration costs in 1991 was, apparently:

Dr Operating costs (I)	21,046	
Cr Future site restoration costs (B)		21,046

(a) What was Cathedral's journal entry to record its 1992 estimate of future site restoration costs?

(b) Explain how the matching concept and the definition of a liability could justify accounting for estimated future site restoration costs.

Depreciation Accounting: Multiperiod Expense Decisions

In Chapter 1, we briefly described how Corel Corporation accounted for its depreciable tangible and intangible capital assets. The accounting decisions involved may be summarized as follows:

- Does a particular expenditure (recall that the term "expenditure" means "an outflow of resources") represent a capital asset, some other asset classification (inventory, perhaps), or an expense or loss?
- If the expenditure is a capital asset, is it a tangible or an intangible capital asset, and is it depreciable (if tangible; amortizable if intangible), or not?
- If the expenditure is a tangible, depreciable capital asset, what depreciation pattern should be used? Over how many future accounting periods should depreciation be accounted for? And what total dollar amount should be depreciated?
- If the expenditure is an intangible, amortizable capital asset, what amortization pattern should be used? Over how many future accounting periods should amortization be accounted for? And what total dollar amount should be amortized?

There are a lot of questions to deal with here; in this chapter we will limit ourselves to describing various depreciation patterns. However, many other accounting decisions related to depreciation accounting will be dealt with throughout this book.

We'll illustrate the various depreciation patterns using the following data:

Suppose that a company's comptroller recommended that a new machine be purchased, and therefore the company made the following expenditures in September 19X1:

Invoice amount of new machine	$25,000
Provincial sales tax and GST (total: 15% of invoice amount)	3,750
Delivery	1,500
Installation	10,500
	$40,750

Unfortunately, the machine was initially installed incorrectly, and the $10,500 incurred for installation (which includes the cost of labour and materials) is twice as much as a single proper installation would cost. The journal entry to record this information is:

Dr	Capital asset, machine (B)	35,500	
Dr	Loss on installation (I)	5,250	
	Cr (Accounts payable, Wages payable, etc.) (all B)		40,750

The machine is expected to have a salvage value of about $5,500 at the end of its expected service life of ten years. Thus, the depreciation base (which is the total cost less the expected salvage value) is $30,000; this is the total amount that will be charged off to depreciation expense over the years. A variety of different depreciation patterns are possible; the following discussion deals with some of the most popular ones.

Straight-line depreciation on a time basis

This pattern accounts for depreciation expense in such a way that each accounting period (year, quarter, month, and so on) receives an equal depreciation expense. If the company prepares monthly financial statements, depreciation expense related to the machine will be computed as follows:

Depreciation base/ expected service life in months	= ($35,500-$5,500)/120 months
	= $250 per month

Therefore, the monthly journal entry to record depreciation expense would be:

Dr Depreciation expense (I)	250	
Cr Accumulated depreciation (B)		250

If the company accounted for depreciation annually, the entry would be:

Dr Depreciation expense (I)	3,000	
Cr Accumulated depreciation (B)		3,000

Straight-line depreciation on a units-of-production basis

This pattern ensures that depreciation falls equally on each unit of product that is produced with the machine. Suppose that instead of defining the machine's expected service life in terms of time, we define it in terms of the expected number of units of output. Let's assume that the company's chief production engineer has determined that about 100,000 units of product will be produced over the expected useful life of the machine. This works out to ($35,500-$5,500)/100,000 units, or $0.30 per unit. If the company prepares financial statements annually, and 11,000 units were actually produced in the first year the machine was in use, depreciation would be 11,000 units × $0.30/unit, or $3,300.

The journal entry would be:

Dr Depreciation expense (I)	3,300	
Cr Accumulated depreciation (B)		3,300

But this journal entry has an implicit assumption hidden on its debit side; it assumes that the $3,300 of depreciation cost should be an expense. This ignores the fact that the machine was being used to add value to the product produced. Thus, a very strong accounting argument could be made that the entry should be:

Dr Inventory (B)	3,300	
Cr Accumulated depreciation (B)		3,300

In this way, the depreciation cost of the depreciable capital asset gets included as part of the cost of the inventory that it helped to produce. When the products are sold, the inventory becomes part of cost of sales, so eventually the $3,300 of first-year depreciation cost winds up as part of an expense on the income statement — next year, perhaps. Notice that this problem of "where to put the depreciation debit" exists only for depreciable tangible capital assets *that are used to produce inventory*. For other depreciable tangible capital assets, such as furniture in a company's sales or central accounting office, accountants usually debit depreciation expense, since sales and accounting activity isn't closely related to adding value to the inventory. For the remainder of our description of depreciation patterns in this chapter, we'll assume that the "machine" is now being used by the sales department (it's turned into a laser printer, perhaps). This will permit us to "assume away" this wrinkle.

Sum-of-years'-digits depreciation

This depreciation method, much more popular in the United States than in Canada, is one of a class of depreciation methods referred to as "diminishing balance methods" or "accelerated depreciation methods." These are characterized by higher depreciation charges earlier in an asset's life. The sum-of-years'-digits, or SYD, method works as follows:

For annual depreciation accounting, we know that the expected service life of the asset is ten years. Now, the sum of years' digits in ten is [1 + 2 + 3 + 4 + 5 + 6 + 7 + 8 + 9 + 10], or 55. The SYD depreciation method computes the first year's depreciation as 10/55 times the depreciation base of $30,000; the second year's as 9/55 times the depreciation base of $30,000; the third year's as 8/55 times the depreciation base of $30,000; and so on. By the end of the tenth year, 55/55, or 100%, of the depreciation base will have been charged off to depreciation. So, the journal entry for the first year is:

Dr Depreciation expense (I)	5454.54	
Cr Accumulated depreciation (B)		5,454.54

which is 10/55 × $30,000. The depreciation charges year by year for the $30,000 depreciation base of the machine (now a printer!) are as at the top of the next column.

Year	Depreciation expense
1	$ 5,454.54
2	$ 4,909.09
3	$ 4,363.64
4	$ 3,818.18
5	$ 3,272.73
6	$ 2,727.27
7	$ 2,181.83
8	$ 1,636.36
9	$ 1,090.91
10	$ 545.45
	$30,000.00

Constant-percentage diminishing balance depreciation methods (also called declining balance methods, and accelerated methods) These methods compute depreciation cost in the following manner: A constant fraction between zero and one (which users of this method often express as a percentage) is multiplied by the net book value (which is, recall from Chapter 1, the cost of the asset less its accumulated depreciation). Varying the constant fraction chosen causes the depreciation to vary. Suppose we choose 0.2, or 20%, as the constant fraction for the machine. Depreciation year by year is then:

Year	Net Book Value, Start of Year [A]	Depreciation Expense (=[A] × 20%]	Net Book Value, End of Year
1	$35,500.00	$ 7,100.00	$28,400.00
2	$28,400.00	$ 5,680.00	$22,720.00
3	$22,720.00	$ 4,544.00	$18,176.00
4	$18,176.00	$ 3,635.20	$14,540.80
5	$14,540.80	$ 2,908.16	$11,632.64
6	$11,632.64	$ 2,326.53	$ 9,306.11
7	$ 9,306.11	$ 1,861.22	$ 7,444.89
8	$ 7,444.89	$ 1,488.98	$ 5,955.92
9	$ 5,955.92	$ 1,191.18	$ 4,764.74
10	$ 4,764.74	$ 952.95	$ 3,811.79
		$31,688.22	

Recall that the expected salvage value of the machine was assumed to be $5,500, so the 20% accelerated depreciation method has overshot by $5,500 - $3,811.79, or $1,688.21. A more precise accelerated rate would be below 20%. However, given that depreciation accounting is replete with estimations and approximations (just look back at the list of all the accounting decisions that must be made for a full depreciation accounting!), most accountants and managers would not be too concerned.

Other depreciation accounting patterns

The methods just described are some of the most popular depreciation methods. In Canada, the most common methods used by companies that prepare financial statements in accordance with GAAP are as follows, based upon a survey of 300 public companies:[4]

	Number of Companies			
	1992	1991	1990	1989
Straight-line	143	137	139	137
Straight-line and				
• diminishing balance	62	65	65	67
• unit of production	46	47	50	49
• other	4	4	3	3
Diminishing balance	16	17	19	17
Unit of production	14	14	8	6
Other	9	9	10	13
Total disclosing methods	294	293	294	292

For financial accounting purposes, managers and accountants should bear in mind the qualitative criteria described in Chapter 4 when choosing a depreciation method. The matching concept becomes very important here; selecting a method which matches the cost of a depreciable capital asset to the revenues the company's use of that asset helped to generate is the key. Of course, this is a very rough process of approximation, given all the assumptions that must be made about capital assets and their depreciation.

Selecting depreciation methods is much easier for income tax purposes than for financial accounting purposes, at least in Canada. The regulations to the Income Tax Act specify that capital assets must be categorized into one of several classes, with generally different depreciation patterns allowable for each class. For example, aircraft are allocated to class 16,[5] and depreciation expense may be recorded up to a maximum of 40% using the declining balance method. Notice that the word "maximum" is used: a company can choose to record no depreciation at all (this would be a rational decision if its taxable income was zero or negative). The depreciation patterns specified in the Income Tax Act's regulations often have very little relationship to matching, or to many of the other desirable qualitative characteristics of financial accounting set out in Chapter 4. This is because the act has purposes far different from those of financial accounting. Say, for example, that a manufacturing or resource company acquires equipment for the purpose of reducing air pollution. The regulations permit the capital asset to be included in class 27, which permits a 50% declining balance depreciation write-off. This very fast depreciation deduction serves to reduce the company's taxable income, and thus the taxes it must pay in the first year or two in which it owns the asset. Here, the government is using the act to accomplish its broad social goals, and not particularly to ensure that a "correct" depreciation number is recorded. This

[4] The survey was conducted by the Studies and Standards Department of the CICA, and is published in *Financial Reporting in Canada* 1993, 20th Edition.

[5] Income Tax Regulations, Schedule II, June 1993.

means that a company may record one depreciation number for a capital asset in its financial accounting records, and a significantly different number on its corporate income tax return. In fact, the number computed for income tax purposes in Canada is so unrelated to the financial accounting depreciation number, both in concept and in amount in any given accounting period, that a special, technical name is used for Canadian income tax depreciation: capital cost allowance (abbreviated as CCA). But just to keep us on our toes, the term "tax depreciation" is used in the United States!

Income Tax Expense

We have seen that CCA and depreciation expense are in general quite different for a given company. In fact, there are many revenue and expense items that are accounted for differently by the financial accounting system and the Canadian income tax accounting system. The differences between these two accounting systems fall into two broad categories: permanent differences, and timing differences.

Permanent differences

These are revenues and expenses that exist in the financial accounting system but not in the income tax accounting system, or vice versa. For example, under Canadian income tax law, interest paid to the government on late income tax instalments is not permitted as a tax deduction, although such interest costs are bona fide business expenses and accounted for as such under GAAP.

Timing differences

These are revenues and expenses that exist in both the financial accounting and income tax accounting systems, but in different accounting periods. Suppose that a landlord receives $1,000 in rent on December 20, 19X1, from a prospective tenant. The payment is for occupying the premises during January 19X2. If the income tax legislation requires that rental payments be accounted for as taxable revenue in the accounting period when received, then income tax is due and a current liability called "Income taxes payable" will appear on the landlord's balance sheet as of December 31, 19X1. But the landlord has not yet earned the revenue, and won't until 19X2 when the tenant actually occupies the premises. So for financial accounting purposes, there is no revenue in 19X1. However, there will be in 19X2.

Income tax expense in financial accounting is derived according to the revenue and expense numbers that financial accounting computes. On the other hand, the actual amount that must, by law, be paid to the government (that is, the income tax payable) is of course derived according to the revenue and expense numbers that are required to be computed under the Income Tax Act. Financial accounting's "net income before income tax expense" (or NIBT, for short), and the act's "taxable income" (or TI for short), in any given year for a particular company are related as follows:

TI = NIBT **plus or minus** permanent differences **plus or minus** timing differences

Let's see how this equation works for the landlord example above, assuming a 40% income tax rate. In 19X1, we have no permanent differences and one timing difference.

TI (taxable Income)	=	NIBT (net income before taxes)	+or- PDs (permanent differences)	+or- TDs (timing differences)
$1,000	=	$0	$0	+$1,000

Since the income tax rate is 40%, we know that income tax of $400 must be paid; therefore, "Income tax payable" on the landlord's December 31, 19X1, balance sheet is $400, and thus a credit of $400 must have gone to that account. But recall that the financial accounting system insisted that no revenue be recognized (it won't be earned until 19X2); therefore, no income tax expense should be accounted for, because there's no revenue against which to match it. If the debit side of the journal entry recording the $400 payable cannot go to "Income tax expense," where can it go? Accountants have come up with an ingenious way of recording this amount: it's accounted for as "Deferred income taxes," a balance sheet account. The journal entry for 19X1 is then:

Dr Deferred income taxes (B)	400	
Cr Income taxes payable (B)		400

Notice that both sides of this entry are to balance sheet accounts; income is not affected at all in 19X1, at least insofar as financial accounting is concerned. Also, note that the debit of $400 is very similar to a prepaid asset (that is, from financial accounting's perspective, the income tax was "paid in advance" of revenue being earned).

In 19X2, taxable income is zero (the revenue was taxed in 19X1), but NIBT is $1,000:

TI (taxable income)	=	NIBT (net income before taxes)	+or- PDs (permanent differences)	+or- TDs (timing differences)
$0	=	$1,000	$0	-$1,000

And the 19X2 journal entry is:

Dr Income tax expense (I)	400	
Cr Deferred income taxes (B)		400

The income tax expense is matched, according to the financial accounting system, to the rental revenue that was recognized in 19X2. In effect, the $400 debit waited on the balance sheet until financial accounting needed it.

Deferred income taxes are an accounting artefact created because of the interaction of two accounting subdisciplines: financial accounting and income tax accounting. Financial accounting (GAAP) principles determine revenues and expenses, which in turn determine NIBT; income tax expense is then derived by multiplying NIBT by the income tax rate.[6] On the other hand, income tax legislation determines tax revenues and deductions; these in turn determine TI, which when multiplied by the tax rate gives income tax payable.

Perhaps the most significant timing difference between the two subdisciplines of accounting arises from the differences between depreciation (a financial accounting number) and CCA (a tax legislation number). Suppose a company has the following results for 19X1:

Net income before income tax expense	$100,000
Depreciation	20,000
CCA	50,000
Interest on late income-tax instalments	5,000
Income tax rate	40%

What is the income tax journal entry for 19X1?

Let's collect all the information in a spreadsheet. This will help us keep track of permanent and timing differences.

[6] This statement is not true under all conditions. More complex situations are examined in intermediate accounting courses.

	"Accounting Income"	"Taxable Income"	"Timing Differences"
NIBT	$100,000	$100,000	
Adjust for permanent differences:			
Add: Interest on late tax instalments (a PD)	5,000	5,000	
NIBT adjusted for permanent differences	$105,000	105,000	
Adjust for timing differences:			
Add: Depreciation		20,000	20,000
Deduct: CCA		(50,000)	(50,000)
TI		$ 75,000	

The spreadsheet column headed "Taxable Income" is simply a reconciliation between NIBT and TI; in effect, it merely adjusts for PDs and TDs. The journal entry to account for income taxes is:

Dr Income tax expense (I)	42,000	
Cr Income tax payable (B)		30,000
Cr Deferred income taxes (B)		12,000

The credit of $30,000 to "Income tax payable" is 40% × the TI of $75,000; the credit of $12,000 to "Deferred income taxes" is 40% × the net timing difference of $50,000-$20,000 (CCA is greater than depreciation, but over the life of the depreciable capital assets that depreciation and CCA relate to, their cumulative sums must be equal, and this creates a timing difference). The $42,000 debit to "Income tax expense" is 40% × $105,000 (which is NIBT after we adjust for the permanent difference of $5,000, which will never be deductible on the company's tax return).

In the landlord example we could interpret the $400 debited to deferred income taxes as being similar to a prepaid asset; the interpretation of the $12,000 credited to deferred income taxes in this example is much more difficult. This is because the $12,000 represents neither a liability, nor part of shareholders' equity. It's not a liability, since it doesn't fit the definition in Chapter 4; after all, it's just an accounting artefact and isn't really owed to the government. And it's not part of shareholders' equity, since if it were, the income tax expense would not be equal to $42,000, the amount we derive by applying GAAP.

Inventory Accounting and the Cost of Goods Sold Expense

Accounting for inventory under GAAP's historic cost model involves a number of decisions:

1. What should be included in inventory? (This is an accounting classification decision.) We refer to this decision regarding what to include in inventory as the "cost inclusiveness decision."
2. How should managers and accountants decide which inventory costs should be reclassified into the expense category as cost of sales (or, as cost of goods sold), when the cost of each unit of inventory is not identical? We refer to this as the "cost flow decision."
3. What happens, under GAAP, if the inventory's balance sheet cost amount exceeds what we may reasonably expect the inventory will be sold or replaced for? (In technical jargon, what happens when *cost* exceeds *market*?) How reasonable is it to continue to account for an asset at a valuation that is known to be overly optimistic? We refer to this as the "lower of cost and market decision."

Let's examine each of these decisions in turn:

1. The cost inclusiveness decision

For purposes of describing the cost inclusiveness decision for inventory accounting under GAAP, it's useful to think of all the costs incurred by an organization as falling into two categories: product costs and period costs. Product costs are those costs which are related to the product that the organization produces and/or sells, while period costs are related to the ongoing ability of the organization to continue operating from accounting period to accounting period. An example of a product cost would be the cost of the wood and other materials included in tables and chairs by a furniture manufacturer. Or, for a retailer, it would be the cost of transporting inventory to the retailer's place of business (a showroom, perhaps). An example of a period cost is the cost of interest on bonds that a company has issued. In practice, the costs that an organization incurs may be thought of as falling along a continuum. "Pure" product and period costs anchor the two ends of that continuum, as follows (using a manufacturing company to illustrate):

The Cost Continuum

A			B			C
• direct material • direct labour	• variable manufacturing overhead	• fixed manufacturing overhead	• R&D costs	• marketing costs	• administrative costs	• financing costs

"Overhead" in this cost continuum is defined as "all production costs other than direct material and direct labour costs ... [Overhead costs] encompass all costs necessary to the operation and maintenance of the plant, including wages of foremen, building and machinery upkeep and depreciation, light, heating, repairs, insurance, taxes, etc."[7]

All the costs between points A and B are accounted for as product costs by most Canadian manufacturers, and therefore are included in inventory. This means that the inventory account is debited when the particular cost is incurred, and it is only in the accounting period in which the manufacturer sells the inventory that the cost winds up as an expense as part of the cost of sales for that particular accounting period. All the costs between points B and C are accounted for as period costs by most Canadian manufacturers; therefore, they are debited to an expense account in the accounting period in which the cost was incurred.

Companies that include all the costs between points A and B as inventory costs are called "full cost" or "absorption cost" companies. Some companies exclude fixed manufacturing overhead from the inventory classification (they debit it directly to expense accounts), and only include direct labour costs, direct material costs, and variable manufacturing overhead costs in inventory. Such companies are called "variable cost" or "direct cost" companies. The vast majority of Canadian companies that prepare GAAP-basis financial statements use the full-cost inventory method. Managers and accountants who favour full-cost inventory accounting argue that all costs related to inventory should be classified as inventory costs, including fixed manufacturing overhead costs. Those who favour variable costing argue that even though fixed manufacturing overhead costs are indeed related to inventory, the magnitude of such costs is unrelated to the volume (number of units) of inventory produced in a given accounting period, since these costs are "fixed" and must be incurred whether inventory is produced or not. They conclude that if variable costing is used, the resulting net income number will be more closely a function of the number of units sold than if full costing were used, and they believe that is a good thing. A small example will illustrate the point:

[7] CICA, *Terminology for Accountants*, Fourth Edition, 1992, p. 150.

Suppose a manufacturing company's accounting records reveal that for Year X1:

- The cost of direct materials per unit of inventory manufactured was $3.00.
- The cost of direct labour per unit of inventory manufactured was $0.50.
- The cost of variable manufacturing overhead per unit of inventory manufactured was $4.00.
- No inventory existed at the start of the accounting period, 10,000 units were produced during the period, and 8,000 were sold at $15.00 each.
- Fixed manufacturing overhead incurred for the accounting period was $20,000, and all other costs (marketing, administrative, and so on) totalled $30,000.
- No taxes were payable.

Income statements under full and variable costing would be as follows:

	Full Costing	**Variable Costing**
Sales	$120,000	$120,000
Cost of goods sold	76,000	60,000
Gross profit	44,000	60,000
Expenses		
Fixed manufacturing overhead	not applicable	20,000
Other	30,000	30,000
	30,000	50,000
Net income	$ 14,000	$ 10,000

Cost of goods sold under the full costing method is computed as follows: Cost of manufacturing one unit of inventory is $3.00 of direct materials plus $0.50 of direct labour plus $4.00 of variable manufacturing overhead plus $20,000/10,000 units (or $2.00 per unit) of fixed manufacturing overhead, for a total of $9.50. But since only 8,000 units were sold, the matching principle requires that only 8,000 units × $9.50 per unit, or $76,000, be transferred from the inventory account to cost of goods sold.

Cost of goods sold under the variable costing method excludes the $2.00 per unit of fixed manufacturing overhead (after all, under this method the entire fixed manufacturing overhead has already been expensed, and we want to avoid double-counting), and is thus just $7.50 per unit, or $60,000 for the 8,000 units sold during the period.

Notice that net income under full costing is greater than under variable costing. This result is usually true when the number of units of inventory produced during the accounting period exceeds the number of units sold during that period. In this situation, full costing defers some of the fixed manufacturing overhead as part of inventory on the balance sheet ($4,000 in our example), while variable costing simply expenses the entire amount of fixed manufacturing overhead.

An illustration of disclosure and accounting for the cost inclusiveness decision is provided by Chai-Na-Ta Corp., a company headquartered in Langley, British Columbia. Chai-Na-Ta is involved in the production, processing, and distribution of North American ginseng. It operates several farms in southern B.C. and has recently expanded into Ontario. Ginseng is harvested only once every three or four years, so costs accumulate over a considerable period of time. In its 1992 Annual Report the company described its accounting policy with respect to ginseng crops as follows:[8]

[8] By permission of Chai-Na-Ta-Corp., Langley, B.C.

The Company uses the full absorption costing method to value its ginseng crops. Included in crop costs are seed, labour, applicable overhead, interest and supplies. Costs are allocated each period based on the total number of acres under cultivation during the period.

Those crop costs relating to the acreage harvested and sold have been charged to cost of sales.

To get a clearer picture of the types of costs that Chai-Na-Ta includes, here is the company's Consolidated Statement of Crop Costs:

Years Ended May 31	**1992**	**1991**	**1990**
Depreciation	$ 580,678	$ 467,578	$ 377,458
Farm equipment operating costs	257,265	206,090	150,263
Interest and financing charges	892,838	167,162	55,744
Land rental	311,383	200,039	69,367
Mulch and fertilizer	561,012	700,394	406,192
Other	53,380	82,491	51,442
Plant science	25,228	26,551	19,501
Salaries and wages	2,525,352	1,488,537	1,048,425
Seed	642,032	388,598	290,210
Small tools and supplies	59,921	64,943	65,319
Warehouse and dryer operations	47,619	—	—
	$ 5,956,708	$3,792,383	$2,533,921
Balance beginning of year	7,244,974	4,332,334	2,840,939
	$13,201,682	$8,124,717	$5,374,860
Less: Cost of crop and seed harvested during the year	2,506,375	879,743	1,042,526
Balance at end of year	$10,695,307	$7,244,974	$4,332,334

2. The cost flow decision

Suppose that a Canadian company buys and sells PC monitors, and that during January 19X1 it made the following purchases:

- January 5: 10 monitors @ $200 each
- January 10: 20 monitors @ $250 each
- January 20: 15 monitors @ $260 each

All monitors are completely identical; the unit prices have changed because of changing supply and demand for monitors generally, and also because the Canadian company must pay its overseas supplier for the monitors in a foreign currency. At the start of January, five monitors were on hand from the previous month, which had been purchased at $190 each.

On January 25 the company sold 30 monitors for $350 each. Assume that all other expenses (marketing, administrative, and so on) total $2,000. Managers and accountants who wish to prepare financial statements according to GAAP in this situation must comply with the *CICA Handbook's* section on inventory accounting,[9] which requires that historic cost be used. But since the unit cost is changing, just how are we to determine historic cost if the monitors are identical and we can't tell which 30 from among the 50 available for sale were the ones actually sold? The *CICA Handbook* describes four alternative ways of dealing with this situation. Provided next are four simple situations (in practice, there are quite a few complications, as well as other variations):

1. Specific identification: "The cost of each item is ascertained. This method can only be used where the items under consideration are of such a nature and value as to make individual identification a practical procedure." Under this alternative, we do away with the problem by keeping track of each monitor separately. This seems worthwhile for high unit-value items (for example, cars in a new car dealership), but not for inventory with really small unit costs of under a few dollars. The monitors are somewhere in the middle of this range. With the advent of computer and telecommunications technology in the field of inventory management and control, the cost of detailed record-keeping has declined enormously over the past decade. In our situation, perhaps each monitor might have its own bar code, which could be scanned when it is sold so that specific information related to its particular cost could be accounted for.

Start of January:	5 units on hand @ $190	$ 950
January 5 acquisitions:	10 units @ $200	2,000
January 10 acquisitions	15 units @ $250	3,750
FIFO cost of goods sold		$6,700

2. Average: "The cost of an item is determined from the weighted average of the cost of similar items at the beginning of the period and of the cost of all similar items acquired during the period. The average may be calculated on an annual, monthly or other periodic basis, or as each additional shipment is received, depending on the circumstances of the business."

   The weighted average unit cost of the monitors is computed as follows:

   [(5 × $190) + (10 × $200) + (20 × $250) + (15 × $260)]/ 50 monitors = $237 per unit

   Cost of sales under this method would be 30 × $237, or $7,110.

3. First In, First Out (FIFO): "For the purposes of income determination, the cost of the first goods purchased or acquired is the cost assigned to the first goods sold. Therefore, the cost allocated to the inventory items on hand at the end of the period is the cost of those items most recently acquired." So, to build up to the cost of goods sold on a FIFO basis, we must go back to the inventory on hand at the start of the accounting period, and keep on adding in costs until we account for the 30 monitors sold. See the chart at the bottom left.

   Notice that even though 20 monitors were acquired on January 10, only the cost of 15 was needed to build up to the FIFO cost for the 30 monitors sold.

4. Last In, First Out (LIFO): "For the purposes of income determination, the cost of the goods most recently purchased or acquired is the cost assigned to the first goods sold ..." On a LIFO cost basis, then, the monitor retailer would compute the following cost of sales (see table, next page):

[9] Section 3030, titled simply "Inventories." The quotations that follow are from paragraph 3030.07.

January 20 acquisitions	15 units @ $260	$3,900
January 10 acquisitions	15 units @ $250	3,750
LIFO cost of goods sold		$7,650

Regarding which cost flow assumption should be used: Income statements for January for the monitor retailer, under each of the weighted average, FIFO, and LIFO cost flow assumptions, are presented below.

	Average	FIFO	LIFO
Sales	$10,500	$10,500	$10,500
Cost of sales	7,110	6,700	7,650
Gross profit	3,390	3,800	2,850
Other expenses	2,000	2,000	2,000
Net income	$ 1,390	$ 1,800	$ 850

Clearly, the variation in reported net income is considerable. What guidance does the *CICA Handbook* provide for making this inventory accounting decision? For this, see paragraph 3030.08:

The selection of the most suitable method for determining the cost will depend upon the particular circumstances of each enterprise and the industry in which it is engaged. In some cases, the choice of method may have little effect on the financial statements. In other cases, where the choice of method of inventory valuation is an important factor in determining income, the most suitable method for determining cost is that which results in charging against operations costs which most fairly match the sales revenue for the period.

And in paragraph 3030.09:

***The method selected for determining cost should be one which results in the fairest matching of costs against revenues regardless of whether or not the method corresponds to the physical flow of goods.*[10]

So the GAAP criterion for deciding how to determine which of the historic cost flow assumptions — average, FIFO, or LIFO — should be followed is the very general matching criterion. In the early 1980s many managers argued that when the costs of labour, materials, and so on were inflating at levels above, say, 5% to 7%, LIFO provided the best matching because it charged off the cost of the most recent, more expensive purchases against a company's revenues, which were inflating also. However, it is rare that accounting decisions, such as choosing an inventory cost flow assumption within the historic cost GAAP model, are resolved by applying only concepts from conceptual framework literature, such as matching.

In Canada back in 1947, the Federal Court of Canada ruled that LIFO could not be used to prepare a corporation's tax return. Now, one of the themes of this book is that even though all the areas of accounting are related (in that they depend on the seven basic ideas described in Chapter 2, and on the concept of a transaction as described in Chapter 3), each has its own separate purposes and constraints; this means that a solution that is optimum in one accounting area may not be optimum for another. By law, LIFO cannot be used to compute a corporation's taxable income in Canada; however, the *CICA Handbook's* section 3030 doesn't prevent LIFO from being used for financial accounting purposes. In fact, application of the matching criterion seems to support its use. But, because virtually all Canadian companies that must comply with GAAP wish to avoid using one accounting method for income tax pur-

[10] In the *CICA Handbook*, the italicized paragraphs (marked in this book with a double asterisk), set out the formal, codified GAAP. The non-italicized paragraphs provide background and clarifying information.

poses (say, FIFO or average), and another for financial accounting purposes (LIFO), almost none use LIFO for financial accounting. In fact, *Financial Reporting in Canada 1993* reports that 48% of the sample companies use FIFO, 35% use weighted average, only 4% use LIFO, and the remaining companies use a variety of other methods.

3. The lower of cost and market decision

The third of the three major categories of GAAP-basis inventory accounting decisions involves two phases. First, we need an answer to this question: "Should inventory be accounted for on a company's balance sheet at (average, FIFO, LIFO, and so on) cost if the cost number exceeds the market value of the inventory?" Let's make this easy to answer by assuming that the difference between the cost and market value numbers is material (recall the materiality criterion from Chapter 4), and that we expect the decline of the market value to be permanent. Under these conditions, if we left the inventory at cost on the balance sheet, the resulting financial statements wouldn't satisfy several of the desirable qualitative characteristics of accounting information as described in Chapter 4. For example, the balance sheet measure of inventory would not be representationally faithful. So writing the inventory down to market value seems to be a reasonable thing to do. For example, suppose that FIFO cost was $1,000 and market value was $800; a journal entry such as the following would record the write-down, in the accounting period in which the market decline below cost was decided by management to be material and permanent:

Dr Loss due to decline in market value of inventory (I)	200	
Cr Inventory (B)		200

where the account "Loss due to decline in market value of inventory" is an expense account appearing on the income statement.

A second question is this: "What 'market value' should be used? The replacement cost of the inventory (an input market number), or the 'net realizable value' (abbreviated NRV) of the inventory (an output market number)?" Canadian GAAP permits either, although most companies use NRV.

The two numbers could, in any given situation, be quite different. NRV is equal to the estimated selling price of inventory under normal business conditions, after estimated costs of completion and sale are deducted. Replacement cost is equal to the cost of replacing the inventory. Both quantities — NRV and replacement cost — must be estimated at the same date.

Let's put the above description of GAAP inventory accounting into perspective by calculating the number of alternatives available, all within GAAP. The inclusiveness decision involved two choices, full costing versus variable costing; the cost flow decision involved three choices (ignoring specific identification); and the lower of cost and market decision involved two decisions. Thus, there are 2 × 3 × 2 for a total of 12 alternatives. Actually, we're understating the number of alternatives here, since each method has one or more variations. Also, companies with more than one product line are under no requirement to use the same methods for each line.

Special inventory approximation methods used by retailers — the retail and gross profit methods

Retail organizations such as Woolworths, Sears, and The Bay often use two accounting methods that approximate historic cost. We can illustrate the *retail inventory accounting* method with the following data:

	Fiscal Year 1995	
	Cost	Retail
Opening inventory	$ 57,000	$ 95,000
Purchases during period	291,000	450,000
Goods available for sale	$348,000	$545,000
Ratio of cost to retail: $348,000/$545,000 =	63.85%	
Deduct: Sales		395,000
Closing inventory, at retail		$150,000
Times ratio of cost to retail computed above		× 63.85%
Equals estimate of closing inventory at cost		$ 95,775

This approximation method of determining inventory (and therefore also cost of sales) requires companies to keep a record of the cost and retail value of opening inventory and current period purchases, as well as retail sales for the period. It assumes that the ratio of cost to retail for the current period's sales is the same as for the goods available for sale for the period. This method permits companies to estimate end-of-period inventories without doing a physical count, and so is useful for interim reporting, or when accounting records must be reconstructed, as in the case of a fire or other insurance loss.

The *gross-profit inventory accounting* method is a cruder approximation method that uses a company's previously estimated gross profit ratio. An example (which assumes that the retailer has estimated its gross profit as 45%) is shown in the table on the lower left.

Opening inventory, at cost		$75,000
Purchases of inventory		300,000
Inventory available for sale, at cost		$375,000
Sales, at retail	520,000	
Deduct: Gross profit @ 45%	234,000	
Therefore, sales @ cost		286,000
Estimated closing inventory @ cost		$89,000

The gross profit method and the retail method are both approximation methods used in accounting for inventory and cost of sales in a retail organization. The retail method is more refined than the gross profit method, and is therefore acceptable under GAAP. The gross profit method assumes that past gross profits can be used in current accounting periods — an assumption that may not hold in volatile markets, such as fashion retail.

Computer Spreadsheets

Computer spreadsheets can help managers and accountants make more informed revenue and expense accounting decisions. The spreadsheet software available at relatively low cost in the mid-1990s has made accountants' and managers' professional lives more interesting and productive. The impact of revenue and expense accounting alternatives can be simulated easily, so as to provide valuable input to those responsible for making accounting decisions. For example, suppose that a company's management wishes to explore the impact of choosing among depreciation accounting methods. Recall that the factors involved in making the depreciation accounting decision under GAAP include the following:

- Estimating the historic cost of the depreciable tangible capital asset.
- Estimating the depreciation base.
- Estimating an expected service life.
- Choosing a depreciation pattern.

Each of these estimates and choices may involve several alternatives. Further, differences in both income statements and balance sheets may result. Also, additional complexity arises because accounting choices in one area (depreciation, say) may well affect other accounting items (depreciation choices affect the NIBT amount, which in turn affects the income tax expense amount, as we saw above). When we model these choices using computer spreadsheets (such as Excel for Windows) we can easily capture and evaluate changes in one or more of any factors.

Accounting, Organizations, and Society "The SkyDome"

Revenue and expense choices are made by management in all sorts of organizations. This section explores some revenue accounting choices made by the management of Toronto's SkyDome.[11]

"To build it today would cost $2 billion ... I don't think it cost too much money ... It was a bargain ... Everyone involved in the project did as much as possible to control costs and meet public expectations." Charles Magwood, former head of SkyDome, quoted in the Toronto Star, *August 2, 1992, A11*

"They made sweetheart deals with everybody from the Blue Jays to McDonald's, [who weren't] required to bid for hamburger rights [and] got them on a platter for 97 years, at a bargain price of $5 million, tax deductible. The stadium gets only 38 per cent of [McDonald's] take; U.S. stadia collect between 45 and 55 per cent. No other hamburger chain is allowed to advertise inside the Dome.

"The whole mess is shrouded in distasteful secrecy. The local press, except for the Star, has treated it gingerly ... The scandal cries out for a public inquiry ..." Pierre Berton, noted Canadian author and journalist, in his column in the Toronto Star, *July 27, 1991, H1*

The Toronto SkyDome, home of the American Baseball League's Blue Jays, bills itself as the "World's Greatest Entertainment Centre," and is "the first urban multi-purpose domed stadium with a fully retractable roof, a hotel, fitness club and other facilities" (1992 Annual Report, note 1). In contrast to the SkyDome's reputation as a sports and entertainment centre, its construction and financing has proven to be very controversial, providing a wealth of material for various newspaper reporters and columnists. Examples of journalists' critical opinions about the SkyDome's financial arrangements include a *Business Week* article by William C. Symonds and a *Toronto Star* article by noted economics writer David Crane. To say that some members of the press have been suspicious of the financial arrangements from

[11] This is a short version of the case "Private Enterprise and the Public Purse: Accounting, Accountability and the Toronto SkyDome," by C. Reed and J. Amernic, *Journal of Accounting Case Research*, in press.

the Dome's inception right up to its impending sale, seems much too mild. The tenor of much of the journalism has been downright hostile, as suggested by the above quote from Pierre Berton's newspaper column.

A Unique Financing Arrangement

"For the millions of Torontonians, SkyDome represents another jewel in the city's crown. But perhaps the more enduring legacy of Toronto's SkyDome story ... is simply that it demonstrates the potential effectiveness of a truly public-private partnership formed to finance urban infrastructure costs and alleviate the direct burden on taxpayers.

"Dare one conclude by suggesting that 'it opens the roof for a sky-is-the-limit approach to future financial ballgames?'" Two senior officers of the Municipality of Metropolitan Toronto, writing in Government Finance Review, *December 1989, p. 12.*

The SkyDome project involved a rather novel combination of public and private funding and ownership, and was felt by many to be a Canadian success story, in spite of its cost having escalated from an initial estimate of $140 million to about $560 million by the time it opened for business in June 1989. As the quotation immediately above suggests, aside from the apparent significant community value of the SkyDome physical plant, the "enduring legacy" of SkyDome was (and still is) thought by many people to lie in the example it provided of a major financing arrangement involving significant co-operation between government and the private sector. Indeed, the two Toronto senior officers quoted above concluded (p. 7) that:

More significantly ... SkyDome is the product of the confluence of vision and power; a unique and unlikely coalition of the public and private sector that galvanized dedicated individuals to seize opportunities, forge alliances and coax the eventual emergence of the necessary political will.

The public-private sector alliance that was forged to finance and oversee the construction of the SkyDome was crystallized in the establishment of Stadium Corporation of Ontario Limited, or Stadco, an Ontario Crown corporation. In Canada, commercial enterprises owned by various levels of government are not uncommon, but both the particular financial design of Stadco and the magnitude of the project it was to undertake, were rather unusual.

One of the important ways in which Stadco's accountability was discharged was via annual audited financial statements. This "Accounting, Organizations, and Society" section focuses on SkyDome management's decision to classify and account for the following three items as revenues on these financial statements:

- SkyBox and club seat rights.
- Preferred rights.
- Facility rental and fees.

1989 was the first year of SkyDome's operations; up until that year, there were no operations, so there was no income statement. Excerpts from the audited financial statements for the year ended December 31, 1989, follow. Question 20 in the end-of-chapter material focuses on these financial statements, especially on the decisions that management made to account for the three items listed above. After attempting this question, perhaps you could offer an opinion as to whether journalists such as Pierre Berton were unfair in their opinions.

Stadium Corporation of Ontario Limited
Incorporated under the laws of Ontario

BALANCE SHEET

As at December 31	1989 $	(M's)	1988 $
ASSETS			
Accounts receivable	15,084		9,235
Prepaid expenses	202		1,097
	15,286		10,332
Project costs	541,859		319,185
Fixed assets	1,196		205
	543,055		319,390
	558,341		329,722
LIABILITIES AND SHAREHOLDER'S EQUITY			
Liabilities			
Bank indebtedness	252,954		54,146
Accounts payable and accrued liabilities	31,063		32,666
Province of Ontario loans (note 6(a))	5,766		5,766
Promissory notes (notes 6(c) and (d))	17,100		14,050
Proceeds from sales of preferred rights (notes 6(c) and (d))	120,527		94,375
Proceeds from sale of SkyBox rights (note 7(a))	43,885		37,950
Proceeds from sale of club seat rights (note 7(b))	19,408		20,269
Deferred revenue	2,729		—
Total liabilities	493,432		259,222
Shareholder's equity			
Share capital (note 8)	30,000		30,000
Contributed capital (notes 6(b) and (d))	40,500		40,500
Deficit	(5,591)		—
Total shareholder's equity	64,909		70,500
	558,341		329,722

Stadium Corporation of Ontario Limited

STATEMENT OF OPERATIONS AND DEFICIT

Seven months ended December 31	**1989** $
	(thousands)
REVENUE	
SkyBoxes, club seats and preferred rights	13,223
Facility rentals and concessions	8,636
Advertising and other	5,223
	27,082
EXPENSES	
Operating and building (net of recoverables)	6,538
General and administrative	6,497
Salaries, wages and benefits	3,413
Marketing, advertising and promotion	499
Interest	8,711
	25,658
Income before depreciation	1,424
Depreciation	7,015
Net loss for the period and deficit, end of period	**(5,591)**

NOTES TO FINANCIAL STATEMENTS

December 31, 1989

1. STADIUM CORPORATION OF ONTARIO LIMITED (THE "CORPORATION")

The Corporation has substantially completed the construction of an entertainment complex (the "Project") which includes the first urban multi-purpose domed stadium with a fully retractable roof, a hotel, health club and other facilities. On June 3, 1989 the stadium portion of the Project commenced operations. Construction continued to proceed on the remainder of the Project.

At a date to be determined, the Corporation will transfer all of its rights, title and interests in the Project to a partnership to be formed between the Corporation and a private company, Dome Consortium Investments Inc. ("Consortium"). The partnership will assume responsibility for the operation of the Project at that time.

2. SUMMARY OF SIGNIFICANT ACCOUNTING POLICIES

...

SkyBox and club seat rights

Proceeds from the sale of rights to SkyBoxes and the use of club seats are amortized over the terms of their respective agreements.

Preferred rights

Proceeds from the sale of preferred rights are amortized over the life of the base stadium.

Facility rental and fees

Facility rentals and fees are recognized as revenue once the related event has occurred. Accordingly, deposits received and expenditures incurred prior to the event are deferred until the event has been completed.

...

6. FUNDING SOURCES

	Prov. of Ontario (a) $	Munici-pality of Metro Toronto (b) $	Consor-tium (c) $	Other Corps. (d) $	Total $
			(thousands)		
Province of Ontario loans	5,766	—	—	—	5,766
Promissory notes	—	—	13,500	3,600	17,100
Proceeds from sale of preferred rights	—	—	121,500	450	121,950
Share capital	30,000	—	—	—	30,000
Contributed capital	—	30,000	—	10,500	40,500
	35,766	30,000	135,000	14,550	215,316
Less accumulated amortization	—	—	1,418	5	1,423
Net	35,766	30,000	133,582	14,545	213,893

(a) Province of Ontario

Prior to 1988, the Province of Ontario subscribed for 30,010 shares of the Corporation for consideration of $30,000,010.

The Province of Ontario has also advanced to the Corporation $5,766,000 which is currently interest-free but will bear interest effective January 1, 1990 at prime rates and will be repayable in seven equal annual instalments starting January 1, 1991.

(b) Municipality of Metropolitan Toronto
The Municipality of Metropolitan Toronto has contributed $30,000,000 to the Corporation.

(c) Consortium
As at December 31, 1989, 27 Canadian corporations ("Consortium Members") have agreed to participate in the financing of the Project. For consideration of $4,500,000 each Consortium Member received certain preferred rights in the supply of goods and services, in the allocation of seating, and in advertising within the stadium for a 10-year period valued at $4,200,000 and an option, valued at $300,000 to extend the period of the preferred rights.

In addition, these Consortium Members have subscribed for shares of the Consortium which will form a partnership with the Corporation. These funds have been loaned to the Project. At December 31, 1989, the Corporation had received $13,500,000 from the Consortium and had issued promissory notes which bear no interest and are repayable on the day prior to the day the partnership acquires the Project.

(d) Other corporations
At December 31, 1989, three other corporations have each made contributions of $3,500,000 as well as loans of $1,350,000 each to the Corporation. The Corporation has issued promissory notes for the loans which bear no interest and are repayable in instalments of varying amounts over 10 years commencing with payments of $450,000 in 1989. In addition, for consideration of $150,000 each, the corporations will receive certain advertising and promotional rights.

7. SKYBOX AND CLUB SEAT FEES

(a) SkyBoxes
The Corporation sold the rights to the use of 113 SkyBoxes for a 10-year period. During the year, the Corporation recognized income of $9,950,000 from the amortization of the proceed from the sale of rights to SkyBoxes.

(b) Club seats
The Corporation received subscription fees of $20,540,000 from the sale of rights to the use of club seats for a 10-year period. In 1989, the Corporation charged an annual fee of $125 per club seat. During the year, the Corporation recognized income of $1,132,000 from the amortization of subscription fees and earned $718,000 in annual fees.

8. SHARE CAPITAL

The following is a summary of the Corporation's share capital as at December 31:

	1989 $	(M's)	1988 $
Authorized			
Unlimited number of common shares			
Issued			
30,000 common shares (1988 – 30,010)	30,000		30,000

9. INCOME TAXES

The corporation is a Crown corporation and is exempt from federal and provincial income taxes.

CHAPTER SUMMARY

The chapter began with a reminder that different businesses generate revenues and incur expenses in different ways, so that accounting decisions must be made with this diversity in mind. Users' needs for high-quality accounting information have a greater chance of being fulfilled if accounting is custom tailored to specific situations.

After reviewing the general criteria for revenue recognition, the chapter went on to illustrate how revenue was accounted for in a variety of industries. As well, expenses incurred by a sample of industries were described and their accounting explained. Depreciation accounting, accounting for income tax expense, and inventory accounting were then described. The chapter finished up with an "Accounting, Organizations, and Society" case study that illustrated some revenue recognition decisions.

Suggested Answers to Accounting and Business Decisions

Decision A

Under the percentage of completion method:

19X2

1. Accounting for construction costs incurred.

Dr Construction in progress (B)	4,750,000	
Cr Various (B) accounts		4,750,000

The amount equals $5,500,000 - $750,000

2. To account for the progress billings.

Dr Accounts receivable (B)	4,000,000	
Cr Billings on construction in progress (B)		4,000,000

3. To account for cash received.

Dr Cash (B)	3,500,000	
Cr Accounts receivable (B)		3,500,000

4. To account for the recognition of revenues and gross profit.

Dr Construction in progress (B)	460,627	
Dr Cost of construction (I)	4,750,000	
Cr Revenues from long-term construction contract (I)		5,210,627

As of the end of 19X2, the percentage completed is estimated as:

$$\frac{5{,}500{,}000}{[5{,}500{,}000 + 3{,}600{,}000]}$$

or 60.44%. Multiplying this by the revised estimate of the total gross profit on the project of $10,000,000 - $9,100,000, or $900,000, gives $543,960 of gross profit earned through 19X1 and 19X2. But $83,333 of this was accounted for in 19X1, so only $460,627 is recorded in 19X2.

19X3

The entries corresponding to #1 to #4 are:

1.

D Construction in progress (B)	3,600,000	
Cr various (B) accounts		3,600,000

Total costs incurred over the life of the project were actually $9,100,000; $5,500,000 had already been recorded in 19X1 and 19X2, so only $3,600,000 needed to be recorded in 19X3.

2.

Dr Accounts 0 receivable (B)	5,300,00	
Cr Billings on construction in progress (B)		5,300,000

3.

Dr Cash (B)	5,900,000	
Cr Accounts receivable (B)		5,900,000

4.

Dr Construction in progress (B)	356,040	
Dr Cost of construction (I)	3,600,000	
Cr Revenue from long-term construction projects (I)		3,956,040

The actual (now known) gross profit over the life of the project is $900,000, but since $543,960 was already recorded in 19X1 and 19X2, only $356,040 may be recorded in 19X3.

In addition to the above four journal entries, a fifth entry is needed this year since the project is now complete. The entry removes the project's accounts from the balance sheet.

5.

Dr Billings on construction in progress (B)	10,000,000	
Cr Construction in progress (B)		10,000,000

Under the completed contract method: For 19X2 and 19X3, journal entries for the percentage of completion method are also required under the completed contract method, except that there is no entry

#4 in either year. Rather, in 19X3 the total actual gross profit on the project is recorded, as follows:

Dr Construction in progress (B)	900,000	
Dr Cost of construction (I)	9,100,000	
Cr Revenue from long-term construction project (I)		10,000,000

Entry #5 in 19X3 under the percentage of completion method would also be required under the completed contract method.

Decision B

(a) Bramalea builds and then rents properties under lease agreements. It also builds and sells land, single homes and townhouses, and condominiums.

(b) The policies are described in the footnote reproduced from Bramalea's 1991 Annual Report. For rental properties, the rental payments are accounted for as revenues only after the properties are no longer classified by management as "under development." Prior to this point in time, the entries appear to be as follows:

Dr Cash (B)	XXX	
Cr Other capitalized costs (B)		XXX

Such an accounting treatment suggests that the rental asset is not yet fully operational, and that these early rental payments are merely offsetting some costs. After the rental properties are reclassified as no longer being under development, rental payments are accounted for as revenues. Notice that Bramalea puts a "reasonable period after substantial completion" limit on the period during which a rental property can be classified as under development.

The criterion that Bramalea uses to reclassify the rental properties is "breakeven point in cash flow after debt service." Since each property is usually financed with its own debt (say, a mortgage), this criterion ensures that the rental properties are expected to at least generate some positive cash flow after payment of interest and other debt costs before revenue recognition begins. It is a conservative approach to revenue accounting, and — if the decisions are made prudently and ethically by management — seems to be in accordance with GAAP for revenue recognition, as described in Chapter 4.

For real estate sales, Bramalea's revenue recognition policies again seem conservative, and in accordance with GAAP. For instance, for single homes or townhouses the policy with respect to the recognition of revenues is to wait until the construction process is completed and the title to the property legally passes over to the purchaser. After this point, the risks and rewards of ownership are no longer Bramalea's (assuming no remaining liability for poor workmanship), so this is a reasonable point in time at which to recognize revenue.

Decision C

Franchisor:

- Franchise fee: recognize revenue as earned, presumably over the life of the franchise agreement of several years.
- Initial assets and services: as provided in agreed-upon condition and quality to the franchisee.
- Ongoing assets and services: as delivered to franchisee under the terms and conditions agreed upon.

In the past, accounting by franchisors was at times "out of control." Some franchisors recorded 100% of franchise fees as revenue in the accounting period in which the franchise agreement was signed with the franchisee, even though the franchisor had not yet provided significant services, little (if any) payment on the franchise fee had been received, and neither the franchisor nor the franchisee looked like a "sure bet" for survival. This inappropriate accounting finally led the Accounting Standards Board to issue, in July 1984, an accounting guideline curbing some of the excesses. Accounting guidelines are not, however, the same as accounting standards; they have less force.

Newspaper:

- "Street sales" are on a cash basis; home delivery accounts for cash received as unearned revenue on the balance sheet until the customer's newspaper has been delivered.
- Advertising revenue is recorded only after the ad has appeared, irrespective of whether it is prepaid.

University:

- Once the nonrefund cutoff date is passed (assuming that the university has provided the course), the total student fee is counted as revenue; the provincial government portion is accounted for as revenue after the verification of student enrolment, even if not yet received.
- For food services and the bookstore, revenue is accounted for as the food or book is sold and cash is received; if credit cards are accepted at the bookstore, only the net amount to be received from the financial institution which sponsors the card should be recorded. Also, a provision for book returns should be deducted from revenue.
- For parking facilities: daily parking is on a cash basis, while prepaid annual or monthly parking revenues are only accounted for after the service has been provided.
- Publishing house: government grants supporting book publishing are counted as revenue after the book is published; commercial book publishing accounts for revenue after the published book has been sold; however, independent book retailers may insist on the right of return.

Decision D

(a)

Dr Future site restoration costs (I)	23,081	
Cr Future site restoration costs (B)		23,081

Cathedral seems to be using the same account name for both the accrued liability and the expense. In the chapter, we used the account name "Operating costs" for the expense, just to reinforce the idea that the debit goes to an expense account.

(b) The company is legally and ethically under an obligation to restore the mining sites that they have exploited. The cost of restoration is one of the operating costs of the mining activity, whether or not the company actually expends cash on restoration during the year. Cathedral in fact did not spend any money, but still incurred the cost. This cost is matched against the revenues it helped generate. Since they have incurred a cost but have not yet paid for it, they must also account for the liability. The definition of liabilities provided in Chapter 4 is "obligations of an entity arising from past transactions or events, the settlement of which may result in the transfer or use of assets, the provision of services or other yielding of economic benefits in the future." Cathedral is the entity so obligated; the past transactions or events are the mining activity and the legal requirement for site restoration; and the transfer of assets in the future is the required payments that Cathedral has estimated.

KEY TERMS

Accelerated depreciation refers to any depreciation method in which higher depreciation charges occur in the early part of a depreciable capital asset's life, and lower depreciation charges occur in the later part.

Average cost, when used in inventory accounting, refers to a cost flow method that determines inventory cost and the cost of sales by computing a weighted average cost of inventory acquired over an accounting period.

Capital cost allowance is the special name given by Canadian income tax legislation to depreciation computed for income tax deduction purposes. CCA, as it is commonly known, must be calculated according to the specific rules set out in the regulations to the Income Tax Act.

Completed contract method accounts for revenue only when all of the goods and/or services have been rendered under a contract.

Constant percentage diminishing balance depreciation is a method of computing depreciation in which the depreciation expense is a constant percentage of the remaining, undepreciated cost. Also called *declining balance depreciation* and *accelerated depreciation*.

Cost flow decision, when accounting for inventory, refers to the choice that must be made about allocating costs between inventory and the cost of sales. Average cost, FIFO, and LIFO are three well-known inventory cost-flow methods.

Cost inclusiveness decision, when accounting for inventory, refers to the decision that must be made about which costs to include as inventory product costs.

Deferred income taxes are balance sheet amounts, often on the liability side of the balance sheet but appearing on the asset side as well, that are created because income tax payable must by law be computed according to the rules of the Income Tax Act, but accountants have chosen to compute income tax expense according to GAAP. Accountants have made this choice because they believe that following GAAP results in a superior measure of income tax expense.

Depletion is the natural resource analogue of depreciation. It is an expense or other cost recorded in a period to account for wasting assets consumed or removed in that period.

Dry holes are gas and/or oil drilling sites that have been identified as not being worthy of commercial exploitation.

First in, first out (FIFO), in accounting for inventory, refers to a cost flow method in which the cost of inventory items sold or consumed during the accounting period is computed as though the items were sold or consumed in their order of acquisition.

Full-cost accounting, in resource industries, is a method of accounting by which all costs (including dry hole costs) of exploration and development of the oil and gas reserves are accounted for as if they were assets.

Full or absorption costing, when referring to inventory accounting, is a method of accounting in which fixed manufacturing overhead costs are included as part of the inventory asset (which includes direct materials, direct labour, and variable manufacturing overhead costs as well).

Future removal and site restoration costs, in extractive industries, and in industries that degrade the environment in general, are costs that an accounting entity expects to incur for dismantling and abandoning a property.

Gross profit method is an approximation method for inventory accounting used by retail organizations. Based upon past experience and any other relevant knowledge, management chooses a gross profit percentage, multiplies this assumed percentage by the total sales at retail prices for the accounting period, and thereby derives estimates of gross profit, cost of sales, and ending inventory.

Last in, first out (LIFO) is an inventory cost-flow method in which the cost of items sold or consumed during the accounting period is assumed to be the cost of the most recent acquisitions.

Lower of cost and market, when used in inventory accounting, refers to a decision in which losses resulting from declines in market prices of inventory below cost are accounted for in the period in which they occur. Most Canadian companies use net realizable value to measure "market," but some use replacement cost.

Net realizable value, when used in inventory accounting, refers to the amount derived when estimated costs of completion and sale are deducted from estimated selling price.

Percentage of completion refers to a method of accounting for revenues and gross profits in industries such as construction, in which contracts relating to a sale run over several periods. The method recognizes the accounting entity's gross profit as being earned and recorded proportionately according to the degree of completion over the life of the contract.

Period cost is a cost accounted for directly as an expense, and not included as part of inventory.

Product cost is a cost included as part of inventory, and therefore eventually as part of cost of sales.

Permanent differences, in accounting for income taxes, are revenues and/or expenses that are accounted for in either the financial accounting system or the income tax accounting system, but never in both.

Replacement cost, when used in inventory accounting, refers to the estimated cost of replacing the inventory on a specific date.

Retail method is a method used by retail organizations to estimate the cost of inventory and cost of sales. The ratio of "cost" to "retail" of inventory acquired during the most recent accounting period is computed; this ratio is then multiplied by the actual (retail) sales during the period to obtain an estimate of the cost of sales.

Specific identification, when used in inventory accounting, refers to a cost flow method in which the cost of items sold or consumed during the period is the cost of the specific items sold or consumed. It makes sense to account for more expensive inventory items using this method; less expensive items are usually accounted for using one of the approximation methods, such as average cost or FIFO.

Straight-line depreciation on a time basis is a method of computing depreciation by which the depreciation base (that is, the capital asset's cost less any estimated disposal value) is divided by the estimated number of periods of service life of the asset.

Straight-line depreciation on a units-of-production basis is a method of computing depreciation by which the depreciation base is divided by the estimated number of units of output expected to be produced by use of the capital asset. The depreciation for any given accounting period is equal to the resulting number multiplied by the actual number of units of output for that period.

Successful efforts accounting, in resource industries, is a method of accounting by which dry hole costs of exploration and development are accounted for as expenses in the period in which a geologist or equivalent expert declares that the wells or other sites are not commercially viable. Only costs associated with successful wells or other sites are accounted for as assets.

Sum-of-years'-digits depreciation is an accelerated depreciation method by which the sum of years' digits in a capital asset's expected life is computed. This amount is then divided into the number of years (or other measure of time, such as months) in the capital asset's expected life. The result is then multiplied by the depreciation base to compute the first accounting period's depreciation. The second period's depreciation is computed in the same manner, except that the sum of years' digits is divided into the capital asset's expected life *minus one*. This process repeats for each succeeding period, until the final period's depreciation is obtained by dividing the sum of years' digits into one, and multiplying the result by the depreciation base.

Timing differences, in accounting for income tax expense, refers to revenues and/or expenses that get into both the financial accounting system *and* the income tax accounting system, but in different accounting periods. Timing differences are what create deferred income taxes on an accounting entity's balance sheet.

Variable or direct costing, in accounting for inventory costs, refers to the method of accounting by which only direct labour, direct materials, and direct or variable manufacturing overhead are included in inventory. Under this method, fixed, or indirect, manufacturing overhead is accounted for as a period cost and expensed immediately in the accounting period.

FACT AND DESCRIPTION QUESTIONS

1. List the accounting decisions involved in accounting for depreciation under GAAP.
2. List the accounting decisions involved in accounting for inventory under GAAP.
3. Explain why accounting for inventory on the basis of its replacement cost would eliminate many of the accounting decisions required for inventory, if GAAP is followed.
4. Explain why timing differences between GAAP-basis financial accounting and income tax accounting under the Income Tax Act and its regulations lead to deferred income taxes.
5. Explain why the completed contract and percentage of completion methods of revenue recognition are both acceptable under GAAP, but are not alternatives.
6. Explain why real estate companies that have rental operations classify rental properties as either operating or under development.
7. Explain the revenue recognition policies banks have for securities and loans.
8. Explain why the Bank of Montreal requires the detailed accounting policies for its "non-accrual" loans as set out in Exhibit 5–1.
9. Describe Canadian Commercial Bank's inappropriate method of accounting for bad loans. Using concepts from Chapter 4, explain why the method was inappropriate. Also discuss whether this is an example of "economic consequences."
10. Is it possible to use the concepts of "asset" and "matching" to justify one or the other of the full cost and successful efforts methods?

Questions for Analysis and Discussion

11. Why might the management of a small petroleum-exploration company prefer the full-cost method, while the management of a large, integrated oil company might be indifferent?
12. Using the matching concept, argue against accruing site restoration costs in the absence of a legal requirement to restore.
13. Justify deferred-income-tax accounting using the matching concept from Chapter 4.
14. "Just equating the income tax expense to the real, actual income tax payable would be a lot less confusing than GAAP is now, since deferred taxes must be accounted for. Also, many people find that interpreting deferred income taxes on the 'liabilities' side of the balance sheet is difficult if not impossible." Discuss.
15. Why might managers of a new, growing company prefer the full or absorption cost method of inventory accounting rather than the direct or variable cost method?

16. (a) Which method gives managers more freedom: LIFO or FIFO?
    (b) Justify the lower of cost and market requirement for inventory accounting under GAAP.
    (c) Could this requirement induce managers to behave against the interests of various stakeholders in the accounting entity?

17. For each of the business types listed below, explain how revenue is generated. Then recommend a revenue-accounting policy that would, in your supported view, comply with GAAP.

real estate broker	transportation company providing school bus services to local school boards
retirement lodge	travel agency
medical practice	destination resort
public accounting firm	law practice
local courier service	highway paving company
international courier service	

18. Recall the illustration in the body of this chapter that focused on the inventory cost inclusiveness decision and Chai-Na-Ta Corp.
    (a) Explain, to the best of your ability given the available information, where along the cost continuum each line item falls in the company's Consolidated Statement of Crop Costs.
    (b) How justified was the company in accounting for each line item as it did?
    (c) The company reported net income of $2,006,000 and $1,039,000 in 1992 and 1991, respectively. If the company's income tax rate was 40%, estimate what net income would have been under direct costing.

19. Many companies must report to their shareholders not only on an annual basis, but also every three months (so-called "interim reporting"). Also, many companies that have a number of operating units (for example, a retailer with 10 or so subsidiaries, each of which has 30 or so stores) require these units to submit financial statements to head office monthly. Explain how the retail and gross profit inventory methods could be used in these situations.

20. (a) Identify the users of Stadco's financial statements (refer to this chapter's "Accounting, Organizations, and Society" section). Be sure to support your answer.
    (b) Reconstruct summary journal entries to account for the balances of SkyBox and club seat rights and preferred rights on the December 31, 1988, balance sheet.
    (c) Reconstruct summary journal entries to account for how these various "rights" affected both the income statement and the balance sheet in 1989. Remember that 1989 was the first year of SkyDome's operations.
    (d) The "preferred rights" become revenues as they are (according to footnote 2, "Summary of Significant Accounting Policies") "amortized over the life of the base stadium." An important accounting policy choice made by SkyDome management was to classify these rights as something other than owners' equity. Do you agree with this choice?
    (e) How, if at all, might SkyDome's audited financial statements be an important factor in public debates about SkyDome?

TECHNICAL QUESTIONS

21. Pigalle Ltd. was established on January 1, 1995, in order to sell lamps and related merchandise. The company carried two lines of lamps: "chic," a luxury lamp intended for the discriminating purchaser, and "nice," intended for the mass market. Purchases and sales over the month of January took place as follows:

January 2	Purchased 100 chic @ \$25.50 Purchased 1,000 nice @ \$10.30
January 5	Sold 2 chic @ \$155.00 Sold 325 nice @ \$19.99
January 10	Purchased 30 chic @ \$22.25
January 11	Sold 10 chic @ \$145.00 Purchased 300 nice @ \$12.50
January 15	Purchased 15 chic @ \$21.00 Sold 10 chic @ \$140.00 Sold 400 nice @ \$19.99
January 20	Sold 10 chic @ \$95.00 Purchased 500 nice at \$10.50
January 31	Purchased 100 chic @ \$15.00

Assume that the income tax rate is 40%.

Required:

(a) Assume that all expenses other than income taxes and cost of sales equal \$3,500. Prepare four income statements: FIFO for both product lines; LIFO for both product lines; FIFO for one line and LIFO for the other; and the latter in reverse.

(b) Suppose each lamp is sold in a separate retail outlet. Irrespective of GAAP, which cost flow assumptions would you prefer for each outlet? Why?

(c) Which is more open to manipulation: LIFO or FIFO?

22. Minitab Limited claimed \$1,250,000 in CCA on its corporate income tax return in 1996. Depreciation expense was \$800,000, and net income before income tax was \$4,200,000. Minitab's income tax rate is 40%.

(a) Prepare a journal entry to record income taxes for 1996, accounting for timing differences.

(b) Prepare a journal entry to record income taxes for 1996, ignoring accounting for timing differences (that is, equate income tax expense to income tax payable).

(c) Which method, (a) or (b), is better?

(d) Oscar Inc. began operations in 1995. Oscar has a 45% corporate income tax rate, and has reported the following for its first four years of operation:

	NIBT	Depreciation	CCA
1995	$330,000	$100,000	$200,000
1996	330,000	100,000	150,000
1997	330,000	100,000	100,000
1998	330,000	100,000	50,000

Compute net income for each of the four years, both accounting for and ignoring timing differences.

23. Miles Trucking Limited (MTL) began operations on January 1, 1996. During the fiscal years ended December 31, 1996, 1997, and 1998, the following activity was recorded in MTL's general ledger account "Capital assets — trucks":

Description	Debit	Credit	Balance
1/01/96 purchase truck #A	17,463.25		17,463.25
15/01/96 purchase truck #B	16,300.90		
10/03/96 purchase truck #C	21,975.00		
11/03/96 tuneup, truck #A	425.50		
25/10/96 purchase truck #D	10,055.50		
10/05/97 sell truck #A: proceeds		$9,600.00	
11/12/97 purchase truck #E	11,514.00		
12/12/98 sell truck #B		16,300.90	

Trucks are depreciated on a straight-line basis, with each truck being accounted for separately. Depreciation is written off over the expected life of the truck, in months, with salvage value set equal to 10% of the original cost of the truck.

The expected lives of the trucks, at time of acquisition, were as follows:

Truck	Expected Life (months)
A	60
B	72
C	72
D	30
E	20

Required:
Prepare all journal entries necessary to account for depreciation for MTL for each of 1996, 1997, and 1998.

CASE

IBM and *WSJ*

On April 7, 1993, the *Wall Street Journal* (the WSJ) ran a front-page article alleging that IBM management had used inappropriate accounting tactics to portray a declining financial position as better than it actually was. The article, "Softer Numbers: As IBM's Woes Grew, Its Accounting Tactics Got Less Conservative," by Michael W. Miller and Lee Berton, made the following comments:[12]

- As IBM's business began to turn sour in the 1980s, it adopted aggressive accounting policies.
- At times, revenue was recorded when product was shipped to dealers who had the right of return ("escape hatches"), and occasionally when product was shipped to IBM's own warehouses. At the time, IBM was under tremendous pressure to maintain its revenue stream. As the WSJ article noted:

  IBM defends its continuing practice of booking revenues as soon as it ships a product and says it makes allowances for returns. "The earnings process is substantially complete upon shipment," IBM contends, adding, "Price Waterhouse was, and continues to be, in full agreement" ...

  However, IBM's approach "can lead to many revenue-booking abuses, particularly in the computer business," says Paul Regan, a leading expert on revenue issues at the Hemmings Morse accounting firm in San Francisco. He offers a more conservative standard for when the "earnings process" is complete: when the products "are functioning properly in keeping with the sales agreement — and that can take a long time."

  IBM isn't the only company that books revenue upon shipment. But many of its high-tech rivals are more conservative.

  "We don't just put it on the floor, then say we can book it," says a spokesman for Amdahl Corp., IBM's leading rival in mainframe computers. "It has to be turned over to our field engineering group. They have to check the machine out, and make sure it's up and running. That's the point we actually take credit for the revenue."

  A middle-ground is used by Xerox Corp. It books revenue from its small copiers immediately upon shipment, but, with its bigger machines, it waits until "everyone says, 'Wow, it's better than sliced bread,'" a spokesman says.

  IBM concedes that it sometimes books revenue when it ships a product to its own warehouse — for "temporary in-transit storage" en route to a customer. But it says it does so only when "installation at the customer" is "expected within 30 days."

- IBM arranged with Merrill Lynch & Co. and others to guarantee the future value of computing and related equipment that IBM had leased to its customers; IBM then recorded all the revenue from these long-term computer leases immediately, just as if it had actually sold the computers. Miller and Berton summarized this issue as follows:

  When companies lease out equipment, they can account for it as an "operating" or a "sales-type" lease. An operating lease is conservative; revenues go on the

[12] Reprinted by permission of *The Wall Street Journal*, 1993, Dow Jones & Company, Inc. All Rights Reserved Worldwide.

books as they actually flow in each year. A sales-type is more liberal; all the revenue that will ever come in is recorded in the first year.

To restrain revenue-hungry companies, the Financial Accounting Standards Board has extensive rules, running to more than 100 pages, about sales-type leases. IBM's accountants zeroed in on a formula in paragraph 7D: Add up all the payments, plus the value of the computer when the lease expires. If the total is 90% of the computer's value today, the lease can be considered a sales-type one.

In the hotly competitive market, IBM was offering terms that didn't add up to the 90% mark. Merrill's solution: It sold IBM "7D insurance" guaranteeing a certain value of the computer at the end of the lease — enough to push IBM over 90% ...

Some accounting experts call 7D insurance a surprising tactic for a conservative company. "Structuring a lease to violate the spirit of the accounting rule ... is weaseling, hokey and totally inappropriate for a company of IBM's stature," says Howard Schilit, an associate professor of accounting at American University in Washington, D.C.

Required:

Adopt the role of special assistant to IBM's corporate comptroller, and prepare a draft press release defending IBM's accounting.

CASE Chambers Development Co. Inc.

The following article appeared in *The Globe and Mail's Report on Business*, March 16, 1992:

Wall Street Dumps Chambers: Accounting Change Devastates Profit

NEW YORK — Wall Street loves growth and until Wednesday it appeared Chambers Development Co. Inc. was providing it, but the landfill developer's stock price fell more than 60 per cent when a change in its accounting policies set profit far below what it previously reported.

The company's class A shares dived from $30.25 (U.S.) each at Tuesday's close to a low of $8.25 Wednesday, before recovering a little to close at $11.25. Trading volume reached 16.6 million shares, about a quarter of the total on the American Stock Exchange.

Yesterday, Chambers's stock closed at $10.62.

Chambers, which is based in Penn Hills, Pa., is involved in refuse collection and disposal, as well as personal protection service. It has grown rapidly, largely through the development of new properties.

The company's accounting change did not affect revenue growth, but it devastated the reported rise in profit.

In the long run, the change will cause some profits to be reported over the next 40 years, rather than right away. Company officials contended Wednesday that nothing, really, had changed. But that was not the way investors saw it.

At issue was how the company treated many of its costs in developing landfills. That development can be a long process, as approval is sought from various government agencies and work is done to make the site acceptable for trash disposal.

As it developed the landfills, the company "capitalized" all costs associated with the development. In other words, those costs were treated not as expenses but as assets.

On Wednesday, the company said it would continue to capitalize "direct costs," such as what it pays for land and development, but not "indirect costs."

Those indirect costs, it turns out, were substantial, and included a large part of the salaries of company administrators.

Richard Knight, the company's chief financial officer, said that if he spent a day on corporate matters, his salary was counted as an expense.

But if he spent the day working on a new project, that part of his pay was capitalized. If the company's public relations staff was working to explain new projects to affected neighbours, the staff salaries were capitalized.

Those costs were generally added to the asset called "land, primarily landfill costs," Mr. Knight said.

He expressed puzzlement that the change had so surprised analysts and investors. "Over the years, in discussions about capitalization with the analysts, with stockholders, with anyone who asked, we've always told them we were capitalizing." But he conceded that even the closest reading of the company's financial statements would not have revealed indirect costs were being capitalized.

Halting the capitalization of indirect costs made a drastic difference. Chambers had previously reported 1991 profit of $49.9-million or 83 cents a share in 1991 on revenue of $322-million. It restated that to $28.8-million (48 cents) and then took an additional writeoff of $27.2-million (45 cents) as a cumulative adjustment to reports from previous periods.

Although most of Wall Street had accepted the earlier profit figures, there had been doubters. "I feel vindicated," said Doug Augenthaler, an analyst at Oppenheimer & Co. who had argued it appeared the company was capitalizing too much in the way of expenses.

Required:

(a) Explain the accounting issues involved, illustrating your response with hypothetical journal entries.

(b) Suggest reasons why the company decided to change its accounting policy.

(c) Does the stock market's reaction prove that the stock market is efficient?

(d) Adopt the role of Richard Knight. Prepare a news release reacting to the drop in Chambers's stock price and setting out the company's point of view.

CASE

Standard Trust Co.

The following article by Konrad Yakabuski appeared in the *Toronto Star* on July 11, 1991:

Huge Losses Not Reported by Standard

Failed Standard Trust Co. was likely losing millions of dollars as early as 1989, despite reporting a record $16.2 million profit to its shareholders.

According to sources inside the trust company, Standard consistently recorded interest payments on all of its delinquent loans, even though no cash was actually coming in from borrowers.

By early 1989, Standard's delinquent loans had ballooned to almost $250 million, or 18 per cent of assets, one insider said.

About $14 million in accrued interest ended up being added to the loans' principal, or capitalized, in turn boosting Standard's assets. All of the uncollected interest — estimated at about $30 million in 1989 — was reflected in the company's income. That created a healthy profit where none really existed.

The almost $50 million in accrued interest recorded in the 18 months to June 30, 1990, would have wiped out Standard's profits back to 1986.

Brian O'Malley, then Standard's chief executive, boasted to shareholders in early 1990 about the company's "strong earnings growth," its "diversified and high quality mortgage portfolio" and "stringent lending requirements."

But recent interviews with sources close to Standard show that the crisis that eventually brought the country's ninth largest trust company to its end in April had probably reached life-threatening proportions a year before O'Malley delivered that upbeat message.

The company's condition deteriorated rapidly until the end of 1990, when, after a $51.4 million asset writedown and O'Malley's resignation in December, borrowers had stopped making payments on fully half of Standard's loans, one company insider said.

However, the seriousness of the situation at Standard, whose $1.4 billion in assets was seized by federal regulators on April 18, had been earlier masked by the company's accounting practices.

Standard's aggressive habit of accruing interest on delinquent loans was approved by its auditors, Peat Marwick Thorne, and a subcommittee of the board of directors.

Federal regulators became increasingly disturbed about Standard's aggressive accounting practices, which they first noticed after examining the trust company's 1987 financial statements. In January, 1989, the office of the superintendent of financial institutions issued the first of several warnings to the trust company, ordering it to end its accrual practices.

Accounting guidelines permit the recognition of unpaid interest only where there is "virtual certainty" that a trust company will be able to collect that money in the future.

But with interest rates rising, property values falling and scores of borrowers walking away from their loans, several sources said Standard was in no position to make such a claim.

"It is well understood in the industry that if a loan goes past due for more than 90 days you stop accruing interest," one source said.

Sources close to Standard, who in recent interviews with The Star requested anonymity, identified a host of dubious business practices at the trust company. These practices included ... classifying loans made against nursing homes, hotels and other commercial properties as part of its residential mortgage portfolio. Such loans were far riskier than residential mortgages, but this practice, unique to Standard, enabled the trust company to circumvent federal guidelines that limit the size of a trust company's commercial loan portfolio.

Between 1987 and 1989, Standard lent more than $50 million against 37 nursing homes. When the borrowers subsequently defaulted, the trust company was left holding every one of the properties...

Reprinted with permission of The Toronto Star Syndicate.

Required:

(a) Explain the accounting policy decisions that are being criticized.

(b) How reliable is this news account?

(c) Was Standard's management unethical?

(d) Attempt to put yourself in the shoes of Standard's CEO; what factors would have been important to you as you participated in making the accounting policy decisions?

CASE

CBC Sports and CTV

Recall the quotes that opened this chapter. The CTV report contained the following information:[13]

CBC CLAIMS IT MAKES MONEY ON SPORTS TO SUPPORT OTHER PROGRAMMING CATEGORIES AND THAT THERE IS NO TAXPAYER SUBSIDY OF PROFESSIONAL SPORTS

In fact, CBC Sports is losing $60-$70 million per year.

Pro Forma Profit and Loss Statement — CBC Sports — 1992/93*

		$ Million
Net Advertising Revenue		$85.3
Production Expense		
— Direct Program Expenditure	$67.0	
— Production/Operational Expense Allocation	52.6	
— Distribution Expense Allocation	11.7	131.3
Income (loss) before Corporate Management, Engineering, and Selling & Merchandising Expense		(46.0)
— Corporate Management/Engineering Expense Allocation	6.7	
— Selling and Merchandising Expense Allocation	13.3	20.0
Income (loss) after Indirect Expense Allocation		$(66.0)

* Based on CBC Annual Report and CRTC filings.

[13] Provided by CTV.

CBC IS RISKING TAXPAYERS' MONEY ON THE ATLANTA OLYMPICS

— Given the high rights costs, CBC will loose in excess of $10 Million on the 1996 Olympics.

CBC Atlanta Olympics

Pro Forma Profit and Loss ($Cdn. Million)

Revenue (air time sales)	$36.8[1]	
Less Agency Commission	(5.5)	
		31.3
Direct Costs		
— Rights	29.6[2]	
— Production	10.5	
— Sales and Promotion	1.5	
		41.6
Direct Program Margin (loss)		(10.3)

[1] Accepts CBC's assertion that they can sell more commercial inventory. Assumes 85% Prime sellout rate; 50% Non-Prime sellout rate; 30 sec. ad rates of $10,000/$5,000 for Prime/Non-Prime. French revenue @ 21% of English revenue (CTV/TVA Lillehammer experience).
[2] Includes conversion to Canadian dollars and financing costs associated with prepayment requirements.

CBC's vice-president, English television networks, responded with the following comments (which were distributed to the press on July 19, 1994):

The CBC and CTV have co-operated where co-operation has served the overall need to strengthen the Canadian broadcasting system, public and private, at a time of increasing competition from abroad ... But, in other areas ... we have competed vigorously ... Occasionally, the public-private relationship has been rocky. But what allowed the balance between co-operation and competition to remain fundamentally healthy was a basic respect the people of both networks held for each other ...

That respect, in turn, has been founded on an underlying civility and professionalism among the people involved, virtually without exception.

The CTV document is not helpful in terms of that on-going relationship.

It was clearly intended to do the CBC damage at a number of levels — with our advertisers, with our audiences, and with our owners, Canadian taxpayers ...

In the aftermath of the document's being leaked, fortunately, even some traditional and acute critics of the CBC have recoiled at the amateurism of CTV's foray into gutter accounting ...

CBC Sports does not lose money. It makes money.

Last year, for example, profits earned by CBC Sports were ploughed back into other programming, including the kind of sports programming that does not draw audiences large enough to pay the freight — such as diving and track and field, for example.

To get around this inconvenient profit, CTV plainly and simply has decided to change CBC profits to losses and announce their decision to the world.

It does so by adopting accounting approaches designed to show what CTV wanted to show, by plucking numbers from the air, by applying them on a worst-case basis, by then asserting the conclusions as fact and by applying a bicycle pump to all the resulting puffery ...

Required:

(a) Identify the users of the CTV-commissioned financial information.

(b) What accounting entities were the CTV-commissioned income statements prepared for?

(c) Was GAAP followed? Did it need to be followed?

(d) Would an independent auditor have had a role to play?

(e) Given the accounting entities involved, suggest some revenue-accounting and expense-accounting issues that might have arisen.

(f) Is what CTV did ethical?

CASE: Burkholder and Eyeshades

Joachim Burkholder graduated with a degree in computer science from a major university in 1989, and spent the first two years of his career working for a large financial institution. Early in 1992 he decided to "strike out on his own," and spent the better part of January and February of 1992 investigating the microcomputer software market. Burkholder was convinced that — with the continuing decline in the cost of fairly high-powered personal computers (even IBM was cloning itself!) — a market niche was developing for high-quality, user-friendly applications software directed toward both the "traditional" and "nontraditional" accounting and tax markets. An example of a particular area of interest in the nontraditional market that Burkholder thought had potential was the assessment of environmental liabilities, compliance, and monitoring.

In March 1992, Burkholder approached his long-time friend, Marvin Eyeshades (who had recently obtained his professional accounting designation), with the following proposition:

- The two would incorporate a new company to be called "Micraccount Software Limited" (MSL), with each partner putting up $150,000 in cash in return for 50% of the common stock.
- Burkholder would act as president and chief programmer; Eyeshades would be vice-president/comptroller and work closely with Burkholder on the development of new accounting and tax software.
- Since the development of new user programs is a costly, labour-intensive, and time-consuming process, MSL would hire three top-flight computer science graduates to assist Burkholder in software development.

The development of new software products, as well as product enhancements, involves two phases: (1) planning and design phase, and (2) construction.

The objective of the planning and design phase is to establish the technological, market, and financial feasibilities of the software product. Costs are incurred in conceptual formulation and design activities. Software firms will develop several plans during this phase, including the following:

- *Product plan* — which defines the business or consumer need, provides a market and environmental analysis, describes the product function and feature requirements, includes technical considerations, specifies the software design, and describes documentation and customer support requirements.
- *Construction plan* — which addresses the physical construction of the prod-

uct, and includes methodologies for developing the detailed program design and for building the product. Resource and time requirements are specified.

- *Financial feasibility plan* — which appraises the expected return on the investment based on a forecast of sales and costs.

Although there is often some overlap between the two phases, the construction phase normally begins after the planning and design phase has been completed. In the construction phase, the actual "manufacturing activities of the product" are conducted in three stages: (1) detailed program design; (2) code and test; and (3) packaging.

Both Burkholder and Eyeshades are concerned about setting accounting policies for the recognition of revenues and costs for MSL. Their concern has two sources: (1) in order to grow, MSL will eventually have to go the bank and, ultimately, the public for additional capital, and (2) reasonable accounting policies will, it is hoped, result in information that will be useful for the two owners in judging MSL's progress, and in minimizing disputes and misunderstandings.

Required:
As MSL's new accountant, outline a set of policies that MSL should follow for its accounting and related systems. Provide reasons.

Zabruski Limited

Zabruski Limited (henceforth ZL) is a small Canadian company specializing in the manufacture of lightweight, relatively low-priced modular office furniture. The company was established in 1985 to take advantage of the shift in the Canadian economy toward self-employment and the resulting increase in demand for furniture that was suitable for home offices. In early 1995, Mr. G. Pack approached the chief executive officer of ZL with the following business proposition:

- ZL and Pack's company, which has operated manufacturing facilities in Eastern Europe for over three decades, will join together to establish a new company, to be called Zablonski/Pack Europe Incorporated (henceforth ZPEI).
- ZL and Pack's company will each own 50% of the common shares of ZPEI. ZL will pay $1.5 million (Canadian) for its 50% of the common shares; for its 50%, Pack's company will transfer the ownership of an office building and the land upon which it is situated to ZPEI.
- ZPEI will purchase Canadian-made office furniture from ZL and market it to private companies and government agencies and departments in Eastern Europe.
- ZPEI will borrow the equivalent of approximately $4 million (Canadian) from a local banking institution to construct a warehouse facility adjacent to the office building. Pack owns a local construction company that will be contracted to build the warehouse.
- A general manager (GM) will be hired to have overall responsibility for ZPEI. Two sales managers will report to the GM.
- Each sales manager will have about ten salespeople on staff. The basic salary that ZPEI will pay its salespeople is rather low; however, a commission equal to 10% of the sales revenue generated by each salesperson is to be paid no later than two weeks after the end of the accounting year. Each sales manager will receive a salary, as will the GM, but they will also receive a bonus based on ZPEI's annual net income.

- Five personnel will be hired to work in the warehouse, in which a state-of-the-art computer system will be used to provide immediate information on inventory levels, orders, and so on. The hardware for the computer system will be rented on a long-term lease arrangement; the software will be purchased.
- Since Pack is thoroughly familiar with the Eastern European market, and has had extensive experience in dealing with both private businesses and governments in the region, he will provide consulting services to ZPEI for an annual fee of $500,000 (Canadian).
- At the end of each accounting year (December 31), ZPEI's net income will be computed by a team of accountants representing both ZL and Pack. If ZPEI's net income is positive, ZL and Pack's company will each receive a dividend equal to 50% of the net income; otherwise, they will receive no dividend.

The CEO of ZL was impressed with Pack's business proposition, and felt that it was very timely, since ZL had been contemplating expansion into an overseas market. However, before making any firm decisions, the CEO has requested that you, an independent consultant, provide advice to ZL regarding accounting and related issues in connection with the determination of net income for ZPEI.

Required:

(a) List, with explanations, the types of revenues and expenses that ZPEI will have on its income statement. For example, the ZPEI GM and other employees will receive salaries, so a "salary expense" will appear on ZPEI's income statement.

(b) Before ZL and Pack's company agree to establish ZPEI, each should have a clear understanding of how the various revenue and expense items will be determined, so that disputes will be minimized. Indicate two items that might lead to dispute, and recommend how they should be measured and accounted for.

CASE: Grosse Point

Grosse Point Inc. (GPI) and the City of Jamestown entered into a contract on January 10, 1993, whereby GPI would construct a prototype rapid transit vehicle specifically for the City of Jamestown's needs. The city had been built on soft shale, so an underground rapid transit system was impossible. The system had to be a monorail-type, with cars designed to be extraordinarily lightweight but at the same time strong enough to endure high speeds.

Under the agreement between GPI and the city, GPI established a wholly owned subsidiary, Rapid Transit Design Corporation (RTDC), to design and build the prototype to the city's requirements. The contract specified:

All costs prudently incurred each year by RTDC, computed according to acceptable accounting principles, will be reimbursed by the City of Jamestown (the City). In addition, the City will pay RTDC an additional amount each year so that RTDC's net income equals $2,170,000 for each year of the three-year contract.

While overall, relations between RTDC and the city ran quite smoothly, and the prototype design and trial schedule met deadline, one aspect of the contract led the two parties to exercise a clause in the contract that required an arbitrator to make a decision. The specific bone of contention involved how the phrase "all costs prudently incurred each year by RTDC, computed according to acceptable accounting principles" was to be interpreted with respect to two issues involving income taxes.

Issue #1: For the period ended December 31, 1993, RTDC's draft income statement showed the following (in $000s):

Net income before provision for income taxes		$4,320
Income taxes		
Current	1,200	
Deferred	950	
		2,150
Net income		$2,170

The deferred tax portion of the 1993 income tax expense was caused by timing differences related to two categories of capital assets ($000s):

Machinery and equipment	$200
Buildings	750
	$950

The buildings (two low-rise structures, adjacent to each other) had been acquired by RTDC from GPI at market value on February 1, 1993, and housed all of GPI's operations.

The City of Jamestown objected to the $950,000 in deferred taxes being included as part of 1993's "costs prudently incurred," and countered with the following alternative:

Net income before provision for income taxes	$3,370
Income taxes — current	1,200
Net income	$2,170

This issue remained in dispute throughout 1994.

Issue #2: For the period ended December 31, 1994, RTDC's draft income statement showed the following (in $000s):

Net income before provision for income taxes		$4,970
Income taxes		
Current	2,100	
Deferred	700	
		2,800
Net income		$2,170

In addition, a "special item" appeared on RTDC's draft retained-earnings statement for the year ended December 31, 1994. It related to the fact that one of the two buildings had been sold early in 1994 for its net book value. RTDC's management had decided that this second building was not needed in their operations, so it was sold to GPI. The reversal of the deferred taxes originally recorded on the building in 1993 was accounted for by means of a journal entry on January 15, 1994 (the day the building was sold), as follows:

Dr Deferred income taxes (balance sheet)	300,000	
Cr Retained earnings (balance sheet)		300,000

The city argued that RTDC was being, at the very least, inconsistent. The city argued that if the $300,000 in deferred taxes that were removed from RTDC's balance sheet in 1994 was not accounted for as an income statement item, then no deferred taxes whatsoever should be accounted for. And thus income tax expense in 1993 should be $1,200,000, as the city had proposed. The city also argued that deferred taxes were not really a cost in any event, since the deferred portion of income tax expense was (to use the city representative's words) "merely an accounting fiction."

RTDC countered by pointing out that income tax expense was computed under GAAP, and that such principles required that such an expense incorporate appropriate timing differences.

Required:
Adopt the role of the arbitrator. It is now early 1995, and the above disputes between the city and RTDC have begun to sour their relationship. Write a brief report outlining the important considerations in this situation and arbitrate the matters in dispute.

CHAPTER 6 six

Accountability: An Introduction to Financial Reporting and Auditing

Learning OBJECTIVES

After you have read, thought about, and discussed this chapter, and completed a selection from the end-of-chapter material, you will have made significant progress in achieving the following learning objectives:

- Explain why ethical decision-making is the core of the financial reporting system.
- Describe the contents of a typical annual report, including the financial statements and footnotes, the audit opinion, and management's discussion and analysis.
- Explain the importance of footnotes, and analyse selected footnote information such as that concerning accounting for bad debts.
- Identify the following participants in the financial reporting system and explain their roles: managers, audit committees, boards of directors, internal auditors, external auditors, users.
- Explain the difference between generally accepted accounting principles (GAAP) and generally accepted auditing standards (GAAS).

Why are annual reports published? Who reads them? What information should they contain? And how can they convey that information more effectively? Raising these questions is easy; finding the answers is not. One reason is that the answers keep changing with the times. But it's also because accountants, with their established expertise in financial disclosure, have not spent enough time addressing these questions — preferring instead to concentrate on financial statements while surrendering the rest of the annual report's contents to the exclusive domain of corporate management ... Misconceptions about the annual report's objectives are common; to some, it is nothing more than a storybook with pretty pictures. Nevertheless, the annual report is first and foremost a financial document. Its primary objective is to communicate timely, reliable and relevant information about an organization. That information — covering past, present and future activities — must be readily understandable because it will be used to make economic decisions.

Gerald R. Trites and J. Paul-Emile Roy, "Dispelling the Storybook Myth," *CAmagazine*, January 1992, pp. 55–58 (an article summarizing their CICA research study *Information to be Included in the Annual Report to Shareholders.*[1]

Along with the singing of birds and the voice of the turtle another vernal sound is being heard in the land this week. It is the scrape, crunch, plod, and plop of the nation's weary postmen, patiently delivering 18,000,000 copies of corporate annual reports to the stockholders of 6,000 publicly owned companies ... Nobody — or almost nobody — will read them.

Reynolds Girdler, "18,000,000 Books Nobody Reads," *Saturday Review*, Vol. 46, no. 15, April 13, 1963, pp. 71, 78.

INTRODUCTION

In Chapter 2, "accountability" was described as one of the basic ideas underlying virtually all areas of accounting. Fulfilling this accountability requirement is accomplished in many ways and in a variety of circumstances. For example:

- A salesperson might submit a weekly summary of travel and related expenditures to a sales manager for approval.
- In a monthly summary of manufacturing costs that a production manager must provide to a corporate vice-president, the actual cost of manufacturing 1,000 computer keyboards might be compared with the expected cost (and the reasons for any difference explained).
- In the James and Gord case in Chapter 2, perhaps senior management required periodic reports comparing the actual sales and expenses of the new product line with expected sales and expenses.
- The senior managers of a university's pension plan might provide the people covered by the plan with an annual set of the pension plan's audited financial statements, as well as details of the investment performance of the plan's assets.

[1] Reprinted with permission from *CAmagazine*, published by the Canadian Institute of Chartered Accountants, Toronto, Canada.

- Corporate management might send an annual report, containing audited financial statements and other information, to a company's shareholders.

Each of these examples of fulfilling accountability requirements involves an accountor *reporting* to an accountee information of a certain type, in a certain form, of a certain quality, and at certain time intervals, in a manner that has been agreed to by both parties. The act of preparing and submitting an agreed-upon report is a crucial link in the accountability cycle. The features mentioned above are all features of an accountability loop. In this chapter, a specific system of discharging accountability via reporting is described: *the financial accounting reporting system*, by means of which an organization's management prepares and issues financial statements and other information to outside users.

Much of this chapter focuses on the annual report published by an accounting entity. The two quotations that opened this chapter offer two contrasting views about the importance of these reports. The first, from Trites and Roy, provides a realistic modern perspective about the annual report — that it is a complex, evolving document that reveals important financial accounting and other information about the accounting entity. The second, from Girdler, though over 30 years old, provides a perspective that we should be alert to today, although for reasons probably not apparent to Girdler.

The image of the scraping, crunching, plodding postman delivering annual reports by hand is of course at odds with modern telecommunications and data storage technology, which permits documents such as annual reports to be accessible not only in hard copy, but also on the Internet. The title of Girdler's article, "18,000,000 Books Nobody Reads," suggests that the entire process of preparing and disseminating annual reports is somewhat of a waste, and it's true that surveys have consistently shown low levels of interest in, and understanding of, annual reports on the part of potential users (much of the information *confirms* previously released information about the accounting entity). That being said, those investors, advisers, and journalists (and others) who do devote time to carefully analysing what's contained (and not contained) in annual and similar reports gain considerable insight into accounting entities and the ways their managers have discharged their accountability obligations.

Financial Reporting as an Accountability System

The relationship between the managers of an accounting entity and the users of that entity's financial accounting information is basically this: management prepares financial reports, such as financial statements, and sends them to the users (shareholders, employees, and others), to whom the managers are accountable. This is the "bare bones" of financial reporting as an accountability system; there are many other important parties and factors that come into play. Next we'll note some of these to make our depiction a bit more realistic.

A general model of financial reporting, to users outside the accounting entity, is shown in Exhibit 6–1. The basic features of an accountability loop are all here; in the real world, however, the system is much more complex, because there are so many players, because the information is disseminated into the public domain, and because many aspects are regulated by law. The system is characterized by checks and balances, which are subject to continuing challenge and change. For example, the managers' right to compete by (among other things) not revealing sensitive information is balanced against the right of shareholders and others to be informed.

We will refer to Exhibit 6–1 several times throughout the chapter as we describe the financial reporting system and its participants.

You have already been introduced to most of the participants in the system shown in Exhibit 6–1; recall especially Chapter 2, where the user orientation of accounting was described. However, audit committees and internal auditors haven't yet been formally introduced, so we will describe them in more detail later in the chapter. Just to suggest their importance to the financial reporting system, however, we will mention here that audit committees are committees that many profit-seeking and not-for-profit entities' boards of directors have established to act as a sort of "buffer" between management and the external auditor. Audit committees are made up of members of the board of directors; ideally, a majority of the members are from outside the organization's management group. Internal auditors are employees of an organization who have the responsibility of (a) checking that accounting and other management systems are working effectively and efficiently, and (b) reporting deficiencies to top management and the audit committee when deficiencies are discovered.

EXHIBIT 6-1
Financial Reporting Accountability and Communication System

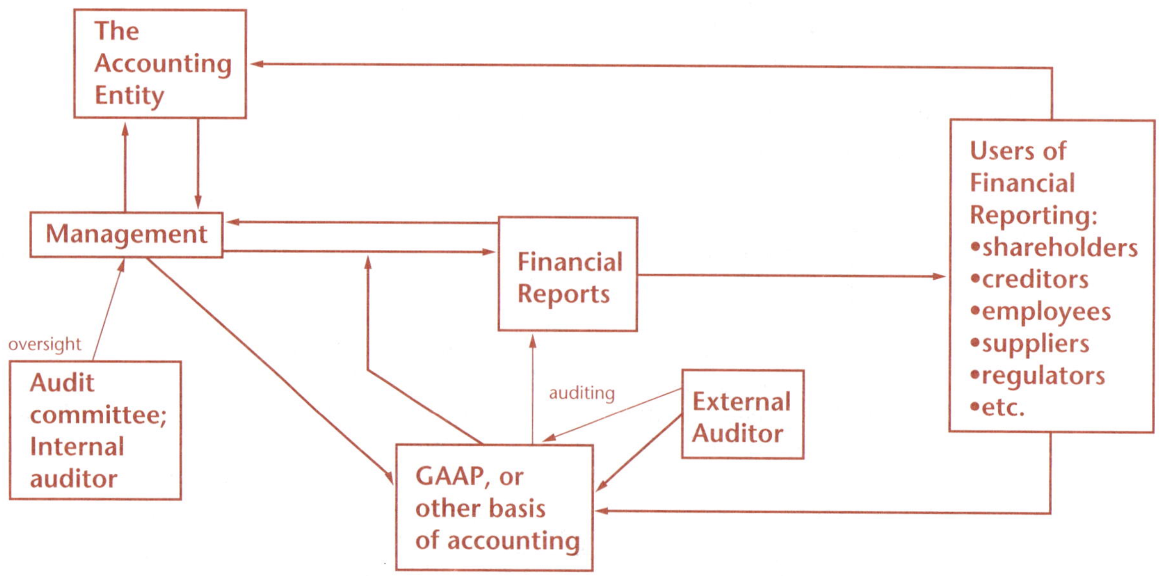

Financial Statements, Financial Reporting, Principals, and Agents

One useful way of explaining the importance of the financial reporting and auditing accountability system is to use the concepts of "principals" and "agents." Assume that individuals make decisions that maximize their personal welfare, given the information they have. Assume also that "agents" (in our example, agents are managers) are hired by "principals" (an organization's shareholders in our financial reporting example) to run the organization. Such an arrangement is an "agency relationship," since it involves the possibility that the agents will make decisions that are in their own best interests but not in the principals'. The principals hire the agent in the hope that the agent will increase the value of the principals' common shares, the assumption being that the agent is an expert in management, or in some technical field that is crucial to the success of the organization. However, a basic conflict of interest arises when managers are hired, since the manager may make decisions benefiting himself or herself at the expense of the principals/shareholders. The managers are close to the organization's operations, and presumably have information that the principals don't have.

Any decision that results in a principal losing wealth results in costs that are called "agency costs." Further, any actions taken by principals to protect themselves against sub-optimal decisions by their agents/managers also result in agency costs. Shareholders are therefore faced with a trade-off: an expected loss in wealth from management actions versus the cost of setting up systems to monitor management and hold management accountable. Rational shareholders, anticipating self-interested behaviour on the part of managers, will tend to reduce managers' compensation accordingly. The agents/managers, anticipating this action on the part of the principals, will have an incentive to demonstrate to the principals that such self-interested behaviour has not occurred, nor will it. In other words, incentives exist for agents/managers to provide audited financial statements to principals/shareholders to help those principals monitor their agents. The accountability concept may be elaborated upon using the above ideas of an agency relationship. Thus, we have several explanations why financial statements and auditing exist:

- For agency reasons, as explained above.
- Also because users of financial information may place a higher value on financial information if it is audited, since auditing provides a degree of quality assurance.
- Also because in some sense it may be possible to shift liability for loss to auditors (an insurance demand for auditing).

Ethical Decision-Making as the Core of the Financial Reporting System

GAAP, external auditing, internal auditing, audit committees, and well-educated users are not in themselves enough to ensure that a financial reporting system will function effectively. Even more fundamentally, there must be a system in place in which all participants internalize the concept that ethical decision-making is at the core of the financial reporting system. All the checks and balances in the world, and all the well-thought-out GAAP in the world, will result in only a second-rate financial reporting system if the participants lack a commitment to ethical behaviour. Even agency theory, which is built upon a self-interest view of individuals' actions, eventually will break down if, say, managers ignore the consequences of limits to self-interested behaviour; after all, there are limits to agency costs. As Exhibit 6–1 indicates, for example, it is managers who select and implement GAAP, make disclosure versus nondisclosure decisions, and generally have the overall responsibility for the quality of financial reporting.

Imagine how enormous the costs of auditing would be (both internal and external) if a reasonable level of ethical behaviour on the part of managers could *not* be assumed! Who would be willing to serve on audit committees of organizations if managers could not be trusted, by and large, to perform their duties ethically? What if unqualified (that is, "clean") audit opinions could be "bought": Would any rational user of financial statements have faith in the quality of the audited information? The whole financial reporting system would eventually break down. So it is no mere whim that in Chapter 2 "ethics" was presented as one of the key ideas in accounting. The structure of the financial reporting system is such that its various participants, its standards such as GAAP, and ethical behaviour all complement one another. The accounting research summarized in this chapter's "Accounting, Organizations, and Society" section presents some interesting and thought-provoking observations about financial reporting and ethics.

Legal Environment

Several aspects of the financial reporting system outlined in Exhibit 6–1 are regulated by law. For example, as we saw in Chapter 2, GAAP itself has been elevated almost to the status of law in Canada, in that the regulations of the Canada Business Corporations Act (the CBCA) state that when financial statements are referred to in the act, it specifically means financial statements prepared in accordance with the *CICA Handbook*. Securities legislation, such as the securities acts of the various provinces, also regulates the type and quality of financial information disseminated. The CBCA also provides that members of the boards of directors of companies incorporated under the act must act in the best interests of the corporation and with due care, subject to criminal proceedings. Several provinces have similar legislation.

In many provinces, laws regulate who may function as an external auditor (see Chapter 2). Also, many pieces of legislation, such as the CBCA, corresponding provincial acts, and acts governing special types of organizations (Crown corporations, condominiums, charities, municipalities, and so on), require organizations falling under their jurisdiction to be externally audited. There are, however, some exemptions for smaller "private" companies if all their shareholders agree to waive the requirement for an audit. Recently, the federal government extended this exemption from an audit to *all* private companies incorporated under the CBCA. This proposal generated considerable commentary in the media, as noted in Exhibit 6–2.

EXHIBIT 6–2
Media Comment on Proposal to Remove the Audit Requirement for Larger Private Companies from the Canada Business Corporations Act

Foreign Subsidiary Bill Is Another Liberal Blunder

by David Crane

The ... government is planning to end the requirement that federally incorporated foreign subsidiaries publish annual reports on their Canadian activities.

This will mean Canadians will no longer have access to financial information on several hundred of the most important companies in the country. Nor will they be able to assess the investment and other behavior of most multinationals in Canada.

Because foreign-controlled subsidiaries played such a large part in the Canadian economy, the Pearson government in the 1960s decided the public needed information on the performance and behavior of these firms.

To accomplish this, the government ... amended the Canada Business Corporations Act by requiring all private companies to file audited financial statements with Ottawa, with public access to this information.

For the first time, companies such as General Motors, Chrysler, IBM, Amoco, Mobil Oil, Kraft, Dow Chemical, DuPont, Goodyear, Unilever, Proctor & Gamble, Pratt & Whitney, Mitsubishi Canada, Marubeni Canada, Nestle, 3M, General Mills, Xerox, General Foods, Kellogg, Nabisco, Chevron, Goodyear, Mitsui, Pepsi-Cola, Digital Equipment, Canadian Safeway, and many others were required to disclose their financial performance in Canada.

Since then, others have been added to the list — Honda, Toyota, Mazda, Canadian General Electric, Price Club and, now, Wal-Mart.

The requirement that these subsidiaries publish annual financial statements not only provided the public with once-secret information on nearly half the manufacturing and resource sectors of the economy but also allowed business publications such as *Canadian Business* and *The Financial Post* to publish much more accurate directories of Canada's top 500 corporations.

In the 1970s, it was the mandatory disclosure rules that allowed Canadians to see how foreign-owned oil and gas companies were siphoning hundreds of millions of dollars out of Canada in special dividends, as oil and gas prices rose ...

Industry Minister John Manley is pushing this wrong-headed change. Manley's weak defence of the move is that disclosure is not required in the United States, so why should we do it in Canada?

It's strange that he should even have to ask the question. The role of foreign-controlled subsidiaries in the Canadian economy is much more significant than the role of foreign subsidiaries in the United States ...

GAAP as a Standard

One of the key items in Exhibit 6–1 is GAAP. This is the set of standards that the financial statements prepared under management's direction must comply with; external auditors assess financial statements in accordance with this set of standards. However, there are many circumstances in which GAAP, for legal or other reasons, is not the relevant standard. The financial statements of some types of organizations — for example, banks and universities — have long been prepared using standards other than GAAP. In Canada, banks' financial statements are prepared in accordance with the Bank Act, which has specified certain accounting treatments that are inconsistent with GAAP. However, in recent years there has been a major push to bring banks, and other institutions that have been following their own accounting principles (such as insurance companies and universities), into the "house of GAAP," either by encouraging these institutions to alter certain aspects of their accounting, or by introducing principles that are custom tailored to the particular type of institution. An example of the latter approach is the attempt to design new sections of the *CICA Handbook* for not-for-profit organizations. Thus, while GAAP represents a very important set of standards in the system summarized in Exhibit 6–1, it may be replaced in certain situations with other sets of accounting principles, by virtue of specific legal requirements or by agreement in certain circumstances.

Since the term "GAAP" is so important in the financial reporting system, the CICA has provided a definition, which is reproduced from the *CICA Handbook* in Exhibit 6–3. The definition contains some features that are important to remember:

- Both specific rules and broad principles (such as the conceptual framework discussed in Chapter 4) are included in the term "generally accepted accounting principles."
- Paragraph 1000.60 of the definition indicates that there is a hierarchy in GAAP.
- Professional judgment, as described in Chapter 4, is crucial.

EXHIBIT 6–3
Generally Accepted Accounting Principles:
A Definition Provided in Section 1000 of the *CICA Handbook*

.59 Generally accepted accounting principles is the term used to describe the basis on which financial statements are normally prepared. There are special circumstances where a different basis of accounting may be appropriate, for example, in financial statements prepared in accordance with regulatory legislation or contractual requirements.

.60 The term generally accepted accounting principles encompasses not only specific rules, practices and procedures relating to particular circumstances but also broad principles and conventions of general application, including the underlying concepts described in this Section.* Specifically, generally accepted accounting principles comprise the Accounting Recommendations in the Handbook and, when a matter is not covered by a Recommendation, other accounting principles that either:

(a) are generally accepted by virtue of their use in similar circumstances by a significant number of entities in Canada; or

(b) are consistent with recommendations in the Handbook and are developed through the exercise of professional judgment, including consultation with other informed accountants where appropriate, and the application of concepts described in this Section. In exercising professional judgment, established principles for analogous situations dealt with in the Handbook would be taken into account and references would be made to:

(i) other relevant matters dealt with in the Handbook;
(ii) practice in similar circumstances;
(iii) Accounting Guidelines published by the Accounting Standards Steering Committee;
(iv) Abstracts of Issues Discussed by the CICA Emergng Issues Committee;
(v) International Accounting Standards published by the International Accounting Standards Committee;
(vi) Standards published by bodies authorized to establish financial accounting standards in other jurisdictions;
(vii) CICA research studies; and
(viii) other sources of accounting literature such as textbooks and journals.

The relative importance of these various sources is a matter of professional judgment in the circumstances.

---

* Textbook author's note: Recall from Chapter 4 that this same section of the *CICA Handbook* documented the CICA's version of a financial accounting conceptual framework.

An Example of the Output of Financial Reporting

Back in Chapter 1 we introduced one of the important outputs of financial accounting — the set of financial statements — by examining the 1991 balance sheet, income statement, retained earnings statement, and cash flow statement of Corel Corporation. We now use the 1993 Annual Report of the same company to describe additional features of financial reporting and how managers may discharge their accountability partly by preparing and disseminating audited financial statements and other material in the Annual Report. Excerpts from the 1993 Annual Report of Corel are reproduced in Appendix A to this chapter. Notice that Corel continues to show increases in sales, and appears to be continuing the strong performance that we noted in Chapter 1.

Annual Reports

Annual reports of Canadian for-profit and not-for-profit organizations have changed significantly over time. For example, compare the 1923 Annual Report of Massey-Harris Limited, a manufacturer of agricultural machinery, which is reproduced in Appendix B, with the Corel Annual Report. Not only is there a much greater wealth of information in the 1993 Annual Report, but even the characteristics of the financial statements themselves have changed, almost beyond recognition. For example, the 1923 balance sheet has its assets in an order opposite to Corel's from 1993. It also has a very cryptic income statement, and doesn't even have a cash flow statement. Financial reporting has certainly evolved over the last 70 years. Let's focus now on Corel's Annual Report.

Notice the wide variety of information in the Annual Report. Some of this information is relatively "soft," qualitative, and unaudited (for example, the "Message to Shareholders" from the company's president; and the product information, which we haven't reproduced); other information is "harder," more quantitative, and audited (for example, the financial statements). Still other information falls somewhere in between these two extremes (for example, "Management Discussion and Analysis"). This variety of information may be categorized as follows (some parts of the Annual Report fit into two categories):

	Audited	**Unaudited**
Quantitative information	Audited financial statements and footnotes.	Management's discussion and analysis of financial condition and results of operations.
Qualitative information	Audited financial statements and footnotes. Audit opinion. Management's report.	Management's discussion and analysis of financial condition and results of operations. Company profile. Message to shareholders. Other information (such as "Year at a Glance"; product information).

Because of the mix of qualitative and quantitative information, and audited and unaudited information, in an annual report, external auditors have an obligation to ensure that there is no inconsistency between the financial statement information they have audited, and the unaudited portions of the annual report, such as the Message to Shareholders and the Management Discussion and Analysis section. An example of a possible inconsistency would be if the president of a company hailed a significant increase in sales as representing a major step forward for the company, even though the audited income statement indicated that most of the increased sales were to only marginally credit-worthy customers, and were unlikely to result in cash inflows.

The quotation that opened this chapter is from an article that summarized the research findings of a CICA study that examined the information content of annual reports. As that quotation indicates, deciding what to include in the annual report (in addition, of course, to the things that legally must be included, such as audited financial statements), what wording to use, how to balance the information needs of diverse users, and so on, presents a considerable challenge to managers and their advisers. The authors of the article went on to note that[2]

Current literature suggests annual reports are expected to be all things to all people. Originally conceived as a timely and thorough presentation of financial results to shareholders, their purposes today are substantially broader. From management's perspective, the main objectives are to report on a company's financial position and operating results, to report on management's stewardship, to facilitate informed investment decisions and to maintain public relations. From an investor/creditor perspective, however, the annual report serves as a general reference, provides background information for meetings with management, verifies information from other sources and is used in forecasting performance ... The goal is to satisfy the perceived information needs of the report's external users and, at the same time, to reflect the messages that management needs to convey, taking into consideration pertinent legal requirements and existing standards for financial reporting.

... One of the most difficult problems faced by management when preparing annual reports is that of balancing the different audiences' information needs — striking a balance between various investor groups, for example, or between investors and other users. Overall, a great many people use annual reports. They look to them for information to help evaluate performance and management quality, to estimate future prospects, to make comparisons, to assess financial strength, stability, adaptability, solvency, liquidity, risk and uncertainty. Annual reports are also used to determine compliance with the law or regulations, to assess contributions to society and to decide on resource allocation. Obviously, meeting all of these needs all of the time would be impossible. As such, the study group felt strongly that it is important to focus on the key users if annual reports are to be manageable and practical. Clearly, shareholders are key users; in fact, their entitlement to receive annual reports from management is protected by law. Creditors come a close second. As a minimum, therefore, annual reports must address the information needs of three primary groups: shareholders (investors), creditors and analysts/advisers who act on their behalf ...

But what of the many other users who also have a legitimate interest in knowing about an organization's activities? It's a long list: suppliers, employees, customers, underwriters, stock exchanges, lawyers, economists, taxing authorities, legislators,

[2] Trites and Roy, "Dispelling the Storybook Myth," *CAmagazine*, January 1992, pp. 55–58. Reprinted with permission from *CAmagazine*, published by the Canadian Institute of Chartered Accountants, Toronto, Canada.

labour unions, trade associations, business researchers, teachers and students, and the public. Nearly all are making economic decisions. Accordingly, annual reports should also help meet their common information needs wherever possible.

Even though much of the information included in an annual report is available before the report is published, the annual report continues to remain an important means of confirming (or disconfirming) and interpreting information, as well as releasing new information. The authors of the CICA research study concluded, in their *CAmagazine* article, that:

Research on the future direction of corporate reporting shows consensus on a number of points:

- *Annual reports will become more complex in response to investors' information needs.*
- *Management will face increasing demands for more detailed disclosure.*
- *There will be pressure on auditors to expand their attest function.*
- *Corporate information releases are likely to be more frequent.*
- *Information sources available to the investor are likely to become more diverse.*
- *Individual investors will become more dependent on stockbrokers.*

To meet the growing challenges of good reporting, therefore, the study concludes that management must approach the task with integrity and openness and be prepared to disclose information that may have been closely guarded in the past — it will be important to give the bad news along with the good. Only with complete, balanced disclosure and thoughtful insight and analysis can annual reports remain relevant in the demanding world of the '90s.[3]

Just a brief comparison of the 1993 Annual Report in Appendix A with the 1923 Annual Report in Appendix B suggests how much more complex and demanding management decision-making with respect to annual reports is today compared with some 70 years ago. Many incentives, such as the need to raise capital at low cost, legal requirements, increasing accountability to diverse user groups, and new types of accountability (to avoid environmental degradation, for example), are combining with the large number of financial accounting requirements and decisions to make the construction of annual reports an extremely interesting management task.

Accounting and Business Decision A

(a) Has Corel controlled costs well? Comment on Corel's profitability over the three-year period. In the process, prepare common-sized income statements for Corel for the three fiscal years 1991 to 1993, for the portion of Corel's income statement up to and including "Net income from continuing operations." Common-sized income statements are income statements in which each item is expressed as a percentage of some base — usually the "sales" number.

[3] Trites and Roy, "Dispelling the Storybook Myth."

(b) Read Michael C.J. Cowpland's "Message to the Shareholders" in Corel's 1993 Annual Report. What is emphasized? What important information, in your supported opinion, has been either de-emphasized or omitted altogether? How skilfully written was this part of the Annual Report?
(c) In your supported opinion, is the "Message to the Shareholders" consistent with the audited financial statements that are also included in the Annual Report?

Footnotes

Corel's audited financial statements included in the company's 1993 Annual Report contain a footnote summarizing the significant accounting policies that the company follows, as well as nine numbered footnotes. The accounting policy note usually precedes the other footnotes, as in the Corel case. All of these footnotes are part of the audited set of financial statements, and provide important information, without which the bare statements would be far less useful. Let's examine the accounting policy note to see just what makes it important.

From the accounting policy note we learn that Corel's financial statements follow Canadian GAAP. That is important: since GAAP differs — sometimes very substantially — from country to country, it's very helpful to know which GAAP the company follows. Since Corel markets much of its product in the United States, and since its common shares trade not only on the Toronto Stock Exchange but also in the United States, the accounting policy note informs American users of Corel's financial statements that the Canadian GAAP followed is "also generally accepted in the United States in all material respects," except for one important difference (described in footnote 8). Canadian companies that either must (because they, like Corel, have issued share or other capital in the United States), or voluntarily choose to, focus on foreign as well as Canadian audiences as users and potential users of their financial statements, typically provide an explanation similar to Corel's. However, there often are many material differences that the company must explain as between Canadian and the particular foreign GAAP. With the signing of the Free Trade Agreement and the North American Free Trade Agreement, and the increasing globalization of both product and capital markets in general, we can anticipate an even greater need to explain the impact of GAAP differences between countries. For example, a study published in December 1994 summarized major differences among the United States, Mexico, and Canada, the three members of NAFTA.[4]

There are many other important pieces of information in Corel's accounting policy note. For example, we're told — under the heading "(b) Sales recognition" — about Corel's policies regarding when revenue is recognized and how discounts and allowances for returns (both potentially very significant items in Corel's business) are treated, at least in a general way. Ensuring that this policy makes sense for Corel, and that Corel's major competitors follow a similar policy, would contribute greatly to our understanding of Corel's impressive increase in revenues over the past several years. Some additional insight is provided in footnote 9, discussed later.

While each of the nine footnotes is very important, we'll limit our discussion

[4] Canadian Institute of Chartered Accountants, Instituto Mexicano de Contadores Publicos, A.C., Financial Accounting Standards Board of the United States, FASB Financial Accounting Series, No. 144-B, *Financial Reporting in North America, Highlights of a Joint Study*, December 1994.

to footnotes 3, 5, and 9. Footnote 3 provides us with the details underlying the share capital section of the shareholders' equity portion of Corel's balance sheet. Note the reference to footnote 3 right on the face of the balance sheet, which is typical. The footnote explains why the share capital total went from $69,130,000 at the end of fiscal 1992 up to $90,510,000 at the end of fiscal 1993. This increase of $21,380,000 occurred because of one factor: under the company's employee stock option plan, certain employees are permitted to purchase common shares of the company at certain set prices. The footnote indicates that 2,683,384 such common shares were purchased by employees in 1993, for a total of $21,380,000. A journal entry to record this set of transactions with the company's employees would be:

Dr Cash (B)	21,380,000	
Cr Share capital (B)		21,380,000

The same footnote indicates that in the previous year there were two factors that caused share capital to increase up to its November 30, 1992, level of $69,130,000:

- As in 1993, certain employees were permitted to purchase common shares under the employee stock option plan, but only 1,119,856 shares were issued, for $7,792,000, in that year.
- There was an initial public offering of common shares in the United States. This raised $30,046,000 for Corel Corporation.

Footnote 5 discloses important information about where the company produces its products (Canada and Ireland), and sells its products, as well as a list of its major customers. Such information may help users answer such questions as these:

- Are the company's production locations positioned to take advantage of opportunities and to ward off potential threats? The signing of the NAFTA suggests that Corel's Canadian location is positioned to serve not only the Canadian market, but the American and Mexican markets as well. The location in Ireland seems to take advantage of the push by European nations to create their own free trade zone.
- Are the company's sales sufficiently diversified geographically, so that declines in any one market will not be an excessive threat, and so that growth markets are being pursued? The footnote suggests very significant growth in all four geographic sectors. Note that while American sales increased significantly in an absolute sense by $7,403,000 from 1992 to 1993, the share of total Corel revenues represented by the American market declined, from 50% in 1992 to 38% in 1993. Thus, diversification is highly welcome, especially in light of the decline in the growth rate of American sales (which grew $15,817,000, or 53.7%, from 1991 to 1992, but only $7,403,000, or 16.3%, from 1992 to 1993).
- Is the company excessively dependent on a small number of customers? The footnote information indicates that in 1993, four major customers accounted for $49,414,000, or 35.2%, of Corel's total sales. In 1992, they accounted for $36,958,000, or 41.0%, of total sales. So, the company is relatively less dependent on this group of customers, but not by much compared to 1992.

Footnote 9 provides some details related to Corel's sales discounts and allowance for returns (recall that we must have this information in order to assess Corel's revenue recognition policy). Let's assume that the "Promotional rebates" mentioned in footnote 9 are the only sales discounts, and that the item "Sales reserve" in the footnote refers to Corel's allowance for software product returned from its customers. The final accounting item mentioned in footnote 9 is Corel's "Allowance for doubtful accounts," which refers to Corel's attempt to account for the business fact of life that not all customers are willing or able to pay their bills. Corel deducts all three of these items from its balance sheet asset account "Accounts receivable — trade"; it then correspondingly reduces its income statement "Sales" number by the first two, and (apparently, but we don't know for sure) increases its income statement expense line item "Selling, general and administrative" by the third item, "Allowance for doubtful accounts." If all this sounds pretty complicated, it is! But let's use the information that Corel has conveniently provided to its financial statement users (that is, us!) in footnote 9 to sort all this out. We are able to do so because Corel has provided the details of the opening balances, additions, deductions, and closing balances of each of these three items from November 30, 1990, to November 30, 1993. Let's first reconstruct what appears to be Corel's accounting for the "Promotion rebates," by tracking the debits and credits in the general ledger account:

	Debits	Credits	Balance
November 30, 1990			0
1991 additions		0	
1991 deductions	0		
November 30, 1991			0
1992 additions		3,087,000	
1992 deductions	552,000		
November 30, 1992			2,535,000 Cr
1993 additions		7,005,000	
1993 deductions	6,491,000		
November 30, 1993			3,049,000 Cr

The corresponding journal entries are, using the activity in 1992 as an illustration:

1992 additions:

Dr Sales (I)	3,087,000	
Cr Accounts receivable (B)		3,087,000

This journal entry reduces both the income statement "Sales" account and the balance sheet asset "Accounts receivable" by the amount of the promotion rebate that Corel negotiated with its customers in 1992. Such an accounting treatment makes sense because otherwise, both of these accounts would be overstated, since the rebates represent offsets to the full sales amount.

1992 deductions:

Dr Accounts receivable (B)	552,000	
Cr Sales (I)		552,000

This journal entry accounts for the fact that perhaps not all of Corel's customers fulfilled the conditions of the rebate agreement.

The corresponding journal entries for 1993 were, apparently:

Dr Sales (I)	7,005,000	
Cr Accounts receivable (B)		7,005,000

This accounts for the original rebates on 1993 shipments of product. Then, to account for unfulfilled rebate agreements:

Dr Accounts receivable (B)	6,491,000	
Cr Sales (I)		6,491,000

We next focus on accounting for the "Sales reserve," or allowance for returns:

	Debits	Credits	Balance
November 30, 1990			2,525,000 Cr
1991 additions		0	
1991 deductions	2,525,000		
November 30, 1991			0
1992 additions		2,738,000	
1992 deductions	1,104,000		
November 30, 1992			1,634,000 Cr
1993 additions		4,267,000	
1993 deductions	2,327,000		
November 30, 1993			3,574,000 Cr

	Debits	Credits	Balance
November 30, 1990			525,000 Cr
1991 additions		541,000	
1991 deductions	0		
November 30, 1991			1,066,000 Cr
1992 additions		946,000	
1992 deductions	922,000		
November 30, 1992			1,090,000 Cr
1993 additions		456,000	
1993 deductions	261,000		
November 30, 1993			1,285,000 Cr

The journal entries year by year appear to be as follows:

1991:

Dr Accounts receivable (B)	2,525,000	
Cr Sales (I)		2,525,000

1992:

Dr Sales (I)	2,738,000	
Cr Accounts receivable (B)		2,738,000

This journal entry reduces both "Sales" and "Accounts receivable" by the dollar amount of product the company expects its customers to return, based on 1992 total sales. Some software product that the company's retail and other distributors have received from Corel during the year will inevitably be returned to Corel; perhaps the product has been superseded by other, competing software, or even one of Corel's newer products. This is just a fact of doing business.

Dr Accounts receivable (B)	1,104,000	
Cr Sales (I)		1,104,000

This second set of accountable events took place in 1992; perhaps some software product that had been returned by certain of Corel's customers was in turn resold to other customers. Perhaps in different markets, or perhaps at a discount.

For 1993, the original returns journal entry is:

Dr Sales (I)	4,267,000	
Cr Accounts receivable (B)		4,267,000

And the possible journal entry accounting for what appears to be subsequent resales:

Dr Accounts receivable (B)	2,327,000	
Cr Sales (I)		2,327,000

The allowance for doubtful accounts portion of all this activity is as at the bottom left of this page.

Accounting for an "Allowance for doubtful accounts" (or, as it is often called, an "Allowance for bad debts") is different from accounting for the promotion rebates and sales reserves, since an expense account ("Bad debt expense") is increased when the allowance is first accounted for. Corel makes life a little more complicated than necessary for users of its financial statements in that it does not explicitly disclose its "Bad debt expense" account; rather, it seems to have grouped it with several other accounts in an income statement line item it calls "Selling, general and administrative" expense. The journal entries appear to be as follows:
1991:

Dr Selling, general and administrative expense (I)	541,000	
Cr Accounts receivable (B)		541,000

Thus, it seems that Corel's management believed that about $541,000 of 1991 sales dollars would ultimately not be received because of customers' inability to pay (perhaps they might become bankrupt).

The matching concept, which was described in Chapter 4, is the theoretical rationale behind this journal entry: Corel's management is matching a cost of doing business on credit — the estimated bad debt expense — to the revenues generated in the year by incurring this expense. One method that many companies use to estimate bad debt expense is illustrated in Appendix C of this chapter.

Let's return to Corel's bad debt expense accounting. Since there are no other journal entries for this item for 1991, we'll move on to 1992.

For 1992, we have:

Dr Selling, general and administrative expense (I)	946,000	
Cr Accounts receivable (B)		946,000

But there is a second journal entry with respect to this item in 1992: footnote 9 tells us that the allowance for doubtful accounts was reduced by *$922,000* in 1992, and thus "Accounts receivable" was increased by this amount. This could mean that $922,000 of the accounts receivable that were previously thought to be bad are now judged to be good (perhaps Corel's management has received new, up-to-date information on certain customers from a credit rating agency):

Dr Accounts receivable (B)	922,000	
Cr Selling, general and administrative expense (I)		922,000

Managers are almost always refining financial accounting estimates with new information. There's nothing wrong with this practice; in fact, it's absolutely necessary if the most relevant, up-to-date information is to be reflected in the financial statements. The necessity to make such estimates in an ethical manner is obvious: management often has the best information about assets, liabilities, revenues, expenses, and other aspects of financial accounting and reporting; thus, even with all the checks and balances built into the system (see Exhibit 6–1), ethical decision-making on management's part is crucial.

The 1993 entries appear to be (in summary form):

Dr Selling, general and administrative expense (I)	456,000	
Cr Accounts receivable (B)		456,000

and,

Dr Accounts receivable (B)	261,000	
Cr Selling, general and administrative expense (I)		261,000

Management Discussion and Analysis

The MD&A, as it has come to be known, is not part of the formal, audited financial statements; however, as may be seen from Corel's MD&A, it can contain a wealth of quite detailed information about products, markets, risks, financial results and position, and so on, all from management's perspective. MD&As are a relatively recent innovation in Canada. Regulatory agencies such as the Ontario Securities Commission (which in 1989 began requiring companies that issued securities in Ontario to publish MD&As) have expressed some dissatisfaction with the overall quality of MD&As, although they acknowledge that there have been improvements in recent years. Some of this criticism has focused on MD&As that merely duplicate information in financial statements and that are not used by management to provide real insight about the company, its environment, and its challenges and risks.

Accounting and Business Decision B

(a) Assess the reasonableness of Corel Corporation's accounting policy with respect to its capital assets, in conjunction with a review of footnote 2 in the 1993 financial statements.

(b) Evaluate the importance of footnote 7, "Discontinued Operations." Suggest why users of financial statements might find it useful if information on a company's discontinued operations were disclosed separately from ongoing operations. In general, and not referring to Corel, might management be tempted to manipulate the classification of operations as between "ongoing" and "discontinued" in certain circumstances, given that GAAP requires information such as set out in Corel's footnote 7 to be disclosed?

(c) Does Corel's MD&A simply repeat the information in the audited financial statements?

Other Reports

Although we focus on annual reports and their make-up in this chapter, we don't by any means wish to give the impression that annual reports are the only output of the financial reporting accountability system. Many organizations publish and disseminate other important reports as well; we will mention briefly two such reports: interim reports and prospectuses.

Corel issues an "interim report" just after the end of each quarter-year. It is much briefer than the Annual Report and the financial information it contains is unaudited. Interim reports are typically cryptic and unaudited because their focus is on disseminating financial information in a timely manner. However, the fact that Corel's Annual Report contains *audited* financial statements lends credence to the financial information contained in the interim reports.

Prospectuses and offering circulars are two other types of financial reports that contain very detailed information about a company's operations, ownership, financing, and future plans, as well as audited financial statements. Under legislation (usually provincial), these reports must be issued by a company when that company wishes to raise capital by issuing new common shares or other securities. Usually, securities legislation specifies that two-year comparative balance sheets, along with five years of income statements, retained earnings statements, and cash flow statements, must be included in these reports. As in the case of annual reports, external auditors must satisfy themselves that there are no inconsistencies between the financial statements they have audited and the rest of the prospectus.

What Do External Auditors Do?

One of the important participants in the financial reporting accountability and communication system set out in Exhibit 6–1 is the external auditor. Simply put, the external auditor performs an audit of the financial statements (which, recall, include the footnotes) and — based upon that audit — judges whether the financial statements comply with GAAP. This is called by some the "attest" role or "attest audit" role of the auditor. Note that auditors may be called upon to perform many other types of audits. For example, they may be called upon to judge whether a set of financial statements is in compliance with a set of accounting standards *other than* GAAP (as set out in special legislation, for example); or to perform special audits of expenditures (for example, candidates contesting a seat in Parliament must have their expenditures audited). There are many other possibilities besides these.

The attest audit involves much more than merely examining the output of the financial accounting process — that is, the set of financial statements that management has prepared. It involves a thorough investigation, examination, and assessment of accounting and disclosure choices, and of the accounting and other management systems used by the company for capturing and summarizing accounting information. All of this requires an understanding of the organization and its context, and an assessment of the degree to which management may be expected to behave ethically. (If the auditor can't trust management to behave ethically, audit procedures will have to be adjusted, and in some extreme circumstances the external auditor may have to resign.) We'll look at some of the important aspects of the auditor's task very soon, when we describe the standards that govern external auditing, referred to as generally accepted auditing standards (which are, as you no doubt expected, abbreviated by accountants, auditors, and their associates as GAAS). We'll also briefly discuss the final output of the external auditor's attest audit, the audit opinion.

Before we turn to GAAS and the audit opinion, however, we must mention how centrally and vitally important it is that the auditor be independent in both fact and appearance. An external auditor may have a superior knowledge of auditing techniques and know the organization being audited in detail, and may perform the audit role with consummate skill with respect to the quality of the audit investigation; but if the external auditor is perceived by users to be *not* independent of management or any other special interests, then the resulting audit will be virtually worthless and the external auditor's audit opinion will not be trusted. This requirement for independence of mind and action on the part of external auditors is another example of the importance of ethics in accounting (see Chapter 2). Ensuring that auditors are independent involves several things, including the following:

- A deep understanding on the external auditor's part of the importance of independence in auditing, and a belief in and a personal commitment to independence in fact and in appearance.

- A professional code of conduct, in which a requirement for independence is a key component. The general platitudes about independence in such a code of conduct should be supported by specific prohibitions against, for example, the external auditor's having more than trivial financial interest in a client. All Canadian provincial accounting professional groups have such a code.
- An arm's-length relationship with the managers, owners, and others involved in the organization being audited, or that the external auditor expects to audit. This may represent a challenge occasionally, especially since it is management that often controls who gets appointed as external auditor, in spite of the requirement in companies acts that the shareholders be formally responsible for such appointments.

Needless to say, there are considerable threats to an external auditor's independence. Many individuals who perform the external audit role with respect to an organization may also (either directly or through their partners in an accounting practice) provide the management of the same organization with advice on other business matters, such as the design of accounting information systems for the company, the selection and implementation of accounting choices, corporate income tax or other tax advice, and other management advisory services (abbreviated MAS). They may even provide consulting services on personal matters such as the manager's personal tax return. Currently, there are no prohibitions against such activities as long as the external auditor's independence is not impaired. But some critics are not happy with this arrangement, and believe that external auditors should restrict their activities to auditing. Those who defend current practice in this area argue that attest audits by themselves are "loss leaders" (in the sense that the total, actual cost of performing an attest audit often exceeds the audit fee that can be charged); thus, external auditors must provide MAS to their audit clients in order to remain economically viable. They also point out that providing MAS to a client improves the external auditor's knowledge of the client's business and organization, and in fact makes the audit more efficient and effective. This remains a controversial area.[5]

One interesting observation related to independence and the credibility of the external auditor's performance as auditor is offered by Philip D. Bougen, a British accounting academic now teaching at the Madrid Business School in Spain. He points out that in the United Kingdom in the latter part of the nineteenth century, financial accounting in general and auditors and accountants in particular were viewed with scepticism and some disdain: "Laughing at accountants for being rogues engaged in assorted deceptive practices was, therefore, a source of 'public amusement'" (p. 328). This was partly because of the rapid expansion of the demand for accounting and auditing services as business expanded, and the corresponding influx of persons with less than adequate training and personal values into the practice of accounting. Bougen reports that earlier in the same century there had been "a client belief in

---

[5] An unabashed critic of current practice is Abraham J. Briloff of the City University of New York. His views are summarized in his article "Accountancy and Society: A Covenant Desecrated," *Critical Perspectives on Accounting*, Vol. 1, 1990, pp. 5–30.

An article in *The Financial Post* by Philip Mathias had a title that shows the continuing concern in this area: "Auditors' loss of independence leaves shareholders wary." The subtitle was even more alarmist: "Increasingly, auditors seen as functionaries giving credibility to management" (Thursday, February 9, 1995).

the personal integrity of the accountant and in the more general values associated with the accountant stereotype" (p. 326), which Bougen describes as:

> *an eye for detail, a somewhat suspicious predisposition and an emphasis on numerical accuracy ... personal honesty, integrity and a commitment to secrecy would presumably have been desirable ...*

EXHIBIT 6–4
EXCERPTS FROM SECTION 5100 OF THE *CICA HANDBOOK* GENERALLY ACCEPTED AUDITING STANDARDS

Standards and Procedures

.01 Auditing standards are different from auditing procedures. Auditing standards relate to the auditor's qualifications, the performance of his or her examination and the preparation of his or her report. Auditing procedures, on the other hand, are the specific acts or steps performed by the auditor to attain his or her objectives in the particular audit engagement.

Generally Accepted Auditing Standards

.02 *Generally Accepted Auditing Standards are as follows:*

General standard

The examination should be performed and the report prepared by a person or persons having adequate technical training and proficiency in auditing, with due care and an objective state of mind.

Examination standards

(i) *The work should be adequately planned and properly executed. If assistants are employed they should be properly supervised.*

(ii) *A sufficient understanding of internal control should be obtained to plan the audit. When control risk is assessed below maximum, sufficient appropriate audit evidence should be obtained through tests of controls to support the assessment.*

(iii) *Sufficient appropriate audit evidence should be obtained, by such means as inspection, observation, enquiry, confirmation, computation and analysis, to afford a reasonable basis to support the content of the report.*

Reporting standards

(i) *The report should identify the financial statements and distinguish between the responsibilities of management and the responsibilities of the auditor.*

(ii) *The report should describe the scope of the auditor's examination.*

(iii) *The report should contain either an expression of opinion on the financial statements or an assertion that an opinion cannot be expressed. In the latter case, the reasons therefor should be stated.*

(iv) *Where an opinion is expressed, it should indicate whether the financial statements present fairly, in all material respects, the financial position, results of operations and changes in financial position in accordance with an appropriate disclosed basis of accounting, which except in special circumstances should be generally accepted accounting principles. The report should provide adequate explanation with respect to any reservation contained in such an opinion.*

Bougen then goes on to argue that in order for accounting and auditing to become a full profession in the United Kingdom in the latter part of the nineteenth century, it had to overcome the negative view of accountants as "rogues," and encourage a return to perceptions common earlier in that century. Leaders in the profession deliberately cultivated the characteristics of the older stereotype — personal honesty, high moral character, and attention to detail — as desirable in accountants and auditors, and encouraged those possessing such characteristics to enter the profession. Thus, the "accounting stereotype" that we introduced in Chapter 2, and from which many of today's leaders are trying to distance the profession, may — according to Bougen — have been one of the crucial factors in the emergence of accounting and auditing as a full profession early in the twentieth century.[6]

Generally Accepted Auditing Standards

To suggest to you the many aspects of the audit and the nature of the general standards that external auditors must follow, we reproduce in Exhibit 6–4 an excerpt from the *CICA Handbook* section on GAAS. The *CICA Handbook* prints its formal standards in italics; other, supporting information is in roman type. The "internal control" to which GAAS refers includes "the policies and procedures established and maintained by management to assist in achieving its objective of ensuring, as far as practical, the orderly and efficient conduct of the entity's business" (*CICA* 5200.03). An example of one such internal control might be a requirement that at least two senior managers of an organization sign all cheques over a certain threshold amount — say, $1,000.

[6] Philip D. Bougen, "Joking Apart: The Serious Side to the Accountant Stereotype," *Accounting, Organizations and Society*, Vol. 19, no. 3, 1994, pp. 319–335.

Accounting and Business Decision C

(a) Why must external auditors be independent in order for the financial reporting accountability and communication system in Exhibit 6–1 to work effectively?

(b) Is it really possible for external auditors to be truly independent in situations in which they provide MAS to their audit client?

The Auditor's Opinion

GAAS's four reporting standards, as set out in Exhibit 6–4, refer to the final product of the external auditor's efforts and judgments — the audit report. Note that the audit report provided with the audited financial statements in Corel Corporation's 1993 Annual Report fulfils all the reporting standards' requirements. Aside from the final sentence of the report, which merely alerts the reader to the U.S.-Canada GAAP similarities and a minor difference, the report is a "clean opinion," or "unqualified." In other words, the auditors, from the firm KPMG Peat Marwick Thorne, have performed sufficient auditing work at Corel Corporation to support their opinion that Corel's financial statements comply with GAAP. In situations where the auditor doesn't judge that the audit evidence permits the granting of an unqualified opinion, other types of audit opinions may be given indicating the concerns the auditor has. These "reservations" in the audit opinion may relate to accounting measurement or disclosure decisions that management has made which, in the auditor's judgment, are inconsistent with GAAP; or they may relate to a situation in which the auditor is unable to collect sufficient evidence to form a judgment about the degree to which the financial statements comply with GAAP. In the vast majority of audits, management has strong incentives to permit the external auditor to perform all the tasks necessary to form an audit opinion (recall the agent–principle discussion), and to make accounting measurement and disclosure decisions consistent with GAAP; in other words, management doesn't want reservations or qualifications in the organization's audit report. There have been rare situations, however, in which less-than-forthright managers have attempted to pull the wool over the auditor's eyes. Such behaviour may result in short-term loss of credibility to the financial reporting system; typically, however, it has a longer-run positive effect in that it stimulates reforms to the system. Similarly, there have been a few instances of management going "opinion shopping" — that is, arranging for an auditor who holds a view contrary to management's self-interested view to be dismissed, and looking for an auditor who will provide an unqualified opinion on management's accounting treatment.

In order for the audit opinion to have credibility, and thus to be an effective part of the financial reporting accountability system shown in Exhibit 6–1, the readers and users of the report must have faith in the auditor's professional and technical competence and independence. The financial reporting accountability system is based heavily on trust: trust in management; trust in auditors; trust in the accountants who design and implement companies' accounting and internal control systems; trust in regulators such as securities commissions; trust in legislators who create laws governing various aspects of financial reporting; trust in the financial and business press, in which journalists often interpret and pass judgment on audited financial information; and so on. It is encouraging that breaches in this web of trust are quite rare. By and large, the system works quite well. (Imagine, just for a moment, the chaos that would result if it didn't!)

Audit Committees

The laws governing incorporation require that many organizations establish audit committees. However, in some legal jurisdictions there are many organizations — for common example, charities, hospitals, and local governments — that are not as yet required to have audit committees. An audit committee is a sort of semi-independent group of individuals, usually selected from an organization's board of directors, who have a high-level oversight responsibility with respect to financial accounting and reporting, and to the overall accountability of the organization. The semi-independence of an audit committee is at least partly ensured by selecting board members who are not members of the organization's management team, and who have well-established outside reputations for personal integrity to maintain. Audit committees, therefore, act in part as a buffer between management and the external auditor, and provide some assurance that the very top level of the governance structure of the organization is closely considering audit and accountability issues.

If the external auditor is experiencing difficulty in dealing with management on a particular accounting issue, he or she has the right to be heard by the audit committee, and the audit committee has the obligation to provide a full and fair hearing, and to exercise due care in acting on the information. The legal requirement to form audit committees is a relatively recent phenomenon; many organizations that are not yet legally required to form such committees do so out of a desire to improve the quality of their overall governance. Some critics, however, are worried that too much may be expected of audit committees. For example, Jean Guertin, the director of L'École des Hautes Études Commerciales in Montreal, writes:

> *Managers ... tell me they ... find that in most cases major problems are identified first by the internal administration, which then seeks the [board of directors'] advice. This is not a reflection of the relative competence of the internal and external groups. Rather, it reflects the fact that managers are involved on a full-time basis and earn most of their income from the organization. It's natural, then, if they have been properly selected, that they would be the first to see things coming, because they know the firm and its industry so well.*
>
> *If the full weight of monitoring financial statements and related reports is pushed onto the shoulders of an audit committee of outsiders, the overall management and monitoring quality of our organizations will be reduced. We would be working against the sacred principle that a decision should be taken where the information is located ... As a manager, I would feel ill-supported by such a committee. Today's companies are simply too complex for their results to be monitored that way ...*[7]

Internal Auditors

Internal auditors are employees of an organization, and have no direct involvement in the attest audit performed by the external auditors (who are independent professionals who are *not* employed by the organization, but are providing a professional service for a fee). Audit committees fulfil a high-level oversight role; internal auditors are actively involved in performing audits of various aspects of the organization. These audits are of two general types:

[7] Jean Guertin, "The Fall Guys," *CAmagazine*, April 1991, pp. 16-20. Reprinted with permission from *CAmagazine*, published by the Canadian Institute of Chartered Accountants, Toronto, Canada.

The first type is very similar to the audit that an external auditor might perform, but the intent is to report to management on whether the procedures and policies as laid down by management are being followed. This is very important in the case of decentralized organizations, as it helps ensure that the accounting information provided by various units in the organization to the central management group is of high integrity. For example, the internal audit group of the University of Toronto conducts audits of the 276 separate colleges, schools, institutes, student organizations, and ancillary for-profit organizations (such as food services and the university press) that make up the university. One thing these internal audits focus on is the degree to which each of these 276 "audit entities" follows approved procedures. They must prove that they do so before, for example, the central Accounts Payable office will disburse cheques for them for the purchase of capital assets. The internal auditors seek answers to questions such as these: Was the capital asset's purchase approved by a senior officer of the college, (or school, or whatever)? Was an approved supplier used? Has the item ordered actually been received? Was it received in good condition? Did appropriate managers of the college (or school, or whatever) approve the request to issue the cheque? Overall, are the accounting and approval systems set up to control the purchase of capital assets working as they were intended? Some of the audit work of the internal auditor may be relied upon by the external auditor, as a means to improve the overall effectiveness of the external audit and reduce costs.

A second type of internal audit might focus on effectiveness and efficiency. Following along with the above example, one of the efficiency concerns of a recent internal audit related to whether or not *all* cheques for payment of capital assets by the 276 audit entities should be approved and disbursed from a central office. Perhaps cheques for the purchase of capital assets below a dollar limit of, say, \$2,000, could be approved and disbursed through the particular college (or school, or whatever) more cheaply and in a more timely manner than through a single, large central office.

The Financial Reporting Accountability System: An Assessment

Accountability is a basic idea in accounting. The system that creates and disseminates an organization's annual report, as outlined in Exhibit 6–1 and described in this chapter, is an important example of how this accountability function is carried out. The system is complex. It involves many participants, each with a unique perspective and with special talents and interests; and it is partially regulated by law. It depends upon professional standards and judgments (GAAP, or some other basis of accounting, and GAAS), and on managers, auditors, and others making good decisions when applying those standards and forming those judgments. Earned trust is vital to the system, and so is the external auditor's independence. The tangible output of the system — the annual report — is a complex document that contains a mix of audited and unaudited information.

Any evaluation of this financial reporting accountability system would require a close, detailed examination of each of its components and participant groups; of the quality of the output of the system; and of the overall effectiveness and efficiency of the system and of its positive and negative impacts on other parts of our society. Obviously, such an evaluation can hardly be started in a single chapter of an introductory book on accounting. However, the descriptions and discussions in this chapter, as well as the experiences of those involved in and affected by the system, indicate that the system works remarkably well, and is adaptable enough to reform and improve itself as failures arise or new challenges appear. But information technology is changing so rapidly that emergent challenges to the system may well cause radical change. For example, the concept of annual financial reports may soon be supplanted by the reality of continuous financial reporting, in which a user at a personal computer logs in via modem to an organization's financial reporting database, and extracts the information needed at whatever level of detail is requested.

Accountability and Financial Reporting via the Internet

More and more organizations are making financial information about themselves available through the Internet. This technology is in its relative infancy, and every accounting entity seems to have adopted a different approach to utilizing it as a means of disseminating financial and other information. For example, the computer giant IBM provides access to its individual financial statements (which may be downloaded in the form of spreadsheets such as Microsoft Excel) as well as to its entire Annual Report. Other companies provide access just to their annual reports, while still others are only at the stage of planning an Internet web site.

In addition to this, government and other information collection agencies are now providing an almost overwhelming amount of accounting and related information over the Internet. For example, the prospectuses and offering circulars that companies must issue when they want to raise equity or debt funds from the public are now becoming available over the Internet. And the Securities and Exchange Commission in the United States provides Internet access to the detailed "10-K" reports that companies issuing debt and/or equity in that country must file annually with the commission. A company's 10-K report contains the entire contents of its annual report as well as additional information about the company, its shareholders, its markets and risks, and so on.

The best way to begin finding out what accounting information is available on the Internet seems to be to just logon and explore. Although most universities and colleges are making Internet access fairly easy and relatively inexpensive for their students, access is still uneven. The situation is changing rapidly and constantly, however. If you do have access, some useful accounting-related sites are shown in the chart to the left.[8]

Organization	Internet Address
Canadian Institute of Chartered Accountants	www.cica.ca
Society of Management Accountants of Canada	www.cma-Canada.org/
Certified General Accountants Association of Canada	www.cga-Canada.org
Securities and Exchange Commission (U.S.)	www.sec.gov/edgarhp.htm
Rutgers University Accounting Web (U.S.)	www.rutgers.edu/Accounting/raw.html
Corel Corporation	www.corel.com/
IBM (U.S.)	www.ibm.com/IBM

[8] Internet addresses ("Universal Resource Locators," or URLs for short) may be changed at any time, so be prepared to do a bit of searching if the URLs in the above list become dated. An overview of the Internet from an accounting perspective is provided in Don Sheehy and Gerald Trites, "Net Recoveries," *CAmagazine*, May 1996, pp. 49–52.

Accounting, Organizations, and Society

What follows is an excerpt from an accounting research article in which the authors attempt to bring together some systematic information about ethics in financial reporting.

The Ethics of Managing Earnings: An Empirical Investigation

by Kenneth A. Merchant and Joanne Rockness

This paper describes the findings of a study designed to explore empirically the controversial issue of earnings management. Earnings management practices probably raise the most important ethical issues facing the accounting profession, yet little research has explored the topic. To assess the prevailing morality regarding earnings management practices, we used a questionnaire comprised of 13 potentially questionable earnings management activities. General managers, staff managers, operating-unit controllers, and internal auditors were sampled. The responses show some areas of general agreement. For example, acceptability was judged to vary with the type, size, timing, and purpose of the actions. But we also found significant areas of disagreement. The paper concludes with a discussion of the implications of this general disagreement and suggestions for future research.

1. Introduction

One thing lawmakers and designers of organizational control systems and professional codes of conduct have in common is their need to distinguish between acceptable and unacceptable forms of behavior. Sometimes these groups' tasks are easy as, for example, conclusions that theft of assets is unacceptable are not controversial. But for many other types of behaviors, deriving these prescriptions is difficult.

One controversial and important area is that of earnings management. Earnings management can be defined as any action on the part of management which affects reported income and which provides no true economic advantage to the organization and may in fact, in the long term, be detrimental ... the National Commission on Fraudulent Financial Reporting ... concluded that earnings management activities can mislead financial-statement users and, sometimes, are precursors of more serious, illegal (fraudulent reporting) activities ...

[The authors of the article go on to review prior research on earnings management, and point out that such research has taken a largely economic perspective, in that it has focused on "the incentives managers have to manage earnings and the consequences of their manipulative actions (i.e., the costs and benefits of allowing discretion in the choice and application of accounting methods)." The authors' research, however, adopts a broader ethical perspective, which they describe as having the following features:]

The ethical perspective raises some interesting and important issues. Most of the earnings management actions which have been studied are legal, not inconsistent with generally accepted accounting principles (GAAP), and within managers' prerogatives. The ethical perspective, however, raises the question as to whether these things are the right things to do. Should we, for example, judge it acceptable for a manager to boost earnings by squeezing reserves? If not, the individuals engaging in these actions are acting in a socially unacceptable way. If the individuals' moral codes do not prevent the actions, it might be beneficial to enact laws or codes of conduct to deter such activities, and to create audit programs and other forms of controls to detect and correct the manipulations before the financial statements are published.

A related question is: Is the intent behind the action relevant? Should our moral judgments depend upon the purpose for which the earnings are being boosted? For example, are managers' actions undertaken to boost earnings to augment their bonuses more heinous than their doing so to prevent their firm from defaulting on the terms of its bank loan? If intent is relevant, the prevention/detection process becomes more complicated ...

How does a society, the accounting profession, or an individual firm draw the line between acceptable and unacceptable earnings management practices? ...

At one extreme are practices which virtually everyone would denounce as unacceptable, such as fraud. At the other extreme ... are practices which most people would view as acceptable such as, perhaps, a fully-disclosed switch from accelerated to straight-line depreciation if the business is in need of more earnings ...

Journal of Accounting and Public Policy, *1994, Vol. 13, pp. 79–94. Reprinted with permission from Elsevier Science Ltd., Oxford, England.*

The authors go on to describe a survey they administered to managers in two companies and to a group of internal auditors. The survey, which is reproduced in question 20 at the end of this chapter, asked respondents to indicate the degree to which they believed several different situations involving accounting and management decisions were ethical or unethical. Specifically, respondents were asked to select one of the following responses on a five-point scale for each of the situations:

- Ethical practice = 1.
- Questionable practice = 2. I would not say anything to the manager, but it makes me uncomfortable.
- Minor infraction = 3. The manager should be warned not to engage in the practice again.
- Serious infraction = 4. The manager should be severely reprimanded.
- Totally unethical = 5. The manager should be fired.

To suggest the types of situations that were in the questionnaire, one situation was as follows:

The general manager "ordered his employees to defer all discretionary expenditures (e.g., travel, advertising, hiring, maintenance) into the next accounting period, so that his division could make its budgeted profit targets. Expected amount of deferral: $150,000. The expenses were postponed from November and December until January in order to make the annual target."

The average of the 308 responses to this situation was 2.09 on the five-point scale, suggesting that this was viewed as a questionable or minor infraction. However, the range of responses was from 1 to 5, and the standard deviation (which is a statistical measure of dispersion) was the highest of all the 13 scenarios presented in the questionnaire — 1.27, suggesting that there was considerable disagreement among the respondents with respect to this item.

It might be interesting to now read the complete questionnaire; see pages 321–322.

CHAPTER SUMMARY

The chapter began by describing how the financial accounting reporting system helps an organization discharge its accountability, then explained how financial statements and auditing arise out of principal–agent theory. The central roles of ethics, the legal environment, and GAAP were then described.

A modern annual report was examined in detail; this included an analysis of selected footnotes. The chapter went on to describe the role of external auditors, audit committees, and internal auditors. The emerging importance of the Internet in financial reporting was mentioned. The chapter finished up with a summary of research on the ethics of managing earnings.

Suggested Answers to Accounting and Business Decisions

Decision A

(a) Common-sized income statements for the three-year period are provided in the Corel Annual Report in Appendix A to this chapter. Note that all income statement items in each year are expressed as a percentage of the particular year's sales number. You might want to verify some of the calculations.

"Cost of sales" seems quite volatile over the three-year period; it jumps from 16% in 1991 to 29% in 1992, and down to 23% in 1993. This has a direct effect on "Gross profit" as well. Corel management offers an explanation of this volatility in the Management Discussion and Analysis section of the Annual Report, under the heading "Gross Profit." The explanation seems quite consistent with the highly competitive, dynamic nature of the industry. Management also offers explanations about the relative changes in other expense items, including the perhaps unexpected relative decrease in R&D between 1992 and 1993. The result of Corel's attempts to control costs (for example, by purchasing some R&D rather than developing it in-house), meet competitive challenges, and ensure that its products meet user expectations, in a very dynamic market, is the significant fluctuation in the number for "Net income from continuing operations" as a percentage of "Sales." From Corel's audited income statements, we can see that sales have been increasing each year (from $52,242,000 in 1991, to $90,140,000 in 1992, up to $140,223,000 in 1993), but the fluctuations in the common-sized numbers suggest how risky the business is.

(b) The Message to the Shareholders is short and to the point, and upbeat. It emphasizes sales and profit growth, cost control, and Corel's product line and new product introductions. The 847 words in this section of the Annual Report are contained in 39 sentences, eight paragraphs; 153 of the words have three or more syllables (18.1% of the total).[9] Only 23% of the sentences are passive. The apparent grade level required to read

[9] Analysis of the Message to the Shareholders was performed using Ami Pro word processing software.

the section is second-year university. This is the type of active, results-oriented message that the CEO of a company like Corel would be expected to write; it emphasizes actions, results, and the taking advantage of opportunities as they arise — an approach that is crucial for success in Corel's industry. Overall, it was written with considerable skill, assuming that the style and packaging of the section were meant to reflect those characteristics which seem desirable for such a company. The relatively high required grade level suggests that the target user groups are better educated than the "average" Canadian; this is in line with surveys which show that Canadians who own shares typically have a university education.

However, the challenges and risks inherent in Corel's industry are not so well revealed. Users must read the entire Annual Report, including such key sections as the Management Discussion and Analysis, to get a more complete picture.

(c) Yes, for information that is included. But, as pointed out in (b), there are significant omissions. This highlights the fact that Messages to Shareholders often represent top management's grand, overall view of recent corporate accomplishments — they are sort of a broad, visionlike statement. The users of an annual report must balance the positive assertions with a more detailed analysis of other sections of the report, such as the MD&A and the audited financial statements.

Decision B

(a) Corel's note summarizing its significant accounting policies provides details about its capital asset accounting:

- "Capital assets are recorded at cost." More precisely, this means total actual historic cost, which is what is required under GAAP. The current replacement cost, or other current value measures, of Corel's various categories of capital assets disclosed in footnote 2, are not accounted for in the audited financial statements, and not disclosed.

- Depreciation and amortization: Both tangible and intangible depreciable capital assets are written off over relatively short periods. For example, furniture and equipment is depreciated at rates ranging from 20% to 33% using the declining balance method. This means that for a desk costing $1,000 with no salvage value and for which the 33% rate is deemed to be appropriate, annual depreciation expense would be:

Year 1	33% of $1,000	= $333.00
Year 2	33% of (1,000 – 333)	= $220.11
Year 3	33% of (1,000 – 333 – 220.11)	= $147.47
Year 4	33% of (1,000 – 333 – 220.11 – 147.47)	= $ 98.81
Year 5	33% of (1,000 – 333 – 220.11 – 147.47 – 98.81)	= $ 66.20
Year 6	33% of (1,000 – 333 – 220.11 – 147.47 – 98.81 – 66.20)	= $ 44.36

and so on.

So, the depreciation expenses for capital assets depreciated or amortized by the declining balance method are "front-end loaded," and decline rapidly (how rapidly depends on the specific declining balance rate). For depreciable assets that provide more benefit to the company in the early years of service life, a declining balance approach would seem to be appropriate. This seems to be a reasonable assumption regarding

Corel's "Furniture and equipment" and "Research and development equipment"; but why not also regarding "Computer equipment and software," which is being depreciated at a rate of 33.3% on a straight-line basis? This expenses one-third of the total each year, suggesting a three-year expected life for such capital assets. This seems sensible for the computer equipment, given the roughly three-year economic life for each new generation of computer hardware that computer users have been experiencing for the past decade or so; but three years may be too long for the software.

(b) Back in Chapter 2, the pervasive importance of classification in accounting was discussed. Corel's financial statement's footnote 7 illustrates another example of classification in accounting. Under GAAP, accounting entities must report the results of their ongoing operations separately from the results of operations they have decided to discontinue, so that users can better understand the profitability and other financial aspects of the ongoing operations of the company. In effect, the accounting entity itself has changed, and the requirement to include details such as those disclosed in footnote 7 contributes toward the achievement of comparability (see Chapter 4) on a year-by-year basis.

In certain circumstances, management may be tempted to manipulate how operations are classified as between "ongoing" and "discontinued," especially if part of an already or soon-to-be discontinued operation is still profitable, and the ongoing part of the company is experiencing tough times. In addition, the timing for classifying an operation as "discontinued" may be susceptible to manipulation. The enforcement of GAAP, a positive corporate ethical culture, an active and alert audit committee and internal audit department, and a vigilant external auditor, will all serve to minimize the risk that such inappropriate decisions will be made.

(c) No. Corel's MD&A provides information that complements the information in the audited financial statements:

- A brief history of the company, its marketing and strategic evolution, and its current major endeavours are described in an even-handed manner in the section titled "Overview."
- While some of the information in the remainder of the MD&A could be derived from the audited financial statements, much of the information in these parts of the MD&A is analytical in nature, and explains the reasons — as Corel's management sees the situation — for important changes.

Decision C

(a) The independence of external auditors ensures that the system diagrammed in Exhibit 6–1 is viewed as credible, so that users — and indeed all stakeholders in the accounting entity — have faith that the information is unbiased and has a high level of the desirable qualitative characteristics described in Chapter 4. We can assess the importance of the external auditor's independence by asking what would happen to Exhibit 6–1 if the auditor was not independent. In such a case, why would anyone bother with the cost of an external audit at all? An external auditor who was not independent of management would in effect be part of management; in such a situation, there would be no one to trust, and the system would fail. Business, like hockey, depends on neutral referees. Auditors are the referees of economic life: If they can't be trusted, no one will want to play, or attend the game.

(b) The MAS independence issue is not an easy one to resolve, especially in the economy of the 1990s, in which many public accountants are finding that competition and other factors have made audits not very profitable. As noted in the chapter, some critics suggest that any MAS whatsoever will taint the appearance, if not the fact, of independence. Defenders of the present system argue that the larger public accounting firms — the ones who audit most Canadian companies — are organized so that MAS is provided by one department, and audit work by another, separate department. Some defenders also argue that providing MAS will not impair independence as long as the MAS provided is not directly related to audit work. For example, if the MAS involved recommending that the client adopt a certain method of revenue recognition for a new type of activity, this would be an example of MAS that was "too close" to what the audit partners in the firm were responsible for auditing.

KEY TERMS

Accounting policy note is a footnote that describes important accounting measurement policies that management is using to prepare the financial statements.

Allowance for bad debts refers to the deduction from accounts receivable that is required to bring the receivables down to the estimated amount that management actually expects will be received. On the balance sheet, the allowance for bad debts is a contra account. Also called **allowance for doubtful accounts.**

Allowance for returns is a reduction in the sales amount due to management's expectation that customers will return a proportion of the products they have purchased from the accounting entity.

Annual report is defined in *Terminology for Accountants* as:

The information provided annually by the directors or management of an organization to the shareholders, owners, members, or other interested parties, concerning operations and financial position. Ususally, it includes the annual financial statements, the auditor's report thereon, and reports by officers or directors.

Audit is both a noun and a verb. A standard dictionary[10] includes the following definitions:

[noun] **1.** *An examination of records or accounts to check their accuracy ...* **4.** *Rare. An audience or hearing ....*

[verb] **1.** *To examine, verify or correct (accounts, records, or claims) ...*

The word comes from the Latin *auditus*, "a hearing," which is derived from the latin *audire*, to hear. Its use today reflects the practice of auditing in ancient times, when the auditor literally listened to, or heard, an official read out the details of the various transactions in which the official had engaged.

In *Terminology for Accountants*, the following general definition is provided:

An examination of evidential matter to determine the relability of a record or assertion or to evaluate compliance with rules or policies or with conditions of an agreement.

[10] *The Houghton Mifflin Canadian Dictionary.*

There are, therefore, several different types of audits, only two of which (external financial statement audit and internal audit) have been described in this chapter.

Audit committee is a committee made up of some of the directors of an organization (for profit-seeking organizations, and not-for-profit organizations that have a board of directors), whose responsibility it is to review the financial statements before the entire board receives and reviews them; to act as a buffer and liaison between the external auditor and management; and to perform duties such as reviewing the appointment of the external auditor, reviewing the external audit and its results, and reviewing the internal financial controls of the organization. In organizations without a board of directors, such as a university, the audit committee may be composed of members of the governing body or council of the organization.

Auditor's opinion is an "opinion expressed by an auditor in the written communication issued at the conclusion of an audit engagement in connection with financial statements or other specified matters" (*Terminology for Accountants*).

Bad debt expense may be computed by two general approaches:

- The *allowance approach*, in which an estimate is made of the bad or uncollectible debts arising from the sales on credit made for the accounting period.
- The *direct write-off method*, in which bad debts are literally written off and expensed only when the customer can no longer be expected to pay. The actual sales to the customer may have been made in accounting periods prior to the write-off decision.

The allowance approach is consistent with accrual accounting and GAAP.

Earnings management is any action taken by management that affects reported income and that provides no benefit to the accounting entity, and that may even harm the company.

Employee stock option plan is an agreement between a company and an employee by which the employee has the right to purchase specified numbers of common or other shares of the company, at a specified price, for a specified period of time, subject to specified conditions.

External audit is an audit of an organization's financial statements or other financial information performed by a person or persons who are independent of the organization. Such persons are called **external auditors**, and are often public accountants.

Footnotes to the financial statements, also called **notes to financial statements**, are defined in *Terminology for Accountants* as:

Explanatory or supplementary information that elaborates on data summarized in the main body of the statements or provides additional information that is important to understanding the situation being reflected in the statements.

Generally accepted accounting principles, in Canada, include the specific requirements and general concepts published in the *CICA Handbook*, and in those situations where a matter is not covered in the *CICA Handbook*, other relevant sources such as accepted industry practice, standards published by authoritative accounting bodies in other jurisdictions, and so on. More broadly, *Terminology for Accountants* defines the term as :

Those accounting principles that have been established in a particular jurisdiction by formal recognition by a standard-setting body, or by authoritative support or precedent.

And the same source defines **accounting principles** as "the propositions that give guidance in the measurement, classification and interpretation of economic information, and communication of the results through the medium of financial statements." Also, **accounting policies** are the "specific accounting principles followed by an organization and the procedures for applying those principles."

Generally accepted auditing standards are standards relating to the auditor's qualifications, performance of the audit, and preparation of the audit report, that have been established in a particular jurisdiction by a standard-setting body.

Interim report contains financial information, including financial statements, for a portion of a year.

Internal audit is an "audit of financial statements, other financial information or operations performed by an employee ... of the organization ..." (*Terminology for Accountants*). An **internal auditor** is the employee who performs the internal audit function within an organization.

Management advisory services are professional business consulting services provided by a public accounting firm or other consultant. MAS services include advice on the design and installation of information systems, accounting advice, and income tax advice.

Management discussion and analysis (MD&A) is a formal report, often included in the annual report, required under securities legislation, that is intended to explain to users the accounting entity's financial situation, performance, risks, and other financial information.

Principals and agents are the two main parties in the following rationale for accounting and auditing: Assume that individuals make decisions that maximize their personal welfare, given the information they have. Assume also that "agents" (in our example, agents are managers) are hired by "principals" (an organization's shareholders in our financial reporting example) to run the organization. Such an arrangement is an "agency relationship," since it involves the possibility that the agents will make decisions that are in their own best interests but not in the principals' best interests. The principals hire the agent in the hope that the agent will increase the value of the principals' common shares (this supposes that the agent is an expert in management, or in some technical field that is crucial to the success of the organization). A basic conflict of interest arises when managers are hired, since the manager may make decisions benefiting himself or herself at the expense of the principals/shareholders. The managers are close to the organization's operations, and presumably have information that the principals don't have.

Any decision that leads to a loss in wealth of a principal results in costs that are called "agency costs." Further, any actions taken by principals to protect themselves against sub-optimal decisions by their agents/managers also result in agency costs. Shareholders are therefore faced with a tradeoff: an expected loss in wealth from management actions versus the costs of setting up systems to monitor management and hold management accountable. Rational shareholders, anticipating this self-interested behaviour on the part of managers, will be prone to reduce managers' compensation accordingly. But the agent/manager, anticipating in turn *this* action on the part of the principals, will have an incentive to demonstrate to the principals that such self-interested behaviour has not and will not occur. In other words, incentives exist for agents/managers to provide audited financial statements to principals/shareholders to help in the principals' monitoring of the agent. So, the accountability concept may be elaborated upon using the above ideas of an agency relationship.

Prospectus is a document provided to potential investors by a company seeking to raise money. It includes a description of securities (common shares, for instance) to be issued, details of the company's business, names of directors and senior managers, financial statements, and other information. The content of propectuses is usually regulated by law.

Reservation in audit opinion is a general term that includes the following:

- An **adverse opinion**, which is an opinion that the financial statements are *not* in compliance with GAAP or another relevant standard.
- A **denial of opinion**, in which the auditor states that he or she is unable to express an opinion about whether the financial statements are in accordance with GAAP. This situation may arise if key information is unavailable — for example, when management prevents the auditor from performing important investigations, or a natural disaster destroys important company records.
- A **qualified opinion** is one in which the financial statements as a whole are in compliance with GAAP, except for a small number of important items.

A reservation in an audit opinion means, of course, that the opinion is *not* an **unqualified audit opinion**.

Unqualified audit opinion is an audit opinion in which the auditor states that the financial statements are in compliance with GAAP or other relevant standards.

FACT AND DESCRIPTION QUESTIONS

1. (a) List the participants in the financial reporting and accountability system.
   (b) How do organizations that are not required to have an audit fit in with the financial reporting and accountability system, if at all?
2. Summarize David Crane's arguments *against* the removal of the financial reporting requirement for federally incorporated foreign subsidiaries (see Exhibit 6–2). Also, develop an argument for the requirement's removal. Do you agree with your argument, or with Crane's?
3. How does GAAS differ from GAAP?
4. (a) Explain why some parts of an annual report contain "soft" information, and other parts contain "hard" information. How hard is the "hard" information?
   (b) How do the various components of the annual report fulfil accountability?
5. How does the theory of agent and principal justify auditing? And how does it justify the preparation of financial statements?
6. Why is ethical decision-making the core of the financial reporting system?
7. Explain how GAAP is a set of standards that the financial statements prepared under management's direction must comply with.
8. Why are footnotes a crucial part of financial statements? Illustrate your answer with reference to Corel's Annual Report.
9. Explain why the allowance method of accounting for bad debts complies with matching.
10. Compare and contrast the roles of external and internal auditors.

Questions for Analysis and Discussion

11. (a) Compare Corel's 1993 Annual Report with Massey-Harris's 1923 Annual Report. You should be able to list at least 20 differences, including the three mentioned in the chapter.
    (b) Speculate on reasons for some of the most important differences.
12. Suppose that you are an executive assistant to the comptroller of a company that is planning to issue its first annual report to the public. Although the company has been in existence for over 20 years, it has just gone public with an initial public offering of common shares. The company manufactures modular homes,

and has captured about 10% of the Canadian market west of Manitoba. Prepare a memo to your boss outlining important factors to consider when planning the annual report.

13. Footnotes are often judged to be poorly written, with lots of jargon. In this regard, assess the effectiveness of Corel's footnotes, being sure to specify the criteria you choose.

14. (a) Read footnote 4 in Corel's 1993 audited financial statements. Are the reconciling items in that footnote timing or permanent differences between net income before taxes per GAAP and taxable income?
    (b) Reconstruct Corel's income tax expense journal entry for 1993.

15. Suppose you are an analyst with a major brokerage firm. Is Corel's footnote 5 useful to you? Explain why, or why not.

16. Explain why it is reasonable to report discontinued operations separately, as Corel has done on its income statement and also in footnote 7.

17. Suppose that a major customer of the company you work for is in some financial difficulty. Your company has an account receivable on its books of $1,075,000 with respect to monies owed by the customer (ABC Company). Total receivables on your balance sheet are $4,500,000, and net income for the year just past (fiscal year ended December 31, 1996) is $4,000,000. Although your company accounts for bad debts using the allowance method, your customer's plight was so sudden and unexpected that no account of its situation was taken in estimating your allowance. In fact, your company's management was unaware of the situation until February 10, 1997, about a month before your 1996 annual report was scheduled to be released. The following discussion took place at a meeting of some of your senior managers on February 15, 1997:

Jones (internal auditor): There's no doubt in my mind that the receivable was impaired as of December 31. We'll have to write it off ... ABC was headed for a fall even last October when they purchased that new factory of theirs ...

Piena (vice-president): But I thought that accounting dealt in facts. How do we know that the receivable was worth less than its face value on December 31? After all, ABC just announced they were shutting down that factory last week, because of lack of demand!

Shuma (president): I think its only fair to do something ... We can't just pretend that ABC still owes us the money when chances are they can't pay it. But to be honest, I'm really worried about the market price of our stock.

Piena: That's just the point! If we write off the receivable in the income statement for the year ended December 31, 1996, and ABC turns out to be all right, at least eventually, I can see some of our shareholders suing if they sold in a panic based on the 1996 financial statements. On the other hand, I guess that if ABC goes under and we don't account for anything, they might want to sue if they *didn't* sell their shares. Looks like a no-win situation for us!

Shuma: Verba, what's your opinion?

Verba (newly-hired executive assistant to Shuma): I ... uh ... I'll get a memo to you on this right after lunch, OK?

Shuma: OK, but I want it in my hands right at 1 p.m.!

Required:
Adopt the role of Verba, and draft the memo.

18. Suppose that you were a member of a national union's research department, and were preparing a report on the usefulness of corporate annual reports from a union's perspective. What would you include in your report?

19. How is the MD&A different from the financial statements?

20. Note: This question is related to the "Accounting, Organizations, and Society" section of the chapter. The questionnaire, which was used to collect the data that was the basis for Merchant and Rockness's article, was first published by William J. Bruns, Jr., and Kenneth A. Merchant under the title "Ethics Test for Everyday Managers" in the *Harvard Business Review*, March–April 1987, pages 220–221. It is reproduced here with permission. Give it a try. Perhaps you will want to compare your answers with those of your classmates, or with those of the seasoned managers in the Merchant and Rockness article. The dates in the questionnaire have been changed to make them more contemporary, and slight wording changes have been made so that the questionnaire is clearer and more gender-neutral. Now the article:

There's more to business ethics than front page scandals about unsafe products, insider trading, and defense contractor fraud. General managers make all kinds of decisions that influence short-term operating results. Some of their decisions are beyond reproach. Others are clearly wrong. Many fall into an ethical gray area.

The following questions reflect these everyday ethical choices. We'd like you to evaluate the practices as they apply to a major division (annual revenues of, say, $100 million) of a billion-dollar public company. Use the following scale to indicate how *you* judge their acceptability.

1. Ethical practice.
2. Questionable practice. I would not say anything to the manager, but it makes me uncomfortable.
3. Minor infraction. The manager should be warned not to do it again.
4. Serious infraction. The manager should be severely reprimanded.
5. Totally unethical. The manager should be fired.

[The following seven situations are totally independent of each other]

1. The division's headquarters building was scheduled to be painted in 1995. But since profit performance was way ahead of budget in 1994, the division general manager (GM) decided to have the work done in 1994. Amount: $150,000

1 2 3 4 5

2. The GM ordered the division's employees to defer all discretionary expenditures (e.g., travel, advertising, hiring, maintenance) into the next accounting period, so the division could make its budgeted profit targets. Expected amount of deferrals: $150,000

a. The expenses were postponed from February and March until April in order to make the first quarter target.

1 2 3 4 5

b. The expenses were postponed from November and December until January in order to make the annual target.

1 2 3 4 5

3. On December 15, a clerk ordered $3,000 of office supplies, and the supplies were delivered on December 29. This order was a mistake because the GM had ordered that no discretionary expenses be incurred for the remainder of the fiscal year, and the supplies were not urgently needed. The company's accounting policy manual states that office supplies are to be recorded as an expense when received. The GM learned what had happened, and to correct the mistake, asked the accounting department not to record the invoice until February.

1 2 3 4 5

4. In September, the GM realized the division would need strong performance in the fourth quarter to reach its budget targets.

a. The GM decided to implement a sales program offering liberal payment terms to pull some sales that would normally occur next year into the current year; customers accepting delivery in the fourth quarter would not have to pay the invoice for 120 days.

1 2 3 4 5

b. The GM ordered manufacturing to work overtime in December so that everything possible could be shipped by the end of the year.

1 2 3 4 5

c. The GM sold some excess assets and realized profit of $40,000.

1 2 3 4 5

5. At the beginning of December 1992, the GM realized the division would exceed its budgeted profit targets for the year.

a. The GM ordered the division's controller to prepay some expenses (e.g., hotel rooms, exhibit expense) for a major trade show to be held in March 1993 and to book them as 1992 expenses. Amount: $60,000

1 2 3 4 5

b. The GM ordered the controller to develop the rationale for increasing the reserve for inventory obsolescence. By taking a pessimistic view of future market prospects, the controller was able to identify $700,000 worth of finished goods that conservative accounting would say should be fully reserved (i.e., written off), even though the GM was fairly confident the inventory would still be sold at a later date at close to full price.

1 2 3 4 5

6. The next year, the division sold 70% of the written-off inventory, and a customer had indicated some interest in buying the rest of that inventory the following year. The GM ordered the controller to prepare the rationale for reducing the reserve for obsolescence by $210,000 (i.e., writing up the previously written-off goods to full cost). The GM's motivation for recapturing the profit was:

a. To be able to continue working on some important product development projects that might have been delayed due to budget constraints.

1 2 3 4 5

b. To make budgeted profit targets.

1 2 3 4 5

7. In November 1994, the division was straining to meet budget. The GM called the engagement partner of a consulting firm that was doing some work for the division and asked that the firm not send an invoice until next year. The partner agreed. Estimated work done but not invoiced:

a. $30,000

1 2 3 4 5

b. $500,000

1 2 3 4 5

21. Exhibit 6–1 is reproduced below, but now the arrows are labelled (a) to (j). Explain the significance of each of the labelled arrows. For example, (f) suggests that external auditors are interested in influencing the development of GAAP, since they are experts in the accounting discipline and also have a stake in exercising some degree of control over GAAP.

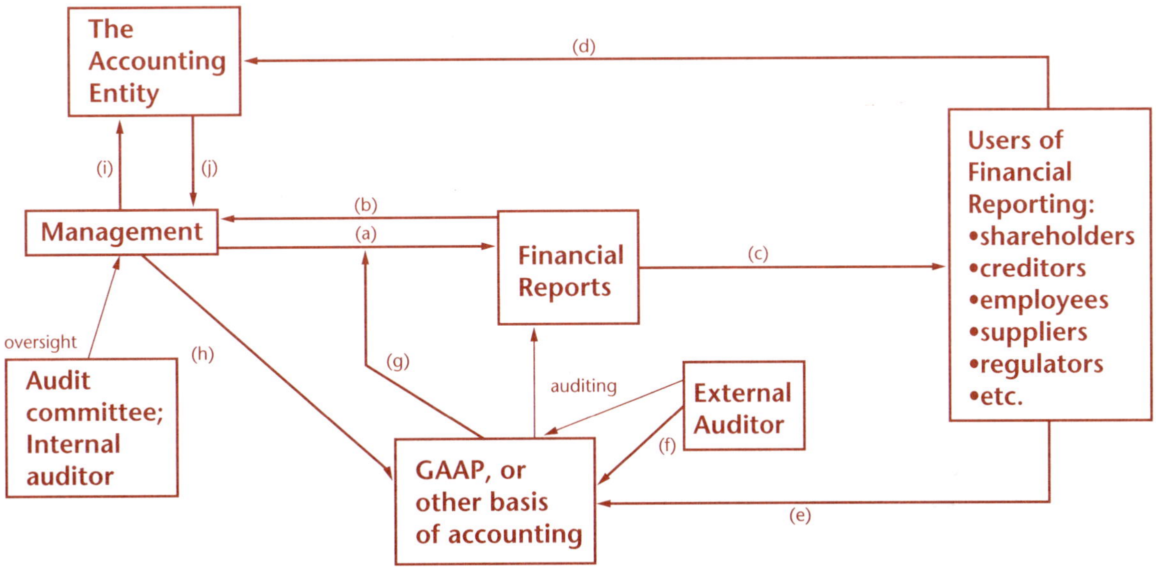

22. Fishery Products International (FPI) is a global seafood company with headquarters in St. John's, Newfoundland. FPI produces and sells a full range of seafood products throughout North America and Europe. It operates six deep-sea trawlers, six scallop draggers, a shrimp freezer trawler, and several processing plants, and employs 2,600 people. Sales for the year ended December 31, 1994, were $665 million, and net income for that year was $13.9 million. For 1993, the corresponding numbers were $602 million and a $15.4 million loss.

The 1993 loss included an "unusual item" on the income statement — a $20 million expense that turned 1993's operating income of $5.4 million into the loss for the year. Footnote 10 of FPI's audited financial statements described this item as follows:

As a result of the imposition of moratoria announced in 1993 and the reduction of quotas on fishing for the Company's key flatfish and other stocks, the Company recorded a provision of $20,000,000 in 1993 to reflect the further revaluation of its Newfoundland-based harvesting and processing assets, and rationalization of operations ...

(a) Suggest what the journal entry to record this unusual item might have been.
(b) The $20 million expense was clearly segregated on FPI's income statement, and was not a determinant of 1993 operating income. Discuss.
(c) Is it ethical for companies to account for such events, even though they do not represent actual transactions?

23. Fionzo Limited began business in early January of 1993. From the beginning, the company's accounting policy with respect to bad debts had been to follow accrual accounting and use an allowance for bad debts account. "Just seems like

a fairer way of estimating the cost of bad debts and its impact on net income," according to Mr. Gordon Fionzo, the company's founder and president. The allowance account had the following activity over the years:

Date	Dr	Cr	Balance
August 30, 1993	3,505		
October 30, 1993	6,210		
December 31, 1993		30,215	20,500
March 12, 1994	2,500		
July 15, 1994		1,500	
December 31, 1994		35,000	54,500
December 31, 1995		15,500	70,000

(a) Suggest journal entries to account for the above activity in the allowance for doubtful accounts account.

(b) If the company's income tax rate has always been 40%, explain how the above information could lead to deferred taxes.

CASE

Arbor Capital Inc.[11]

On April 22, 1988, the Ontario Securities Commission (OSC) published its decision on an application by Arbor Capital Inc. (ACI) to be allowed to exceed the 140-day time limit for filing its annual audited financial statements. In granting Arbor an extension, the OSC explained that it felt that the company had been "put in a difficult position almost two months after its fiscal year end." The difficulty arose because of a serious difference of opinion between ACI management and its firm of public accountants (or independent accountants), Coopers & Lybrand (C&L), concerning the accounting method the company was using to recognize certain of its revenues. At one point, the risk of ACI receiving a qualified audit report was quite real, and since the OSC does not accept filings accompanied by qualified opinions, Arbor's management was very concerned.

The Company

ACI is a Canadian public company that is listed on the Toronto Stock Exchange. At the time of this case, the company was controlled by its chairman, who owned about 53% of the class A voting shares. The company's fiscal year end is October 31. Through its subsidiary companies in Canada and the United States, ACI has been engaged in cemetery operations for more than 40 years. The principal sales activities of the company arise from two types of transactions:

- "At-need" sales, which occur at the time of death.
- "Pre-need" sales, which are made at any time to people who wish to make cemetery or funeral arrangements in advance of need.

Historically, about 80% of sales have been pre-need in nature. The rate of at-need sales had been increasing at the time of this case because of ACI's expansion into the funeral service sector; even so, pre-need sales were still roughly 60% of total sales. Sales are made on account or on an instalment basis. For sales made on an instalment basis, a service charge is applied to the outstanding balance.

[11] This is a short version of a case written by Joel Amernic and Martha Dunlop.

Revenue from at-need and pre-need sales has been recognized at the date of the sales agreement, less an appropriate provision for cancellation and doubtful accounts. Historically, the company has experienced a cancellation rate of not more than 9% of contracts. To match costs to pre-need revenues, provision is made, using actuarial techniques, for the discounted amount of the estimated future cost to ACI of delivering all services and merchandise.

The Disagreement

In December 1987, questions as to the appropriateness of the revenue recognition policy for pre-need sales were raised by C&L. Although C&L had issued unqualified audit opinions on the financial statements of ACI for several years, they were of the opinion that a change in the revenue recognition policy for pre-need sales was now required. This argument was based on a newly issued pronouncement on revenue recognition by the CICA in September 1986.

ACI's management disagreed with C&L's position on the basis that they believed the current policy reflected economic reality. The issue was complicated by the fact that adherence to the revenue recognition policy required by C&L could lead to technical breach of certain debt covenants. At the same time, *lack* of adherence could lead to a reservation in the audit opinion — something unacceptable to both ACI's management and the OSC.

Applying Professional Judgment

On January 25, 1988, C&L set out its reasoning about ACI's method of revenue recognition in a letter to ACI's president. ACI decided to seek outside, independent advice, and to that end retained two international public accounting firms: Touche, Ross (TR) and Deloitte, Haskins & Sells (DH&S).[12] The positions (with supporting arguments) of ACI management, C&L, TR, and DH&S are summarized in Appendix A to this case.

On March 10, 1988, after the TR and DH&S letters had been written and sent, a lawyer acting on behalf of ACI sent a letter to C&L. This letter urged the firm "to complete its audit and provide an unqualified auditor's report," and pointed out that C&L's reports had been unqualified in the past and that, further, other public accounting firms disagreed with C&L. The letter continued: "You are ... a professional and, surely, you cannot expect that your opinions are always infallible ... If you believe that you cannot change your opinion, then, on behalf of Arbor, I would ask you to resign graciously."

On June 15, 1988, after receiving the OSC's permission to delay filing its financial statements and sending them to its shareholders, ACI held an "annual and special meeting of shareholders." This meeting was called to present shareholders with unaudited financial statements for the year ended October 31, 1987, and to consider removing C&L as auditor of the company, appointing DH&S in its place.

The financial statements presented to the shareholders at the meeting of June 15, 1988, adopted a policy that defers the recognition of revenue from pre-need funeral arrangements until the time of delivery. Revenue from pre-need cemetery sales is recorded at the date of the sales agreement. Comparative financial statements for 1986 were retroactively restated to conform with this new policy. Selected financial information from the previously issued audited 1986 financial statements of ACI, together with comparative unaudited financial information applying management's proposed new recognition policy and C&L's proposed revisions, is included in Case Appendix B.

[12] Because of mergers, the names of large public accounting firms have changed over the years. For example, the current firm of Deloitte Touche was at the time of this case two separate firms: Touche Ross and Deloitte Haskins and Sells.

Required:

(a) Evaluate the arguments made by ACI management and the three public accounting firms in connection with revenue recognition. Of the various positions taken by the parties involved, which do you consider is the most defensible? Explain.

(b) Analyse the effect of the above positions on ACI's financial information for 1986.

(c) Assess the quality of professional judgment exercised by the three public accounting firms. How is it possible that each came to a different conclusion while applying the same accounting standard of revenue recognition? What does this suggest about accounting standards?

(d) Evaluate the relationship between ACI management and C&L. Under what pressures does an independent auditor operate? How might these pressures be controlled so as to enhance the apparent and substantive effectiveness of financial reporting?

(e) If the TSE market for equity securities is at least fairly efficient, is the entire case "much ado about nothing"?

Case Appendix A

Position of ACI Management — Supported by TR

In a "statement of facts concerning the corporation and its accounting policies for revenue recognition" (February 1988), ACI defended its policy of recognizing revenue on the sale of pre-need contracts at the date of the sales agreement. Its main arguments were these:

- The amount to be collected is clearly established and the amount of bad debts and/or cancellations can reasonably be estimated by experience.
- Burial services have been identified, constructed, deeded, and completed to a deliverable state.
- Merchandise sold is either acquired (and stored) prior to delivery or is readily available at point of need. Cost of merchandise to be acquired is reasonably determinable.
- Services are an integral part of the burial space and therefore should be recognized as part of the sale. Furthermore, ACI's system is established and has both the capacity and the capability to deliver the service at all times.
- ACI's performance situation is comparable to that of a life insurance company when such a company is required to deliver on a claim to a life insurance policy. Life insurance companies are permitted to recognize revenue at the time of issuing a life insurance policy.

Position of C&L

C&L suggested that revenue should be deferred until performance has been achieved. This position was supported with reference to the operations of the company as follows:

- For sales of merchandise, completion of performance would occur when goods are available for the exclusive use of the buyer, or when title has passed to the buyer. At this point, risks and rewards of merchandise are transferred to the owner, and the amount of consideration to be received is estimable and reasonably assured.

- Recognition of revenue from pre-need services at the date of the sales agreement is in advance of activities promised in consideration of payments received. The appropriate point of revenue recognition is when the services have been rendered.

Position of DH&S

DH&S suggested that different revenue recognition policies be established in line with the corporate structure. That firm supported ACI's revenue recognition policy for pre-need cemetery plans but could not support the policy of recognizing revenue on pre-need funeral contracts at the date of the sales contract.

- DH&S's support for the revenue recognition policy with respect to pre-need cemetery plans was based on the comparison to life insurance companies, on the fact that it is the prevailing industry practice, and on a belief that such a policy produced a more appropriate picture of the economic reality of the business. Furthermore, this method of revenue recognition is less subjective than deferral and produces financial statements that are more readily understandable to the average reader.
- DH&S indicated that it could not support the current method of revenue recognition on pre-need funeral services, as this ran counter to industry practice, and as there was no apparent reason for not following predominant industry practice. However, the firm did not specifically suggest a method of revenue recognition on pre-need funeral contracts.

Case Appendix B

ARBOR CAPITAL INC.
Selected Financial Data — 1986
($000s omitted)

	C&L Position	ACI Proposal	Previously Issued
Income:			
Revenue	$58,125	$62,138	$73,495
Net earnings	2,275	2,759	3,656
Cash flow:			
From operations	4,825	4,825	4,825
From financing	13,732	13,732	13,732
From investing	(23,266)	(23,266)	(23,266)
Balance sheet:			
Total assets	173,555	183,113	183,113
Total liabilities	139,375	139,432	136,456
Shareholders' equity	34,180	43,681	46,657
Per share data:			
EPS ($ per share)	.29	.35	.47
Operating ratios:			
Debt to equity	80/100	76/100	73/100
Return on assets plus care funds	1.11	1.29	1.71

CASE Woolworth Corporation[13]

On March 30, 1994, Woolworth Corporation, one of the largest retail chains in the world, issued the following news release from its New York headquarters:

> ***FOR IMMEDIATE RELEASE***
>
> *NEW YORK, MARCH 30 — Woolworth Corporation (NYSE: Z) announced today that it will restate its interim financial results for the fiscal year ended January 29, 1994 and may have to restate its interim financial results for the fiscal year ended January 30, 1993. The restatements, to the extent necessary, are not expected to have an impact on the full-year results for such fiscal years, and will reflect the correction of gross margins. The company is not in a position at this point to estimate the amount of any required interim restatements.*
>
> *The Board of Directors has appointed a Special Committee of outside directors to investigate allegations of accounting irregularities, including the accounting procedures that resulted in the need to restate the interim financial results for the fiscal year ended January 29, 1994. While the company cannot at this time evaluate the accuracy of the allegations, it believes that nothing in the allegations will materially adversely affect the company's financial position.*
>
> *The Special Committee is chaired by Mr. John W. Adams, Chairman of the Audit Committee, and has retained the law firm Paul, Weiss, Rifkind, Wharton & Garrison, and Paul, Weiss has retained the accounting firm KPMG Peat Marwick, to assist in the investigation.*

Two weeks later, a second news release was issued from corporate head office:

> ***FOR IMMEDIATE RELEASE***
>
> *WOOLWORTH CORPORATION SAYS INDEPENDENT ACCOUNTANTS CONFIRM 1993 AND 1992 YEAR-END RESULTS*
>
> *—Company Restates Quarterly Results for 1993*
>
> *NEW YORK, April 13 — Woolworth Corporation (NYSE: Z) said today that Price Waterhouse, its independent accountants, confirmed that the company's previously reported full-year results for the years ended January 29, 1994, and January 30, 1993, were correct as previously reported and will not be restated.*
>
> *Based on a review initiated by the Special Committee of the company's Board of Directors, Woolworth has restated quarterly (interim) financial results for the year ended January 29, 1994. Quarterly results for the year ended January 30, 1993, are unchanged. The restated 1993 quarterly results are presented in the table that follows.*
>
> *The restated 1993 quarterly results reflect a correction of gross margins and certain selling, general and administrative expenses and a decision to record in the third quarter the previously announced fourth quarter reversal of $145 million of the repositioning reserve.*
>
> *The company also said that the Special Committee of the Board of Directors is proceeding with its investigation of the events that resulted in the need to restate the quarterly financial results. That remaining part of the investigation is expected to be completed within the next few weeks.*
>
> *"This concludes that part of the investigation which impacts the company's financial results, and should put to rest any concern about those results," said John W. Adams, interim Chairman of the Board and Chief Executive Officer. "Our associates, suppliers, shareholders and others can have confidence in our financial position as we*

[13] Prepared from public information and information provided by Woolworth Corporation.

move ahead with the day-to-day business of the corporation and its operations."

In other actions today, the Board of Directors declared a cash dividend of $.29 per share on the company's common stock, and a cash dividend of $.55 per share on the company's $2.20 Series A Convertible Preferred Stock. These dividends will be paid on June 1, 1994, to shareholders of record on May 2, 1994.

WOOLWORTH CORPORATION
1993 Quarterly Results
Year Ended January 29, 1994

Earnings (loss) per share

Quarter	As Previously Reported	As Restated
First	$ .01	$(.18)
Second	.01	(.08)
Third	(3.43)	(2.66)
Fourth	(.35)	(.84)
Year	$(3.76)	$(3.76)

Net Income (loss) in Millions

Quarter	As Previously Reported	As Restated
First	$ 1	$(24)
Second	2	(10)
Third	(452)	(350)
Fourth	(46)	(111)
Year	$(495)	$(495)

In an update of May 27, 1994, the investor advisory service Value Line urged investors to be cautious about Woolworth stock, and indicated that this advice was based on several factors, including these:

- Pressure on revenues and gross margins.
- Insecure dividends.
- Alleged accounting irregularities, as noted in the above news releases.

The Company

Woolworth Corporation and its subsidiaries operate a multinational retailing business selling a wide range of merchandise in over 8,000 locations in the United States, Canada, Europe, and Australia. Among the company's many well-known chains are Woolworth, Woolco, Randy River, Northern Reflections, Foot Locker, and Lady Foot Locker. The company operates five factories that manufacture footwear and accessories, and has purchasing offices in Mexico and Asia. Woolworth Corporation is the successor to a company that was founded in 1879, and is headquartered in New York City. Sales for the year ended January 29, 1994, were $9.626 billion, and for the year ended January 30, 1993, were $9.962 billion. The table on the left provides some financial statistics for the company, in millions of U.S. dollars:

	1993	1992	1991
Revenues	9,626	9,962	9,914
Operating (loss) profit	(653)	574	53
Repositioning/restructuring charges (pretax)	558		390
Loss on sale of Woolco stores (pretax)	168		
Net (loss) income	(495)	280	(166)

The Special Committee

On May 18, 1994, the Special Committee of the board of directors lodged its report with Woolworth Corporation's full board. A copy of the report was sent to the Securities and Exchange Commission (SEC). The executive summary of the report is reproduced below.

May 18, 1994

The Board of Directors
Woolworth Corporation
Woolworth Building
233 Broadway
New York, New York

To the Board:

The following is the Report of the Special Committee (the "Special Committee") of the Board of Directors of Woolworth Corporation (the "Company") regarding its investigation of certain alleged accounting irregularities and related issues at the Company.

PART ONE
GENERAL
I
DESCRIPTION OF THE REPORT

Part One of this Report sets forth a summary of the Special Committee's findings; a chronology of the circumstances that led to the appointment of the Special Committee; the allegations that formed the basis of the Special Committee's Investigation (the "Investigation"); and a description of the scope of the Investigation and the procedures employed. Part Two is a detailed summary, by topic, of the evidence (specifically, the results of the interviews with Company personnel and the review of documents, which form the basis for the Special Committee's findings). Part Three sets forth the Special Committee's conclusions and recommendations.

II
EXECUTIVE SUMMARY

The Special Committee was formed on March 29, 1994, by the Company's Board of Directors (the "Board") to investigate certain alleged accounting irregularities and related issues at the Company. During the next four weeks, the Special Committee, through its independent counsel (Paul, Weiss, Rifkind, Wharton & Garrison) and counsel's accounting expert (KPMG Peat Marwick), conducted an extensive investigation, which was completed the first week in May.

During the Investigation, based on the Special Committee's recommendation, the Company restated its quarterly results for fiscal year 1993. The Company's decision to restate was announced on March 30, 1994, and the actual restatement was announced April 13, 1994, once KPMG Peat Marwick and the Company's outside auditors (Price Waterhouse) had computed the amounts involved. The Company's restated quarterly results for fiscal 1993 were filed with the United States Securities and Exchange Commission ("SEC") on Form 8-K on April 13, 1994, and were included in the Company's 1993 Annual Report and the Company's Form 10-K for 1993, both dated April 28, 1994 ...

In addition, based on the Special Committee's recommendation and the work of KPMG Peat Marwick, and with the concurrence of Price Waterhouse, the Company announced on April 13, 1994, that its quarterly results for fiscal **1992** did not require restatement; that the Company's **year-end** financial results for fiscal years 1992 and 1993 did not require restatement; and that the results of the Investigation would **not** have a material adverse impact on the Company's financial position.

The Company further determined, based on the Special Committee's recommendation, (i) to record in the third quarter of fiscal 1993, $145 million which had been reversed from the Company's 1993 repositioning reserve and previously credited against the fourth quarter of fiscal 1993, and (ii) to reduce the repositioning reserve by an additional $72 million, and to record that amount instead against operations for fiscal 1993.

Having now concluded the Investigation, the Special Committee reaffirms the foregoing determinations and makes the following additional findings, which are only summarized here, and which should be read in the context of the entire Report:

First, the Investigation disclosed interim financial reporting practices and other activity at two of the Company's subsidiaries (Kinney and Woolworth Canada) that resulted in inaccurate reporting of quarterly financial results during fiscal 1992 and 1993, but which did not affect year-end results. The interim reporting practices involve a failure to use the best internally available data at the time. Additionally, and apart from the foregoing, inaccurate numbers were reported to corporate headquarters by the two subsidiaries during certain quarters of fiscal 1993. Consequently, a restatement of the Company's fiscal 1993 quarterly results was required. No restatement of quarterly results for fiscal 1992 was required because of certain offsetting credits that rendered the reporting variances in that year immaterial.

The need to restate the Company's 1993 interim results was the core issue that gave rise to this Investigation. All of the other matters, while of great concern, did not affect prior public reporting and could have been dealt with by the Board in the course of its regular oversight activities. But the question of inaccurate interim reporting opened the company to public and regulatory scrutiny and criticism, thereby requiring the Board to convene a special investigation of the allegations.

The process was a painful one for all members of the Special Committee, particularly given the seriousness of the issues, the admissions by high-level subsidiary executives of inaccurate reporting activity, the allegations directed at senior corporate financial management, and the intractable conflict of recollections regarding who was responsible.

In the end, the Special Committee was unable to resolve the conflicting recollections and differing stories regarding who or what may have caused the inaccurate interim reporting in 1993. Nevertheless, the evidence has persuaded the Special Committee that senior corporate management failed to create an environment in which it was clear to employees at all levels that inaccurate financial reporting would not be tolerated. To the contrary, the environment apparently led certain otherwise conscientious and able financial personnel to conclude just the opposite in 1993.

The investigation indicated that the Company's relevant accounting systems and controls were adequate and sufficient to their task. But no system can function properly unless the environment is supportive; and any system is vulnerable to "management override." In the Special Committee's view, "management override," even if only perceived, played a significant role in what happened at Woolworth in 1993, opening the door to the inaccurate reporting that required the Company to restate its 1993 quarterly results. For this outcome, senior corporate management bears ultimate responsibility, even if senior corporate financial management did not instruct, request or authorize the employees who admittedly reported the inaccurate numbers to do so.

It is particularly disturbing that such an environment existed, and that improper reporting activity occurred, despite the Company's long-standing and clearly articulated commitment to the highest business standards. The Company's Statement of Corporate Policy has long provided that no employee of the Company may

> "... directly or indirectly, cause to be entered in, or to be omitted from, any of the Company's books or records any transaction that would lead to an improperly recorded asset, liability, revenue or expense. Similarly, [no employee] may ... make or cause to be made any false or knowingly inaccurate entry in any of the Company's books or records."

Violations of this policy for any reason are not acceptable, and it is senior corporate management's responsibility to make certain that this point is well understood and enforced throughout the Company.

To underscore the importance that the Company's directors attach to fulfillment of this responsibility, and to monitor the implementation of all proposed actions arising out of this Investigation, the Special Committee respectfully recommends to the Board that the Special Committee remain in existence after issuing this Report, and that it consult at least monthly for the balance of the year and, if need be, regularly thereafter with senior corporate management and regularly with other appropriate Committees of the Board on the proposed actions hereinafter set forth and other such matters as may be appropriate.

Second, the Investigation disclosed that a principal assumption underlying the Company's 1993 repositioning reserve of $775 million was not adequately supported. The evidence established also that senior corporate management adopted an aggressive accounting strategy, hoping to write off significant inventory markdowns at continuing stores against the repositioning reserve. The Board was not informed of this strategy until after the SEC inquired into the Company's reserve in February 1994. Management then reevaluated its position and advised the Board that it had decreased the reserve by $145 million, and had also charged $164 million in accumulated markdowns to fourth quarter operations rather than to the reserve. Further, the Special Committee concluded earlier in this Investigation, based on KPMG Peat Marwick's analysis, that an additional $72 million items still remained in the reserve that could, without regard to their materiality or other possible offsetting factors, be considered (or used to accrue for) normal operating costs. Accordingly, as noted, the Company further reduced the repositioning reserve by that amount.

Third, the Investigation disclosed that senior corporate management directed certain changes to the Company's 1994 budget that were not supported, and in a manner that was inconsistent with the Company's budgeting process. This activity, too, reflects a "management override" environment unacceptable to the directors.

Fourth, the Investigation also considered allegations that senior corporate management intentionally understated the expected loss on the Company's sale of its Woolco Canada stores to Wal-Mart. These allegations were not supported by the evidence. Although the eventual loss on the transaction was significantly greater than originally estimated, this does not establish that the original estimate was deliberately flawed.

Fifth, the Investigation found no material inventory problems arising out of any of the allegations or other matters discussed in this Report.

Sixth, the Special Committee found no evidence that any officer, director or employee of the Company engaged in self-dealing, or sought or obtained any personal gain or enrichment.

Required:

(a) Identify the financial reporting and related ethical issues in this case, and explain their importance.

(b) Although the annual financial results for the fiscal year ended January 29, 1994, were unaffected by the alleged irregularities, and only interim financial accounting results were misstated, the parties involved judged that the situation was important enough to issue several news releases and establish a special committee to investigate the situation. Why?

(c) After the Special Committee began its investigation, a member of management of one of Woolworth's subsidiaries told that committee that Woolworth's most senior managers in effect ordered that inaccurate interim financial results be reported. What ethical dilemmas does this member of subsidiary management face?

Appendix A
Excerpts From Corel Corporation's 1993 Annual Report:[14]

The following excerpts from the 1993 Annual Report of Corel Corporation are reproduced with the permission of the company:

[14] Reprinted with permission from Corel Corporation.

COMPANY PROFILE

Corel Corporation, a world leader in the development of graphics and SCSI (Small Computer System Interface) software, was founded in June, 1985, by Dr. Michael Cowpland. Originally, the Company was engaged primarily in the systems integration business, and provided customers with turnkey PC-based desktop publishing systems and local area networks by combining hardware and software products from various manufacturers with the Company's proprietary software enhancements.

As a result of its experience in developing software enhancements, Corel began to devote additional resources to developing a separately packaged graphics software program. In January, 1989, the Company introduced its first version of CorelDRAW. CorelDRAW 2.0 was introduced in November of 1990; CorelDRAW 3 became available in May of 1992. CorelDRAW 4, the most recent upgrade, was launched in May of 1993.

In 1993, our acquisition of Ventura Publisher and DataBase Publisher, and subsequent launch of Corel Ventura 4.2, further increased Corel's visibility as a provider of a complete software solution for desktop publishing.

In 1991, Corel launched CorelSCSI, which allowed SCSI users to connect up to seven PC peripherals to a single host adapter. In May of 1992, Corel launched a software-only version of CorelSCSI, which has become one of the most popular SCSI software solutions on the market today. Corel currently markets CorelSCSI Version 2 for DOS, Windows and OS/2 and CorelSCSI Network Manager for control of peripherals on a Novell Network. Late in 1993, Corel also launched Corel CD PowerPak, a CD-ROM utilities package for sound and photos, in response to the growing CD-ROM market.

The multi-volume Corel Professional Photos on CD-ROM Series has also greatly increased Corel's range of products and visibility. Accessible by both PC and Macintosh users, this premier source of royalty free stock photography and screen saver images is helping to revolutionize the digital stock photo industry.

Corel Corporation ships its products through a network of more than 100 distributors in 60 countries worldwide. Corel is traded on The Toronto Stock Exchange (symbol: COS) and the NASDAQ National Market System (symbol: COSFF).

To strengthen Corel's presence in the European and Asian marketplace, the company recently established Corel Corporation Limited, a subsidiary in Ireland, with the assistance of the Industral Development Authority (I.D.A.).

COREL FINANCIAL HIGHLIGHTS

		1993	1992	1991
INCOME STATEMENT	Sales	$140,223	90,140	52,242
	Net income	27,841	11,186	11,357
	Net income per share	0.90	0.87	0.96
BALANCE SHEET	Working capital	113,247	79,961	42,017
	Total assets	176,623	105,313	59,358
	Shareholders' equity	148,511	98,793	49,769
KEY RATIOS	Current ratio	5.5	13.3	5.4
	Return on sales	19.9	12.4%	21.7

(Amounts in thousands, except per share data and key ratios)

1993 was an excellent year for Corel — sales grew by 56% to $140 million, while after tax profit grew by 149% to $27.8 million. We continued our focus on keeping a lean, high-performance team, and achieved these results with only 300 employees. 1993's sales per employee of $465 thousand and profit per employee of $84 thousand are among the highest in the industry. Our flagship product continued to be CorelDRAW, known worldwide as the market leader in PC graphics, with almost one million units installed. With over 150 first place awards from industry magazines, the amazing popularity of CorelDRAW is largely ascribed to its power, ease of use and value. Our strategy to improve our lead even further is to develop new releases annually based upon customer feedback and our own ideas. In addition to our own high-powered software team, we also draw on software talent around the world through the purchase of technology and development sub-contracts. Our lead on the competition allows us to continue to concurrently market earlier versions of the software. CorelDRAW 3 is still selling strongly as our entry-level product at $199, even though CorelDRAW 4 has been on the market since May 1993, priced at $595. Valuable clipart and font libraries containing tens of thousands of images and hundreds of fonts are included in CorelDRAW on CD. In order to access these libraries, our customers have been increasingly adopting CD-ROM drives. Corel is further encouraging this trend by offering a $50 to $200 discount on the "CD-ROM only" versions of CoredDRAW, a price reduction which is offset by not including costly floppy disks.

Our strong balance sheet, including 76.1 million in cash with zero debt, was a major asset during the year as it facilitated a straightforward cash purchase of the Ventura product line from Xerox when the opportunity arose in August. We were able to produce and ship Corel Ventura 4.2 by November, and sales were off to a fast start thanks to the high value and lower price point positioning. Ventura has a strong worldwide reputation as the most powerful and automated desktop publishing software for longer, complex documents, providing an excellent complement to CorelDRAW's shorter document emphasis. By May 94, we plan to launch CorelDRAW 5, which will include advanced, tightly integrated versions of both Ventura and CorelDRAW to provide unmatched power and versatility for virtually all graphics and desktop publishing tasks.

During the year we launched our Photo CD-ROM series which offers hundreds of CD photo collections on CD-ROM on a royalty free basis. We are using the Kodak Photo CD-ROM format, recently established as the world's leading standard for digital images. Each disc provides 100 high-resolution images on CD that provide razor-sharp full page photos for publishing applications. We feel this approach will fill a rapidly growing international appetite for digital photos. Corel has assumed a leadership role in this market with over 200 titles now in production and new ones being added at a rate of 20 per month. As the first major company to take this approach, we have been able to enlist the talents of some of the world's top photographers. These photos can be imported to CorelDRAW for enhancement, special effects and incorporation in DTP documents.

During the year our CorelSCSI line continued to increase its market lead. CorelSCSI is rapidly becoming the standard software for connecting up to seven peripherals to a single PC SCSI card. The combination of a highly experienced engineering team and our unique SCSI testing lab is unmatched anywhere in the industry.

Our finance and administration team is highly computerized, using client server LAN architecture which continues to improve in efficiency. Our customer support, technical support and manufacturing teams use a combination of in-house expertise and a high level of sub-contracting to keep our fixed operating costs low, while achieving the highest customer satisfaction ratings.

In 1993, Corel opened a new center for manufacturing, marketing and support in Dublin, Ireland, a city that has become one of the most popular locations for software companies in Europe. Dublin has excellent infrastructure, a well trained labor pool, easy access to European markets, and substantial tax incentives.

Our dynamic and effective marketing team continues to penetrate new distribution channels around the world and build our brand names using one of the largest advertising budgets in the industry. Our prolific in-house creative agency has generated several thousand advertisements and collateral marketing materials during the year.

The annual CorelDRAW $1,000,000 World Design Contest is our way of celebrating the exciting world of art and technology. This past year we received over 3,000 entries from 35 countries. These entries were judged by a blue ribbon panel of 140 industry luminaries of the computer, media and entertainment industry. The spectacular results are captured in ArtShow 4, a multimedia best-seller. As we enter the 1994 fiscal year, Corel is well positioned for continued success. Our leadership in the core technologies of Graphics, SCSI, and CD-ROM applications, combined with our strong balance sheet and highly motivated and talented employees, promises yet another great year to come.

[signed]
Dr. Michael C.J. Cowpland
Chairman, President and CEO

[Pages 6 to 24 are omitted. These pages focus on Corel's product lines, with liberal use of colour graphics]

COREL CORPORATION

INDEX TO CONSOLIDATED FINANCIAL STATEMENTS

COREL CORPORATION

MANAGEMENT'S DISCUSSION AND ANALYSIS OF FINANCIAL CONDITION AND RESULTS OF OPERATIONS

Overview

From its inception in 1985 until 1987, the Company was engaged primarily in the systems integration business and provided customers with turnkey PC-based desktop publishing systems and local area networks by combining hardware and software products from various manufacturers with the Company's proprietary software enhancements. As a result of its experience in developing proprietary software enhancements, and as a result of declining margins in the systems integration business, the Company began, in 1987, to devote additional resources to developing a separately packaged illustration software program, which became CorelDRAW. In 1989, the Company introduced its first version of CorelDRAW. CorelDRAW 2.0 was introduced in November 1990, CorelDRAW 3.0 was introduced in May 1992 and CorelDRAW 4, the current version, was introduced in May 1993. Also in connection with its system integration business, the Company developed SCSI interface software for optical peripherals in 1987. Subsequently, the Company enhanced the capabilities of its software to interface with a greater number of SCSI peripherals, including non-optical devices. Until fiscal 1992, the Company's strategy was to provide a range of SCSI products, some of which included hardware and software, for customers desiring optical storage solutions. During fiscal 1992, the Company's SCSI strategy was to phase out the products with lower margin hardware components and concentrate on the higher margin software products. In June 1992, the Company commenced shipment of CorelSCSI, a software only product. In May 1993, the Company commenced shipment of CorelSCSI-Pro, an enhanced version of CorelSCSI, and CorelRAID, a software solution for automatic and independent back-up of network disk drives.

In November 1991, the Company decided to concentrate its efforts on the higher margin graphics and SCSI software markets and, consequently, discontinued its system integration business. In connection with the discontinuation of the systems integration business, the Company incurred charges in the fourth quarter of fiscal 1991 and the first and second quarters of fiscal 1992. The financial statements of the Company have been restated to reflect this discontinuation.

In January 1992, the Company introduced its Blockbuster bundle, a limited time promotion, which included a third party CD-ROM drive, CorelSCSI interface software, a SCSI host adapter card and CorelDRAW 2.0 on CD-ROM. The objective of Blockbuster was to increase awareness and promote the use of CD-ROM technology, thereby potentially increasing demand for the Company's graphics and SCSI software products. Production of the Blockbuster bundle was discontinued in the third quarter of fiscal 1992 and the blockbuster promotion was completed in the fourth quarter of fiscal 1992.

Upon the launch of CorelDRAW 3.0 in May 1992, the Company released only a full kit into the distribution channel. Consistent with prior new product releases, in June 1992, in order to encourage existing users of CorelDRAW to upgrade to CorelDRAW 3.0, the Company introduced an existing user upgrade package of CorelDRAW 3.0 at a lower price than the full kit. The Company believes that during the third quarter of fiscal 1992, new users may have been able to purchase existing user upgrade packages from distributors and dealers despite precautions (including the requirement that purchasers return disks and/or the front page of the user manual for the prior version of CorelDRAW to the dealer or distributor) intended to limit such purchases to existing CorelDRAW users. In August 1992, in an effort to expand the installed base of CorelDRAW users and to lessen the effects of leakage, the Company introduced a competitive upgrade program which permitted users of graphics software products produced by other companies to buy CorelDRAW 3.0 at a price lower than that of the full kit, but higher than that of the existing user upgrade. Additionally, the Company no longer sold existing user upgrade packages of CorelDRAW 3.0 through distributors or, except in limited circumstances, to dealers, and end users could generally purchase such upgrades only directly from the Company. During the fourth quarter of fiscal 1992, the Company introduced seven foreign language versions of CorelDRAW 3.0 (including full kit, existing user upgrade and competitive upgrade). During the first and second quarters of fiscal 1993, the Company introduced a further six foreign language versions of CorelDRAW 3.0 (including full kit, existing user upgrade and competitive upgrade). Each version of CorelDRAW 3.0 - full kit, existing user upgrade and competitive upgrade - had approximately the same unit production cost. The introduction of the existing user upgrade and of the competitive upgrade each had a negative impact on the gross margins in the third and fourth quarters of fiscal 1992. In connection with the launch of CorelDRAW 3.0 in May 1992 and the introduction of the competitive upgrade program and the introduction of several foreign language versions of CorelDRAW 3.0 in the fourth quarter of fiscal 1992, advertising expenses increased by 107% to $20.1 million in fiscal 1992 from $9.7 million in fiscal 1991. Although sales increased by 72.5% to $90.1 million in fiscal 1992 from $52.2 million in fiscal 1991, gross margin as a percentage of sales decreased to 71% in fiscal 1992 as compared to 84% in fiscal 1991 and net income from continuing operations increased 1.9% to $12.3 million in fiscal 1992 from $12.1 million in fiscal 1991.

Upon the launch of CorelDRAW 4 in May 1993, the Company released a full kit version of CorelDRAW 4 into the distribution channel as well as continuing to market the full kit version of CorelDRAW 3.0 at a reduced price. Consistent with prior new product releases, in May 1993, in order to encourage existing users of CorelDRAW to upgrade to CorelDRAW 4, the Company introduced an existing user upgrade package of CorelDRAW 4 at a lower price than the full kit. As Corel's installed base grows, the percentage of sales attributable to existing user upgrade packages is expected to increase, particularly in the periods immediately following the launch of a new version of CorelDRAW. From the launch of CorelDRAW 4 through the end of June 1993, the existing user upgrade package of CorelDRAW 4 was only available directly from the Company. Subsequent to June 1993, the existing user upgrade package of CorelDRAW 4 was available through distribution as well as directly from Corel. During the third and fourth quarters of fiscal 1993, Corel introduced eight foreign language versions of CorelDRAW 4 (including full kit and existing user upgrade). Unit sales of CorelDRAW to new users grew 99.8% from fiscal 1991 to fiscal 1992 and 103.7% from fiscal 1992 to fiscal 1993. Each version of CorelDRAW 4 — full kit and existing user upgrade — had approximately the same unit production cost. In connection with the launch of CorelDRAW 4 in May 1993, the continued marketing of CorelDRAW 3.0 and the introduction of several foreign language versions of CorelDRAW 4 in the third and fourth quarters of fiscal 1993, advertising expenses increased by 37% to $27.5 million in fiscal 1993 from $20.1 million in fiscal 1992. Sales increased by 56% to $140.2 million in fiscal 1993 from $90.1 million in fiscal 1992, gross margin as a percentage of sales increased to 77% in fiscal 1993 as compared to 71% in fiscal 1992 and net income from continuing operations increased 127% to $27.8 million in fiscal 1993 from $12.3 million in fiscal 1992.

In August 1993, the Company introduced Corel Professional Photos on CD-ROM. Corel Professional Photos is a complementary product line for the Company's increasing involvement in CD-ROM publishing. It also is the Company's first entry in the Macintosh graphics and desktop publishing market. As of November 30, 1993, the Company was publishing approximately 140 photo titles. The suggested retail price for this product is US$49.95 per unit.

On September 30, 1993, the Company purchased Ventura Publisher, Ventura Database Publisher and all related technologies from Ventura Software Inc. The Company acquired ownership of all platform and localized versions in both source code and object code form of these products as well as trademarks and customer base associated with the software. Effective October 1, 1993, Corel assumed full responsibility for customer service for these products and, effective October 29, 1993, Corel assumed full responsibility for technical support for these products. Ventura Publisher has an installed base of approximately 400,000 users. Corel did not hire any of Ventura Software Inc.'s employees and did not assume any of Ventura Software Inc.'s liabilities, except for limited product returns.

On October 20, 1993 the Company announced Corel Ventura 4.2, the first release of the product since the acquisition. Corel Ventura combines Ventura Publisher and Database Publisher, together with extensive font, photo and clipart libraries, for US$249. The product began shipping in early November of 1993. As of November 30, 1993, the Company is manufacturing only the Windows version of Corel Ventura. However, the Company will continue to monitor the market and may introduce versions that support other platforms in the future, although there is no assurance that it will do so.

The Company believes that inflation has not had a material effect on the Company's results of operations, liquidity or capital resources.

COREL CORPORATION

Results of Operations

The following table presents certain statement of income data expressed as a percentage of sales for the years ended November 30, 1991, 1992 and 1993:

	Year ended November 30,			Period to Period Increase (Decrease)	
	1991	1992	1993	1992 compared to 1991	1993 compared to 1992
Sales	100%	100%	100%	72.5%	55.6%
Cost of Sales	16%	29%	23%	207.2%	24.9%
Gross profit	84%	71%	77%	46.5%	68.0%
Expenses					
Advertising	19%	22%	20%	106.7%	36.6%
Selling, general and administration	19%	20%	17%	74.9%	35.7%
Research and development	8%	8%	6%	62.9%	16.5%
Depreciation and amortization	3%	4%	4%	173.6%	45.2%
Loss (Gain) on foreign exchange	1%	(3%)	(1%)	*	*
	50%	51%	46%	74.2%	41.9%
Income from operations	34%	20%	31%	5.5%	132.0%
Interest and dividend income	5%	2%	2%	(37.1)%	94.3%
Income before income taxes	39%	22%	33%	0.0%	129.0%
Income taxes	16%	8%	13%	(2.8)%	132.6%
Net income from continuing operations	23%	14%	20%	1.9%	126.6%

* not meaningful

Sales

Sales are net of allowances for returns. Prior to 1993, these allowances include reserves established by the Company at the time of introduction of new versions of CorelDRAW which were based on management's best estimate of the expected returns of previous versions of CoredDRAW upon the launch of a new version of CorelDRAW. Upon the launch of CorelDRAW 4 in May 1993, the Company continued to market the full kit version of CorelDRAW 3.0 at a reduced price and no reserve was established in fiscal 1993 for returns of CorelDRAW 3.0 upon the launch of CorelDRAW 4. The table below shows sales for fiscal years 1991, 1992 and 1993, consisting of new licenses (full kits and competitive upgrades), existing user upgrades and other sales (including sales from the Company's peripheral interface software business, which had historically also included hardware sales, and Professional Photo-CDs):

	Year ended November 30,		
	1991	1992	1993
	(in thousands of Cdn$)		
CorelDRAW - new licenses	$41,158	$60,668	$ 93,958
CorelDRAW - existing user upgrades	4,453	18,916	35,880
Total graphics software	45,611	79,584	129,838
Other	6,631	10,556	10,385
Total sales	$52,242	$90,140	$140,223

COREL CORPORATION

Sales increased 72.5% to $90.1 million in fiscal 1992 from $52.2 million in 1991 and 55.6% to $140.2 million in fiscal 1993. Sales increased in each of the periods presented due to increased aggregate unit sales of Corel's products (primarily CorelDRAW) and, to a lesser extent, price increases. Unit sales of CorelDRAW to new users grew 99.8% from fiscal 1991 to fiscal 1992 and 103.7% from fiscal 1992 to fiscal 1993. The increase in fiscal 1992 was primarily due to an increase in unit volume sales of CorelDRAW, including the continued market acceptance of CorelDRAW 2.0 and the introduction of CorelDRAW 3.0 (including full kits in May 1992, existing user upgrades in June 1992, competitive upgrades in August 1992 and seven foreign language versions during the fourth quarter of fiscal 1992) and also due to the Blockbuster promotion (which represented 6% of sales in the period). The growth in sales attributable to the introduction of CorelDRAW 3.0 was partially offset by a decline in average selling price due to the greater proportion of sales of existing user upgrades and due to sales of competitive upgrades. The increase in fiscal 1993 was primarily due to an increase in unit volume sales of CorelDRAW, including the continued market acceptance of CorelDRAW 3.0 and the introduction of CorelDRAW 4 (including full kits and existing user upgrades in May 1993, the German foreign language version in August 1993 and nine other foreign language versions during the fourth quarter of fiscal 1993) and the continuation of CorelDRAW 3.0 at a lower than full kit price after the launch of CorelDRAW 4. The growth in sales attributable to the introduction of CorelDRAW 4 was partially offset by a slight decline in average selling price due to the significant proportion of sales of CorelDRAW 3.0 at the lower price of US$199. Corel believes that, as of the end of fiscal 1993, its distributors and dealers held significant inventories of CorelDRAW 3.0 and CorelDRAW 4. Corel has not experienced to date any adverse consequences from the levels of unsold stock held by distributors and dealers at the end of fiscal 1993.

Corel's products are sold in US dollars in all countries other than Canada and, commencing in 1992, in US dollars to Canadian distributors. Sales in US dollars as a percentage of total sales were 90%, 92% and 97% in fiscal 1991,1992 and 1993, respectively.

Corel sells its products primarily through distributors. Three distributors accounted for $17.5 million (34%), $32.7 million (36%) and $38.5 million (27%) of Corel's sales in fiscal 1991, fiscal 1992 and fiscal 1993, respectively. The Company allowed its distributors approximately 90 to 120 days from the launch of CorelDRAW 3.0, in May 1992, to return versions of CorelDRAW 2.0.

Sales outside North America, principally in Europe, were 34%, 39% and 54% of Corel's sales for fiscal 1991, 1992 and 1993 respectively. The increases in sales outside North America as a percentage of sales in 1991, 1992 and 1993 were primarily due to the introduction of numerous foreign language versions of CorelDRAW and the Company's increased marketing efforts outside North America.

Gross Profit

Corel includes in cost of sales all costs associated with the acquisition of components, the assembly of finished products, the amortization of software acquisition costs and shipping. Costs associated with warehousing are included in general and administration expenses. Acquired software has been capitalized and is being amortized over a 36-month period commencing with the month of first shipment of the product incorporating such acquired software.

Gross profit as a percentage of sales decreased from 84% of sales in fiscal 1991 to 71% in fiscal 1992, and increased to 77% in fiscal 1993. The decrease in fiscal 1992 reflected the lower margins associated with sales of hardware products, including the Blockbuster bundle which had margins of less than 40%, the larger than anticipated sales of CorelDRAW 3.0 existing user upgrades (21% of fiscal 1992 revenues) which carry a margin that is less than 80% of the margin of CorelDRAW 3.0 full kit sales, and, to a lesser extent, sales of competitive upgrades which commenced in August 1992. The increase in fiscal 1993 reflected the termination in 1992 of sales of lower margin hardware products offset partially by the lower margins associated with the low priced full kit version of CorelDRAW 3.0 after the launch of CorelDRAW 4 in May 1993.

Advertising Expense

Advertising expenses include all marketing, advertising and trade show expenses. Advertising expenses increased by 107% to $20.1 million in fiscal 1992 from $9.7 million in fiscal 1991 and by 37% to $27.5 million in fiscal 1993. The increase in fiscal 1992 was due to increased marketing efforts, such as advertising in trade publications and preparation of marketing materials, the hiring of additional marketing personnel associated with growth in Corel's sales as well as increased advertising expenses related to the introduction of CorelDRAW 3.0 and CorelSCSI in May 1992, foreign language versions of CorelDRAW 3.0 during the fourth quarter of fiscal 1992 and Blockbuster in the first quarter of fiscal 1992. The increase in fiscal 1993 was due to the hiring of additional marketing personnel associated with growth in Corel's sales as well as increased advertising expenses related to the introduction of CorelDRAW 4 in May 1993, foreign language versions of CorelDRAW 4 during the third and fourth quarters of fiscal 1993, the introduction of Corel Professional Photos on CD-ROM in August 1993 and the launch of Corel Ventura in November 1993. Advertising expenses as a percentage of sales have increased from 19% in fiscal 1991 to 22% in fiscal 1992 and decreased to 20% in fiscal 1993. Corel anticipates that in the next 12 to 18 months, advertising expenses will continue to be incurred in amounts equal to or greater than the amounts incurred in the most recent corresponding periods.

Selling, General and Administration Expense

Selling, general and administration expenses include all selling expenses (except for advertising expenses) and general administrative expenses as well as expenses associated with warehousing. Selling, general and administration expenses increased by 75% to $17.7 million in fiscal 1992 from $10.1 million in fiscal 1991 and by 36% to $24.0 million in fiscal 1993. The increase in fiscal 1992 was due to the hiring of additional customer support and management and administrative personnel associated with growth in Corel's sales. The increase in fiscal 1993 was due to the contracting to third parties of significant portions of Corel's customer support functions as well as, to a lesser extent, the hiring of additional customer support and management and administrative personnel associated with growth in Corel's sales. General and administration expenses as a percentage of sales were 19%, 20% and 17% in fiscal 1991, 1992 and 1993 respectively. The Company anticipates that in the next 12 to 18 months, selling, general and administration expenses will continue to be incurred in amounts equal to or greater than the amounts incurred in the most recent corresponding periods.

Research and Development Expense

The Company has expensed all of its internal software development costs as incurred, in accordance with Canadian GAAP. Research and development expenses are reported net of Canadian investment tax credits. The table below shows gross research and development expenses, related tax credits and gross research and development expenses as a percentage of sales for the periods indicated:

	Year ended November 30,		
	1991	1992	1993
	(in thousands of Cdn$, except percentage data)		
Gross research and development expenses	$5,408	$8,315	$10,026
Research and development tax credits	1,008	$1,148	1,673
Net research and development expenses	$4,400	$7,167	$ 8,353
Gross research and development expenses as a percentage of sales	10%	9%	7%

Net research and development expenses increased by 63% to $7.2 million in fiscal 1992 from $4.4 million in fiscal 1991 and by 17% to $8.4 million in fiscal 1993. These increases were primarily attributable to increased staffing and costs associated with the continued maintenance and enhancement of Corel's products. Net research and development expenses as a percentage of sales were steady at approximately 8% in fiscal 1991 and fiscal 1992 and decreased to 6% in fiscal 1993. The decrease in fiscal 1993 reflects Corel's strategy of purchasing suitable technology, where available, rather than developing technology in-house from conception. Corel anticipates that net research and development expenses will remain relatively constant as a percentage of sales in the next 12 to 18 months.

Depreciation and Amortization Expense

Depreciation and amortization expenses, which do not include the amortization of purchased software, increased by 174% to $3.8 million in fiscal 1992 from $1.4 million in fiscal 1991 and by 45% to $5.4 million in fiscal 1993. These increases were due in part to purchases of additional office and computer equipment over these periods. The increase in fiscal 1992 was also due to the reclassification of certain computer hardware from inventory to capital assets in connection with the discontinuation of the Company's systems integration business.

Loss (Gain) on Foreign Exchange

Foreign exchange gains or losses on US dollar transactions are due to fluctuations in the value of the Canadian dollar relative to the value of the US dollar between the time sales are recorded and the collection of the account receivable. The fiscal 1992 foreign exchange gain of $3.2 million reflected the weakening of the Canadian dollar from US$0.88 at the beginning of fiscal 1992 to US$0.78 at the end of fiscal 1992. The fiscal 1993 foreign exchange gain of $0.6 million reflected the further weakening of the Canadian dollar from US$0.78 at the beginning of fiscal 1993 to US$0.75 at the end of fiscal 1993.

Interest and Dividend Income

Interest and dividend income decreased by $1.0 million to $1.6 million in fiscal 1992 from $2.6 million in fiscal 1991 and increased by $1.6 million to $3.2 million in fiscal 1993. The decrease in fiscal 1992 from fiscal 1991 was primarily due to declining interest rates during fiscal 1992. The increase in fiscal 1993 was due to the increased cash and short term investments at the beginning of fiscal 1993, primarily resulting from the Company's initial public offering in the United States which raised $30.0 million and the increase in cash and short term investments of $26.4 million during fiscal 1993, offset by declining interest rates during fiscal 1993. The interest and dividend income received by Corel resulted from weighted average interest and dividend rates of 11% in fiscal 1991, 6% in fiscal 1992, and 5% in fiscal 1993.

Income Taxes

Corel's effective tax rates for fiscal 1991, 1992 and 1993 were 40%, 39% and 40%, respectively. These rates vary from the Company's statutory tax rate of 44% primarily due to the application of research and development tax credits and manufacturing and processing deductions in fiscal 1991 and fiscal 1992. The fiscal 1993 rate varies from the Company's statutory tax rate of 44% primarily due to foreign tax rate differences associated with Corel's operations in Ireland and the application of research and development tax credits. Corel expects that, under current tax laws, it will continue to generate additional tax credits or allowances directly related to Corel's ongoing research and development efforts and continue to benefit from foreign tax rate differences associated with Corel's operations in Ireland.

Liquidity and Capital Resources

As of November 30, 1993, Corel's principal sources of liquidity included cash and short-term investments of approximately $76.1 million, accounts receivable of $51.4 million and an undrawn bank credit facility in the amount of $2.0 million. Corel has had no long-term debt and has no present commitments or agreements which would require any long-term debt to be incurred. Corel believes that the existing sources of liquidity and anticipated funds from operations will satisfy Corel's projected working capital and capital expenditure requirements for at least the next 12 months. Corel anticipates that subsequent to that time, its working capital and capital expenditures will be satisfied by existing sources of liquidity, funds from operations and, if necessary, additional financings.

Corel has used funds generated from operations and from the exercise of employee stock options to fund its operations and the growth in its working capital and to acquire capital equipment, products and technology. Corel's operating activities provided cash of approximately $6.8 million in fiscal 1991, $2.6 million in fiscal 1992 and $32.4 million in fiscal 1993. Non-cash working capital (current assets net of cash and short-term investments and current liabilities) increased by $14.3 million to $31.5 million at November 30, 1992 from $17.2 million at November 30, 1991 and by $5.6 million to $37.1 million at November 30, 1993. Major components of non-cash working capital include accounts receivable, inventories, accounts payable and income taxes payable or recoverable.

Accounts receivable increased by $12.6 million in fiscal 1992 to $30.9 million at November 30, 1992 from $18.3 million at November 30, 1991 and by $20.5 million in fiscal 1993 to $51.4 million at November 30, 1993, primarily due to increased sales in fiscal 1992 and fiscal 1993.

Inventories decreased by $1.7 million in fiscal 1992 to $5.0 million at November 30, 1992 from $6.7 million at November 30, 1991 and increased by $4.8 million in fiscal 1993 to $9.8 million at November 30, 1993. The decrease in fiscal 1992 reflected the Company's decisions to discontinue its systems integration business in the fourth quarter of 1991 and subsequently to concentrate solely on the software business in the second quarter of 1992. The increase in fiscal 1993 reflects the Company's decisions to maintain CorelDRAW 3.0 as a separate product line, initiate the manufacture of CorelDRAW at a second location in Ireland and introduce Corel Professional Photos on CD-ROM.

Accounts payable and accrued liabilities increased by $0.1 million in fiscal 1992 to $5.2 million at November 30, 1992 from $5.1 million at November 30, 1991 and by $10.1 million in fiscal 1993 to $15.3 million at November 30, 1993 primarily due to the increased sales levels and expenses during these periods.

Income taxes payable decreased by $3.5 million in fiscal 1992 to a recoverable position of $0.5 million at November 30, 1992 and increased by $10.4 million in fiscal 1993 to $9.9 million at November 30, 1993. The decrease in fiscal 1992 is due to the payment in the first quarter of 1992 of income taxes payable of $3.0 million at November 30, 1991 and the higher than anticipated investment tax credits generated by the higher level of research and development spending in fiscal 1992. The increase in fiscal 1993 is due primarily to the increase in income from continuing operations before income taxes.

The exercise of employee and other stock options provided cash of approximately $4.5 million in fiscal 1991, $13.1 million in fiscal 1992 and $21.4 million in fiscal 1993.

Corel's capital expenditures totaled $6.5 million in fiscal 1991, $15.5 million in fiscal 1992 and $28.4 million in fiscal 1993, including expenditures for acquired software ($7.6 million in fiscal 1992 and $21.4 million in fiscal 1993), for computer equipment and for computer hardware, in fiscal 1991 and fiscal 1992, reclassified in connection with the discontinuation of the systems integration business. At November 30, 1993, Corel had no material commitments for capital expenditures.

COREL CORPORATION

MANAGEMENT'S REPORT

Management is responsible for the preparation of the Company's consolidated financial statements. Management believes that the consolidated financial statements fairly reflect the form and substance of transactions and that the consolidated financial statements reasonably present the Company's financial condition and results of operations in conformity with generally accepted accounting principles. Management has included in the Company's consolidated financial statements amounts based on estimates and judgements that it believes are reasonable under the circumstances.

KPMG Peat Marwick Thorne, the independent auditors appointed by the shareholders of the Company, have audited the Company's consolidated financial statements in accordance with generally accepted auditing standards and they provide an objective, independent review of the fairness of reported operating results and financial position.

The Board of Directors of the Company has an Audit Committee which meets with financial management and the independent auditors to review accounting, auditing, internal accounting controls, and financial reporting matters.

[signed]
Dr. Michael C.J. Cowpland
Chairman, President and CEO

[signed]
Charles A. Norris
Chief Financial Officer and Controller

AUDITORS' REPORT

We have audited the consolidated balance sheets of Corel Corporation as at November 30, 1993 and November 30, 1992 and the consolidated statements of income, retained earnings and changes in financial position for the years ended November 30, 1993, 1992 and 1991. These financial statements are the responsibility of the Company's management. Our responsibility is to express an opinion on these financial statements based on our audit.

We conducted our audit in accordance with generally accepted auditing standards. Those standards require that we plan and perform an audit to obtain reasonable assurance whether the financial statements are free of material misstatement. An audit includes examining, on a test basis, evidence supporting the amounts and disclosures in the financial statements. An audit also includes assessing the accounting principles used and significant estimates made by management, as well as evaluating the overall financial statement presentation.

In our opinion, these consolidated financial statements present fairly, in all material respects, the financial position of the Company as at November 30, 1993 and 1992 and the results of operations and the changes in financial position for the years ended November 30, 1993, 1992 and 1991 in accordance with generally accepted accounting principles.

Generally accepted accounting principles in Canada differ in some respects from those applicable in the United States (note 8).

[signed]
KPMG Peat Marwick Thorne
Chartered Accountants

Ottawa, Canada
January 14, 1994

COREL CORPORATION

CONSOLIDATED BALANCE SHEETS

	As at November 30, 1992	1993
	(in thousands of Cdn$)	
ASSETS		
Current assets:		
Cash and short-term investments	$ 49,720	$ 76,102
Accounts receivable		
Trade (note 9)	28,879	48,501
Other	2,028	2,917
Inventory (note 1)	4,973	9,828
Prepaid expenses	385	1,084
Income taxes recoverable	496	—
	86,481	138,432
Capital assets (note 2)	18,832	38,191
	$105,313	$176,623
LIABILITIES AND SHAREHOLDERS' EQUITY		
Current liabilities:		
Accounts payable	$ 1,299	$ 7,197
Accrued liabilities	3,949	8,108
Income taxes payable	—	9,880
	5,248	25,185
Deferred income taxes	1,272	2,927
Shareholders' equity:		
Share capital (note 3)	69,130	90,510
Contributed surplus	470	470
Accumulated foreign currency translation adjustment	—	497
Retained earnings	29,193	57,034
	98,793	148,511
	$105,313	$176,623

Commitments (note 6)

On behalf of the Board:

[signed]
Dr. Michael C.J. Cowpland
Director

The Honourable William G. Davis, P.C., C.C., Q.C.
Director

(See accompanying Notes to Consolidated Financial Statements)

COREL CORPORATION

CONSOLIDATED STATEMENTS OF INCOME AND RETAINED EARNINGS

	Year ended November 30,		
	1991	1992	1993
	(in thousands of Cdn$, except per share data)		
Sales	$52,242	$90,140	$140,223
Cost of sales	8,458	25,980	32,457
Gross profit	43,784	64,160	107,766
Expenses:			
Advertising	9,732	20,116	27,474
Selling, general and administrative	10,127	17,712	24,039
Research and development	4,400	7,167	8,353
Depreciation and amortization	1,371	3,751	5,446
Loss (gain) on foreign exchange	546	(3,159)	(641)
	26,176	45,587	64,671
Income from continuing operations	17,608	18,573	43,095
Interest income	2,609	1,641	3,189
Income from continuing operations before income taxes	20,217	20,214	46,284
Income taxes:			
Current	7,798	7,758	16,788
Deferred	362	170	1,655
	8,160	7,928	18,443
Net income from continuing operations	12,057	12,286	27,841
Loss from discontinued operations, net of income taxes (note 7)	(700)	(1,100)	—
Net income	11,357	11,186	27,841
Retained earnings beginning of year	6,650	18,007	29,193
Retained earnings at end of year	$18,007	$29,193	$ 57,034
Earnings per share: (note 3)			
Net income from continuing operations:			
Basic	$ 0.54	$ 0.52	$ 0.99
Fully diluted	$ 0.51	$ 0.47	$ 0.90
Net income			
Basic	$ 0.51	$ 0.47	$ 0.99
Fully diluted	$ 0.48	$ 0.43	$ 0.90
Weighted average number of Common Shares outstanding (000s):			
Basic	22,300	23,610	28,134
Fully diluted	23,626	25,778	30,764

(See accompanying Notes to Consolidated Financial Statements)

COREL CORPORATION

CONSOLIDATED STATEMENTS OF CHANGES IN FINANCIAL POSITION

	Year ended November 30,		
	1991	1992	1993
	(in thousands of Cdn$)		
CASH PROVIDED BY (USED FOR):			
Operations:			
Net income from continuing operations	$12,057	$12,286	$ 27,841
Items which do not involve cash:			
Depreciation and amortization	1,371	4,415	8,578
Deferred income taxes	362	170	1,655
Increase in accounts receivable	(6,727)	(12,607)	(20,511)
(Increase) decrease in inventory	(845)	1,702	(4,855)
(Increase) decrease in prepaid expenses	(633)	327	(699)
Increase (decrease) in accounts payable	303	(887)	5,898
Increase in accrued liabilities	687	995	4,159
Increase (decrease) in income taxes payable/recoverable	(113)	(3,518)	10,376
Increase (decrease) in other current liabilities	372	(325)	—
Net cash provided by operations	6,834	2,558	32,442
Loss from discontinued operations	(700)	(1,100)	—
	6,134	1,458	32,442
Financing:			
Issue of share capital	4,532	37,838	21,380
Investments:			
Purchase of capital assets	(6,467)	(15,495)	(28,428)
Proceeds on disposal of assets	—	—	491
	(6,467)	(15,495)	(27,937)
Effect of foreign currency translation on cash flow	—	—	497
Net increase in cash	4,199	23,801	26,382
Cash at the beginning of year	21,720	25,919	49,720
Cash at end of year.	$25,919	$49,720	$ 76,102

Cash is defined as cash and short-term investments

(See accompanying Notes to Consolidated Financial Statements)

COREL CORPORATION

NOTES TO CONSOLIDATED FINANCIAL STATEMENTS

Summary of Significant Accounting Policies

The consolidated financial statements have been prepared in accordance with accounting principles generally accepted in Canada. These principles are also generally accepted in the United States in all material respects except as disclosed in Note 8.

(a) Basis of Consolidation

The consolidated financial statements include the accounts of the Company and its wholly-owned subsidiary, Corel Corporation Limited (Ireland).

(b) Sales recognition

Sales are recognized when the products are shipped to the customer, and are net of discounts and allowances for returns.

(c) Research and Development Costs

All research and development costs are expensed as incurred. Acquired software is capitalized and amortized over its expected useful life, generally three years.

(d) Inventory

Inventory is valued at the lower of cost, determined on a specific identification basis, and realizable value.

(e) Capital Assets

Capital assets are recorded at cost. Amortization of licenses commences with the market release of each new software product and versions. Depreciation and amortization are calculated using the following rates and bases:

Furniture and equipment	20-33% declining balance
Computer equipment and software	33.3% straight-line
Research and development equipment	20% declining balance
Software licenses and purchased software, clipart libraries and Photo CD libraries ...	Shorter of the life of the license or 20.0-33.3% straight-line
Leasehold improvements.	Straight-line over the term of the lease

(f) Cash and Short-term Investments

Short-term investments are stated at the lower of cost and market. Short-term investments of $52,114,000 and $68,629,000 at November 30, 1992 and 1993, respectively, included with cash consisted principally of government securities, commercial paper, bankers' acceptances, letter loan agreements, term deposit certificates and bearer deposit notes. The carrying amount approximates fair value because of the short maturity of those instruments.

(g) Foreign Currency Translation

The consolidated financial statements are prepared using Canadian dollars. The operations of the wholly-owned foreign subsidiary which are undertaken in currencies other than Canadian dollars are considered self-sustaining.

The assets and liabilities of the self-sustaining subsidiary are translated at the fiscal year end exchange rates and the resulting unrealized exchange gains or losses are accumulated as a separate component of shareholders' equity described in the consolidated balance sheets as "Accumulated foreign currency translation adjustment". The income statement of the self-sustaining foreign operation are translated at exchange rates prevailing during the fiscal year.

Other monetary assets and liabilities, which are denominated in a foreign currency, are translated into Canadian dollars at the rate of exchange in effect at the balance sheet date. Revenue and expense items are translated at exchange rates prevailing during the period. Exchange gains and losses resulting from the translation of these amounts are included in the consolidated statements of income.

1. Inventory

	As at November 30, 1992	1993
	(in thousands of Cdn$)	
Raw materials	$2,720	$6,139
Finished goods	2,253	3,689
	$4,973	$9,828

2. Capital Assets

	November 30, 1993 Cost	Accumulated Depreciation and Amortization	Net	Net November 30, 1992
	(in thousands of Cdn$)			
Furniture and equipment	$ 6,148	$ 2,749	$ 3,399	$ 3,567
Computer equipment and software	13,274	6,113	7,161	6,316
Research and development equipment	4,275	1,529	2,746	2,097
Leasehold improvements	502	276	226	285
Software licenses and purchased software, clipart libraries and photo CD libraries	28,966	4,307	24,659	6,567
	$53,165	$14,974	$38,191	$18,832

The cost at November 30, 1992 amounted to $25,721,000 and accumulated depreciation and amortization at November 30, 1992 amounted to $6,889,000. The carrying amount of licenses not being amortized at November 30, 1993 and 1992 amounted to $3,697,000 and $2,420,000 respectively.

3. Share Capital

	As at November 30, 1991	1992	1993
	(in thousands of Cdn$)		
(a) Authorized and issued share capital			
Authorized			
Unlimited preferred shares, issuable in series, no par value			
Unlimited common shares			
Issued (as at November 30)			
Number of shares (000s)	22,636	27,350	30,034
Stated capital	$31,292	$ 69,130	$ 90,510
(b) Common Shares issued during the year			
Employee share plan			
Number of shares (000s)	760	1,114	2,684
Cash consideration	$ 2,999	$ 7,792	$ 21,380
Other			
Number of shares (000s)	464		
Cash consideration	$ 1,533		
U.S. Initial public offering			
Number of shares (000s)		3,600	
Cash consideration		$ 30,046	

(c) Stock Split

On November 22, 1993, the Board of Directors declared a two for one stock split, effected in the form of a stock dividend, payable December 8, 1993 to shareholders of record on December 1, 1993. All references in the consolidated financial statements with regard to shares outstanding and per share amounts have been restated to reflect the stock split.

(d) Earnings per common share

The calculations of the earnings per common share are based on the weighted daily average number of shares outstanding during the year. The calculation of fully diluted earnings per common share assumes that all outstanding options have been exercised at the later of the beginning of the fiscal period or the option issuance date.

(e) Employee stock option plan

The Company's Employee Stock Option Plan is administered by the Compensation Committee which is a subcommittee of the Board of Directors. The Compensation Committee will designate employees to be included under the Plan and will designate the number of options and share price pursuant to the new options, subject to applicable securities laws and stock exchange regulations. Information with respect to stock option activity for 1992 and 1993 follows:

	Number of Shares	Option Price Range per Share
Outstanding at November 30, 1991	1,513,560	\$0.50-\$10.42
Granted	2,300,764	\$8.20-\$11.19
Exercised	(1,119,856)	\$2.13-\$10.42
Cancelled	(453,856)	\$5.00-\$11.19
Outstanding at November 30, 1992	2,240,612	\$0.50-\$11.19
Granted	5,874,676	\$7.00-\$22.32
Exercised	(2,683,384)	\$0.50-\$15.88
Cancelled	(2,560,744)	\$8.20-\$11.19
Outstanding at November 30, 1993	2,871,160	\$2.13-\$22.32

The outstanding options expire between May 10, 1994 and October 12, 1997.

4. Income Taxes

Income tax expense varies from the amount that would be computed by applying the basic federal and provincial income tax rated to income from continuing operations before income taxes, as shown in the following table:

	Year ended November 30,		
	1991	1992	1993
	(in thousands of Cdn\$)		
Basic rate applied to income from continuing operations before income taxes	\$8,964	\$8,963	\$20,522
Increase (decrease) in taxes resulting from:			
Manufacturing and processing deduction	(430)	(458)	—
Provincial research and development deduction	(237)	(320)	(403)
Amortization of share costs	(137)	(405)	(410)
Foreign tax rate differences	—	—	(1,378)
Other items	—	148	112
	\$8,160	\$7,928	\$18,443

5. Segmented Information

In the opinion of management, the Company operates in one industry segment, being the PC software development business. The Company distributes those products worldwide from two geographic regions.

	Canada	Ireland	Total
		(in thousands of Cdn$)	
Sales	$109,070	$38,912	$147,982
Inter-segment Revenue	(7,759)	—	(7,759)
Net Sales	101,311	38,912	140,223
Net Income	22,329	5,512	27,841
Identifiable Assets	$140,115	$36,508	$176,623

A summary of sales by region and by major customers from consolidated operations is as follows:

	Year ended November 30,		
	1991	1992	1993
		(in thousands of Cdn$)	
By Region:			
U.S.A	$ 29,453	$45,270	$ 52,673
Europe	14,600	30,856	66,011
Canada	5,161	9,803	12,337
Other	3,028	4,211	9,202
	$ 52,242	$90,140	$140,223
By Major Customer:			
Ingram Micro Inc.	$ 8,121	$18,710	$ 16,944
Kenfil Distribution	6,038	7,704	11,144
Merisel Inc	3,361	6,328	10,459
Computer 2000	1,616	4,216	10,867

6. Commitments

The Company rents office premises under long-term operating leases which expire between 1996 and 1998. Rent expense (in thousands) for these leases aggregated $1,641, $1,750, and $2,257 during the years ended November 30, 1991, 1992 and 1993, respectively. At November 30, 1993, the minimum lease payments (in thousands), are approximately as follows:

1994	$1,285
1995	1,612
1996	1,439
1997	754
1998	55
	$5,145

7. Discontinued Operations

On November 30, 1991, the Company adopted a formal plan to discontinue the operations of its Systems Division, a systems integration business. Accordingly, the financial statements of the Company have been reclassified to report separately the operating results of this discontinued operation.

Net assets of the discontinued operation were $3,206,000 and NIL at November 30, 1991 and 1992, respectively. These amounts consisted of current assets and current liabilities.

For the periods ended November 30, 1991 and 1992, the Company recorded a loss from discontinued operations of $700,000 and $1,100,000 net of income tax recoveries of $485,000 and $797,000, respectively. Sales applicable to the Systems Division for November 30, 1991 and 1992 were $8,824,000 and $1,682,000 respectively.

8. Significant Differences Between Canadian and United States GAAP

The Company's financial statements are prepared on the basis of Canadian GAAP, which is different in some respects from US GAAP. Significant differences between Canadian GAAP and US GAAP are set forth below:

Calculation of earnings per share

Under Canadian GAAP, the basic earnings per share data are computed using only the weighted daily average number of shares outstanding during the year. Under US GAAP, the weighted average number of shares is computed including dilutive options, and as if the funds obtained from the assumed exercise of the options were used to purchase common shares at the average market price during the period.

The calculation of fully diluted earnings per share for US GAAP purposes is not significantly different from the primary calculation for US GAAP and therefore is not presented.

	Year ended November 30,		
	1991	1992	1993
		(in Cdn$)	
US GAAP–Primary			
Net income from continuing operations per share	$0.51	$0.52	$0.98
Net income per share	$0.48	$0.47	$0.98
Weighted average number of Common Shares outstanding (000s)	22,564	23,704	28,446

9. Supplementary Financial Statement Information

Included in accounts receivable trade are the following reserves and related activity:

Period Ended	Description	Opening Balance	Additions	Deductions	Ending Balance
			(in thousands of Cdn$)		
November 30, 1993	Promotional Rebates	$2,535	$7,005	$6,491	$3,049
	Sales reserve	1,634	4,267	2,327	3,574
	Allowance for doubtful accounts	1,090	456	261	1,285
November 30, 1992	Promotional Rebates	—	3,087	552	2,535
	Sales reserve	—	2,738	1,104	1,634
	Allowance for doubtful accounts	1,066	946	922	1,090
November 30, 1991	Sales reserve	2,525	—	2,525	—
	Allowance for doubtful accounts	525	541	—	1,066

Appendix B
1923 Annual Report of Massey-Harris, Limited

ANNUAL REPORT

FOR THE YEAR 1923

of

MASSEY-HARRIS COMPANY, LIMITED

ESTABLISHED 1847

Implement Makers to H. M. the King

Toronto, Canada, February 16th, 1924

MASSEY-HARRIS COMPANY, LIMITED

Directors

Honorary President
C. D. Massey

President
Vincent Massey

Vice-President and Chairman of the Board
Jos. N. Shenstone

Sir Edmund Walker, C.V.O.
T. Bradshaw
George Valentine
E. R. Wood
A. S. Patterson
J. G. Hossack
Lloyd Harris
C. L. Wisner
W. J. Verity

Officers

T. BRADSHAW,	General Manager
C.L. WISNER,	Ass't Gen. Manager Foreign Sales
GEORGE VALENTINE,	Ass't Gen. Manager Manufacturing
J. G. HOSSACK	General Solicitor
LEO SMYTH	Secretary

Head Office

915 King Street W., Toronto, Canada

MASSEY-HARRIS COMPANY, LIMITED

REPORT OF THE PROCEEDINGS

of the

ANNUAL MEETING OF SHAREHOLDERS

16th February, 1924

The Annual Meeting of the Shareholders of Massey-Harris Company, Ltd. was held at the Head Office of the Company in Toronto on the 16th of February, 1924, at 11 a.m.

The President, Mr. Vincent Massey, having taken the chair, Mr. Leo Smyth was appointed to act as secretary.

The President called upon the Secretary to read the Annual Report of the Massey-Harris Company, Limited, and the following Directors' Report of the combined companies:—

REPORT

To the Shareholders:

Your Directors beg to present the following statement of the affairs of the Massey-Harris Company, Limited, and its subsidiary companies — Verity Plow Company, Limited, and The Bain Wagon Company, Limited, — the entire capital stock of both of which companies is owned by your Company, for the year ended 30th November, 1923:

Income Account

The Income Account, from the year's operations including profit realized from sale of timber lands, but before deducting interest and appropriations was		**$1,120,937.07**
From this there has been deducted:		
Interest on borrowing	$616,087.19	
Appropriation for depreciation of plants, etc.	174,708.59	
Appropriation for possible losses on receivables	233,308.71	
Appropriation for foreign exchange and taxes	95,834.14	
Appropriation for Pension and Insurance funds	23,446.95	**1,143,385.58**
Leaving a Net Loss for the Year of		**$ 22,448.51**

Surplus Account

The surplus at 30th November, 1922, was	**$772,601.24**
Deducting the Net Loss for 1923	**22,448.51**
The Surplus at 30th November, 1923, was	**$750,152.73**

The Total Assets now amount to $42,379,815.71, of which $31,819,642.72 or 75 per cent are current, or quick assets. Deducting from the latter the current liabilities of $11,209,983.66, the net liquid surplus or working capital at 30th November, 1923, was $20,609,659.06.

Sales for the year exceeded those of the previous year by 16 per cent., but they are still only about two-thirds of what may be termed normal. The necessarily increased production enabled the factories to operate upon a more economical and uniform basis than in 1922.

Capital Outlay for new properties and equipment was strictly limited to pressing necessities with the object of reducing operating costs. As a result of a decision not to operate the timber lands situated in Arkansas, U. S. A., these were sold, as well as several small properties which were not required for business purposes.

Factories. Branch premises and other properties have been maintained in a sound state of repair, all expenditure in connection therewith having been charged to the year's operations. In addition there has been reserved for the depreciation of buildings and equipment the amount usually set aside for that purpose.

The Balance Sheet submitted herewith is accompanied by the certificate of the Auditors appointed by the shareholders, Messrs. Clarkson, Gordon & Dilworth, and Mr. H. L. Gillson. Every Canadian and Foreign Branch was audited during the past year.

Serious Losses have been generally experienced by practically all makers of farm implements in Canada and the United States during the past three years. Your combined companies have been no exception, since they suffered a net loss in 1921 of $1,456,000, in 1922 $643,000, and in the year just closed $22,448. Due to the close relationship which exists between agriculture and the implement industry, its present condition is but a reflex of the unfavorable position at home and abroad of its only customer — the farmer. While the outlook is not entirely clear, it is hoped that a turning point has been reached for both the farmer and the implement maker, and that hereafter their operations may be carried on upon a more profitable basis.

Your Directors desire to place on record their grateful appreciation of the loyalty and efficiency of the members of the organizations at home and abroad, in these trying times and especially during the past year.

THOMAS BRADSHAW
General Manager

VINCENT MASSEY,
President.

Toronto, February 12th, 1924

MASSEY-HARRIS COMPANY, LIMITED
AND SUBSIDIARY COMPANIES
CONSOLIDATED BALANCE SHEET, 30TH NOVEMBER, 1923

ASSETS

Capital Assets		
Factories — real estate and equipment — Toronto, Brantford, Woodstock and Weston	$ 5,667,875.66	
Branches — real estate, buildings and equipment	2,194,692.07	
Massey-Harris Harvester Co. Inc. 22,702 shares Common stock at cost	2,680,041.62	
Patents	17,563.64	10,560,172.99
Current Assets		
Inventories of raw materials, goods in process and finished goods (valued at cost, not exceeding replacement value)	14,912,537.44	
Expenditures on account of next year's operations	2,102,591.23	
Bills and accounts receivable (accrued interest not taken into account)	14,507,366.01	
Cash on hand and in banks	297,148.04	31,819,642.72
TOTAL		**$42,379,815.71**

LIABILITIES

Capital		
Common — authorized $25,000,000.00 — issued and fully paid up		$24,179,800.00
Current Liabilities		
Bills and accounts payable		11,209,983.66
Reserves and Funds		
Taxes — foreign branches	$280,505.30	
Foreign exchange, etc.	636,823.94	
Pension fund	207,573.33	
Buildings and equipment	1,894,366.73	
Possible branch losses on receivables	2,351,570.33	

Fire indemnity fund	489,039.69	5,859,879.32
Contingent account as called for by charters and by-law of companies	380,000.00	
Profit and loss account	750,152.73	1,130,152.73
TOTAL		**$42,379,815.71**

CONTINGENT LIABILITIES: — Joint Debenture Note issue with the Massey-Harris Harvester Company Inc., (now reduced to $2,800,000.00) and loans of that Company guaranteed by this Company $1,035,000.00

VINCENT MASSEY, ***President***
THOMAS BRADSHAW, ***General Manager***

We have examined the Head Office books and accounts of Massey-Harris Company Limited, The Bain Wagon Company Limited, and Verity Plow Company Limited, as of 30th November, 1923, and have accepted the returns from the Branches.

The above figures include the Australian and Argentine Branch accounts as at 30th June, 1923.

The officials have assured us that the Reserves for possible losses on collections and for depreciation are sufficient, and accepting this we certify that in our opinion the above Balance Sheet is properly drawn up to show the true position of the combined Companies at 30th November, 1923, according to the best of our information, the explanations given to us and as shown by the books of the Companies.

We have obtained all the information and explanations we have required.

CLARKSON, GORDON & DILWORTH, C.A.
H. L. GILLSON,
Auditors.

Toronto, 11th February, 1924.

The Meeting was addressed by the President, the Vice-President and the General Manager, after which, upon motion of the President, seconded by the Honorary President, the Report was adopted.

Upon motion duly made, seconded and carried, Messrs. Clarkson, Gordon & Dilworth and Mr. H. L. Gillson were appointed Auditors until the next Annual Meeting.

The following Directors were elected: —

C. D. Massey, Vincent Massey, J. N. Shenstone, Sir Edmund Walker, C.V.O., T. Bradshaw, George Valentine, E. R. Wood, A. S. Patterson, J. G. Hossack, Lloyd Harris, C. L. Wisner, W. J. Verity.

At a meeting of the Board of Directors, held later, Mr. C. D. Massey was appointed Honorary President, Mr. Vincent Massey, President, Mr. J. N. Shenstone, Vice-President and Chairman of the Board.

ASSETS

Capital Assets

Factories - real estate and equipment, being cost of land, buildings and equipment of the following manufacturing plants: — Toronto, Ont., main plant, 28 acres. Brantford, Ont., binder and mower plant, 28 acres. Brantford, Ont., plow plant, 21 acres. Woodstock, Ont., wagon plant, 20 acres. Weston, Ont., gas engine plant (closed) 20 acres - Total 117 acres $5,667,876

Against these properties there is a reserve, provided under liabilities, of $1,454,290.

Sales Branches — real estate and equipment, being cost of land, buildings, etc., as follows:—

Ontario Branch — 2 distributing and 2 agency warehouses.

Quebec Branch — Headquarters building, Montreal, Que., and 4 distributing warehouses.

Maritime Branch — Headquarters building, Moncton, N.B., and 2 distributing warehouses

Winnipeg, Man. Branch — Headquarters building, Winnipeg, 1 distributing warehouse and 21 local agency warehouses.

Brandon, Man., Branch — Headquarters building, Brandon, 1 distributing warehouse and 37 local agency warehouses.

Saskatoon, Sask. Branch — Headquarters building, 1 distributing warehouse and 6 local agency warehouses.

Regina, Sask., Branch — Headquarters building, Regina, 2 distributing warehouses and 15 local agency warehouses.

Yorkton, Sask. Branch — Headquarters building, Yorkton and 4 local agency warehouses.

Swift Current, Sask. Branch — Headquarters building, Swift Current, and 1 distributing warehouse.

Calgary, Alta. Branch — Headquarters building, 2 distributing warehouses and 12 local agency warehouses.

Edmonton, Alta. Branch — Headquarters building, Edmonton, and 12 local agency warehouses.

European Branch — Distributing warehouse, Manchester, England, Branch Headquarters, Paris, and distributing warehouses, Lyons and Nantes, France.

Australasian Branch — Branch Headquarters building at Melbourne, warehouse and other property at Melbourne; and warehouse and other property at Sydney. Branch Headquarters building at Brisbane.

Assets—Continued

Branch Headquarters building at Perth and warehouse at Fremantle. Warehouse and other property at Dunedin, Lyttleton and Auckland, New Zealand. A reserve of $422,513 covering depreciation and amortization on foregoing Branch properties is included in "Buildings and Equipment" reserve under liabilities.	$2,194,692
Massey-Harris Harvester Co., Inc., Batavia, N.Y. (This represents 82 per cent. of the paid-up capital stock)	2,680,042
Patents — The valuable patents and rights of the Companies are carried at the nominal value of A reserve for the same amount, is included in the liabilities.	17,564

Current Assets

Inventories — Raw Materials are valued at cost not exceeding replacement prices. Finished goods and goods in process are taken at bare factory cost.	14,912,537
Expenditures incurred on account of next year, 1924, include cost of material received and all charges directly incurred between time of stock taking (August and September) and the close of the Company's fiscal year, 30th November, 1923	2,102,591
Bills and Accounts Receivable — comprising notes and accounts due by farmers in Canada, Australasia, Argentine and by certain jobbers and dealers elsewhere. Credit has not been taken for accrued interest, which amounts to over $1,300,000. A reserve of $2,351,570 has been provided, under liabilities, for possible losses.	14,507,366
Cash — mainly bank balances at Branches	297,148
Total Assets	**$42,379,816**

The value of the Companies' factories, equipment and Sales Branches has never been written-up. On the contrary, the amount in the balance sheet $7,862,568 represents actual cost, less substantial write-offs. In addition, reserves for depreciation, amounting to no less than $1,894,367 have been accumulated and set up against these properties (see liabilities). An independent appraisal made in 1921 determined the value of factory property and equipment, apart from the many sales branch properties, at $13,873,993 or $9,479,828 in excess of the net amount at which they were carried.

The aggregate of fire insurance maintained on factories and branch properties is approximately $9,553,000.

LIABILITIES

Capital		
The Company has no funded debt and only one class of stock — common. The authorized capital is $25,000,000, of which there has been issued and paid up		$24,179,800
Current Liabilities		
Bills and Accounts payable — including borrowings from banks and current open accounts		11,209,984
Reserves and Funds		
Taxes — provision for taxes not levied, but anticipated, for all branches	$ 280,505	
Foreign exchange, etc. — estimated provision for loss in exchange in the transfer of funds and receivables from branches outside of Canada	636,824	
Pension Fund — Actuarial liability for pensions granted to factory employees	207,573	
Buildings and equipment — covering depreciation on Factories and Branch properties, also on factory and other equipment	1,894,367	
Possible losses on Receivables — estimated after a careful classification of receivables at all branches	2,351,570	
Fire Indemnity Fund — accumulations of the Company's self-insurance fund instituted in 1899, which carries limited risks on certain of the Company's properties	489,040	5,859,879
Contingent Account — as required by Companies' Charters and by-law — this is an entirely free surplus	380,000	
Profit and Loss Account	750,153	1,130,153
Total Liabilities		**$42,379,816**

Factories

R. W. Gifford, General Superintendent of Factories.
B. S. Harris, General Superintendent Experimental Departments.
O. H. Shenstone, Superintendent, Toronto Factory.
S. B. Chadsey, Manager, Brantford Factory.
W. J. Verity, Pres. and Gen'l Man. Verity Plow Co., Ltd., Brantford.
E. B. Terryberry, Gen'l. Manager Bain Wagon Co., Ltd., Woodstock.

Branch Houses

Europe

C. W. Dawkins, European General Manager, London.
R. O. McDonald, European Ass't. General Manager, London.
J. S. Duncan, Sr., Manager French Branch, Paris.
Wm. Magladery, Ass't Manager, French Branch, Paris.

Australasia

A. S. Patterson, General Manager for Australia, Melbourne.
C. Cornell, Secretary-Treasurer, Melbourne.
W. A. Shields, Manager for Victoria and Tasmania, Melbourne.
G. B. Mitchel, Asst. Manager for Victoria, Melbourne.
E. G. Grant, Manager for New South Wales, Sydney.
W. H. Pardey, Manager for New Zealand, Christchurch.
J. Ure, Manager for Western Australia, Perth.
H. Latimer, Manager for Queensland, Brisbane.
J. C. Knox, Acting Manager for Queensland, Brisbane.

Argentine

A. E. Shields, Manager Argentine Branch, Buenos Aires.

Canada

W. E. Greig, Manager Ontario Branch, Toronto.
Thos. Magladery, Associate Manager Ontario Branch, Toronto.
O. F. Vaughan, Asst. Manager Ontario Branch, Toronto.
F. L. Spoor, Manager Quebec Branch, Montreal, Que.
George Ballantyne, Manager Maritime Branch, Moncton, N. B.
C. H. Whitaker, Manager Winnipeg Branch, Winnipeg, Man.
A. A. Campbell, Manager Brandon Branch, Brandon, Man.
J. A. Graham, Manager Regina Branch, Regina, Sask.
John Nichol, Manager Saskatoon Branch, Saskatoon, Sask.
W. H. Horsfield, Manager Yorkton Branch, Yorkton, Sask.
D. B. McPherson, Manager Swift Current Branch, Swift Current, Sask.
A. W. Trickey, Manager Calgary Branch, Calgary, Alta.
Herbert Baker, Manager Edmonton Branch, Edmonton, Alta.

Appendix C
Accounting For Bad Debt Expense

In this appendix we'll illustrate how a company accounts for bad debt expense. Suppose that Verbatim Inc. (VI) begins operations to sell camping equipment in large retail outlets across the country in early 1996. For the accounting period ended December 31, 1996, VI had sales of $17,500,000. VI does not accept any credit cards, but sells for cash or on credit terms of 30 days. At December 31, 1996, the company had $3,210,000 in accounts receivable, and an aged *accounts receivable trial balance* of the receivables showed the following age distribution:

Age of Accounts Receivable	$ amount
Current (0 to 30 days)	$1,050,000
31 to 60 days	825,000
61 to 90 days	1,200,000
over 90 days old	135,000
Total, December 31, 1996	$3,210,000

Suppose that the managers of VI know that industry experience indicates that 99% of current receivables are collected eventually, against 80% of receivables 31 to 60 days old, 60% of receivables 61 to 90 days old, and just 30% of those over 90 days old. Applying these percentages to the data in the aged accounts receivable trial balance gives:

$.99 \times 1{,}050{,}000 + 0.80 \times 825{,}000 + 0.60 \times 1{,}200{,}000 + 0.30 \times 135{,}000 = \$2{,}460{,}000$

This suggests that $3,210,000 - $2,460,000, or $750,000, of VI's accounts receivable will be uncollectible. Thus, the matching principle supports the recording of an adjusting entry for the year ended December 31, 1996, as follows:

Dr Bad debt expense (I)	750,000	
Cr Allowance for doubtful accounts (B)		750,000

The bad debt expense is matched against the revenue that the granting of credit helped generate, and is accounted for in 1996, which is the same year in which that revenue is accounted for. The allowance for doubtful accounts is a contra account, which is shown on the balance sheet as a deduction from VI's accounts receivable.

Now let's move into 1997: Suppose this year that sales are $21,000,500, and year-end accounts receivable have the following aging:

Age of Accounts Receivable	$ amount
Current (0 to 30 days)	$2,500,000
31 to 60 days	1,000,000
61 to 90 days	300,000
over 90 days old	1,400,000
Total, December 31, 1996	$5,200,000

Also, during fiscal 1997 VI's accountant learned that accounts receivable totalling $110,000 had to be written off since the debtors had gone bankrupt or could no longer be located. These "write-offs" are accounted for as follows:

Dr Allowance for doubtful accounts (B)	110,000	
Cr Accounts receivable (B)		110,000

The $110,000 in worthless accounts receivable dollars are removed from the balance sheet account, and the allowance is also reduced. Notice that both sides of this entry are to balance sheet accounts; in effect, this entry is just confirming a part of the allowance that was originally recorded as the year end 1996 adjusting entry, and is another example of estimation in accounting.

At year end, December 31, 1997, the aged accounts receivable trial balance calculation suggests that the following receivables will be collected:

0.99 × 2,500,000 + 0.80 × 1,000,000 + 0.60 × 300,000 + 0.30 × 1,400,000, or $3,875,000

Therefore, an allowance for doubtful accounts of $5,200,000 - $3,875,000, or $1,325,000, is needed at the end of 1997. The balance in "Allowance for doubtful accounts" is the $750,000 credit recorded at the end of 1996, less the $110,000 debit due to the write-offs that was recorded during 1997, or $640,000. Therefore, VI needs to increase (or credit) "Allowance for doubtful accounts" by $685,000 in order to bring it up to its required end-of-year 1997 amount of $1,325,000. The adjusting entry to do this is:

Dr Bad bebt expense (I)	685,000	
Cr Allowance for doubtful accounts (B)		685,000

The method of accounting for bad debts that we have illustrated is often called the "allowance" method. It is an attempt to match the cost of incurring bad debts to the benefit obtained by offering credit to customers. The particular approach to estimating the amount required in the contra account "Allowance for doubtful accounts," based upon an aged accounts receivable trial balance, is used quite often in practice. Since estimation and judgment are involved, this is susceptible to expedients and other shortcuts, so auditors, managers, and users of accounting information incorporating bad debt expense based on the allowance method must be on the alert for less-than-optimum data. Abrupt changes in the ratio of the allowance for doubtful accounts to accounts receivable might be one indicator of problems.

Many smaller organizations don't bother setting up "Allowance for doubtful accounts," and just write off bad debts when they judge that the debtor isn't able (or willing) to pay. This is called the direct write-off method; it makes no attempt to match expense with revenue and so is not consistent with GAAP. Since no receivables were written off by VI management in 1996, no bad debt expense would have been accounted for under this method in that year. In 1997, $110,000 in bad debts were written off, resulting in the following journal entry under the direct write-off method:

Dr Bad debt expense (I)	110,000	
Cr Accounts receivable (B)		110,000

The direct write-off method is the method of accounting for bad debts permitted under income tax legislation.

A comparison of bad debt expense under the two methods for VI for 1996 and 1997 follows:

Method	**1996**	**1997**
Allowance	$750,000	$685,000
Direct write-off	0	$110,000

The difference in expense between the two methods is most extreme usually when an organization is growing or declining. When an organization is operating at a steady state, the difference in expense should be immaterial.

Aside from being in accordance with GAAP and providing a more accurate measure of bad debt expense than the the direct write-off method, the allowance method forces management to exert better control over accounts receivable. When something is accounted for, when managers are held accountable for something, attention and effort are allocated to management of the item.

CHAPTER 7 seven

Accounting Information About Cash and Cash Flows

Learning OBJECTIVES

After you have read, thought about, and discussed this chapter, and completed a selection from the end-of-chapter material, you will have made significant progress in achieving the following learning objectives:

- Describe what accountants mean when they say "cash" and "cash equivalents."
- Describe how cash is disclosed in balance sheets.
- Prepare a bank reconciliation.
- Explain the working capital cycle and operating cash flow.
- Explain why it is important for managers to monitor working capital.
- Identify the differences among the following three categories of cash flows: operating, investing, and financing.
- List eight cash flow patterns, and explain their importance.
- Prepare a cash flow statement from accrual accounting information for a simple situation.
- Prepare a cash flow statement from accrual accounting information for a more complex situation, using T-accounts and reconstructed journal entries.
- Form judgments about an accounting entity's quality of earnings in a simple situation.
- Be able to prepare a cash budget for a small business.
- Describe differences in how cash is defined in financial statements of accounting entities in different countries.

In Wall Street — where styles in investing change as often as they do for women's clothes on the Rue de la Paix — a new fad is appearing: "cash flow analysis."

"Cash Flow is the New Fad," *Business Week*, November 4, 1961

In the last decade the users of financial statements have become increasingly interested in analyzing the cash flows generated by a company. It is almost standard practice for stock market analysts, commercial bankers, credit managers, and other investors to evaluate cash statements as well as accrual statements when making decisions ... The long term survival of a company requires that it be profitable. It also requires that the company be able to meet its cash obligations as they become due. Profitable activities do not necessarily generate cash at the time it is needed and cash-generating activities are not necessarily profitable. A cash analysis therefore provides useful information in addition to that provided by traditional financial statements prepared on an accrual basis. A cash analysis shows how cash funds have been used in the past. Usually, it is a first step towards making cash projections that enable the statement user to assess the company's ability to service debt, pay dividends, and meet other future obligations.

John Hull, "Monitoring a Company's Operating Cash Flow Using Variance Analysis," *Accounting Horizons*, September 1990, pp. 50–57

Talk about stretch targets: Could any corporation operate without working capital? A fast-growing number of companies are setting that audacious goal because pursuing it — even if they never attain it — unleashes efficiencies and savings that can dramatically improve corporate performance. In an era when global competition makes raising prices difficult and when companies need hefty cash flow to expand overseas, invest in new technologies, and pay down debt, this newly articulated discipline represents a managerial tool whose time has come.

Shawn Tully, "Raiding a Company's Hidden Cash," *Fortune*, August 22, 1994

INTRODUCTION

Up till now, we've spent an awful lot of time describing accrual accounting, in which revenues and expenses, and assets and liabilities, are accounted for. We stressed the point that there isn't always a correspondence between an accounting entity's cash inflows and outflows on the one hand, and its revenues and expenses on the other. Now we shift our focus to examine accounting information that centres explicitly on cash and cash flows. After all, accrual accounting information is important, but cash information is very often equally or even more important, as the quotations that opened this chapter point out. Ultimately, actual cash represents an entity's command over goods and services.

Our examination of accounting information about cash and cash flows is built around the various cash-oriented reports that an accounting entity may prepare. Reports may deal with the amounts of cash that an entity has on hand, as in published balance sheets. Other reports, such as bank reconciliations and published statements of changes in financial position, may provide the user with information about past cash inflows and outflows. Still others may deal with forecasted cash flows, which of course have not yet occurred. Cash reports may be prepared for management's use (for example, a cash budget, or capital expenditure proposals like the one in the Gord and James case in Chapter 2), or for shareholders and other outsiders (for example, future-oriented financial information about corporate cash flows).

Disclosing Cash in Published Balance Sheets

The CICA's *Terminology for Accountants* defines "cash" as "coin, bank notes, money orders, cheques ... and (by extension) the balances in respect of demand and saving deposits at banks or other financial institutions." And it defines "cash equivalents" as "financial instruments [such as readily marketable investments in common shares] that are subject to no more risk than is cash and that are readily convertible to cash on short notice."

Usually, organizations group cash and cash equivalents together for purposes of financial statement presentation (the term "cash and cash equivalents" will be abbreviated as CCE in this book). This is because cash equivalents are very close to being cash in terms of their economic characteristics, and usually represent a short-term use of temporarily "excess" cash. For example, a company could take the cash it is planning to spend on new capital asset purchases in the next quarter, and invest it in guaranteed investment certificates (commonly called GICs), the rationale being that the purchase of capital assets won't be made for some months, and meanwhile the company will earn interest on the GICs.

On its balance sheet, Corel Corporation discloses cash and short-term investments as one item (see Chapter 6, Appendix A); in its Summary of Significant Accounting Policies, it explains the composition of the cash equivalents portion of CCE as consisting of government securities and similar financial instruments. Clearly, management has some discretion about how to present CCE on the balance sheet and in other financial statements. For this reason, users must be sure about what's included in CCE, so that they understand the significance for any given company of changes in CCE. This theme of caution is pursued in the "Accounting, Organizations, and Society" section later in the chapter, where an article is summarized that describes how CCE is defined in different countries.

Bank Reconciliations

Every person or organization that has a bank account upon which cheques may be issued is interested in ensuring that everything is all right with the account — that there is sufficient money in the account to cover any uncashed cheques, that the bank's service charges are reasonable and for services actually received, and that all deposits (especially those made by night drop boxes or by electronic data interchange, or EDI) have been properly recorded by the bank. It follows that the monthly (or other time interval) bank statement we receive from the bank is important to us as an accounting and decision-making tool. In this section we will illustrate how the user of such a report — the person or organization that has opened the bank account — can gain some insight and control over cash by preparing an analysis called a bank reconciliation.[1]

First, let's be clear about what a bank statement is. Suppose Ms. Zanga, who owns and operates a small boutique, has a bank account with the local branch of a hypothetical financial institution, which we'll call the Western National Bank. In effect, she has loaned the bank some money (that's why her bank account is "credited" when she makes a deposit). The bank is doing the accounting from *its* perspective, so when it receives Zanga's deposit, it accounts for it in the following way:

Dr Cash (B)	XXX	
Cr Loan payable — Ms. Zanga (B)		XXX

EXHIBIT 7–1
BANK STATEMENT
Branch No. 135; Account No. 1234-56789

WNB WESTERN NATIONAL BANK

Description	Debits	Credits	Date	Balance
Balance forward-09/01/95			SEP01	1,236.22
CHQ#158	31.49		SEP05	1,204.73
CHQ#164	40.00		SEP06	
CHQ#161	76.29		SEP06	
CHQ#150	140.00		SEP06	948.44
CHQ#155	350.00		SEP11	598.44
CHQ#151	53.01		SEP12	
CHQ#152	429.39		SEP12	
CHQ#156	151.12		SEP12	OD 35.08
Presentment charge	5.00		SEP13	
Deposit		50.00	SEP13	9.92
CHQ#153	111.44		SEP14	OD 101.52
Presentment charge	5.00		SEP15	
Deposit		150.00	SEP15	
CHQ#154	61.88		SEP15	OD 18.40
Monthly deposit		4,556.69	SEP18	4,538.29
CHQ#149	594.99		SEP19	3,943.30
CHQ#165	400.00		SEP20	3,543.30
CHQ#163	167.00		SEP22	3,376.30
CHQ#166	61.58		SEP26	
CHQ#167	250.00		SEP26	
CHQ#168	400.00		SEP26	
CHQ#170	500.00		SEP26	2,164.72
CHQ#171	600.00		SEP28	1,564.72
Bank service charges	10.46		SEP30	1,554.26

[1] Accountants, ever in search of jargon, love to call a bank reconciliation a "bank rec," but we'll avoid the temptation.

At the end of a typical month (September 1995, say), Zanga receives the report, reproduced in Exhibit 7–1, from the Western National Bank. This report is called a bank statement, and summarizes the inflows and outflows in her business's bank account *from the bank's perspective*. But Zanga also keeps track of the inflows and outflows of cash for her business in her company's general ledger "Cash" account. These are two independent records of the boutique's cash flows. The records, however, are almost always out of sync: when she issues a cheque, Zanga prepares a journal entry that credits her general ledger "Cash" account; but to reduce, or debit, Zanga's boutique's bank account, the bank must wait until the cheque is presented to it for payment. Also, although Zanga receives cash each day in her boutique from sales, she only makes a deposit once in a while — usually just once per month.

So the two records are almost always out of sync. On top of this, one may contain information that the other does not. For example, it is not until she receives the bank statement that Zanga knows what the bank service charges are, at which point she can prepare a journal entry to record those charges in the boutique's accounting system, as we will illustrate below.

Let's look at the story the boutique's bank statement tells us. Because Zanga waited until September 18 to deposit the boutique's cash receipts, her business has incurred $10.00 of "presentment" charges. The bank makes these charges to customers who have issued cheques for which there are insufficient funds. To avoid such charges in the future, perhaps she should make her deposits more often. Also, more frequent deposits would mean less money on-site at the boutique, and less likelihood of theft. And avoiding overdrafts might make her bank manager more congenial. But perhaps the trip to the bank is difficult for her, so she prefers to make it just once a month (some small Canadian communities are underserviced by banks). The point is that there is some useful management information in even this very simple small-business bank account. But there is useful *control* information as well.

The bank statement acts as an independent control on the accuracy of Zanga's general ledger "Cash" account, or on the raw list of cash received and cheques issued from which such a general ledger account may be constructed. This control function is carried out by preparing a bank reconciliation, which Zanga should do at least every time she receives her boutique's bank statement. The boutique's bank reconciliation for September 1995 is shown below:

Balance according to bank statement, Sept. 30		$1,554.26
Add: Cash receipts as yet unrecorded by bank		1,010.00
		2,564.26
Deduct: Cheques issued but not yet presented to bank:		
Chq#157; Jones Supply	$ 14.04	
Chq#159; Lobe Limited	90.46	
Chq#160; Newton Inc.	102.43	
Chq#169; Municipality–taxes	1,420.79	1, 627.72
		936.54
Add: Bank charges not yet recorded in accounts		
Bank service charges	$ 10.46	
Presentment charges	10.00	20.46
Balance according to general ledger "Cash" account, before adjustment for as yet unrecorded bank charges, Sept. 30		$ 957.00

Zanga had $1,010.00 of cash receipts on hand at the boutique that had already been accounted for in the general journal and ledger by means of the following journal entry:

Dr Cash (B)	1,010.00	
Cr Sales (I)		1,010.00

However, the bank had no way of knowing this, and besides wouldn't have cared because it did not yet have the hard, cold cash. So, this not yet deposited amount is a reconciling item on the bank reconciliation.

Further, of the over 20 cheques that Zanga had issued in September, four (#'s 157, 159, 160, and 169) had not yet been cashed by the recipients and processed through the bank clearing system. But since she had issued them, she had already recorded journal entries, which resembled the following:

Dr Various expense accounts or asset (perhaps inventory) accounts	XX	
Cr Cash		XX

So, these issued cheques that have not yet appeared on the bank statement are also reconciling items on the bank reconciliation.

The new information she received in the bank statement is about the presentment charges and other bank charges. She must now account for these in the boutique's accounting system. The journal entry required to adjust the "Cash" account is:

Dr Bank charges (I)	20.46	
Cr Cash (B)		20.46

This journal entry adjusts the "Cash" account in the company's general ledger to its correct balance of $936.54, as of September 30, 1995.

Accounting and Business Decision A

(a) Most companies prepare bank reconciliations at least once a month. Why bother?

(b) If Zanga issued a cheque for $100.00 in August 1995, and it has not yet been cashed by the time she receives the September bank statement, what should she do?

(c) Many individuals and companies arrange for cash to be transferred automatically each month to suppliers' accounts. How would such transfers be treated in a bank statement? How would they be treated on a bank reconciliation?

Operating Cash Flow and the Working Capital Cycle

The quotation from Shawn Tully near the beginning of this chapter referred to the efforts many companies are making to increase their operating cash flow and net income by reducing their working capital as much as possible. Working capital is defined in *Terminology for Accountants* as the "excess of current assets over current liabilities. It is an indicator of the ability to finance current operations and meet obligations as they fall due."

In other words, an accounting entity's working capital at any point in time is its current assets less its current liabilities. In more detail:

Current assets	Cash and cash equivalents
	+ Inventories
	+ Accounts receivable
	+ Prepaid assets
	+ Other current assets
	= ***Total current assets***
Current liabilities	Wages payable
	+ Taxes payable
	+ Accounts payable
	+ Accrued liabilities
	+ Deferred revenue
	+ Other current liabilities
	= ***Total current liabilities***
WORKING CAPITAL	***Total current assets - Total current liabilities***

Tully (see this chapter's opening quotations) used the phrase "working capital" in a slightly different way: "It consists of inventories — raw materials, work-in-process, and finished goods — as well as a company's receivables ... minus its payables" (p. 82). In other words, the author excluded cash and cash equivalents, and so was really talking about working capital *net* of cash and cash equivalents. The article pointed out that while, on average, Fortune 500 companies[2] have 20 cents of working capital for each dollar of sales, many companies are aggressively reducing that ratio. For example, Quaker Oats' working capital was $339 million as of December 31, 1993, but that was only $0.07 per dollar of the company's revenues.

Corel Corporation's working capital net of CCE compared to its sales is shown in the following table for two recent fiscal years ended November 30 (in thousands of dollars; derived from Corel's financial statements in Chapter 6):

	1992	**1993**
Sales	90,140	140,223
Working capital net of CCE	31,513	37,145
WC, net of CCE, per sales dollar	0.35	0.26

Corel's working capital per dollar of sales seems high when compared with the 20 cents average of the Fortune 500 companies, but we must keep in mind that many of the latter companies are more traditional manufacturers, rather than "knowledge-based" companies, of which Corel is one. (Further, Corel has loads of CCE.)

Why has monitoring this ratio become so important? Tully gives this answer:[3]

Reducing working capital yields two powerful benefits. First, every dollar freed up from inventories or receivables rings up a one-time $1 contribution to cash flow. Second, the quest for zero working capital permanently raises earnings. Like all capital, working capital costs money, so reducing it yields savings. In addition, cutting working capital forces companies to produce and deliver faster than the competition, enabling them to win new business and charge premium prices for filling rush orders. As inventories evaporate, warehouses disappear. Companies no longer need forklift drivers to shuttle supplies around the factory or schedulers to plan production months in advance.

[2] Fortune 500 companies are the largest 500 corporations.
[3] Shawn Tully, "Raiding a Company's Hidden Cash," *Fortune*, August 22, 1994.

Over the 12 months that ended last May, Campbell Soup pared working capital by \$80 million. It used the cash to develop new products and buy companies in Britain. Campbell also expects to harvest an extra \$50 million in profits over the next few years by lowering overtime, storage costs, and other expenses — savings that will persist year after year.

The most important discipline that zero working capital necessitates is speed. Many companies today produce elaborate long-term forecasts of orders. They then manufacture their product weeks or months in advance, creating big inventories; eventually they fill orders from the bulging stocks.

Minimizing working capital forces organizations to demolish that system. Scrapping forecasts, companies manufacture goods as they are ordered. The best companies start producing an auto braking system or cereal flavor after receiving an order and yet still manage to deliver just when the customer needs it.

The system, known as demand flow or demand-based management, builds on the familiar idea of just-in-time inventories but is far broader. Most companies achieve just-in-time in one or two areas. They demand daily shipments from suppliers, for example, or dispatch finished products the hour the customer wants them. But just-in-time deliveries don't guarantee efficiency. To meet the rapid schedule, many companies simply ship from huge inventories. They still manufacture weeks or months in advance.

Achieving zero working capital requires that every order and part move at maximum pace, never stopping. Orders streak from the processing department to the plant. Flexible factories manufacture each product every day. Finished goods flow from the assembly line onto waiting trucks. Manufacturers press suppliers to cut inventories as well, since minimal stocks translate into lower raw material prices to the manufacturer. Instead of cluttering plants or warehouses, parts and products hurtle through the pipeline. As velocity rises, inventory — working capital — dwindles. That's why working capital levels are such a useful yardstick for efficiency and why, in the 1990s, manufacturers with the least working capital per dollar of sales will reign as the world's best-run companies.

In sum, monitoring working capital levels and the components of working capital is an important management function that complements the monitoring of cash flows. The article just excerpted urges managers to take steps that will lead to lower or even negative working capital — for example, requiring suppliers to deliver raw materials "just in time" (that is, just as needed). Doing so shifts the cost of storing inventory backwards onto the supplier, who presumably will then have an incentive to reduce *its* inventory, and so on. The ultimate goals are improved cash flow and profits for the company farther downstream.

Published Cash Flow Statements: An Early Look at Corel's Statement of Changes in Financial Position

Refer to Corel Corporation's consolidated statements of changes in financial position for the years ended November 30, 1991 through 1993, in Appendix A of Chapter 6. The information in these financial statements is summarized in the table on the next page.

In terms of the three broad categories

Cash Provided by (used for):	Year Ended November 30 1991	1992 (in thousands of dollars)	1993
Operations	$ 6,134	$ 1,458	$32,442
Financing	4,532	37,838	21,380
Investments	(6,467)	(15,495)	(27,937)
Other	—	—	497
Net increase in cash	4,199	23,801	26,382
Cash at the beginning of year	21,720	25,919	49,720
Cash at end of year	$25,919	$49,720	$76,102

of cash flows, Corel has maintained a pattern over the past three years such that net cash flow from operations is positive, net cash flow from financing is also positive, and net cash flow from investing is negative. Overall, Corel's total net cash flow has been positive ("Net increase in cash" has in fact increased each year). This pattern is consistent with what an analyst might expect of a growing, successful company in terms of its cash flows:

- Operating cash flows are positive, which signals that the company's day-to-day business activities related to its ongoing operations are generating more cash receipts than expenditures.
- Financing cash flow is also positive, which suggests that investors have enough confidence in the company's future that they are willing to invest their money in it.
- Investing cash flow is negative, indicating that the company is investing in capital assets and perhaps expanding.

Of course, this very broad-brush look at Corel's cash flow pattern is only suggestive; other features of Corel's results, plans, and environment are crucial. For example, analysts might question the apparent volatility of operating cash flows over the three-year period (down in 1992 compared to 1991; up in 1993 compared to 1992). Nevertheless, gaining a bit of insight into a company's success or failure by examining its overall cash-flow pattern is a good way to start financial analysis.

Accounting and Business Decision B

Suggest actions that a management could take to reduce working capital. Analyse the consequences of these actions. Consider three types of actions: (a) actions related to the management of the business, such as attempts to improve productivity and efficiency, and quality; (b) actions related to the speeding up or slowing down of purchases, payments, collections, and so on; and (c) actions related specifically to the portfolio of *accounting* choices.

Patterns of Cash Flows

Since each of a company's operating, financing, and investing cash flows can have only one of two algebraic signs — positive or negative — there are 2 × 2 × 2, or eight, cash flow patterns that are possible. These eight patterns are set out in Exhibit 7–2.

EXHIBIT 7–2
PATTERNS OF CASH FLOWS*

	Cash Flow from Operating Activities	Cash Flow from Investing Activities	Cash Flow from Financing Activities	POSSIBLE EXPLANATION
1.	+	+	+	A rare pattern: capital assets are being sold off, while operating activities are generating positive cash flows, and additional capital is being raised from the capital markets. Perhaps the company is undergoing a strategic change into a new business whose technology is less capital-asset intensive. A cash-rich company; may be in search of an acquisition.
2.	+	–	–	Company is using (apparently significant) operating cash flow to acquire capital assets and pay down debt or pay owners. Pattern consistent with a mature, successful company.
3.	+	+	–	The company is using its positive operating cash flow, plus cash flow generated from disposal of capital assets, to pay down debt or pay owners. Company is not reinvesting in new capital assets; perhaps is undergoing a restructuring, by which a heavy debt load must be reduced.
4.	+	–	+	The company's positive operating cash flow and its positive cash flows from new debt or equity are being invested in new capital assets. An apparently healthy, growing company.
5.	–	+	+	Company has operating cash flow problems; the disposal of capital assets and issue of debt and/or equity are being used to cover the shortfall. Investors seem optimistic; perhaps operating cash flow will turn positive soon.
6.	–	–	+	A growth company, but perhaps rapid growth in sales is using up cash as both inventories and accounts receivable increase rapidly. Perhaps a young, fast-growing company that investors have a lot of confidence in.
7.	–	+	–	A down-sizing pattern; perhaps the company is in a declining industry, and has not been successful in strategically diversifying.
8.	–	–	–	All three activities show negative cash flows; therefore, the company must be drawing down on previously established cash reserves. Not a sustainable pattern.

* Adapted from M.T. Dugan, B.E. Gup, and W.D. Samson, "Teaching the Statement of Cash Flows," *Journal of Accounting Education*, Vol. 9, 1991, pp. 33–52.

Corel falls into pattern 4 of Exhibit 7–2, and has been there for each of the three years noted in its 1993 Annual Report for which statements of changes in financial position information have been provided.

Another way of analysing a company is to compare operating cash flows with the company's net income from continuing operations. Operating cash flows and net income from continuing operations may each be positive or negative, and operating cash flows may either exceed or be less than net income. The situations are portrayed as follows:

Net Income from Continuing Operations	Operating Cash Flow	Net Income from Continuing Operations > Operating Cash Flow	Net Income from Continuing Operations = Operating Cash Flow	Net Income from Continuing Operations < Operating Cash Flow
positive	**positive**	**cell 1**	**cell 2**	**cell 3**
positive	negative	**cell 4**	not possible	not possible
negative	positive	not possible	not possible	**cell 5**
negative	negative	**cell 6**	**cell 7**	**cell 8**

In Corel's case, we have the following (for years ended November 30; dollar amounts in thousands):

	1991	1992	1993
Net income from continuing operations	+$12,057	+$12,286	+$27,841
Operating cash flow	+$6,834	+$2,558	+$32,442

In 1991 and 1992, Corel fell into cell 1, and in 1993 it fell into cell 3. The statements of changes in financial position in Appendix A of Chapter 6 disclosed the reconciliations between these two numbers for each of the three years. In 1991 and 1992, net income from continuing operations — the accrual accounting number — exceeded cash flow from operations, mainly because of the significant increases in accounts receivable that occurred in each of these years. Recall that the general form of the journal entry for a sale on credit is:

Dr Accounts receivable (B)	XX	
Cr Sales (I)		XX

Thus, such sales increased net income, but they did not increase cash flow. In 1991, $6,727,000 in increased accounts receivable was not supported by cash flows; in 1992, it was $12,607,000.

However, the 1993 increase in accounts receivable (which was $20,511,000), and that year's increase in inventories (which was $4,855,000) were offset by significantly larger than prior years' increases in accounts payable, accrued liabilities, and income taxes payable. By year-end 1993, Corel had $76,102,000 in cash (defined as cash and short-term investments) on its balance sheet; this represented 43.1% of its total assets of $176,623,000, so the company appeared to be very liquid indeed. Cash flow had increased from 1992, as had the absolute amount of cash, but cash as a percentage of total assets had actually *declined* from 47.2% the previous year.

Accounting and Business Decision C

What is Corel's cash flow for 1993? If Corel had defined CCE as just including cash, but no cash equivalents, what would its 1993 cash flow have been?

Preparing a Simple Cash-Flow Statement

Cash flow and accrual information provide insight into different but complementary aspects of an organization's results. In this section, we illustrate how a cash flow statement may be prepared from accrual financial statements: specifically, the balance sheet, income statement, and information from the statement of retained earnings. Suppose a small fictional company in the office supply business — we'll call it Rondo, Inc., or RI for short — began business early in 1994. Balance sheets as at December 31, years 1994, 1995, and 1996 (the current year), are shown in Exhibit 7–3, as are income statements and retained earnings statement dividend information for the years then ended.

EXHIBIT 7–3
RONDO INC.'S FINANCIAL STATEMENTS
(not including a cash flow statement)

Balance Sheets: December 31 ($000s)	**1996**	**1995**	**1994**
Cash and cash equivalents	320	150	100
Accounts receivable	300	600	200
Inventories	675	300	300
Prepaid expenses	75	60	50
Capital assets — gross	1,200	1,000	1,000
Accumulated depreciation	–600	–400	–200
Intangible assets	110	20	30
ASSETS	2,080	1,730	1,480
Wages payable	100	100	0
Accounts payable	200	100	300
Taxes payable	50	0	0
Deferred revenue	50	100	100
Debt — current portion	100	100	100
Deferred taxes	150	100	10
Debt	300	400	300
Common shares	630	480	470
Preferred shares	100	0	0
Retained earnings	400	350	200
LIABILITIES AND OWNER'S EQUITY	2,080	1,730	1,480
Income Statements: Year Ended Dec. 31 ($000s)	**1996**	**1995**	**1994**
Revenues	2,750	2,000	1,200
Cost of sales	1,350	900	500
Gross profit	1,400	1,100	700
Depreciation	200	200	200

	1996	1995	1994
Amortization	10	10	10
Selling	300	150	100
Administrative	215	115	90
Interest	40	40	40
Income taxes	200	185	60
	965	700	500
Net income	435	400	200
Dividend Information ($000s):			
Dividends	385	250	0

For the year ended December 31, 1996, the total cash flow (or, total *net* cash flow) is +$170,000 (= $320,000 - $150,000). We know that:

Total cash flow = Cash flow from operating activities + Cash flow from investing activities + Cash flow from financing activities

Or, in symbols,

TCF = CFO + CFI + CFF

That is,

170,000 = CFO + CFI + CFF

We'll begin our construction of RI's statement of changes in financial position — or as many managers and accountants call it, the SCFP — by focusing on cash flow from operating activities, symbolized as CFO, and start from the net income number. Our goal is to "undo" all the accrual accounting that separates net income from CFO. In effect, we're preparing a reconciliation between the two. The only way we can derive CFO, given the information we have, is through this "indirect" approach. Refer to Exhibit 7–4.

We begin with net income. But we know that net income is an accrual accounting number, and doesn't by any stretch of the imagination purport to represent cash flow from operations. In RI's case, there are ten reconciling items, as follows:

1. The 1996 journal entry to record depreciation on RI's books was, we know, as follows:

Dr	Depreciation expense (I)	200	
	Cr Accumulated depreciation (B)		200

This entry includes no impact on "Cash"; it does, however, reduce net income. Since we are beginning our derivation of CFO with the net income number, this item — depreciation expense — is an item that we must add back as we travel from net income to CFO.

2. The journal entry to record amortization on RI's books is as follows:

Dr	Amortization expense (I)	10	
	Cr Intangible assets (B)		10

In a way totally analogous to depreciation, we must add amortization back to the net income number, since it doesn't use up any cash. Remember, we're performing a reconciliation here.

3. From RI's income statements, we see that income tax expense for the three years was $60,000 (for 1994), $185,000 (for 1995), and $200,000 (for 1996). However, in Chapter 5 we showed how income tax expense is based on accrual accounting, and how a portion of it (the deferred tax portion) is a bookkeeping amount with no impact on cash flow. The change in the balance sheet account "Deferred taxes" each year must be equal to that particular year's addition or deduction to deferred taxes. As shown in the general ledger account, the "Deferred taxes" balance sheet account has changed as follows over the three years of RI's operations:

Deferred Taxes

	Dr	Cr	Balance
Opening balance, January 1, 1994			0
December 31, 1994, entry		10	
Balance, December 31, 1994			10 Cr
December 31, 1995, entry		90	
Balance, December 31, 1995			100 Cr
December 31, 1996, entry		50	
Balance, December 31, 1996			150 Cr

All the amounts in the "Cr" column were "plugged out"; we knew the final balances each year from the balance sheets we were given in Exhibit 7–3, so the changes (credits, in this case) were relatively easy to get. Thus, we are able to deduce that the journal entries recording income taxes in RI's accounting system each year must have been:

1994:

Dr Income tax expense (I)	60,000 [from the income statement]	
Cr Income taxes payable (B)		50,000 [plug]
Cr Deferred taxes (B)		10,000 [from the above ledger account we reconstructed]

1995:

Dr Income tax expense (I)	185,000	
Cr Income taxes payable (B)		95,000 [plug]
Cr Deferred taxes (B)		90,000

1996:

Dr Income tax expense (I)	200,000	
Cr Income tax payable (B)		150,000 [plug]
Cr Deferred taxes (B)		50,000

So, in our reconciliation of net income to CFO, we must adjust for the fact that only a portion of the income tax expense that was charged against net income actually gets to eventually reduce cash. In the above entries, it's only the credit to income taxes payable that ultimately will be a cash flow out of the firm. Therefore, in Exhibit 7–4, the 1994 change in deferred taxes, the $10,000, is added back; analogously, $90,000 is added back in 1995, and $50,000 in 1996.

4. In Exhibit 7–4, we *deduct* the accounting period's *increase* in accounts receivable of $200,000 for 1994 (the amount changed from an opening balance of zero to $200,000 by the end of 1994), since this increase accounts for revenues

that, while bona fide and acceptably recorded in accrual accounting, are not yet in cash form. Notice that accounts receivable *declined* in the year ended December 31, 1996, so this results in an *addition* of $300,000. Accounts receivable were $600,000 at the start of 1996, and declined to $300,000 by year end; this must mean that $300,000 of receivables from prior years were collected this year. Of course, under accrual accounting the revenues for those prior years' receivables were recorded in those prior years, not in the revenue or net income numbers for 1996. So to convert from accrual to cash in this situation, we add back the decrease in receivables to net income in order to head toward CFO.

5. An increase in inventories is — like an increase in accounts receivable — deducted in Exhibit 7–4. Think of the increase in this operating asset as using up cash. More on this below.

6. The accountant must have recorded the increase in prepaid expenses by means of journal entries as follows:

Dr Prepaid expenses [for insurance, say] (B)	XX	
Cr Cash (B)		XX

Cash is used up, but the income statement is not affected. Therefore, in order to convert the accrual net income number to a cash flow number, we must deduct the increase in prepaids as we go from net income to CFO. A decrease in prepaids would, of course, have the opposite effect.

7. Exhibit 7–4 tells us to add back increases in wages payable. When we think of the accrual journal entry recording wages expense, this makes sense:

Dr Wages expense (I)	XX	
Cr Cash (B)		XX
Cr Wages payable (B)		XX

It's only the cash portion of wages expense that affects cash flow; the other portion — the portion that changes wages payable over the accounting period — does not affect cash flow. But the entire wages expense was charged against revenues to determine net income, so the increase in wages payable must be added back in our reconciliation. A reduction in wages payable would have the opposite effect.

8. Accounts payable operates much like wages payable, insofar as Exhibit 7–4 is concerned. An increase means that cash was not used up to the extent of the increase. Looking at the "Inventory" and "Accounts payable" accounts together may shed a slightly different and also helpful light on these reconciling items. Let's assume that it is only inventory purchases that get credited to accounts payable in RI's accounting system. Now, recall that:

Cost of sales = Opening inventory + Purchases - Closing inventory [A]

and that

Opening Accounts Payable + Purchases - Payments = Closing Accounts Payable [B]

Let ΔI represent (Closing inventory - Opening inventory), and ΔA/P represent (Closing accounts payable - Opening accounts payable).

Then [A] becomes

ΔI + Cost of Sales = Purchases

and [B] becomes

ΔA/P + Payments = Purchases

Therefore,

ΔI + Cost of sales = ΔA/P + Payments

and,

Payments = Cost of sales + ΔI - ΔA/P

This last equation explains how the cost-of-sales number, which is an accrual number, is converted to the actual cash outflows, or payments. If inventories increased over the accounting period (that is, if ΔI is greater than zero), this has the effect of making payments exceed the accrual cost-of-sales number, and helps us understand why, in reconciling item #5 in Exhibit 7–4, an increase in inventory is *deducted* as we go from net income to CFO.

Also, if accounts payable increased over the accounting period (that is, if $\Delta A/P$ is greater than zero), actual cash payments will be *less than* cost of sales — this explains reconciling item #8. Of course, the net of [+ ΔI - $\Delta A/P$] will determine whether payments exceed or are less than cost of sales.

9. Taxes payable didn't change over 1994 and 1995, but over 1996 they increased by $50,000. This represents cash not yet paid out, even though it was charged as an expense. So it is added back.

10. Recall that deferred revenue arises when a company receives a cash payment in advance of earning it. The journal entry is as follows, in general:

Dr Cash (B)	XX	
Cr Deferred revenue (B)		XX

It is only in the future, when the revenue is earned, that the amount in the "Deferred revenue" account is transferred to the "Revenue" account on the income statement. In 1994, deferred revenue increased by $100,000; this means that RI received this amount of cash in excess of the revenues it recorded. So net income does not include this $100,000, and it must be added back to the net income number as we travel toward CFO. In 1995, there was no change in deferred revenue, so no reconciling item is necessary. But deferred revenue decreased by $50,000 in 1996; this means that the following journal entry was recorded by RI:

Dr Deferred revenue (B)	50,000	
Cr Revenues (I)		50,000

Revenues, and therefore net income, contains $50,000 of revenues whose cash flows occurred in *prior* years. Therefore, the decrease in deferred revenue is *deducted* as a reconciling item in Exhibit 7–4.

The end product of these ten reconciliations is "Cash flow from operations," or CFO, which was $705,000 in 1996, $190,000 in 1995, and $270,000 in 1994.

We now turn to the two other components of total cash flow: cash flow from investing activities, and cash flow from financing activities.

Cash flow from investing activities is derived by examining the changes in noncurrent assets, year by year. RI started up business on January 1, 1994, with no assets. On December 31, 1994, capital assets costing $1,000,000 were on its balance sheet, which indicates that capital assets to this amount were acquired during the year. There was no change in 1995, but $1,200,000 appears on the December 31, 1996, balance sheet, suggesting that capital assets to the amount of $200,000 were acquired in 1996.

Similarly, intangible assets were also acquired. In 1994, it seems that $40,000 of intangible assets were purchased ($30,000 on the December 31, 1994, balance sheet; but recall that $10,000 was amortized in 1994). Nothing was acquired in 1995 (the account changed by -$10,000, but we have already taken that change into consideration as reconciling item #2 in the derivation of CFO). In 1996, however, $100,000 of new intangible assets were acquired (the change over 1996 is only $90,000, but again we must take into consideration the $10,000 amortization). So cash flows from investing activities (CFI) are as follows ($000s):

	1996	1995	1994
Acquisition of capital assets	(200)	0	(1000)
Acquisition of intangible assets	(100)	0	(40)
Cash flow from investing activities	(300)	0	(1040)

Examination of changes in the non-operating liability accounts and the owners' equity accounts provides us with information to develop a summary of cash flows from financing activities (CFF). First, let's examine the "Debt" accounts. The total debt as at December 31 for each of the three years was:

Debt (as at December 31; $000s)	1996	1995	1994
Debt — current portion	100	100	100
Debt (noncurrent portion)	300	400	300
Total Debt	400	500	400

During 1994, total debt increased from zero up to $400,000; this information is captured by the following journal entry:

Dr Cash (B)	400,000	
Cr Debt (B)		400,000

This was a financing source of cash for 1994 — a positive cash inflow. For 1995, the corresponding entry is:

Dr Cash (B)	100,000	
Cr Debt (B)		100,000

However, in 1996 total debt decreased by $100,000, so a financing cash outflow occurred. This is captured as follows:

Dr Debt (B)	100,000	
Cr Cash (B)		100,000

Common shares went from zero to $470,000 during 1994, then increased a further $10,000 during 1995. In 1996, common shares increased again by $150,000, to $630,000. Summarizing this information in journal entry form:

	1996	1995	1994
Dr Cash	150,000	10,000	470,000
Cr Common shares	150,000	10,000	470,000

No preferred shares were issued until 1996, at which time an entry such as the following would have been recorded:

Dr Cash (B)	100,000	
Cr Preferred shares (B)		100,000

This was another financing cash inflow.

The only balance sheet account that remains is "Retained earnings." Recall that our reconciliation of net income to CFO already took into account the impact of net income on cash flow. Retained earnings increased by $200,000 in 1994, and net income was also $200,000, so dividends were zero (which agrees with the information we were given in Exhibit 7-3). In 1995 and 1996, respectively, retained earnings increased by $150,000 and $50,000. Net income in those years was $400,000 and $435,000, so dividends were $250,000 and $385,000. The impact of dividends on financing cash flows is captured by the following entries:

	1996	1995	1994
Dr Retained earnings (B)	385,000	250,000	0
Cr Cash (B)	385,000	250,000	0

EXHIBIT 7–4
RECONCILIATION BETWEEN RONDO'S NET INCOME AND CASH FLOW FROM OPERATIONS — 1994 TO 1996 ($000s)

	1996	1995	1994
Begin with net income	435	400	200
Add (from income statement) items not using up cash:			
1. (+) Depreciation	+200	+200	+200
2. (+) Amortization	+10	+10	+10
3. (+) The current year's deferred taxes	+50	+90	+10
Deduct (from balance sheet) increases in noncash operating assets:			
4. (-) Increases in accounts receivable	+300	–400	–200
5. (-) Increases in inventories	–375	0	–300
6. (-) Increases in prepaid expenses	–15	–10	–50
Add (from balance sheet) increases in noncash operating liabilities			
7. (+) Increases in wages payable	0	+100	0
8. (+) Increases in accounts payable	+100	–200	+300
9. (+) Increases in taxes payable	+50	0	0
10. (+) Increases in deferred revenue	–50	0	+100
Wind up with cash flow from operations	705	190	270

The final statement of changes in financial position is set out in Exhibit 7–5.

The above preparation of RI's SCFP may be seen as based on an expansion of the basic accounting identity:

Assets = Liabilities + Owners' equity

For RI, if we let the various assets, liabilities, and components of owners' equity be represented by the following symbols:

Cash and cash equivalents	CCE
Accounts receivable	A/R
Inventories	Invor
Prepaid expenses	Ppd
Capital assets—gross	CapAssets
Accumulated depreciation	AccumDep
Intangible assets	Intang
Wages payable	W/P
Accounts payable	A/P
Taxes payable	T/P
Deferred revenue	D/R
Debt—current portion	Debt/Curr
Deferred taxes	D/T
Debt	Debt
Preferred shares	PfdShs
Common shares	ComShs
Retained earnings	R/E

we have the following expanded version of the basic accounting equation:

CCE + A/R + Invor + Ppd + CapAssets - AccumDep + Intang = W/P + A/P + T/P + D/R + Debt/Curr + D/T + Debt + PfdShs + ComShs + R/E

If we let the symbol "Δ" signify "the change over the accounting period in" the various items, then we have the following:

ΔCCE + ΔA/R + ΔInvor + ΔPpd + ΔCapAssets - ΔAccumDep + ΔIntang = ΔW/P + ΔA/P + ΔT/P + ΔD/R + ΔDebt/Curr + ΔD/T + ΔDebt + ΔPfdShs + ΔComShs + ΔR/E

When we isolate the change in CCE on the left-hand side, we arrive at an expression — derived from the basic accounting equation — that helps explain what caused the change in CCE over an accounting period:

$$\Delta CCE = -\Delta A/R - \Delta Invor - \Delta Ppd - \Delta CapAssets + \Delta AccumDep - \Delta Intang + \Delta W/P + \Delta A/P + \Delta T/P + \Delta D/R + \Delta Debt/Curr + \Delta D/T + \Delta Debt + \Delta PfdShs + \Delta ComShs + \Delta R/E \quad [C]$$

Without explicitly mentioning it, this was the basis on which we prepared the SCFP for RI. Let's see how this works for RI for 1996: We'll set up a table, as in Exhibit 7–6, with the various "change" items from the right-hand side of equation [C] down the rows. The three columns represent the three components of ΔCCE (that is, CFO, CFI, and CFF). Since we're interested in these components, one of the things we must do as we analyse the effect of each change item on cash flow is decide which of the three classifications of cash flow the particular change item affects. Notice that some of the change items affect two cash flow categories; for example, "ΔIntang" in total was +$90,000 (recall the change in this account over 1996 from the balance sheets in Exhibit 7–3), which was the net of $10,000 to be added back to net income as a reconciling item to help travel toward CFO, and $100,000, which was an actual purchase of new intangible assets. In general, and not referring to the RI case, each change item could affect any or all of the three cash flow categories.

EXHIBIT 7–5
RI'S STATEMENT OF CHANGES IN FINANCIAL POSITION, OR CASH FLOW STATEMENT ($000s)

	1996	1995	1994
Operations			
Net income	435	400	200
add: depreciation	200	200	200
add: amortization	10	10	10
add: increase in deferred taxes	50	90	10
less: increase in prepaids	–15	–10	–50
less: increase in A/R	300	–400	–200
less: increase in inventory	–375	0	–300
add: increase in wages payable	0	0	100
add: increase in A/P	100	–100	200
add: increase in taxes payable	0	0	0
add: increase in deferred revenue	0	0	100
Other	0	0	0
Cash flow from operations:	**705**	**190**	**270**
Investing			
Net increase in capital assets	–200	0	–1000
Net increase in intangible assets	–100	0	–40
Cash flow from investing	**–300**	**0**	**–1040**
Financing			
Issue debt	–100	100	400
Issue common shares	150	10	470
Issue preferred shares	100	0	0
Dividends	–385	–250	0
Cash flow from financing	**–235**	**–140**	**870**
TOTAL CASH FLOW	170	50	100

EXHIBIT 7-6
EQUATION [C] AND RI's 1996 CASH FLOW ANALYSIS ($000s)

	ΔCFO	ΔCFI	ΔCFF
–ΔA/R	–(–300)		
–ΔInvor	–375		
–ΔPpd	–15		
–ΔCapAssets		–200	
+ΔAccumDep	+200		
–ΔIntang	+10	–100	
+ΔW/P	0		
+ΔA/P	+100		
+ΔT/P	+50		
+ΔD/R	+(–50)		
+ΔDebt/Curr			0
+ΔD/T	+50		
+ΔDebt			+(–100)
+ΔPfdShs			+100
+ΔComShs			+150
+ΔR/E	+435		+(–385)
	+705	–300	–235

Accounting and Business Decision D

(a) Prepare tables similar to that in Exhibit 7–6 for RI's 1995 and 1994 cash flows.
(b) Critically assess RI's cash flow and net income patterns.

Corel Corporation: Further Cash Flow Analysis

Be prepared to refer back again to Corel's consolidated SCFP in Appendix A of Chapter 6. We've already examined some aspects of these statements; now we're going to examine them a bit further, from a somewhat different perspective. This perspective draws from the work of two accounting educator/researchers, Kochanek and Norgaard,[4] who urged financial statement users to analyse CFO by taking a look at its components in the following way.

First, we use Corel's financial statement information to prepare the following table:

[4] Richard F. Kochanek and Corine T. Norgaard, "Analyzing the Components of Operating Cash Flow: The Charter Company," *Accounting Horizons*, March 1988, pp. 58–66.

Corel Corporation Year end, November 30		1989	1990	($000s) 1991	1992	1993
Net income from continuing operations	NICO	2,193	7,071	12,057	12,286	27,841
Cash provided by operations	CFO	-2,204	4,701	6,834	2,558	32,442
Working capital provided by operations	WCFO	2,518	7,878	13,790	16,871	38,074
Change in operating current assets — effect on cash	ChOCA	-7,075	-7,329	-8,205	-10,578	-26,065
Change in operating current liabilities — effect on cash	ChOCL	2,353	4,152	1,249	-3,735	20,433

Income from continuing operations and cash provided by operations are given in Corel's annual reports. The other numbers have been derived. "Working capital provided by operations" is equal to net income from continuing operations ($27,841,000 in 1993), plus depreciation and amortization ($8,578,000 in 1993), plus deferred income taxes ($1,655,000 in 1993), for a total of $38,074,000. This is the portion of the change (an increase, in this case) in working capital due to everyday operations (that is, excluding things such as the issue of common shares for cash). "Change in operating current assets" and "Change in operating current liabilities" were computed as seen in the chart at the bottom left, from Corel's consolidated SCFP (using 1993 as an example).

Change in operating current assets:	
Increase in accounts receivable	$20,511,000
Increase in inventory	4,855,000
Increase in prepaid expenses	699,000
Impact on cash flow in 1993	–$26,065,000

Change in operating current liabilities:	
Increase in accounts payable	$5,898,000
Increase in accrued liabilities	4,159,000
Increase in income taxes payable	10,376,000
Impact on cash flow in 1993	$20,433,000

Kochanek and Norgaard argue that changes in current operating assets and current operating liabilities should be examined in order to assess the ability of an organization to alter its short-term investment behaviour (operating assets) and short-term financing behaviour (operating liabilities) in response to rapidly changing business conditions. Corel experienced flat growth in net income from continuing operations from 1991 to 1992, in contrast to rapid growth in this number both before (in 1989 to 1991) and after (1992 to 1993) this period. What short-term response was Corel able to make in 1992, in response to hitting this plateau of earnings that year? Operating current assets *increased* by a record amount, using up cash of $10,578,000, while operating current liabilities *decreased*, using up further cash of $3,735,000. The total of these two numbers, $14,313,000, equals the difference between the working capital provided by operations of $16,871,000 and cash provided by operations of $2,558,000. Kochanek and Norgaard (p. 63) suggest that a company that is able to respond rapidly and flexibly to changing business conditions would display the opposite results:

The reduction in investments in operating current assets during a period of decreasing profits and the ability to generate increasing amounts of cash provided by operations can be interpreted as an indication of financial flexibility in response to changing economic conditions.

Accounting and Business Decision E

(a) Explain why Corel's 1992 results were opposite to what Kochanek and Norgaard would have preferred.
(b) Do you think Corel was in any danger in 1992, or was this merely a "blip"?

Using T-Accounts to Prepare the SCFP From Accrual Information

In this section, we will illustrate how T-accounts and journal entries may be used as analytical devices to help prepare an SCFP, or cash flow statement. The T-accounts we will be using do not represent formal accounts in the organization's general ledger, nor do the journal entries we will be deriving represent formal journal entries in the general journal: we are using these only as tools to help us prepare the cash flow statement. Now we will describe the hypothetical company we will use in our demonstration:

Office Equipment Inc. (OEI, for short) is a small company whose common shares are held by 31 members of the Relack family. OEI, which sells high-quality office furniture, was founded 20 years ago by Ms. S. Relack. She had the reputation among her relatives of being a sharp businesswoman, if occasionally a little idiosyncratic, so they pretty much left the business in her hands. Relack owned 40 percent of the shares up to the start of 1995. The remaining 60 percent were owned equally by each of the 30 relatives, and for them, the effort it would have taken to watch out for their individual 2% interests didn't seem worthwhile. In fact, they even thought that a shareholders' agreement would be too much bother.

Abruptly last month (January 1996), Ms. Relack sold her share of the company, resigned her position as CEO and also her position on the board of directors, and moved to a South Sea island. As one of the relatives exclaimed: "Why, she didn't even leave an e-mail address where she could be reached!" The remaining Relack cousins have asked you (a financial consultant who has met a few of the Relacks socially) to assess the financial condition of the company, before they begin their search for a new CEO. You have been provided with the information in Exhibit 7–7 for the most recent two fiscal years, and have decided to begin your analysis by preparing a cash flow statement.

EXHIBIT 7–7
OFFICE EQUIPMENT INC.
Balance Sheets and Other Information

	December 31 (Canadian $)	
	1995	1994
Cash	0	40,000
Accounts receivable	400,000	200,000
Inventory, at FIFO cost	600,000	250,000
Investments	10,000	110,000
Land	100,000	150,000
Buildings and equipment	1,000,000	1,060,000
Accumulated depreciation	(760,000)	(800,000)
Patents	10,000	15,000
	1,360,000	1,025,000
Accounts payable	160,000	80,000
Accrued wages	80,000	0
Notes payable	300,000	320,000
Common shares	600,000	500,000
Retained earnings	220,000	125,000
	1,360,000	1,025,000

For 1995:

- Net income was $250,000; there were no extraordinary gains or losses, and everything was accounted for as being due to operations.
- Issued $100,000 in common shares for notes payable; a major supplier had accepted the notes payable last year in lieu of payment.
- Land was sold for $70,000 cash.
- Depreciation expense of $20,000 was recorded.
- Depreciable capital assets that were fully depreciated were sold for $30,000.
- The "Investments" account consisted mainly of blue-chip common shares that provided a steady if unspectacular stream of dividend income to OEI over the years. They were sold for $75,000 just after the stock market went into a tailspin in July.
- Sales were $1,500,000, 10 percent higher than in 1994. The increase was attributable to Ms. Relack's new policy of granting extended credit terms of 18 months to selected customers. All of the $1,500,000 in sales was on account.

Step 1: Compute the total change in CCE for the year; this is the number we must "explain," and it acts as a check number for our calculations. For OEI, this amount is $(40,000).

Step 2: Set up T-accounts for CFO, CFI, and CFF, and also for each noncash account on the balance sheet. For each of these noncash T-accounts, compute the change that occurred over the year and enter it in the first line of the T-account; this is the number whose analysis will help determine how cash was generated or expended during the accounting period. These T-accounts are shown in Exhibit 7–8.

Step 3: Go through each one of these noncash T-accounts, and reconstruct journal entries to explain the changes in the specific accounts. While reconstructing the journal entries, keep on the lookout for items that reconcile net income to CFO. "Post" each journal entry's debits and credits to the appropriate T-account, as shown below.

Step 4: After completing your analysis of all the noncash T-accounts, ensure that each one balances; that is, ensure that all the debits and credits representing the changes net out to the change you computed in Step 2 for the particular account.

Step 5: Compute the net change in each CFO, CFI, and CFF T-account, and then check that their sum equals the original total change in CCE that you computed in Step 1.

EXHIBIT 7–8
T-ACCOUNT WORKSHEET

Cash Flow from Operations

Comment	Dr	Cr	Balance
1. Net income	250,000		
2. A/R increased		200,000	
3. Inventory increased		350,000	
4. Loss on investments	25,000		
5. Gain on land sale		20,000	
6. Gain on B&E sale		30,000	
7. Depreciation	20,000		
8. Amortization	5,000		
9. A/P increased	80,000		
10. Accrued wages increased	80,000		
TOTAL CFO			140,000 Cr

Cash Flow from Investing

Comment	Dr	Cr	Balance
4. Sell investments	75,000		
5. Sell land	70,000		
6. Sell B&E	30,000		
TOTAL CFI			175,000 Dr

Cash Flow from Financing

Comment	Dr	Cr	Balance
12. Issue notes	80,000		
13. Pay dividends		155,000	
TOTAL CFF			75,000 Cr

ΔA/R

Comment	Dr	Cr	Balance
change	200,000		
2.	200,000		

ΔInventory

Comment	Dr	Cr	Balance
change	350,000		
3.	350,000		

ΔInvestments

Comment	Dr	Cr	Balance
change		100,000	
4.		100,000	

ΔLand

Comment	Dr	Cr	Balance
change		50,000	
5.		50,000	

ΔBuilding & Equipment

Comment	Dr	Cr	Balance
change		60,000	
6.		60,000	

ΔAccumulated Depreciation

Comment	Dr	Cr	Balance
change	40,000		
6.	60,000		
7.		20,000	
Net change	40,000		

ΔPatents

Comment	Dr	Cr	Balance
change		5,000	
8.		5,000	

ΔAccounts Payable

Comment	Dr	Cr	Balance
change		80,000	
9.		80,000	

ΔAccrued Wages

Comment	Dr	Cr	Balance
change		80,000	
10.		80,000	

ΔNotes Payable

Comment	Dr	Cr	Balance
change	20,000		
11.	100,000		
12.		80,000	
Net change	20,000		

ΔCommon Shares

Comment	Dr	Cr	Balance
change		100,000	
11.		100,000	

ΔRetained Earnings

Comment	Dr	Cr	Balance
change		95,000	
1.		250,000	
13.	155,000		
Net change		95,000	

Reconstructed journal entries

The journal entries that portray the events that occurred and their impact on cash flows are as follows:

1. Begin reconciliation with net income:

Dr CFO	250,000	
Cr Retained earnings		250,000

2. Accounts receivable increased:

Dr A/R	200,000	
Cr CFO		200,000

3. Inventory increased:

Dr Inventory	350,000	
Cr CFO		350,000

4. Sell off long-term investments:

Dr CFI	75,000	
Dr CFO	25,000 [this reverses the accounting loss]	
Cr Investments		100,000

5. Sell off land:

Dr CFI	70,000	
Cr CFO		20,000 [this reverses the accounting gain]
Cr Land		50,000

6. Sell off building and equipment:

Dr CFI	30,000	
Dr Accumulated depreciation	60,000	
Cr Building and equipment		60,000
Cr CFO		30,000 [reverses accounting gain]

7. Depreciation expense is a reconciling item:

Dr CFO	20,000	
Cr Accumulated depreciation		20,000

8. Patent amortization is a reconciling item:

Dr CFO	5,000	
Cr Patents		5,000

9. Accounts payable increased:

Dr CFO	80,000	
Cr Accounts payable		80,000

10. Accrued wages increased:

Dr CFO	80,000	
Cr Accrued wages		80,000

11. Debt–equity swap:

Dr Noted payable	100,000	
Cr Common shares		100,000

12. Additional notes payable issued; deduced by "plugging" the amount needed to balance the account:

Dr CFF	80,000	
Cr Notes payable		80,000

13. Dividends paid out; deduced by "plugging" the amount needed to balance the account:

Dr Retained earnings	155,000	
Cr CFF		155,000

The completed SCFP is shown in Exhibit 7–9.

EXHIBIT 7–9
OFFICE EQUIPMENT INC.
Statement of Changes in Financial Position
Year Ended December 31, 1995

Operations:		
Net income	$250,000	
Loss on sale of investments	25,000	
Depreciation	20,000	
Amortization	5,000	
Gain on land sale	(20,000)	
Gain on buildings and equipment sale	(30,000)	
Change in working capital from operations	250,000	
Increase in accounts payable	80,000	
Increase in accrued wages	80,000	
Increase in accounts receivable	(200,000)	
Increase in inventories	(350,000)	
Net cash flow (used in) operations		(140,000)
Investing:		
Sale of long-term investments	75,000	
Sale of land	70,000	
Sale of building and equipment	30,000	
Net cash flow from investing activities		175,000
Financing:		
Issue notes payable	80,000	
Dividends	(155,000)	
Net cash flow from financing activities		(75,000)
Net cash flow		$(40,000)

There is one more important wrinkle that we have to point out in connection with OEI's SCFP. Recall Exhibit 7–6, in which we allocated all the changes in RI's balance sheet accounts *other than cash* to the three cash flow categories, CFO, CFI, and CFF. We do the same thing for OEI in Exhibit 7–10, but this time we have four categories: the previous three cash flow categories, plus one that represents the disclosure of important financing and investing transactions that do not affect cash flows. In the case of OEI, the transaction is the exchange by those who held OEI's notes payable for OEI common shares. Two other important noncash transactions (in general; they didn't occur in the OEI case) that might merit disclosure are these:

- The acquisition of capital assets in exchange for other capital assets.
- The acquisition of capital assets in exchange for debt (for example, a mortgage is assumed by a company to finance a building).

The SCFP for OEI in Exhibit 7–9 would be modified by the addition of the information about the noncash financing and investing activities, as the case may be, as illustrated for OEI in Exhibit 7–11.

EXHIBIT 7–10
MODIFIED EQUATION [C] AND OEI'S 1995 CASH FLOW ANALYSIS AND SCFP DISCLOSURE
($000s)

	Worksheet Entry	ΔCFO	ΔCFI	ΔCFF	Disclosure Item?	
–ΔA/R	2	–200				
–ΔInvor	3	–350				
–ΔInvestments	4	25	75			
–ΔLand	5	–20	70			
–ΔCapAssets	6	–30	30			
+ΔAccumDep	7	20				
–ΔIntang	8	5				
+ΔA/P	9	80				
+ΔAccWages	10	80				
+ΔNotesPayable	11				–100	Yes
	12			80		
+ΔComShs	11				100	Yes
+ΔR/E	1	250				
	13			–155		
		–140	175	–75		

EXHIBIT 7–11
OFFICE EQUIPMENT INC.
STATEMENT OF CHANGES IN FINANCIAL POSITION
Year Ended December 31, 1995

Operations:		
Net income	$250,000	
Loss on sale of investments	25,000	
Depreciation	20,000	
Amortization	5,000	
Gain on land sale	(20,000)	
Gain on buildings and equipment sale	(30,000)	
Change in working capital from operations	250,000	
Increase in accounts payable	80,000	
Increase in accrued wages	80,000	
Increase in accounts receivable	(200,000)	
Increase in inventories	(350,000)	
Net cash flow (used in) operations		(140,000)
Investing:		
Sale of long-term investments	75,000	
Sale of land	70,000	
Sale of building and equipment	30,000	
Net cash flow from investing activities		175,000
Financing:		
Issue notes payable	80,000	
Dividends	(155,000)	
Net cash flow from financing activities		(75,000)
Net cash flow		$(40,000)
Other financing activities:		
Exchange of notes payable for common stock		$100,000

The Quality of Earnings and Cash Flows: A Further Look at OEI

Now that we've prepared a cash flow statement for OEI, let's step more fully into the shoes of the consultant hired by the Relack relatives. We want to learn as much about the business and Ms. Relack's decisions as possible. Our assessment will be based on the two general questions that follow:

1. **"The accounting policies that management chooses may provide an insight into management's attitudes, philosophies, and so on. Critically evaluate the accounting policies used at OEI."**

Some comments on OEI's accounting policies:

- Depreciation is $20,000 per year, but building and equipment assets cost about $1,000,000; this implies a 50-year average service life. Doesn't this seem excessively long? So, is the $20,000 excessively understated, perhaps to inflate reported net income?
- Should the accounting gains on the sale of land and B&E, and the accounting loss on the sale of the investments, be classified as non-operating items? If "yes," then the net income number misstates sustainable income from continuing operations.
- Why is there apparently no allowance for doubtful accounts, especially since there is now a new, looser, credit-granting policy? Is this another overstatement of net income? Accounts receivable have increased by 100%, but sales are up by only 10%.
- Inventory has increased by $350,000, but sales are up by 10%. How saleable is the inventory on hand? What would a "lower of cost and market" approach to inventory valuation do in this case? A FIFO cost flow assumption is being used; is this inflating net income as well?
- Is the revenue recognition point for "selected" customers appropriate? Since they were granted extended credit terms, should we either delay revenue recognition, or at the very least account for possible sales returns?
- Why was no cash flow statement prepared and distributed to the owners?
- It seems that an audit was not performed. Why not?

Overall, the array of accounting policies chosen by Ms. Relack leads to serious questions about OEI's "quality of earnings." That is, how well does the income number, taking into consideration all the decisions that are behind it, represent the results of operations of the organization? Recall that CFO is $(140,000), while net income is $250,000. The accounting decisions behind OEI's net income, along with the highly negative CFO, strongly suggest that Ms. Relack was selecting accounting alternatives in an unethical manner, and that the quality of OEI's earnings is very poor indeed.

2. **"What management decisions made over the year are questionable?"**

Of course, we have just finished complaining quite loudly about Ms. Relack's accounting decisions, which are an important type of management decision. We now turn to the business decisions that were made:

- CFO was negative, CFI was positive, and CFF was negative. From Exhibit 7–2, this cash flow pattern (#7) is consistent with that of a downsizing company. Why were capital assets being sold off? To generate cash flow when operations were not doing so?
- Why were the blue-chip stocks sold off, especially just after the market declined? Another attempt to generate cash flow when operations were not?
- Was CFO overstated by the deferring of both accounts payable and (possibly) accrued wages?
- Why was the new credit policy adopted?
- Why was so much inventory purchased? Was there a link between Ms. Relack and certain suppliers? If so, were the prices OEI paid fair?
- Why was such a large dividend paid out, in relation to CFO and the change in CCE? This becomes especially troublesome if CFO was artificially overstated by the deferring of payments, and total cash flow by the

selling off of possibly productive capital assets.

- Why were some suppliers not paid last year? Apparently, they accepted notes payable in exchange for accounts payable. This year, they exchanged their notes payable for common shares, so that the Relacks' shareholding was diluted.

There are plenty of upsetting things to worry about in this short case. Perhaps the Relack relatives should think about hiring a lawyer. For our purposes, the case is a nice little illustration not only of the preparation of a cash flow statement, but also of how such an activity can provide some extra insight into an organization.

Accounting Principles Governing the Cash Flow Statement: Alternatives in Practice

The *CICA Handbook* section 1540, "Statement of Changes in Financial Position," provides the authoritative GAAP for cash flow statements in Canada. The material in this chapter illustrating the preparation of the SCFP is consistent with this section; however, the section permits management considerable discretion regarding the details in, format of, and disclosure required by the SCFP. For example, although the section requires that the components of CCE be disclosed, it does not significantly constrain the definition of CCE that a particular management may select.

Also, although the reconciliation approach for deriving CFO is used by the vast majority of companies (it is also called the *indirect* approach), a few companies use the *direct* approach, in which the actual operating cash inflows and operating cash outflows are disclosed. The direct approach doesn't confound the cash flow statement with accrual numbers; its disadvantage is that it does not disclose the items that account for the difference (if any) between an accounting entity's CFO and net income. Such disclosure may be useful in an assessment of an organization's quality of earnings.

Accounting and Business Decision F

Management is responsible for making numerous accounting measurement and disclosure decisions. Some decisions in connection with the SCFP are:

- How prominent should the cash flow statement be in relation to the accrual statements?
- How detailed should the statement be?
- How should CCE be defined?
- Should the direct or indirect approach be used in disclosing CFO?

In making each of these decisions, what might management be concerned about?

Cash Budgets

Another important type of cash flow report is the cash budget. This is a forecast, based on reasonable assumptions and negotiations among managers, of expected cash flows over a certain future time period. The report may be in the form of an SCFP, or in any other form that the manager or user finds useful. An example of a cash budget for a small business — a bed-and-breakfast operation called Leanne and Margo's — is shown in Exhibit 7–12. It provides some insight for the operators of the business about such things as when a short-term bank loan might be required. It shows that between February and May, the owners will need to draw from their personal savings or arrange for a loan.

Cash Budget Sensitivity Analysis: Electronic Spreadsheets

Since people make plans in the form of cash budgets, it is crucial to assess the sensitivity of such reports. What would happen, say, if Leanne and Margo were too optimistic about June room rentals, and they were only about 50% of normal (perhaps the weather might be bad)? Electronic spreadsheet modelling of cash budgets makes this a fairly standard management activity.

Project Cash Flow Forecasts

A special type of cash budget is the project cash flow forecast. One of these was prepared in the Gord and James case in Chapter 2. Since that time, we've seen that forecasting cash flows can get very complicated:

- Tax effects must be taken into account. For example, the new CCA created by capital asset expenditures for a proposed project will reduce income taxes, while the new taxable income generated by increased revenues will increase it.
- Most cash flows are uncertain, to a greater or lesser degree. We saw this with the controversy surrounding salvage value in the Gord and James case. Simulation using electronic spreadsheet models helps managers cope with such uncertainty. Uncertainty is reflected in the assumptions that managers must make about future product prices, sales volumes, and so on. Some of these assumptions may be backed up by considerable research, while others may be "informed guesstimates."

Once a project has been approved (recall in the Gord and James case that approval depended in part on the project's net present value), it becomes part of the organization's capital expenditure budget. Such a budget is similar to the one that Leanne and Margo prepared for their bed-and-breakfast business, except it contains information only about approved capital asset acquisitions.

EXHIBIT 7–12
LEANNE AND MARGO'S BED AND BREAKFAST
CASH FLOW BUDGET 1995

ITEM	JAN	FEB	MAR	APR	MAY	JUN	JUL	AUG	SEP	OCT	NOV	DEC	TOTAL
1 Room rentals	$ 0	$240	$320	$1,120	$1,680	$3,120	$3,120	$3,120	$3,120	$1,600	$880	$0	$18,320
2 Extra meals	0.00	30.00	45.00	90.00	112.00	125.00	125.00	125.00	125.00	45.00	45.00	0.00	867.00
3 Services	0.00	0.00	0.00	0.00	0.00	0.00	0.00	0.00	0.00	0.00	0.00	0.00	0.00
4 Other	0.00	0.00	0.00	0.00	0.00	0.00	0.00	0.00	0.00	0.00	0.00	0.00	0.00
5 Total cash receipts	0.00	270.00	365.00	1210.00	1792.00	3245.00	3245.00	3245.00	3245.00	1645.00	925.00	0.00	19187.00
6 Booking fees	0.00	7.20	9.60	33.60	50.40	93.60	93.60	93.60	93.60	48.00	26.40	0.00	549.60
7 Guest food	0.00	45.00	60.00	210.00	315.00	585.00	585.00	585.00	585.00	300.00	165.00	0.00	3435.00
8 Utilities	105.00	155.00	122.00	155.00	105.00	172.00	105.00	155.00	122.00	155.00	105.00	172.00	1628.00
9 Property taxes	0.00	0.00	324.00	0.00	0.00	324.00	0.00	0.00	324.00	0.00	0.00	324.00	1296.00
10 Mortgage interest	40.00	40.00	40.00	40.00	40.00	40.00	40.00	40.00	40.00	40.00	40.00	40.00	480.00
11 House repairs	30.00	30.00	30.00	30.00	30.00	30.00	30.00	30.00	30.00	30.00	30.00	30.00	360.00
12 House insurance	0.00	0.00	0.00	0.00	150.00	0.00	0.00	0.00	0.00	0.00	0.00	0.00	150.00
13 Bank charges	15.00	15.00	15.00	15.00	15.00	15.00	15.00	15.00	15.00	15.00	15.00	15.00	180.00
14 Office expense	30.00	30.00	30.00	30.00	30.00	30.00	30.00	30.00	30.00	30.00	30.00	30.00	360.00
15 Accounting and legal	0.00	0.00	180.00	0.00	0.00	0.00	0.00	0.00	0.00	0.00	0.00	0.00	180.00
16 Business insurance	0.00	0.00	0.00	0.00	100.00	0.00	0.00	0.00	0.00	0.00	0.00	0.00	100.00
17 Advertising	200.00	200.00	200.00	200.00	0.00	0.00	0.00	0.00	0.00	0.00	0.00	0.00	800.00
18 Agents listing fees	0.00	0.00	0.00	0.00	0.00	0.00	0.00	0.00	0.00	0.00	0.00	100.00	100.00
19 Licences	100.00	0.00	0.00	0.00	0.00	0.00	0.00	0.00	0.00	0.00	0.00	0.00	100.00
20 Loan repayments	250.00	250.00	250.00	250.00	250.00	250.00	250.00	250.00	250.00	250.00	250.00	250.00	3000.00
21 Other expenditures	0.00	0.00	0.00	0.00	0.00	0.00	0.00	0.00	0.00	0.00	0.00	0.00	0.00
22 Total expenditures	770.00	772.20	1260.60	963.60	1085.40	1539.60	1148.60	1198.60	1489.60	868.00	661.40	961.00	12718.60
23													
24 Monthly net cash flow	($770)	($502)	($896)	$246	$707	$1,705	$2,096	$2,046	$1,755	$777	$264	($961)	$6,468
25													
26 Cash at start of month	$1,000	$230	($272)	($1,168)	($921)	($215)	$1,491	$3,587	$5,633	$7,389	$8,166	$8,429	
27 Cash at end of month	$230	($272)	($1,168)	($921)	($215)	$1,491	$3,587	$5,633	$7,389	$8,166	$8,429	$7,468	

Accounting, Organizations, and Society

Two British accounting professors, Wallace and Collier, looked at how CCE is defined in different countries. The objective of their accounting research was:

> *to highlight the inadequacies of the definitions of cash provided by standard-setters and to determine how reporting enterprises use the standard-setters' definitions of cash in their [cash flow statements].*

Their article on this topic is excerpted below.

The "Cash" in Cash Flow Statements: A Multi-Country Comparison

by R. S. Olusegun Wallace and Paul A. Collier

Cash is a loose term with many different definitions. In strict legal sense, cash is legal tender which represents ready money in one's pocket or safe such as bank notes and coins acceptable as a medium of exchange. Traditionally, economists define cash (or money) as anything that combines the attributes of a medium of exchange, a store of value and a unit of account. This extends the legal definition to include other money such as balances in current and deposit accounts at a bank. As a business term, "cash" represents the medium of exchange in common and daily use for transactional, precautionary and speculative purposes. What people understand as cash may include (a) "narrow cash" which is money available for ordinary use in the form of legal tender such as coins, bank notes in one's wallet; (b) "broad cash" which includes negotiable instruments such as money orders, cheques, and accepted sight drafts and balances on demand and time deposits with banks and/or other financial institutions after deducting uncleared cheques and adding unpresented (but not likely to be dishonoured) cheques; and (c) "near cash" items (or cash equivalents) that fulfil the store of value function and are readily convertible into a medium of exchange but are not themselves narrow or broad cash. "Cash equivalents" can include marketable securities, the cash surrender value of life policies and treasury bills ...

Table 1 [shown on the following page] presents a comparative summary of the differences in the definitions of cash and cash equivalents in the pronouncements of [five countries and the International Accounting Standards Committee] ...

In reality, cash is not an objective construct ...

The cash spectrum

... The pronouncements ... cover several positions within the cash and cash equivalents definitional spectrum. Consider an enterprise with cash of 200 units, cash equivalents of 2,500 units, a bank overdraft of 500 units and other short-term borrowings of 300 units. The cash position could be as follows:

Possible Cash Positions

	1	2	3
Cash	200	200	200
Cash equivalents	2,500	2,500	2,500
Bank overdraft		(500)	(500)
Short-term borrowings			(300)
Reportable cash positions	2,700	2,200	1,900

Table 1
DIFFERENCES IN THE DEFINITION OF CASH AND CASH EQUIVALENTS

	Canada	New Zealand	U.S.	South Africa	U.K.	IASC
Treatment of cash and cash equivalents						
(a) net of short-term borrowings	x	x				
(b) net of short-term bank borrowings					x	
(c) gross			x*	x*		x
Treatment of equity securities as cash equivalents						
(a) specifically excluded		x				x+
(b) not specifically excluded	x		x	x	x	
Specific guidelines on maturity periods for cash equivalents						
(a) yes	x		x			x
(b) no		x		x	x	
Cash flow statement should disclose components of						
(a) cash and cash equivalents	x					x
(b) cash equivalents			x		x	
(c) no disclosure is required		x		x		

* netting is not mentioned
+ unless they are in substance cash equivalents

Position 1 is the stance of the U.S. and South African pronouncements. Position 2 is permissible under the U.K. pronouncement. Position 3 is presently acceptable in Canada and New Zealand ...

Survey of Annual Reports

The cash flow reporting practices in the annual accounts of 20 large non-financial listed companies, selected ... from each of [Canada, South Africa, the United States, and New Zealand] were examined ... The results reported in Tables 2 and 3 show considerable variation in the positions adopted along the spectrum ...

The positions taken by reporting companies do not necessarily adhere to the national pronouncements ...

The preceding analysis shows international as well as domestic differences ...

Table 2
DEFINITIONS OF CASH RESOURCES USED IN CASH FLOW STATEMENTS
(by country)

	Canada	New Zealand	U.S.A.	South Africa	Total
Cash	1	—	—	—	1
Cash and temporary or short-term cash investments	8	—	5	4	17
Cash and cash equivalents	2	11	12	7	32
Cash, short-term investments, and deposits less bank overdrafts	9	2	—	4	15
Cash and cash equivalents, less bank advances/overdrafts and notes payable	—	7	3	5	15
	20	20	20	20	80

Table 3
DEFINITIONS OF CASH RESOURCES USED IN CASH FLOW STATEMENTS
(by industry)

	Consumer Goods	Capital Goods	Basic Goods	Other	Total
Cash	1	—	—	—	1
Cash and temporary or short-term cash investments	10	3	2	2	17
Cash and cash equivalents	15	8	5	4	32
Cash, short-term investments, and deposits, less bank overdrafts	6	4	3	2	15
Cash and cash equivalents, less bank advances/overdrafts and notes payable	8	5	2	—	15
	40	20	12	8	80

Accounting Horizons, *December 1991, pp. 45–52.*

CHAPTER SUMMARY

The chapter focused on a variety of reports that accountants may construct that deal with "cash." We began with a description of how cash was disclosed on balance sheets, and then examined the bank reconciliation report. The relationship between cash and working capital was described, and the importance of management's monitoring of cash flows was emphasized. Next, the components of cash flow were discussed, and eight cash flow patterns were identified and described.

The preparation of cash flow statements using accrual accounting information was explained initially with an introductory example, and then with a more complex example using the T-account worksheet approach. The concept of quality of earnings was introduced and related to cash flow analysis. The chapter ended with a brief description of the GAAP regulating cash flow disclosures; a cash budget was outlined, and research was presented illustrating the international diversity of the misleadingly simple term "cash."

Suggested Answers to Accounting and Business Decisions

Decision A

(a) Regular bank reconciliations are one means of exerting control over the asset "cash," since the bank statement input to the reconciliation is prepared by an independent outside organization. Most companies except the very smallest have many bank accounts (a general account for each location, and also perhaps a payroll account); for them, preparing bank reconciliations for all the accounts is a part of regularly scheduled operating procedures. It is also a way of catching errors in cheques and deposits; further, it provides input for the journal entry that records bank service and other charges. If the usefulness of bank reconciliations as a control device is to be maximized, they shouldn't always be assigned to the same person.

(b) The $100.00 has already been credited to the boutique's "Cash" general ledger account. This was done when the cheque was issued. However, it has not yet been cashed by the recipient, and therefore does not appear as a debit on the September bank statement. Consequently, it is one of the items on the bank reconciliation that reconciles the September 30 cash balance according to the boutique's general ledger "Cash" account with the September 30 balance according to the bank statement.

(c) Preauthorized automatic cash transfers appear as debits on a bank statement, often with quite cryptic descriptions. Since they have been preauthorized, it's unlikely that they would appear as reconciling items on a bank rec because the authorizing company would most likely have already accounted for them as a credit to the "Cash" general ledger account. If the company hasn't yet done this, then the debit on the bank reconciliation might serve as input to a general journal entry recording the decrease in cash; but this reduces control, since the independent information on the bank statement is being used as a *source* of the entry and not to corroborate the entry. This becomes even more dangerous if either the bank or the payee company makes errors and sometimes "double-debits" the pre-authorized amounts.

Decision B

Assume that we're talking about a manufacturing business.

(a) Actions related to the management of the business:

- Improving product quality by, for example, purchasing higher-quality components and raw materials. Error rates and spoilage would decrease, as would product returns. The higher purchasing costs might be offset by lower levels of work in process and finished goods inventory, and by increased sales to more satisfied customers, so profits and cash flow might increase. The net impact on working capital would be hard to predict, since inventories would decrease but accounts receivable would increase (unless the more satisfied customers paid more quickly).
- Switching to a just-in-time inventory management system, so that components and raw materials were ordered and received from the company's supplier "just in time" as they were needed in the production process. Inventory levels would decrease, but so would accounts payable. Costs of storing inventory would decline, so profits and cash flow might increase.
- Hiring employees with skills and abilities better suited to the company's management approach. For example, employees who could adapt quickly and effectively to a just-in-time inventory management system might better help achieve the assumed benefits of JIT.

(b) Actions related to speeding up collections and slowing down payments:

- Speeding up collections of accounts receivable. This might improve cash flow and reduce working capital, but might be only a short-run benefit if customers became upset. Perhaps if implemented in combination with other changes, such as improving product quality, it might have long-run benefits.
- Slowing down payments. Again, in the short-run cash flows might improve and working capital might decrease, but there is a risk that suppliers might rebel against being treated as a continuing source of financing.

(c) Actions related to accounting choices:

- Switching from weighted average or FIFO inventory costing to LIFO. If costs were increasing, this would usually serve to reduce the inventory amount on the balance sheet, so working capital would decrease. But this change in accounting principles, if motivated solely by the desire to reduce working capital, is virtually unethical unless there are other compelling circumstances supporting such an action.
- Switching from an accounting policy of deferring prepaid expenses such as insurance premiums, to expensing them as incurred. This would reduce working capital, but would also breach the matching concept. As above, it must be justified on firmer grounds than financial expediency.

The message here is that suggestions, such as the one by Shawn Tully (see page 375) to reduce working capital to zero, must be evaluated on a costs-versus-benefits basis. Management actions related to the operations of the business and to the speeding up or slowing down of payments and collections can have unintended cash flow, profit, and other consequences. Also, focusing too narrowly on a single measure, such as working capital, can lead management to start managing the *measure* (by making switches in accounting policies) instead of the *business*.

Decision C

If someone asks you what a company's cash flow is for a particular time period, suggest that he or she be more precise. Corel noted several types of cash flows for 1993: its operating cash flow was +$32,442,000; its financing cash flow was +$21,380,000; its investing cash flow was -$27,937,000; and its total cash flow for 1993 was +$26,382,000. Notice that Corel also separated out "Effect of foreign currency translation on cash flow," which was zero in 1991 and 1992, but +$497,000 in 1993.

If Corel had defined CCE as just including cash, but no equivalents, its cash flow numbers would have been different. Corel's "Summary of Significant Accounting Policies" footnote reveals that short-term investments (the "equivalents" part of CCE in Corel's case) were $52,114,000 and $68,629,000, at the beginning and end respectively of the fiscal year ended November 31, 1993. Thus, they changed by +$16,515,000. But since total cash flow based on CCE was reported as +$26,382,000, this means that "just cash" changed by only +$9,867,000.

Decision D

(a)

For RI's 1994 cash flow analysis:

	ΔCFO	ΔCFI	ΔCFF
–ΔA/R	–200		
–ΔInvor	–300		
–ΔPpd	–50		
–ΔCapAssets		–1000	
+ΔAccumDep	+200		
–ΔIntang	+10	–40	
+ΔW/P	0		
+ΔA/P	+300		
+ΔT/P			
+ΔD/R	+100		
+ΔDebt/Curr			
+ΔD/T	+10		
+ΔDebt			+400
+ΔPfdShs			
+ΔComShs			+470
+ΔR/E	+200		
	+270	–1040	+870

For RI's 1995 cash flow analysis:

	ΔCFO	ΔCFI	ΔCFF
–ΔA/R	–400		
–ΔInvor			
–ΔPpd	–10		
–ΔCapAssets			
+ΔAccumDep	+200		
–ΔIntang	+10		
+ΔW/P	+100		
+ΔA/P	+(–200)		
+ΔT/P			
+ΔD/R			
+ΔDebt/Curr			
+ΔD/T	+90		
+ΔDebt			+100
+ΔPfdShs			
+ΔComShs			+10
+ΔR/E	+400		+(–250)
	+190	0	–140

(b) RI's net income is positive and increasing over the three-year interval, so this seems all right. The only caution is that the *rate* of increase has gone down, from (400-200)/200, or 100%, in 1994–95, to (435-400)/400, or 8.75%, in 1995–96. A more in-depth analysis would inquire into the causes of this decline. Perhaps it simply represents the levelling off of a dramatically high growth in earnings as the company's market matures. We won't go into a detailed analysis now, but perhaps when you've finished reading Chapter 8's discussion of financial statement analysis, you may want to for practice.

RI's pattern of cash flows has changed as follows:

	1996	1995	1994
CFO	+	+	+
CFI	–	n/a	–
CFF	–	–	+
TOTAL CF	+	+	+

CFO began positive in 1994, and remains so. In fact, from Exhibit 7–5 we can see that 1996's CFO is almost three times as large as 1994's. This growth in CFO seems like a very positive indicator. However, CFO did decline in 1995 from its 1994 level, even though net income did not. Could this indicate that CFO is excessively risky? Or perhaps the increase in accounts receivable and the decrease in accounts payable in 1995 was just a one-time phenomenon.

The pattern of the algebraic signs for the CFO, CFI, and CFF cash flows in 1994 is pattern 4 in Exhibit 7–2; this suggests a healthy, growing company. As of 1996, the pattern has changed to pattern 2, which suggests a mature, successful company. In 1996 the company is still issuing new equity, but is paying out dividends in excess of this new equity. Also, it is reducing its debt. The negative CFI and CFF are able to be financed by the very significantly positive CFO.

Decision E

(a) The main factor behind the increase in Corel's operating current assets in 1992 (which used up cash) was the increase in accounts receivable of $12,607,000. The main factor behind the decrease in Corel's operating current liabilities in 1992 (which also used up cash) was the decrease in income taxes payable/recoverable. Corel's gross profit percentage went down from 1991's 84% to 71% in 1992. Sales increased by 72.5%, but gross profit was negatively impacted by a large increase in advertising expenses; this kept income at about 1991 levels, and resulted in a significant decline in CFO. Perhaps in order to keep its dealer distribution channels and market share, Corel wasn't able to speed up its collections.

Going by Kochanek and Norgaard, it might have been better if Corel had been able to react quickly to its 1992 gross profit, expense, and cash flow problems by requiring its customers to remit cash faster. But either Corel couldn't do so and keep its customers, or it chose not to do so as part of a longer-term strategy of maintaining customer relationships, and perhaps helping those customers who had their own cash flow problems.

(b) This was, apparently, a "blip," since 1993 showed not only a dramatic increase in net income, but also a rebound in gross profit percentage to 77%. One result was the very positive CFO in 1993. But what if the gross profit percentage had not improved in 1993? The increase of six percentage points in gross profit percentage over 1992's results provided an additional 6% × $140,223,000, or $8.4 million in gross profit (where the $140,223,000 is the 1993 sales number). The increase in accounts payable, accrued liabilities, and income taxes payable provided about $20 million, so perhaps Corel was more capable of "matching" its operating cash inflows and outflows in 1993 than it was in 1992.

Decision F

- How prominent should the cash flow statement be in relation to the accrual statements?

Management might hope for both types of accounting statements, since they provide equally important information, to be treated with equal prominence. However, sometimes real-life pressures interfere with normative ideals, and one or the other type might be downplayed. For example, when the multinational manufacturing company Varity Corporation was having little success in producing accrual earnings, management urged readers of the company's financial statements to use cash flow to judge the company's progress.

- How detailed should the statement be?

We saw that Corel's SCFP was not detailed enough for us to reconstruct its investing cash flows. This is neither "bad" nor "good"; it merely illustrates that decisions to disclose more than the minimum required by GAAP (if GAAP "rules") are trade-offs. Excessive disclosure may overwhelm the (mythical?) average reader; but avid users of financial statements, and certainly professional analysts, will thrive on it. Excessive disclosure may also give the impression that each disclosed item is of equal importance, when this is not the case.

- How should CCE be defined?

The "Accounting, Organizations, and Society" excerpt in this chapter demonstrated that "cash" is not as objective and straightforward a concept as might be thought, and that accounting standards-setters in different countries have defined it differently for financial reporting purposes. Perhaps full and fair disclosure is the key here; this would mean informing the user that alternative definitions of CCE are possible.

- Should the direct or indirect approach be used in disclosing CFO?

The direct approach has this benefit: it discloses the actual operating cash inflows and operating cash outflows of the company for the accounting period. It is less confusing than the indirect approach, since it doesn't confound cash flow presentations with a reconciliation between accrual income and CFO. However, it does have drawbacks, in that the resulting SCFP no longer ties in, or "articulates," with the income statement, and useful information that might assist the user in forming a judgment about the company's quality of earnings is not explicitly provided. It may be that *both* approaches should be used.

KEY TERMS

Bank reconciliation is a specific type of **reconciliation statement**. The latter is defined in the CICA's *Terminology for Accountants* as follows:

Any statement that accounts for the differences between two related records, e.g., the statement drawn up to account for the difference between a bank balance as reflected in the books of the bank and the balance of the same account as reflected in the books of the bank's customer.

Therefore, a bank reconciliation is a report (called a "statement" in the above CICA definition) that accounts for the differences between an accounting entity's own record of cash in its general ledger account and the bank's record of the entity's cash as it appears in the bank statement.

Bank statement is a statement or record prepared and issued by an accounting entity's bank or other financial institution, such as a trust company, that sets out the opening balance, and specific increases and decreases, in the accounting entity's cash on deposit at the financial institution, *from the perspective of the financial institution.*

Cash is defined in *Terminology for Accountants* as "coin, bank notes, money orders, cheques ... and (by extension) the balances in respect of demand and savings deposits at banks or other financial institutions." This definition is broader than a general dictionary definition, which is "Ready money; currency or coins,"[5] which is probably closer to the everyday meaning of the word.

Cash and cash equivalents (CCE) includes cash as defined by accountants, as above, plus assets — such as readily marketable investments in common shares — that are both low in risk and disposable for cash on short notice. Users of financial statements must make sure they know what cash equivalents an accounting entity has included in its CCE.

Cash budget is a forecast, based upon reasonable assumptions, of an accounting entity's expected cash inflows (or cash receipts) and expected cash outflows (or cash payments or disbursements), over a specific period of time.

Cash flow is defined in *Terminology for Accountants* as the "net change in cash position during a period." It is also referred to as **net cash flow**. The phrase "cash flow" could also be used to refer to specific cash inflows or outflows, so practice caution when you come across this term.

Cash flow pattern, as used in this book, refers to the particular pattern of cash flow from operations (positive or negative), cash flow from investing activities (positive or negative), and cash flow from financing activities (positive or negative), that is displayed by an accounting entity for a specific accounting period. Since three types of cash flows are involved, and each type may be either positive or negative (ignoring the case of zero cash flows), there are eight possible cash flow patterns.

Cash flow statement, also called a **statement of changes in financial position**, is a formal financial statement that discloses the details of operating, investing, and financing cash flows for an accounting entity, for a period. The statement is a reconciliation statement, since it enables users to reconcile the accounting entity's opening and closing CCE balances.

Cash flows from financing activities. See **financing cash flows.**

Cash flows from investing activities. See **investing cash flows.**

Cash flows from operating activities. See **operating cash flows.**

Financing cash flows, also called **cash flows from financing activities**, are cash inflows and outflows of an accounting entity that arise from financing activities, such as the receipt of cash when common shares are issued.

Investing cash flows, also called **cash flows from investing activities**, are cash inflows and outflows of an accounting entity that arise from investing activities, such as the payment (or disbursement) of cash upon the acquisition of a capital asset such as a building.

Operating cash flows, also called **cash flows from operating activities**, are cash inflows and outflows of an accounting entity that arise from operating activities, such as the receipt of cash in respect of a customer's payment of an accounting entity's accounts receivable recorded when the entity's product was sold.

Presentment refers to charges made by a bank or other financial institution to a customer when that customer has issued a cheque for which there are insufficient funds in the customer's bank account. Also referred to as an **NSF charge**, since there are "not sufficient funds" in the bank account.

[5] *The Houghton Mifflin Dictionary of the English Language*, p. 208.

Quality of earnings refers to a judgment assessing the degree that an accounting entity's income number, taking into consideration all the decisions that are behind it, represents the results of operations of the entity. Organizations that adopt "liberal" accounting policies, such as recognizing revenue before the revenue recognition criteria are reasonably fulfilled, are said to have low-quality earnings, all other things being equal.

Reconstructed journal entry is a journal entry that a user of financial statements has deduced by analysing the statements and any related footnotes. Such entries are not formal journal entries that record transactions and adjustment information (see Chapter 3); but in the context of this chapter, they are useful tools for preparing cash flow statements.

Statement of changes in financial position (SCFP). See **cash flow statement**.

Working capital is the excess of current assets over current liabilities of an accounting entity, both measured at the same point in time.

Working capital cycle, also called **operating cycle**, is the time interval between the acquisition of raw materials or merchandise and the receipt of cash from the sale of the organization's product.

Worksheet T-account is a T-account that can assist a user of accounting information in understanding the inflows and outflows through a specific account or group of accounts. It should be distinguished from the T-accounts used in Chapter 3, which represented an accounting entity's formal general-ledger accounts. In this chapter, worksheet T-accounts were used to help prepare a cash flow statement.

FACT AND DESCRIPTION QUESTIONS

1. (a) What are cash equivalents, and why are they included in CCE for purposes of preparing an SCFP and a balance sheet?
   (b) Are cash equivalents used in preparing a bank reconciliation?

2. Describe what a bank statement is, who prepares it, and how it is related to a bank reconciliation.

3. (a) Describe operating cash flow, and explain how it differs from net income from operations.
   (b) Suppose that Bingo Company pays out $1,000,000 in interest expense in 1996. The journal entry to account for this is:

Dr Interest expense (I)	1,000,000	
Cr Cash (B)		1,000,000

   If an SCFP is being prepared using the direct method (in which the actual cash sales and cash expenditures are disclosed), will this amount appear as an operating cash outflow?

4. On SCFPs, why are cash flows classified into three categories?

5. Why is the operating portion of an SCFP prepared according to the indirect method really a reconciliation? Is it a bank reconciliation?

6. Explain how cash flow information might be useful for managers in planning. And in discharging, at least in part, their accountability.

7. (a) Explain the difference between reconstructed worksheet entries and formal journal entries.
   (b) Explain the difference between worksheet T-accounts and general ledger accounts.

8. Explain why the following items may be reconciling items in an SCFP:
   (a) depreciation
   (b) amortization

(c) deferred income taxes
(d) unearned revenue

9. (a) Explain why a company's purchases of inventory may often not be equal to its payments to the suppliers of the inventory.

(b) Explain Kochanek and Norgaard's concept of "financial flexibility." What are its strengths and weaknesses?

10. Describe the concept of "quality of earnings," and why it is useful.

Questions for Analysis and Discussion

11. Agra Industries Limited is an international company, headquartered in Canada, that provides management and engineering services in industries ranging from oil and gas pipelines to hazardous materials handling. It employs more than 5,000 people in over 140 offices in 17 countries. Revenues for the fiscal year ended July 31, 1993, were over $593 million. Agra's consolidated statements of cash flow for 1993 and 1992 are presented below. The increase in cash in 1993 was significantly lower than in 1992. Explain why.

Consolidated Statement of Changes in Cash

For the year ended July 31, 1993 (in thousands of dollars)	1993	1992
Cash Provided By (Used in) Operating Activities		
Earnings (loss) from continuing operations	$7,928	(931)
Items not affecting cash flow	4,540	20,505
Changes in non-cash working capital		
Accounts receivable	(18,336)	(11,056)
Contracts in progress and inventory	(4,809)	11,139
Prepaid expenses	(73)	(463)
Accounts payable	19,378	5,800
Income taxes recoverable	8,775	(5,281)
	17,403	19,713
Discontinued operations	(8,102)	(5,079)
	9,301	14,634
Investing Activities		
Purchase of fixed assets	(16,482)	(12,326)
Proceeds on disposal of fixed assets	2,224	2,283
Investment in non-consolidated entities	(1,707)	(1,486)
Increase in other investments	(5,367)	—
Net proceeds from condominium projects	46	5,355
Acquisition of subsidiary operations	(1,411)	(39,113)
Proceeds from investments	35,714	585
	13,017	(44,702)

(continued...)

Financing Activities		
Proceeds from debenture issue	—	40,000
Proceeds from other long-term debt	42,910	41,468
Deferred financing charges	(298)	(3,037)
Retirement of long-term debt	(55,365)	(23,844)
Issue and redemption of share capital	108	506
	(12,645)	55,093
Payment of Dividends		
By the Company	(2,768)	(2,753)
By subsidiaries to minority shareholders	(500)	—
	(3,268)	(2,753)
Increase in Cash	6,405	22,272
Cash Position, Beginning of Year	5,652	(16,620)
Cash Position, End of Year	$12,057	5,652
Represented By:		
Cash and short-term investments	42,201	38,063
Bank indebtedness	(30,144)	(32,411)
	$12,057	5,652

12. Contrans Corp. is a publicly traded company listed on the TSE. Its operating subsidiary, Laidlaw Carriers, Inc., is one of largest truck load carriers based in Ontario. In 1992, revenues were over $62 million. The company's consolidated SCFPs for 1991 and 1992, along with footnotes 9, 10, and 11 of the 1992 financial statements, are presented next. Explain, to the best of your ability, each line item in the SCFPs.

Consolidated Statements of Changes in Financial Position
(000s omitted)

Year Ended August 31	1992	1991
Operating Activities		
Loss before discontinued operations	$ (1,652)	$(20,820)
Items not affecting cash:		
Depreciation and amortization	4,656	5,894
Deferred income taxes	(1,429)	(1,952)
Other expenses (Note 10)	901	17,871
Other	89	(173)
Working capital provided from operations	2,565	820
Prior period adjustment (Note 9)	—	(1,524)

Decrease in non-cash working capital balance relating to operations	4,905	588
Net Cash provided by (used in) continuing operations	7,470	(116)
Net Cash provided by (used in) discontinued operations	1,504	(555)
Net Cash provided by (used in) Operating Activities	8,974	(671)
Investing Activities		
Proceeds from sale of fixed assets	2,282	2,246
Purchase of fixed assets	(60)	(1,348)
Reclassification between fixed assets and inventory	426	(1,095)
Decrease in long-term receivables and investments	23	216
Net Cash provided by (used in) Investing Activities	2,671	19
Financing Activities		
Proceeds of long-term debt	4,591	4,679
Repayment of long-term debt	(7,473)	(7,581)
Net Cash used in Financing Activities	(2,882)	(2,902)
Increase (decrease) in Net Cash	8,763	(3,554)
Bank Indebtedness—Beginning of Year	(10,858)	(7,304)
Bank Indebtedness—End of Year	$ (2,095)	$(10,858)

The accompanying notes are an integral part of these statements.

9. **Prior Period Adjustment** *(000's omitted)*
   a) In 1992 management concluded that its objection to a Revenue Canada reassessment relating to prior years could not be negotiated without proceeding to litigation. Management felt it was appropriate to reflect the financial impact of the reassessment for the period reassessed and the impact these items have on subsequent periods, retroactively. The Company's deficit for periods prior to 1992 was increased in the amount of $1,654,000. Of this amount, $130,000 is applicable to fiscal 1991 and was charged to income for that year. The remaining $1,524,000 is applicable to years prior to 1991 and the balance of the opening deficit for 1991 was increased accordingly.
   b) As a result of audits conducted by Retail Sales Tax and the Worker's Compensation Board, the Company's deficit for periods prior to 1991 was increased in the amount of $400,000. Of this amount $50,000 is applicable to fiscal 1990 and was charged to income for that year. The remaining $350,000 is applicable to years prior to 1990 and the balance of the opening deficit for 1990 was increased accordingly.

10. **Other Expenses** *(000's omitted)*

Year Ended August 31	1992	1991
Write-off of goodwill relating to trucking operations	$ —	$17,871
Loss on long-term receivables under independent contractor truck program	590	423
Write-down of equipment	901	—
Other	119	404
	$1,610	$18,698

a) During 1992 management reviewed the estimated useful life of the Company's fixed assets and determined that a write-down would be appropriate in the amount of $901,000.

b) Management determined that there was a permanent impairment in the value of goodwill originally acquired on the purchase of trucking businesses. The Board of Directors therefore approved a write-off of goodwill as at August 31, 1991.

11. Discontinued Operations *(000's omitted)*

On August 31, 1992, management adopted a formal plan to sell the New Products Division. The disposition of this operation is expected to be substantially complete by February 28, 1993.

The results of discontinued operations are summarized below:

	1992	1991
Revenue	$6,847	$ 9,884
Loss from operations prior to measurement date of August 31, 1992	1,439	447
Recovery of income taxes	(637)	(198)
	802	249
Provision for loss on disposal and results of operations subsequent to measurement date of August 31, 1992	795	—
Recovery on income taxes	(257)	—
	538	—
Loss from discontinued operations, net of related income taxes	$1,340	$249

Reported results from discontinued operations include an allocation of interest expense.

The net assets of the discontinued operations are detailed as follows:

	1992	*1991*
Working capital	$ 407	$ 1,888
Long-term receivables	90	734
Fixed assets, net	1,051	2,768
Deferred income taxes	1,045	196
	$2,593	$5,586

The net assets are being carried at the lower of their existing net book value and estimated net realizable value.

13. Mitsui & Co., Ltd., is a Japanese-based global company engaged in activities ranging from iron and steel to foodstuffs. 1991 revenues exceeded the equivalent of $147 billion U.S. dollars. Mitsui's 1991, 1990, and 1989 statements of consolidated cash flows are presented below. Describe, to the best of your ability, Mitsui's broad financing and investing strategies.

Mitsui & Co. Ltd. and Subsidiaries
For the Years Ended March 31, 1991, 1990, and 1989

	Millions of Yen			Translation into Thousands of United States Dollars
	1991	1990	1989	1991
Cash Flows from Operating Activities:				
Net income	¥ 40,990	¥ 36,414	¥ 40, 338	$ 290,709
Adjustments to reconcile net income to net cash provided by (used in) operating activities:				
Depreciation and amortization	46,958	40,643	31,340	333,035
Provision for doubtful receivables	12,092	8,835	9,542	85,759
Provision for estimated losses on foreign investment	43,905	36,583	1,533	311,383
Equity in earnings of associated companies – net	(8,559)	(3,241)	(893)	(60,702)
Deferred income taxes	2,730	21,826	11,585	19,362
Profit on sale of investment securities – net	(21,981)	(23,142)	(12,411)	(155,894)
(Profit) loss on property and equipment – net	(22,340)	(6,115)	195	(158,440)
Provision for pension and severance indemnities	5,239	6,215	5,473	37,156
(Increase) decrease in marketable securities	11,548	(24,300)	(2,750)	81,901
Increase in trade receivables	(222,921)	(402,830)	(249,935)	(1,581,000)
Increase (decrease) in inventories	59,166	(89,041)	(24,350)	419,617
Increase in trade payables	224,159	224,186	217,399	1,589,780
Increase (decrease) in agency accounts	(25,869)	460,800	—	(183,468)
Other—net	67,645	(268,904)	(22,878)	479,752
Net cash provided by operating activities	212,762	17,929	4,188	1,508,950
Cash Flows from Investing Activities:				
Net (increase) decrease in other time deposits	27,423	(976,601)	—	194,489
Investments in and advances to associated companies	(47,872)	(20,407)	(35,526)	(339,518)
Collection of advances to associated companies	2,796	1,986	9,219	19,830
Acquisition of other investments	(378,002)	(294,556)	(172,480)	(2,680,865)
Proceeds from sale of investments	252,614	84,462	55,981	1,791,589
Increase in long-term loan receivables	(121,885)	(145,869)	(104,325)	(864,433)

Collection of long-term loan receivables	41,793	42,852	64,863	296,404
Additions to property leased to others, and property and equipment	(138,693)	(97,068)	(109,118)	(983,638)
Proceeds from sale of property leased to others, and property and equipment	36,965	20,634	18,899	262,163
Net cash used in investing activities	(324,861)	(1,384,567)	(272,487)	(2,303,979)
Cash Flows from Financing Activities:				
Net increase (decrease) in short-term borrowings	(261,905)	1,381,694	535,396	(1,857,482)
Incurrence of long-term debt	719,205	1,160,055	554,613	5,100,744
Reduction of long-term debt. other than conversion of convertible bonds and notes	(296,944)	(465,758)	(344,606)	(2,105,986)
Issuance of common stock in public offering	—	118,400	—	—
Issuance of common stock upon exercise of warrants	4,497	4,383	32,697	31,894
Net proceeds ascribed to warrants	—	—	19,216	—
Payment of cash dividends	(10,753)	(8,262)	(6,347)	(76,262)
Net cash provided by financing activities	154,100	2,190,512	790,969	1,092,908
Effect of Exchange Rate Changes on Cash and Cash Equivalents	(96,779)	13,252	(10,431)	(686,376)
Net Increase (Decrease) in Cash and Cash Equivalents	(54,778)	837,126	512,239	(388,497)
Cash and Cash Equivalents at Beginning of Year	1,967,361	1,130,235	617,996	13,952,915
Cash and Cash Equivalents at End of Year	¥1,912,583	¥1,967,361	¥1,130,235	$13,564,418
Cash paid during the year for:				
Interest	¥453,332	¥314,861	¥216,662	$3,215,121
Income taxes	41,791	58,703	44,376	296,390
Non-cash investing and financing activities:				
Conversion of convertible bonds and notes 3 into common stock	4,621	46,528	9,324	32,77

14. In an effort to increase cash flow and earnings, many companies are striving to reduce working capital. A measure suggested to track the progress of this effort is "working capital per sales dollar." Following is a sample of knowledge companies and their working capital per sales dollar for a recent year:

Company	Sales ($000s)	Working Capital ($000s)	Working Capital per Sales Dollar
Microsoft: a large, U.S.-based multinational; well known for "Windows" and related products	$3,753,000	$2,287,000	61 cents
Intera Information Technologies: a Calgary-based software development company focusing on the resource sector	$73,702	$5,422	7 cents
Knowledge House: a Halifax-based developer of interactive medical education software	$1,018	$787	77 cents

(a) The three companies range from the very large to the very small. Does size have anything to do with the adequacy of this measure?
(b) Can this measure be manipulated?
(c) Is it possible for this measure to show "improvement," even while cash flow is deteriorating?
(d) Are there any ethical implications to setting a zero or negative objective for working capital? *Fortune* published the following letter in its issue of October 3, 1994:

NEGATIVE WORKING CAPITAL
I am surprised that you recommend a negative working capital as something to be proud of ("Raiding a Company's Hidden Cash," August 22). Negative working capital can only mean that the business is conducted at the expense of the suppliers by stretching payments beyond the terms agreed to. When receivables are less than payables ... there is no way bills can be paid on time. That is certainly nothing to be proud of, and outright dangerous for small business.

CARL E. ROSENFELD
Senior Vice-President, Walter W. Cribbins Co.
San Francisco

15. Explain how the following ideas are related to information about cash and cash flows:
    - accountability
    - accounting entity
    - user orientation
    - classification

16. Suppose that a labour arbitrator is assigned to decide how much of a wage increase a company must pay. Before deciding on the actual amount of the increase, the arbitrator must first decide which financial measures, if any, provide a reasonable indication of the employing company's ability to pay. The union plans to argue that cash flow provides the best measure, while management will argue that net income does.

(a) Adopt the role of a member of the union negotiating team, and draft a submission to the labour arbitrator about the superiority of cash flow as a measure of ability to pay.
(b) Adopt the role of a member of the management negotiating team, and draft a submission to the labour arbitrator about the superiority of net income as a measure of ability to pay.
(c) Adopt the role of the labour arbitrator, and decide (with reasons) whether either of the submissions is convincing.

17. Morton Lachance owns 100 lottery and fresh fruit kiosks across the city. He carefully investigates the background of the people he hires to operate each of the kiosks, and requires them to remit a $1,000 security deposit with him on the day they begin work. They are paid a relatively low base monthly salary and receive a monthly bonus equal to 10% of the previous month's total sales of fresh fruit. Each kiosk operator is responsible for ordering fresh fruit from local suppliers, and for hiring any relief workers. Turnover of personnel is high, with 20 or 30 operators leaving each month, most after working for just a couple of months. "The lottery ticket business and the fresh fruit business have a lot in common," according to Morton. "They're both cash businesses, and the products have a short shelf life, and it's not that easy to track them down when they're stolen."

Required:

Morton can't be in 100 different places at once, so he needs a good system of internal control to ensure that all cash received for both lottery sales and fresh fruit sales is ultimately transferred to him, and that his inventory (lottery tickets and fresh fruit) — which is in 100 different locations — doesn't "shrink."

(a) Suggest some accounting and management systems that might be of use to Morton.
(b) Morton doesn't own the kiosk operations directly; rather, he owns 100% of the common shares of Mort's, Inc., the legal entity that in turn owns and operates the kiosks. How should Mort's account for the cash flows from the security deposits? How would these cash flows be shown on Mort's SCFP? Even though you don't know much about the financial results of Mort's, prepare an SCFP, using X's to represent the unknown numbers.

18. Up until the mid-1980s, most published SCFPs were prepared on a working capital basis. The statements disclosed the following:

- Change in working capital from operations.
- Change in working capital from investing activities.
- Change in working capital from financing activities.
- Total change in working capital.

Suggest why SCFPs are now prepared on a cash flow basis rather than a working capital basis.

19. "The eight patterns of cash flows in Exhibit 7–2 might provide a useful overview of a company's situation, but they mask detail, and that could be misleading." Comments?

20. For this question, refer to this chapter's "Accounting, Organizations, and Society" article.

(a) Examine a sample (say, ten) of published financial statements. What definition of cash is used by each organization?

(b) What impact (if any) does altering the definition of cash have on the financial statements?

TECHNICAL QUESTIONS

21. Saga Ventures Inc. manufactures customized fibreglass boat shells. The company began operations early in January 1994. Based upon the following balance sheet and income statement information, prepare SCFPs for Saga for 1994, 1995, and 1996. Comment on the company's cash flow experience.

Balance Sheets:
December 31 ($000s)

	1996	1995	1994
Cash and cash equivalents	640	300	200
Accounts receivable	600	1,200	400
Inventories	1,350	600	600
Prepaid expenses	150	120	100
Capital assets — gross	2,400	2,000	2,000
Accumulated depreciation	–1,200	–800	–400
Intangible assets	220	40	60
Total Assets	4,160	3,460	2,960
Wages payable	200	200	0
Accounts payable	400	200	600
Taxes payable	100	0	0
Deferred revenue	100	200	200
Debt — current portion	200	200	200
Deferred taxes	300	200	20
Debt	600	800	600
Common shares	1,260	960	940
Preferred shares	200	0	0
Retained earnings	800	700	400
Total liabilities and owner's equity	4,160	3,460	2,960

Selected income statement information:

- Depreciation each year was $400,000.
- Amortization each year was $20,000.

22. Newberry Sales Incorporated buys and sells used office equipment. On March 5, 1997, Newberry's accountant received the company's February bank statement, shown below. At the beginning of the month, both the bank statement and the company's cash accounting records were in agreement, except for $35.12 in bank charges not yet recorded in the accounts but shown on the January bank statement. Using information in the February bank statement and also in the company's records of cheques disbursed, the accountant prepared the following:

Cheques Issued	**Amount**	**Cheque Cashed?**
#150 Apex Supplies	140.00	Y
#151 Simplon Ltd	53.01	Y
#152 Apex Supplies	429.39	Y
#153 Wilson's Office Supplies	111.44	Y
#154 Mitchell's Inc	222.30	N
#155 Chang Inc	350.00	Y
#156 Simplon Ltd	100.05	N
#157 Franco Inc	90.90	N
#158 Apex Supplies	31.49	Y, but twice?
#159 Change Inc	17.63	N
#160 Apex Supplies	125.89	N
#161 Cyril Long	76.29	Y
#162 T. E. Smith Ltd	39.95	N
#163 Consumers Sales Inc	6,267.00	Y
#164 Charles Riley	40.00	Y
#165 Fred Leung	594.97	Y
#166 Myron Lystak	261.58	Y
#167 Mitchell's Inc	50.00	Y
#168 Chang Inc	400.00	Y
#169 Apex Supplies	310.98	N
#170 P. Jones	90.35	N

The accountant also noted that a deposit of $1,205.75 made on February 25 did not appear on the bank statement. When she phoned the bank, she was told that it would appear on the March statement.

bestBank Inc Branch No. 12; Account No. 1234-56789

Description	Debits	Credits	Date	Balance
Balance forward-FEB01/97			FEB01	3,500.25
CHQ#158	31.49		FEB05	3,468.76
CHQ#164	40.00		FEB06	3,428.76
CHQ#161	76.29		FEB06	3,352.47
CHQ#150	140.00		FEB06	3,212.47
CHQ#155	350.00		FEB11	2,862.47
CHQ#151	53.01		FEB12	2,809.46
CHQ#152	429.39		FEB12	2,380.07
CHQ#158	31.49		FEB12	2,348.58
Deposit		750.00	FEB13	3,098.58
CHQ#153	111.44		FEB14	2,987.14
Monthly deposit		5,556.70	FEB18	8,543.84
CHQ#165	594.97		FEB19	7,948.87
CHQ#163	6,267.00		FEB22	1,681.87
CHQ#166	261.58		FEB26	1,420.29
CHQ#167	50.00		FEB26	1,370.29
CHQ#168	400.00		FEB26	970.29
Bank service charges	23.95		FEB28	946.34

Required:

(a) How did the accountant know whether cheques had been cashed?

(b) Prepare a bank reconciliation as of February 28, 1997.

CASE

NewTech Inc.[6]

Fazia Jones had been an engineer with a large multinational for over ten years when she was "de-hired" during the economywide corporate downsizing of the mid-1990s. A creative person who had always had an entrepreneurial flair, Jones didn't let the grass grow under her feet, and within months had established NewTech Inc., a company devoted to profiting from innovations in niche areas related to communications technology.

Her strategy was this: intensively research the need for a new product; make it usable (that is, as easy and convenient as possible for the product's user) and simple to manufacture (that is, both low in cost and high in quality); then market the product through a distribution channel that could expect next-day order fulfilment and liberal payment terms. She wanted to focus her R&D, manufacturing, and marketing energies on one new product at a time. By January 31, 1996, NewTech's first innovation — an inex-

[6] Based on "Fun 'n' Games Company," by Robert N. Anthony and James S. Reece.

pensive but effective monitor lens — had been on the market for three months.

Cost information

NewTech employs the variable costing approach. Each monitor lens cost NewTech $28, broken down as follows:

Standard cost of one monitor lens		
Direct costs	direct materials	$15
	direct overhead	10
	direct labour	3
		$28
Selling price		$44

NewTech, of course, also incurred other, fixed costs of being in business; these totalled $8,000 per month.

Financial results for the three months ended January 31, 1996

Jones had invested her life savings of $200,000 in establishing the company and getting it up and running. NewTech's balance sheet as at November 30, 1995, was:

NewTech Inc.
Balance Sheet
November 30, 1995
(unaudited)

Cash	$148,000
Inventory	28,000
	$176,000
Common shares	$200,000
Retained earnings	(24,000)
	$176,000

During the first three months of operations, NewTech had just broken even, so that retained earnings as of January 31, 1996, were zero (Jones had not declared any dividends, since she wanted all resources ploughed back into the business). Aside from the monthly fixed costs of $8,000, expenditures of $16,000 had been made in November 1995 to establish the company.

The number of monitors sold had climbed from none in November, to 1,000 in December, and up to 1,500 in January, at which time a profit was reported as follows:

Income Statement
January 1996
(unaudited)

Sales	$66,000
Cost of sales	42,000
Contribution margin	24,000
Deduct fixed costs	8,000
	$16,000

For this case, assume that NewTech is exempt from paying taxes.

Sales projections, customer relations, and just-in-time philosophy

Jones was delighted to have broken even after only three months. In a February 1 interview with the features writer of a magazine directed toward new entrepreneurs, she noted: "Being able to cover all my monthly fixed costs and leave $16,000 over for profits after only a few months is absolutely terrific! I firmly expect that we'll ship 2,000 monitors in February, and orders will increase by 500 monitors per month thereafter."

When asked about her business philosophy, Jones replied, "It's very customer-oriented. The customer is king. The only way we can ever hope to make our mark in this crazy economy is if the market thinks of us first when they need our product. That's why our policy is 'just-in-time' delivery, with no order or billing foul-ups. Now, this means that we need to schedule our production one month in advance of predicted sales orders, so since we anticipate shipping 2,500 monitors in March, that's the number we'll produce in February. It also means that we give our customers a break in paying us; the industry standard is 'net 30,' but our customers pay in sixty days. They get the best-quality product when they need it, and we help their cash flow a bit, too. In addition, it means that we treat our suppliers like kings also, so that they provide us with the best-quality raw materials and parts exactly when we need them. So, we pay all our bills in cash each month as they're incurred."

Late May, 1996

Jones's February 1 sales forecast had proved to be almost too accurate to be true. Actual monitors sold versus her predictions for the four-month period February to May, 1996, was as shown in the table, at the bottom of the page.

In late May 1996, Jones received an urgent call on her cellular phone as she was sitting in a traffic jam on the beltway. It was from NewTech's banker, whose friendly tone of just a few weeks before had turned strangely cold. "I'm afraid that we won't be able to honour any of NewTech's cheques if you go into overdraft, and that's coming up virtually as we speak. Can you come in right away?" Jones pressed END on her cell phone. "What the heck's going on?" she muttered, as she spotted a hole in the traffic, darted off the beltway, and headed toward the bank.

Required:

(a) Prepare monthly income statements and balance sheets for each month from November 1995 to December 1996.
(b) For each month from November 1995 to December 1996, prepare a reconciliation between NewTech's net income and cash flow from operations.
(c) Explain the root cause of NewTech's cash crisis. Suggest, with reasons, ways that it could have been avoided.

Month	Forecasted Units Sold	Actual Units Sold
February	2,000	2,000
March	2,500	2,500
April	3,000	3,000
May	3,500	unavailable*

*This table was prepared mid-May, 1996; a revised forecast made at the start of May agreed with the original forecast of 3,500.

Merchison Metal Coatings

Merchison Jones established Merchison Metal Coatings Limited (henceforth MMCL) in 1985, as a means of pursuing what he believed was a growing demand for coated sheet metal. An engineer by training, Jones was convinced that he could develop and successfully market cheaper and better sheet metal coating technologies than were currently available. He obtained a $300,000 loan from his wealthy uncle to begin the business, in return for a note payable. At first, things went extraordinarily well for Jones, as the demand for coated sheet metal took off. However, the recession of the early 1990s was a severe blow to MMCL, as many longtime customers either went bankrupt or sharply curtailed their orders.

In late 1994, Jones was forced to issue common shares to a new investor who agreed to put $500,000 into the business. Now Jones owned 50% of the common shares and the new investor owned 50%. The $500,000 was used to pay suppliers and employees in December 1994 (a month that Jones described later as "the worst time of my business career"), and to build up MMCL's cash balance to $80,000 by December 31, 1994.

Part of the agreement between the two owners was that the new investor had the right to appoint a general manager to run MMCL for a period of one year, beginning January 1, 1995; Jones would focus his efforts on improving the coating technology the company used. The general manager was to receive a salary of $160,000 per year, plus a bonus equal to 30% of MMCL's net income. At the end of the one-year period, Jones had the right to evaluate the success (or lack thereof) of MMCL; as the shareholders' agreement put it, "Merchison Jones may at that time repurchase the 50% of the common shares for its original $500,000 issue price if there has not been at least a 100% increase in retained earnings over the year. However, if retained earnings as at December 31, 1995, is at least 200% of retained earnings as at December 31, 1994, Merchison Jones must purchase the 50% of common shares at a price equal to 50% of the balance in shareholders' equity on MMCL's balance sheet as of December 31, 1995."

It is now January 1996, and Jones has approached you for advice on MMCL's financial progress over 1995. He supplies you with the information shown in the table at the top of the next page.

"I'm not sure," Jones tells you, "but I'm really astounded by how those two turned the company around. I know we've got a great coating process — after all, I invented it myself — but profits, they tell me, went up to $550,000. That's after a loss of $100,000 in 1994! Here, I found this on the floor after they left the office last night ... maybe you can make some sense out of it." Jones then hands you a piece of paper, which is reproduced at the bottom of the next page. Unfortunately, because of a muddy shoeprint, much of the document is unreadable.

Required:

Advise Jones on MMCL's financial progress over 1995.

BALANCE SHEETS
(unaudited)

	December 31 (Canadian $)	
	1995	1994
Cash	100,000	80,000
Accounts receivable	800,000	400,000
Inventory, at FIFO cost	1,100,000	500,000
Investments	20,000	220,000
Land	100,000	300,000
Buildings and equipment	2,100,000	2,120,000
Accumulated depreciation	(1,520,000)	(1,600,000)
Patents	20,000	30,000
	2,720,000	2,050,000
Accounts payable	320,000	60,000
Accrued wages	160,000	100,000
Notes payable	600,000	640,000
Common shares	1,200,000	1,000,000
Retained earnings	440,000	250,000
	2,720,000	2,050,000

Summary of cash deposits, December 29

Proceeds of disposal	Land	$200,000
	Machinery	60,000
	Common shares & bonds	150,000
		$410,000

Expense calculations

Depreciation on buildings & equipment	40,000
Amortization of patents on coating pro	

CHAPTER 8 eight

User Orientation: Analytical Uses of Financial Accounting Information

Learning Objectives

After you have read, thought about, and discussed this chapter, and completed a selection from the end-of-chapter material, you will have made significant progress in achieving the following learning objectives:

- Describe financial statement analysis.
- Explain why effective financial statement analysis requires knowledge and experience.
- List and explain six steps in financial statement analysis.
- Give examples of how accounting choices may mask similarities or differences in underlying performance.
- Describe the derivation and purpose of 21 representative financial statement ratios and other measures.
- Explain why ratios based upon cash flow information may complement other financial statement ratios.
- Describe three "new economy" ratios.
- Describe the purpose of multivariate financial statement ratio models.
- Derive earnings per share numbers, and explain their use and deficiencies.
- Explain the importance of future-oriented financial information.

In the old economy, the most impressive companies were the ones with the best physical and financial assets — machinery, equipment, land, buildings, cash on their balance sheets. A whole convention of financial ratios and accounting methods evolved to measure these attributes. They could tell us whether a corporation was growing rapidly or not; whether it had genuine value; whether, in fact, it had a future.

But today, key players in the new economy have different kinds of assets. Software companies don't have giant football-field-size assembly plants or vast fleets of trucks. Their best assets are two-legged, human, very mobile — and impossible to evaluate using the old measurements. Start running phenomenally successful software-developer Microsoft through the old financial drills and you'll soon be exclaiming, "Holy cow! This company doesn't make any sense! Why would anyone want to invest in it? It can't possibly survive!"

Nuala Beck, *Shifting Gears — Thriving in the New Economy*, HarperCollins, 1992, pp. 146–147

The effective analysis of a set of financial statements requires an understanding of (1) the economic characteristics and current conditions of a firm's businesses, (2) the particular strategies the firm selects to compete in each of these businesses, and (3) the accounting principles and procedures underlying the firm's financial statements. Equipped with these three essential building blocks, the analyst can assess the success of the strategies as measured by profitability, relative to the level of risk incurred. This three-fold approach to financial statement analysis elevates it from one involving the mechanical calculation of a long list of financial statement ratios to one where the analyst has an opportunity to integrate concepts from economics, business strategy, accounting, and other business disciplines. This synthesizing experience rewards the student both intellectually and practically.

Clyde P. Stickney, *Financial Statement Analysis: A Strategic Perspective*, 2nd Edition, The Dryden Press, 1993, p. vii

ACCOUNTING

INTRODUCTION

This chapter focuses on the analytical uses of the financial statement output of accounting. It follows that this chapter has a strong user orientation, and deals with a variety of analytical tools that may be derived from financial statement information. This approach was taken in many places in earlier chapters — for example, even way back in Chapter 1, we were interested in interpreting Corel Corporation's performance using ratio analysis as we illustrated some of the basic aspects of financial accounting. In Chapter 7 our discussion of cash flow statements stressed methods for interpreting accounting information by evaluating an organization's pattern of cash flows.

It is important to emphasize that *all* the outputs of accounting systems — the financial statements, other reports, financial statement–based ratios, and so on — must be considered with great care, challenged if need be, and rejected if necessary. The two quotations that led off this chapter stress that users of financial accounting information should be intelligent skeptics:

- Nuala Beck argues that companies in the "new economy" — high-tech, software development, medical, professional services, and so on — are knowledge based, and therefore cannot be evaluated using the same financial measures as applied to the "old economy" companies in manufacturing and the more traditional industries. This is an important point, and is a restatement of the more general observation that any information used in making a decision should be relevant to that particular decision. Corel is a member of the new, knowledge-based economy: Do its financial statements as prepared according to GAAP reveal enough about the company's human capital — its most important asset? Very little about the knowledge base of the company is captured and reported in the formal financial statements.
- Clyde Stickney expands on this idea by suggesting that the user as analyst of financial statements cannot analyse in a vacuum. The analyst must understand not only the key economic characteristics of the organization being studied and the characteristics of its industry, but also the strategies the organization has selected to reach its goals, and the various accounting alternatives it has chosen when measuring and reporting its results. If you sense that there's some circularity here, you're right. What Stickney implies is that effective financial statement analysis requires considerable background knowledge and understanding — in a word, *experience*. But that's all right, because it's the purpose of books like this to provide you with some of that experience.

For purposes of this chapter, we'll define financial statement analysis as the systematic evaluation of an accounting entity's financial statements, often in conjunction with other information, with the goal of making decisions about the entity. Financial statement analysis requires knowledge and experience; the importance of these is illustrated in the next section of this chapter.

Financial statement analysis may be viewed as consisting of the following steps:

1. Decide why the financial statement analysis is being performed. This is important, because it may reduce the effort and extent of the subsequent analysis. However, many reasons for analysing a company's financial statements require common approaches, so be careful of reducing the scope of the analysis too much at this early stage.
2. Learn as much as possible about the accounting entity under examination: its industry, the types of business operations it is engaged in, how it generates its revenues and incurs its expenses, the nature of its assets and how it finances those assets, and so on. The Management Discussion and Analysis (MD&A) may be useful here.
3. Learn about the accounting entity's accounting policies, and check the audit report to see if it is unqualified. If the company has chosen accounting policies different from those of its competitors, or has changed accounting policies, attempt to learn why. Are such differences and/or changes justified? Learn about how accounting choices may affect reported net income and financial position. Has the entity's management generally made conservative choices, or not? Does the extent and depth of disclosure appear to be high or low? These questions are related to the concept of quality of earnings that we discussed in Chapter 7.
4. Choose standards of comparison. Such standards may relate to the same company in prior years, other typical companies in the same industry, the best-performing companies in the same or other industries, or goals that you (or perhaps

the company's management, as announced in its annual report) have decided the company must achieve. For example, an analyst searching for companies to include in a growth-oriented mutual fund may require that companies have at least a 20% annual increase in sales after adjusting for inflation.

5. Select the various ratios and other measures that you judge will best suit the purposes of your analysis. Compute or otherwise obtain the ratios and other measures for the company under examination, as well as the standards of comparison. A number of organizations sell such information on computer-accessible media such as CD-ROM[1] and, increasingly, over the Internet. Of course, the hardcopy annual report is also usually available from the company, and many larger companies are now providing their financial statements on the World Wide Web. Don't be confounded by differences in accounting principles; many financial statement ratios are constructed differently by different analysts and organizations that maintain and market ratio and similar information.
6. Evaluate the information, perhaps search for more information, and (hopefully) come to a decision that you and others have confidence in.

Importance of Knowledge and Experience in Financial Statement Analysis

Let's take a brief, preliminary look at the importance of background knowledge and experience in financial statement analysis. We'll choose as our example a situation involving a company in the "old economy"; this way, we'll avoid (at least for the moment) Nuala Beck's concern about the relevance of traditional financial ratios. The company is hypothetical, but the situation is based on a realistic scenario.[2] It involves two American financial analysts evaluating a Japanese manufacturer of machine tools called Tanaguchi Corporation. They are concerned about whether Tanaguchi's common shares would make a good addition to the portfolio of the mutual fund they work for. One analyst, after computing various financial statement ratios based on Tanaguchi's published financial statements prepared according to Japanese accounting principles, says to the other:

Tanaguchi Corporation does not appear to be as profitable as comparable U.S. firms. Its operating margin and rate of return on assets are significantly less than the median ratios for U.S. machine tool operators. Its rate of return on common equity is only slightly less than its U.S. counterparts, but this is at the expense of assuming much more financial leverage and therefore risk. Most of this risk is in the form of short-term borrowing. You can see this in its higher total liabilities to total assets ratio combined with its lower long-term debt ratio ...[3]

[1] Statistics Canada publishes industrywide financial statement ratio information. Companies such as Micromedia Limited and Disclosure Incorporated maintain Micromedia's Cancorp database, which includes accounting and other information on more than 8,500 Canadian companies and public, private, and Crown corporations.

[2] This example is based on Paul R. Brown and Clyde P. Stickney, "Tanaguchi Corporation," *Issues in Accounting Education*, Spring 1992, pp. 57–79.

[3] Brown and Stickney, p. 57. All the financial statement ratios mentioned in this quotation are defined in this chapter.

Ultimately, the two analysts decide that there are two general explanations for the apparently poor performance of the Japanese company relative to the American machine tool industry, when performance is measured using financial statement ratios:

1. Japanese and American accounting principles are often different for similar transactions or other events. For example, most Japanese companies use accelerated depreciation, while straight-line is the most popular depreciation method in the United States.
2. Business practices and relationships differ significantly between the two countries. Such differences have a significant impact on the way financial statement ratios should be interpreted. For example, a Japanese company often belongs to a group of corporations, known as a *keiretsu*. Such a group may consist of companies in ten or so industries, such as banking, chemicals, manufacturing, retailing, and so on. The individual companies in a given *keiretsu* may own 20 to 30 percent of each others' common shares; however, ownership of common shares is not intended to permit the owner to exercise control or exert influence over the individual company whose shares are owned. Rather, the share ownership provides a means of establishing working links between the companies in a group. Companies within a *keiretsu* buy a significant proportion of their raw materials and sell a significant proportion of their output to other companies within the group, and the group typically includes a bank that provides financing to group members. The bank would not normally permit a fellow group member to go bankrupt; thus, the analysts' American-oriented judgment — that the risk of short-term borrowing is high for Tanaguchi because of "its higher total assets to total liabilities ratio combined with its lower long-term debt ratio" — is misplaced.

An analyst's understanding of important nuances and differences in business situations may be enhanced by knowledge and experience. In the future, the two analysts will probably conduct their "offshore" evaluations more intelligently, based in part on their experience with Tanaguchi.

Who Is Interested in Analyses of Financial Accounting Information?

All of the financial statement users identified in Chapter 2 are potentially interested in analysing financial statements. Understanding the particular user's perspective and needs is the first important step in financial statement analysis, since this determines the objectives of the analysis. For example, potential investors in the common shares of a publicly traded company (a company whose shares trade on a stock exchange) may be interested in the company's ability to pay dividends, and in the likely future value of the shares. They may want answers to questions such as these:

- How risky is the company's operating cash flow?
- How profitable are its various businesses?

- How well does it perform relative to its competitors?

Headquarters management of a decentralized company might be interested in how profitable each of its businesses is compared to its budget, how profitable each is as a percentage of total assets employed, and so on.

The managers of a company might be interested in performing a financial statement analysis of their company's leading competitors, in order to gain insight into the differences between their company and the industry leaders. Such ongoing attempts by an organization to monitor and emulate the business practices of leading competitors are called "benchmarking," and have become widespread.

Accounting and Business Decision A

(a) The North American Free Trade Agreement has created the potential for a common market among Canada, the United States, and Mexico. The intent is to expand the agreement to other Western Hemisphere countries, such as Chile. Suggest some implications for financial statement analysis.

(b) Provide some reasons why the Tanaguchi example supports the contention that knowledge and experience are important in financial statement analysis.

Financial Statement Ratios and Accounting Differences

A ratio depends on the numbers in its numerator and its denominator. Accounting information used in deriving financial statement ratios must be assessed carefully in order to eliminate any misleading inferences about an organization arising merely from accounting choices. For example, consider the selected information in Exhibit 8–1 about two companies that have completed one year of operations; they are identical in every way except that Company A uses FIFO to account for its inventory, while Company B uses LIFO.

We are going to examine the current ratio for each company. Recall that the current ratio is derived by dividing an organization's current assets by its current liabilities.

EXHIBIT 8–1
TWO "ALMOST IDENTICAL" COMPANIES

Selected Financial Information	Company A (uses FIFO)	Company B (uses LIFO)
Sales	$1,000,000	$1,000,000
Cost of goods sold	750,000	800,000
Net income	100,000	50,000
Current assets	300,000	250,000
Current liabilities	200,000	200,000

The cost of replacing inventory is increasing for these two companies; that is, prices are going up. So the LIFO company (B) reports a higher cost of goods sold than the FIFO company (A).

The current ratio for Company A is \$300,000/\$200,000, or 1.5, while it is \$250,000/\$200,000, or 1.25, for Company B. The only difference between the two companies relates to inventory accounting methods; the difference in current ratios is due merely to the "noise" created by differences in accounting, and not to any real underlying differences. However, this apparently trivial accounting difference could have unintended real consequences for the two companies:

1. Users of financial statements who employ the ratios to make decisions about the two companies may come to the apparently naïve conclusion that the companies are different. Potential investors, for example, may conclude that Company B, with its lower current ratio and net income, is a less desirable investment opportunity. We know this seems silly, but poor decisions based on accounting differences are bound to occur at times, since humans have a finite capacity for processing information.

2. Contracts may be written based on the accounting numbers. Say, for example, that each company has arranged for debt financing, and that each financing agreement stipulates that the company must always maintain a current ratio that exceeds a certain amount — say, 1.2. Requirements such as this are intended to protect the lender from imprudent behaviour by the borrowing company's management. Notice that because of the difference in accounting methods used, Company B's management appears to have far less flexibility than Company A's management. A has a 0.30 cushion, while B has only a 0.05 cushion. So B's management might make operating and other business decisions that would reduce the likelihood of their violating the agreement, while A's management might not be particularly concerned about the ratio and make decisions as usual. Thus, an *apparent* difference arising from accounting choices can become a *real* difference as people react to the information.

To avert errors in comparing two or more companies that are using different accounting methods, it makes sense to convert to a common accounting method, unless the different methods are justified by differences in circumstances. Unfortunately, this conversion is often very difficult and at times impossible for those analysts who must rely on publicly available financial statements, since companies don't usually disclose sufficient information so that financial statements can be readily coverted from one accounting method to another. The caveat here is that we do not want to be imposing an artificial uniformity on the companies if there were good reasons for the original accounting differences. After all, even in our Company A and Company B example, in which the only difference was that one company used LIFO to account for its inventories while the other used FIFO, we must keep in mind that management managed the LIFO firm keeping an eye on the accounting numbers based on LIFO, and may have made its decisions on that basis; ditto for the FIFO firm. This is especially important when management compensation contracts are tied into the accounting numbers. For example, a LIFO firm's manager who has a compensation contract based on net income may hesitate before approving a year-end purchase of inventory if the per unit cost of inventory from the supplier has increased, since such a purchase will have an immediate negative impact on net income and therefore on the manager's compensation. This is so even when making the purchase would be in the company's overall interest (perhaps a shortage is anticipated). So adjusting for accounting artifacts is much more complex than just changing the LIFO firm's accounting to FIFO or vice versa — human behaviour in the presence of a management control system that uses accounting information must also be considered, when possible.

Accounting and Business Decision B

Explain how the following accounting alternatives could be expected to affect a company's current ratio and the ratio of total liabilities to total assets:

(a) Straight line versus accelerated depreciation.
(b) "Too aggressive" accounting for sales revenues. The *Wall Street Journal* reported on September 7, 1994, that Knowledgeware Inc., among a number of other similar software companies, appeared to be stretching revenue recognition practices to unreasonable lengths, and accounting for revenue much too quickly in the earnings process.
(c) Accounting for capital leases as if they were operating leases.

Traditional Ratio Analysis: Derivation, Uses, and Limitations

A Canadian research study published in 1993 observed that it is possible to compute innumerable ratios based on financial statements and that there is little standardization in how ratios are defined and labelled.[4] In fact, the only ratio whose calculation has been standardized by the accounting profession is the earnings per share ratio,[5] and unfortunately the Canadian standard differs from foreign (including American) standards for this ratio.

In this section we will provide a sample of ratios and other measures that may be derived from financial statements, and discuss some of their strengths and weak-

[4] CICA, *Research Study: Using Ratios and Graphics in Financial Reporting*, Toronto, 1993.
[5] *CICA Handbook*, section 3500.

nesses. We encountered a number of these ratios and measures at earlier points in this book, but gather them here in a convenient summary.

Exhibit 8–2 shows 21 financial statement–based measures, which are classified into five analytical groups:

- ratios measuring overall performance
- profitability ratios
- measures of investment utilization
- measures of financial condition and short-term risk
- measures of financial condition and longer-term risk

Along with the name of each ratio or other measure, the exhibit also indicates how it is derived, and describes its purpose. An illustration of how each of these measures is computed begins just after this exhibit, so you'll have to keep referring back to Exhibit 8–2.

EXHIBIT 8–2
A REPRESENTATIVE LIST OF RATIOS AND OTHER MEASURES

MEASURES	DERIVATION	PURPOSE
Ratios measuring overall performance		
1. Return on total assets	$\dfrac{\text{Net income + Interest (1 – income tax rate)}}{\text{Average total assets for the period}}$	Provides a relative measure of how well all of the resources under control of the company have been used.
2. Return on common shareholders' equity	$\dfrac{\text{Net income – Preferred share dividends}}{\text{Average common shareholders' equity for the period}}$	Provides a relative measure of how much the company has earned on its common shareholders' equity.
3. Price/earnings ratio	$\dfrac{\text{Price per common share}}{\text{Earnings per common share}}$	Companies with very high-quality earnings may have relatively high "P/E" ratios. This means that the stock market is setting a price on the company's common shares that reflects a great deal of respect for each dollar of earnings. On the other hand, companies whose earnings are perceived by the stock market as being risky, or overstated, may have very low P/E ratios.
Profitability ratios		
4. Gross margin percentage	$\dfrac{\text{Gross margin}}{\text{Sales}}$	This ratio is important to manufacturers and retailers, since it provides information to management about how businesses, or even individual product lines, provide gross margins to cover nonproduct, or period, costs.
5. Profit margin or operating margin	$\dfrac{\text{Net income}}{\text{Sales}}$	This ratio is computed in order to assess the net income provided by each dollar of sales revenue. The numerator should be net income from continuing operations, and before extraordinary items.
6. Earnings per share	$\dfrac{\text{Portion of net income that goes to common shareholders}}{\text{Weighted average number of common shares outstanding over the period}}$	Provides an overall measure of accounting entity performance on the basis of each common share.
Measures of investment utilization		
7. Asset turnover	$\dfrac{\text{Sales}}{\text{Average total assets for the period}}$	Provides a broad measure of the asset base needed to support each dollar of sales.

Ratio	Formula	Description
8. Capital intensity	Sales / Average total capital assets for the period	Similar to the asset turnover ratio, but includes only capital assets in the denominator.
9. Days' receivables	Accounts receivable / Sales/365	Provides information on how quickly receivables are being collected.
10. Accounts receivable turnover	Sales / Average accounts receivable for the period	Measures the number of times during the accounting period that accounts receivable "turn over," or go through a cycle of being created and then reduced to zero.
11. Days' inventory	Average inventory / Cost of goods sold/365	Provides a measure of the average number of days of inventory that was on hand over the period.
12. Inventory turnover	Cost of goods sold / Average inventory	Provides a measure of the number of times an accounting entity's inventory has turned over during the period.
Measures of financial condition and short-term risk		
13. Current ratio	Current assets / Current liabilities	Provides a very rough measure of liquidity — that is, how well a company is able to pay off its currently maturing obligations.
14. Quick ratio	Quick assets / Current liabilities	Some analysts believe that this ratio provides a better measure of liquidity than the current ratio, since only quick assets (such as cash and cash equivalents, accounts receivable, and marketable securities) are included in the numerator.
15. Accounts payable turnover	Purchases / Average accounts payable	Provides a measure of the frequency with which a company pays off its current year's purchases.
16. Days' payables outstanding	Average accounts payable / Purchases/365	Provides a measure of the number of days, on average, between a company's incurrence of an accounts payable obligation, and its payment.
Measures of financial condition and longer-term risk		
17. Long-term debt to total assets	Average long-term debt for the period / Average total assets for the period	Provides a measure of the proportion of total assets that are financed with long-term debt.
18. Long-term debt to owners' equity	Average long-term debt for the period / Average total common shareholders' equity for the period	Provides a measure of the relative proportion of long-term debt to common shareholders' equity in a company's capital structure.
19. Times interest earned	Net operating income before income tax expense + Interest expense / Interest expense	Provides a measure of whether a company has a sufficient "cushion" to pay its interest expense (which, unlike common share dividends, must be paid).
20. Dividend yield	Dividends declared during the period / Price per common share	Provides a measure of the current dividend return to holders of a company's common shares. Ignores capital gains due to increases in the price of the common shares.
21. Dividend payout	Dividends declared during the period / Net income	Indicates what proportion of the current year's net income has been declared as a dividend.

Examples of the calculation of the ratios and measures described in Exhibit 8–2 are provided in Exhibit 8–3; the examples are based on the 1993 financial statements of Corel (from Chapter 6), supplemented by other information as needed. Please keep in mind that many of these ratios may be computed in ways *other than* those described here; when someone tells you that a particular ratio for a particular company has such-and-such a value, be sure to find out exactly how the ratio was derived. Now let's describe each of these ratios and measures in more detail.

Ratios Measuring Overall Performance

1. Return on total assets

This ratio, often abbreviated as ROA, provides a measure of how much the company has earned on the totality of its resources. Since we know that the total assets of an organization must be equal to the sum of current liabilities, long-term liabilities, and shareholders' equity, this ratio suggests how well *all* the funds or resources under the control of the company have been used. Not only are external financial analysts interested in this ratio, but so also are the managers of decentralized companies. A multidivisional company's top management can employ this ratio to evaluate its individual business units, since although the divisional managers may be able to exert considerable control over the assets under their care, they often have little influence over how those assets were financed, because such decisions are made by headquarters management. Thus, the ROA ratio may be an important part of an organization's management control system.

Return on total assets is computed by first adding together the company's net income and its interest expense. The interest expense is adjusted for income tax effects by multiplying it by one minus the company's income tax rate. So if a company's 1996 net income was \$500,000, its total assets at the start and end of the year were \$4,000,000 and \$6,000,000 respectively, its interest expense was \$80,000, and its income tax rate was 40%, ROA would be:

$$\frac{500{,}000 + 80{,}000(1 - 0.40)}{(4{,}000{,}000 + 6{,}000{,}000)/2}$$

or 0.1096, about 11%.

Thus, the overall return to *all* sources of financing for this company in 1996 was 11%, according to the calculation.

Notice that the numerator of this ratio includes the term "Interest(1–income tax rate)." This serves to increase net income by the interest expense, after adjusting for income taxes. The reason for this adjustment to the numerator of this ratio is that the denominator is made up of all sources of financing, both debt and equity, so to be consistent the numerator must be made up of the return not only to shareholders (that is, net income), but also to all forms of debt (that is, interest). Unfortunately, sometimes this adjustment is not made to this ratio by analysts, so a bias is introduced. So the ratio "Net income/Average total assets" is also often referred to as ROA. This bias may not be important when a company has little debt and insignificant interest expense, as in the case of Corel. Corel's 1993 ROA, calculated as shown in Exhibit 8–3, was 19.7%.

Like all accounting-based information, the ROA ratio must be used with care. One reason is that both its numerator and its denominator are most often based on financial statement information that has been prepared in accordance with GAAP, and we know that such data have weaknesses as well as strengths. For example, suppose that the ROA ratio is being used by the top manager of a company with two divisions in order to assess how well the divisional managers are performing against each other. The divisions are in the same industry but in different geographic locations; also,

Division A was established many years ago while Division B was established quite recently. Since GAAP requires that tangible depreciable capital assets be accounted for on the basis of their total laid-down historic cost, and since replacement costs have increased over time, depreciation expense for Division B will exceed depreciation expense for Division A, and the net book value of B's capital assets will be also be larger. Therefore, B's ROA will be biased lower than A's, since B's numerator will be lower (higher depreciation expense), and its denominator will be higher (higher net book value).

In the early part of the twentieth century, large, capital-intensive industrial firms such as the Dupont Powder Company (a chemical processing company) and General Motors achieved vast size and scope, and accounting measures had to be developed that would provide corporate managers with a means of controlling and managing their new, vast organizations. The managers at Dupont are credited with developing an analysis based on dissaggregating one version of the ROA ratio into two components: profit margin and total asset turnover. Thus:

ROA = [Net income/Sales] × [Sales/Average total assets for the period]

This dissaggregation was performed for each of the many company divisions. In this way, top management was able to monitor and control profit margins and asset turnover.[6] These companies were capital intensive in the "old economy" sense of having major investments in tangible capital assets such as land, buildings, and machinery; management focused on managing such assets by applying the disaggregated ROA formula. Selling and Stickney point out that the appeal of this formula "was the linking of [profit margin and asset utilization] to a single index of profitability which, when disaggregated into various subindexes, embodies all items on the balance sheet and the income statement."[7]

The disaggregating of the ROA measure in this way points out two major business strategies for creating wealth. One strategy is represented by a company such as Potash Corporation of Saskatchewan Inc., headquartered in Saskatoon, which mines potash and markets it globally. With its heavy investment in land, buildings, machinery, mines, and other capital assets, Potash Corporation, like many capital-intensive businesses, has a rather low ratio of sales to total assets, so it concentrates on increasing its profit margin in order to obtain a satisfactory ROA.

A second strategy is illustrated by a company in the retail food distribution business, such as Safeway or Loblaws. Such companies typically have very low profit margins, and so attempt to obtain a satisfactory ROA by increasing total asset turnover as much as possible. Keeping inventories down by utilizing computer-based inventory management systems is one such way these companies control asset levels.

These two strategies, each arising from the nature of the particular business, are illustrated below with the following accounting information (the food retailer is a hypothetical company, while Potash Corporation is a real Canadian company):

---

[6] H. Thomas Johnson and Robert S. Kaplan, *Relevance Lost: The Rise and Fall of Management Accounting* (Boston; Harvard Business School Press), 1987.

[7] Thomas I. Selling and Clyde P. Stickney, "Disaggregating the Rate of Return on Common Shareholders' Equity: A New Approach," *Accounting Horizons*, December 1990, pp. 9–17.

Hypothetical Company Limited
(52 weeks ended December 31, 1994; millions of dollars)

	1994	1993	1992
Sales	999.9	935.6	
Net income	12.6	11.2	
Total assets, end of year	294.7	274.2	247.4
Total assets, average for the year	$\frac{294.7 + 274.2}{2}$	$\frac{274.2 + 247.4}{2}$	
	= 284.5	= 260.8	
Net income/Sales	12.6/999.9 = 1.3%	11.2/935.6 = 1.2%	
Sales/Total assets, average for the year	999.9/284.5 = 3.5	935.6/260.8 = 3.6	
ROA	1.3% × 3.5 = 4.6%	1.2% × 3.6 = 4.3%	

Potash Corporation of Saskatchewan Inc.
(year ended December 31, 1994; millions of dollars)

	1994	1993	1992
Sales	596.7	374.6	
Net income	128.0	62.7	
Total assets, end of year	1,441.8	1,453.9	1,283.6
Total assets, average for the year	$\frac{1{,}441.8 + 1{,}453.9}{2}$	$\frac{1{,}453.9 + 1{,}283.6}{2}$	
	= 1 ,447.9	= 1,368.8	
Net income/Sales	128.0/596.7 = 21.5%	62.7/374.6 = 16.7%	
Sales/Total assets, average for the year	596.7/1,447.9 = 0.41	374.6/1,368.8 = 0.27	
ROA	21.5% × 0.41 = 8.8%	16.7% × 0.27 = 4.5%	

Potash Corporation's ratio of net income to sales was 16.7% in 1993; for the food retailer the figure was just 1.2%. Retail food chains are under constant pressure to offer discounts and "specials"; competition is fierce, and so profit margins are razor-thin. On the other hand, Potash Corporation is in an industry in which sales prices are able to cover all costs, and provide a comfortable profit.

The asset turnover ratios also reflect the differences in the two industries. In 1993 this ratio was only 0.27 for Potash Corporation, because of the enormous required investment in capital assets. For Hypothetical Company Limited, the food retailer, the ratio was 3.6, reflecting the fact that in food retailing a far smaller relative investment in total assets is necessary. When ROA was computed for 1993 for the two companies, the combined impact of profit margin and total asset turnover resulted in somewhat similar ROAs: 4.5% for Potash Corporation and 4.3% for the food company.

2. Return on common shareholders' equity

This ratio is often abbreviated as ROE, even though ROCE (for "return on common equity") would seem to be more accurate. The ROE ratio is intended to provide a measure of how much the company has earned on its common shareholders' equity, and is of interest to current and potential shareholders. Common shareholders' equity includes everything in shareholders' equity on a company's balance sheet, except for preferred shares, so the numerator of this ratio is computed by reducing net income by preferred dividends (if any). Keep in mind that ROE, like ROA, is based on GAAP numbers, and thus the denominator is *not* the market value of common shareholders' equity that might be obtainable from stock market listings.

ROE equals the ratio derived by dividing net income, *less any preferred share dividends*, by the average common shareholders' equity for the accounting period. For example, if a company's net income for 1996 was \$500,000, preferred share dividends were \$60,000, and common shareholders' equity was \$2,000,000 and \$4,000,000 at the start and end of the year respectively, ROE would be:

$$\frac{500{,}000 - 60{,}000}{(2{,}000{,}000 + 4{,}000{,}000)/2}$$

or 0.1466, about 14.7%.

The calculation of ROE for Corel as shown in Exhibit 8–3 is relatively simple, since Corel has no preferred shares and therefore no preferred dividends.

It is useful for analysts to examine how an accounting entity's ROA and ROE are related over several periods. This is done in Exhibit 8–4 for Varity Corporation, a major international farm implement and engine manufacturer headquartered in Buffalo, New York, for a five-year period. As can be seen, ROE seems to be more volatile than ROA, with higher peaks and lower troughs. This is a result of the "leverage effect." This effect is explained by the impact of debt, in the capital structure of an accounting entity, on the entity's return on common shareholders' equity. During profitable periods, when profits are sufficient to cover interest costs and more, ROE is greater than ROA, since the excess goes to shareholders. But when profits are low, interest costs still have to be paid, and ROE falls below ROA.

This effect is amplified as the proportion of debt in the capital structure of a company increases. For this reason, some analysts argue that a company with relatively lots of debt (a "highly levered" or "highly leveraged" company) is riskier for shareholders than a company with less debt. However, they also point out that in more profitable years, the leverage effect can result in greater returns to the shareholders of a highly leveraged company, so there seems to be a trade-off between risk and return.

3. Price-earnings ratio

This is one of the most widely cited ratios, and is often mentioned in the financial press. It is referred to as the "P/E ratio," and is monitored closely by financial analysts and by others who are interested in the performance of companies whose shares trade on stock exchanges. The ratio is only relevant for such companies. Corel's P/E ratio for 1993, computed by dividing its quoted common share price on the Toronto Stock Exchange at the close of trading at the end of Corel's 1993 fiscal year (namely, $15.33), by its reported 1993 earnings per share of $0.99 (obtained from Corel's financial statements in the appendix to Chapter 6), was 15.48.

The numerator of the P/E ratio is the market price of the company's common shares, which is set by the actions of those who buy and sell the shares on the stock exchange. If a company's P/E ratio declines to a greater degree than can be explained by general market and industry trends, management is usually concerned.

Companies with very high-quality earnings may have relatively high P/E ratios. This means that the stock market is setting a price for the company's common shares that reflects a great deal of respect for each dollar of earnings. On the other hand, companies whose earnings are perceived by the stock market as being risky, or overstated, may have very low P/E ratios.

Profitability Ratios

4. Gross margin percentage

In the "Results of Operations" section of Corel's MD&A in Chapter 6, the income statement is shown with each line item as a percentage of sales. Management tends to monitor the gross profit, or gross margin, percentage quite closely. In periods of intense price competition, this number may decrease, but total dollar gross margin may be maintained or even increase as the total volume of units sold increases. As shown in Exhibit 8–3, Corel's gross margin percentage was 76.9% in 1993.

This ratio is important to manufacturers and retailers, since it provides information to management about whether businesses, or even individual product lines, are providing sufficient gross margin to cover nonproduct, or period, costs. External users are also interested in this ratio, for similar reasons. The higher the ratio, the greater the gross margin provided by each dollar of sales revenue.

5. Profit margin

The return on sales, or profit margin, is calculated by dividing an organization's net income number by its sales number. In Corel's case this is straightforward; but when a company has extraordinary items, or a gain or loss from shutting down one of its businesses, it may want to adjust both the numerator and the denominator of the ratio by these effects in order to focus on ongoing operating results. This ratio was 19.9% for Corel in 1993, as shown in Exhibit 8–3.

Companies in industries with relatively low profit margins (such as the food industry) typically have relatively high asset turnover; companies in industries with relatively high profit margins (such as mining, or chemicals and chemical products) often have relatively low asset turnover because of their heavy investment in capital assets. The comparison of the food retailer and Potash Corporation of Saskatchewan, presented earlier in this chapter, illustrated this relationship.

The profit margin measure provides an overall indicator of operational performance, and may suggest, in general terms, where managerial actions might strengthen a company's results. For example, suppose that an organization's profit margin is lower than the industry average (where the "industry" is defined as the organization's peer companies in terms of products, customers, and size). Management should consider whether some or all of the following factors help explain this shortfall: average unit selling prices too low; average unit cost of sales too high, perhaps because of production inefficiencies; overall sales volume in units too low, resulting in a low absolute gross margin; relatively high administrative or marketing expenses; and so on.

The table below shows profit margins for companies in a sample of Canadian industries for the years 1991 through to 1994. Clearly, profit margins differ by industry, as well as over time (1991 and 1992 were recession years).

6. Earnings per share

Accountants consider the earnings per share, or EPS, ratio to be so important — since it receives so much publicity in the newspapers and financial press — that accounting standards-setting bodies have developed GAAP especially for it. Since these standards are rather complex, they are described in their own section later in this chapter. In Chapter 6's appendix, Corel's 1993 EPS information is disclosed just below "Consolidated Statements of Income and Retained Earnings." As you'll notice, *four* EPS numbers are disclosed for 1993 and also for each of the two other years, 1992 and 1991. The "Basic" EPS ratio for Corel, computed using Corel's 1993 net income, was $0.99 per common share — a significant increase from the $0.47 per common share from 1992.

Measures of Investment Utilization

7. Asset turnover

This ratio provides a broad measure of the asset base needed to support each dollar of sales. A company with a lower asset turnover will need a higher profit margin to achieve a target ROA than a company with a higher asset turnover. In Exhibit 8–3, we can see that for Corel, this ratio was about 1.0 in 1993.

Profit Margin

	Industry	1991	1992	1993	1994
1	Food (except retailing)	3.0%	2.8%	2.8%	3.2%
2	Forestry	–7.1%	–9.3%	1.7%	3.7%
3	Petroleum and natural gas	6.3%	6.3%	9.4%	10.5%
4	Chemicals and chemical products	5.8%	6.2%	6.8%	7.1%
5	Iron, steel, and related products	0.8%	–.0.5%	4.0%	8.4%
6	Electronic equipment and computer services	2.0%	3.1%	2.2%	4.1%
7	Telecommunication carriers	25.2%	25.1%	22.2%	21.1%
8	Entertainment, recreation, and amusement services	1.8%	–1.5%	0.6%	0.4%
9	Chartered banks and other deposit-accepting intermediaries	11.5%	3.9%	7.1%	10.9%
10	All nonfinancial	3.6%	3.2%	3.9%	5.3%
11	All financial	9.5%	6.1%	9.1%	10.7%

Source: Statistics Canada publications. "Profit margin" is defined by Statistics Canada as "Operating profits/Operating revenue."

8. Capital intensity

A special subset of asset turnover is the capital intensity ratio, which attempts to measure the *capital assets* needed to support each dollar of sales revenue. Companies in traditional manufacturing industries typically have relatively low capital-intensity ratios; service-oriented companies have higher such ratios. Notice the significant spread between Corel's asset turnover ratio (1.0 times) and its capital intensity ratio (4.9 times). This spread is an indication of operating flexibility: since the costs associated with tangible capital assets such as production machinery are often quite fixed, a company with a large spread between these two ratios, or a service-oriented business that has a very high capital-intensity ratio to begin with, may be better able to downsize and reduce costs during a recession than a company with a low ratio, which indicates significant dependence on tangible capital assets.

9. Days' receivables

This ratio, which measures the number of days on average that it takes the company's customers to pay, is 126 days for Corel, using the year-end trade accounts receivable balance of $48,501,000. Perhaps the average of the 12 month-end accounts receivable should be used, if available, to arrive at a more representative number. Also, the sales number should exclude any sales on a cash basis. To ensure that this measure is useful, financial analysts should make certain that the company's revenue-recognition policy doesn't overinflate the sales number, and that accounts receivable are not misstated.

This measure should be evaluated in the context of the credit terms offered by the company to its customers, or compared with the industry average. The number provides information on how quickly receivables are being collected: the lower the number, the less resources a company has tied up in accounts receivable — and that's good, unless the company is losing sales because of its insistence on collecting too quickly, relative to the competition.

10. Accounts receivable turnover

This ratio is closely related in terms of information content to the days' receivables measure. It was 3.6 in 1993 for Corel. The higher the ratio, the more frequently receivables are turning over, and the fewer resources a company has tied up in receivables.

11. Days' inventory

As seen in Exhibit 8–3, Corel has about 83 days' worth of its product in inventory. Many companies are applying just-in-time (JIT) production management techniques in an effort to reduce this ratio as much as possible. Whether a particular company's days' inventory number is "good" or "bad" depends on how the number has changed over the last few accounting periods, and on what has happened to the number in competing companies. High-tech companies with short product life cycles would be expected to have relatively low days' inventory numbers.

12. Inventory turnover

This ratio is closely related to the days' inventory number. Corel's inventory turned over about 4.4 times in 1993 (see Exhibit 8–3). Perhaps the ultimate JIT target in connection with this ratio is 365, or once per day! The logistics of maintaining such a ratio may well be impossible, however. More realistic inventory turnover targets would seem to be more advisable.

As with all ratios and other measures based on accounting, inventory turnover varies significantly between industries. For example, inventory turnover for a butcher shop would be very high, but for a manufacturer of nuclear turbines it would be quite low. Manufacturing companies in most industries have strived to increase this ratio in recent years by reducing their inventory levels. Increasing this ratio lowers the costs of holding inventory (fewer storage and security needs, for example), but may result in inventory shortages and unfulfilled orders.

Measures of Financial Condition and Short-Term Risk

13. Current ratio

Corel's current ratio was 5.5 times in 1993, as shown in Exhibit 8–3. This ratio is intended to provide a measure of liquidity, or how well a company is able to pay off its currently maturing obligations. Earlier in this chapter we saw how a company's accounting policy choices for inventory could bias this ratio (see Exhibit 8–1 and the related discussion). Ensuring that current assets such as accounts receivable (with an appropriate allowance for doubtful accounts) and inventories (watching that cost doesn't exceed market, for example) are fairly measured is crucial in deriving a useful estimate for this ratio. Also, current liabilities such as accruals must be accounted for.

Another concern is the "window dressing" phenomenon, which arises when a company whose current ratio is above 1.0 takes actions to simultaneously reduce a current asset and a current liability by an equal amount just before a reporting date, such as a year end. The actions have no purpose other than to show an improvement in the current ratio; the current asset and current liability are restored just after the reporting date. For example, suppose that Q Company has current assets of $1,000,000 and current liabilities of $800,000 as at December 30, 1997. Management pays off a short-term loan of $200,000 on December 31, with the result that the current ratio goes from 1,000,000/800,000, or 1.25, to 800,000/600,000, or 1.33. Management then borrows the money again just after the new year starts. The result is an increase in the current ratio as at the year end, but clearly, this is not in the least representationally faithful.

Such window dressing only increases the current ratio if the ratio is greater than 1.0. The ratio is reduced by such actions if the ratio is less than 1.0.

14. Quick ratio

This ratio, 5.1 times for Corel in 1993, eliminates some of the possible measurement biases associated with the current ratio, since only quick assets are included in the numerator. Quick assets are current assets *excluding* those current assets such as inventory and prepaid expenses that cannot quickly be turned into cash.

15. Accounts payable turnover

Corel's accounts payable turned over about 8.8 times in 1993. Notice the calculation of the numerator portion of this ratio in footnote b of Exhibit 8–3.

16. Days' payables outstanding

In 1993 there was an average of 41 days between the time Corel incurred a liability for an account payable and the time it paid off that liability (Exhibit 8–3). If we add up the days' receivables plus the days' inventory, and subtract the days' payables, we obtain a measure of the "cash conversion cycle" — that is, the average number of days in the company's operating cycle of cash to cash. For Corel, this is 126 + 83 - 41, or 168 days. Changes in the cash conversion cycle indicate changes in an organization's liquidity, and also suggest how long additional financing may be needed as sales volume increases.

Measures of Financial Condition and Risk: Longer Term

17. Long-term debt to total assets

Corel has no long-term debt, so this ratio is zero for the company. For Electrohome

Limited, a Canadian company with operations in broadcasting and electronics, long-term debt was $33,407,000 and $51,322,000 as at the end of the company's fiscal years August 31, 1993 and 1992; total assets were $100,621,000 and $95,843,000 on those same dates. So the ratios were 33.2% and 53.5% at the years ending August 31, 1993 and 1992. This ratio states the percentage of total resources that is financed with debt: the higher the ratio is, the greater a company's ROE is in good times, but the lower it is in bad times. This is the leverage effect that we mentioned earlier.

What is the optimum ratio of long-term debt to total assets for a company? Is Corel's management wise in not including long-term debt as part of its capital structure? Answers to these questions are not simple, and involve concepts from corporate finance that you may study later in your career. Many observers suggest that some long-term debt benefits common shareholders, but that "too much" creates excessive financial risk.

18. Long-term debt to equity

This ratio is closely related to the previous ratio, and provides another measure of financial risk. Again, it is zero for Corel. Since Electrohome's shareholders' equity was $26,350,000 at August 31, 1993, and $17,404,000 at August 31, 1992, the long-term debt to equity ratio for that company was 126.8% and 294.9% at those two dates — an apparently excessive amount that Electrohome's management was eager to reduce.

19. Times interest earned

Again, zero for Corel, but a concern to Electrohome. We will derive this ratio based on Electrohome's 1993 and 1992 income statements, which are reproduced on the following page.

Ignoring Electrohome's discontinued operations, since they will not be representative of the company's future operations, the times interest earned ratio is calculated as shown in the table at the bottom of this page.

So it appears that Electrohome's very heavy debt in 1992, as measured by its 294.9% ratio of long-term debt to equity, resulted in the 1.35 times interest earned ratio in that year, and that management action in 1993 reduced the ratio of long-term debt to equity and helped increase the times interest earned ratio to 1.85.

20. Dividend yield *and* 21. Dividend payout

Since Corel did not declare dividends, these two ratios are zero for the company. It is fairly common for high-growth companies such as Corel not to pay dividends: investors in the common shares of such companies are purchasing the *expectation* of high and increasing dividends at a later time. For more mature, dividend-paying companies, however, these ratios are closely monitored, and changes may be interpreted as either good or bad news by participants in the capital markets.

in $ thousands	1993	1992
Earnings before income taxes and discontinued operations	4,912	2,459
Interest expense	5,808	7,125
	10,720	9,584
Interest expense	5,808	7,125
(Pretax operating income + interest)/Interest	1.85	1.35

Consolidated Statements of Earnings and Retained Earnings (as adapted)

For years ended *(thousands except per share amounts)*	**August 31 1993**	**August 31 1992**
Revenue		
Broadcast	$ 58,448	$ 61,339
Electronics	71,134	63,186
	129,582	124,525
Expenses		
Operating expenses	109,982	103,691
Research and development expenses	4,796	4,575
Depreciation and amortization	3,415	3,701
Operating income	11,389	12,558
Interest expense	(5,808)	(7,125)
Other income	1,085	1,118
Earnings before unusual items, income taxes and discontinued operations	6,666	6,551
Refinancing and restructuring expenses	(2,927)	(4,092)
CTV debt forgiveness	1,173	—
Earnings before income taxes and discontinued operations	4,912	2,459
Income taxes	(103)	297
Earnings before discontinued operations	5,015	2,162
Discontinued operations	3,566	(3,608)
Net earnings (loss) for the year	8,581	(1,446)
Retained earnings at beginning of year	9,770	11,240
	18,351	9,794
Dividends on preference shares	30	24
Retained earnings at end of year	$ 18,321	$ 9,770

Reprinted courtesy of Electrohome Limited.

EXHIBIT 8–3
EXAMPLES OF RATIO CALCULATIONS

Measures	As Computed for Corel Corporation for 1993[a]
Ratios measuring overall performance	
1. Return on total assets	\$27,841,000/ [(\$105,313,000 + \$176,623,000)/2] = 19.7%
2. Return on common shareholders' equity	\$27,841,000/ [(\$148,511,000 + \$98,793,000)/2] = 22.5%
3. Price/earnings ratio	15.48
Profitability ratios	
4. Gross margin percentage	\$107,766,000/ \$140,223,000 = 76.9%
5. Profit margin	\$27,841,000/ \$140,223,000 = 19.9%
6. Earnings per share	So-called "basic" EPS was \$0.99 per common share in 1993, based on Corel's net income. See text explanation for EPS.
Measures of investment utilization	
7. Asset turnover	\$140,223,000/ [(\$176,623,000 + \$105,313,000)/2] = 1.0 times
8. Capital intensity	\$140,223,000/ [(\$38,191,000 + \$18,832,000)/2] = 4.9 times
9. Days' receivables	\$48,501,000/ \$140,223,000/365 = 126 days
10. Accounts receivable turnover	\$140,223,000/ [(\$48,501,000 + \$28,879,000)/2] = 3.6 times
11. Days' inventory	[(\$4,973,000 + \$9,828,000)/2]/ \$32,457,000/365 = 83 days

12. Inventory turnover	\$32,457,000/ [(\$4,973,000 + \$9,828,000)/2] = 4.4 times
Measures of financial condition and risk — short-term	
13. Current ratio	\$138,432,000/ \$25,185,000 = 5.5 times
14. Quick ratio	[\$138,432,000 – \$9,828,000 – \$1,084,000]/ \$25,185,000 = 5.1 times
15. Accounts payable turnover	\$37,312 ,000[b]/ [(\$1,299,000 + \$7,197,000)/2] = 8.8 times
16. Days payables outstanding	365/8.8 = 41 days
Measures of financial condition and risk—longer-term	
17. Long-term debt to total assets	0
18. Long-term debt to equity ratio	0
19. Times interest earned	n/a
20. Dividend yield	0
21. Dividend payout	0

[a] Corel's 1993 tax rate is computed as follows:
Reported income tax expense/Income from continuing operations before taxes
= \$18,443,000/\$46,284,000
= 39.85%
All balance sheet quantities used in ratios involving income statement numbers are computed as averages of opening and closing balances. For example, TA (or total assets) in the ROA ratio is [\$105,313,000 + \$176,623,000]/2 = \$140,968,000. This averaging is done in order to account for the fact that the income in the numerator of the ROA ratio was earned over the whole year.

[b] Purchases are derived as follows:
We know that COGS = Opening inventory + Purchases – Closing inventory, and that COGS, opening inventory, and closing inventory can be obtained from the financial statements, as follows:

COGS = \$32,457,000
Opening inventory = \$4,973,000
Closing inventory = \$9,828,000
So, Purchases = COGS + Closing inventory – Opening inventory
= 32,457,000 + 9,828,000 – 4,973,000
= 37,312,000

EXHIBIT 8–4 RELATIONSHIP BETWEEN ROA AND ROE FOR VARITY CORPORATION*		
Year	Return on Closing Total Shareholders' Equity	Return on Total Closing Assets (measured by $NI/TA_{closing}$)
1992	4.9%	1.3%
1991	(36.0)%	(5.6)%
1990	13.1%	2.7%
1989	15.2%	2.8%
1988	24.0%	5.6%

*Source: Varity Corporation 1992 Annual Report, for years ended January 31.

Cash Flows and Financial Statement Analysis

Cash flows and some methods for analysing them were described in Chapter 7. There are several additional ways that cash flow information may be analysed. Cash flow statement information may be developed into financial ratios, either on its own or in combination with accounting information from the income statement or balance sheet. In Exhibit 8–5, the first two ratios combine cash flow and accrual accounting information, while the third ratio is constructed solely from the cash flow statement.

Figlewicz and Zeller[8] explain the usefulness of the "operating cash return on sales" ratio in Exhibit 8–5 as follows (p. 69):

[It] represents a "quality of sales" measure. For example ... a common practice is to shift inventory from the firm's to the customer's books by offering relaxed credit requirements and attractive discounts. Such economic events may not be reflected in [the traditional profit margin] measure because of accrual accounting techniques. [The operating cash return on sales ratio] may serve as a complementary measure to directly capture the impact of a changing credit policy. Specifically, by comparing [the traditional and cash-basis ratios], the analyst can identify the extent to which a business enterprise relies on noncash items to generate sales. Consequently, as economic, industry, and/or firm specific operating conditions change (e.g., slowing cash collections), [the cash-flow based ratio] will change, whereas the [traditional ratio] may be stable.

[8] Raymond E. Figlewicz and Thomas L. Zeller, "An Analysis of Performance, Liquidity, Coverage, and Capital Ratios from the Statement of Cash Flows," *Akron Business and Economic Review*, Vol. 22, No. 1, Spring 1991, pp. 64–81.

EXHIBIT 8–5
TABLE OF SOME CASH FLOW RATIOS

Ratio	Derivation	Comments
Operating cash return on sales ratio	Cash flow from operations / Sales	For Corel in 1993, this ratio is $32,442,000/$140,223,000 = 23.1%
Cash flow liquidity ratio	Cash flow from operations / Current liabilities	For Corel in 1993, this ratio is $32,442,000/[($5,248,000 + $25,185,000)/2] = 2.1 times
Operating cash flow as a percentage of total cash flow	Cash flow from operations / Total cash flow	For Corel in 1993, this ratio is $32,442,000/$26,382,000 = 123%

They explain the usefulness of their cash flow liquidity ratio as follows (p. 70):

> *It does provide a measurement that the current and quick ratios miss. Theoretically, traditional ratios assume current assets can be liquidated to meet current liabilities. However, the true economic value of current assets may be substantially different from amounts reported on accrual based financial statements ... A need for cash from nonoperating sources to meet critical current needs would be indicated by values < 1 ...*

Clearly, there are many possible ratios and other measures available to the analyst of financial statements. It cannot be stressed enough that all of us must exercise considerable care when constructing and interpreting ratios and other measures based on financial statements. *Caveat emptor* — or an appropriate analogue for "user" — should be the catchphrase of financial statement analysis.

But what about those "new economy" companies that Nuala Beck said were being done a disservice by traditional ratios? Well, traditional ratios are still used, but with increasing caution and skepticism, and new ratios — often based on nonfinancial statement data — are being developed.

A Sample of "New Economy" Ratios

Nuala Beck, in *Shifting Gears: Thriving in the New Economy* (which was the source of the quotation that led off this chapter), writes that "knowledge is the asset of the nineties" (p. 125). She has suggested a series of ratios for measuring the degree to which individual companies and whole industries have been successful in the new economy. Many of these ratios are radically different from the more traditional financial statement–based ratios discussed earlier. Samples of these new ratios are provided in Exhibit 8–6.

EXHIBIT 8–6
A SAMPLE OF "NEW ECONOMY" RATIOS

Ratio	How Derived	Comments
Knowledge ratio™	Number of knowledge workers as a percentage of total employment	Engineering, architecture, research, consulting, broadcasting, and so on, have knowledge ratios of 40% or higher.
Patent to share price ratio	Number of patents per year divided by share price	For two companies in the same industry, the one with the higher ratio is generating more patents per dollar of share price, and has a relatively greater chance of enjoying commercial discoveries.
Technology spending ratio	Spending on technological capital assets (especially information processing–related assets) as a percentage of total capital asset spending	The higher this ratio, the more the company is shifting into the information economy.

In the MD&A section of its Annual Report (in Chapter 6), Corel emphasizes ratios such as "net research and development expenses as a percentage of sales." For this knowledge-based company, this ratio indicates the impact that each R&D dollar has on company sales. The ratio for Corel has declined, from about 8% in 1991 and 1992 to about 6% in 1993. This means that a relatively greater number of sales dollars are being generated by each R&D dollar expended. There is a limit below which this ratio should not sink; starving the R&D department would probably have negative sales consequences in future years.

As you might expect, some financial statement ratios are peculiar to specific industries. For example, the following ratio is often computed for property and casualty insurance companies:[9]

$$\frac{\text{Underwriting expenses}}{\text{Net premiums earned}}$$

Extensions of Ratio Analysis: Multivariate Financial Statement Ratio Models

Extensive research has been published in the accounting, finance, and other business literature assessing the usefulness of financial ratios for such purposes as these:

- Predicting the financial distress and bankruptcy of companies.
- Identifying companies that would make suitable takeover targets (that is, companies whose common shares should be purchased with the intent of gaining control).
- Bond-rating.
- Determining which companies are suitable investment opportunities.

Much of this research has focused on the use of individual ratios. However, considerable research has also focused on the use of ratios in combination, applying various statistical methods to develop equations consisting of a variety of ratios weighted by coefficients. For example, Edward Altman was among the first to apply a statistical method known as discriminant analysis for predicting financial distress.[10] He matched pairs of failed and successful manufacturing companies on criteria such as total sales, and ran a discriminant analysis computer program using five financial ratios to see which combination of these ratios best discriminated the failed from the successful firms. The program output the following multivariate, ratio-based equation:

$$Z = 1.2X1 + 1.4X2 + 3.3X3 + 0.6X4 + 1.0X5$$

where

X1 = Working capital/Total assets

X2 = Retained earnings/Total assets

X3 = Earning before interest and taxes/Total assets

X4 = Market value of preferred and common equity/Book value of total liabilities

X5 = Sales/Total assets

For example, if

X1 = 0.30

X2 = 0.10

X3 = 0.10

X4 = 1.50

X5 = 2.0,

then,

Z = 3.73.

---

[9] Statistics Canada, *Quarterly Financial Statistics for Enterprises, First Quarter 1994,* Catalogue 61–008 Quarterly, July 1994, p. 47.

[10] E.I. Altman, "Financial Ratios, Discriminant Analysis and the Prediction of Corporate Bankruptcy," *Journal of Finance*, September 1968, pp. 589–609, and E.I. Altman, *Corporate Financial Distress: A Complete Guide to Predicting, Avoiding and Dealing with Bankruptcy*, New York: John Wiley and Sons, 1983.

The computer program suggested to Altman that when Z was less than 1.81 there was a high probability of bankruptcy, and that scores higher than 3.00 indicated a low probability of bankruptcy. Scores in the range 1.81 to 3.00 were in a grey area in which the model's predictions were not that striking.

Altman's original Z-score equation was based on research done almost 30 years ago; both Altman and others have developed many refinements to the approach since then. Of course, since there have been tremendous changes in the economy over time, these original equations may not be good diagnostic tools today, and they and all other similar approaches to financial statement analysis must be used with care. Nuala Beck's opening comment would seem to reinforce this criticism.

The Special Case of the Earnings Per Share Family of Ratios

The earnings per share, or EPS, ratio is the only ratio whose calculation is regulated by official pronouncements from authoritative accounting bodies. This is partly because of abuses in how this ratio used to be calculated. In this section, the calculation of the EPS ratio is illustrated for Canada; other rules apply in other jurisdictions, such as the United States.

Suppose that Alphonso Corporation reported net income of $6,500,000 in the year ended December 31, 1995, and that this included an extraordinary gain of $500,000. The company's capital structure as at December 31, 1995, included the following securities, all of which were outstanding throughout 1995, except for 500,000 of the common shares, which were issued on July 1, 1995:

Long-term debt

8% bonds, due 2010, convertible into common stock at the rate of 3 shares for each $100 bond; 100,000 bonds outstanding.

Shareholders' equity

- Preferred stock, cumulative as to dividends of $4.50 per share; callable at $100; convertible into common stock at the rate of 2 shares of common for each share of preferred; 200,000 shares of preferred outstanding.
- Common stock, 1,500,000 shares outstanding.
- Warrants to purchase common shares. There were two categories of warrants: $20 warrants to purchase up to 100,000 shares, and $60 warrants to purchase up to 200,000 shares. Warrants are documents that give those who own them the right to purchase a prespecified number of a company's common shares.

We also assume that the company is subject to a 40% income tax rate, and that its return on equity is 6%.

Using the above data, the calculation of what the Canadian EPS accounting GAAP calls "basic EPS" proceeds as follows:

Step One

Compute the net income that accrues to the holders of residual equity (that is, to the common shareholders). To this end, adjustments must be made for things such as cumulative preferred dividends, since the common shareholders do not receive any dividends unless all cumulative preferred dividends are up to date. This calculation is made both before and after extraordinary items.

	Before Extraordinary Items	After Extraordinary Items
Net income	$6,000,000	$6,500,000
Deduct preferred share dividends	(900,000)	(900,000)
Residual income	$5,100,000	$5,600,000

Step Two

Compute the weighted average of common shares outstanding over the accounting period.

	Actual Shares	Weighting	Weighted Shares
Shares outstanding throughout the year	1,000,000	1	1,000,000
Shares issued July 1	500,000	0.5	250,000
Total weighted average of common shares			1,250,000

Step Three

Compute basic EPS.

	Before Extraordinary Items	After Extraordinary Items
Residual income	$5,100,000	$5,600,000
Divided by total weighted average of common shares	1,250,000	1,250,000
Basic EPS	$ 4.08	$ 4.48

Thus far we have two EPS ratios for Alphonso Corporation — but we're far from finished! Canadian accounting standards for EPS require that additional EPS ratios be computed whenever a company has "contingent securities" in its capital structure — that is, securities that may cause additional common shares to be issued. Alphonso Corporation has four such securities: the convertible preferred shares; the convertible bonds; and the two sets of warrants. The additional EPS ratios collectively go by the name "fully diluted" EPS, and of course must also be computed both before and after extraordinary items. For ease of exposition, we'll just illustrate the "before extraordinary items" calculations. The objective of this set of calculations is to estimate the minimum value that EPS could take on (hence the term "fully diluted"), assuming that the contingent securities were exercised. The calculation for Alphonso Corporation proceeds as shown in the table at the top of the next page.

Step Four

Compute the marginal effect on EPS of each of the potentially dilutive securities.

Step Five

Test the impact of each potentially dilutive contingent security on EPS. That is, does the presence of its marginal effect cause the basic EPS number to decrease? If it does, then the potentially dilutive security is indeed dilutive; if it does not, we ignore it in the computation of fully diluted EPS. The first marginal effect we test is that of the security with the lowest marginal EPS number — the $20 warrants. Then we test the next lowest, and so on, as shown in the bottom table on the next page.

Step Four

Contingent Security	Hypothetical Number of Common Shares	Hypothetical Increase in Residual Income	Marginal Impact on EPS	Rank Order (lowest to highest)
8% convertible bonds	3 × 100,000 bonds = 300,000 common shares	8% × $100 × 100,000 bonds × (1– 0.40) = $480,000	$\frac{\$480{,}000}{300{,}000\text{ shares}}$ = **$1.60** per share	2
$4.50 convertible preferred shares	2 × 200,000 convertible preferred shares = 400,000 common shares	$4.50 × 200,000 = $900,000	$\frac{\$900{,}000}{400{,}000\text{ shares}}$ = **$2.25** per share	3
$20 warrants	100,000 common shares	$20 × 100,000 new common shares = $2,000,000 in new equity; at a return on equity of 6%, this generates $120,000	$\frac{\$120{,}000}{100{,}000\text{ shares}}$ = **$1.20** per share	1
$60 warrants	200,000 common shares	$60 × 200,000 new common shares = $12,000,000 in new equity; at 6%, this generates $720,000	$\frac{\$720{,}000}{200{,}000\text{ shares}}$ = **$3.60** per share	4

Step Five

	Number of Shares	Residual Income	EPS
Basic EPS (based on original calculation, above)	1,250,000	$5,100,000	$4.08
First, add in the marginal impact of the $20 warrants	100,000	$ 120,000	
Subtotal	1,350,000	$5,220,000	$3.87
EPS is declining, so add in the effect of the next-lowest marginal EPS — the 8% convertible bonds	300,000	$ 480,000	
Subtotal	1,650,000	$5,700,000	$3.45
EPS is still declining, so add in the effect of the next-lowest marginal EPS — the convertible preferreds	400,000	$ 900,000	
Subtotal	2,050,000	$6,600,000	$3.22
EPS is still declining, so add in the effect of the final marginal EPS — the $60 warrants	200,000	$ 720,000	
Subtotal	2,250,000	$7,320,000	$3.25

Since the EPS increased when the impact of the $60 warrants was included, those warrants are ignored because they are *antidilutive* — that is, they cause the EPS number to increase. The fully diluted EPS for Alphonso Corporation for 1995, before extraordinary items, is therefore $3.22.

Accounting and Business Decision C

Using the information contained in Corel Corporation's financial statements in Chapter 6, verify the company's 1993 and 1992 basic EPS from continuing operations and for net income. Use the information in footnote 3 of Corel's 1993 financial statement to verify the weighted average number of shares outstanding during the two years.

Deriving EPS numbers in even our relatively simple Alphonso Corporation example was a bit of a bother, and the calculations can become even more complex for real companies. Does EPS really provide useful information to users of accounting information? Well, there's no doubt that this is probably the most popular financial statement ratio (just scan today's copy of a major newspaper's business section, or a publication such as the *Financial Post*); even so, popularity is no guarantee that something is worthwhile. The deficiencies of EPS include the following:

- Its numerator is based on GAAP-based net income, with its historic cost bias and other problems.
- It is oriented toward the past.
- It is merely a single measure (albeit with many variations, as we saw in the Alphonso Corporation example), and so cannot be expected to capture the richness and complexity of an accounting entity.

We can rail against accounting EPS all we want, but users and the business press will continue to demand overall, single, simple, essentially past-oriented measures of corporate success, and therefore managers will continue to be required to pay heed to it. And probably, they will continue to be tempted to make accounting and business decisions at least partly on the basis of what a "good" EPS number should be.

We now turn to financial accounting information that looks explicitly toward the future, and offers the financial statement analyst management's view of what the accounting entity's financial statements will look like as that future unfolds.

Future-Oriented Financial Information

For those interested in analysing an entity's financial statements, future-oriented financial information would seem to be of potentially great value. After all, forecasting the future is a key objective of financial statement analysis. Indeed, financial statement ratio analysis may be applied to future-oriented financial information as well as to an entity's actual financial statements.

The *CICA Handbook* in section 4250 defines future-oriented financial information as "information about prospective results of operations, financial position and/or changes in financial position, based on assumptions about future economic conditions and courses of action."

Interestingly, accounting standards-setters did not issue GAAP in Canada on future-oriented financial information until 1989. Public accountants and auditors were loathe to have their professional reputations associated with forecasts or projections. Their worry was that if the future didn't unfold as forecast, or their projections were alleged to be misleading, they might well be held liable by aggrieved users. However, the demand for some standards for future-oriented financial information prompted the CICA to issue its section 4250 in 1989.

The standard is written quite carefully, with a view to ensuring that future-oriented financial information is constructed with reasonable assumptions and full disclosure, and even includes "a cautionary note to the effect that actual results achieved for the period covered will vary from the information presented and that the variations may be material" (4250.24). When we consider the power of information — especially information that is located in an annual report associated with an auditor's professional opinion — this careful approach seems understandable. Sometimes, however, events are so far from expectations that accounting entities must engage in a major effort to explain why future-oriented financial information was so far off the mark. Such was the case with ATI Technologies Inc., a company based in Thornhill, Ontario, whose graphics accelerator cards and other personal computer enhancement products are well known. Excerpts from a press release issued by the company on July 7, 1994, are reproduced in Exhibit 8–7.

EXHIBIT 8–7
PRESS RELEASE TO DEAL WITH FUTURE-ORIENTED FINANCIAL INFORMATION THAT DID NOT COME TRUE

For Immediate Release
July 7, 1994

ATI ANNOUNCES THIRD QUARTER FINANCIAL RESULTS AND REVISED 1994 FORECAST

Thornhill, Ontario — ATI Technologies Inc. today announced its financial results for the third quarter and nine months ended May 31, 1994. Sales for the third quarter totaled $51.6 million with an after-tax loss in the quarter of $7.4 million, after deducting a pre-tax provision for inventory write downs of $11.5 million related principally to excess *mach32* product inventories. This after-tax loss in the quarter amounts to $0.16 per common share. The sales, net loss and loss per common share for the quarter are below the Company's forecast for the third quarter of sales of $98.2 million, net income of $9.6 million and earnings per common share of $0.22 contained in its prospectus dated November 19, 1993.

Sales for the nine months ended May 31, 1994 of $171.7 million and net income of $215,000, amounting to $0.01 per common share, are also below the forecast for the same nine month period of $215 million in sales and $16.4 million in net income, amounting to $0.37 per common share.

ATI's third quarter business was affected by a two month delay in shipments of its *mach64* graphics and multimedia products, coupled with an industry supply shortage of PCI-based systems which adversely affected OEM and Distribution sales, as well as substantially lower than anticipated sales of *mach32* products, particularly in Europe.

The Company has revised its fiscal 1994 forecast to reflect the shortfall in third quarter sales and lower than anticipated OEM and European sales in the fourth quarter. Total revised 1994 forecast sales are $231.5 million and net income is forecast at $957,000, amounting to $0.02 per common share. This compares to the original forecast contained in ATI's prospectus of sales of $315 million and net income at $26 million, amounting to $0.57 per share. A summary of the revised forecast and significant forecast assumptions is attached.

"The Company's third quarter results and fourth quarter forecast are unacceptable to me personally and to the Board of Directors" said K.Y. Ho, President and Chief Executive Officer. "The Company is taking the following actions: a) commencing a search for an industry knowledgeable Chief Operating Officer; b) strengthening our sales management; c) maintaining and expanding OEM relationships and sales channels; and d) strengthening the financial and management controls within the Company. I don't underestimate the challenges that lie ahead, but I believe ATI's continuing concentration on product quality, leading technology and customer satisfaction, coupled with the dedication of our employees, will justify my continued confidence in ATI's prospects."

ATI is one of the world's leading manufacturers of graphics enhancement products for personal computers. The Company's main product lines — components and board level graphics accelerators — increase the speed at which graphics can be displayed on PC monitors and improve the resolution and colour definition.

Accounting, Organizations, and Society

The following excerpt, from a CICA research report, is included here because it provides a comprehensive assessment of the benefits and limitations of financial statement ratios, and complements the introduction to financial statement analysis and the use of ratios presented in this chapter.

The Role of Ratio Analysis in Financial Accounting

A CICA Research Report

A ratio is a measure of relative size determined by dividing one number into another. Financial ratios depict the relationship between two numbers, for example, 2:1. A ratio is converted to a percentage when multiplied by 100. Ratios may relate two items in the balance sheet, such as current assets to current liabilities, or two items in the income statement, such as interest charges to net income. Ratios may also relate a balance sheet item to an income statement item, such as accounts receivable to sales. In addition, ratios may relate capital market data to information in the financial statements, such as market price per share and earnings per share.

Financial ratios are often used to interpret and explain financial statements. Indeed, the primary benefit of ratio analysis is that it provides a benchmark to measure performance, target future goals, and help identify actual or potential problem areas. Used properly, it can be an effective tool in evaluating the liquidity, debt position and profitability of an entity. It can also be used to evaluate, for investment purposes, such matters as market price in relation to earnings.

There is a common misconception, however, that ratio analysis provides secret knowledge about an entity and its operations. This is not so. [Ratios] are only a starting point for evaluating future performance. Because they may give conflicting signals, ratios must be used with caution. A review of the benefits and limitations of ratio analysis follows.

Benefits of Ratio Analysis

Financial ratio analysis is probably the most effective technique to evaluate where an entity has been financially and to project its financial future through the examination of trends. There are two principal uses of financial ratios. First is the traditional, normative use. Typically, this involves the assessment of an entity's ratio against a benchmark, and comparison with the planned ratio for the current period, the corresponding ratio for the preceding period, the corresponding ratio for a similar entity or the average ratio for the industry. Second is the predictive use in estimating relationships. Accountants and analysts use financial ratios to forecast certain variables, such as future profits, whereas researchers use financial ratios in statistical models for mainly predictive purposes, such as corporate failure, credit rating and risk assessment.

Financial ratios are used for all kinds of purposes, such as assessing the ability to pay debts and evaluating management performance. Concern for the bottom line is paramount when looking at financial statements because profits provide a basis for increase in investor wealth and encourage creditors to risk their money. Since it is largely profits that determine future expansion and since future profits are uncertain, ratio analysis provides an analytical tool for interpreting the key trends and relationships which give insight into current and future profitability.

Some benefits of using financial ratios are set out below.

- Ratios can provide a greater awareness of the interrelationship of individual financial statements and a greater understanding of the financial statements themselves by summarizing data in a form that is more easily understood, interpreted and compared.
- Ratios can facilitate comparisons with external measurements, such as industry-wide norms, and help identify an entity's strengths and weaknesses.
- Ratios can facilitate comparisons over time, such as changes in long-term trends of financial position, operations and cash flows.
- Ratios can provide an informed basis for making investment-related decisions by comparing an entity's financial performance in relation to another entity in the same industry and the industry as a whole.
- Because they are determined by dividing one financial variable by another, ratios downplay the impact of size and allow evaluation over time or across companies without undue concern for the effect of size differences.
- Ratios can identify the stability of relationships within an entity over time and common relationships among entities within a given industry.
- Ratios can be used to support the viability of extending credit. For example, a small closely-held entity may ask a supplier for trade credit or approach a bank for a loan. In such cases, credit managers and bank loan officers may be able to use ratio analysis on the financial statements to gain insights into the past, present, and future prospects of the individual applicants. These insights may help potential creditors predict the future cash flows of prospective borrowers and make credit decisions on a more rational basis.
- Ratios can serve as benchmarks against which the financial strength of an entity is measured; for example, debt covenants often specify limits in terms of financial ratios.
- Ratios can be used as an initial indicator to determine if there are specific problems that need to be investigated further, such as aging of accounts receivable and inventory turnover.
- Ratios can assist auditors and other users in evaluating the reasonableness of the amounts shown in the financial statements. Analytical review procedures can help the auditor in gaining an understanding of the client's business, plan the engagement, identify unexpected relationships among accounting data and provide substantive audit evidence.

Limitations of Ratio Analysis

The limitations of ratio analysis are closely interrelated with the limitations of financial statements. Therefore, when preparing or using ratios for financial statement analysis, users should be aware of the pitfalls.

Some of the more important limitations are set out below.

- An extensive number of ratios can be calculated from available financial data. Yet, there exists no *theoretical foundation* for financial ratio analysis that identifies the utility of individual ratios or provides a basis for selecting appropriate ratios for decision-making. In addition, few ratios have been developed for effective evaluation of the statement of cash flows. As a result, the decision-maker may be at a loss in selecting appropriate ratios for the task at hand.
- Ratios have limitations because of their *mathematical composition*. A ratio is the result of a numerator divided by a denominator. If either figure is suspect for any reason (such as failing to use an average or weighted average), the ratio may be of doubtful use. Furthermore, magnitude may pose a problem for the unwary (for example, one thousand divided by ten thousand will give the same ratio as one million divided by ten million).
- Ratios are usually based on *financial statement data* which are the result of conventional accounting principles and are subject to the limitations of the accounting process; for example, assets are generally reported in the balance sheet at historical cost rather than market value. Also, most information sources do not disclose the *accounting methods* used by the entities from which the comparative figures or ratios have been compiled. Users must, therefore, consider the potential impact that different accounting methods might have on their ratio analysis. In addition, *accounting classifications*, such as the distinction between current versus non-current assets and liabilities, are very important in the calculation of many ratios. If there is any inconsistency in such classifications from one period to another, the trend comparison expressed in ratios will be distorted and judgment may be influenced in an unrealistic way.
- Ratios calculated for only one year in the life of an entity have limited value. To be meaningful, they must be compared with similar ratios of the entity over a period of years. If historical analysis covers an insufficient number of years, the user may misinterpret *trends* and current performance; for example, due to substantial capital investments in the current year.
- Ratios are informative if there is *some external basis for comparison*. A ratio by itself is often meaningless until it is compared to projections and industry averages, as well as to similar ratios of other companies in the same industry. Furthermore, the relevance of certain ratios will vary according to the industry.
- *Fundamental differences* are inherent in any comparative analysis; consequently, differences in the nature and size of the business, geographic location, product lines, seasonal sales patterns, business practices, objectives and constraints may impact on the ratio results.

In summary, the major caveats to consider when performing financial ratio analysis are:

- ratios are meaningful only if there is a clear understanding of the purpose of each relationship;
- ratios are only as valid as the data in the financial statements themselves;
- ratios require a basis for comparison;
- ratios are only a clue to areas needing further investigation — they rarely supply answers.

In the end, the most significant drawback to financial ratio analysis may well be that the average investor has neither the time nor the inclination to calculate a series of ratios for each security being considered for purchase or disposal.

CICA Research Report: Using Ratios and Graphics in Financial Accounting, *1993, pp. 12–15.*

CHAPTER SUMMARY

After first describing financial statement analysis, the chapter explained the importance of knowledge and experience, outlined some uses of financial statement analysis, and warned about the impact of accounting differences.

Traditional financial ratios and other measures were then described, and the importance of cash flow information, "new economy" ratios, and multivariate financial statement models were briefly introduced. The special case of the earnings per share family of ratios was presented in detail. The chapter finished up by describing future-oriented financial information.

Suggested Answers to Accounting and Business Decisions

Decision A

(a) Different countries have different GAAP, and often have different ways of conducting business affairs (the *keiretsu* in Japan, for example). It follows that the ratios of companies in different countries must be adjusted in light of different accounting principles. Then the different ways of doing business must be incorporated into the analysis; for example, Japanese companies' high debt-to-equity ratios may be quite reasonable, since the banking member of a *keiretsu* would not usually permit a fellow *keiretsu* member company to go bankrupt.

(b) Knowledge and experience are important in financial statement analysis:

- Knowledge of the measurement decisions behind accounting numbers.
- Knowledge of the impact of those decisions on the numerator and denominator of financial statement ratios.
- Knowledge of differences between countries in GAAP and business practices.
- Experience in interpreting ratios and other financial information

Decision B

	Current Ratio	Ratio of Total Liabilities to Total Assets
(a)	No effect	Total assets lower under accelerated during the earlier part of the asset's life, so the ratio is higher under accelerated.
(b)	Accounts receivable overstated, so "aggressive" companies show a higher ratio	"Aggressive" companies show a lower ratio.
(c)	No effect	Both lease assets and liabilities are missing from the operating lease accounting company's balance sheet, so the effect is uncertain.

Decision C

From footnote 3 (number of common shares, in thousands):

	1992	1993
Common shares, start (A)	22,636	27,350
Issued during year:		
Employees	1,114	2,684
U.S. initial public offering	3,600	—
Assume issued halfway through year (B)	4,714/2 = 2,357	2,684/2 = 1,342
Estimated weighted average	**24,993**	**28,692**
Reported weighted average, from financial statements	**23,610**	**28,134**

If the reported weighted average common shares are used in each year, the calculations of basic EPS from continuing operations and for net income are correct.

KEY TERMS

Accounts payable turnover is the ratio derived by dividing an accounting entity's purchases of inventory for an accounting period, by its average accounts payable for the period.

Accounts receivable turnover is the ratio derived by dividing an accounting entity's sales for an accounting period, by its average accounts receivable for the period. The sales should be credit sales.

Altman's Z-score equation is an equation made up of financial statement ratios and other financial information, obtained through statistical methods, that helps analysts form judgments about the likelihood that a company will experience financial distress.

Asset turnover is the ratio derived by dividing an accounting entity's sales for an accounting period by its average total assets for the period.

Basic earnings per share is a ratio obtained by dividing an accounting entity's net income for an accounting period, after subtracting cumulative preferred dividends, by its weighted average number of common shares over the period. If there are extraordinary items in net income, basic EPS must be computed both before and after extraordinary items.

Capital intensity ratio is derived by dividing an accounting entity's sales for an accounting period by its average total capital assets for the period.

Cash conversion cycle is the sum of days' inventory plus days' receivables, less days' payables.

Cash flow liquidity ratio is derived by dividing an accounting entity's cash flow from operations for an accounting period by its average current liabilities over the same period.

Contingent securities include convertible preferred shares, convertible bonds, and warrants. Such securities, if converted or exercised, result in the issuance of common shares.

Current ratio is derived by dividing an accounting entity's current assets by its current liabilities, both measured as of the same date.

Days' inventory is derived by dividing an accounting entity's average inventory over an accounting period by the entity's cost of sales (cost of goods sold) for the period, and multiplying the result by 365.

Days' payables outstanding is derived by dividing an accounting entity's average accounts payable over an accounting period by its cost of sales (cost of goods sold) for the period, and multiplying the result by 365.

Days' receivables is derived by dividing an accounting entity's average accounts receivable over an accounting period by its sales for the period, and multiplying the result by 365.

Dividend payout ratio is derived by dividing the common share dividends declared by an accounting entity for an accounting period by the net income for the period.

Dividend yield ratio is derived by dividing the common share dividends declared by an accounting entity for an accounting period by the price per common share as obtained from the stock market. The common share price used is often the period-end price.

Earnings per share ratio is derived by dividing a number based upon an accounting entity's net income for an accounting period by a number based upon the entity's weighted average number of common shares outstanding over the period. It is a general term that refers to a set of EPS ratios computed and disclosed by the accounting entity. By itself, it is very imprecise, and should be modified by adjectives such as basic, or fully diluted, or similar.

Fully diluted EPS is a ratio that is an EPS number in which the assumed exercise of any contingent securities in the accounting entity's capital structure has been taken into account. Fully diluted EPS, if it exists for a particular accounting entity, is always less than basic EPS for that entity for the period.

Future-oriented financial information is defined in the *CICA Handbook*, section 4250, as "information about prospective results of operations, financial position and/or changes in financial position, based on assumptions about future economic conditions and courses of action."

Gross margin percentage is a ratio derived by dividing an accounting entity's gross margin for an accounting period by its sales for the period. It is usually expressed as a percentage, but may also be expressed in decimal form (gross margin ratio).

Inventory turnover is derived by dividing an accounting entity's cost of goods sold for an accounting period by its average inventory over the period.

Keiretsu refers to a group of Japanese companies that have a long-term co-operative relationship. Many different types of companies may be in the group — for example, electronics, heavy manufacturing, chemical, banking, and so on. Such companies typically own some small percentage of common shares of other members of the *keiretsu* and supply each other with goods and services.

Knowledge ratio is a ratio published by Nuala Beck[11] that is derived by dividing an accounting entity's number of knowledge workers by its total number of workers, both measured as of the same date.

Leverage effect refers to the impact of debt, in the capital structure of an accounting entity, on the entity's return on common shareholders' equity. During profitable periods, when profits are sufficient to cover interest costs and more, ROE is greater than ROA, since the excess goes to shareholders. But in those periods when profits are low, interest costs still have to be paid, and ROE falls below ROA.

Long-term debt to equity ratio is derived by dividing an accounting entity's average long-term debt for an accounting period by its average total common shareholders' equity for the period.

Long-term debt to total assets ratio is derived by dividing an accounting entity's average long-term debt for an accounting period by its average total assets for the period.

Operating cash flow as a percentage of total cash flow ratio is derived by dividing an accounting entity's cash flow from operations for an accounting period, by its total cash flow for the same period.

Operating cash return on sales ratio is derived by dividing an accounting entity's cash flow from operations for an accounting period by its sales for the period.

[11] Nuala Beck, *Shifting Gears — Thriving in the New Economy*, HarperCollins, 1992.

Patent-to-stock-price ratio is a ratio published by Nuala Beck[12] that is derived by dividing the number of patents that an accounting entity receives in an accounting period, by its share price.

Price-earnings ratio is derived by dividing an accounting entity's price per common share by its earnings per common share. The numerator of this ratio is often the period-end share price; the denominator is almost always the accounting entity's basic EPS before extraordinary items for the period.

Profit margin ratio is derived by dividing an accounting entity's net income for an accounting period by its sales for the period. The numerator that should be used is net income from continuing operations, but sometimes other numerators are used, such as the final net income number, which may not be representative of operations if there are discontinued operations and/or extraordinary items.

Quick assets are cash and cash equivalents, plus current accounts receivable and notes receivable.

Quick ratio is derived by dividing an accounting entity's quick assets by its current liabilities, both measured as of the same date.

Return on common shareholders' equity ratio is derived by dividing an accounting entity's net income (less any preferred share dividends) for an accounting period by its average common shareholders' equity over the period. Variations in how this ratio is computed involve whether the final net income is used, or net income before any discontinued or extraordinary items.

Return on total assets ratio is derived by dividing an accounting entity's net income for an accounting period plus its interest expense adjusted for income tax effects, by its average total assets over the period.

Technology spending ratio is a ratio published by Nuala Beck[13] that is derived by dividing an accounting entity's spending on technological capital assets for an accounting period, by its total capital asset spending for the period.

Times interest earned ratio is derived by dividing an accounting entity's net income before income tax expense plus interest expense for an accounting period, by its interest expense for the period.

FACT AND DESCRIPTION QUESTIONS

1. Describe the steps in financial statement analysis that are suggested in this chapter.
2. Suggest at least three reasons why financial statement ratios may be biased. Why are such ratios still useful?
3. Explain what is meant by "accounting differences." Describe how accounting differences may impair financial statement analysis.
4. Describe how disaggregating the ROA ratio into its profit margin and total asset turnover components could assist top management of a large, divisionalized company.
5. Explain why standards of comparison are important in financial statement analysis.
6. The profit margin of a food retailer is relatively low, while that of a manufacturing company is relatively high. Explain. Could both companies have the same ROA? How?
7. Explain why earnings per share ratios, as computed by accountants, may be misleading.
8. Explain the difference between "basic" and "fully diluted" EPS.
9. Why are accountants so cautious about becoming involved with future-oriented financial information?
10. Are ratios derived from the statement of changes in financial position more objective than ratios derived from the income statement and balance sheet?

[12] Nuala Beck, *Shifting Gears*.
[13] Nuala Beck, *Shifting Gears*.

Questions for Analysis and Discussion

11. Suppose you are an analyst employed by a not-for-profit group that identifies companies which it believes are harming the public interest. Suggest ways that financial statement analysis might be of use to you.

12. Explain how overall measures of corporate performance such as EPS might influence (for good or ill) a company's managers when they must make ethical decisions regarding the following:

    - Actions that may harm the environment but that may result in significant short-run profits.
    - Actions affecting employment during a recession.
    - The choice from among accounting alternatives for, say, revenue recognition.
    - The decision whether to write inventory down to market, where market is materially less than cost.

13. Explain the leverage effect. Why is the optimum amount of debt in a company's capital structure probably greater than zero? Financial statement ratios measuring financial leverage are usually based on accounting numbers. Is this a problem?

14. Explain why financial statement ratios for companies from different countries may not be comparable. How does this affect financial statement analysis?

15. The following references are to two recent articles that are critical of the more traditional tools of financial analysis. Look up the articles in your library and critically evaluate them.

    - Thomas A. Stewart, "Your Company's Most Valuable Asset: Intellectual Capital," *Fortune*, October 3, 1994, pp.68–72 and 74.
    - Alan Willis, "For Good Measure," *CA Magazine*, December 1994, pp. 16–22, 24, 27.

16. VF Corporation is an international apparel company headquartered in Wyomissing, Pennsylvania. Its brand names include Wrangler jeans and other popular lines of clothing. Estimates of ROE and ROA for the period 1983 to 1993, based upon VF's published financial statements, are as follows:

Year	ROE	ROA
1983	33.9	23.1
1984	29.8	19.7
1985	28.4	16.2
1986	21.5	12.3
1987	19.8	9.4
1988	16.8	9.1
1989	17.4	9.3
1990	9.9	4.1
1991	18.8	8.0
1992	23.0	9.7
1993	16.9	8.5
Average	**21.5**	**11.8**
Standard deviation	**6.9**	**5.6**

Required:

Suggest why the above "average" and "standard deviation" results for VF Corporation might be expected.

17. Michael Globe, a research analyst with the firm of Nesbitt Thomson (now Nesbitt Burns), prepared an analysis of Wal-Mart Stores Inc. on August 25, 1994. It is provided below.

Required:

(a) Suggest why Globe chose to analyse the financial ratios in his report. Be sure to consider the nature of Wal-Mart's business.
(b) Critically assess Globe's "Outlook and Recommendation." Conduct some research and find out what happened to Wal-Mart.

Second-Quarter and First-Half 1994 Review

The Company:
Wal-Mart is the fastest growing retailer in the U.S. and the largest retailer in the world. Net sales in the year ended January 31, 1994 totalled $67.3 billion. There are about 250 million people in the U.S. On average, each of them, including babies in prams, grannies in nursing homes and convicts in prison, spent $270 at Wal-Mart last year. There are a lot of countries in the world where the gross national product per capita is less than $270. The company opened 103 new Wal-Mart variety stores during the year, bringing the total to 1,953; it added 38 Supercenters, which are larger stores incorporating a food section, bringing the number to 68, and it opened 163 Sam's Clubs, bringing the number to 419 at year-end.

The Second Quarter—Summary:
Wal-Mart's reported second-quarter earnings per share number of $0.25, up from $0.22 a share in the previous corresponding period, was on target with street expectations. The latest figure includes approximately $0.01 from the sale of the Western Merchandising division.

Second Quarter Revenues, Earnings and Financial Ratios:
In the following table we show the second quarter revenue and earnings numbers for 1993 and 1994. Wal-mart's aggressive expansion continues unabated, so as well as showing the percentage gains in revenue for the various retail components, we also show the increase on a same-store basis in the comparable store change (Comp. Change) column.

Wal-Mart Stores Inc.
Financial Analysis:

Second Quarter **Period to July 31, 1994**	**1993**	**1994**	**Change**	**Comp. Change**
Sales: ($ million)				
Wal-Mart	11,608	14,172	22.1%	9.7%
Sam's Clubs	3,606	4,775	32.4%	–3.6%
McClane	1,022	995	–2.7%	n.a.
Total Sales:	$16,237	$19,942	22.8%	6.4%
Other Income	156	252		
Total Revenue:	$16,393	$20,195	23.2%	
Cost of Sales	12,963	15,960	23.1%	
Operating Earnings	$3,430	$4,234	23.5%	
S.G.&.A.	2,520	3,169	25.8%	
Interest - Debt	77	123		
Interest - Leases	48	52		
Total Interest	125	174	40.0%	
Earnings before Tax	$786	$891	13.4%	
Tax	290	326	12.5%	
Net Income	$496	$565	13.9%	
Earnings ($ per share)	$0.22	$0.25	13.6%	

Financial Ratios		
Operating Margin	21.1%	21.2%
S.G.&A./Sales	15.5%	15.9%
EBIT/Sales	5.6%	5.3%
Pre-tax Margin	4.8%	4.5%
Net Margin	3.1%	2.8%
Tax Rate	36.9%	36.6%

Back in 1980, when revenues were running out at about $1 billion a year, the cautious were concerned that the pace of growth, which had taken the company from zero to $1 billion in less than 20 years, was unsustainable. A reasonable concern at the time, although it looks a little silly now that the company is running at over $1.5 billion a week, and is likely to reach $2 billion a week in the near future.

In any event, retail revenues in the second quarter rose 24.5% over year-earlier levels, while total revenue, which includes the McLane division, which distributes food and other merchandise to convenience stores, and other income, expanded by 23.2%. Excluding outlets opened over the past year, Wal-Mart revenues increased by 9.7%, Sam's Clubs' revenues declined by 3.6% and total retail revenues increased by 6.4%.

The decline in revenues at Sam's and McClane's reflects, in part, lower cigarette prices and some other deflationary pricing, including an increase in private label goods. A change in sales mix due to the faster growth in wholesale club sales (up 32.4%) than in Wal-Mart store sales (up 22.1%) led to a slight decline in gross margins. Selling, general and administrative expenses grew at a faster rate than sales as the company integrated the Pace warehouse chain in the U.S. and the Woolco chain in Canada.

During the quarter, the company opened 19 new Wal-Marts and closed three, expanded or relocated five Wal-Marts, relocated 10 Wal-Marts to Supercenters and opened seven Sam's Club stores for a total of 38 additions. At the end of the quarter the company was operating 1,969 Wal-Marts, up from 1,879 last year; 87 Supercenters, up from 56; 434 Sam's Clubs up from 310, and 122 Canadian Wal-Marts, up from zero. In Canada, 35 Wal-Marts were remodeled during the quarter, bringing the total to 57 since the acquisition, and all the remainder should be finished by the end of November, in time for the Christmas selling season.

Outlook and Recommendation:
We expect to see continuing strong growth in revenues as the company's expansion domestically and overseas continues, and we look for an improvement in margins due to (1) less competition in the warehouse segment following the recent rationalization, (2) a reduction in percentage SG&A expense as the PACE and Woolco units are fully integrated into the system, (3) a return on the $5 billion-plus in capital investment and acquisitions made in 1993, and (4) a greater relative contribution from the higher-margin Supercenters. This all adds up to extremely attractive prospects for a company that has been as successful as Wal-Mart and is continuing to grow revenues rapidly.

We believe earnings per share growth could be in the high-teens to low-twenties over the next few years. Since peaking at $34 in early 1993, the share price has been as low as $22 3/8. It now stands at $24 1/2. Given that the shares are only trading at just over 16 times our estimate of next year's earnings, and at below our estimate of future earnings growth, we believe they represent excellent value and recommend a purchase.

Michael Globe, CFA
August 25, 1994

Reprinted courtesy of Nesbitt Burns.

18. Accounting students are sometimes tempted to assume that a standard, large, publicly traded manufacturing company is the "typical" financial accounting and reporting case. (Of course, nothing could be further from the truth, especially in a country such as Canada, which has a resource-based, service-dominated economy.) Consequently, it is useful to think about the different accounting choices, users, and so on that are important factors in evaluating the performance of, and selecting accounting policies for, different types of companies.

    This exercise focuses on the impact that *industry* membership has on outputs of the financial accounting process (financial statements, selected ratios, and other selected data). The case was inspired by Harvard Business School case 261–001 (Rev. 1971), "The Case of the Unidentified U.S. Industries."

    Because of diversification, differences in accounting policies, and so on, companies in similar industrial classifications show variations in financial statement patterns; however, the between-industry differences are usually greater than the within-industry differences.

Required:

(a) Match each lettered data set in Exhibit 1 with the appropriate Canadian company from the list in Exhibit 2. Explain your choices in detail.

(b) Discuss the differences in asset structure and operating patterns (that is, cash flows from operations, revenues, expenses), and the resulting need for and source of funds, for each of the companies in Exhibit 2.

EXHIBIT 1
FINANCIAL DATA SETS

	A	B	C	D	E	F	G	H	I	J
Balance Sheets[a] *(in %)*										
Cash and marketable securities	0.6	—	—	27.0	11.1	—	—	1.7	—	1.1
Receivables	15.9	24.6	7.4	15.1	52.9	23.5	7.6	12.1	7.1	17.2
Inventories	34.4	—	14.8	—	3.1	13.3	—	24.8	—	9.5
Other current assets	3.3	—	5.4	2.8	4.6	0.4	16.0	0.4	1.5	5.9
Plant and equipment, net (including capitalized leases)	40.4	12.8	63.0	3.0	23.9	58.7	39.6	59.9	88.1	41.2
Other assets (including investments)	5.4	62.6	9.4	52.1	4.4	4.1	36.8	1.1	3.3	25.1
ASSETS	100.0	100.0	100.0	100.0	100.0	100.0	100.0	100.0	100.0	100.0
Accounts payable	15.6	10.9	9.2	6.6	47.1	11.7	19.6	14.1	4.0	12.8
Notes payable and bank indebtedness	—	44.8	—	—	5.0	—	3.1	—	—	3.2
Taxes payable	—	1.0	1.0	—	1.2	4.1	—	2.9	1.1	2.0
Other current liabilities	6.6	16.1	4.9	—	8.7	1.2	4.1	—	6.9	—
Long-term debt	34.4	—	5.3	3.2	10.0	26.1	29.6	22.1	35.1	33.1
Deferred taxes	5.5	6.6	7.4	1.2	2.4	9.3	5.9	17.6	14.3	5.7
Other liabilities	1.0	1.0	3.6	62.6	0.1	—	—	—	3.4	—
Capital stock	16.2	9.7	4.2	16.0	18.1	14.6	25.4	26.3	18.0	41.5
Retained earnings[b]	20.7	9.9	64.4	10.4	7.4	33.0	12.3	17.0	17.2	1.7
LIABILITIES AND OWNERS' EQUITY	100.0	100.0	100.0	100.0	100.0	100.0	100.0	100.0	100.0	100.0

Ratios and other data										
Current ratio	2.42	—	1.83	—	1.15	2.16	0.88	2.30	0.71	1.86
Inventory turnover	4.12	—	n/a[d]	—	—	6.04	—	4.91	—	11.99
Net revenue/total assets	1.82	1.43	1.26	0.30	2.50	1.22	0.48	1.60	0.44	1.38
Net profits[c]/net revenue	0.05	0.05	0.07	0.02	0.01	0.10	0.13	0.11	0.11	0.01

[a] These account titles are general, and may not be used by particular companies in Exhibit 2.
[b] Includes foreign currency translation adjustments.
[c] Before extraordinary items.
[d] Not available, since "cost of goods sold" not disclosed.

EXHIBIT 2
THE COMPANIES AND THEIR INDUSTRIES

1. National Sea Products Limited: harvesting, processing, delivering, and marketing sea products.
2. Greyhound Lines of Canada Ltd.: intercity bus line operator and motor coach manufacturer.
3. CFCF Inc.: diversified communications company.
4. Royal LePage Limited: a diversified real estate services organization.
5. Simcoe Erie Investors Limited: a management and holding company whose subsidiaries and other companies operate in the general insurance business.
6. St. Lawrence Cement Inc.: cement producer and related businesses.
7. Banister Continental Ltd.: construction company.
8. Crestbrook Forest Industries Ltd.: logging and wood products.
9. Maritime Telegraph and Telephone Company, Limited: telecommunications.
10. T.C.C. Beverages Ltd.: produces, packages, distributes, and markets Coca-Cola and related soft drink brands.

19. (a) In his most recent book,[14] Edward Altman comments on his Z-score model as follows (p. 179):

The Z-score model has proven to be quite accurate over these last 25 years and remains an objective, established tool to be combined with other means to assess the health of companies. There certainly is some question of the model's continued applicability since the corporate environment has changed, and the original model's coefficients remain the same ...

Compute Z-scores for Corel Corporation for 1991, 1992, and 1993. Assume that the appropriate share prices to use in the formula for these three years were $6.00, $6.50, and $10.00.

(b) Suggest some benefits and costs of using a multivariate model such as Altman's Z-score model in the following situations:

(i) A new manager wishes to gain insights into the business, and computes Z-scores for the past five years.

(ii) A financial analyst interested in screening investment possibilities for clients computes Z-scores for several hundred companies.

20. Briefly summarize the main points that were made in the CICA research study that was excerpted in the "Accounting, Organizations, and Society" section of this chapter.

21. Recent financial statements for VF Corporation are shown on the next four pages. In the company's 1993 Annual Report, top management made the following comments:

- While net sales increased by 13% to a record $4.3 billion in 1993, earnings performance was disappointing.
- A major challenge is reducing our product cost. The combination of a low-inflation economy and consumers who are value-conscious makes it difficult to pass on increased costs through higher prices.
- Although VF competes in several mature, slow-growth markets, the active, casual lifestyles of the 1990s will continue to drive demand for VF's basic and fashion apparel. We give consumers an unbeatable combination of brands, price, and quality.
- Diversification into related product categories, such as our recent entry into licensed sports apparel, will contribute to growth.
- Both jeanswear and intimate apparel are contributing to our growth. Our success abroad in jeanswear is a testament to the appeal of genuine American brands such as Lee and Wrangler.
- The most compelling reasons to hold VF stock include these: our diversified portfolio of brands; our excellent retail relationships; our market response system, or MRS, which cuts cycle times, inventories, and costs; and our dedicated and aggressive management team.

Required:

You are an analyst employed by a major bank that has been approached by VF Corporation for a $50 million loan to assist the company in its expansion into the Mexican market. Perform an analysis that will provide useful information to your superiors.

[14] Edward I. Altman, *Corporate Financial Distress and Bankruptcy*, 2nd Edition, John Wiley and Sons, 1993.

Consolidated Statements of Income

In thousands, except per share amounts *Fiscal year ended*	*January 1, 1994*	*January 2, 1993*	*January 4, 1992*
Net Sales	$4,320,404	$3,824,449	$2,952,433
Costs and Operating Expenses			
Cost of products sold	2,974,861	2,603,726	2,039,787
Marketing, administrative and general expenses	913,734	791,343	608,592
	3,888,595	3,395,069	2,648,379
Operating Income	431,809	429,380	304,054
Other Income (Expense)			
Interest income	35,284	17,453	13,432
Interest expense	(72,671)	(71,068)	(68,587)
Miscellaneous, net	5,565	8	14,298
	(31,822)	(53,607)	(40,857)
Income Before Income Taxes	399,987	375,773	263,197
Income Taxes	153,572	138,742	101,867
Net Income	$ 246,415	$ 237,031	$ 161,330
Earnings Per Common Share			
Primary	$ 3.80	$ 3.97	$ 2.75
Fully diluted	3.71	3.85	2.62
Cash Dividends Per Common Share	$ 1.22	$ 1.11	$ 1.02
Average Number of Common Shares Outstanding	64,011	58,608	57,152

See notes to consolidated financial statements.

Sales and Operating Profit by Business Group *(Unaudited)*

In thousands	*Fiscal year ended*	*January 1, 1994*	*January 2, 1993*	*January 4, 1992*
Net Sales				
Jeanswear		$2,097,509	$1,896,258	$1,371,978
Casual/Sportswear		638,986	652,571	505,804
Intimate Apparel		436,500	420,200	452,899
International		641,827	420,278	272,524
Other Apparel		505,582	435,142	349,228
		$4,320,404	$3,824,449	$2,952,433
Operating Profit				
Jeanswear		$ 266,680	$ 274,256	$ 173,640
Casual/Sportswear		24,265	52,184	37,889
Intimate Apparel		40,214	53,425	42,289
International		70,891	34,253	35,937
Other Apparel		67,842	46,483	42,103
		469,892	460,601	331,858
Corporate Expenses		(38,083)	(31,221)	(27,804)
Interest, net		(37,387)	(53,615)	(55,155)
Other Income, net		5,565	8	14,298
Income Before Income Taxes		$ 399,987	$ 375,773	$ 263,197

Consolidated Balance Sheets

In thousands	*January 1, 1994*	*January 2, 1993*
Assets		
Current Assets		
Cash and equivalents	$ 151,564	$ 86,320
Accounts receivable, less allowances of $28,808 in 1993 and $30,275 in 1992	511,887	493,030
Inventories	778,767	742,474
Deferred income taxes	38,138	21,788
Other current assets	19,824	21,961
Total current assets	1,500,180	1,365,573
Property, Plant and Equipment	712,759	711,087
Intangible Assets	575,359	554,703
Other Assets	89,050	81,017
	$2,877,348	$2,712,380
Liabilities and Shareholders' Equity		
Current Liabilities		
Short-term borrowings	$ 35,648	$ 125,822
Current portion of long-term debt	110,119	54,195
Accounts payable	246,503	248,592
Accrued liabilities	267,578	255,393
Total current liabilities	659,848	684,002
Long-term Debt	527,573	767,641
Other Liabilities	126,978	95,248
Redeemable Preferred Stock	63,309	63,900
Deferred Contribution to Employee Stock Ownership Plan	(47,760)	(52,382)
	15,549	11,518
Common Shareholders' Equity		
Common Stock, stated value $1; shares authorized 150,000,000; shares outstanding, 64,488,660 in 1993 and 59,519,239 in 1992	64,489	59,519
Additional paid-in capital	543,165	301,336
Foreign currency translation adjustments	(12,865)	4,244
Retained earnings	952,611	788,872
	1,547,400	1,153,971
	$2,877,348	$2,712,380

See notes to consolidated financial statements.

Consolidated Statements of Cash Flows

In thousands *Fiscal year ended*	*January 1, 1994*	*January 2, 1993*	*January 4, 1992*
Operations			
Net income	$246,415	$237,031	$161,330
Adjustments to reconcile net income to cash provided by operations:			
Depreciation	106,678	90,866	76,292
Amortization of intangible assets	19,087	17,415	14,699
Other	(3,177)	(19,215)	(1,124)
Changes in current assets and liabilities:			
Accounts receivable	(24,094)	(95,027)	(18,342)
Inventories	(41,797)	(160,511)	(55,317)
Accounts payable	421	48,608	95,767
Other, net	(9,782)	3,893	13,867
Cash provided by operations	293,751	123,060	287,172
Investments			
Capital expenditures	(209,494)	(207,202)	(110,762)
Business acquisitions	(17,629)	(133,857)	(60,806)
Sale of outlet facilities	62,000	—	—
Other, net	45,840	8,513	10,476
Cash invested	(119,283)	(332,546)	(161,092)
Financing			
Increase (decrease) in short-term borrowings	(86,756)	55,751	(27,632)
Proceeds from long-term debt	98,557	331,900	100,325
Payment of long-term debt	(283,560)	(231,708)	(51,656)
Sale of Common Stock	232,068	—	—
Cash dividends paid	(82,831)	(69,552)	(62,712)
Other	13,298	47,123	15,872
Cash provided (used) by financing	(109,224)	133,514	(25,803)
Net Change in Cash and Equivalents	65,244	(75,972)	100,277
Cash and Equivalents—Beginning of Year	86,320	162,292	62,015
Cash and Equivalents—End of Year	$151,564	$86,320	$162,292

See notes to consolidated financial statements.

22. Recent income statements and balance sheets based on Mohawk Oil Canada Limited are shown below. The company markets automotive fuels through over 250 retail and bulk sales outlets in Western Canada; its corporate head office is in Burnaby, B.C. Partly as a result of its corporate philosophy of offering environmentally responsible fuels and lubricants under its slogan "Mother Nature's Gas Station," Mohawk had become a public company by 1994.

Mohawk had the following common shares issued and outstanding:

Date	Common Shares
September 30, 1992	9,994,765
September 30, 1993	9,995,844
September 30, 1994	12,115,228

Mohawk Canada Limited 1994 Annual Report.

Required:

(a) Prepare common-sized income statements and balance sheets for 1994 and 1993.

(b) Derive as many of the ratios described in the chapter's Exhibit 8–2 as you can, for Mohawk.

Consolidated Statements of Earnings

Years Ended September 30 (in thousands of dollars)

	1994	1993
Sales	$ 307,713	$ 307,817
Cost of Sales	256,753	259,352
Gross Profit	50,960	48,465
Expenses and Other Income		
Operating, administrative and general	30,739	30,896
Depreciation and amortization	4,940	5,246
Interest on long-term debt	3,719	4,633
Other interest	324	1,071
Share of equity income of partially-owned entities	(812)	(1,077)
Other	495	362
	39,405	41,131
Operating earnings from continuing operations before the undernoted	11,555	7,334
Unusual expenses	182	1,264
Earnings from continuing operations before income taxes	11,373	6,070

(Provision for) Recovery of Income Taxes		
Current	(6,178)	(2,937)
Deferred	1,115	891
	(5,063)	(2,046)
Earnings from continuing operations	6,310	4,024
Earnings from discontinued operations	25	2
Net earnings	$6,335	$ 4,026
Basic earnings per share		
Earnings from continuing operations	$ 0.65	$ 0.42
Net earnings	$ 0.65	$ 0.42

Mohawk Canada Limited 1994 Annual Report.

Consolidated Balance Sheets

September 30, 1994 and 1993 (in thousands of dollars)

	1994	1993
Assets		
Current Assets		
Cash	$ 16,177	—
Accounts receivable		
Trade	15,741	13,993
Other	1,444	1,664
Inventories of crude oil and products	12,252	9,825
Prepaid expenses and other	5,006	3,119
Current assets of discontinued operations	—	868
	50,620	29,469

	1994	1993
Non-current assets of discontinued operations	—	540
Agreements and notes receivable	2,585	4,626
Investments in and advances to partially-owned entities	3,727	9,896
Property, plant and equipment	43,460	52,627
Deferred financing costs	1,885	56
Other assets	1,873	1,216
	$ 104,150	$ 98,430

Liabilities and Shareholders' Equity

Current Liabilities		
Bank indebtedness	—	$ 11,281
Accounts payable and accrued liabilities	26,649	22,152
Income taxes	2,716	3,836
Current portion of long-term debt	6,431	14,136
Current liabilities of discontinued operations	—	783
	33,796	52,188
Non-current liabilities of discontinued operations	—	45
Long-term debt	33,794	28,811
Other liabilities	645	635
	68,235	81,679
Deferred income taxes	216	1,771
Deferred gains on sale and leaseback of property	5,651	1,134
Convertible debentures and shareholders' equity		
Convertible debentures	6,500	—
Shareholders' equity		
Share capital	12,589	3,926
Retained earnings	10,959	11,032
	23,548	14,958
Less share purchase loans to Mohawk employee trust	—	(1,112)
Total shareholders' equity	23,548	13,846
	$ 104,150	$ 98,430

Mohawk Canada Limited 1994 Annual Report.

23. ATI Technologies Inc., based in Thornhill, Ontario, is an innovative Canadian company in the personal computer enhancements industry. Its *mach64* graphics and multimedia accelerator products were considered leading edge. The company's sales for the fiscal year ended August 31, 1994, exceeded $230 million. Unfortunately, 1994 was a disappointing year for ATI, because of delays in shipping new products, heavy competition, and the cannibalization of the company's older products by its newer product lines.

Financial statements for ATI for 1994 and 1993 are shown on the next few pages. 40,000,000 common shares were outstanding on September 1, 1993; 7,250,000 additional shares were issued in fiscal 1994. The company's common shares, which are listed on the Toronto Stock Exchange, closed at 16 1/2 on August 31, 1993, and at 5 1/8 on August 31, 1994.

Required:

(a) Compute Altman's Z-scores for ATI for 1993 and 1994.

(b) Adopt the role of a financial analyst, and advise a large corporate client in a related business whether ATI appears to be an attractive takeover target. List other information that would make your job easier.

(c) Recall from the chapter that ATI's original 1994 FOFI income statement was revised in a press release dated July 7, 1994. The original forecast and the July 7 revision were as follows. Suggest why the actual 1994 results were different from the revised forecast.

Forecast Consolidated Statement of Operations

	Year Ending August 31, 1994 (thousands of dollars, except per share amounts)	
	Revised	Original
Sales	$231,549	$315,000
Cost of goods sold	178,853	218,000
Gross margin	52,696	97,000
Expenses		
Selling	17,093	23,333
Administrative and other	20,213	23,613
Research and development	16,331	13,882
	53,637	60,828
Other income	2,359	2,480
Income before income taxes	1,418	38,652
Income tax expense	461	12,583
Net income	$957	$26,069
Net income per common share	$0.02	$0.57

Financial Statements for 1993 and 1994:

ATI TECHNOLOGY INC.
Consolidated Statement of Operations and Retained Earnings

(Thousands of dollars, except per share amount)

	Year Ended August 31 1994	1993
Sales	$232,280	$221,668
Costs of goods sold	183,712	148,593
	48,568	73,075
Expenses		
Selling	22,859	20,330
Research and development net of investment tax credits of $3,300 (1993—$2,100)	15,820	10,478
Administrative	15,028	11,079
Management bonus	—	27,200
Interest	972	678
	54,679	69,765
	(6,111)	3,310
Interest and other income	2,228	777
Income (loss) before income taxes	(3,883)	4,087
Income taxes		
Current	240	42
Deferred	(1,432)	1,316
	(1,192)	1,358
Net income (loss)	($2,691)	$2,729
Loss per share	($0.06)	n/a
Retained earnings		
Retained earnings, beginning of year		
As previously stated	$ 17,836	$15,107
Settlement of prior years' income taxes	(9,800)	(9,800)
As restated	8,036	5,307
Net income (loss)	(2,691)	2,729
Retained earnings, end of year	$ 5,345	$ 8,036

ATI 1994 Annual Report.

Consolidated Balance Sheet

(thousands of dollars)

	August 31	
	1994	**1993**
Assets		
Current assets		
Cash and short-term investments	$ 29,275	—
Accounts receivable	33,005	16,402
Current portion of investment tax credits recoverable	1,700	3,960
Inventories	52,000	42,255
Prepayments and sundry receivables	3,377	2,284
	119,357	64,901
Capital assets	19,479	15,480
Long-term portion of investment tax credits recoverable	6,162	—
Deferred income taxes	1,702	—
	$146,700	$80,381
Liabilities and shareholders' equity		
Current liabilities		
Bank indebtedness	$ 23,734	$14,712
Accounts payable and accrued liabilities	19,459	15,328
Due to shareholders	—	27,200
Income taxes payable	204	9.918
	43,397	67,158
Mortgage payable	—	3,300
Deferred income taxes	—	1,878
Shareholders' equity		
Share capital	97,958	9
Retained earnings	5,345	8,036
	103,303	8,045
	$146,700	$80,381

24. It is December 1994, and Canada's largest banks have just reported profits ranging up to $1 billion for their fiscal years ended October 31, 1994. This is prompting some observers to allege that bank profits are obscenely high; others are pointing out that current profit levels are no more than reasonable compensation, and that banks have also had their lean years. In its 1994 annual reporting package, Bank of Montreal, which describes itself as "a Canadian bank with a North American future," included a supplement titled "Financial Goals and Measures," in which the company stated:[15]

Bank of Montreal's financial objective is to maximize long-term shareholder value through consistently superior, that is above industry average, earnings growth and return on common shareholders' equity (ROE). The Bank will achieve this objective through differentiation, superior productivity, well-managed risk-taking and strategic investment in the future. To assess its financial performance and condition, the Bank constantly monitors a set of eight key financial measures which balance profitability and prudential concerns.

The graphs and statistics on the following pages assess the Bank's performance on these measures in comparison to the six largest chartered banks in Canada and the 24 largest banks in North America. The bank's goal is to achieve consistently superior performance relative to its peer groups across the primary measures of financial performance and condition, thereby achieving top tier return on common shareholders' investment (ROI) over the long term. Top tier means being in the top two of the six Canadian banks and in the top six of the 24 North American banks.

Excerpts from the bank's special Annual Report Supplement are provided below, along with its 1994 balance sheet and income statement.

Required:

(a) Critically evaluate Bank of Montreal's choice of performance measures, and the peer groups it has chosen.
(b) Verify the earnings growth of 16.4% for 1994. Suggest some factors that might affect this number.
(c) Verify the productivity measure of 62.0% in 1994. Some patience and trial-and-error is required here. Suggest some factors that might affect this number.
(d) Can you verify any other measures from the eight published by the bank?
(e) Are there additional ratios that the bank should have included?
(f) Suggest some strategies and actions that the bank might take.

[15] Published with permission of Bank of Montreal.

Description of the Eight Measures

Return on Common Shareholders' Investment
Bank of Montreal measures return on common shareholders' investment (ROI) as the total return earned on an investment made at the beginning of the fiscal year in Bank of Montreal common shares. The total return includes the effect of the change in share price, dividends received and the assumed reinvestment of dividends in additional Bank of Montreal common shares. The Bank also measures a five-year return on common shareholders' investment (five-year ROI) calculated as the annualized total return earned on an investment made at the beginning of a five-year period in Bank of Montreal common shares.

The ROI for 1994 was negative 2.3% as compared to 0.8% for the average of the Canadian peer group. Bank of Montreal common stock closed at $25.125, 6.5% below the closing price in 1993 of $26.875, compared to an average decline in bank share prices for the six major Canadian banks of 3.0%.

The Bank's five-year ROI, at 14.3% in 1994, exceeded the Canadian and North American peer group averages of 8.2% and 10.2% respectively, and achieved top tier performance in both cases ...

Profitability
Profitability, as measured by return on average common shareholders' equity (ROE), was 14.9% for 1994 and its ranking in the Canadian peer group, at second, remained unchanged from last year. The Bank has consistently earned a ROE above the Canadian peer group average each year from 1991 to 1994.

The Bank's five-year average ROE was 14.5% and ranked first in its Canadian peer group and exceeded the North American peer group average of 13% ...

Earnings Growth
Earnings growth, at 16.4%, ranked fourth in the Canadian peer group.

The Bank ranked eleventh in earnings growth in its North American peer group.

The Canadian and North American peer group averages benefited from a large decline in the provision for credit losses relative to 1993 as indicated in the Asset Quality section ...

Productivity
Productivity is measured by the ratio of non-interest expense to total revenue; a lower ratio indicates better productivity. Bank of Montreal's expense-to-revenue ratio was 62.0% in 1994, marginally above the Canadian peer group average of 61.9%. Non-interest expense included a special charge related to losses incurred by the Special Lending Unit of Harris. Excluding this special charge, the Bank's expense-to-revenue ratio was 60.7%.

The Bank's expense-to-revenue ratio was better than the North American peer group average of 62.5%.

Asset Quality
Asset quality is measured by the ratio of the provision for credit

losses to average loans and acceptances; the lower the ratio, the better. Bank of Montreal's asset quality ratio in 1994 improved significantly to 0.63% and ranked second in the Canadian peer group. Over the last five fiscal years, the Bank's provisioning ratio averaged 0.62%, better than the Canadian peer group average of 0.83%.

The Bank's asset quality ratio was above the North American peer group average of 0.60%, which reflects a large decline in provisioning by U.S. banks relative to 1993. The Bank's five-year average provisioning ratio is better than the North American peer group average of 1.26% ...

Capital Adequacy*

Capital adequacy is measured by the ratio of Tier 1 capital to the level of risk-weighted assets. Tier 1 capital consists of common shareholders' equity; non-cumulative perpetual preferred shares; and controlling interest in subsidiaries, less goodwill.

The Bank's Tier 1 capital ratio continued to be the strongest in its Canadian peer group and was well above the minimum statutory requirement of 4% ...

Liquidity

Liquidity is measured by the proportion of cash resources and securities to total assets. The Bank, at 29.8%, continues to have the highest level of liquidity in its Canadian peer group which reported an average of 26% ...

Credit Ratings

External credit rating agencies closely monitor an organization's financial performance and rate its financial strength relative to other borrowers on a regular basis. These ratings affect the organization's cost of borrowing and ability to access debt markets. Bank of Montreal measures its credit rating as the composite of Standard & Poor's and Moody's ratings of its senior debt. The result is expressed in terms of Standard & Poor's ratings. All major credit rating agencies maintained their strong rating of Bank of Montreal during fiscal 1994. The Bank's credit rating remained constant at AA-, equal to the average of the Canadian peer group.

Strong financial condition and long-term earnings stability contributed to the Bank's above average ranking in its North American peer group ...

Bank of Montreal's performance ranking in its Canadian peer group in 1994 was equal to or better than the peer group average on five of the eight financial measures: return on common shareholders' equity, asset quality, capital adequacy, liquidity and credit ratings. Consistently strong performance has resulted in the Bank achieving top tier status on four of these measures.

** [Textbook author's note: The Office of the Superintendent of Financial Institutions (OSFI) requires Canadian banks to maintain at least a specified minimum capital adequacy ratio, in order to protect depositors against possible losses from banks' activities. The "risk-weighted assets" used in the construction of the ratio include "off-balance sheet assets," such as commitments, foreign exchange rate contracts, and interest rate contracts.]*

Consolidated Balance Sheet

As at October 31 (Canadian $ in millions)

	1994	1993
Assets		
Cash resources		
Cash and deposits with Bank of Canada	$ 840	$ 1,158
Deposits with other banks		
Interest-bearing	12,873	9,190
Non interest-bearing	946	1,048
Cheques and other items in transit, net	—	685
	14,659	12,081
Securities		
Investment (Market value $15,906 in 1994 and $15,003 in 1993)	15,733	14,599
Trading	10,481	8,560
Loan substitute	321	169
	26,535	23,328
Loans		
Residential mortgages	24,215	21,261
Non-residential mortgages	2,086	1,888
Consumer instalment and other personal loans	11,013	9,399
Credit card loans	3,261	2,896
Loans to businesses and governments	34,515	32,842
Securities purchased under resale agreements	14,572	7,658
	89,662	75,944
Allowance for credit losses	(1,028)	(1,916)
	88,634	74,028
Other		
Customers' liability under acceptances	3,430	3,555
Premises and equipment	1,575	1,458
Other assets	3,342	2,419
	8,347	7,432
Total Assets	$138,175	$116,869

	1994	1993
Liabilities and Shareholders' Equity		
Deposits		
Banks	$ 22,301	$ 20,807
Businesses and governments	28,741	22,675
Individuals	47,199	44,377
	98,241	87,859
Other		
Acceptances	3,430	3,555
Securities sold but not yet purchased	8,145	6,442
Securities sold under repurchase agreements	13,524	6,452
Other liabilities	6,079	4,512
	31,178	20,961
Subordinated Debt	2,218	2,363
Shareholders' Equity		
Share capital		
Preferred shares	860	852
Common shares	3,002	2,632
Retained earnings	2,676	2,202
	6,538	5,686
Total Liabilities and Shareholders' Equity	$138,175	$116,869

The accompanying notes to consolidated financial statements are an integral part of this statement.

[Footnotes not included]

[signed]
Matthew W. Barrett
Chairman and
Chief Executive Officer

[signed]
F. Anthony Comper
President and
Chief Operating Officer

Published with permission of Bank of Montreal.

Consolidated Statement of Income

For the Year ended October 31 (Canadian $ in millions except per share amounts)

	1994	1993	1992
Interest, Dividend and Fee Income			
Loans	$5,618	$5,505	$5,620
Securities	1,260	1,200	1,322
Deposits with banks	481	420	540
	7,359	7,125	7,482
Interest Expense			
Deposits	3,367	3,316	3,900
Subordinated debt	189	169	148
Other liabilities	423	428	424
	3,979	3,913	4,472
Net Interest Income	3,380	3,212	3,010
Provision for credit losses	510	675	550
Net Interest Income After Provision for Credit Losses	2,870	2,537	2,460
Other Income			
Operating services	422	415	390
Lending fees	178	147	118
Card services	211	208	193
Investment and securities services	424	312	241
Trust income	197	183	165
Foreign exchange	149	170	161
Other fees and commissions	168	146	97
	1,749	1,581	1,365
Net Interest and Other Income	4,619	4,118	3,825
Non-Interest Expense			
Salaries and employee benefits	1,795	1,664	1,549
Premises and equipment	600	580	555
Communications	180	165	167
Other expenses	546	477	458
	3,121	2,886	2,729

Goodwill and other valuation intangibles	31	30	36
Special charge	71	—	—
Total non-interest expense	3,223	2,916	2,765
Income Before Provision for Income Taxes	1,396	1,202	1,060
Provision for income taxes	560	487	416
Income Before Non-Controlling Interest in Subsidiary	836	715	644
Non-controlling interest	11	6	4
Net Income	$ 825	$ 709	$ 640
Preferred dividends	$ 69	$ 68	$ 64
Net income available to common shareholders	$ 756	$ 641	$ 576
Average common shares outstanding (in thousands)	251,307	247,727	242,079
Net Income Per Common Share			
—basic	$ 3.01	$ 2.59	$ 2.38
—fully diluted	2.97	2.55	2.36

The accompanying notes to consolidated financial statements are an integral part of this statement.
[Footnotes not included]

CASE

Metals Ltd.[16]

Jack Delance slumped down in his office chair, thinking about the assignment that his boss, Myron Peters, had just given him. Peters was the comptroller of Metals Ltd. (ML), and Delance had been hired six months earlier as his assistant. It was a great opportunity, working directly for a senior corporate executive while at the same time gaining experience credits toward a professional accounting designation. The opportunity, however, did not seem so great to Delance at times like right now — Peters had just given him yet another open-ended assignment. Jack now looked over his notes and recalled their conversation of the last half-hour:

MYRON PETERS (Comptroller, ML): Jack, I'm really pleased with your work on the new equipment proposal policy that you gave me last week — great job! You're a real self-starter!

JACK DELANCE (Special Assistant to the Comptroller): Thanks, Mr. Peters. I learned a lot on that job and it also gave me a chance to apply some of the theory I learned at school.

PETERS: I'm glad to hear you say that — that's exactly why I called you in this morning, so you can apply

[16] Prepared with Professor Russell Craig.

some more of the ideas you learned at business school, only this time it's not a policy I need your input on — it's much more pressing than that. You know that our industrial relations manager, Frank Alta, begins the current round of labour negotiations with the workers' union next month, don't you?

DELANCE: I guess I'm not too clued in on ML's labour relations — I wasn't aware that the contract was up for renewal soon.

PETERS: Well, it is, and Frank tells me that the union really wants to make up what they see as lost ground this time, especially since they co-operated over the last few years by agreeing to relatively small wage increases during the time that our sales and profits were hit.

DELANCE: That's interesting, but what can we do to help?

PETERS: Jack, Frank and his bargaining team need solid numbers, solid backup support based on ML's financial statements, to help them at the bargaining table. He wants us to work up some numbers that'll provide some indication of just how much we can afford to pay the union this year.

DELANCE: Sure, I'd be glad to provide as much support as I can, but I really don't know too much about collective bargaining.

PETERS: Frank just wants our financial and accounting experience, Jack. Look, he gave me some background information on the bargaining history at ML [Exhibit 1], and here's another copy of the company history that I gave you when you joined [Exhibit 2].

Required:

Using the techniques of financial statement analysis, prepare a report that you believe will be useful to Frank Alta. Exhibits 3 and 4 contain financial information about ML.

EXHIBIT 1
COLLECTIVE BARGAINING HISTORY AT ML

- Local 100 of the Sheet Metal Workers Union (SMWU) was certified as the exclusive bargaining agent in 1965.
- Union/management relations have been very positive over the years (even during the severe economic crisis of the middle to late 1970s); however, strain began to show three years ago, when ML profits nosedived and the union agreed to forgo wage increases and benefit improvements. Up until the current round of negotiations, contracts had always been for two years; this time, the union is only willing to sign a one-year contract.
- The key issue this year (1997) is "catch-up." About 50% of the cost of goods sold represents SMWU labour. The total wage increase demanded is expected to be about 10%, plus a cost of living allowance equal to 50% of the expected increase in the general price index.
- ML's top management has always worked hard to maintain good labour relations; this has involved the open sharing of information.
- Top management is concerned that ML's turnaround will be harmed by an excessive wage settlement. In 1994, ML had suffered a loss, and the $9 million profit in 1995 represented only a 9.6% return on total assets of $93,300,000 — far below the target return of 14%.

EXHIBIT 2
A SHORT HISTORY OF METALS LTD.

- 1949 — ML (founded by two army veterans) is established to produce metal parts for automobiles, industry, and so on.
- 1950 to 1955 — ML develops a reputation for quality, cost control, and reliability.
- 1955 — ML signs contracts to produce sheet metal parts for four suppliers to the automobile industry. This leads to a major expansion of plant and workforce (now at 30).
- 1960 — Further major expansion (to 200 employees); most of the business involves producing sheet metal and related products.
- 1965 — ML's employees organize Local 100 of the SMWU.
- 1970 — ML now has 1,000 employees. Major expansion is financed by going public. The two founders and their families keep 40% of the voting shares; the remaining 60% are widely dispersed.
- 1974 to 1982 — Severe economic problems are encountered, arising from the oil crisis, a drop in the demand for automobiles, and so on.
- 1983 to 1993 — ML profits recover; ML is "leaner and meaner"; the workforce is now about 600.
- 1994 to 1996 — OML records losses in 1993 and 1994, profits in 1995 and 1996. By 1995, ML has established a strong niche in a competitive, cyclical market. The company's tradition of emphasizing quality and reliability (including on-time delivery), and strong focus on cost control, have enabled it to become a strong force in the much-reduced, riskier market of the 1990s.
- 1997 and beyond — The company's strategy involves entering the government contract market (perhaps on a cost-plus basis), as well as expanding its product line and diversifying its customer base so that by the year 2000 sales to the automobile industry will represent only 50% of total sales.

EXHIBIT 3
METALS LTD. FINANCIAL STATEMENTS

Balance Sheets
as at December 31, 1996 and 1995, in $000,000s

	1996	1995
Shareholders' equity		
Common shares	10.0	10.0
Preferred shares (10% non-participating)	1.0	1.0
Retained earnings	35.6	31.3
	46.6	42.3
Represented by:		
Assets		
Current:		
Cash	1.6	0.8
Accounts Receivable (net)	26.0	20.0
Inventory, at FIFO cost	34.0	33.6
Noncurrent:		
Property, plant, and equipment (net)	36.7	33.9
Investment in Newcastle Products Ltd.	2.0	2.0
Intangible:		
Goodwill	2.0	3.0
	102.3	93.3
Less:		
Liabilities		
Current:		
Bank overdraft	7.7	5.0
Accounts payable	16.0	14.0
Income taxes payable	6.0	6.0
Current portion of long-term debt	2.0	2.0
Noncurrent:		
Long-term debt	14.0	16.0
Deferred Credits:		
Deferred income taxes	10.0	8.0
	55.7	51.0
Equals		
Net Assets	46.6	42.3

Statement of Net Income

	1996 ($m)	1995 ($m)
Sales	169.0	137.0
Cost of goods sold, excluding deprec'n	116.0	96.0
Depreciation	8.0	7.1
Selling, general & admin. expenses	20.9	14.9
Amortization of deferred charges	1.0	1.2
Interest	3.9	2.8
Loss on sale of property, plant & eqpt.	(0.8)	.0
	149.0	122.0
Profit before income taxes	20.0	15.0
Income taxes — current	6.0	6.0
— deferred	2.0	.0
	8.0	6.0
Net profit	12.0	9.0
Retained earnings at January 1	31.3	28.1
	43.3	37.1
Less:		
Dividends		
Common	7.6	5.7
Preferred	0.1	0.1
	7.7	5.8
Retained earnings at December 31	35.6	31.3

EXHIBIT 4
OTHER INFORMATION
(pertaining to Metals Ltd.)

1. Debt Redemption Schedule

(a) Long-term debt

repayable 1–1–1998	$5.0m
repayable 1–1–2000	6.0m
repayable 1–1–2002	3.0m

(b) A contingent liability arising from litigation over breach of a product warranty is noted in the accounts. The suit is for a maximum damages payment of $10m. A decision is expected before 30–6–1997.

2. Debt Covenant

The company is required to maintain a ratio of working capital to long-term debt of at least 1.0 in order not to default on its borrowing obligations.

3. The dramatic increase in selling, general, and administrative expenses in 1996 is an aberration arising from the substantial set-up costs involved in providing the necessary selling and administrative infrastructure to accommodate the company's plan to expand into new markets.

4. For 1997 and 1998:
   - All operating expenses (other than depreciation), and selling, general, and administrative expenses are expected to increase at 10% p.a.
   - Sales revenue is expected to grow at 5% p.a.
   - Dividend policy is to declare 50% of net historic cost–based income as a common stock dividend, with the remainder retained to fund preferred stock dividends, asset replacement, and growth.
   - Income taxes are expected to be constant at about $7.5m p.a. There are no deferred income taxes arising for activities in 1997 and 1998.
   - Inventories of work in process, finished goods, and raw materials are expected to remain at about current levels. Cash receipts and cash payments arising from all relevant income statement items are received or paid in the period in which they accrue.

5. Plant purchased in 1987 will be retired on 30–6–1997. It is expected to fetch $2.5m on the used machinery market. A replacement machine costing $10m is to be installed. Funding for the new machine is to be generated internally. Twelve monthly payments of $1m, commencing in July 1997, are required.

6. General price index data, actual and forecasted, reveal the following (other indices that may be required are available from government publications):

	Actual Index 1996	Forecasted Index 1997
1 January	200	220
Average for year	210	227
31 December	220	232

7. ML expects to face intense price competition from importers in the later part of the 1990s.

8. ML's principal domestic competitor recently agreed to increase the contract wages of its employees by 5% p.a. in fiscal year 1996.

10. All outstanding deferred charges for goodwill are to be fully amortized in 1997.

11. Investment in Newcastle Products Ltd: In early December 1995, ML and Cyril Lee, a prominent venture capitalist, concluded an agreement to establish Newcastle Products Ltd. (NPL). ML invested $2.0 million for 40% of the common shares, plus 100% of the preferred shares; Lee invested $3.0 million for the remaining common shares. The preferred shares could, at the option of the holder, be converted into common not less than two years after their original issue, thereby increasing the total number of common shares outstanding from the 1,000,000 originally issued to 1,300,000.

    In late December 1995, NPL purchased $4.2 million of state-of-the-art production equipment. The idea was that the NPL facility would be a sort of "experiment" for ML — a means to assess the feasibility of converting the bulk of ML's operations to JIT management techniques. The intent was to staff NPL with a small group of ML managers, who could run the entire pilot operation by themselves, since the equipment was highly automated.

    On the same day the new equipment was purchased, NPL signed an agreement to rent a small building suitable for its needs. The lease agreement specified the following:

    - Effective date of lease to be January 1, 1996.
    - Term of lease 60 months; renewal for an additional 60 months at NPL's option.
    - Rental: $50,000 monthly, in advance, for 60 months; renewal terms (if option exercised) $5,000 monthly, in advance.

    Unfortunately, technical problems with the new equipment delayed the planned start-up of the NPL test facility from June 1996 to June 1997.

Mr. Lean

In early January 1993, Ann Lee, the manager of the branch where Peter Lean did his banking, put Lean in touch with Orem Green, who was representing a group of Western Canadian entrepreneurs who had joined forces in 1982 to establish Organic Products Inc. (OPI). Lean was an extremely successful businessman who was on the lookout for "an interesting, high-potential investment opportunity" in which to invest the considerable amount of cash he had recently received from the sale of two companies he had established many years ago. As Lean put it:

I want to sit on the sidelines as far as a new investment is concerned — I took this so-called early retirement so that I could devote my energies to helping those less fortunate than me start up businesses in Eastern Europe, so I'd expect a new investment to provide me with cash flow for that purpose.

OPI was an integrated company based in British Columbia that was engaged in the production, processing, and distribution of North American ginseng, a root crop with unique medicinal and therapeutic properties. The primary market for ginseng is in Asia. The acceptance of OPI's North American ginseng in the Asian market strongly suggested that profits would grow without bound even in a generally weak economy. Thus, Lean immediately became quite interested in exploring whether an arrangement to invest in the business could be worked out.

The OPI group, according to Green, felt that the cash which Lean could inject into OPI could be used partly to pay down OPI's debt and partly to acquire further acreage for ginseng cultivation in southern British Columbia.

In late January 1993, Lean and the OPI group tentatively agreed on an arrangement whereby Lean would acquire 51% of the group's 100% holding of OPI common stock, for a total consideration equal to "five times the OPI annual net income." Lean engaged an independent accountant to assess OPI's accounting records and advise him as to the reasonableness of OPI's accounting information. He wanted to know whether he could rely on OPI's net income number. The available information for OPI follows.

Required:

Adopt the role of the independent accountant.

(a) As the first step in your analysis of OPI's financial accounting information, you have decided to reconstruct as well as you can the transactions in which OPI participated in 1992. This will, you feel, provide you with an understanding of the nature of OPI's business. You begin by computing the change in each balance sheet account, and seeing if you can understand what caused the changes.

(b) Summarize briefly OPI's business and the major risks that it faces.

(c) Do you feel that Lean should rely on OPI's net income number for 1992? Explain.

EXHIBIT 1
EXCERPTS FROM OPI'S ANNUAL REPORT

Corporate Profile

OPI has several active farms in southern B.C. The ginseng crop is harvested after the fourth year of growth and is exported to the Orient. 1992 was a year of record profits and sales, in which the company successfully secured much of the financing needed to meet the anticipated requirements for our operations and expansion. It was also the year in which we successfully launched a joint venture with the Peoples' Republic of China which established Canadian Natural Ginseng Ltd (CNGL), in which we have a 51% interest. CNGL owns and operates a processing facility in mainland China, which will enable OPI to exert control over important marketing channels, and also to benefit from the high profit margins available in the value-added market for ginseng products.

The $6.3 million in new long-term financing placed in 1992 consists of a $4.3 million private placement and a $2 million debenture. Management is actively looking for an additional $6 million to finance the company's expansion in order to take advantage of anticipated attractive market opportunities. Management expects the rapid growth and high profitability of the past several years since the company's inception to continue, with a strategic focus on our goals of expanding farm operations in Canada and developing value-added products in the Orient.

Interest costs increased significantly in 1992. Total interest was $1.3 million, which includes $0.9 million capitalized as part of root costs. The major component of interest expense was in relation to the root loan arranged in May 1991, and which was replaced by the $2 million debenture. Up until April 1992, when the most recent financing was completed, the company was required to finance expansion through expensive non-conventional methods since conventional lenders were reluctant to make large loans to an unproven new industry.

The economics of our business are summarized by the following:

- ginseng has a relatively stable world price;
- our acreage under cultivation continues to expand significantly, with 550 acres in 1992;
- demand for ginseng continues to grow, and Canadian ginseng is finding acceptance equal to the overseas domestic product;
- we are experiencing significant economies of scale from the Canadian farm operations;
- our Chinese joint venture is making inroads into marketing and value-added;
- recent events in mainland China bode well for business confidence, and Hong Kong investors are expanding their investments on the mainland. These two factors are expected to make the transition by the mainland to a more market-oriented economy much easier — since China is the world's largest market for ginseng, the increasing wealth will stimulate the demand for our product.
- a strong commitment to improving root quality through plant research and expansion of acreage under cultivation have been our keys to success (the commitment to quality through research — at all phases from selection of land through to the drying of the root — has led to greater acceptance of our product in the Orient, especially in mainland China).
- the benefits of being an industry leader: The company does not perceive any serious threats from competitors due to new entrants' inability to successfully control risks, market large volumes of root, and overcome barriers to entry (the ability to raise capital, the availability of expertise, and the availability of seed). The availability of seed is the most important barrier to entry into the market — seed is not available in large amounts since most growers are quite small and they either use their seed or destroy surplus seed to discourage new competition. Seed also needs a twelve-month germination period after it is harvested to

allow the embryo to mature, after which it must be planted within a short time or it will die. Further, seed costs about $10,000 per acre or about 25% of total costs. OPI is now fully self-sufficient in seed, which is a major competitive advantage.

- the availability of more conventional financing should lower financing costs.

Operating Results

	1992	1991
— Acres harvested	42	16
— Crop yields per acre (pounds)	3,125*	3,600
— Total acres under cultivation	550**	350
— Total number of farm sites	10	8

— Of the 550 acres currently under cultivation, 65 acres are to be harvested in 1993, 125 in 1994, 160 in 1995, and 200 in 1996.

(*The decline was due to record setting poor weather throughout the entire growing season. The cold temperatures caused lower than average yields per acre.)

(**Current plans are to level off at 900 acres in 1996. There is a need to geographically diversify crop sites so as to organize farm operations into manageable units and limit the risk of crop loss, while at the same time retaining the benefits of economies of scale.)

EXHIBIT 2
EXCERPTS FROM OPI'S BALANCE SHEETS
May 31
($000s)

	1992	1991
Assets		
Cash	507	92
Short-term investments	804	1,048
Accounts receivable	1,432	39
Inventory	549	150
Investment in CNGL	865	145
Ginseng crops	10,695	7,245
Property, plant, and equipment	5,608	4,759
	20,460	**13,478**
Liabilities		
Trade accounts payable	409	153
Accrued liabilities	147	73
Term debt	2,635	3,000
Deferred income taxes	3,550	1,970
	6,741	**5,196**
Shareholders' equity		
Share capital	10,129	6,424
Retained earnings	3,590	1,858
	13,719	8,282
	20,460	**13,478**

EXHIBIT 3
EXCERPTS FROM OPI'S INCOME STATEMENTS AND RELATED INFORMATION
for Year Ended May 31
($000s)

	1992	1991	1990
Sales	7,990	3,484	3,730
Cost of sales	2,404	767	936
Gross margin	5,586	2,717	2,794
General & administrative*	947	701	658
Interest & financing charges	448	72	18
Marketing	587	76	133
	1,982	849	809
Operating income	3,604	1,868	1,985
Other income (expense)	29	(50)	44
Earnings before income taxes	3,633	1,818	2,029
Income taxes	1,580	779	833
Net income	2,053	1,039	1,196
Dividends declared & paid	NIL	NIL	683
Private placement costs	321	NIL	NIL

* Note that G&A expenses include depreciation as follows: $52 in 1992, $48 in 1991, and $25 in 1990.)

EXHIBIT 4
STATEMENT OF CROP COSTS
For Year Ended May 31
($000s)

	1992	1991	1990
Depreciation	581	468	377
Farm equipment operating costs	257	206	150
Interest & financing	893	167	58
Land rental	311	200	69
Mulch & fertilizer	561	700	406
Other	53	82	51
Plant science	25	27	20
Salaries & wages	2,525	1,489	1,048
Seed	642	389	290
Small tools & supplies	60	65	65
Warehouse & dryer operations	48	NIL	NIL
	5,956	3,793	2,534
Balance at start of year	7,245	4,332	2,841
	13,201	8,125	5,375
Deduct: cost of crop & seed harvested during the year	2,506	880	1,043
Balance at end of year	10,695	7,245	4,332

EXHIBIT 5
EXCERPTS FROM FOOTNOTES
1992 FINANCIAL STATEMENTS

1. ACCOUNTING POLICIES

(a) The company complies with accounting principles as generally accepted in Canada ...

(d) Sales are recognized when ginseng products have been delivered to customers ...

(f) Inventory, consisting of ginseng seed, is valued at the lower of cost and net realizable value ...

(h) ... Included in crop costs are seed, labour, applicable overhead, interest and supplies. Costs are allocated each period based on the total number of acres under cultivation during the period. Crop costs related to the acreage harvested and sold have been charged to operations ...

(l) Assets and liabilities have not been segregated into current and non-current since the company's business cycle is longer than one year ...

2. CHANGE IN ACCOUNTING POLICY

During the year, the company changed its method of accounting for interest expense, from expensing all amounts in the current year, to the inclusion of the portion relating to expenditures on ginseng crop costs in the ... valuation of ginseng crops.

It had become apparent that the interest component of costs associated with the four year investment in the crop was not being properly reflected. Management believes that the new policy provides a better matching of costs against the associated revenues. The change has been applied retroactively. Interest of $893 (1991: $167; 1990: $58; 1989 and prior: $75) has been capitalized to crop during the year. Previously capitalized interest of $39 (1991: $40; 1990: $20) has been expensed in the year. The income tax effect of the change was to increase deferred income taxes by $54 in 1991 (1990: nil) ...

7. TERM DEBT

	1992	1991
Debenture payable*	2,000	—
Root loan**	588	3,000
Other	47	—
	2,635	3,000

*NOTE: During the year, the company issued $2 million in debentures bearing interest at prime plus 1.5%, secured by a floating charge over all assets of the company. In addition, warrants were issued to the holders of the debentures, entitling them to purchase up to 15% of the capital stock of the company, for $2 million, between June 1, 1993 and May 31, 1997.

The debentures are repayable in four equal annual instalments, plus accrued interest, beginning May 31, 1994.

**NOTE: In May, 1991, the company received funds for the assignment of proceeds on the sale of 75,000 pounds of ginseng root, of which 27,500 pounds was to related parties. The contract amount was set at the lesser of $40 per pound or $10 below the market price of ginseng as at December 31, 1991 (which was $55 per pound). At May 31, 1992, a balance of $588 thousand was outstanding, with repayment to be made within the next fiscal year ...

10. RELATED PARTY TRANSACTIONS

(a) Sales of $1.995 million (1991 and earlier: nil) were made to CNGL, of which $1.261 million was unpaid at year-end ...

CHAPTER 9 nine

Pushing the Boundaries of Accounting

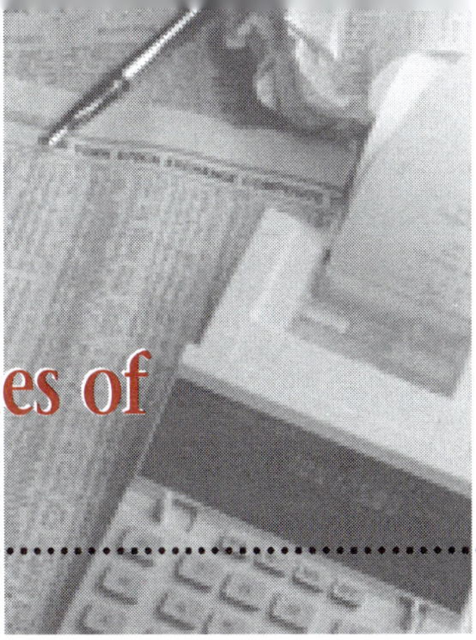

Learning OBJECTIVES

After you have read, thought about, and discussed this chapter, and completed a selection from the end-of-chapter material, you will have made significant progress in achieving the following learning objectives:

- Explain why the things that financial accounting measures and discloses change as the economy and society change.
- Explain why environmental accountability is important to all parties concerned with accounting and business.
- Describe current examples of environmental accounting.
- Describe possible future directions of environmental accounting.
- Explain why accounting for pension costs and liabilities is important.
- Describe differences between defined benefit pension plans and defined contribution pension plans.
- List strengths and weaknesses of existing pension accounting GAAP.
- Describe post-employment benefits other than pensions, and explain how they are accounted for.
- Describe employee stock option plans, and explain how they are accounted for.
- Describe derivative financial instruments and some of their accounting implications.

Different social values (and the varying views of business's place in society, which they give rise to) will result in the computation of different costs and liabilities, as well as different definitions of assets.

Daniel Blake Rubenstein, "Beyond the Clear-cut," *CAmagazine*, October 1994, pp. 23–29

ACCOUNTING

INTRODUCTION

An important point made in Chapter 3 was that the boundary between events that are accountable and events that are not accountable is continually changing. In that chapter, capital leases and environmental liabilities were introduced briefly as examples of this phenomenon (lease accounting is dealt with in more detail in the appendix at the end of the book). Environmental accounting is dealt with in much more detail in the present chapter. As well, pension plans, post-employment benefits other than pensions, employee stock option plans, financial instruments, and derivative securities are included in this chapter as further examples of business and economic arrangements that have become so important that they are now being given accounting recognition.

This theme — that what is considered to be accountable is ever-changing — is captured succinctly in this chapter's opening quotation from Daniel Rubenstein, who is a professional accountant with a special interest in environmental accounting. There seems to be no steady state in accounting — no final, perfect accounting system — since business and social activities, relations, and expectations are always changing. And the law changes too, to catch up — albeit more slowly and always imperfectly. When public opinion was more or less blithely unaware of the negative environmental impact of many business and government activities, and the law reflected the view that such insults were inconsequential or were externalities for which the offending accounting entity was neither responsible nor accountable, there was little perceived need for environmental accounting of any sort. When pensions and other post-employment benefits were informal arrangements granted almost at the whim of the employer, and cost relatively little, there wasn't the pressure to develop comprehensive accounting standards in these areas. And before the days of "creative financial engineering," when debt was debt and equity was equity and the two forms of long-term financing could easily be distinguished from each other, and swaps were what you did with baseball cards, there wasn't a need for accounting measurement and disclosure for these "sophisticated" financial instruments. But the world doesn't stand still, and if accounting did so it would quickly become irrelevant. Managers, accountants, users of accounting information, and indeed all those involved in the financial reporting and accountability process, must continually be pushing the boundaries of accounting.

Environmental Accountability

Have you ever driven past an area thick with chemical industry and regretted doing so because of the foul smell? Or wandered through the outskirts of a mining town and wondered how the terrain could be so barren? Or discovered that most sizes and species of fish from many (most?) of our lakes, even the remote ones, are unfit to consume because they contain unsafe levels of toxic substances such as mercury? Slowly — much too slowly, it seems — stakeholders in our modern economy are beginning to acknowledge that the ways we organize ourselves for economic activity, and many of the products we produce, create shocking environmental insults and impair the quality of life for us all. Indeed, some observers fear that this recognition has come too late for at least certain parts of spaceship Earth. For example, a report in *The Globe and Mail* of Saturday, December 24, 1994, said that Banff National Park in Alberta:

> *is in danger. A number of internationally respected biologists are finding that the environment of Banff National Park — and especially the crucial montane wintering ground around the town of Banff — is now so severely degraded by encroaching development that it may be difficult or impossible to repair ... Varius Geist, the University of Calgary's elk expert, calls it "almost a black hole."*

EXHIBIT 9–1
EDITORIAL CARTOON
JUST AFTER THE EXXON VALDEZ DISASTER

Toronto Star Thursday, March 30, 1989. Reprinted with permission of The Toronto Star Syndicate.

The ethical and accountability ideas embedded in accounting make it imperative that managers and others take meaningful steps to develop ways to redirect the various accounting subdisciplines *away from* contributing to environmental crises, and toward preventing or reversing such crises. Since the late 1980s, accounting professional groups worldwide have become heavily involved in exploring ways that accounting might be so redirected; to this end, they have commissioned and published a number of research and other studies. The accounting community's relatively late stirrings of awareness of its environmental duties and opportunities have inspired a fair degree of cynicism on the part of the media and others. For example, when the now-(in)famous *Exxon Valdez* oil tanker disaster befouled the Alaska coast in 1989, an editorial cartoonist for the *Toronto Star* drew the cartoon shown in Exhibit 9–1. It strongly implied that the professional "spin doctors" — accountants among them — were much more important to Exxon's view of the crisis than were the biologists, medical personnel, and others who could help with the *real* ecological crisis. In other words, accountants (and, by extension, accounting) were seen as part of the problem rather than part of the solution.

Accounting academics as a group have been no less negligent and tardy than their practitioner cousins when it comes to developing processes for ensuring environmental accountability, and to developing accounting curriculum that incorporates environmental accounting. Even so, some academics have made useful observations. For example, Keith Maunders and Roger Burritt, in their 1991 article "Accounting and Ecological Crisis," suggested that basic accounting ideas resulted in a "mismatch between accounting information and its application to ecological issues."[1] They went on to point out:

For the most part, ecological "problems" concern what are termed externalities *in welfare economics; i.e., impact outside the originating entity ... Such effects are excluded from conventional measurements of the entity's performance.*

So if up until now environmental accountability has not been included in accounting systems and reports, in a very real sense such an accountability may be said not to have existed, since accounting information does so much to create perceptions of reality. Ruth Hines, another accounting professor, put it this way when writing about the power of accountants and accounting:[2]

We create a picture of an organization, or the economy ... whatever you like, and on the basis of that picture (not some underlying "real" reality of which no-one is aware) people think and act. And by responding to that picture of reality, they make it so: it becomes "real" in its consequences.

These academics are suggesting that when environmental costs and liabilities weren't accounted for, they didn't exist for all practical purposes. They weren't visible as part of the "official" account of an accounting entity, and thus no one was held accountable for them.

But the picture of an entity's impact on the environment as portrayed by accounting is changing. For example, two recent studies supporting environmental accounting have been published by the CICA:

- *Environmental Costs and Liabilities: Accounting and Financial Reporting Issues*, 1993.
- *Reporting on Environmental Performance*, 1994.

Excerpts from the conclusions of the first study are reproduced in the appendix to this chapter. That study focuses on developing financial accounting and disclosure principles for reporting to those outside the accounting entity, as its foreword makes clear:

The objective of the project was to discuss the information needs of various user groups ... relating to the impact of an entity's operations on the environment, and to develop proposals for consideration by the Accounting Standards Board on accounting for and reporting on environmental measures (past, present and those contemplated for the future) within the existing financial reporting framework.

The second study, published in 1994, had a broader mandate and a "primary objective ... to develop a basis for a

[1] Keith T. Maunders and Roger L. Burritt, "Accounting and Ecological Crisis," *Accounting, Accountability and Auditing Journal*, Vol. 4, no. 3, 1991, pp. 9–26.

[2] Ruth D. Hines, "Financial Accounting: In Communicating Reality, We Construct Reality," *Accounting, Organizations and Society*, Vol. 13, no. 3, 1988, pp. 251–261.

framework for the reporting of information relating to the performance of an organization in accordance with standards and expectations relating to environmental conduct and responsibility" (p. ii). It recognizes that companies must develop information systems, including management accounting, management control, and financial reporting systems, that incorporate in a comprehensive manner environmental issues, such as targets for reducing noxious effluent from production processes. Indeed, there is now a movement to require companies to have such systems in place; for example, the International Organization for Standardization (ISO) is working on environmental management systems standards (the ISO 14000 series) that may eventually be mandatory for organizations wanting to serve as suppliers to leading companies.

What Might Environmental Accountability Be Like?

To illustrate, here are two current examples of environmental accounting from the financial accounting subdiscipline. There are also important implications of environmental accountability for other areas of accounting, such as management accounting, management control, and taxation.

1. Cott Corporation: In its annual report for the fiscal year ended January 29, 1994, Cott Corporation, a leading supplier of retailer-branded beverages with 1994 sales of $665,370,000, disclosed the following in the MD&A section of its 1994 Annual Report:[3]

ENVIRONMENTAL MATTERS
The Environmental Protection Act (Ontario) and certain regulations thereunder (collectively the "Act") provide that a minimum of 30% of sales of soft drinks, by volume, have to be sold in refillable containers. In order to comply, the Company, like other industry participants, would have to significantly increase its sales in this package. While attempts to improve this ratio are being undertaken primarily through significant price discounting of this package relative to other packages, it is apparent that this requirement will not be met by the company.

The requirements of the Act, if enforced, could result in significantly reduced margins in the 750mL refillable glass package as well as potential fines for non-compliance and possibly the prohibition of sales of soft drinks in non-refillable containers in Ontario. The Company is continuing to work directly and through industry associations to minimize the potential financial impact of these requirements.

2. Electrohome Limited: In the MD&A section of its Annual Report for the fiscal year ended August 31, 1994, Electrohome Limited, the Canadian electronics and broadcasting company that we encountered in Chapter 8, included the following environmental information:[4]

Unusual Items
...
Environmental Expense
The Company discovered some environmental contamination at one of its properties in 1991. As a result of recent testing, the Company in 1994 provided for potential remediation costs of approximately $2.5 million.

And in its consolidated statements of earnings and retained earnings, it included environmental expense as an unusual item, as shown in Exhibit 9–2.

[3] Cott Corporation, Annual Report.
[4] Reprinted courtesy of Electrohome Limited.

EXHIBIT 9–2
ELECTROHOME LIMITED'S 1994 INCOME STATEMENT

Consolidated Statements of Earnings and Retained Earnings

(thousands except per share amounts)	**August 31 1994**	**August 31 1993**
Revenue		
Electronics	$ 93,522	$ 71,134
Broadcast	57,616	58,448
	151,138	129,582
Expenses		
Operating expenses	127,385	110,063
Research and development expenses	6,140	4,796
Depreciation and amortization	3,527	3,415
Operating income	14,086	11,308
Interest expense	(3,757)	(5,808)
Other income	972	1,085
Earnings before unusual items, income taxes and discontinued operations	11,301	6,585
Investment tax credits on research and development	3,000	—
Environmental expense	(2,535)	—
Refinancing and restructuring expenses	—	(2,927)
CTV debt forgiveness	—	1,173
Earnings before income taxes and discontinued operations	11,766	4,831
Income taxes	175	(103)
Earnings before discontinued operations	11,591	4,934
Discontinued operations	487	3,566
Net earnings for the year	12,078	8,500
Retained earnings at beginning of year, as restated	16,574	8,104
	28,652	16,604
Dividends paid	747	30
Retained earnings at end of year	$ 27,905	$ 16,574
Earnings per class X and Y share		
Basic		
Before discontinued operations	$ 1.68	$ 0.88
Net for the year	1.75	1.53
Fully diluted		
Before discontinued operations	$ 1.63	$ 0.86
Net for the year	1.70	1.47

Reprinted courtesy of Electrohome Limited.

In the footnotes to its 1994 audited financial statements, Electrohome stated the following:

16. Commitments and contingencies
(a) In 1991, the Company became aware of some contamination at one of its properties. Testing is continuing. Based on information currently available as a result of tests conducted during 1994, the Company has estimated that the present value of the potential costs associated with remediation of this site may amount to approximately $3.0 million. The increase in the provision of approximately $2.5 million over amounts previously expensed has been charged to earnings in the current year ...
(b) In 1993, a claim was filed against the Company by Scotia Mortgage Corporation in connection with contaminated soil at a property sold by the Company to a third party in 1987. The claim seeks up to $1.5 million for clean up costs and an additional amount for unspecified damages. The Company has filed a Statement of Defence. Examinations for discovery are scheduled for late 1994. Any costs and/or damages which might be found by a court to be the responsibility of the Company will be accounted for as prior period adjustment ...

Although the disclosures made by both Cott Corporation and Electrohome provide some insight into environmental accountability, they also illustrate that the development of financial accounting and disclosure in this area is in its very early stages. Cott's disclosure was a little defensive, and didn't offer any details about the positive actions that the new law would encourage the company to take. Also, no environmental information was provided about the many other geographic regions in which the company operates; this seems inadequate, when one considers the nature of the company's product and its containers.

Electrohome's provision of an "environmental expense" classification on its income statement is useful, because it lets users know that this is an unusual expense and not part of everyday earnings; but again, very little in the way of proactive information is provided. For example: What programs does the company have in place to monitor soil contamination? What targets for reducing contamination (if discovered) does it have? And why was the increase in costs of $2.5 million not established until 1994, some three years after the company became aware of the contamination? By the way, Electrohome's footnote 16(b) doesn't represent anything innovative in environmental disclosures; this is just a fairly standard contingency disclosure.

The Cott and Electrohome examples represent at most slight extensions of the status quo. Some critics of the current accounting model have proposed more far-reaching changes. One interesting approach is described by Rubenstein, who conducted a project for the United Nations Center on Transnational Corporations that explored methods of accounting for sustainable development. Sustainable development is defined as "development that meets the needs of this generation without compromising the needs of the next."[5]

Rubenstein was interested in developing accounting models that would serve both financial accounting and management accounting needs. With the co-operation of a forest products company, he attempted to design experimental accounting systems and reports that had the following objectives:

- To estimate the cost of implementing sustainable development by the forest products company.
- To estimate the cost (including the cost of possible damage to the environment) of *not* implementing sustainable development. "The object was to determine the company's 'sus-

[5] Daniel Blake Rubinstein, "Beyond the Clear-cut," *CAmagazine*, October 1994, pp. 23–29.

tainable income' (its reported bottom line income adjusted to reflect the potential cost of damage to the company's natural capital.)"[6]

- To expand the definition of an asset so that it would include the resources and environment that the forest products company depended on to stay in business. As Rubenstein explains: "Here, I wanted to experiment with putting a dollar value on natural capital and recording the potential impairment of these assets in the same way that a company would calculate depreciation."[7]
- To design a series of reports that would both summarize the information collected during the course of the United Nations–sponsored project, and help management of the company report on its stewardship of the company and the natural assets for which it was accountable.

With such an ambitious set of objectives, it is not surprising that his project was only partly successful. Still, it represents a worthwhile direction for further exploration, in the sense that what is accounted for becomes accountable. However, there are critics of this approach to environmental accounting. These critics object to assigning money measures to aspects of nature. For example, Ruth Hines (whom we met just above), in writing about nature as a "friend," says:

To reduce a friend to a number or, worse, a money equivalent is likely to have even worse consequences than excluding them from accounts altogether. Nature can be given prominence in accounting reports without reducing it to a number. Quantifying our environment must inevitably further alienate people from nature.[8]

How Far Have We Come in Environmental Accounting?

Environmental accounting might be considered part of the social accounting or corporate social reporting movement. Back in July 1979, the U.S. Department of Commerce published "Corporate Social Reporting in the United States and Western Europe — Report of the Task Force on Corporate Social Performance," in which the term "social reporting" was defined as follows: "the reporting of information to the public about the impacts of day-to-day business activities on the physical environment, on employees, consumers, local communities and other affected interests" (p. 3). A bit earlier, in 1975, the American Accounting Association (an American-based international association of accounting academics) had suggested that introductory accounting textbooks contain the description of social accounting set out in Exhibit 9–3.

Aside from the now rather quaint and probably unintentional gender bias, the striking thing about this suggested description of social accounting is the astonishing lack of progress we've made over the past 20 years. The two CICA research studies mentioned earlier show that the accounting profession is beginning to move, at least on the environmental side of the social accounting issue. But when you examine the social (which includes the environmental) accountability information in a sample of annual reports in your school's library, the lack of progress will seem immense. Both Cott and Electrohome really had very little in the way of environmental information in their annual reports; and much social accounting information is more or less platitudes (for example, Cott's Annual Report says, "We have a

---

[6] Rubenstein, p. 23.
[7] Rubenstein, p. 24.
[8] Ruth Hines, "On Valuing Nature," *Accounting, Auditing & Accountability Journal*, Vol. 4, no. 3, 1991, pp. 27–29.

responsibility to contribute to communities in which we operate through the creation of quality employment, by protecting the environment, and by doing our share to support community service organizations" (p. 5). Perhaps the need to compete in the "lean and mean" global marketplace of the 1990s is blunting the environmental and social accounting movement.

EXHIBIT 9-3
AMERICAN ACCOUNTING ASSOCIATION'S SUGGESTED INTRODUCTION TO SOCIAL ACCOUNTING*

Accountants have long been viewed as the advocates of big business and the well-to-do; concerning themselves with maximization of net income and stockholder wealth. However, in recent years an area of accounting has been developing that concerns itself with the evaluation of a firm's contribution to society as a whole. Rather than determining a net income figure the accountant tries to represent the firm's effect on the quality of life.

The public has come to realize that any decision of a corporation has social impact. A decision to build a paper mill in a community not only provides more jobs, but may also affect the allocation of scarce resources and cause a noticeable difference in the purity of the air and water in the area. A firm's decision to sponsor a job training program not only affects the profits available to the stockholders, but may drastically alter the lives of the participants, their families, and even the community.The results might be considerably different than if the firm utilized the funds in a welfare-type program.

Social responsibility occurs when a firm recognizes that it is not merely accountable to its stockholders but to all of society. Many groups are concerned how well corporations are meeting this responsibility. All firms under SEC jurisdiction must make certain disclosures on expenditures for anti-pollution programs. Many organizations (churches, universities, etc.) include a firm's social responsibility in the criteria for investment decisions.

It is all well and good for a firm to feel it has implemented a socially responsible program, but it is essential that they communicate the efforts and results to the public so that they can make their own evaluation. The accountant is a natural choice as a communicator in this process since he already performs the task of presenting the firm's economic activities in a useful manner. Of course, it is a much easier thing to represent social program expenditures than results; but even in supplying this information, the accountant is supplying data which is nowhere else to be found. As the accepted measurer of corporate efforts, you can look to the accounting profession to develop the techniques needed to represent a firm's social responsibility.

* *Report of the Committee on Accounting for Social Performance*, American Accounting Association, 1975, pp. 61–2. In the material that follows, "SEC" refers to the U.S. Securities and Exchange Commission.

Accounting and Business Decision A

(a) Why is it useful for financial statement users to know Electrohome's environmental expense? Does separate classification of this item on the income statement make sense?

(b) Suggest how the idea of the accounting entity might be used to include environmental liabilities and costs.

Accounting For Pensions

Accounting for pension plans has been a controversial area for the past 40 years or so, ever since such arrangements became an important part of employee compensation. The *CICA Handbook* provides a good working definition of "pension plan" in section 3460, "Pension Costs and Obligations." This definition, and a few more we'll need, are in the following paragraphs.

A *pension plan* is "any arrangement (contractual or otherwise) by which a program is established to provide retirement income to employees." So a pension plan may exist, at least according to this definition, even when a written contract for one does not, as long as the accounting entity/employer has an established program in place. There are two general types of pension plans: defined benefit and defined contribution.

A *defined benefit pension plan* is a pension plan that "specifies either the benefits to be received by employees after retirement or the method for determining those benefits." For example, many organizations have a defined benefit pension plan that determines the annual pension benefits according to the following formula:

[Number of years employed by the organization × 2%; up to a maximum of 70%] × [Average of salary for the last 36 months of employment before retirement]

According to this formula, an employer who retired after working for the employer for 20 years, and whose average salary for the last 36 months before retirement was $60,000, would be entitled to a pension of $24,000 per year.

A *defined contribution pension plan* is a pension plan "in which the employer's contributions are fixed, usually as a percentage of compensation, and allocated to specific individuals. The pension benefit for each employee is the amount that can be provided at retirement based on the accumulated contributions made on that individual's behalf and investment earnings on those contributions." So under this type of pension plan, the pension a retiree gets depends greatly on what the interest rates are in the economy at the point in time when he or she retires. Generally speaking, employees bear more risk under defined contribution plans than they do under defined benefit plans. In the sometimes brutal economy of the 1990s, it isn't hard to understand why many employers are attempting to renegotiate their pension plans in order to convert defined benefit plans to defined contribution plans. And it also isn't hard to understand why some employers are attempting to terminate defined benefit plans, or to spin off divisions of their company that have such plans.

An *actuarial valuation* is an assessment of the financial status of a pension plan. It consists of the valuation of assets held by the fund and the calculation of the actuarial present value of benefits to be paid under the plan. The valuation results in a calculation of the required future contributions and a determination of any gains or losses since the last valuation. These measurements are performed by an accredited professional known as an actuary. By law in most Canadian jurisdictions, such valuations must be performed at least once every three years. Actuaries measure the assets of the pension plan, which are under the control of an independent trustee, using conservative assumptions about how much the assets (financial securities such as bonds, shares, and so on) will earn. So the actuary's measure of the plan's total assets tends to be biased downwards. The actuary's measure of the present value of the employer's defined benefit pension obligations tends to be conservative as well (because of conservative assumptions about employee turnover, future salaries, and the like); this results in an upward bias in the obligation measure. These biases are perfectly legitimate when we realize that the actuary's main job is to inform management how much cash the employer company needs to transfer to the pension plan trustee each year. Thus, the actuary is concerned with the *funding* of the plan, not with accounting for it. Prudence is the catchphrase for the actuary, because both the employing company's cash flow and the security of the employee's pension plan are at stake.

Accounting for versus funding defined benefit pension plans

Accounting principles under section 3460 of the *CICA Handbook* require that pension plan information included either in financial statements or disclosed in the footnotes be based on "best estimates," or "a set of actuarial assumptions each of which reflects management's judgment of the most likely set of conditions affecting future events." The accountant's "best estimate" measures of pension plan assets and pension plan obligations, then, may be quite different from the actuary's "conservative" measures, because the accountant and the actuary have such different roles. Their activities intermingle, however, because the actuary provides management with information that determines how much cash must be paid out to the pension plan's trustee, which in turn determines the credit to the "Cash" general ledger account.

Interestingly (or perhaps, confusingly), a defined benefit pension plan may be overfunded (so that plan assets exceed plan obligations) for actuarial purposes, and underfunded for accounting purposes, or vice versa. It is the accounting information, of course, that is disclosed in financial statements.

Accounting entities and defined benefit pension plans

The defined benefit pension plan itself may be regarded as a separate accounting entity, with its own assets and obligations and with the difference between them being the plan's net worth or equity. Indeed, a relatively new section of the *CICA Handbook*, section 4100, sets out Canadian GAAP for pension plans. Such financial statements provide useful information about plan performance for users, including the management of the employer company, and the employees covered by the plan. However, it is the impact of the plan on the employer company itself (often referred to as the plan sponsor) that is of crucial interest to the stakeholders in the company. And since defined benefit pension plans may have such a strong impact on plan sponsors, management has been extremely reluctant to account for the complete impact of (especially) plan obligations on the sponsor's balance sheet. Therefore, section 3460 of the *CICA Handbook*, which sets out Canadian GAAP for the impact of such plans on the employer's financial statements, is a compromise. The American analogue of section 3460 (known as Statement of Financial Accounting Standards No. 87, "Employers' Accounting for Pensions"), is a compromise as well, but requires much more disclosure than the Canadian standard. The two standards are otherwise quite similar. To see what we mean by a compromise, refer to Exhibit 9–4, which contains footnote information on the defined benefit pension plan sponsored by VF Corporation, a leading American apparel manufacturer.

The first paragraph of the footnote describes the plan in general terms. It is a defined benefit plan, so we know that VF is responsible for fulfilling obligations related to the promised pensions. It is also "noncontributory," which means that VF's employees do not contribute to, or pay into, the plan's assets.

The first of the two numerical schedules in the footnote describes the "effect of the defined benefit plan on income" — that is, on VF's pension expense for the year. From elsewhere in the financial statements, we know that VF's income before income taxes for the year ended January 1, 1994 — that is, the 1993 fiscal year — is $399,987,000, so the 1993 pension expense of $10,164,000 is just 2.5% of this number. But pension expense as a percentage of income before income taxes may also be significant; for example, for the Canadian company Electrohome in 1994, the $1,140,000 pension expense was 9.7% of before-tax income. This numerical schedule presents the components making up pension expense, at least according to the requirements of American (and Canadian) GAAP. The $10,337,000 of expense described as "Service cost — benefits earned during the year" is an estimate of the increase in the present value during the current year of the employer's pension promise made to the

EXHIBIT 9–4
VF CORPORATION'S PENSION FOOTNOTE

• Note H • Benefit Plans

The Corporation sponsors a noncontributory defined benefit pension plan covering substantially all full-time domestic employees. Benefits are based on employees' compensation and years of service. The Corporation annually contributes amounts, as determined by an actuary, that provide the plan with sufficient assets to meet future benefit payments. Plan assets consist principally of common stocks, corporate obligations and U.S. government obligations.

The effect of the defined benefit plan on income is as follows:

In thousands	*1993*	*1992*	*1991*
Service cost—benefits earned during the year	$ 10,337	$ 8,568	$ 8,343
Interest cost on projected benefit obligation	22,148	18,934	16,750
Actual return on plan assets	(34,895)	(19,646)	(42,530)
Net amortization and deferral	12,574	(1,884)	23,448
Pension expense	$10,164	$ 5,972	$ 6,011

The funded status of the defined benefit plan is as follows:

In thousands	*1993*	*1992*
Present value of vested benefits	$265,457	$203,763
Present value of accumulated benefits	$285,390	$217,087
Plan assets at fair value	$289,324	$254,191
Present value of projected benefits	332,656	241,514
Funded status	(43,332)	12,677
Unrecognized net loss	42,147	978
Unrecognized net asset	(20,580)	(24,958)
Unrecognized prior service cost	33,169	19,371
Pension asset recorded in Other Assets	$ 11,404	$ 8,068

The projected benefit obligation was determined using an assumed discount rate of 7.5% in 1993 and 9.0% in 1992 and 1991. The assumption for compensation increases was 5.0% in 1993 and 5.5% in 1992 and 1991, and for return on plan assets was 8.75% in 1993 and 1992 and 8.5% in 1991.

employees, arising from the fact that the employees have provided another year of work. The particular dollar amount of service cost depends on assumptions that actuaries make. The matching concept discussed in Chapter 4 may be used to rationalize classifying this component of VF's pension expense as an expense: VF's employees have provided their labour services during fiscal 1993, and these labour services helped generate VF's revenues that year. One of the employee-related compensation costs incurred by VF during the year was the current year's service cost. Under the matching principle, costs that help to generate revenues should be accounted for as expenses in the same accounting period that the revenues they helped generate are accounted for as revenues. So the service cost is a matched expense of fiscal 1993.

The next line item — "Interest cost on projected benefit obligation" of $22,148,000 — is a component of pension expense that arises because time is passing and the pension obligation or liability is growing from its present value to its larger future value. The "Actual return on plan assets" of a negative expense of $(34,895,000) accounts for the fact that the assets of the pension plan itself — that is, the common shares, corporate obligations (such as bonds), and U.S. government obligations — are earning interest, dividends, and the like. This serves to reduce the company's pension expense, except when the assets in the pension plan meet a bad year and perhaps incur a loss.

The last line item making up VF's pension expense is the $12,574,000 titled "Net amortization and deferral." This is really several items grouped together. To illustrate, assume that in fiscal 1993 VF learned that the present value of its pension obligation had increased by, say, $25,000,000 because of new information about interest rates, expected employee turnover, and so on. Under GAAP as it now exists, this $25,000,000 is not accounted for by increasing 1993 pension expense by the full amount. Rather, GAAP permits the $25,000,000 to be slowly brought into pension expense by deferring it and amortizing it over the number of years equal to the expected average remaining service life of the existing employees covered by the pension plan. This could be ten or more years; thus, only about $2,500,000 would get into pension expense in any given year because of this pension obligation revaluation.

This same deferral and amortization approach to accounting is permitted for revaluations of plan assets, increases in pension obligations when plans are renegotiated, and so on. In fact, the second numerical schedule in VF's footnote contains information on these unrecognized amounts. For instance, the "Unrecognized prior service cost" refers to the fact that VF's pension obligation increased because VF and its employees agreed to a more generous pension plan. So the first compromise in GAAP's accounting for pension plans is this deferral and amortization approach. To be even-handed, many observers of the pension accounting scene wouldn't label this as a compromise, since they believe that the accounting for long-term arrangements such as defined benefit pension plans should be smoothed out over time.

Note that Canadian GAAP does not require companies to disclose the components of pension expense as VF does, although many Canadian companies do so. Also, pension expense itself need not be disclosed. Given the potentially material size of pension expense, this qualifies as the second compromise in GAAP's pension accounting.

Now let's focus on the schedule in the footnote labelled "The funded status of the defined plan is as follows." The line item "Present value of vested benefits" of $265,457,000 represents the present value of benefits that are irrevocably due to the employees covered by the plan; that is, these benefits are vested in the employees. Several jurisdictions have legislation that specifies that after a certain number of years of employment, defined benefit pension benefits vest in an individual. The next line item, "Present value of accumulated benefits" of $285,390,000, represents all the benefits that employees have accumulated up to the end of the 1993 fiscal year, and not just the ones that have vested.

"Plan assets at fair value" of $289,324,000 is fairly self-explanatory. It represents all the financial assets in the plan, measured at approximately their current market value. "Present value of projected benefits" of $332,656,000 is an estimate of the value as at January 1, 1994, of the amount that the pension obligation of VF will grow to in the future, taking into account expected future salaries, turnover, and so on. Notice that:

Present value of projected benefits >
Present value of accumulated benefits >
Present value of vested benefits

VF discloses that the difference between the plan assets at fair value and the present value of projected benefits is a deficiency of $43,332,000 as at the end of fiscal 1993; that is, the plan is underfunded, on an accounting basis. The previous year, it was overfunded by $12,677,000; that is, it had a surplus. Part of the reason for this drastic swing in funding status is found in the bottom part of the footnote excerpt, where VF explains that the interest rate used to present-value the projected benefit obligation went down by 1.5 percentage points — a huge drop — thereby increasing the measure of the obligation considerably. By the way, many companies had pension surpluses on an accounting basis until quite recently, and one of the controversies that resulted involved the question of who "owned" such surpluses, the employer or the employees covered by the plan. Some employers attempted to "withdraw" the surpluses by various means, such as by terminating overfunded plans, using the surplus to avoid paying the actuary's determination of the current year's service cost, and so on.

The next three line items refer to the unrecognized, deferred amounts that we mentioned earlier. The sum of these three amounts, plus the net difference between the plan assets and the present value of projected benefits, is $11,404,000, as is recorded on VF's balance sheet as part of a balance sheet category that VF calls "Other Assets." This leads to the third compromise in GAAP pension accounting: neither the plan assets nor the plan obligations are recorded on the sponsoring organization's balance sheet. The number that is recorded — the $11,404,000 in VF's case — is an artificial construction that has no easy interpretation.

After all this churning about, let's reconstruct the actual journal entry that VF must have recorded to account for its defined benefit pension plan in 1993. We know that the debit to pension expense was $10,164,000, and we know that the artificial construct labelled "Pension asset" went from a debit of $8,068,000 at the start of the year to $11,404,000 at the end of the year — a change of $3,336,000 in the debit direction. So the journal entry must have been:

Dr	Pension expense (I)	10,164,000	
Dr	Pension asset (B)	3,336,000	
	Cr Cash (B)		13,500,000

The credit to cash was plugged out. This is the amount of cash that VF sent to the trustee of the pension plan.

Evaluation of accounting for pension plans

The numerous compromises and the need for a wide variety of estimates and disclosures make pension accounting under current GAAP quite contentious. The April 1992 issue of the monthly financial and accounting newspaper *The*

Bottom Line screamed out this headline: "CICA's Rules for Pension Plan Accounting Judged Inadequate for Times." Accounting researchers have alleged that not including pension assets and liabilities in sponsor's financial statements has led to misleading measures of financial position and results of operations. For example, Paul Miller and Rodney Redding show that the ratio of liabilities to equity for Chrysler Corporation using 1987 data increased by 141.6% when pension information was more fully included in the automaker's financial statements.[9]

However we may criticize current pension accounting GAAP, it represents a significant improvement over pension accounting GAAP as it existed before the mid-1980s. The general extent and quality of pension accounting information disclosed has increased; no longer are pension plans virtually unobservable. Until the late 1960s, pension accounting GAAP permitted sponsors of defined benefit pension plans to account for such plans on a cash basis, so that pension expense was set equal to the cash amount that was paid to the trustee. If the amount was, say, $1,000,000, the journal entry would have been:

Dr	Pension expense (I)	1,000,000	
	Cr Cash (B)		1,000,000

The actuary informed the company's management how much cash had to be paid to avoid underfunding the plan, but the amount involved was subject to fairly wide estimates. At times, some managements who wished to boost net income and cash flow either convinced their actuary to approve a lesser cash payment, or ignored the actuary and paid a smaller than required amount to the trustee. The pension accounting GAAP now in place largely prevents such behaviour, since it measures pension expense on (at least approximately) an accrual basis.

Accounting and Business Decision B

Suppose you are the chief negotiator for the union representing the employees of VF Corporation. Prepare a list of questions to ask management about VF's defined benefit pension plan.

[9] Paul B.W. Miller and Rodney J. Redding, "Measuring the Effects of Political Compromise on Employers' Accounting for Defined Benefit Pensions," *Accounting Horizons*, March 1992, pp. 42–61.

Post-Employment Benefits Other Than Pensions

Business practices and social expectations change. Until fairly recently, pensions were virtually the only post-employment benefit provided by an employer to retirees. However, it has become more common for employers to provide other benefits to their retirees, such as dental care, insurance, health care to supplement provincial health plans, eyecare and eyeglass plans, and so on. In 1989, the CICA's Emerging Issues Committee wrote:

There appears to be at least three methods of accounting for these plans currently being used in practice. These are as follows:

- *The current accrual method whereby a current service cost is actuarially determined and accrued in the accounts.*
- *The "pay as you go" method under which costs are recognized as incurred by the retirees and paid by the employer.*
- *A third method under which an estimated liability for benefits to be provided is accrued at the time an employee retires.*[10]

The matching concept can be used to justify that the current service costs associated with defined benefit pension plans should be accounted for as an expense of the accounting period during which employees provided labour services; it can also be used to make a similar argument for the cost of post-employment benefits other than pensions. Thus, the first of the three methods described in the preceding quotation seems to be the most consistent with accounting concepts, and GAAP seems to be moving in this direction. The Americans issued an authoritative pronouncement in this regard, effective February 1, 1993 (SFAS No. 106, "Employers' Accounting for Postretirement Benefits Other Than Pensions"), that requires the cost of such benefits to be recognized over the employees' working lives, including the interest cost on any accumulated postretirement obligation relating to such benefits.

Although the CICA has not yet issued an analogous pronouncement, companies such as Electrohome have already begun to account for post-employment benefits on this more complete basis. Excerpts from Electrohome's 1994 Annual Report dealing with this issue are shown in Exhibit 9–5.

EXHIBIT 9–5
ACCOUNTING FOR POSTEMPLOYMENT BENEFITS OTHER THAN PENSIONS: ELECTROHOME'S ACCOUNTING CHANGE

Notes to Consolidated Financial Statements

Years ended August 31, 1994 and 1993

1. Summary of significant accounting policies

(g) *Postemployment benefits*

The Company provides supplementary health benefits to its former employees during their retirement. To date, these benefits have been recognized when paid. In anticipation of a change in generally accepted accounting principles that will require the Company to account for postemployment benefits on an actuarially determined basis, the Company has changed its accounting policy in the current year to reflect this basis. See note 17 for the effect of the change on earnings and retained earnings. ...

17. Change in accounting policy

As described in note 1(g), the Company has changed its accounting policy with respect to postemployment benefits. Opening retained earnings at September 1, 1992 has been reduced by $1,666,000 representing the cumulative amount of the postemployment benefit obligation accrued to that date. $81,000 is applicable to 1993 and $73,000 to 1994. These amounts have been charged to earnings for those years.

Actuarial estimates indicate that the present value of the accrued postemployment benefits as of August 31, 1994 and August 31, 1993 were $1,820,000 and $1,747,000 respectively. The amount of accrued postemployment benefits is included in "Other liabilities".

[10] CICA's Emerging Issues Committee, Abstract of Issues Discussed, "Postemployment Benefits Other Than Pensions," October 24, 1989.

Accounting and Business Decision C

(a) A company provides supplementary health benefits to its former employees during their retirement years. The following journal entry is recorded by the company when such benefits are paid:

Dr Compensation expense (I)	XXX	
Cr Cash (B)		XXX

Explain how accounting concepts described in Chapter 4 can be used to criticize such a practice.

(b) Do you expect that requiring the cost of post-employment retirement benefits to be recorded over employees' working lives will have a "chilling" effect on a company's willingness to agree to such employee benefits?

Employee Stock Option Plans as Compensation Cost

Designing compensation plans for management and other employees is a very important part of administering an organization. Rewarding people fairly and providing them with incentives to do a good job is in the interest of all stakeholders. An increasingly common feature of management and employee compensation plans is the employee stock option plan, or ESOP. An ESOP is an arrangement by which certain employees of a company are granted an option to purchase a certain number of the company's shares over a certain period of time at a fixed price — usually the market price at the time the option is granted. If you look at Corel Corporation's financial statements in Chapter 6, you'll see information about that company's ESOP in footnote 3(e).

Here are some things to notice about Corel's ESOP:

- It is administered by a very senior group in the company; thus, it is considered to be an important part of the company's management control system.
- Only employees designated by this senior group qualify under the plan, so it is intended to provide rewards and incentives for key personnel.
- Options are granted for specific numbers of shares, at specific prices, and for specific time periods.

Disclosure of ESOPs, such as Corel has made, provides useful information for other users of financial statements. For example, in Corel's case we can see from footnote 3 that the 2,871,160 shares outstanding under the company's ESOP represent almost 10% of the total 30,034,000 common shares outstanding on that same date. So if a significant proportion of the options were excercised — presumably at exercise prices below the current market price — Corel's EPS might be diluted and its share price might be a bit lower.

An ESOP is one way for a company's board of directors to ensure, to the extent possible, that management's interests are aligned with the interests of the company, as represented by the shareholders. If a significant proportion of management's potential compensation is in the form of ESOPs, then management may be motivated to make decisions that are likely to increase the value of the company's shares on the stock exchange. That's the theory; however, it doesn't always work out like that, since share prices are affected by so many things.

The rise in popularity of ESOPs over the past 30 years or so has led to an awareness that the granting of an ESOP may be an accountable event. Typically, ESOPs are merely disclosed in footnotes (as in Corel's case), and have no impact on the financial statements until, of course, they are exercised. At that time, "Cash" is debited and "Common shares" is credited with the amount of the proceeds. But recently, accounting standards-setters in the United States have argued that ESOPs have value (otherwise, why would a seemingly intelligent manager accept an ESOP as part of a compensation package?), and that:[11]

- The value of stock options issued to employees is compensation.
- Compensation is a cost that should be recognized in the income statement.
- The value of the stock options should be measured at their fair, or market, value.
- "The amount to be attributed to employee services to be received as consideration for equity instruments shall be recognized as a cost ... as employees render the related services."[12]
- Just disclosing the details of ESOPs in footnotes, while useful, is not a substitute for actually recording costs associated with them in the financial statements.

One of the thorny problems here is how to measure the ESOP's fair value, and we're going to avoid dealing with it in this introductory book. The hypothetical situation that follows makes the heroic assumption that fair value has already been determined.

Alpha Company's common shares trade on a public stock exchange. The company established an ESOP for its senior managers and other key employees on January 1, 1996. The exercise price has been set equal to the stock's market price on that date (which was $50 per share), and the option period is three years. All the employees covered by the ESOP have agreed not to leave the company for the three-year period. We assume that the fair value of each option is $18. Options to purchase a total of 100,000 shares were involved. The options were all exercised on December 31, 1998. Keep in mind that the suggested journal entries to follow are not as yet part of GAAP, since ESOPs are only just now at the boundary between that which is accountable and that which is not. That this boundary is contested terrain in the case of ESOPs may be seen by the newspaper article reproduced in Exhibit 9–6.

The journal entries are as follows:

January 1, 1996:

Dr Prepaid compensation cost (B)	1,800,000	
Cr Options outstanding (B)		1,800,000

The account "Prepaid compensation cost" is an intangible asset that strictly speaking should be divided one-third to

[11] Financial Accounting Standards Board, Exposure Draft, Proposed Statement of Financial Accounting Standards, "Accounting for Stock-Based Compensation," June 30, 1993.
[12] FASB, "Accounting for Stock-Based Compensation, p. 3.

current assets and two-thirds to long-term assets. The account "Options outstanding" is a new subdivision of shareholders' equity.

December 31, 1996, 1997, and 1998 (assuming straight-line amortization):

Dr Compensation expense (I)	600,000	
Cr Prepaid compensation (B)		600,000

December 31, 1998:

Dr Cash (B)	5,000,000	
Dr Options outstanding (B)	1,800,000	
Cr Common shares (B)		6,800,000

EXHIBIT 9–6
RECOGNIZING ESOPS AS CONTESTED TERRAIN

Congress Fits New Company Options Rule

Jay Matthews

Special to the Star

The edicts of the Financial Accounting Standards Board (FASB), a kind of supreme court for accountants tucked away in the Connecticut hills, are usually ignored in Washington. But since April, when FASB endorsed a rule spoiling payday for many high-tech company executives and others, the board has gotten the attention of Congress.

"I believe that the global pre-eminence of America's vital technological industries could be damaged by the proposal FASB has put forward," said Sen. Joseph I. Lieberman, D-Conn., in submitting a bill to block the board's action. A companion measure has been introduced in the House and legislators with high-tech constituents are spending August gathering sponsors.

The controversy revolves around stock options — the authority granted to favored employees to buy a certain number of company shares over a certain period of time at a fixed price, usually the market price at the time the option is granted.

Such options are an important reason why the average large-company chief executive's pay rose 42 per cent, to $3,494,296 (all in U.S. dollars), last year, according to *Business Week*. They also explain some of last year's stratospheric CEO compensation packages, including $125 million for Thomas F. Frist Jr. of Hospital Corp. of America and $64.9 million for Sanford I. Weill of Primerica Corp.

Despite the gasps these figures draw from ordinary wage earners, stock options are popular with many corporate boards and shareholders, because they are thought to help motivate executives to increase the value of the company's stock and thus guarantee themselves a profit when they exercise their options.

Until now, companies have not had to deduct options from profits on their earnings statements, because accountants could not agree on how to value them. Instead, options plans are disclosed in footnotes on corporate profit-and-loss statements. But FASB, the accounting industry's seven-member rulemaking board in Norwalk, Conn., voted April 7 to require that companies begin deducting option costs from reported profits by 1997.

FASB let companies decide what formula to use to calculate the options' worth. The change only affects earnings statements and does not have any immediate significant impact on how much companies pay in taxes.

Business and investor groups have been lobbying FASB for years not to go ahead with a charge on options. Now that the clock has begun ticking toward 1997, they have become very upset, and very active in Washington.

Leaders of the 32-member coalition worked closely with congressional staff members to produce Lieberman's bill. Called the Equity Expansion Act of 1993, it would not only void FASB's order to charge options against earnings, but also create a new category of option that would be tax-free to employees if companies agreed to give up some tax deductions so that there would be no drain on the Treasury.

Sen. Carl Levin, D-Mich., whose goading helped lead to the FASB rule, has warned he will fight Lieberman's efforts to defend a policy "that encourages runaway executive pay by disguising the true cost of stock option compensation."

Toronto Star, August 15, 1993, H5. Reprinted with permission of The Toronto Star Syndicate.

Derivative Financial Instruments: Accounting for and Disclosing New Risks

In a recent edition of an American accounting practitioner publication, two employees of the FASB wrote:[13]

Swaps, forwards, futures, puts, calls, swaptions, caps, floors, collars, captions — the rapid growth of these useful but complex and poorly understood financial instruments, known collectively as derivatives, has propelled them into the spotlight as one of today's hottest financial topics. Accountants — preparers, auditors, and standard-setters — are struggling to keep pace with this innovative and increasingly important market.

The terms used in the first sentence of the above paragraph sound like the product of a creative but perverse mind. In fact, they refer to some of the financial contracts that have been designed over the past few years allegedly to help companies manage some of the risks they bear when they raise money or conduct their operations in the global marketplace. Some features of financial instruments and derivative securities are described in the following paragraphs.

A *financial instrument* "is any contract that gives rise to both a ... financial asset [for example, cash or the right to receive cash] of one entity and a ... financial liability [for example, an obligation to deliver cash] or equity instrument of another entity."[14]

Derivative securities are financial instruments whose value depends on or is derived from the value of an underlying asset, specified rate (such as an interest rate), or index (such as an index of share prices).

Derivative financial instruments may be grouped into two broad categories:

(a) *Forward contracts*, which require one party to the contract to buy, and the other party to sell, a specific asset at a specific future date for a specific price. To illustrate, suppose that a Canadian company building a warehouse in the United States to take advantage of exporting opportunities under the North American Free Trade Agreement is required to pay all its construction bills in U.S. currency. Assume that its bills are due and payable one year hence. Since the company has not yet started operations in the United States, all its money is in Canadian dollars. In order to protect itself (or "hedge") against the risk of an increase in the value of the American dollar versus the Canadian dollar, the company enters into a forward contract with another accounting entity in which the company agrees to buy the number of U.S. dollars it needs one year hence at a price that is fixed now. The risk associated with U.S. dollar–Canadian dollar exchange rates has been eliminated, and there is even the possibility of a gain for the company if the U.S. dollar's exchange rate exceeds the fixed rate negotiated in the forward contract.

(b) *Options* are contracts that involve one party paying another party for the right (but not the obligation) to acquire a specific asset or to benefit in some other way in the future. The

[13] Halsey G. Bullen and Laura J. Porterfield, "Derivative Financial Instruments: Time for Better Disclosure," *The CPA Journal*, July 1994, p. 18.
[14] CICA Accounting Standards Board, Proposed Accounting Recommendations, Re-exposure Draft, "Financial Instruments," April 1994, paragraph .006.

amount paid is often called a "premium." After the inception of the contract, the value of the option depends on the value of the underlying asset or other agreed-upon item. ESOPs, which we introduced earlier in this chapter, are a type of option. Recall that the option price in our ESOP example was $18; the greater the underlying share price exceeds $18, the greater the value of the option.

Let's look at an example of a derivative transaction entered into by a bank. Suppose some of a bank's corporate customers wish to deposit money in the bank at high fixed interest rates, while other customers wish to borrow at low variable interest rates. In fact, in the economy of the mid-1990s, this is what often happens. Consequently, if interest rates fall, the income that the bank receives on the variable-rate loans it makes falls faster than the interest expense it incurs on the fixed-rate deposits of its customers (which are liabilities from the bank's perspective). If interest rates increase, the opposite situation occurs. In order to protect itself against the risk of falling interest rates and the resulting losses, the bank might enter into contracts, called "swaps," with other financial institutions in which the bank agrees to receive a fixed interest rate and pay a floating rate. The bank is thus said to be "hedging" its original position. As Bullen and Porterfield describe it:

A swap contract works likes a series of forward contracts, each covering a specified period. At the end of each period, the parties to the swap contract settle up based on what has happened to interest rates during the period. For example, a bank uncomfortable with having variable-rate-loan assets and fixed-rate liabilities might enter into a swap in which it "pays" the floating rate and "receives" the fixed rate, applied quarterly to a "notional principal" amount. The bank makes or receives a net payment depending on the way interest rates went during the period. This counteracts the effects of the rate change on its interest income from variable rate loans.[15]

Derivatives can get quite complex, and may be used not only for managing a company's risk by hedging, but also for risky speculations. There have been some high-profile cases in which companies heavily into derivative contracts for more speculative purposes lost enormous amounts of money when the underlying assets or rates went in an unexpected direction. For example, Proctor & Gamble Co. in the United States incurred hundreds of millions in losses due to their derivative contracts, and the German company Metallgesellschaft A.G. almost went bankrupt after losing about $1 billion in 1993 in oil futures and other derivative contracts.

Metallgesellschaft's management had intended to hedge its long-term fixed-price contracts to supply customers with petroleum products, by entering into short-term future contracts to purchase oil. Such a hedging policy would have been wise had oil prices increased or decreased gradually, but they fell abruptly after the Organization of Petroleum Exporting Countries (OPEC) failed to agree on limiting exports.

Those who set accounting standards have been hurrying to develop disclosure and measurement GAAP for derivatives, so that users of financial statements will be better able to understand the risks they may bear by investing in and/or doing business with companies having such contracts. The development of such standards, some observers argue, will also have a "chilling effect" on the more reckless use of derivatives, and encourage companies to establish systems of internal control

[15] Bullen and Porterfield, "Derivative Financial Instruments," pp. 18–19.

over derivative activity. In addition, there is some activity in the U.S. Congress to put legal controls on the activities of banks, securities firms, and others who are engaged in the derivatives market.

In the United States, the SEC has recently proposed that companies engaged in certain complex swaps be required to recognize gains and losses on their income statements as changes in the market value of those contracts occur (so-called "mark-to-market accounting"), instead of carrying those contracts on their books at historic cost, as many companies do now. With interest rates increasing, this would result in massive write-downs for such companies.

Writers for the *Wall Street Journal* (August 25, 1994, A6) estimated recently that the worldwide derivatives market exceeds US$35 trillion in terms of the value of the underlying assets, so the potential for misunderstanding or abuse is significant. Clearly, the need to extend accountability in this area is rather urgent. The *Financial Post* reported on May 19, 1994, that the value of derivatives traded in Canada in 1992 was over $1.2 trillion. The CICA has issued accounting standards that encourage companies to do the following:

- Identify the extent, nature, and significant terms of financial instruments, including interest-rate risk and fair value.
- Disclose management's policies for controlling risk.

Other Canadian regulatory agencies are also active. For example, the federal Office of the Superintendent of Financial Institutions has issued draft guidelines to require banks, trust companies, and other financial institutions to cut the risks they take in derivatives and disclose the impact of such derivatives on their financial position.

Accounting, Organizations, and Society

In January 1994, Thomas Scott of the University of Alberta published a research article in *The Accounting Review* titled "Incentives and Disincentives for Financial Disclosure: Voluntary Disclosure of Defined Benefit Pension Plan Information by Canadian Firms." He was interested in examining two theories that purported to help explain why companies voluntarily disclose information. The information he focused on was the voluntary pension plan disclosures that some Canadian companies that sponsored defined benefit pension plans made after the current pension accounting GAAP became effective in 1987. Canadian GAAP requires that only the actuarial present value of projected pension benefits and the market-related value of pension fund assets be disclosed; but certain Canadian companies were voluntarily disclosing additional information, to the extent that their pension disclosure was very similar to that of the American company VF Corporation (see Exhibit 9–4).

Scott developed testable hypotheses based on the two theories, only one of which we will describe here. This is the proprietary cost theory, which suggests that managers will weigh the costs versus the benefits of disclosing information that is not required by GAAP or by law to be disclosed. Proprietary costs are defined as any potential reductions in the company's expected future cash flows that are attributable to disclosure. The information may be good news or bad news about the company;

and even if the news is good, there may be proprietary costs. For instance, if a company voluntarily discloses that it expects record profits next quarter, the unions representing its employees may well demand high wage settlements, and the company's share price may drop as a result! Scott concluded that the more favourable the news, the more positive the expected influence on share price and the greater the incentive managers have to disclose the information. On the other hand, the larger the expected proprietary costs of disclosing the information, the greater will be the decrease in share price upon disclosure and the greater will be the incentive for managers not to disclose. Scott pointed out that in the absence of proprietary costs, all relevant news is disclosed, but as proprietary costs increase only more favourable information is disclosed. He also pointed out that as proprietary costs increase, investors in the company's shares may be expected to be less upset by lack of disclosure, since management's motive for not disclosing information becomes less certain.

Scott developed the following two hypotheses from the theory:

1. "The probability of a firm disclosing information is negatively associated with the proprietary costs attached to the disclosure, *ceteris paribus*" (p. 28).
2. "The probability of a firm disclosing information is positively associated with the favorableness of the news in the disclosure, *ceteris paribus*" (p. 28).[16]

He went on to argue that the Canadian situation involving pension accounting provides an almost ideal setting to test these two hypotheses, for these reasons:

- Pension accounting information is relevant to investors, and thus should be an important input in setting the price of a company's shares in the secondary equity market (the stock exchange).
- Preparing a sample of companies with defined benefit pension plans is made possible because Canadian GAAP requires that companies disclose the pension asset and liability. Further, the subset of this sample that is made up of the voluntary disclosers of additional pension information is easily obtained by a review of financial statement footnotes, so two groups of Canadian companies — the voluntary disclosers and the nonvoluntary disclosers — can be prepared.
- The financial statement footnote information on pension plans is virtually the only source for such information in Canada.
- Pension disclosures probably have potential proprietary costs. For example, such disclosures have been alleged to likely undermine a company's future labour relations and wage negotiations.

Based on a variety of statistical tests on a sample of 288 Canadian companies, 102 of which disclosed at least some voluntary pension information over and above the required, and 186 of which did not, Scott found that the proprietary cost theory could not be dismissed, and provided at least some tentative explanatory ideas about those Canadian companies that voluntarily disclosed pension information above and beyond what Canadian GAAP requires.

[16] The phrase *ceteris paribus* in the two hypotheses translates from the Latin as "all other things being equal." It is a standard condition that social science researchers strive for, and has been roundly criticized as artificial and rarely if ever achievable.

CHAPTER SUMMARY

After pointing out that the boundaries of accounting keep changing, we provided environmental accounting as an example of an important new area in financial accounting and reporting. Progress, however, has been relatively slow in the matter of including environmental costs and liabilities in reports.

The chapter then described pension plans, and their impact on employer accounting entities, as another evolving area in accounting. Employee stock option plans, derivative securities, and retirement benefits other than pensions provided additional cases of society extending the boundaries of accounting and the resulting accountability.

Suggested Answers to Accounting and Business Decisions

Decision A

(a) Financial statement users would benefit because they could assess the relative magnitude of environmental expenses versus other expenses, and also track the trend in environmental expenses over time. They could thus determine whether such expenses should be considered an operating expense; and whether management is enjoying success in controlling and reducing such expenses (perhaps investment in capital equipment is required; perhaps better investigation should be carried out before sites are purchased; and so on). When such expense is separately disclosed, management may be held accountable for it — it is now visible and can be monitored.

(b) By defining the accounting entity to exclude the portion of the environment that the entity pollutes, accounting has traditionally ignored the costs and liabilities of environmental degradation. The costs and expenses incurred by the accounting entity thus exclude the costs of restoring the environment. Also, if the price charged for the entity's products is at least partly influenced by the costs the entity incurs, perhaps the products will be priced too low, and excessive consumption will be encouraged, leading to ever greater environmental degradation.

If the entity is expanded to include the environment, as Rubenstein suggests, then such costs will be accounted for. But perhaps a more practical approach is the rigorous development and enforcement of environmental laws that impose stiff penalties on polluters. The costs and liabilities resulting from those penalties, or incurred to avoid the penalties, that the accounting entity must then account for will serve as rough proxies for the environment. But will this amount to a "licence to pollute"?

Decision B

Based on VF's pension footnote reproduced in Exhibit 9–4, some questions are:

- What does "covering substantially all full-time domestic employees" mean? Who is not covered? What about non-domestic employees?
- What is the formula that determines the benefits "based on employees' compensation and years of service"?

- How well has the plan asset portfolio been performing, especially compared to similar funds?
- What accounts for the significant increase in service cost over the two prior years?
- Why has the actual return on plan assets been so volatile?
- What are the details behind the "Net amortization and deferral" component of pension expense?
- Why has the plan gone from an overfunded to an underfunded status?
- Why have the discount rate, compensation increase, and return on plan assets assumptions changed as they have?
- How much was paid out to retirees during the year?

Many other questions could also be asked.

Decision C

(a) The company is using a cash-basis approach to accounting for the supplementary health benefits it provides for its retired employees. The accrual approach, based on matching the total costs of employee compensation to the revenues the employees helped generate and recognizing those costs in the same accounting period in which the revenues were recognized, would require that the costs of supplementary health care be recorded over the employees' working lives.

The company is also not providing for the systematic funding of these benefits on an actuarial basis; rather, it is using a "pay as you go" approach. Consequently, there might be material unaccounted-for projected benefit obligations, as well.

Using a full accrual approach, and at least disclosing any unrecorded projected benefit obligations, would probably result in more relevant and representationally faithful financial statements. Then, measures of company achievements such as net income, EPS, and so on would not be overstated.

(b) Perhaps such a requirement could have a "chilling" effect on a company's willingness to agree to such plans, since financial statement performance numbers could be adversely affected if (for example) the cash-basis expense were less than the accrual-basis expense. Also, any management compensation and other contracts (such as financial ratio limitations imposed on the company by lenders or lessors) might be adversely affected. However, the union's bargaining power, competitive pressures, and/or evolving legislation might compel the company to supply such benefits anyway.

KEY TERMS

Actuarial valuation of a pension plan is performed by an actuary. It is an assessment of the financial status of the plan, including the valuation of the assets held by the pension fund and the calculation of the actuarial present value of benefits to be paid under the pension plan.

Defined benefit pension plan is a pension plan in which either the pension benefits to be received under the plan are specified in advance, or the method for determining the benefits is specified.

Defined contribution pension plan is a pension plan under which benefits are determined by the accumulated employee and employer contributions to the plan and the interest rates in the economy at the employee's retirement date.

Derivative financial instruments, also called **derivative securities**, are financial instruments whose value depends upon, or is derived from, the value of an underlying asset, specified rate (such as an interest rate), or index (such as an index of share prices).

Employee stock option plan is an arrangement by which certain employees of an accounting entity are granted an option to purchase a certain number of the entity's common shares (usually) over a certain period of time at a fixed price.

Environmental accounting spans a range of possible ways of accounting for the impact of the accounting entity's actions on the environment. At the rudimentary end, some companies are providing disclosure of environmental matters, including the impact of legislation. Other companies are classifying environmental costs separately in financial statements. More sophisticated environmental accounting is illustrated by the environmental reports published by a few companies, that provide details of the degree of achievement of pollution abatement and other environmental goals. Ultimately, some companies may adopt environmental accounting models that serve both financial accounting and management accounting needs, and implement fundamental changes in accounting, such as incorporating the environment into the definition of the accounting entity.

Financial instrument is a contract that gives rise to both cash or the right to receive cash (that is, a financial asset) of one accounting entity, and an obligation to deliver cash (that is, a financial liability) of another accounting entity.

Forward contract requires that one accounting entity buy and another accounting entity sell a specific asset at a specific future date for a specific price. The term is often used when the asset involved is currency, such as Japanese yen.

Options are contracts that involve one accounting entity paying another accounting entity for the right to acquire a specific asset or to benefit in some way in the future.

Pension plan is any arrangement (contractual or otherwise) by which a program is established to provide retirement income to employees. The CICA's *Terminology for Accountants* defines the term as "an arrangement, usually contractual, under which a program is established to provide for the payment of pension benefits."

Post-employment benefits other than pensions may include dental care, insurance, health care to supplement provincial health plans, eyecare and eyeglass plans, and so on. The specific benefits included in any particular situation depend on the agreement between the employer and the employee or union.

Present value of projected benefits of a defined benefit pension plan is an estimate, provided by an actuary, of the present value of the amount that the pension obligation will grow to in the future, taking into account expected future salaries, turnover, and the like.

Service cost of a defined benefit pension plan is an estimate, provided by an actuary, of the increase in the present value during the current year of the employer's pension promise to the employees, arising from the fact that the employees have provided another year of work.

Social reporting has been defined as "the reporting of information to the public about the impacts of day-to-day business activities on the physical environment, on employees, consumers, local communities and other affected parties."[17] Social reporting is therefore broader in scope than environmental accounting.

Sustainable development refers to corporate and governmental use of the environment that meets the needs of this generation without compromising the needs of the next generation.

FACT AND DESCRIPTION QUESTIONS

1. Explain why the boundary between accountable and nonaccountable events keeps changing.
2. (a) Distinguish between a defined benefit and a defined contribution pension plan.
   (b) What are the costs and benefits of each type of plan for employees? for the plan's sponsor?
3. Suggest why postretirement benefits other than pensions are becoming accountable events.
4. Explain why derivative financial instruments might be useful to a company. Explain why they might create significant risks.
5. Justify categorizing the incurrence by a company of environmental liabilities as accountable events. Give an example, and suggest an approach to measuring such events.
6. Explain why managers and other stakeholders in a company that has a material unfunded defined benefit pension plan might be reluctant to disclose such information. Explain why they might want to disclose such information.
7. Could a projected benefit obligation exist for postretirement benefits other than pensions?

Questions for Analysis and Discussion

8. In 1993 KPMG Peat Marwick Thorne published a document titled "International Survey of Environmental Reporting," in which 810 companies from ten countries were questioned about their current practice on environmental reporting.

   (a) One of the questions explored by the survey focused on what KPMG called the "honesty factor," which was explained as follows:

   Disclosing the bad news as well as good is very important if companies want to gain credibility for their reports. Otherwise, the reports can appear biased and akin to public relations tools. Even if there is considerable data, an otherwise "good" report will invite suspicion on all its disclosures if companies are not "up front" about the problems they are facing, including fines and prosecutions. One argument for not doing so, which is perhaps more relevant to the U.S., is the fear of litigious or other adverse consequences that might arise.

[17] Department of Commerce, Government of the United States, *Corporate Social Reporting in the United States and Western Europe — Report of the Task Force on Corporate Social Performance*, July 1979, p. 3.

Only 63 of the companies in the sample disclosed bad news as well as good. Do you have any comments? Perhaps adopting the perspective of various stakeholders might help in responding to this question.

(b) Explain how, if at all, the "honesty factor" is related to ethics in accounting.

9. The article on ESOPs reproduced in Exhibit 9–6 illustrates that setting accounting standards is not merely a technical exercise of discovering which accounting method, if any, best complies with the conceptual framework described in Chapter 4. Identify the issues raised by the article, and adopt and defend a position on them.

10. Read the excerpt from the 1993 CICA research study reproduced in the appendix to this chapter. Adopt the role of an executive of a Canadian forest products company, and prepare reasonable and convincing arguments against the research study's proposals on disclosure.

11. Suppose you are a researcher with a national union who has been requested to appear before the CICA's Accounting Standards Board to provide input into its deliberations on accounting for postretirement benefits other than pensions. Prepare a position paper supporting a cash-basis method of accounting, based on your desire for such benefit programs to be expanded.

12. (a) Referring to the material in the "Accounting, Organizations, and Society" section of this chapter, explain why managers might find Scott's research useful.
    (b) Suppose Scott's research was available to the CICA's Accounting Standards Board when they were considering whether to modify the Canadian pension accounting GAAP. Should it have any influence on the board's deliberations?

13. (a) Suggest why companies whose shares trade on public stock exchanges might wish to adopt an ESOP as part of their compensation package for key personnel.
    (b) Would treating the granting of an ESOP as an accountable event encourage or discourage such companies from adopting an ESOP?

14. Recall the quotation from Maunders and Burritt earlier in the chapter. The article from which the quotation came was concerned with the adverse impact that existing financial accounting methods might have on the quality of land in Australia. Read the following excerpt from the article, and answer the questions at the end.

The Case of Land Degradation in Australia

Australia, like other countries, faces a range of ecological and environmental problems. Of these, land degradation has been identified as the most serious ... Land degradation is the process by which land deteriorates through the actions of natural agents, such as water, wind, gravity and temperature, and/or land use and management practices, so that it is less useful for human beings ...

In Australia land degradation is evidenced by landscape features reflecting soil erosion, soil salinity, soil structure decline, mass movement, soil acidity and woody shrub invasion.

In spite of at least 17 reports between 1944 and 1983 concerned with land conservation and the need for national action there is still no co-ordinated approach to land use policy ... The mere presence of technical solutions has not been enough to make farmers use them ... Appropriate technology is now portrayed as a necessary but insufficient condition for solving land degradation problems ... social and economic analysis is being used to examine reasons why land users do not adopt technically optimal solutions available to them ...

Accounting helps convey information to land users about valuation and changes in valuations related to land use decisions. Because land users operate subject to financial constraints and with some concern for their wealth, a connection can be made between accounting information, financial management and decisions which lead to land degradation. Consequently, if inappropriate accounting information is provided, it can act as a barrier to the adoption of sound land conservation practices by land users ...

Land Degradation and Accounting — An Exploratory Set of Ideas

Given the above background, there seems to be a number of ways for accounting to have an adverse impact upon land degradation decisions and policies:

(1) Accounting rules permit a number of methods for measuring an entity's income and financial position. It is to be expected that land users would use this flexibility to create appropriate accounting results, if it assisted them to attain short-term gains. To take a hypothetical example, when dry conditions persist land users might be expected to choose accounting methods which reduce accounting earnings, in order to gain political sympathy for the declaration of drought areas. In the past, Government drought policy has been seen as synonymous with the implementation of a suitable financial assistance package for primary producers in times of financial hardship ... Once a drought area is declared, land users can obtain available assistance from fodder, water and restocking transport facilities. Thus creative accounting techniques can be used to bolster arguments for Government financial assistance which may help land users to keep marginally productive land overstocked in drought conditions. Any overstocking would exacerbate degradation pressures on the land through removal of further vegetation and through increased soil erosion caused by the action of wind on bare soil or by the result of intensive drought-breaking rains. Consequently, the flexibility of accounting measurement rules could be used in a way which promotes land degradation.

(2) Accounts are conventionally drawn up based upon historical cost measurements. These do not provide a useful basis for land degradation decisions ... In a multi-period setting, accounts which do not in general measure wealth and changes in wealth using discounted cash flow notions ... will not provide useful feedback as a basis for monitoring the relative success of land conservation and other decisions even if off-site costs are included. For external reporting and taxation purposes, use of historic cost and not current market values is the norm. As a result, accounting reports are likely to provide misleading information, leading to incorrect decisions about the financial capacity of a land user to undertake land conservation practices.

(3) Accounts reflect only transactions, transformations and events directly affecting the accounting entity (say a farm). Hence off-site effects for which there are often no market values, such as the costs of depositing soil in rivers, reservoirs and ditches, of dredging commercial waterways, of purifying water for drinking, of lost recreational use of streams and lakes and of lost aesthetic qualities of the environment, are not incorporated in information about periodic income and financial position of the land user because there is no legal relationship between off-site parties and the land user. Thus with current institutional arrangements accounting will provide only limited financial information to land users for decision making about land degradation.[18]

[18] Keith T. Maunders and Roger L. Burritt, "Accounting and Ecological Crisis," *Accounting, Accountability and Auditing Journal*, Vol. 4, no. 3, 1991, pp. 9–26.

Required:

(a) Briefly summarize Maunders and Burritt's arguments in your own words.

(b) Maunders and Burritt allege that accounting has probably contributed to environmental crises involving land degradation in Australia. Are their allegations credible?

(c) Would the recommendations they offer improve the situation? From whose point of view?

Strategic's Disclosure

Strategic Inc. (SI) is a large, diversified construction and industrial chemical manufacturer operating in Canadian and international (mostly American and British) markets. Through a number of subsidiaries acquired over time, it is active in industrial, commercial, and pipeline construction, in producing a variety of chemical products for industrial customers such as the steel industry, and in manufacturing plastic pipe. Revenues in 1996 were $795 million, of which 25% were in Canadian markets. Its shares were actively traded on the stock exchange until about a year ago, when analysts more or less stopped following the stock. Common share price has fallen from $21 in late 1993 to the $4 range recently.

The recession of the 1990s has hit SI hard, and the small profit that the company enjoyed in 1993 has turned into three straight loss years in the $20 million range. Top management expects that 1997 revenues will decline by about 10% from 1996, mainly for the following reasons:

- In commercial and industrial construction, the volume of new work is not expected to replace the volume of work completed in 1996.
- In pipeline construction, the rigorous application of new environmental assessment practices has slowed (and in the case of one major project, curtailed) a number of projects, so that the subsidiary's continuing fixed costs are supported by considerably less revenue than previously, in spite of continued strong demand.
- In industrial chemical manufacturing, soft markets combined with significant expenditures on pollution abatement programs have dampened profits.

It is now January 1997, and top management's 15-member Senior Executives Committee is holding its annual four-day retreat. This retreat is an important planning and communications mechanism; functional and other managers make themselves available to help the committee develop strategies to deal with various issues and problems. Thus, when production issues are being discussed, production management and the VP–engineering join the meeting; when accounting and financial reporting topics are dealt with, the corporate comptroller and senior subsidiary comptrollers are invited, as well as corporate counsel.

On the evening of the fourth day, three hours are devoted to a discussion of SI's 1996 Annual Report. Four of the 20 main agenda items involve situations with which the committee does not have extensive experience; for this reason they have been classified as "emerging issues":

Issue 1: SI's legal counsel was notified early in January 1997 that Construct Limited (CL) had filed suit, alleging that SI had interfered with CL's definite merger arrangement with Aggressive Construction Inc. (ACI). SI had agreed to pay US$200 million for 100% of ACI's common shares early in March 1996. The acquisition turned out to be a good one for SI, since ACI subsequently won (in April 1996) a major airport construction contract for which it had special expertise, and on which the expected gross profit was expected to make a material contribution to SI's consolidated bottom line.

CL is alleging that in February 1996, it had an agreement to purchase 100% of ACI's common shares for US$175 million. The CL suit is seeking damages of approximately $225 million.

The discussion of this item at the committee meeting centres around the merits of CL's claim, and the report of counsel that "we have a strong case, but there's always some uncertainty in these things." After debating "who did what when" for about 20 minutes, the discussion turns to managing the disclosure of the lawsuit, both in the media and in SI's more formal filings with securities commissions and in its annual and quarterly reports. One member of the committee expresses concern that "if we lose and they get the $225 million in damages, our shareholders' equity goes from $120 million into the garbage." Counsel has prepared a preliminary analysis as follows:

- January 1997 — suit launched
- remainder of 1997 — pretrial activity
- early 1998 — probable trial date; expect trial court judgment after about 2 to 3 months; expect that chances of negative judgment are 50–50; interest of about 8–10% would be accrued by the judge from the date the alleged action took place
- mid-1998 — if trial court judgment goes against us, we launch an appeal
- rest of 1998 — appeal process
- early 1999 — appeal court judgment — outcome uncertain

Issue 2: SI's Canadian Pipe Manufacturing Limited subsidiary (CPML) has two major plastic-pipe manufacturing operations, one in Alberta and the other in Quebec. The subsidiary's top management has just decided to shut down the Quebec operation and source all of its supply from the Alberta plant; no announcement has yet been made. The employees in the two plants are represented by the same union, as are many other employees in other SI subsidiaries. Overall, labour relations in the past have been "adversarial," partly because of top management's resentment (at both the SI and the operating unit level) that "their" employees opted to join unions beginning about 15 years ago. There have been occasional strikes and lockouts over the past ten years.

Management is emphatic in its decision to shut down the Quebec operation, and has already, privately, finalized the sale of the facilities. Its rationale is that the present value of the increased transportation and other out-of-pocket costs is probably much less than the present value of the costs that will be escaped by shutting down the plant; thus, the value of SI's shares will probably rise a bit. Total CPML employment will decrease by 40% (which translates into 10% for the SI group as a whole), although some of the workers in the Quebec plant will be offered jobs in Alberta.

Over the past few years, SI's corporate industrial relations function has matured, and so has top management's attitude toward unions. Top management wishes to improve its relations with the unions across all SI operations, and has already begun to do so, as evidenced by the significant decline in grievances, absenteeism, and spoilage rates in manufacturing over the past year.

Unfortunately, with the impending announcement of the shutdown, and all the dislocation and layoffs that decision will entail, the recent gains made in labour relations may quickly evaporate. Top management feels that it is in the long-run interests of the shareholders to maintain the improvements it has achieved in labour relations; however, doing so during a recessionary period will be difficult, and thus SI's Senior Executives Committee views the CPML shutdown decision as an important "demonstration case."

From the perspective of information disclosure, the issue has been defined in the following terms by SI's corporate comptroller:

The key corporate concern here is how to develop a union and general public disclosure policy with respect to the shutdown. Perhaps this issue should have been addressed back when the original shutdown analysis was performed by CPML management, but unfortunately it was not. Obviously, we'll need to develop a corporate-wide policy on this, and I'll work with the corporate director of industrial relations on it. The way I see it, we have four broad options insofar as disclosure policy is concerned —

1. *To announce the decision has been made, and disclose all the supporting analyses, thereby opening up the analyses and their assumptions to debate.*
2. *To announce that the decision has been made, and disclose the supporting analyses only to the union leadership, assuming they take an oath of confidentiality, so that they can better understand and explain in broad, general terms some of the overall reasons to their membership.*
3. *To announce that the decision has been made, and refuse to disclose any information on the grounds of confidentiality and management rights.*
4. *To announce that a feasibility study will be undertaken to assess whether or not one of the plants will be shut down. Management can then either ask for or ignore union inputs.*

Issue 3: SI's industrial-chemical and pipeline-construction subsidiaries are subject to increasing scrutiny by both environmental monitoring groups and governmental agencies concerned with pollution and sustainable development. Top management — at the urging of an outside member of the corporate audit committee — has recently decided that a policy in this area is probably overdue, and has placed the following item on the agenda of the Senior Executives Committee meeting:

Need for a Framework for Corporate Reporting on Sustainable Development and Pollution: *Since the traditional financial accounting and reporting model — which forms the basis for generally accepted accounting principles — was not conceived with the intent of measuring exchanges between an organization and its environment, an SI corporate policy on this matter is needed.*

At about ten in the evening, just as the meeting is about to break up, and as members of the committee prepare to race for their flights home or their rides to the suburbs, a short discussion ensues about the desirability of such a policy. One senior manager (from the British industrial construction subsidiary) says that "pollution effects and the things we do to destroy the natural environment are not well measured, if at all, in financial statements, and that's just plain wrong, because then it's not visible to our shareholders early enough, and then they get hit with a big surprise when we're sued. Also, it doesn't get incorporated into our management incentive and control systems." Another member of the committee offers the opinion that "production costs are, probably, significantly understated in some cases — perhaps some of our product-line contribution information is out of whack."

The corporate comptroller agrees with these comments, but reminds the members of the committee that the costs as well as the benefits of new, innovative accounting measurement and disclosure systems have to be considered. She then distributes some "practical suggestions" based on a research study that she has read:[19]

- *Improving the classification of environmental expenditures in financial statements to more clearly reflect the results of sustainable development programs (e.g., separate classification of operating and capital expenditures related to environmental issues);*

- *Assessing whether present accounting standards for distinguishing capital assets and expenses are appropriate for environmental and sustainable development programs;*
- *Strengthening accounting standards for estimating and allocating the costs of restoration programs and other related environmental commitments over the useful life of the business operations;*
- *Re-examining the measurement and accounting issues for contingent liabilities that relate to environmental problems.*

A further, and more difficult, step would be to develop better techniques for measuring the environmental and social costs/benefits of corporate activities that are presently not incorporated into performance measurements.

As SI's comptroller is about to explain how such concepts might be applied to SI's various business activities, the chair announces, "It is now ten-thirty, and since we're thirty minutes past our ten o'clock cutoff, I'm afraid that our good comptroller will have to follow up with overnight faxes to everyone if we're to catch our various flights." As the committee members say their goodbyes, the comptroller overhears the head of the Canadian pipeline manufacturing subsidiary muttering to no one in particular (but ensuring that the mutter is just loud enough to be audible): "What a crock ... hamstring us with more constraints, just when we're trying to work our way out of a recession ... just what we need, along with employment equity, women's issues, and everything else ... whatever happened to the good old market reacting for itself?"

Issue 4: The fourth emerging issue was prompted by the common disclosure implications of the previous three issues, as well as by other important disclosure questions that often arise. This agenda item is titled "The Need to Perceive Corporate Disclosure Strategically — Is a Policy Necessary?" Unfortunately, the meeting adjourns before this item can be discussed.

Required:

Identify the important accounting and ethical issues in this case, and recommend tentative, practical policies to deal with them, based on the information available.

[19] *Framework for Corporate Reporting on Sustainable Development — Discussion Paper*, a research project sponsored by the International Institute for Sustainable Development, the Business Council for Sustainable Development, and DRT International, August 1991. The quotation is from pp. 25–26.

Appendix
Excerpts from CICA Research Study[20]

Disclosure

Environmental expenses

- Total environmental expenses, excluding the amortization of capital assets related to environmental concerns, should be disclosed in financial statements.
- It is desirable to disclose in financial statements the dollar amount and nature of each category making up the total environmental expense shown, particularly if one category is a significant component of the total. It is also desirable to indicate where each category (or part thereof) is reflected in the income statement, if not obvious.
- There should be separate disclosure in financial statements of a particular environmental expense if it is likely to differ in the future.
- Known trends with respect to environmental matters that have had a favourable or unfavourable impact on net sales, revenues or income from continuing operations should be disclosed in financial reports, but outside financial statements. Further, it is desirable to similarly disclose information that explains any significant change from year to year in any disclosed environmental expense figures.

Capital assets related to environmental concerns

- If current environmental expenditures on capital assets represent a significant component of current expenditures on capital assets or if they are likely to differ significantly in the future, their nature and amount should be disclosed in the financial statements.
- It is not necessary to segregate or disclose in financial statements the cost of capital assets related to environmental concerns.

Other assets related to environmental concerns

- If current expenditures on other assets related to environmental concerns are significant in relation to total current expenditures on capital and other assets, or if they are likely to differ significantly in the future, their nature and amount should be disclosed in the financial statements.
- The major categories of other assets related to environmental concerns should be separately disclosed, together with the basis of amortization, if any.

[20] CICA, Research Report, "Environmental Costs and Liabilities: Accounting and Financial Reporting Issues," 1993, pp. ix–xii.

Impairment of assets as a result of environmental concerns

- If the impairment of assets as the result of environmental concerns is recognized through a loss accrual under *Handbook* Section 3290, the accrued loss should be shown as a liability and should be distinguished from other liabilities.

Environmental liabilities

- There should be separate disclosure in financial statements of environmental liabilities.
- Environmental liabilities that are individually material should be disclosed separately. If a counter-claim or claim against a third party has been deducted in determining the amount recognized, it is desirable that the gross amount of the liability and the amount deducted be disclosed separately.
- Any deferred charge that has resulted from the recognition of a liability for expected future environmental expenditures may be presented in the financial statements as a deduction from that related liability, provided there is note disclosure of the full amount of the liability and the disposition of the deferred charge.
- The nature of any significant measurement uncertainties relating to a recognized liability that is disclosed separately, and the range of reasonably possible outcomes, should be disclosed.
- Changes in the amount of the recorded environmental liability would not normally be disclosed.
- As a minimum, the aggregate of payments to be made in each of the next five years for future environmental expenditures that have been recognized as a liability should be disclosed. If such disclosure cannot be made because there is considerable uncertainty about the timing of the future expenditures, this fact should be disclosed.
- For environmental liabilities that have not been recognized in financial statements because no estimate can be made of them, the following should be disclosed:
    - the nature of the expected future expenditure or loss, including an indication of the likelihood of the expenditure being made or the loss being suffered;
    - a statement that an estimate of the expected future expenditures or loss cannot be made;
    - the timing of the expected future expenditure or loss, including an indication of any uncertainties related to timing.

Any unrecognized liabilities that are individually material should be disclosed separately.

Commitments

- Significant future environmental capital expenditures that involve "contractual obligations" or commitments, and that are abnormal in relation to financial position or usual business operations, should be disclosed in accordance with *CICA Handbook* Section 3280, "Contractual Obligations."

- Significant future environmental expenditures required because of environmental legislation or regulations and that are abnormal in relation to financial position or usual business operations should be disclosed. Such expenditures should also be disclosed if required by proposed legislation or regulation that it is virtually certain will come into force.
- If an entity has made a commitment with respect to significant future environmental operating expenditures that will govern the level of expenditures for a considerable period into the future, the particulars of the commitment should be disclosed (as required by Section 3280). Similarly, if existing environmental legislation or regulations will require significant future environmental operating expenditures for a considerable period into the future, the particulars of the regulations and related expenditures should be disclosed.
- It is desirable that there be disclosure in the financial report, but not necessarily in the financial statements, of environmental capital expenditures that are planned or are expected to be required under new legislation or regulations, for at least the following year.
- It is desirable that there be disclosure in the financial report, but not necessarily in the financial statements, of the environmental operating expenditures that are planned or are expected to be required under new legislation or regulations, for at least the following year.

Accounting policies

- An entity's accounting policies with respect to the following should be disclosed:
  - what is included in the definition of "environmental costs";
  - the basis on which environmental costs are expensed or capitalized;
  - how environmental costs are amortized to income;
  - the basis on which environmental liabilities are recognized.

Possible future environmental expenditures and impairment losses

- "Reasonably possible" future environmental expenditures related to past events or transactions or "reasonably possible" asset impairment losses that could have a significant impact on future cash flows should be disclosed in financial statements.
- If the probability of an environmental loss related to past events or transactions is remote, but the impact could have a significant adverse effect on the financial position of the entity, it is desirable to disclose this possibility.
- With respect to possible future environmental expenditures or losses that are disclosed in financial statements, the following details should be provided:
  - the nature of the expected future expenditure or loss, including an indication of the likelihood of the expenditure being made or the loss being suffered;

- the size of the expected future expenditure or loss: an estimate of the expenditure or loss; or an estimate of the range of possible outcomes or a statement that an estimate cannot be made;
- the timing of the expected future expenditure or loss, including an indication of any uncertainties related to timing.

- Possible future environmental expenditures, or losses due to asset impairment, that are individually material should be disclosed separately. Others with similar characteristics may be grouped.

Possible future environmental losses relating to future events or transactions

- There is normally no need to disclose normal business risks with respect to environmental concerns, unless the possibility of loss is imminent or could be very significant.
- An entity should disclose, in its financial statements, the industry in which it operates, the basic nature of its operations within that industry, and the particular circumstances of the entity, such as location of operations.
- If possible future environmental losses relating to future events or transactions and resulting from the public's concerns about the environment, as expressed either through legislation, regulation or public pressure, could have a significant adverse effect on the future cash flows of the entity, the nature and possible effect of these concerns should be disclosed in the financial report.
- If there is little or no risk related to environmental concerns, it may be desirable to disclose this fact in the financial report, along with an appropriate explanation.
- If the possibility of a future environmental loss exists because of a specific action by the entity or because of a specific action by others, the nature of the action and the possible effect should be disclosed in the financial report.
- If the possibility of a future environmental loss exists, but the probability of its occurrence has been reduced by actions taken by the entity, such actions should be disclosed in the financial report.

CHAPTER 10 ten

The Accounting Entity and Substance over Form: Debt, Equity, and Intercorporate Investments

Learning OBJECTIVES

After you have read, thought about, and discussed this chapter, and completed a selection from the end-of-chapter material, you will have made significant progress in achieving the following learning objectives:

- Explain why debt and owners' equity are accounted for separately.
- Describe ten features that a bond might have.
- Explain how a simple bond issue is accounted for, including the preparation of journal entries.
- Describe in-substance defeasance transactions, and explain why they became popular.
- Identify the characteristics of hybrid securities, and explain accounting issues they create.
- Describe how the control and ownership by one accounting entity of another may affect how the accounting entity itself may change.
- Distinguish among the cost, consolidation, and equity methods of accounting for intercorporate investments.
- Explain how the cost method works, including the preparation of journal entries.
- Explain how the equity method works, including the preparation of journal entries.
- Explain why the consolidation method may provide representationally faithful financial statements for most parent–subsidiary relationships.

- Demonstrate the preparation of a consolidation worksheet and consolidated financial statements in simple situations.
- Be aware that accounting principles such as consolidation are not universal.

Alternatives to equity financing affect future cash flows. Hence, the distinction between debt and equity should continue ...

Myrtle W. Clark, "Entity Theory, Modern Capital Structure Theory, and the Distinction Between Debt and Equity," *Accounting Horizons*, Vol. 7, no. 3, September 1993, p. 14

How should a parent company report its investment in one or more subsidiaries in its financial statements?

Ross M. Skinner, *Accounting Standards in Evolution*, Holt, Rinehart and Winston of Canada, 1987, p. 342

INTRODUCTION

In Chapter 2 the accounting entity concept was identified as one of the key ideas underlying all of accounting. In this chapter we explore some further aspects of the accounting entity concept in financial accounting, focusing first on accounting for debt versus equity. How we view the accounting entity determines whether we should be concerned about the classification between debt and equity on the balance sheet. Since many financial securities have recently been designed that have a combination of debt and equity characteristics, such a classification is becoming more and more challenging.

The chapter continues its examination of the accounting entity concept by discussing the impact of one entity investing in the common shares of another. Once we change the focus of accountability, we find that other accounting ideas have to be adjusted as well.

Entity Theory and the Distinction Between Debt and Equity

The opening quotation from Myrtle Clark's article seems to suggest that accountants, managers, and others interested in financial accounting information have not always agreed that it is useful to classify long-term sources of financing as either debt or owners' equity. Indeed, at one time back in the early part of the twentieth century, the eminent accounting theoretician W.A. Paton argued that the separation of debt from equity, and calculation of the debt-to-equity ratio, was irrelevant to an investor's decision-making. Clark summarizes this argument by suggesting that it:

relied on two basic assumptions: (1) investment and financing decisions are independent and (2) the value of the firm is unaffected by the type, or types, of capital employed in its capital structure. Paton argued that the particular source, or sources, of capital have no effect on the company's performance. If debt is substituted for stock, the cost of factors of production remains the same. Operating profits are unaffected by the amount of leverage in the corporate capital structure ... [1]

This view would regard a company's assets as belonging to the corporate entity itself, not to its shareholders, and therefore interest would not be deducted as an expense on the income statement, but rather would be accounted for as dividends are accounted for: as a distribution of earnings via the statement of retained earnings. However, this is not the currently accepted view among accountants and others; for that reason it remains important to carefully classify sources of long-term financing as either debt or equity. This is fairly easy to do with financial instruments that are clearly debtlike (such as the bonds described below), or clearly equitylike (such as common shares); but it becomes quite difficult and controversial when the financial instrument we are examining has characteristics of both debt and equity. One example of such an instrument, the adjustable rate convertible note, is described later.

Accounting for Bonds and Other Long-Term Debt

In this section we'll describe some of the accounting aspects of bonds and other long-term debt. In *Terminology for Accountants,*[2] the CICA defines a bond as a "certificate of indebtedness issued by a government or corporation ... In a corporation, the term usually implies that specific assets have been pledged as security." If specific assets have not been pledged as security, the term *debenture* is usually used. However, in practice the two terms are often used interchange-

[1] Page 15 of Clark's article, which was cited in the introductory quotation. Paton's work was published in *Accounting Theory*, New York: The Roland Press, 1922.

[2] *Terminology for Accountants*, CICA, 1992.

ably. Bonds may be registered with provincial and national securities commissions and be issued to the public. They may be bought and sold after they have been issued by a borrower.

Bonds

Companies usually attempt to raise long-term capital by issuing either capital stock, or debt, or both. Bonds are the most common type of debt, and most companies have some bonds on their balance sheet. The steps a company must take to raise money by issuing bonds include the following:

- Management decides that funds are needed for a long-term purpose, such as the construction of a new factory, expansion, or similar use.
- The chief financial officer and other management agree that raising the funds by means of issuing bonds is the best course of action.
- The board of directors gives its approval to the bond issue, including the principal amount of the bonds, the interest rate, and so on.
- Legal requirements are satisfied; lawyers, accountants, underwriters, and other advisers may be involved. The underwriters purchase the bonds from the company and then resell them for a profit; they are specialists helping companies to successfully issue bonds.
- The bonds are issued.

EXHIBIT 10–1
A BOND'S LIFE

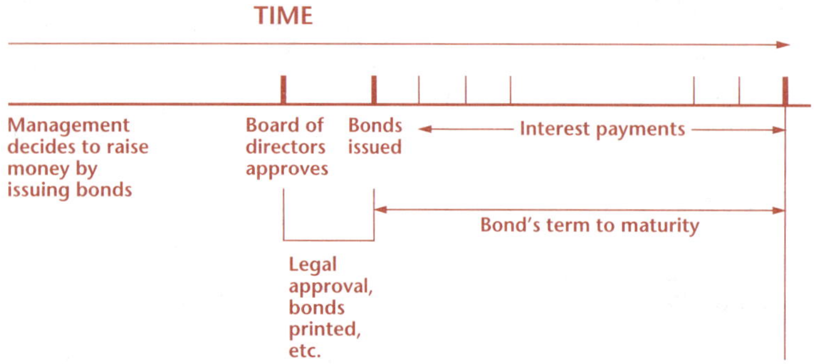

Exhibit 10–1 highlights some of the key points in a bond's life.

There are a wide variety of bonds, containing features that permit the issuer and borrower to accommodate their needs and constraints. A powerful issuer (or borrower) may be able to issue bonds that have relatively low interest rates and that give the investor (lender) few privileges; a weak issuer that is in dire need of funds may be virtually compelled to offer lenders all sorts of special features. Some of the most common types of features are these:

- *Callable bond:* This type of bond has a contractual feature that permits the issuer (that is, the company or other organization borrowing money) to redeem the bond prior to the bond's maturity date (that is, the date that the borrower has agreed, by contract, to repay the money) under certain conditions that are prespecified in the contract between the lenders and the borrower (this contract is called the bond indenture).
- *Convertible bond:* The individual or organization investing in this type of bond (the lender) has the option to exchange the bond for other securities of the organization that issued the bonds (the borrower), under certain prespecified conditions. These other securities are usually capital stock.
- *Coupon bond:* This type of bond contains detachable coupons, which the investor must present to the issuer on specified dates for payment of interest.
- *Income bond:* With this type of bond, the amount of interest to be paid depends on the income of the issuer.
- *Indexed bond:* With this type of bond, the interest and/or the principal is linked to an index specified in the bond indenture. The index is usually a published one, such as the consumer price index.

- *Mortgage bond:* This type of bond is secured by a mortgage.
- *Retractable bond:* The holder (lender, investor) has the option of redeeming the bond prior to maturity, under specified conditions.
- *Serial bonds:* Such bonds mature in instalments.
- *Sinking fund bond:* A bond indenture that contains this clause requires that the issuing organization set aside funds on a regular basis so that the funds set aside, plus any interest that such funds earn, will provide for redemption of the bonds. Clearly, this feature is intended to protect the lender.
- *Stripped bond or zero-coupon bond:* This type of bond is a coupon bond from which the coupons for future interest payments have been removed; the bond is issued for a discount from its face value prior to maturity.

Example of Accounting for a Bond Issue

We are going to focus on the issuer of the bonds; we will not deal with the holder of the bonds, or the investor in the bonds. Suppose that the board of directors of MultiSync Inc., a company that manufactures small appliances, has approved a proposal by operating management that the company invest $25,000,000 in new manufacturing facilities. The chief financial officer of the company has recommended that the funds be raised through an issue of debenture bonds, and the firm of underwriters has agreed. The proposed bonds have the following characteristics:

- Face value of the bonds is $26,000,000.[3]
- Interest of 10% per annum is payable each January 1.
- Term to maturity is ten years.
- Market interest rate (for bonds of same risk and term to maturity) on the date of bond issue (January 1, 1997) is 11% per annum.

The bond interest rate (also called the bond face rate) of 10% determines the amount of interest payments each January 1 — in this case 10% of $26,000,000, or $2,600,000. The interest rate demanded by the market in this example, 11%, is the return that lenders require; they are unwilling to lend their money (that is, invest in MultiSync's bonds) unless they receive an 11% return.

Bond face interest rates are almost always different from market rates, since market rates are very volatile and change daily. The face rate, however, must be set in advance as management and their advisers design the details of the bond issue.

In the MultiSync example, the difference between the face rate and the market rate is 1% (or 100 "basis points," each 1/100 of a percent being referred to as a basis point). This is unusually large.

The first step in accounting for the bonds is to prepare a time line tracking the exact cash flows. See the table on the left.

Point in time	Exact cash flows
January 1, 1997	+NPV (net present value)
January 1, 1998	–$2,600,000: interest payment
January 1, 1999	–$2,600,000: interest payment
January 1, 2000	–$2,600,000: interest payment
January 1, 2001	–$2,600,000: interest payment
...	...
January 1, 2007	–$2,600,000: final year's interest payment
	–$26,000,000: repay principal

[3] Although only $25,000,000 is needed for the investment, management realizes that transactions costs and other factors may reduce the amount actually received, so they have set the face value of the bonds at $26,000,000.

There are ten payments of $2,600,000 interest, plus a final repayment of the principal of $26,000,000. The net present value of these future cash flows, using the market interest rate at the time of the bond issue as the interest rate by which to compute the NPV, is what the "market" (that is, the investors in the bonds) would be willing to pay for the bonds. This NPV equals $24,468,799.68, and is computed as follows:

$$NPV = \sum_{p=1}^{10} 2{,}600{,}000/(1.11)^p + 26{,}000{,}000/(1.11)^{10}$$

MultiSync's accountant records the following journal entry when the bonds are first issued:

Dr Cash (B)	24,468,799.68	
Dr Bond discount (B)	1,531,200.32	
Cr Bonds payable (B)		26,000,000.00

The "Bond discount" account is a contra account, and is shown on the balance sheet as a deduction from "Bonds payable," as follows:

Long-term liabilities section of balance sheet (excerpt)	
Bond	$26,000,000
Less: Bond discount	1,531,200
	$24,468,800

As an alternative, many companies simply disclose the net amount of the bonds payable.

To make the example a little more realistic, suppose that the underwriters, lawyers, and other professionals associated with helping MultiSync issue the bonds charged a total fee of $400,000. The above journal entry would then be:

Dr Cash (B)	24,068,799.68	
Dr Unamortized bond issue costs (B)	400,000.00	
Dr Bond discount (B)	1,531,200.32	
Cr Bonds payable (B)		26,000,000

The account "Unamortized bond issue costs" is grouped on the assets side of the balance sheet.

Both "Bond discount" and "Unamortized bond issue costs" are amortized (that is, expensed) over the life of the bonds to which they relate. In effect, they represent part of interest expense. We'll illustrate this with "Bond discount" only, pretending that there were no bond issue costs (and ignoring pennies).

Let's assume that MultiSync has a December 31 fiscal year end. This means that on December 31, 1997, and for the following nine years, the company must record the following adjusting journal entry:

Dr Interest expense (I)	2,753,120	
Cr Interest payable (B)		2,600,000
Cr Bond 0 discount (B)		153,12

The $153,120 is simply the bond discount of $1,531,200 divided by ten years. Of course, after ten years' amortization, the balance in the "Bond discount" account will be zero.

On January 1, 1998, the first interest payment of $2,600,000 is disbursed to the holders of the bonds. The entry to account for this on MultiSync's books is:

Dr Interest payable (B)	2,600,000	
Cr Cash (B)		2,600,000

An identical entry must be made each January 1 until and including the year 2007, at which time the bond principal will also be repaid:

Dr Bond payable (B)	26,000,000	
Cr Cash (B)		26,000,000

Another way of accounting for the bond discount is the "effective interest" method, in which each year's interest expense is computed by multiplying the net carrying value of the bond by the market interest rate that was in effect when the bond was issued (in our example, 11%), as follows:

For 1997:

11% × $24,468,799.68 = $2,691,568

and the journal entry would then be

Dr Interest expense (I)	2,691,568	
Cr Cash (B)		2,600,000
Cr Bond discount (B)		91,568

where the $91,568 is a plug.

The bond's net carrying value for 1998 is:

Face amount of bond		$26,000,000
Less: Bond discount at issue date	$ 1,531,200	
Deduct: 1997 amortization	91,568	1,439,632
Net carrying value during 1998		$24,560,368

Interest Expense Comparison
Straight-line Versus Effective Interest Rate Methods of Amortization of Bond Discount

Year	Straight-line Method	Effective Interest Rate Method
1997	$ 2,753,120	$ 2,691,568
1998	2,753,120	2,701,640
1999	2,753,120	2,712,821
2000	2,753,120	2,725,231
2001	2,753,120	2,739,007
2002	2,753,120	2,754,297
2003	2,753,120	2,771,270
2004	2,753,120	2,790,110
2005	2,753,120	2,811,022
2006	2,753,120	2,834,233*
Totals	**$27,531,200**	**$27,531,200**

* 89 added due to rounding.

And the 1998 journal entry to account for the interest expense and bond discount amortization under the effective interest method is:

Dr Interest expense (I)	2,701,640	
Cr Cash (B)		2,600,000
Cr Bond discount (B)		101,640

where the interest expense is 11% × $24,560,368 = $2,701,640.

And the credit to "Bond discount" of $101,640 is, as in 1997, a plug.

Over the ten-year life of the bond, the two methods give the results shown in the table at the bottom left.

Both of the above methods used to account for bond amortization are acceptable within GAAP; of course, neither accounts for the bond on a current or market value basis, since both focus on accounting for the historic cost of the bond, which was fixed when the bond was first issued on January 1, 1997.

Since the interest rate demanded by the market on the date the bonds were issued (that is, 11%) was higher than the face interest rate of the bonds (which was 10%), the NPV was, as we saw, less than the $26,000,000 face value of the bonds. We say that bonds issued under this condition were issued "at a discount." If the market rate at the time of issue had been less than the face rate, the bonds would have been issued "at a premium," since the NPV would have been greater than the face value of the bonds. Bonds are almost always issued at a discount or premium, because it takes several months to plan a bond issue, obtain the necessary approvals from government agencies, and arrange for the issue's marketing. Since the market interest rate changes continuously, the face rate chosen for the particular bond issue will inevitably differ from the market rate by at least a little.

Accounting and Business Decision A

(a) Suppose MultiSync's bond was issued when the market demanded a 9% rate of interest. Prepare all journal entries associated with the bond issue.
(b) Suppose MultiSync's bond was issued when the market demanded a 10% rate of interest. Prepare all journal entries associated with the issue.

Accounting for bonds is based on the historic cost of the bond — that is, on the money received by the issuer when the bond was first issued. But when you look up bond prices in the newspaper, what you see is current market price information. In effect, the market is discounting all the remaining cash flows associated with a bond issue, using as a discount (or interest) rate the rate of return that the market, in its collective wisdom, requires on that day. So bond prices go up and down on a daily basis. Should accounting for bonds be based on such a current value approach? Perhaps disclosure in footnotes of the current market value of the company's bonds would be a good idea. It might even discourage management from making decisions about their existing bond issues for what could largely be accounting reasons — that is, based on a desire to report "good" results.

For example, in the 1980s many companies did the following: They observed that market interest rates for bonds had risen significantly above the rates at which they had issued their bonds that were currently outstanding and thus on their balance sheets. This meant that the current value of their bonds was significantly below carrying value (since as market interest rates go up, the present value of future cash flows must go down). Now, if the bonds they had issued could not be redeemed earlier under conditions they considered reasonable, they entered into a sequence of transactions described as an "in-substance defeasance." This involved the following steps:

1. Issuing new debt — perhaps new bonds — at the current high interest rates.
2. Purchasing government bonds with the funds generated by the new debt issue. Government bonds are low-risk, low-yield financial securities. The companies ensured that the government bonds they purchased were such that the cash inflows from the government bonds matched the cash outflows required to service their old, low-interest bonds.
3. Arranging with an independent trustee to make all the necessary payments on the old bonds from the government bonds, which they then irrevocably transferred to the trustee. Of course, the trustee received a fee for this.
4. Finally, removing both the government bonds (which were a financial asset of the company) and the old bonds (which were, of course, a long-term financial liability) from the balance sheet, justifying such a journal entry by arguing that the old bonds were "in substance" defeased, or that the obligations under the old bonds were satisfied. In order to balance, the journal entry usually needed a credit, which was accounted for as a gain on the company's income statement.

The company was, however, still liable for interest and principal repayments of the old bonds. As well, such a sequence of transactions was costly, since the trustee, lawyers, accountants, and other specialists had to be paid, and the money invested in the government bonds might well have had a more profitable use in the company (perhaps had it been invested in new machinery, or research and product development). Many observers of the business scene thought that such a sequence of transactions was just another example of the "economic consequences" we described in Chapter 4 as driving accounting and business decisions.

Accounting and Business Decision B

Suppose that MultiSync's bonds were repurchased in the marketplace by MultiSync on January 1, 1999, when the bonds were trading at a price reflecting the market interest rate on that day of 15%. Prepare the journal entry to account for the transaction. Assume that straight-line amortization was used.

Other Long-Term Debt

Long-term notes payable are issued by smaller companies to raise cash, whereas bonds are used by larger companies. Long-term notes payable are often backed (or secured) by a mortgage, which is a legal document that pledges the borrower's property as security for the loan. Some companies in resource-based industries issue long-term debt based on commodities. For example, in 1988 LynnGold Resources Inc., a small, public gold-mining company, issued a "gold loan," whereby it borrowed gold from a bank, immediately sold it to raise cash, and promised to repay the gold to the bank at a specified time in the future. Accounting for such transactions has been the subject of some controversy.[4]

Hybrid Securities: "A Bit of This, a Bit of That"

Hybrid securities have some features that resemble debt, and some that resemble shareholders' equity. This creates a problem for accountants and managers, who must classify securities on the accounting entity's balance sheet as either debt or equity. The two categories are mutually exclusive. Misclassification could cause financial statement ratios to be misstated; and since debt interest is an expense but the cost of equity is not accounted for as an expense in accounting, such misclassifications could also affect income measurements. Hybrid securities have become more and more popular, with companies and their financial advisers continually striving to raise funds at the lowest possible cost in highly competitive global capital markets. Let's examine a hybrid security, and see how accounting practice and accounting theory would deal with it.

The particular example of a hybrid security that we are going to look at is an adjustable-rate convertible note, or ARCN for short.[5] ARCNs used to be issued by such American companies as Borg-Warner and Hercules. ARCNs had the following characteristics:

---

[4] Claude P. Lanfranconi and Darroch A. Robertson, "Instructional Case: LynnGold Resources, Inc.," *Issues in Accounting Education*, Vol. 9, no. 2, Fall 1994, pp. 385–400.

[5] This section is based on Thomas E. King and Alan K. Ortegren, "Accounting for Hybrid Securities: The Case of Adjustable Rate Convertible Notes," *The Accounting Review*, July 1988.

- Cash payments to the investors in such securities (the "holders") were set to provide a yield in excess of the dividend yielded by the issuing company's common shares, and adjusted as needed in order to maintain this spread.
- Maturity values of ARCNs were significantly less than their face amounts — about 50%.
- At maturity, ARCNs were convertible into the issuing company's common shares at a conversion rate that was fixed; and this conversion rate was such that the ARCNs were convertible into common shares having a total market value equal to the ARCN's face amount at the time the ARCNs were issued.

These characteristics tended to make the value of ARCNs dependent on the value of the issuing company's common shares. As the share price increased, the ARCNs became more valuable, and in addition they had a yield slightly greater than the shares' yield. At maturity, holders of the ARCNs opted to convert to common shares, because the ARCNs themselves had a very low maturity value.

Let's look at an example of an ARCN and its accounting possibilities. Suppose that Pete Corporation issued 25-year ARCNs for $45,400,000, with a maturity value of $22,700,000. Annual payments to holders were $119.46 per $1,000 note, so the total annual cash payment to holders was $119.46 × 45,400 notes, or $5,423,484. One way that ARCNs were accounted for in practice was to record the following journal entry on Pete's books on the date the notes were issued:

Dr Cash (B)	45,400,000	
Cr Notes payable (B)		22,700,000
Cr Contributed capital (B)		22,700,000

"Notes payable," which was of course a long-term liability here, was credited with the maturity value of the ARCNs, and the residual was allocated to the shareholders' equity account "Contributed capital." When annual payments of $5,423,484 were made by Pete, it accounted for them under this method as follows:

Dr Interest expense (I)	5,423,484	
Cr Cash (B)		5,423,484

This method led to misleading accounting results. For example, a reader of Pete's financial statements would estimate that the interest rate Pete Corporation was paying on its ARCN debt was:

$$\frac{5,423,484}{22,700,000}$$

or 23.9%, which was much higher than actual rates on debt.

A second way ARCNs were accounted for in practice was to initially record the debt as being equal to the sum of the present values of the periodic payments of $5,423,484 plus the present value of the maturity or redemption value of $22,700,000. The interest rate chosen to perform the present value calculation was the rate at which Pete could issue "straight debt" — that is, debt with no fancy hybrid or conversion characteristics, just a bond such as we described earlier in the chapter. Suppose that Pete Corporation's interest rate on such an obligation would have been 15.75%. Using common spreadsheet software such as Excel, the present value of a 25-year annuity in arrears (or ordinary annuity) of $5,423,484, at 15.75%, is $33,545,674, and the present value of $22,700,000, discounted over 25 years, is $586,139. The sum of these two amounts is $34,131,813, so the journal entry that Pete would have recorded under this method when the ARCNs were issued was:

Dr Cash (B)	45,400,000	
Cr Notes payable (B)		22,700,000
Cr Premium on notes payable (B)		11,431,813
Cr Contributed capital (B)		11,268,187

The total of the credit of $22,700,000 of the face value of the debt plus the $11,431,813 premium on the debt, equals the $34,131,813 debt carrying, or book, value.

Interest expense under this method is accounted for as 15.75% × the book value of the debt. The book value is reduced each year by amortizing the premium, until by the end of year 25, the book value equals the $22,700,000 redemption or maturity value. The first year's interest expense and premium amortization results in the following journal entry:

Dr Interest expense (I)	5,375,761	
Dr Premium on notes payable (B)	47,723	
Cr Cash (B)		5,423,484

This interest expense is equal to 15.75% × $34,131,813. The debit to "Premium on notes payable," representing the amortization, is a plug to make the entry balance.

King and Ortegren[6] disagree with the two approaches to accounting for ARCNs that were found in practice, and argue that neither is consistent with the substance of these hybrid securities. They point out that it is very likely that the issuer will make the periodic payments until maturity, but that it is very unlikely that the maturity amount will be paid out, since holders will opt to convert to Pete Corporation's common shares at maturity (unless, of course, the common share price takes a nosedive). They then claim that the stream of periodic payments represents a liability according to the definition set out in Chapter 4, and conclude that ARCNs should be accounted for by crediting the "Notes payable" account with the present value of these payments when the note is initially issued, with the remainder of the credit side of the journal entry to the "Contributed capital" account, as follows:

Dr Cash (B)	45,400,000	
Cr Notes payable (B)		33,545,674
Cr Contributed capital (B)		11,854,326

where the $33,545,674 is the present value of the 25 annual end-of-year payments of $5,423,484, discounted at Pete's "pure" debt rate of 15.75%. Notice that under this approach the redemption amount is not accounted for, because it is not likely to be paid. Interest expense at the end of the first year would be accounted for as follows:

Dr Interest expense (I)	5,283,444	
Dr Notes payable (B)	140,040	
Cr Cash (B)		5,423,484

The $140,040 debit to "Notes payable" is a plug, and represents amortization.

King and Ortegren suggest that their preferred method is more consistent with GAAP, at least in terms of conceptual framework literature, since:

in effect, the ARCN represents two securities: (1) an equity security with a "bailout" or put feature (i.e., the redemption amount); and (2) a debt security entitling the holder to receive a stream of periodic cash payments.

[6] Thomas E. King and Alan K. Ortegren, "Accounting for Hybrid Securities: The Case of Adjustable Rate Convertible Notes," *The Accounting Review*, July 1988.

Treating the present value of the periodic payments as debt is justified because these payments will be made by the issuer until conversion of the note, and conversion cannot be assumed to be probable until immediately prior to maturity. Not treating the redemption amount of the note as debt is justified because the notes seldom will mature; they generally will be converted immediately prior to maturity.

ARCNs are just one of a number of securities that have both equity and debt characteristics. Other such securities include:

- Term-preferred shares, which have the legal form of preferred shares but are issued with a limited life.
- Subordinated perpetual debt, whose principal is only payable upon the liquidation of the issuing corporation. Air Canada has issued such securities.

We now turn from considering some aspects of accounting for long-term debt and equity by the accounting entity, to examine how the very idea of the accounting entity *itself* may change under certain circumstances.

Accounting and Business Decision C

Prepare journal entries for Pete Corporation accounting for the second year of the ARCN issue, using the three approaches described above.

The Intercorporate Investment Continuum: Control and Ownership

Consider the following diagram, which illustrates the percentage ownership that one company (Investor Co.) may have in the common shares of another company (Investee Co.):

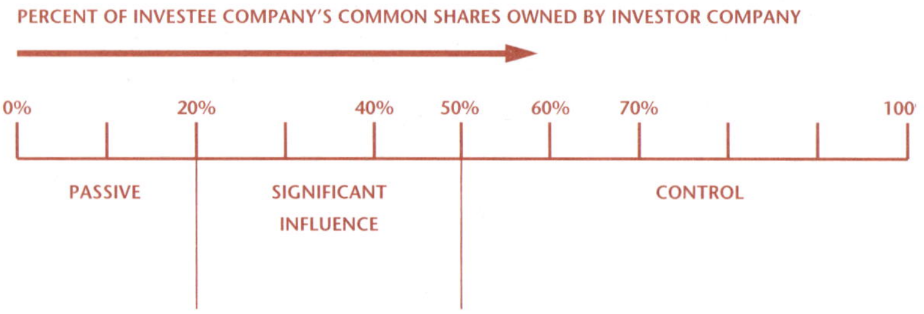

Investor Co. may own none of the common shares of Investee Co., or it may own all the way up to 100% of Investee's issued and outstanding common shares. If Investor owns just a small percentage of Investee's common shares, that investment represents a passive financial asset from Investor's point of view. Investor is able to exert no influence over strategic or operating decision-making at Investee.

As the percentage of voting common shares that Investor owns increases, so does the likelihood that Investor will be able to influence strategic and operating decisions at Investee. This is especially true if no other investors own large blocks of Investee's common shares. For example, if another investor owned 55% of Investee's shares, then probably Investor wouldn't be able to exert much influence even if it owned the entire remaining 45%: it could always be outvoted at Investee shareholder meetings. Assuming that this is not the case, then as Investor's share ownership goes above, say, the 20 percent level, some degree of significant influence is possible.

When Investor owns more than 50% of Investee's common shares, it is highly likely that Investor will be able to exert control over Investee. There are some exceptions to this general situation, of course. (What would accounting be like without exceptions?) For example, if Investee Co. is legally bankrupt, then the courts and creditors may control Investee, even when Investor owns 100% of Investee's common shares.

Actually, accounting principles have recently extended the concept of "control" to encompass more than just common share ownership. In 1991 the CICA issued *Handbook* section 1590, which states that one company "is presumed to control another enterprise when it owns, directly or indirectly, an equity interest that carries the right to elect the majority of the members of the other enterprise's board of directors" (1590.08). This usually means greater than 50% common share ownership. However, the Accounting Standards Board goes on in section 1590 to say that control may be exercised "through factors other than ownership of an equity interest" (1590.13), such as "ownership of rights, options, warrants, convertible debt, convertible non-voting equity such as preferred shares, or other similar instruments that, if converted or exercised, would give the enterprise the majority voting interest" (1590.13). This broadening of the concept of control is modified slightly by the following qualification: "Exercises and conversions are only taken into account when the economic cost is not so high as to make them unlikely for the foreseeable future" (1590.13).

So, the impact of one company on another may extend from (1) virtually nil (a passive investment), through (2) significant influence, up to (3) control. The way that financial accounting information about Investor Co. and Investee Co. is constructed depends greatly on which of these three categories matches the situation at hand. If Investor has merely a passive relationship with Investee, a method of accounting for Investor's common share ownership called the "cost" method is used (this is a specific, technical use of the term "cost"). If the relationship is such that Investor Co.'s management, while not able to exercise control over Investee, has significant influence over Investee's activities, then the "equity" method is used (this is a specific, technical use of the term "equity"). And if Investor controls Investee, the consolidation method is used. Here, then, is another example of classification in accounting! And this classification is very important since, as we'll see below, the cost, equity, and consolidation methods give greatly different financial statement results.

By the way, Canadian GAAP has set a 20% ownership level as the cutoff point for using the cost method rather than the equity method (3050.04). However, this is not a hard-and-fast rule; it's merely a guideline, and each situation should be evaluated on its own merits.

Now, let's look at how the three accounting methods work.

Passive and Active Relationships, and Substance over Form

Cost method

This accounting method reflects the passive relationship by accounting for dividends received (or receivable) by Investor upstream from Investee, as income to Investor. Investor's management does not have control over Investee, and so cannot tell Investee's management what to do — for example, when to declare dividends. The only economic benefit that Investor enjoys from the relationship (aside from any gain or loss when it ultimately sells its Investee common shares) is the upstream dividends, over which it has no control as to amount and timing.

The cost method accounts for upstream dividends as income to Investor and in this way accounts for the substance of the passive relationship. We'll illustrate the details of this method a little later.

Equity method

When Investor is able to exert significant influence over the strategic operating, investing, and financing policies of Investee, upstream dividends are accounted for not as Investor income, but rather as a partial return of Investor's investment in Investee. This reflects the substance of the relationship, since Investor's management could significantly influence Investee's declaring of the dividend, and thus inappropriately manipulate its own income if the dividends were accounted for as income. Under the equity method, Investor also accrues its pro rata share of Investee's net income or loss, since it had significant influence in Investee's earning of the income or incurrence of the loss. The details of the equity method are illustrated later.

Consolidation methods

When Investor can exercise control in virtually all aspects of Investee's strategic operating, investing, and financing decisions, two separate accounting entities no longer exist. We now have, in substance, one *consolidated* accounting entity (even though two legal corporations are involved), and the consolidation accounting method reflects this fact. The consolidated accounting entity has one set of financial statements that it presents to users, in which all transactions between the two companies have been eliminated; the transactions are now treated as occurring within the (enlarged) accounting entity. The graphic in Exhibit 10–2 at the bottom left represents the situation.

EXHIBIT 10–2
EGGSHELL MODEL OF A CONSOLIDATED ENTITY

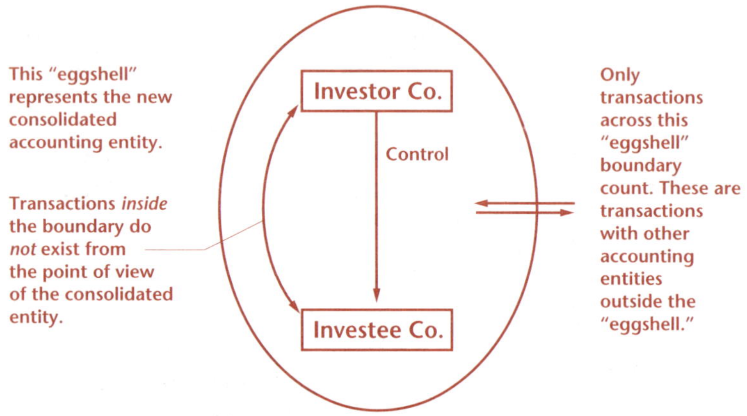

The "eggshell" represents the boundary between the consolidated accounting entity and the rest of the world. It is only transactions which cross this boundary that may be accounted for; all transactions between Investor Co. and Investee Co. are inside the boundary, and therefore do not exist as far as the consolidated financial statements are concerned. Suppose Investee sold a parcel of land to Investor for $150,000. The land cost Investee $100,000, and this is the amount that Investee carries it at on its individual company balance sheet. After the sale, Investee records a nonoperating gain on its individual company income statement of $50,000 from the sale of land. Also, Investor now accounts for the land at $150,000 on its individual company balance sheet. The $50,000 profit has been realized from Investee's individual company perspective, and the cost of the land from Investor's individual company perspective is $150,000, so these numbers are recorded in the respective general ledgers of the two companies. But from the perspective of the consolidated entity, no transaction ever took place. Thus, our view of when a transaction takes place changes as we alter the accounting entity.

The historic cost of the land on the consolidated entity's balance sheet is $100,000, and the consolidated entity earned no profit on a land sale since no transaction took place between it and an accounting entity outside the eggshell. When consolidated financial statements are prepared from the two sets of individual company financial statements, such items must be dealt with. The consolidation is performed by means of a spreadsheet, in which the two sets of legal company financial statements are modified for items such as the "inside the eggshell" land sale by means of "consolidation worksheet entries." These entries don't appear in either company's books of account, but only on the consolidation spreadsheet. The consolidation worksheet entry for the land sale, for example, would be (ignoring any tax implications for simplicity):

Dr	Gain on sale of land (I)	50,000	
	Cr Land (B)		50,000

We'll illustrate consolidation accounting with a more comprehensive example later on, after we describe how companies account for passive common share investments using the cost method. We will leave the equity method illustration until after we illustrate the consolidation method because it duplicates many of the calculations that are performed under consolidation.

The Cost Method

Suppose that on March 10, 1997, Hypothetical Inc. (henceforth HI), a manufacturer of kitchen furniture, acquired 10,000 common shares of FAS Ltd. on the stock exchange, with the intent of including the FAS shares as part of its long-term investment portfolio. HI paid $21.00 per share, plus a brokerage fee of $10,000, for a total of $220,000 in cash. FAS Ltd. has 900,000 common shares issued and outstanding, so HI's investment, at about one percent of the total, is definitely a passive one.

The journal entry on HI's books to record this acquisition of a financial asset is:

Dr	Investment in common shares (B)	220,000	
	Cr Cash (B)		220,000

The account "Investment in common shares" is a long-term asset.

HI has a December 31 year end. In early December 1997, HI's chief accountant received a notice that FAS had declared a cash dividend of $1.00 per share of common stock, payable to shareholders of record as of November 30, 1997; and on December 20, HI received a cheque for $10,000 from the financial institution that looked after FAS's share-related affairs. The entry to record the cash receipt is:

Dr	Cash (B)	10,000	
	Cr Investment income (I)		10,000

So, on its income statement for fiscal 1997, HI will show nonoperating investment income of $10,000. This entry accounts for the dividend as an income item from HI's perspective, and under "normal" circumstances this is just what the cost method requires. However, if the $10,000 in dividends were out of FAS's preacquisition earnings (in other words, if FAS had had a loss this year), then the credit side of the entry would go to the balance sheet account "Investment in common shares," as a return *of* (not *on*) the investment.

Consolidation Methods

Consolidation accounting can become quite complex when several subsidiaries are involved with all sorts of cross-ownerships. We'll keep it fairly simple in this introductory book, and illustrate a straightforward consolidation with only a single subsidiary. That way, we'll be able to point out the main ideas without getting caught up in more advanced technical subjects.

The example we'll use to illustrate consolidation accounting is based on the following hypothetical scenario: Atlantic Telecommunications Supply Inc. (ATSI) is a supplier of equipment to the Maritime telecommunications industry. Sales for 1996 were over $250 million. On January 1, 1997, ATSI purchased 100% of the outstanding common shares of Technology Limited (TL), an engineering company engaged in developing new applications. TL was founded in the mid-1970s by Joachim Delance, whose family sold the shares to ATSI.

ATSI's management had decided to acquire a controlling interest in TL in the belief that ATSI would be able to make good use of TL's engineering expertise. During 1997, ATSI purchased $10 million worth of engineering services from TL. The cost of these services to TL was $4 million, and the price that TL charged was the same as it charged its other corporate clients. ATSI accounted for the purchased engineering services as a product cost, since they were related to improvements of existing product lines of ATSI telecommunications equipment. By December 31, 1997 (ATSI's year end), 50% of the services purchased from TL were still in ATSI's inventory as part of the cost of as yet unsold equipment. Thus, 50% of the profit of $10 million minus $4 million, or $3 million, was left in ATSI's year end inventory. ATSI also had not yet paid TL for any of these services. ATSI's board of directors declared and paid $10,000,000 of dividends on common shares during the year, while TL's board declared and paid dividends of $5,000,000.

Balance sheets and income statements for ATSI and TL for the year ended December 31, 1997, are shown in Exhibit 10–3. ATSI accounted for its investment in TL using the cost method on its individual-company financial statements. ATSI has no other subsidiaries. One of the reasons that ATSI was interested in TL was the fact that TL had developed and patented innovative new encryption code to ensure telecommunications message security. The patent was valued at $1,500,000 by ATSI's finance department; in keeping with GAAP, TL had not accounted for the patent as an asset on its balance sheet.

The consolidation worksheet entries are developed below, and are shown in Exhibit 10–4 under the heading "Consolidation entries."

EXHIBIT 10–3
BALANCE SHEETS AND INCOME STATEMENTS FOR ATSI AND TL*

Balance Sheets (condensed)
as at December 31, 1997
($000s)

	ATSI	TL
Cash	$ 6,000	$ 3,000
Accounts receivable (net)	35,000	47,000
Inventories	80,000	10,000
Capital assets (net)	127,000	20,000
Investment in subsidiary	22,000	—
	$270,000	$80,000
Accounts payable	$ 41,000	$25,000
Other current liabilities	15,000	17,000
Bonds payable	25,000	6,000
Common stock	100,000	14,000
Retained earnings	89,000	18,000
	$270,000	$80,000

Income Statements (condensed) Year Ended December 31, 1997 ($000s)	ATSI	TL
Sales and services	$255,000	$110,000
Cost of sales and services	205,000	70,000
Gross margin	50,000	40,000
Other operating expenses	30,000	5,500
Net operating income	20,000	34,500
Other revenues and (expenses)	10,000	—
Net income before income taxes	30,000	34,500
Income taxes	15,000	17,250
Net income	$ 15,000	$ 17,250

*TL's assets and liabilities approximate current values.

Developing the consolidation worksheet entries[7]

1. *Accounting for aquiring 100% of TL's common shares on January 1, 1997:*

Since ATSI uses the cost method of accounting for its investment in TL common shares on its individual-company financial statements, the 100% interest must have cost ATSI $22,000,000. Therefore:

Cost of 100% interest in TL common shares		$22,000,000
Deduct: Book value of 100% interest, as of January 1, 1997:		
• Common shares of TL	$14,000,000	
• Retained earnings of TL (see below)	5,750,000	
	$19,750,000 x 100% =	19,750,000
Excess of price paid for shares over book value acquired		2,250,000
Deduct: Fair value of unrecorded asset (patent)		1,500,000
Residual, equals goodwill acquired on share purchase		$750,000

[7] The particular method of consolidation accounting that we're going to illustrate is called *purchase consolidation accounting*, and is used in virtually 99% of consolidations in Canada. Another method, called *pooling consolidation accounting*, is rarely used, and leads to far different consolidated financial statements. Purchase and pooling are not alternatives for the same fact situation; purchase is used when it is clear that one of the companies in the corporate group is the parent and the other is the subsidiary. Pooling is used in situations, usually involving a share exchange, in which identifying who is the parent and who is the subsidiary is not possible.

The retained earnings of TL at the time ATSI made its share purchase were:

TL's retained earnings as at December 31, 1997	$18,000,000
Add back: Dividends TL declared during 1997	5,000,000
	23,000,000
Deduct: TL's 1997 net income	(17,250,000)
Equals: Retained earnings, January 1, 1997	$5,750,000

"Goodwill" in the above calculation, and in the consolidated worksheet entry that follows, represents the excess of the amount that ASTI was willing to pay for the TL shares — that is, $22,000,000 — over the fair value of all the net assets it acquired ($19,750,000 + $1,500,000 for the patent). This goodwill amount, which was $750,000 as of January 1, 1997, indicates that TL has a value as an ongoing, operating company that exceeds the value of all of its individual assets less liabilities.

The consolidation worksheet entry to account for all this activity is:

Dr	Common stock	14,000,000	
Dr	Retained earnings	5,750,000	
Dr	Patent	1,500,000	
Dr	Goodwill	750,000	
	Cr Investment in subsidiary		22,000,000

This entry accomplishes the following:

- It prevents TL's common shares of $14,000,000 from appearing on the consolidated balance sheet, since these shares are now owned *inside* the consolidated group or eggshell boundary.
- It does the same to TL's retained earnings that existed at the date ATSI made its share purchase; only income earned after the share purchase date now counts.
- It records the patent asset.
- It records the goodwill asset.
- It prevents the account "Investment in subsidiary" from appearing on the consolidated balance sheet, since the assets and liabilities represented by this account are now fully portrayed on the consolidated balance sheet, and we don't want to double-count.

This first consolidation spreadsheet entry is important; it is a little like beginning the process of getting the two companies ready for their first public appearance together as one corporate group, with one commanding board of directors (ATSI's) that really runs the whole show.

2. *Accounting for the $10,000,000 ATSI still owes TL for services purchased:*

Dr	Accounts payable	10,000,000	
	Cr Accounts receivable		10,000,000

This entry ensures that both consolidated "Accounts receivable" and consolidated "Accounts payable" are not overstated by the amount of money owed *inside* the eggshell.

3. *Accounting for TL's $10,000,000 in services sold to ATSI:*

Dr	Sales and services	10,000,000	
	Cr Cost of sales and services		10,000,000

This entry prevents consolidated "Sales and services" from being $10,000,000 too high. It also does the same to consolidated "Cost of sales and services." This is so since ATSI's purchases over the year were increased by the $10,000,000, and recall that:

Cost of goods sold = Opening inventory + Purchases – Closing inventory

If we permitted the entire $205,000,000 of ATSI's "Cost of sales and services" to get onto the consolidated income statement, we would be overstating this expense from a consolidated perspective.

4. *Accounting for the 50% of the purchased services still in ATSI's inventory at year end:*

Dr Cost of sales and services	3,000,000	
Cr Inventory		3,000,000

The profit on the 50% of services that still remains as part of ATSI's inventory at year end arises from the fact that the inventory to which it was debited when ATSI purchased it remains unsold. Using the same cost-of-goods-sold equation that we used for entry 3, we can see that the $3,000,000 must be eliminated if we wish to prevent consolidated "Inventory" and consolidated "Cost of sales and services" from being overstated. After all, merely shuffling costs around between members of a corporate group shouldn't lead to higher assets on the balance sheet, nor should it result in higher gross margins and reported profits.

5. *Accounting for the TL dividends that ATSI counted as an income item on its individual-company financial statements:*

Recall that ATSI uses the cost method to account for its investment in TL's common shares on its own individual-company financial statements. That's all right, since these are not the statements that must be presented to ATSI's various stakeholders under GAAP; it is consolidated financial statements that must be. But we have seen that in order to prepare these consolidated financial statements, a variety of things that appear on the individual-company statements must be changed. This is simply another. Under the cost method of accounting for intercorporate equity investments, ATSI accounts for dividends as "Other revenues." These upstream dividends from TL totalled $5,000,000 in 1997; so the following spreadsheet entry is therefore required:

Dr Other revenues	5,000,000	
Cr Retained earnings		5,000,000

This entry does two important things. First, it prevents the $5,000,000 dividend from TL to ATSI from being counted on the consolidated income statement. It shouldn't be counted, since we know it just went from one part of the consolidated group (TL) to another (ATSI), and nothing has happened that affects the group in terms of its relations with any accounting entity outside the eggshell.

Second, the entry adds back the dividends that had been removed from TL's "Retained earnings" account on its individual-company balance sheet; from a consolidated entity point of view, no such dividends have been declared!

6. *Accounting for amortization of the now-accounted-for patent:*

Since we are now accounting for the patent, we must also account for its amortization. Patents are usually amortized over the lesser of their remaining legally protected life (a maximum of 17 years in Canada) and economic life. Let's assume that 10 years is the amortization period in this case, and that straight-line amortization is used:

Dr Amortization of patent	150,000	
Cr Patent		150,000

7. *Accounting for amortization of goodwill arising on consolidation:*

The *CICA Handbook* requires that goodwill arising on consolidation be amortized on a straight-line basis over not more than 40 years, but we'll choose 10 years and charge off $750,000/10 years, or $75,000 per year:

Dr Amortization of goodwill	75,000	
Cr Goodwill		75,000

The consolidation spreadsheet is shown in Exhibit 10–4; the final consolidated income statement and balance sheet are shown in Exhibit 10–5.

EXHIBIT 10–4
CONSOLIDATION SPREADSHEET

	A	B	C	D	E	F	G	H	I	J	K	L	M
1													
2	ATSI AND TL CONCOLIDATION SPREADSHEET												
3													
4	BALANCE SHEETS ($000'S						New accounts created	Consolidation entries					CONSOLIDATED
5					ATSI	TL	by consolidation	#	Dr	#	Cr		AMOUNTS
6		Cash			6,000	3,000							9,000
7		Accounts receivable (net)			35,000	47,000		2			10,000		72,000
8		Inventories			80,000	10,000				4	3,000		87,000
9		Capital assets (net)			127,000	20,000							147,000
10		Investment in subsidiary			22,000	0				1	22,000		0
11							Patent	1	1,500	6	150		1,350
12							Goodwill	1	750	7	75		675
13					270,000	80,000							317,025
14		Accounts payable			41,000	25,000		2	10,000				56,000
15		Other current liabilities			15,000	17,000							32,000
16		Bonds payable			25,000	6,000							31,000
17		Common stock			100,000	14,000		1	14,000				100,000
18		Retained earnings			89,000	18,000		1	5,750	5	5,000		98,025
19								8	*8,225*				
20					270,000	80,000							317,025
21													
22	INCOME STATEMENTS ($000'S)												
23		Sales and services			255,000	110,000		3	10,000				355,000
24		Cost of sales and services			205,000	70,000		4	3,000	3	10,000		268,000
25		Gross margin			50,000	40,000					87,000		
26		Other operating expenses			30,000	5,500							35,500
27							Amortization of patent	6	150				150
28							Amortization of goodwill	7	75				75
29		Net operatiing income			20,000	34,000							51,275
30		Other revenues (expenses)			10,000	0		5	5,000				5,000
31		Net income before income taxes			30,000	34,500							56,275
32		Income taxes			15,000	17,250							32,250
33		Net income			15,000	17,250							24,025
34									18,225		10,000		
35													
36								8			*8,225*		

*Note: Consolidation entry 8 balances the consolidated balance sheet by transferring the *net* of all the income statement changes to retained earnings.

EXHIBIT 10–5
CONSOLIDATED INCOME STATEMENT AND BALANCE SHEET

Atlantic Telecommunications Supply Inc.
Consolidated Balance Sheet (condensed)
as at December 31, 1997
($000s)

Cash	$ 9,000
Accounts receivable (net)	72,000
Inventories	87,000
Capital assets (net)	147,000
Patent	1,350
Goodwill	675
	$317,025
Accounts payable	$ 56,000
Other current liabilities	32,000
Bonds payable	31,000
Common stock	100,000
Retained earnings	98,025
	$317,025

Consolidated Income Statement (condensed)
Year Ended December 31, 1997
($000s)

Sales and services	$355,000
Cost of sales and services	268,000
Gross margin	87,000
Other operating expenses (including patent and goodwill amortization)	35,725
Net operating income	51,275
Other revenues	5,000
Net income before income taxes	56,275
Income taxes	32,250
Net income	$ 24,025

Minority interest

In our consolidation accounting example, ASTI purchased 100% of the common shares of TL. But what if ASTI were able to exercise control over TL by purchasing *less than* 100% of TL's common shares, but still more than 50%? In this case, a minority interest in the Investee company would exist.

Say, for example, that ASTI had originally purchased 80% of TL's common shares. The holders of the other 20%

would represent a class of owners whose power over TL's affairs was much less relative to that of ASTI.

On a consolidated balance sheet, minority interest is usually located between long-term debt and owners' equity. In simple situations, its amount is equal to the percentage of common shares owned by the minority shareholders, times the owners' equity of the subsidiary.

The "Equity" Method

The equity method of accounting for intercorporate investments in common shares is often informally called "one-line consolidation," because even though only the one line of the investment account appears on the investor's balance sheet, the impact on the investor company's net income is the same as if the investor and investee companies had been consolidated. They haven't under this method, of course, so the balance sheet of the investor wouldn't contain the assets and liabilities of the investee — just a single line representing its investment asset. Also, the investor's income statement wouldn't include the investee's sales, cost of sales (if any), and other expenses, on a line-by-line basis; it would simply show a single line labelled (often) "Investment income." However, if the investee that is being accounted for by the equity method has an extraordinary gain or loss on its individual-company income statement, and if the amount involved is material from the investor company's perspective, the investor's pro rata share of the extraordinary item will be disclosed separately on the investor's income statement.

Cost of 25% interest in TL common shares	$7,000,000
Deduct: Book value of 25% interest (recall that we had determined earlier that 100% of TL's book value at the time of purchase was $19,750,000)	
$19,750,000 × 25%	4,937,500
Residual (equals goodwill on the 25% of TL acquired by ASTI)	$2,062,500

25% of TL's 1997 net income of $17,250,000	$4,312,500
Deduct: Goodwill amortization (2,062,500/10 years)	206,250
	$4,106,250

Let's use the same facts as in the ASTI and TL case above, except now we assume that ASTI purchased just 25% of TL's common shares, and paid $7,000,000 cash. To simplify the illustration, we'll also assume that TL doesn't have an unrecorded patent and the ASTI inventory, which includes purchased services, has all been sold.

On ASTI's books, this investment in common shares is accounted for as follows:

Dr	Investment in common shares	7,000,000	
	Cr Cash		7,000,000

An analysis of the purchase is shown in the upper table on the left.

TL's 1997 net income was, as before, $17,250,000. Under the equity method, ASTI must accrue its 25% share of TL's net income, but must also account for the goodwill amortization. The calculation is shown in the bottom left table.

And the entry that ASTI records is:

Dr	Investment in common shares	4,106,250	
	Cr Investment income		4,106,250

This entry accrues ASTI's pro rata share of TL's 1997 income, after any adjustments that are required to make the impact on ASTI's net income the same as if TL had been consolidated.

But we mustn't forget to also account for the dividend that TL declared; we'll continue to assume that it totalled

$5,000,000. ASTI's 25% is $1,250,000. Under the equity method, this dividend is accounted for not as ASTI income (we've already accrued that, and to treat the dividends as income would be double-counting), but rather as a return of ASTI's investment in TL:

Dr Cash	1,250,000	
Cr Investment in common shares		1,250,000

Accounting, Organizations, and Society

Does Consolidation Accounting Travel Well? The Case of Japan

With all the talk of globalization and the breaking down of international barriers to trade and the flow of capital, there has been a strong push to develop international accounting standards. However, even stronger forces seem — at least at times — to be pulling in the other direction. A case in point involves consolidation accounting, as Jill McKinnon explains in the article we summarize below: "Application of Anglo-American Principles of Consolidation to Corporate Financial Disclosure in Japan," (*Abacus*, Vol. 20, no. 1, 1984, pp. 16–33).

McKinnon writes that consolidation accounting was introduced in Japan because of three factors:

- The entry of Japanese corporations into foreign capital markets in the early 1960s; as a result of this, Japanese firms' parent-only financial statements were no longer acceptable.
- The bankruptcy of Sanyo Special Steel Company in 1965, in which fictitious intercompany sales between the parent company and its subsidiaries were recorded at inflated prices.
- The entry of foreign corporations, with their consolidated financial statements, into the Japanese capital markets in the early 1970s.

However, the *nature* of company-to-company relationships differs significantly between Japan and the West; because of this, Anglo-American style consolidation practices are misleading in countries like Japan. Japan has a long history of "corporate groups." These groups originated among the leading merchant families of the seventeenth century. When the corporate form of organization was introduced to Japan in 1899, these groups made a smooth transition, forming a few dominant *zaibatsu*, or corporate groups. These *zaibatsu* were formally dissolved during the postwar Allied occupation, but rose again immediately after the occupation. By the 1970s they dominated the Japanese economy.

Each corporate group consists of a number of listed and unlisted companies that are aligned with one another. Following are some features of these groups:

- Share ownership follows a complex pattern of cross-ownership, in contrast to Anglo-American patterns:

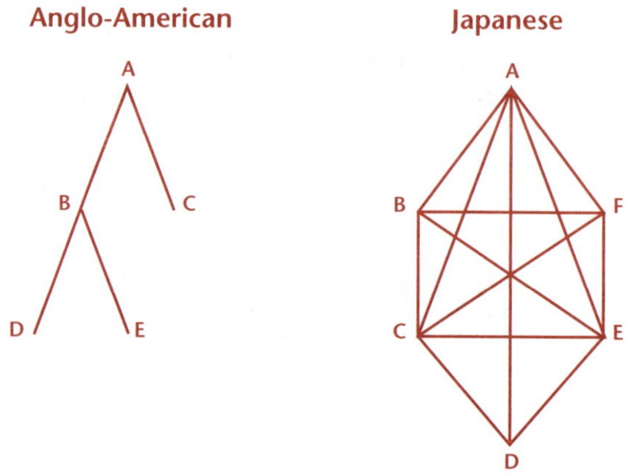

- Total share ownership within a group averages less than 50% of total share capital of the listed group companies.
- Japanese corporate groups are often referred to as *keiretsu*, or headless combines, since there is an absence of holding companies, and thus an absence of what we think of as controlling boards of directors. Instead, a council of presidents meets regularly to exchange views.
- Great importance is attached to nonshare relationships, such as debt relationships, historical associations, and interdependences based on raw materials, technology, and so on.

Thus, the concept of "control," which underlies consolidation accounting, is not generalizable to all other cultures. In Anglo-American countries, share ownership seems to be the primary criterion for deciding whether consolidation is appropriate; in Japan, share ownership is only one of many criteria linking corporations within a group. That's why importing the shareholding criterion for consolidation to Japan may result in misleading financial statements. McKinnon goes on to write that:[8]

[The following] conclusions may be reached in respect of the introduction of the requirement for consolidated financial statement reporting in Japan. First, historical and cultural determinants provide significant contrasts between corporate group associations in Japan and Anglo-American nations. These contrasts include the decentralized cross-holding pattern of share ownership, the predominance of small shareholdings, and the relative importance of non-share criteria in maintaining corporate group associations. The cultural characteristics of dantai ishiki *(group consciousness) and interdependence underlie the contemporary perceptions and attitudes of group relatedness in Japan, and are reflected in the close relationships in finance, raw materials, markets and technology that form and maintain group associations.*

Second, and therefore, the assumptions underlying consolidation practices in Anglo-American nations, including group associations based primarily on share ownership criteria, the

[8] Jill McKinnon, *Abacus*, Vol. 20, no. 1, 1984, p. 30. © Accounting and Finance Association, University of Sydney. Reprinted with permission.

notion of control through direct or indirect share ownership, and the presence of a holding or ultimate parent company, are less appropriate to the corporate context in Japan ...

Anglo-American practices of consolidation, when superimposed on the corporate groups which have functioned in Japan for many years, serve only to "break up" the complex and dynamic reality of those groups into a number of "Anglo-American type" corporate groups, and to portray an Anglo-American perspective of something that is uniquely Japanese ...

It must be concluded, therefore, that Anglo-American methods of consolidation fail to reflect adequately the nature of corporate group associations in Japan.

CHAPTER SUMMARY

The chapter began by pointing out that the accounting distinction between debt and equity should be kept, and then went on to illustrate accounting for a bond issue. Next, the classification problems created by hybrid securities were described, and accounting for a hybrid security was illustrated.

A continuum of intercorporate ownership was introduced, and the concept of control was described. The three methods of accounting for intercorporate investments were then explained: cost, consolidation, and equity. The chapter ended with an "Accounting, Organizations, and Society" section that provided evidence that accounting principles are often more appropriate to one culture than to another. The specific case involved consolidation accounting in Japan.

Suggested Answers to Accounting and Business Decisions

Decision A

(a) If the market rate is 9%, then the cash flow pattern created by a $26,000,000 face value bond with annual 10% interest payments and a ten-year term to maturity has a present value of:

$$NPV = \sum_{p+1}^{10} 2{,}600{,}000/(1.09)^{p} + 26{,}000{,}000/(1.09)^{10}$$

or $27,668,591.00.[9] Thus, there is a premium of $27,668,591 - $26,000,000, or $1,668,591. The entry to account for the issuing of the bonds is:

Dr Cash	27,668,591	
Cr Bonds payable		26,000,000
Cr Bond premium		1,668,591

If the premium is amortized on a straight-line basis over the ten-year life of the bonds, then its annual amortization will be $166,859, and the December 31 entry for each of the ten years will be:

[9] The Microsoft Excel (version 4.0) formula for the present value is:

= PV(0.09,10,2600000) + 26000000/(1.09)∧10

where the 0.09 refers to the periodic 9% interest rate, the 10 refers to the number of periods (years in the case of this bond), and the ∧ is Microsoft Excel's way of indicating that the (1.09) is to be raised to the power of 10.

Dr Interest expense	2,433,141	
Dr Bond premium	166,859	
Cr Interest payable		2,600,000

The January 31 entries accounting for the cash flows will be:

Dr Interest payable	2,600,000	
Cr Cash		2,600,000

And the January 1, 2006, entry accounting for the repayment of the principal will be:

Dr Bonds payable	26,000,000	
Cr Cash		26,000,000

(b) If the interest rate demanded by the market had equalled the bond face interest rate of 10%, then the bond would have been issued at its face amount of $26,000,000. There would have been no premium or discount; and the journal entry for January 1, 1997, would have been (ignoring the $400,000 of issue costs):

Dr Cash	26,000,000	
Cr Bonds payable		26,000,000

And the journal entry each December 31 for the next ten years would be:

Dr Interest expense	2,600,000	
Cr Interest payable		2,600,000

Of course, each January 1 following this accrual entry, an entry accounting for the actual cash outflow would be necessary:

Dr Interest payable	2,600,000	
Cr Cash		2,600,000

And on January 1, 2006, when the bond was paid off:

Dr Bond payable	26,000,000	
Cr Cash		26,000,000

Decision B

On January 1, 1999, the remaining cash flows associated with the original bond issue are (assuming the January 1, 1999, payment has already been made):

- Seven remaining $2,600,000 interest payments due January 1, beginning January 1, 2000, and ending January 1, 2006.
- The principal repayment of $26,000,000, to be made on January 1, 2006.

At a market interest rate of 15%, the present value of these remaining cash outflows (using Microsoft Excel) is $20,591,454.35.

As of January 1, 1999, three years of amortization have been recorded on the discount created by the original bond issue. Assuming straight-line amortization, this means that the carrying value of the original bond issue as at January 1, 1999, is:

Bonds payable		$26,000,000
Less: Bond discount	$1,531,200	
Deduct: Amortization for three years	459,360	1,071,840
		$24,928,160

The company pays the bondholders $20,591,454 on January 1, 1999. The journal entry to record the purchase of the bonds by the issuer, MultiSync, is:

Dr Bonds payable	26,000,000	
Cr Bond discount		1,071,840
Cr Cash		20,591,454
Cr Gain on retiring bond issue		4,336,706

The credit of $1,071,840 to the account "Bond discount" removes the remaining discount.

The $4,336,706 is a plug to balance the journal entry. Should this item be a gain item on MultiSync's income statement? If the bonds had been accounted for on a current-value basis since they were issued, this "gain" would have been recorded over the 1996 to 1998 period — perhaps a bit each year. But of course, such current value accounting for bonds is not GAAP.

Decision C

First approach:

Dr Interest expense	5,423,484	
Cr Cash		5,423,484

Second approach:

Dr Interest expense	5,368,244	
Dr Premium on notes payable	55,240	
Cr Cash		5,423,484

where the second year's debit to "Interest expense" is 15.75% × [$34,131,813 – $47,723], or $5,368,244, and the debit to "Premium on notes payable" is a plug accounting for the second year's amortization.

Third approach:

Dr Interest expense	5,261,387	
Dr Premium on notes payable	162,097	
Cr Cash		5,423,484

where the second year's debit to "Interest expense" is 15.75% × [$33,545,674 – $140,040], or $5,261,387, and the $162,097 debit to "Premium on notes payable" is a plug accounting for the second year's amortization of the ARCN's issue premium under this method.

KEY TERMS

Bond, as used in Chapter 10, is defined in the CICA's *Terminology for Accountants* as follows: "a certificate of indebtedness issued by a government or corporation ... In a corporation, the term usually implies that specific assets have been pledged as security."

The term also refers to the financial liability itself, in the sense that a company may be referred to as having bonds on its balance sheet. Bonds may have a variety of characteristics (callable, convertible, and so on). The structure of a bond — that is, the timing and amount of cash flows that must be paid out by the issuing company — is determined by the coupon, or face, interest rate, the face value of the bond, and the specific dates on which interest payments must be made.

Bond discount is the difference between the face value of a bond and the market value or proceeds obtained by issuing the bond, if the proceeds are *less than* the face value. Bond discount is amortized over the term to maturity of the bond.

Bond premium is the difference between the face value of a bond and the market value or proceeds obtained by issuing the bond, if the proceeds are *greater than* the face value. Bond premium is amortized over the term to maturity of the bond.

Callable bond is a bond that, under prespecified conditions, may be redeemed by the issuing company before maturity.

Consolidated financial statements, according to *Terminology for Accountants*, refers to the set of "financial statements of a parent company and one or more of its subsidiaries, combined so as to ignore the separate legal entities of the corporations and show the financial position and operating results of the group as one economic unit." The accounting entity, for purposes of accounting for transactions, is therefore redefined as a consolidated group of companies, instead of remaining as individual-company legal entities.

Control, as used in Chapter 10, refers to the ability of one company to elect the majority of the board of directors of another company. The first company is said to control the second company.

Convertible bond is one that the investor (lender) has the option to exchange for other securities of the organization that issued the bonds, under certain prespecified conditions. These other securities are usually capital shares.

Cost method, when used in connection with accounting for intercorporate investments, is defined in *Terminology for Accountants* as follows:

> *A basis of accounting for long-term intercorporate investments whereby the investment is initially recorded at cost and the post-acquisition earnings of the investee are recognized only to the extent received or receivable as dividends; dividends in excess of the investor's pro rata share of post-acquisition earnings reduce the recorded cost of the investment.*

Coupon bond is one that contains detachable coupons, which the investor must present to the issuer on specified dates, for payment.

Coupon or face interest rate is the interest rate specified in the bond indenture for a bond issue. This rate determines the amount of the periodic interest payments. It should not be confused with the market rate.

Debenture usually refers to a bondlike arrangement, except that specific assets of the issuer are not pledged as security or collateral.

Equity method, when referring to accounting for long-term intercorporate investments, is defined in *Terminology for Accountants* as follows:

> *A basis of accounting ... whereby the investment is initially recorded at cost and the carrying value adjusted thereafter to show the investor's pro rata share of the post-acquisition earnings or losses of the investee computed on a consolidated basis; dividends reduce the recorded carrying value of the investment.*

In simple English, this means that the investing company's net income is computed *as if* the investee company had been consolidated.

Holder of a bond is an individual or organization that has either provided money to a company issuing bonds in exchange for the bonds, or acquired the bonds from another holder.

Hybrid securities have a blend of both debt and equity characteristics.

In-substance defeasance occurs when a company that has issued bonds, or other debt, deposits financial assets such as cash or low-risk government securities in an irrevocable trust — that is, gives over forever the financial assets to another party, the trustee, who then assumes responsibility for using the financial assets to pay the interest and principal on the debt. However, the issuer is still contingently liable for the interest and principal, and the holders of the bonds are not party to the arrangement.

Income bond is one in which the amount of interest to be paid depends on the income of the issuer.

Indenture is a written agreement between parties that specifies their respective rights and obligations. An example is a **bond indenture**.

Indexed bond is one on which the interest and/or principal is linked to an index specified in the bond indenture.

Issuer of a bond is the company that raises funds by means of issuing bonds.

Market interest rate is the interest rate demanded by the market. When the future interest and principal payments of a bond are discounted by the market interest rate at the date of issue, the resulting present value is equal to the bond proceeds to be received by the issuer.

Mortgage bond is a bond secured, or backed up, by a mortgage.

One-line consolidation means the same thing as "equity method of accounting for intercorporate investments."

Retractable bond is one that the holder (lender) has the option of redeeming before maturity, under prespecified conditions.

Serial bond is a bond issue that matures in installments.

Significant influence exists when Company A is able to exert power over the operating and strategic decisions of Company B, which Company A has an equity investment in but does not control.

Sinking fund bond is one in which the bond indenture contains a clause requiring the issuer to set aside funds on a regular basis so that the funds set aside, plus any interest that such funds earn, will provide for the redemption of the bonds.

Stripped or zero-coupon bond is a coupon bond from which the coupons for future interest payments have been removed.

Term to maturity refers to the time period between the date of issuance of a financial security such as a bond, and its maturity date, on which the principal must be fully repaid.

Upstream dividends are dividends paid or payable by an investee company to an investor company.

FACT AND DESCRIPTION QUESTIONS

1. Explain why a bond discount or premium exists, and why such premium or discount should be amortized.
2. Explain why the first step in accounting for bonds is to prepare a time line tracking the exact cash flows.
3. Why is an accrual necessary to account for bond interest, even if the interest payment is not due until the next fiscal year?
4. Describe and justify King and Ortegren's approach to accounting for ARCNs.
5. Air Canada disclosed the following information in a footnote in its 1990 audited financial statements:[10]

Subordinated perpetual debt
In November 1989, the Corporation concluded a Japanese yen subordinated perpetual debt financing. The interest rate is 6.55% until 1994 and it will be reset for each subsequent five-year reset period based upon a capped spread over the Japanese long-term prime lending rate ...

	[millions of Cdn. dollars]	
December 31	1990	1989
60 billion Japanese yen at 6.55% until 1994		
Callable in year 1994 and every fifth year thereafter at par	$498	$498

... The maturity of this subordinated perpetual debt is only upon the liquidation, if ever, of the Corporation. Principal and interest payments on the debt are unsecured and are subordinated to the prior payment in full of all indebtedness for borrowed money. Since it is not probable that circumstances will arise requiring redemption of the debt and since, under present circumstances, it is not probable that the Corporation will call the debt, it is valued at the historical exchange rate and no provision is made for foreign exchange fluctuations ...

[10] Copyright Air Canada.

Required:

(a) Is the "subordinated perpetual debt" debt, or equity, or a hybrid security?

(b) Explain why your answer to part (a) is important.

6. (a) Explain the difference between significant influence and control.
   (b) Explain how significant influence may exist when the investor company owns considerably less than 20% of the investee company's common shares.
   (c) Explain how significant influence may not exist when the investor company owns just under 50% of the common shares of the investee company.
   (d) Explain how control may not exist even when the investor company owns more than 50% of the common shares of the investee company.

7. (a) Explain why the cost method is regarded as a passive method of accounting for intercorporate equity investments.
   (b) Explain how the equity method is an accrual approach, while the cost method is more consistent with a cash approach.

8. Explain why the accounting entity changes when one company controls another.

9. (a) Explain why transactions between a parent and its subsidiary are ignored when consolidated financial statements are prepared.
   (b) Recall from this chapter the land sale example between Investor Co. and Investee Co. Describe the implications if an income tax on individual companies had been taken into account, with a tax rate on land sale profits of 25%.

10. (a) Explain why debt and owners' equity are classified separately on an accounting entity's balance sheet.
    (b) Alpha Company issued the bond represented by the following diagram. If the market interest rate for bonds similar to Alpha's with respect to term to maturity and risk is 8%, what proceeds can Alpha expect to receive from the bond issue, ignoring transactions costs?

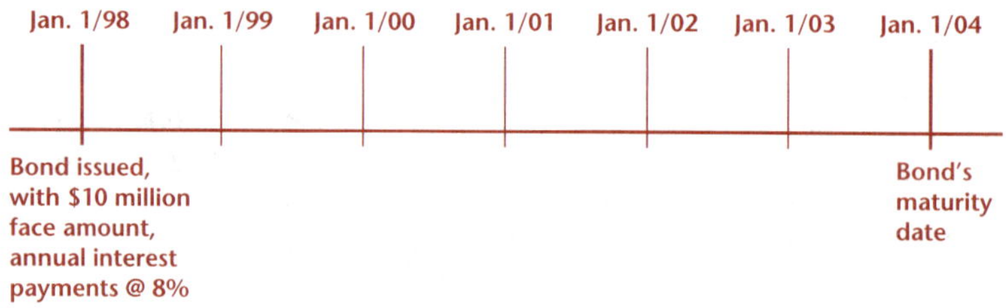

    (c) If the market rate on the issue date was 9%, prepare all the journal entries that Alpha would require over the life of the bond issue.

Questions for Analysis and Discussion

11. In 1972, Ross Skinner (author of one of the quotations that began this chapter) presented the following arguments against consolidated financial statements:[11]

[11] R.M. Skinner, *Accounting Principles: A Canadian Viewpoint* (Toronto: CICA, 1972), pp. 175–177.

- Aggregation of different businesses leads to meaningless asset and liability totals on the consolidated balance sheet. For example, the current ratio for a manufacturer is different from that of a public utility; if the utility is the parent of the manufacturer and the two are consolidated, the current ratio based on the consolidated balance sheet information is difficult to interpret because it is a weighted average.
- The user may overlook important information about legal restrictions on the free movement of assets within the consolidated group, such as restrictions on dividends imposed by the creditors of a subsidiary.
- If some member companies of a consolidated group are profitable and have strong balance sheets, but others are incurring operating losses and have weak balance sheets, creditors of the weaker subsidiaries may be misled if they refer only to the group's consolidated financial statements.

Required:

(a) Evaluate the above arguments. Are they sufficient to eliminate the rationale for consolidation accounting?

(b) Until recently, many manufacturing companies that had so-called "sales finance" subsidiaries did not consolidate these subsidiaries. The subsidiaries, which were often 100% owned by the manufacturer, provided financing to purchasers of the manufacturer's product (say, a tractor bought by a farmer). Top management of the manufacturer would argue that the two businesses were so different that consolidated financial statements would have been misleading. However, the CICA now requires that all subsidiaries be consolidated, except in certain specific instances, such as when the subsidiary is bankrupt. Comments?

12. (a) Suggest how investment income should be treated on a cash flow statement prepared using the indirect method, if the investment income arises because the company issuing financial statements is using the equity method to account for its investments in common shares.

(b) Why is the equity method of accounting for intercorporate investments in common shares informally referred to as "one-line consolidation"?

(c) If Invest Inc. owns 5% of the common shares of Cup Ltd., is it a foregone conclusion that the cost method of accounting for intercorporate common share investments should be used?

13. Managers and accountants are required to decide whether an intercorporate equity investment in common shares is passive, or one of significant influence, or one of control. Having done so, they must use the cost method for passive investments, the equity method for significant influence investments, and the consolidation method for controlling investments. Explain how all of this is an example of substance over form.

14. Explain how the approach to accounting for ARCNs suggested by King and Ortegren may be viewed as an example of substance over form.

15. Explain why recording an in-substance defeasance may *not* be an example of substance over form.

16. The cost of debt (that is, interest) is accounted for as an expense on the income statement, but the cost of equity such as common shares and retained earnings is not. One explanation for this asymmetric treatment of these two costs of long-

term financing is that accountants have rejected Paton's view that we are accounting for an entity that raises its financing and owns its assets, in favour of the view that regards the shareholders as proprietors (a proprietory view of the accounting entity). Under this proprietory view, the basic accounting equation becomes:

$$A - L = E$$

and costs such as interest on debt are appropriately expensed, whereas the cost of shareholders' equity is not an expense but rather a distribution of income *after* income has been determined.

(a) Is this asymmetric accounting treatment of these two costs justified, in your view?

(b) Adopt the role of a corporate treasurer (a manager whose job it is to raise funds for the company). You must raise $10,000,000 to invest in a new manufacturing process. You must decide whether to raise the funds by issuing common shares or by issuing bonds. How would these two alternatives affect the corporate income statement? (Keep in mind that bond interest is tax deductible, whereas dividends are not.) Should this difference in accounting treatment affect your decision?

17. (a) Explain why hybrid securities create accounting problems.

(b) Parent companies do not, of course, always own 100% of the common shares of their subsidiaries. Suppose that Shifty Limited owned 90% of the common shares of Pirate Limited. The 10% of Pirate not owned by Shifty is called the minority interest in Pirate, and appears on the consolidated balance sheet of Shifty and its subsidiary Pirate as an item with a credit balance on the right-hand side of the balance sheet, in between consolidated shareholders' equity and liabilities. It represents a bit of the subsidiary owned *outside* the corporate group. Suppose that Pirate declared a dividend on its common shares totalling $1,000,000; how would the existence of the minority interest affect the consolidation worksheet accounting for this intercorporate upstream dividend?

18. Alpha Company owns 90% of the common shares of Omega Company, which in turn owns 80% of the common shares of Beta Company. A member of Alpha's board of directors suggests that Alpha could increase its consolidated net income by purchasing a 10% block of the 80% of Beta's shares that Omega now holds (that is, one-eighth of Omega's holdings). Is this true, assuming that each of the companies earned a net income of $100,000 on an individual-company basis before any accounting for intercorporate holdings?

19. For this question, refer to the "Accounting, Organizations, and Society" section of this chapter.

(a) The *CICA Handbook* states that an *"enterprise should consolidate all of its subsidiaries"* (1590.16), and defines the key term "subsidiary" as "an enterprise controlled by another enterprise ... Control ... is the continuing power to determine its strategic operating, investing and financing policies without the co-operation of others" (1590.03). The *Handbook* goes on to say that "control ... though normally acquired through an equity interest in the subsidiary, may be acquired by other means. The form in which a parent controls a subsidiary ... does not determine the substance of their relationship" (1590.06); also, that "the level of equity interest in one enterprise held by another leads to a presumption regarding control" (1590.08).

Is the objection to consolidation raised by McKinnon more apparent than real?

(b) Assuming for the purposes of this part that McKinnon's objections to consolidation are valid in many situations, how would consolidation result in misleading financial statements?

(c) Are international common accounting standards possible? Are they desirable?

TECHNICAL QUESTIONS

20. Silverado Limited entered into the following transactions:

- February 10, 1996: Purchased 2,000,000 common shares of Pinkus Inc., a publicly traded company, at $1.05 per share. Broker's fees were $94,000. Pinkus has 25,500,000 common shares issued and outstanding, of which 15,000,000 are held by the Pinkus family. The remaining shares are actively traded. Siverado's management intends to hold the Pinkus shares in a portfolio of long-term investments. The current value of Pinkus's assets and liabilities is about equal to book value.
- February 20, 1996: The board of directors of Pinkus Inc. issued a press release announcing a $0.05 per share dividend to shareholders of record as of February 20, 1996. On February 21, Silverado purchased 1,000,000 more common shares at $1.13; brokerage fees were $47,000. The current value of Pinkus's assets and liabilities is still about equal to book value.
- August 17, 1996: Silverado sold 50,000 shares of Pinkus at $1.31; brokerage fees were $3,000.

Like most retailers, Silverado has a January 31 year end. On January 15, 1997, Silverado's chief accountant read in the financial press that Pinkus Inc.'s net income for the year ended December 31, 1996, was $72,545,000, after an extraordinary gain (net of income tax) of $8,300,000. Silverado is a private company owned 100% by the Silverado family.

Required:

(a) What accounting policy should Silverado select in order to account for its Pinkus common share investment? Why?

(b) Prepare journal entries accounting for Silverado's investment in the common shares of Pinkus, following the policy you selected in (a).

(c) Assume that no shareholder other than Silverado owns more than 5% of the publicly issued and outstanding common shares of Pinkus, and that the Pinkus family has invited Silverado's management to fill three places on the board of directors of Pinkus Inc. Would your response to (a) and (b) change?

21. Recall the bond that MultiSync Inc. issued, which was described in the body of the chapter.

(a) Compute the amount of cash that MultiSync could raise by issuing the bond at market interest rates varying from 5% to 15%, in increments of 0.5 percent. Assume that issue costs are still $400,000, as in the chapter. (If you have access to spreadsheet software, this would be a good time to use it.)

(b) If the market rate was 11% when MultiSync issued the bonds, but interest on the bonds is payable every half-year, beginning on July 1, 1997, what will the journal entries be for the life of the bond issue?

(c) Suppose that the original annual-interest-payment bonds were issued when the market rate was 11%, but that the issue date was April 1, 1997, rather than January 1, 1997. Prepare journal entries accounting for the life of the bond issue.

(d) Suppose that MultiSync arranges to buy back all the original annual-interest-payment bonds on January 1, 1998. If the market interest rate is 10% on that date, what will MultiSync have to pay to repurchase its bonds? As in the original situation, assume that the issue date was January 1, 1997. Prepare a journal entry to account for the buy-back from MultiSync's perspective.

(e) Suppose that you had invested in the bonds described in part (d) to this question. You had purchased MI's bonds having a face value of $5,000,000 on January 1, 1997. Prepare journal entries accounting for the events described in part (d), from your point of view.

22. Pietro Inc. (henceforth PI) had the following condensed balance sheet as of its year end January 31, 1997 (all amounts in $000s):

Balance sheet	**as of January 31, 1997**
Cash	25,500
Accounts receivable	37,200
Allowance for doubtful accounts	(1,500)
Inventory, weighted average	67,000
Equipment, at cost	105,000
Accumulated depreciation	(85,000)
	148,200
Accounts payable	5,000
Other current liabilities	3,000
Bonds	45,000
Preferred shares	10,000
Common shares	30,000
Retained earnings	55,200
	148,200

PI was an old-line manufacturer of office furniture and accessories. Although it had accumulated a significant amount of cash, its management was certain that it had to modernize or else, and so a decision was made to use the cash to acquire 100% of the common shares of Lethbridge Limited (LL), a smaller but technically more advanced competitor. On February 1, 1997, all 100,000 common shares of LL were purchased from Jim Lethbridge, the founder and sole shareholder, for $250.00 per share. Since it was a private transaction, no fees were involved.

LL's balance sheet as of February 1, 1997, along with information about the current values of its assets and liabilities, is shown next (all amounts in $000s):

	Actual Balance Sheet	Current Value
Cash	100	100
Accounts receivable (net)	2,500	2,200
Inventory, FIFO cost	8,000	9,200
Equipment	16,000	16,000
Accumulated depreciation	(1,600)	(1,600)
Patent	0	1,000
	25,000	
Accounts payable	3,500	3,500
Note payable, due December 31, 1997	2,000	1,800
Common shares	15,500	
Retained earnings	4,000	
	25,000	

Required:

(a) Prepare a journal entry from PI's perspective recording its acquisition of LL common shares.

(b) Prepare a consolidated balance sheet as of February 1, 1997, assuming that the February 1, 1997, balance sheet for PI is identical to its January 31, 1997, balance sheet, except for the LL common share acquisition.

CASE

Weston

Before 1973, the CICA had no formal accounting standard relating to consolidation. Even after the standard was issued, it met with some resistance, as evidenced by the following description of how George Weston Limited accounted for its subsidiary Loblaw Companies Limited.

Back in 1972, George Weston Limited was a large Canadian corporation engaged in retailing, manufacturing, and wholesaling. Its 1972, its sales were $1.1 billion, its assets were $500 million, and its net income was $30 million. GWL ranked ninth in sales, twenty-ninth in assets, and thirty-third in net income, according to *The Financial Post's* 1972 survey of Canadian industrial firms. Approximately 55% of the outstanding voting shares of the company were owned directly or indirectly by the Weston family.

Of its $500 million in assets, $27 million represented the company's 64% ownership (at cost) of the voting shares of Loblaw Companies Limited (LCL), a holding company whose major interests included control of Loblaws Limited (a major Canadian supermarket chain), Loblaw Inc. (an American supermarket chain), and National Tea Company.

In 1972, LCL had consolidated assets of $548 million, sales of $2.6 billion, and net income of $7.8 million, and was ranked among the top ten merchandisers in Canada by *The Financial Post*. For the fiscal year ending March 31, 1973, LCL reported a net loss of $14.8 million, or $1.40 per share. Loss per share *before* "special items" was $0.67.

Weston had not consolidated LCL prior to 1973, since the CICA had issued no hard-and-fast rule concerning consolidation in such circumstances. In its recommendations effective January 1973, however, the CICA *required* consolidation, except "i) where the subsidiary or the parent is in a regulated industry ..., ii) where the subsidiary is a corporate joint venture ..., iii) where control is temporary or the subsidiary is in legal reorganization, or in bankruptcy ..., [and] iv) where the subsidiary is in a foreign country (with exchange or earnings repatriation restrictions, or an unstable social climate)" (3050.07).

Since none of these exceptions apparently applied to Weston's interest in LCL, it was required to consolidate under the then-new CICA rules. Unfortunately, if Weston, which had been accounting for its investment in LCL at cost (and which had therefore been recording upstream dividends as revenue) were to consolidate LCL, Weston's earnings per share would *decrease* by about $0.60, according to newspaper reports.

After the new CICA rules on consolidation were issued, Weston issued public statements to the effect that it did not intend to consolidate its LCL holdings in its December 31, 1973, report (see the accompanying article). The essence of Weston's argument was that consolidation would not present fairly the financial position and results of operations for George Weston Limited, and thus, in order to provide "fair disclosure," unconsolidated statements should be presented. Weston did indeed not consolidate LCL for the fiscal year ending December 31, 1973, and received a qualified audit report. For the year ending December 31, 1974, however, Weston *did* include its LCL holdings on a consolidated basis. The 1974 earnings per common share (before extraordinary items) on a consolidated basis were $3.55; if LCL had not been consolidated (and the cost method retained), 1974 EPS would have been $3.88. Thus, consolidating LCL in 1974, thereby complying with the CICA recommendations, led to a $0.33 *decrease* in Weston's EPS for its LCL holding. In the following excerpt from the 1973 Annual Report of George Weston Limited, some data on the effect of *not* consolidating in 1973 is shown.

Required:

(a) Describe in words the effect on Weston's balance sheet and income statement of the change from the cost to the consolidation method. (See the Annual Report data that follow.)

(b) Do you feel that G.E. Creber's argument had merit? (See the article from the November 10, 1973, issue of *The Financial Post* that follows.) Consider the uses of the financial statements in your answer.

(c) By not consolidating LCL, and by using the cost method to report to its shareholders and other users, was Weston in a position to "smooth" its income? Explain in detail.

George Weston Limited
Notes to Financial Statements, 1973

George Weston Limited December 31, 1973

1. Summary of significant accounting policies

(a) Basis of consolidation

(i) the accompanying financial statements consolidate all subsidiary companies except Loblaw Companies Limited and its subsidiary companies ("Loblaw") which is carried at cost.

George Weston Limited ("Weston") has voting control of Loblaw through ownership of 67.7% of that company's outstanding class B voting shares. The Weston holding of the combined Class A non-voting shares and the class B voting shares represent 60.3% of the total participating shares outstanding. Because of the large minority interests in

Loblaw, as well as the substantial minority interests in the Loblaw subsidiary companies themselves, management has felt that consolidation of the Loblaw accounts with those of Weston's would not be the most informative presentation.

Effective January 1, 1973, the Canadian Institute of Chartered Accountants has recommended that, with rare exceptions, all subsidiaries should be fully consolidated. The effect of this recommendation is that the practice followed in the accompanying financial statements of carrying the investment in Loblaw at cost can no longer be said to be in accordance with generally accepted accounting principles.

In view of this it is the company's intention to include the accounts of Loblaw in the Weston consolidated financial statements for the year commencing January 1, 1974, the earliest practicable period for which such a step could be taken. To provide a proper starting point for the consolidation, the fiscal year-end of Loblaw has been changed to coincide with that of Weston, effective December 31, 1973. The Company proposes to first publish operating results on a fully consolidated basis commencing with the quarter ending March 31, 1974.

The following information has been extracted from the audited consolidated financial statements of Loblaw for the fifty-two weeks ended March 31, 1973 (with comparative figures for the previous year as restated by Loblaw):

		1973	1972
		($000s)	
Working capital		$71,527	$ 99,588
Total assets		531,282	547,109
Minority interests in subsidiaries		90,266	111,267
Shareholders' equity		95,585	117,099
Sales		2,560,283	2,592,748
Income (loss) before special items		(6,539)	4,095
Net income		(14,764)	7,261
Weston's share of the above consolidated earnings (loss) of Loblaw (after eliminating an inter-company gain of $340,000 in 1973) is as follows:			
Net income (loss)	— total	(9,097)	3,177
	— per share of Weston common stock	(83c)	(29c)
Weston has reflected in its net income the dividends received from Loblaw as follows:			
Dividends received during the year ended December 31	— total	2,510	2,274
	— per share of Weston common stock	23c	21c

Weston's share of the undistributed earnings of Loblaw from date of acquisition to March 31, 1973 (after retained earnings adjustments) amounts to $19,705,000.

Source: Annual Report, George Weston Limited, 1973.

Weston's Ted Creber Bucks the Tide

by Charles Davies

In his usual unimpassioned style, George Edgar (Ted) Creber, president and managing director of **George Weston Ltd.**, faced a luncheon gathering of the Toronto Society of Financial Analysts last week and dealt with some very contentious investor questions about the company.

Contrary to guidelines established earlier this year by the Canadian Institute of Chartered Accountants, he said, Weston will not provide a full consolidation of 60%-owned Loblaw Cos. at the end of the current fiscal year ...

In this frontal assault on the accounting profession, Weston believes it is on firm ground. Creber has maintained all along that its comparatively small, $31-million equity holding in Loblaw Cos. doesn't justify a consolidation that would double Weston's assets to roughly $1,000 million by adding those of Loblaws.

The call of the Canada Corporations Act for fair disclosure overrides the CICA guidelines, he thinks, and, in any event, information detailing the impact of Loblaw Cos. will be given in the notes to the annual report.

Loblaw Cos., of course, has been a notable loser. On the basis of red-inkstained performances by components such as **Loblaw Inc. and National Tea Co.** in the U.S., it had a deficit — including extraordinary items — of $17.34 a share for its 1973 fiscal year. Consolidated with Weston's 1973 earnings, this would reduce earnings per share by 60 cents, Creber says.

Despite such forthright disclosures to assembled analysts, the problem about not consolidating isn't merely the depressing effect it would have on Weston's earnings.

What will happen among other things, is that company auditors **Clarkson, Gordon & Co.** will be left in an awkward spot. Knowing that Weston is presenting its statement in conflict with generally accepted accounting principles, about all they can do is give a qualified signature to the annual report. Clarkson, Gordon also has to wonder about Weston's long-term intentions — will consolidation come in 1974? — and the effect they could have on the audit treatment done this year.

There could also be problems for Weston in bucking the tide. Douglas Thomas, research director of the CICA, agrees that although the CICA guidelines on accounting practice represent moral suasion rather than law, the provincial securities commissions across Canada make it a point to adhere to them as a matter of policy.

Thomas thinks that Weston may recant on consolidation once it has to come to market for further debt or equity financing.

It gets very hypothetical at this point, but it seems clear that the Ontario Securities Commission could make life miserable if Weston doesn't consolidate.

According to H.S. Bray, vice-chairman of the OSC, prospectuses could be refused for failure to comply with accounting principles and even a qualified balance sheet — such as Weston plans to produce at its year end — could raise questions.

And, if it really wanted to be nasty, the OSC could issue a stop-trading order.

These, however, are what Bray terms "ultimate sanctions" and they are "highly improbable."

"If they came forward with a filing," he says, "I doubt very much if these questions would arise. They'd consolidate and that would be that."

What it all adds up to is that, despite public statements, Weston may not have fully made up its mind on consolidation. Bray, echoing the sentiments of others in the accounting field, says he is "awaiting with interest" the Weston annual report for 1973 and it would also be a fair guess that the company is having ongoing discussion about it with the auditors ...

The Financial Post, *November 10, 1973.*

CASE

Fortis Inc.

Fortis Inc.'s 1994 Annual Report contained the following corporate profile:[12]

Fortis Inc. is a holding company with two electric utility subsidiaries, Newfoundland Power and Maritime Electric, the principal distributors of electricity in the Province of Newfoundland and the Province of Prince Edward Island, respectively. Through two non-utility subsidiaries, Fortis also has investments in financial services, real estate and telecommunications.

Newfoundland Power serves approximately 205,000 customers, or about 85% of the electrical consumers in the Province of Newfoundland. It owns and operates 33 generating plants with a combined capacity of 148 Mws, but purchases most of its energy from another utility. Newfoundland Power is regulated by the Board of Commissioners of Public Utilities of Newfoundland.

Maritime Electric serves approximately 54,000 customers, or about 90% of the electrical consumers in the Province of Prince Edward Island. It has approximately 110 Mws of installed capacity but purchases most of its energy from utilities in other provinces. Its activities are regulated under the Maritime Electric Company Limited Regulation Act (Prince Edward Island) and are monitored by the Island Regulatory and Appeal Commission.

Fortis Inc. has two non-utility subsidiaries which operate in the Province of Newfoundland. Fortis Trust is a deposit-taking institution which lends primarily on residential mortgages. Fortis Properties owns and manages commercial real estate. It also holds a 50% interest in Unitel Newfoundland which, through Unitel Communications, provides long distance telecommunications in Newfoundland as part of the national Unitel system.

The common shares of Fortis Inc. are traded on The Montreal Exchange and The Toronto Stock Exchange. The preferred shares of Fortis are traded on The Toronto Stock Exchange.

In August 1994, Fortis acquired the 68% of the outstanding common shares of Maritime Electric Company Limited that it did not already own. Fortis' 1994 financial statements, including footnote 1, which describes how the share acquisition was accounted for, are shown on the following pages.

Required:

(a) Reconstruct, as best as you are able based on the information provided, the journal entries that account for Fortis's acquisition of the 68% of outstanding common shares of Maritime Electric that it did not already own.

(b) Critically assess Fortis's accounting and its presentation of the Maritime Electric acquisition.

[12] Reprinted courtesy Fortis Inc.

FORTIS INC.

(Incorporated under the laws of the Province of Newfoundland)

Consolidated Balance Sheet

As at December 31

Assets	1994	(in thousands) 1993
Current Assets		
Cash	$ 9,866	$ 9,366
Accounts receivable	52,357	35,400
Income taxes receivable	215	
Materials and supplies	7,651	4,192
Prepaid expenses	2,667	3,664
Rate stabilization account	5,165	4,882
	77,921	57,504
Long Term Investments	14,652	36,574
Other Assets		
Mortgages receivable—Fortis Trust	47,899	43,981
Deferred charges	16,779	13,417
	64,678	57,398
Fixed Assets	650,551	508,213
Goodwill	28,216	
	$ 836,018	$ 659,689

Liabilities	1994	1993
Current Liabilities		
Bank indebtedness	$ 51,926	$ 21,582
Accounts payable and accrued charges	60,746	46,802
Deposits payable—Fortis Trust	27,987	18,860
Dividends payable	6,363	4,396
Income taxes payable		4,693
Interest accrued on long term debt	3,917	3,952
Current installments of long term debt	9,689	2,375
	160,628	102,660
Long Term Debt	264,699	221,988
Deposits Due Beyond One Year—Fortis Trust	18,172	19,683
Deferred Credits	47,030	25,621
Non-Controlling Interest	20,702	10,905

Shareholders' Equity		
Shareholders' Equity		
Common shares	**113,893**	76,177
Earnings retained and invested in the business	**160,894**	152,655
Common shareholders' equity	**274,787**	228,832
Preference shares	**50,000**	50,000
	324,787	278,832
	$ 836,018	$ 659,689

Reprinted courtesy Fortis Inc.

FORTIS INC.

Consolidated Statement of Retained Earnings

For the Year Ended December 31

	1994	*(in thousands)* **1993**
Balance at Beginning of Year	**$ 152,655**	$ 142,435
Net income for the year	**31,313**	30,633
	$ 183,968	$ 173,068
Dividends		
Preference Shares	**4,350**	4,350
Common Shares	**18,724**	16,063
	23,074	20,413
Balance at End of Year	**$ 160,894**	$ 152,655

Consolidated Statement of Income

For the Year Ended December 31

	1994 (in thousands)	1993
Operating Revenues	$ 381,937	$ 343,252
Operating Expenses		
Purchased power	205,776	186,142
Other expenses	61,590	55,168
Depreciation	31,259	27,513
	298,625	268,823
Operating Income	83,312	74,429
Interest Charged to Construction	1,302	411
Interest Earned	1,395	1,714
	86,009	76,554
Finance Charges	31,378	28,010
Income Before Income Taxes	54,631	48,544
Income Taxes	23,074	18,827
Income Before Underlisted Items	31,557	29,717
Equity Income	818	2,396
Income Before Non-Controlling Interest	32,375	32,113
Non-Controlling Interest	1,062	1,480
Net Income for the Year	31,313	30,633
Dividends on Preference Shares	4,350	4,350
Earnings Applicable to Common Shares	$ 26,963	$ 26,283
Average Common Shares Outstanding	10,948,849	10,269,857
Earnings Per Common Share	$ 2.46	$ 2.56

FORTIS INC.
Consolidated Statement of Changes in Financial Position
For the Year Ended December 31

	1994 (in thousands)	1993
Cash from operations		
Net income for the year	**$ 31,313**	$ 30,633
Items not affecting (generating) cash		
Depreciation	**31,259**	27,513
Deferred income taxes	**(1,683)**	(1,128)
Weather normalization account	**(413)**	1,681
Other deferred charges	**2,371**	1,233
Equity income	**(818)**	(2,396)
Non-controlling interest	**1,062**	1,480
	63,091	59,016
Change in non-cash working capital	**2,052**	7,528
	65,143	66,544
Cash from external financing		
Net proceeds from common shares	**37,716**	3,569
Net proceeds from long term debt		5,529
Repayment of long term debt	**(1,989)**	(2,281)
Redemption of preference shares of subsidiary	**(3)**	(11,391)
Increase in bank indebtedness	**30,344**	2,582
Increase (decrease) in deposits payable	**(1,511)**	6,166
	64,557	4,174
Cash used in investing		
Acquisition of Maritime Electric Company, Limited	**(66,677)**	
Capital expenditures (net)	**(35,554)**	(43,752)
Contributions in aid of construction	**3,962**	887
Mortgages	**(3,918)**	(5,811)
Long term investments	**485**	1,165
Increase in deferred charges	**(3,362)**	(1,413)
	(105,064)	(48,924)

Dividends		
Common shares	**(18,724)**	(16,063)
Preference shares	**(4,350)**	(4,350)
Subsidiaries to minority shareholders	**(1,062)**	(1,480)
	(24,136)	(21,893)
Increase (decrease) in cash	**500**	(99)
Cash, beginning of year	**9,366**	9,465
Cash, end of year	**$ 9,866**	$ 9,366

1. Acquisition of Maritime Electric Company, Limited

In August, 1994, pursuant to a take-over bid, the Corporation acquired all the outstanding common shares of Maritime Electric Company, Limited ("Maritime Electric") not already owned by Fortis, thereby making Maritime Electric a wholly-owned subsidiary. Prior to the acquisition of the additional shares, Fortis owned approximately 32% of the outstanding shares of Maritime Electric. For financial reporting purposes, Maritime Electric has been accounted for on the equity basis to July 31, 1994 and has been consolidated subsequent thereto. Maritime Electric is an electric utility based in Prince Edward Island.

Details of the acquisition, which has been accounted for using the purchase method, are as follows:

Assets acquired	
Fixed assets	**$137,988**
Deferred charges	**3,689**
	141,677
Liabilities assumed	
Working capital deficiency	**(1,754)**
Long term debt	**(52,000)**
Deferred credits	**(20,794)**
Non-controlling interest	**(9,800)**
	(84,348)
Net assets	**57,329**
Equity position at date of acquisition	**(18,882)**
	38,447
Goodwill	**28,230**
Total acquisition cost	**$ 66,677**
Consideration	
Cash	**$ 33,002**
Common Shares	**33,675**
	$ 66,677

CHAPTER

11

eleven

Accounting and Change: Past, Present, and Future

Learning OBJECTIVES

After you have read, thought about, and discussed this chapter, and completed a selection from the end-of-chapter material, you will have made significant progress in achieving the following learning objectives:

- Be able to identify several emergent issues in accounting.
- Describe how accounting has changed over time, and identify ways in which accounting is changing in the present and into the future.
- Describe implications of technological change for accounting.
- Explain electronic data interchange and its importance for accounting.
- Explain how the Internet may affect accounting and financial reporting.
- Describe accounting for not-for-profit organizations.
- Explain why generally accepted accounting principles and their historic-cost focus may need reform.

> *After a long period of cogitation I am convinced that the main subject-matter in accounting is not numbers, but human activity and the results of some particular aspects of human activity. Human activity and the (human) relationships leading up to and arising from activity between individuals and groups of people are what the accounting processes focus attention on.*
>
> Louis Goldberg, Emeritus Professor, University of Melbourne, "Whither Accounting Research? A Personal View," *Asia-Pacific Journal of Accounting*, Vol. 1, December 1994, pp. 2–17

INTRODUCTION

Well, this is it — the last chapter in an introductory accounting textbook. We have introduced plenty of ideas and concepts, and many technical tools as well. Above anything else, we hope you are beginning to appreciate the importance of accounting to organizations and society, and especially to you as an individual. Our theme has been that there are common principles underlying all areas of accounting (see Chapter 2), but our focus has been on financial accounting, and even here there is much more to tell.

In this final chapter, we will discuss a few important emerging issues to give you a sense of where accounting may be going. We consider the impact of technological change, the widening of the scope of GAAP to include not-for-profit organizations, and (very briefly in the Appendix) accounting for changing prices. The issues selected are just some of the many we could have chosen. A more comprehensive list of emerging issues in the accounting discipline and its profession would include these three as well as at least the following (some of which we've discussed in previous chapters):

- Designing and implementing environmental accounting and accountability systems and reports (see Chapter 9). This includes measuring costs and benefits in ways that don't ignore the rights of stakeholders. For example, the cost of a unit of nuclear-generated electricity should include the expected costs of decommissioning the nuclear facility, as well as the costs of environmental degradation caused by nuclear power generation.
- As a general extension of the first point, extending the boundary of what is accountable — for example, accounting for post-employment benefits other than pensions and derivative securities (see Chapter 9).
- Ensuring that the demographic composition of the accounting profession fairly reflects our society.
- Designing and implementing fair and humane management control systems that are effective in helping accounting entities achieve fair objectives.
- Designing and implementing fair tax systems, including measurements of taxable income.

- Establishing ways to make audits more effective, while controlling their costs.
- Encouraging more common ground in international accounting standards, while at the same time recognizing that in different countries are found different social, legal, and religious factors that affect how economic activity takes place and therefore what accounting is like.

This list could continue for several pages. All of these issues relate to the human activities that Louis Goldberg was talking about in the quotation that opened this chapter.

The Impact of Technological Change

The clay tokens described by Mattesich and Young back in Chapter 1 (refer to the opening quotations to that chapter, and to the "Accounting, Organizations, and Society" article at the end of that chapter) provided the basis for a system of accountability that is now many thousands of years old. With the advent of paper and double-entry bookkeeping, this system evolved into the complex system of accounting that we have today. The financial reporting part of that system was described in Chapter 6.

Technology has been a constant companion of accounting, and accounting has both influenced and been affected by technology. In the opening quotation to Chapter 3, the chief financial officer of Microsoft Corporation linked the success of the personal computer industry to Luca Pacioli's popularization of double-entry bookkeeping. It is obvious that the personal computer has revolutionized how accounting is done. Examples: the accounting cycle introduced in Chapter 3 is handled by PC-based accounting systems in even the smallest of organizations; electronic spreadsheets permit a wide variety of simulations and what-if analyses; and relatively complex accounting such as consolidations can now be modelled using such spreadsheets, as shown in Chapter 10. PCs and related telecommunications have become just another working tool of managers and accountants.

Electronic data interchange

In this section we'll focus our attention on the implications for accounting of one aspect of computer technology: electronic data interchange, or EDI. EDI is a communication network that links the computer system of one organization (say, a supplier) to the computer system of another organization (say, a customer). A customer can place an order through the network directly to a vendor's system, which reduces both paperwork and the time needed to initiate and process transactions. The vendor acknowledges the order, issues a delivery notice, and dispatches an invoice to the customer electronically through the telecommunications network. By mutual agreement, the supplier can even arrange access to its customer's inventory status file so that it can replenish its customer's inventory automatically.

The benefits of EDI are so great that many organizations, such as General Motors Canada (which has thousands of suppliers), make it a criterion for doing business, citing the following as justification:[1]

[1] *Issues for Canada's Future: EDI or DIE*, June 1992, published by Kelly Lavoie Inc., on behalf of the EDI Council of Canada.

- EDI is cost-effective to the extent that a transaction costs just 13 cents.
- It's fast, eliminating mailing time.
- It's reliable.
- It's flexible. Previously, when transactions were processed using paper forms, adding new information required often costly form redesign; with EDI, information may be easily and cheaply added as needed.
- EDI is expandable: additional transactions can easily be added to the system linking a supplier and a customer.

Let's see how accounts payable and accounts receivable can be affected by EDI. Assume that the organization we're discussing — call it FG Inc., or FGI — makes hundreds of purchases each day. In order to validate an account payable as legitimate, FGI's accounts payable department must match up three supporting documents: a purchase order, which was originally issued by FGI (this provides proof that the organization did in fact make the order, and that it was properly authorized); a receiving report, which provides proof that the items ordered were in fact received by the organization; and the invoice issued by the supplier, so that the purchaser can verify prices and other details of the transaction. The first two documents are internally generated by FGI's operational accounting system, which is a computer-based system. The suppliers transmit their invoices through an EDI network. Thus, FGI must integrate its EDI system with its internal operational accounting system so that it can access and match the vendor invoices to purchase orders and receiving reports.

At the same time, the supplier's accounts receivable must be verified with a customer order and shipping report. The customer order is transmitted through the EDI network from FGI to the supplier. By properly matching the customer order to an internally generated shipping report, the supplier's accounts receivable department can produce an invoice and transmit it back through the EDI telecommunications network to FGI.

With little human involvement, FGI's and the supplier's integrated EDI-operational accounting systems can update both customer and vendor accounts, and record necessary journal entries on a real-time basis. And if FGI's bank also participates in the EDI network, the payment that FGI makes to the supplier may be processed through the bank's electronic funds transfer system; in this way, the complete cycle of ordering, receiving, and paying becomes virtually automatic.

So EDI can be a very important means of processing the many routine transactions that accounting entities engage in every day (and night, since EDI is global, and "normal business hours" don't mean much to an international telecommunications system). But with the technology there come additional challenges, some of which are explained in the article excerpted in Exhibit 11–1.

A database approach to financial accounting: Will A = L + OE join the dinosaurs?

We can think of computer technology as going through several phases, as far as accounting is concerned:

- In the 1960s, 1970s, and early 1980s, expensive mainframes and minicomputers processed large quantities of an organization's routine transactions, such as payroll, on a batch basis. A "batch basis" meant that several transactions — perhaps a month's payments — were processed during one computer run.
- In the 1980s, more decentralized, distributed data processing was introduced, and there was a move toward PC-based networks, "real-time" processing of transactions in organizations, and the use of stand-alone personal computers.

EXHIBIT 11–1
SOME CHALLENGES POSED BY EDI TO ACCOUNTING*

System integrity
How reliable is the information prepared through an integrated EDI-EDP ["EDP" refers to electronic data processing] system? Traditional accounting control focuses on internal activities. Under an EDI system, internal controls alone cannot ensure the integrity of a company's information system, particularly for data coming from external sources. Therefore, external controls based on mutual agreements between trading partners are necessary to ensure the system's integrity. When a third-party network is used, another contract between traders and the network administrator is required. Controls must be clearly resolved and delineated in both the trading partners' contract and the network contract in a number of areas.

Trade authentication
When an electronic document replaces paper, the parties' signatures used to prove its authenticity are no longer available. Thus, trading partners must specify in their contracts what elements are needed to authenticate a trade. Some experts suggest using digital signatures instead. These are algorithms governing the encryption and decryption of messages. The messages can be protected from alterations by either the sender or the receiver. If trading partners agree on this approach, how exactly will they implement it? How should they resolve disputes?

Audit trail
A complete, reliable audit trail of all messages transmitted through a network is vital to corporate accountants and auditors. Besides helping to authenticate trades, this trail provides a history of record transmission, allowing the accountant to uncover any problem and, possibly, the responsible party.

Establishing an effective audit trail requires the cooperation of both trading partners and network administrators. The network contract must specify the administrator's responsibility to set up a satisfactory trail. It must also describe what network members should do to make such an audit trail available. In most cases, what's needed are a history log, access log and transaction log maintained by the administrator in an electronic database for all messages transmitted through the network.

Network members and the administrator must also agree on how the records of the audit trail can be used. For example, is the administrator responsible for disclosing the records of the audit trail? Must the administrator protect the records' confidentiality? Who owns the records in case of disputes? Is the administrator liable for damages if the required audit trail fails?

Data encryption
For security reasons, some trading partners may want to transmit only encrypted messages. They must agree with their network administrator on how messages will be encrypted and decrypted.

External audit
To ensure a network's integrity during EDI communication, a company might obtain a right to audit its partners or the administrator. Or a network administrator might want to audit its members to ensure that all procedures are properly implemented. Thus, another external audit is desirable. The right to audit, and the obligation to be audited by other EDI trading parties, must be established through mutual agreements. The contracts must clearly define the nature and extent of allowable audits.

An integrated EDI-EDP system permits source data automation beyond the bounds of individual companies. Not only can its participants substantially cut their data processing costs, but they can prepare timely information for operating and decision support. In order to reduce risks to the accounting system's integrity, accountants must consider external control measures to ensure the validity of data from outside sources. These measures can be implemented through mutual agreements between trading partners and between a network's administrator and its members. EDI provides opportunities and challenges for management accountants. To keep up with changing information technology, accountants must update their knowledge with continuous professional development.

*From Bor-Yi Tsay, "Electronic Data Interchange: A Challenge for Management Accountants," *CMA Magazine*, July–August 1993, pp. 19–22. Reprinted with permission from The Society of Management Accounts of Canada.

- In the 1990s, with the introduction of EDI and the rise of the Internet, it became possible for a variety of outside users to access accounting entities' databases by modem.

It is this most recent phase which suggests that some very fundamental changes may be store for financial accounting. We shouldn't be at all surprised by this: the clay tokens of the Sumerians and the ledgers of fifteenth-century Renaissance Italy each in their turn changed people's conceptions regarding what should be accounted for, how the accounting should be done, and who was entitled to the information. With computer and telecommunications technology making access to accounting and related data and its analysis relatively easy, concepts such as the accounting entity, the accounting reporting period, a transaction, and even financial statements themselves, must be rethought.

For example, if all the events (including transactions) entered into by an organization are being continuously updated in a computer-accessible database on a real-time basis, perhaps users just need the events data and not the balance sheets, income statements, and other financial statements that pre-process this data. Chapter 5 was devoted almost entirely to the various revenue recognition and expense judgments and decisions that different companies make when converting transactions information into financial statements. And a substantial portion of GAAP is concerned with such issues. Is technology now pointing toward a new, "events-based" type of financial accounting, and making irrelevant all the debates about which inventory cost flow to choose (FIFO, LIFO, and so on), whether deferred tax accounting makes sense, what depreciation method to choose, when to recognize revenue, and so on?[2]

Accounting and Business Decision A

(a) Many managers responsible for cash management closely monitor their company's cash "float" — that is, the lag between the time a cheque is mailed to a supplier and the time it clears the bank. A large float means that cash outflow is delayed, and may reduce a company's costs. EDI systems that include banks process cash payments instantaneously, so companies lose their cash float. Is this good or bad?

(b) One argument in support of a database approach to financial reporting is provided by Cushing:[3]

Continuous updating of the events data base would enable investors to monitor significant transactions and trends on a real-time basis, and to respond quickly whenever circumstances called for a revision of their investment portfolio. Furthermore, investors would not be forced to wait for quarterly and annual reports ...

Put yourself in the shoes of a senior manager of a company that has two divisions; one division has a fairly stable product line, the other has relatively risky, innovative products. Suggest how Cushing's observation might have a bearing on your management approach.

[2] If you wish to explore this fascinating topic further, a good place to start is an article by B.E. Cushing, "On the Feasibility and the Consequences of a Database Approach to Corporate Financial Reporting," *Journal of Information Systems*, Spring 1989, Vol. 3, no. 2, pp. 29–52.
[3] Cushing, "On the Feasibility ...," p. 39.

Accounting, accountability, and the Internet

In Chapter 6 we briefly described the emerging importance of the Internet as a means through which organizations are beginning to disseminate accounting and other information about themselves. The technology is changing almost week to week, it seems, so making definitive conclusions about financial reporting via the 'Net is premature. But since the publishers of many academic journals and magazines are now seriously implementing Internet distribution, and even textbook publishers "expect that by the end of the decade, they will be sending the contents of their textbooks across a nationwide campus network, possibly to be printed in campus bookstores,"[4] and textbooks are now appearing that have a Web homepage, can we expect that financial reporting will be far behind?

We'll briefly explore one aspect of the potential impact of the Internet on accounting: financial reporting and accountability via the Internet.

In the *1996 Canadian Internet Handbook*, Jim Carroll and Rick Broadhead concluded:

For organizations, the Internet represents a new method to reach existing and potential customers, shareholders, the general public, government bodies, and other third-party groups. The reality of the Internet for many organizations is that it is changing business such that an organization can have an "information relationship" with those people and organizations with which it already has a business relationship.[5]

This Internet-based information relationship has three dimensions:

- *Marketing.* The Internet is used to target specific consumer groups with product and lifestyle information, and perhaps includes interactive features designed to appeal to the organization's customers. Carroll and Broadhead (p. 45) suggest that Molson's site (**www.molson.com**) is "a good example of a sophisticated marketing initiative ... that contains national information about Canadian concerts, a unique hockey pool, and other information."
- *General.* This includes information for suppliers, prospective employees, and so on.
- *Financial.* This includes financial data and more general information about accountability. It is this dimension we're interested in.

Back in Chapter 6, we mentioned that many organizations are now making some or all of their accounting and related information available over the Internet. While technical obstacles to establishing effective corporate websites are continually falling, many companies are just beginning to deal with the *strategic* issues relating to this new information relationship with their various user groups. What accounting information should be made available? Should the information be identical to the traditional "hardcopy" information, or should management provide additional interpretations? What if management believes that the formal, hardcopy audited financial statements do not fairly present the company's results of operations and financial position, perhaps because of a generally accepted accounting principle with which management disagrees (say, the requirement to expense all R&D expenditures as they are incurred)? Could management provide *alternative* financial statements through the Internet, and still be in compliance with all the legal requirements because the hardcopy statements were in agreement

[4] Robert E. Jensen and Petrea K. Sandlin, *Electronic Teaching and Learning: Trends in Adapting to Hypertext, Hypermedia, and Networks in Higher Education*, Trinity University, 715 Stadium Drive, San Antonio TX, 78212-7200, pp. 5–11.
[5] Prentice Hall Canada, 1996, p. 21.

with GAAP? After all, "at the moment, there are few rules in cyberspace."[6] Here, we'll look at three examples of what companies are doing with respect to financial reporting and accountability via the 'Net, as of mid-1996.

First, Adidas, the popular German-based sports equipment company. At their website users can download their recent financial statements, in what is identical to hardcopy form. No additional analysis is provided. This approach is perhaps best described as a first step in using the Internet for financial reporting and accountability; undoubtedly, the company will adopt a more strategic approach and go beyond merely duplicating what's available to shareholders and other users in hardcopy form.

Our next example is Maple Leaf Foods Inc., "the largest food processing company in Canada, with annual revenues in excess of $3 billion."[7] According to corporate head office, the company doesn't have a website. Carroll and Broadhead (p. 486) point out that large companies spend up to $1 million in designing and implementing websites, so it's not hard to understand why "everyone" doesn't have a web presence as yet. But the competitive pressure to use the Internet as a means of developing information relationships will spur companies such as Maple Leaf Foods to join in.

Our third and final example is The Body Shop, a British-based company that researches, manufactures, and markets a wide variety of skin preparations, creams, and the like. The company's website does not include the traditional financial statements (in contrast to Adidas); however, it does include a very extensive set of linked pages detailing the company's concern with the environment and social causes. The main web page is **www.think-act-change.com/**. The environmental and social responsibility material posted on the Internet by The Body Shop includes:

- The Body Shop approach to ethical auditing.
- The company's animal protection statement.
- The company's environmental statement.
- An independent social assessment of The Body Shop by Kirk Hanson, professor of business ethics and social responsibility, Stanford University.

Bringing NFP Organizations into GAAP

An enormous amount of human activity takes place through not-for-profit (NFP) organizations. Charities, clubs, hospitals, universities, and religious organizations are just some of the organizations in the NFP sector. The CICA has suggested the following definition of an NFP organization:[8]

Not-for-profit organizations are organizations in which there is normally no transferable ownership interest and from which the members or contributors do not receive any financial return which directly results from membership or contribution, and that are formed, for example, for social, educational, professional, religious, health or philanthropic purposes.

[6] Debra Spar and Jeffrey J. Bussgang, "Ruling the Net," *Harvard Business Review*, May–June 1996, pp. 125–133.

[7] RBC Dominion Securities, Maple Leaf Foods Inc., May 10, 1996, p. 3.

[8] Re-exposure Draft, *Not-For-Profit Organizations*, CICA Accounting Standards Board, December 1993.

Financial accounting for NFPs has tended to be quite different from that for profit-seeking accounting entities for a number of reasons, including the following:

- NFPs by definition are not established for profit, so there is no need to measure net income; for this reason, the concepts of revenue recognition and matching that are so important in the profit-seeking sector become irrelevant.
- Instead of income statements, many NFP organizations prepare statements that are a mixture of accrual accounting and cash flow accounting. For example, receivables are accrued, but no depreciation is accounted for. This isn't as silly as it may seem: accruing accounts receivable is a useful way to exert control over them, while not accounting for depreciation just acknowledges the fact that many NFP organizations in the past had little need to account for the cost of the services they provided.
- Many NFP organizations report their financial statements on a fund accounting basis, which the CICA defines as "the collective accounting procedures resulting in a self-balancing set of accounts for each fund established by legal, contractual or voluntary actions of an organization. Elements of a fund can include assets, liabilities, net assets, revenues and expenses. Fund accounting involves an accounting segregation, although not necessarily a physical segregation of resources" (paragraph .102 of the re-exposure draft). A fund-accounting-basis set of financial statements for a university is shown in Exhibit 11–2; an explanation of the various funds being accounted for is set out in Exhibit 11–3.

Over the past decade there has been a move to integrate NFP organizations into GAAP, while still providing for their uniqueness. This movement has suffered one or two false starts, as the article excerpted in this chapter's "Accounting, Organizations, and Society" section suggests. But in December 1993, the CICA's Accounting Standards Board issued a series of re-exposure drafts on NFP accounting, and these have been incorporated into the *CICA Handbook*. In part, these new generally accepted accounting standards set NFP accounting principles as follows:

- They state that "a clear and concise description of a not-for-profit organization's purpose, its intended community of service, its status under income tax legislation and its legal form should be included as an integral part of its financial statements."
- They suggest that NFPs normally produce a statement of financial position, a statement of operations and changes in net assets, and a statement of cash flows.
- If an NFP reports its financial accounting information on a fund accounting basis, it "should provide a brief description of the purpose of each fund reported."
- Capital assets should be accounted for at cost, and amortized over their useful lives.
- An NFP organization should consolidate other accounting entities that it controls, or at least present information in its financial statements about the controlled organizations' assets, liabilities, purpose, and relationship to the NFP. For example, a university may own a university press, or a foundation that raises money from alumni and the community.

EXHIBIT 11–2
A UNIVERSITY'S FINANCIAL STATEMENTS ON A FUND-ACCOUNTING BASIS

Balance sheet, April 30, 1994 ($000s)

	Operating Fund*	Ancillary Fund*	Capital Fund*	Restricted Fund*	1994 Total	1993 Total
ASSETS:						
Cash and cash equivalents	97	9			106	238
Accounts receivable	23,532	6,952		411	30,895	27,517
Inventories	2,726	7,323			10,049	11,081
Deferred pension charge						11,949
Investments	86,192	5,283	8,005	532,357	631,837	586,454
Property, plant & equipment		47,347	307,451		354,798	330,948
Advances to university press	6,462	(6,462)				
Total assets	119,009	60,452	315,456	532,768	1,027,685	968,187
LIABILITIES:						
Bank indebtedness	7,472				7,472	11,299
Accounts payable	51,054	12,491	2,906		66,451	55,672
Accrued pension liability	2,618				2,618	
Unearned income	6,816	2,039			8,855	9,702
Long-term debt		24,998	8,274		33,272	34,865
Total liabilities	67,960	39,528	11,180		118,668	111,538
NET ASSETS:						
Operating deficit	(16,173)	14,549			(1,624)	(2,944)
Endowment funds				398,712	398,712	374,006
Reserves	67,222	6,365	273,455	134,056	481,098	454,756
Equity in land		10	30,821		30,831	30,831
	51,049	20,924	304,276	532,768	909,017	856,649
	119,009	60,452	315,456	532,768	1,027,685	968,187

*The operating, ancillary, capital, and restricted funds are defined in Exhibit 11–3.

Operating statement for the year ended April 30, 1994 ($000s)

	Operating Fund*	Ancillary Fund*	Capital Fund*	Restricted Fund*	1994 Total	1993 Total
REVENUES:						
Government grants	386,277		5,439	88,089	479,805	515,162
Student fees	138,490	3,515	385		142,390	128,779
Sales and services	23,476	57,692			81,168	84,777
Investment income	19,567	1,228	968	35,740	57,503	52,501
Contract research	4,716			19,930	24,646	28,801
Other grants				37,919	37,919	33,280
Donations		460	1,383	22,494	24,337	21,042
Other income	925				925	1,410
Total revenues	573,451	62,895	8,175	204,172	848,693	865,752

EXPENSES						
Compensation:						
Academic salaries	224,609			11,296	235,905	244,716
Staff salaries	134,555	2,928		76,606	214,089	215,721
Benefits	43,221	292		8,286	51,799	52,141
Total compensation	402,385	3,220		96,188	501,793	512,578
Physical plant—repairs & maint.	58,270	6,279			64,549	67,766
Cost of sales/services		44,502			44,502	46,979
Amortization		2,119	36,193		38,312	37,609
Contract research				21,394	21,394	22,194
Scholarships	15,852			6,555	22,407	21,704
Supplies & other	58,755	2,147		29,429	90,331	83,140
Renovations	2,291		6,356	1,144	9,791	3,744
Interest expense	792	2,444			3,236	2,472
Total expenses	538,345	60,711	42,549	154,710	796,315	798,186
EXCESS OF REVENUES OVER EXPENSES	35,106	2,184	(34,374)	49,462	52,378	67,566

Statement of cash flows for the year ended April 30, 1994 ($000s)

	1994 Total	1993 Total
OPERATING ACTIVITIES		
Excess of revenues over expenses	52,378	67,566
(Increase) decrease in assets:		
Accounts receivable	(3,378)	(761)
Inventories	1,032	94
Deferred pension charge	11,949	(2,978)
Increase (decrease) in liabilities:		
Accounts payable	10,779	(2,535)
Accrued pension liabilities	2,618	
Unearned income	(847)	(4,132)
Non-cash components:		
Amortization expenses	38,312	37,609
	112,843	94,863
INVESTING AND FINANCING ACTIVITIES:		
Purchase of investments, net	(45,383)	(61,088)
Additions to property, plant and equipment, net	(62,162)	(53,184)
Increase (decrease) in long-term debt	(1,593)	8,924
	(109,138)	(105,351)
Increase (decrease) in bank indebtedness during the year	(3,705)	10,488
Bank indebtedness, beginning of year	11,071	583
Bank indebtedness, end of year	7,366	11,071

Accounting and Business Decision A

(a) Many NFP organizations own profit-seeking operations that make a contribution to the general goals of the NFP. For example, universities operate textbook and computer shops, hospitals operate cafeterias and parking lots, and so on. In your opinion, should such activities be consolidated in with the NFP's financial statements?

(b) Explain why the operating fund's operating statement in Exhibit 11–2 is not an income statement.

(c) The accounting policy footnote to the university's financial statements is excerpted in Exhibit 11–3. List the accounting decisions that the footnote indicates university management has made, and comment on the reasonableness of the decisions as best as you can.

EXHIBIT 11–3
EXCERPT FROM UNIVERSITY'S ACCOUNTING POLICY FOOTNOTE (as adapted)

The accounts of the University are maintained in accordance with the principles of fund accounting in order that any limitations and restrictions placed on the use of available resources may be observed. Under fund accounting, resources held for various purposes are classified into funds in accordance with the specified objectives. For financial reporting purposes, the University has combined funds with similar characteristics into four groups: Operating fund; Ancillary fund; Capital fund; and Restricted fund.

The operating fund accounts for the costs of academic, administrative and other operating expenditures of the University funded by fees, grants and other general income. It also records the assets (other than property, plant and equipment which are recorded as assets of the capital fund), liabilities, funds committed for specific purposes and cumulative surplus or deficit relating to regular academic and administrative operations.

Expenditures for ancillary operations include both direct and indirect costs. Parking, residences, food and beverage services are operated on a fee-for-service basis. Ancillary operations include buildings and equipment used exclusively for its operations.

The capital fund accounts for amounts expended and funds available to be spent on the capital building program. The capital fund includes land, buildings, and equipment and investments held in the capital renewal fund for future building projects.

The restricted funds account for funds received which are earmarked for research and other special purposes, either by the donor of such funds or the governing body of the University.

Accounting: A Final Comment

We hope that you're now both more aware of how accounting affects your life, and better able to evaluate accounting information, than you were when you began this book. Perhaps you will choose to study accounting and its various subdisciplines in more depth, and go on to become a professional accountant. Or you may decide, "This is enough!" Whatever you do, never take accounting for granted, because with advances in technology and increasing demands by business and government for accountability, accounting surely won't take *you* for granted, and almost everything you do in your personal and work life, and every transaction you enter into, will be accounted for in some way. Understanding the strengths, weaknesses, and assumptions of accounting information, financial statements, and accounting systems is clearly important.

This makes Louis Goldberg's opening quotation all the more poignant. After a life spent engaged in the scholarly study of accounting, his conclusion that "the main subject-matter in accounting is not numbers, but human activity ..." seems obvious, though really it isn't. Accounting, with its objectivity, precise numbers, and balance sheets that always balance, *seems* to be a highly technical subject. There is no doubt that accounting has a highly technical side — after all, debits and credits, trial balances, and spreadsheets are all technical in nature. And constructing accrual and cash flow statements is a technical activity. And the tools accountants use — computers, applications software, and the like — are technical in nature.

But it is how you *use* the technical apparatus of accounting, and the *impact* of these "merely" technical choices on people, that is the main subject matter of accounting. At the same time, you cannot know how to use accounting, nor can you understand the impact of accounting choices, unless you also have an appreciation for the technical aspects of accounting. So the two go hand in hand. Knowing the technical becomes the means to the end of knowing the impact of accounting on organizations and society, and on individuals.

We finish this book by providing an illustration, in this chapter's "Accounting, Organizations, and Society" section, of the "human activity" that Goldberg mentions.

Accounting, Organizations, and Society

The following article focuses on the attempt by the CICA's Accounting Standards Board to extend GAAP to NFP organizations, and suggests the general flavour of power struggles in accounting standards-setting.

CICA Exposure Draft: A Comment

by L.S. Rosen, York University

A small group within the Canadian Institute of Chartered Accountants (CICA) has suggested that several major changes be made to financial reporting by non-profit organizations (CICA, Exposure Draft, "Non-Profit Organizations.") For example, they want long-lived items such as equipment set up as assets and then amortized each year. These changes will tend to be costly to implement and maintain, thereby diverting scarce funds away from charitable programs into very questionable accounting and reporting expenses.

An even greater problem with many of the proposed changes is that their purpose is at best unclear or remote and, at worst, that the proposals are outdated, misleading, or pointless. Charitable organizations are strongly urged to study the Exposure Draft carefully (ideally through a small *independent* study group) and respond forcefully to all of those sections that they find objectionable. Otherwise, the Exposure Draft will become approved practice and auditors who are chartered accountants will be compelled to, in effect, force it upon each charity they serve. In an age of deregulation the CICA group's proposals are difficult to fathom.

In broad terms, the suggested changes are bringing to the boiling point a much larger issue in financial reporting in Canada. Unfortunately, the nonprofit organizations are being caught in the middle of a fight among chartered accountants that has been raging for about 10 years. Until recently, the debates have primarily covered government reporting. Some even-handedness existed because organized groups of government officials could raise objections and receive satisfaction. Now with charities being targeted, many letters of complaint from volunteers will have to be sent to achieve suitable results, with the ideal being a withdrawal of the proposed changes.

Some History

Charities are being told by the Exposure Draft advocates to, in effect, report in accordance with GAAP (generally accepted accounting principles). GAAP for the most part are 60-year-old "technology". They are a vague and largely uncatalogued number of accounting and reporting approaches that developed mainly after the 1929 stock market crash. Contrary to popular belief, GAAP are prone to extensive manipulation.

GAAP have to be contrasted with *cash basis* accounting (recording only cash receipts and cash disbursements) and *accrual* accounting (cash basis modified for the recording of short-term transactions such as receivables and payables). Each — cash, accrual, and GAAP — has its usefulness or legal necessity in the vast array of Canadian organizations. (Given the existence of differing ownerships, differing industries, differing sizes, and other variations, more than one approach is necessary.)

Should GAAP be used for charities? In order to respond to this question it is necessary to look at what GAAP were designed for, and whether this old technology still stands up in the 1990's in most, or any, organization(s).

GAAP are based on a series of fundamental *assumptions*, primarily derived from the 1930s and 1940s, many of which do not fit a large number of organizations and their environment in the 1990s. A few of these GAAP *assumptions* are:

1. The need to *match* costs to revenues in a time period so that the organization can *calculate profit.* (Given this matching assumption alone, one has to wonder how a system designed for profit-seeking organizations and taxation could possibly make any sense for non-profit organizations.) Clearly implied in "matching" is the practical ability of accountants to be able to match in an unbiased manner. Obviously, matching can be difficult to achieve in organizations with long-lived assets, research and development, and changing information technologies. Matching is wide open to manipulation of numbers. Hence, the validity of the matching concept is being seriously questioned today, in an era of longer-term investments and increasing litigation from readers of financial reports.

   GAAP matching could have an impact on nonprofit organizations in peculiar and unfortunate ways. One example would be that the initial setting up of previously unrecorded equipment and similar items would give the appearance of sudden wealth, which might convince prospective donors that the organization no longer required support. The subsequent writing down of these so-called assets could then create non-cash deficits. This in turn, could lead to donors feeling a need to contribute more cash to eliminate the deficit or, more probably, a management decision that important charitable programs would have to be curtailed so as to eliminate the (artificial) deficit. Who knows how donors may react to the accounting changes? But, why force them away from cash thinking unless there are overwhelming benefits to the charities? Experience has shown that many people are baffled by GAAP. Why confuse or annoy charitable donors?

2. Historic, original-transaction, cost must be used in GAAP accounts and financial statements. That is, current replacement costs of assets, or their current resale prices, are *not* to be accounted for under GAAP as long as the asset is still owned. In brief, if you want information about the cost of replacing one of the charity's assets, or what the asset may be sold for, do not expect the GAAP records to tell you. Indeed, the GAAP figures could be quite misleading for a decision about asset replacement. Of what relevance are historic costs to managers of charities? The CICA Exposure Draft appears to ignore this type of user/use question and presses on with what could easily be called arbitrary allocations of historic cost, for unspecified uses. Probably most charitable organizations will find that adherence to historic cost GAAP incurs significant accounting cost with no discernible benefit, or creates confusion. Those not trained in accounting, for example, could easily be confused by the historic numbers and might well not understand why the managers of the charity are using them. Decisions to curtail a charitable program could be erroneous because historic numbers were used in arriving at the cost of the program.

3. Long-run continuity (often referred to as the going-concern assumption) is assumed by GAAP, with the outlook often being towards long-term profitability. Current liquidity or current cash flows are downplayed under GAAP because they tend to assume stability in the organization and the economy. (With such an assumption, and the use of GAAP, it is hardly surprising that in the past 10 years in Canada we have seen banks fail because they ran out of cash, i.e., failure occurred in cases where the current GAAP financial statements showed that operations were profitable.) Supreme Court of Canada Justice Willard Estey in his report on the Alberta bank failures made the liquidity versus profitability contrast a highlight of his criticisms of GAAP accounting. Like banks, charities have to focus on cash, both to survive and to comply with Revenue Canada requirements. GAAP deflect the cash and liquidity emphasis that is essential to management if it is to ensure organizational survival. Often, what GAAP may claim to do is actually accomplished more cost-effectively through cash management or accounting — which tend to be in the realm of certified management accountants and not those chartered accountants who perform audits.

4. The presumption of bargained, arm-length, objective transactions is another underpinning of GAAP. Does this make sense in the operations of a charity, especially smaller ones that rely on the good intentions of donors, volunteers who provide services, and difficult-to-quantify guarantees from supporters for any bank loans? Does a bank actively seek GAAP financial statements of a charity or is it content with other documentation such as cash budget? These types of questions do not seem to have been addressed by the advocates of the CICA Exposure Draft. Sometimes they want fair market value figures;

mostly they do not. The inconsistency is puzzling, given that proponents of the changes are seeking comparable accounting among charities.

Current Canadian GAAP deal with non-arm's-length transactions such as the provision of assets or services between related parties in a highly questionable manner. That is, readers of financial statements of large corporations are not provided with either the current market value of the asset or service or the difference from whatever non-arms-length figures are shown in the financial statements. Yet, this Exposure Draft is trying to hold charities to higher standards than chartered accountants require from their large corporate clients.

GAAP's Deficiencies

At our university we often teach students that Canadian GAAP primarily apply to large, public, audited, widget corporations at the plateau of their life cycle. GAAP often do not apply (unless a group forces them upon the organization) to small private corporations, unincorporated businesses, governmental bodies and similar enterprises. GAAP have severe limitations for readers of financial statements when they are used for many resource companies: logging, mining, oil, gas, farming, and others where historic cost bears little relationship to current worth. For the most part GAAP exist because of corporate, and some income-tax, legislation. GAAP financial statements do not tend to be helpful tools in decision-making by managers of organizations because GAAP intermingle cash, accrual receivables, historic costs and similar items that are measured in different ways.

As we move from the industrial era to an information-technology era, assets will tend to be computer software, trained people, patents, copyrights, investments in research, and related intangibles. The historic cost and matching assumptions of GAAP will continue to be less and less applicable to the organizational reality of the 1990s and the next century. What charities do not need is 60-year-old technology that was designed for large, public, profit-seeking companies — unless some clear benefits can be identified.

Unfortunately, the Exposure Draft does not set forth specific benefits but relies on vague generalities such as section 305 where the purpose is described as "... enables users of the financial statements to make comparisons with other organizations". But who are these users? Are they donors who would benefit the charity? What sort of comparison would make any sense given the diversity of size, purpose and method of operation of Canadian charities?

Much of the thinking underlying the Exposure Draft can be traced to what is called in accounting the "general purpose user/reader". From a validation or research point of view a concept of "general purpose reader" is meaningless. A person who is trying to evaluate the benefits of an accounting proposal cannot test for relevance or benefit because "general purpose" is a fiction, an unknown character. Hence, supporters of "general purpose" can advocate anything, because there is no way of dealing with the amorphous "general".

Rejections of General Purpose

Why should managers of charities have to tolerate the "general purpose" mentality? As stated, more beneficial management tools can be found in the fields of cash and management accounting (e.g., cash budgets). The purpose of financial reporting by charities is not to please a school of accounting thought that praises "general purpose" and illogical beliefs about the need to compare.

Fortunately, "general purpose" has recently lost several battles. In dealing with accounting litigation cases in Canada, most courts have adopted a specific user/use orientation. Public accountants owe a duty of care to specific individuals or similar classes of individuals who are "foreseeable" as users, with a "proximate" or close connection between accounting figures and the suffering of damages. The judges have to assess whether a specific complainant, and not a "general purpose" one, was misled.

The court interpretations are consistent with a concept in accounting called "materiality". A material transaction is one that will influence the decision of a foreseeable user. For some reason the concept of "materiality" does not appear within the Exposure Draft. Materiality requires the identification of the specific users/readers of financial statements.

"General purpose" has also not fared well with the Ontario Securities Commission (OSC). In 1972, the OSC gave chartered accountants a chance to develop more effective financial statements for investors. Opinions will differ, but I believe the chartered accountants have dropped the ball badly. Apparently, the OSC is not overly impressed with GAAP financial statements for public companies because it has introduced a "Management Discussion and Analysis" (MD&A) requirement. MD&A involves extensive supplementing of GAAP figures and presentations in order to overcome GAAP deficiencies and disclosure limitations. Each year the OSC publishes a commentary on GAAP reporting and identifies GAAP deficiencies and manipulations.

Other jurisdictions and regulators are currently taking a second look at general purpose GAAP requirements and their usefulness to the Canadian public. It is too early to say, but there may also be federal Business Corporations Act changes that reflect poorly on GAAP reports.

In the United States, GAAP has been severely criticized by senior officials of the Securities and Exchange Commission for its role in many Savings and Loan failures. A number of lawsuits have been launched against public accountants for losses that are alleged to be in the billions. Several public accountants have been settling out of court by providing multi-million-dollar payments.

Meanwhile, a group in Canada wants charities to adopt the GAAP model of reporting. To serve whom?

This article first appeared in "The Philanthropist," Vol. 11, no. 2.

Although L.S. Rosen in the long article just excerpted was particularly concerned with GAAP's application to not-for-profit organizations, his more general displeasure with the historic cost and matching assumptions of GAAP is evident. In fact, there have been several attempts to reform GAAP, and relax the historic cost concept, not only in Canada but elsewhere. These attempts are most vigorous when inflation is significant, and tend to lose steam when inflation rates are in the 1% to 2% range. The appendix to this chapter illustrates how one Canadian company dealt with the issue of accounting when prices were changing significantly, and also outlines some other aspects of this subject.

CHAPTER SUMMARY

A sample of important emerging issues in accounting were identified. Two of these issues were described in more detail in the chapter: the impact of technological change on accounting, and the widening of the scope of GAAP to include not-for-profit organizations.

Suggested Answers to Accounting and Business Decisions

Decision A

(a) This is good, because managers responsible for cash management would have "real-time" information on the cash inflows and outflows of the organization, and perhaps be better able to plan for expenditures, short-term loans, and the like. On the other hand, if they no longer have the cash float, they may have to seek out other sources of cash, especially if their customers are not yet part of an EDI arrangement that includes a bank (consider that the company loses its float because its payments go through the EDI system to its suppliers, but its customers still have their float).

(b) Put yourself in the shoes of a manager whose every decision is almost instantly visible by a company's shareholders (and the public at large). You might shie away from risky projects in general — especially those that have longer-term payoffs. It's like having someone looking over your shoulder, second-guessing your every move. Now, of course many shareholders would not act like this, but some may, and as long as you believed that quick, positive results were now needed, you might perhaps choose projects in the riskier division only if they had quick profits and cash flows, and a positive net present value. And you might ignore innovative projects with longer-term payoffs — perhaps the most innovative ones. Perhaps the division with the stable product line would become more important to the manager.

Experimentation, learning from error, and the willingness to take a chance — all so important in nurturing innovation and entrepreneurship — might be dampened under such an accountability system, unless specific provision was made to shield such activities from punishment if they did not immediately prove profitable.

Decision B

(a) The use of fund accounting permits such operations to be shown separately in an ancillary operations fund, as well as being consolidated in the "totals" column. Some university operations are very close to typical profit-seeking operations (a bookstore or computer shop, for example), while others (such as student residences) are more closely aligned to the basic educational objectives of the university, and may incur operating losses. The clearly profit-seeking operations should probably be expected to "stand on their own two feet," and make a profit; other, less commercially oriented activities would normally be expected to be "subsidized" by general university funds. So perhaps the clearly commercial operations should be grouped into their own fund, so that their profit or loss status will be more visible and they can accordingly be held more accountable. But this raises the issue of how the "indirect" costs mentioned in Exhibit 11–3 are to be determined. For example, are ancillary operations charged a fair fee for the university's computer-based payroll services?

(b) The operating fund's operating statement in Exhibit 11–2 is not an income statement for the following reasons:

- The government grants and student fees are not revenues generated from selling services in a market environment. The government sets per-student grants and also controls fees.
- The concept of "net income" has no meaning in this environment.

- Certain operating costs, such as amortization (depreciation), are accounted for in other funds (the capital fund for amortization).

(c) The accounting decisions involve classification, measurement, and disclosure, as well as the decision to use fund accounting. A list of the decisions follows:

- Fund accounting is used, and for financial reporting purposes similar funds are grouped together into one of the four fund groups chosen.
- The operating fund accounts for academic and related activities, except for property, plant, and equipment, which are accounted for in the capital fund.
- Ancillary, or commercial, operations are accounted for separately.
- The capital fund includes not only capital assets, but also investments that are intended to be used to finance the acquisition of future capital assets.
- Depreciation accounting is followed.
- Assets whose use is restricted, either by the outside provider of the assets or by the university's governing body, are accounted for separately in the restricted fund.

KEY TERMS

Database approach to financial reporting. If all the events (including transactions) entered into by an organization are being continuously updated in a computer-accessible database on a real-time basis, perhaps users just need the events data and not the balance sheets, income statements, and other financial statements that pre-process this data in a variety of ways. A database approach to financial reporting would be based on the following:

- Events, including transactions, are stored in an easily accessible, low-cost manner, such as on a compact disk.
- The database is updated continuously.
- Users have access to this database via links such as a personal computer and modem.
- The cost users must bear is relatively small.
- Users may extract data in a wide variety of ways. For example, a potential shareholder in a company might wish to know what sales were by product line for each of the geographic regions in which the company operated. This also raises the issue of what portions of the database should be confidential and *not* accessible to all users.

The spreadsheet introduced in Chapter 1 to account for Devo Green's On Ice business is a simple sort of database.

Electronic data interchange, or EDI, is a communication network that links the computer systems of one organization (say, a supplier) to the computer systems of another organization (say, a customer). A customer can place an order through the network directly to a vendor's system; this reduces paperwork as well as the time needed to initiate and process transactions. The vendor acknowledges the order, issues a delivery notice, and dispatches an invoice to the customer all electronically through the telecommunications network. By mutual agreement, a supplier can even arrange for access to its customer's inventory status file so that it can replenish its customer's inventory automatically.

Fund accounting refers to accounting on the basis of a self-balancing set of accounts for each fund established by legal, contractual, or voluntary actions of an organization. Elements of a fund can include assets, liabilities, net assets, revenues, and expenses. Fund accounting involves an accounting segregation, although not necessarily a physical segregation of resources. For example, many universities publish financial statements containing information based on the following funds:

- Operating fund.
- Ancillary fund.
- Capital fund.
- Restricted fund.

Not-for-profit organization is an organization in which there is normally no transferable ownership interest; and from which the members or contributors do not receive any direct financial return from membership or contribution; and that is formed, for example, for a social, educational, professional, religious, health, or philanthropic purpose.

FACT AND DESCRIPTION QUESTIONS

1. What features are common to all areas of accounting (see Chapter 2)? Are these features also common to NFP accounting?
2. List costs and benefits of EDI for a manufacturing company that wishes to implement a JIT philosophy.
3. Explain how accounts payable accounting might be affected by the adoption of EDI for a company that makes hundreds of purchases daily, and that makes these purchases for 100 retail stores located across the country.
4. Describe a database approach to financial reporting, and explain how it could lead to the elimination of financial statements as we now know them.
5. Explain how the basic accounting concept of "accountability" could be fulfilled in an era of a database approach to financial reporting.
6. Explain why an organization's choices concerning financial reporting and accountability via the Internet are not merely technical choices, but strategic as well.
7. (a) Explain what fund accounting is, and why it may be appropriate for discharging accountability in NFP organizations such as universities and charities.

   (b) "Even though an NFP organization might set up its general ledger accounts on the basis of fund accounting, it still might report its financial statements in a more familiar, non-fund manner." How is this possible?
8. Explain why revenue recognition and matching may be irrelevant for the major activities of an NFP organization, while these two accounting concepts may be very relevant for ancillary activities of the NFP organization, such as operating a cafeteria.
9. Explain why following accrual accounting is important for an NFP organization's accounts receivable, accounts payable, and accrued liabilities, while following depreciation accounting may not be.
10. Suggest some typical transactions entered into by the following NFP organizations:
    - Big Brothers and Big Sisters.
    - A large, provincially funded university.
    - A small, local health clinic.
    - A church, mosque, synagogue, or other local religious institution.
    - A hockey club that operates leagues for youths of various ages, from 5 to 17.
    - A general hospital.
    - A social club.
    - United Appeal.

Questions for Analysis and Discussion

11. (a) In your opinion, who are the users of a university's financial statements?
    (b) Suppose that fund accounting was *not* used in reporting the financial results of the university in Exhibit 11–2, but that all funds were "consolidated," and only the "total" column was reported. What are the advantages and disadvantages of such a financial statement presentation? Do you believe that users of the university's financial statements — for example, potential donors — would make different decisions depending upon whether fund accounting or a "consolidated" financial statement presentation was used?

12. Travel electronically to The Body Shop homepage at URL **www.think-act-change.com.** The information made available by The Body Shop at its website is quite extensive, and focuses on the company's concerns about social and environmental responsibility. How objective is this information? How credible is it? Is it merely self-serving? Identify the direct and indirect costs of preparing and disseminating this information. Could the company's resources be used in a better manner?

13. (a) It has been observed that managers of NFP organizations (i) prefer their organization's operating fund to show a deficit on the balance sheet, and (ii) prefer their organization's operating statement to always show that revenues and expenses are about equal. Put another way, both too great an excess of revenues over expenses, and too great an excess of expenses over revenues, are "bad." Comments?
    (b) Suppose that an NFP organization's management makes accounting decisions such that the two accounting objectives mentioned in part (a) of this question are achieved. Is this ethical? Would it be ethical if the NFP provided a crucial service (say, meals to seniors in rural areas), and needed to raise funds and also show that it was being run efficiently?

14. Locate the Internet home pages of the following organizations:

    - Canadian National Railways.
    - Air Canada.
    - Alberta Energy Corporation.

    For each company:

    (a) List the financial reporting and accountability information provided at the company's website.
    (b) Identify information and reports that you believe should have been provided, but were not, given the nature of the company's activities.
    (c) Evaluate the quality of the financial reporting and accountability at the website, using the following scales (circle the appropriate number in each row):

	Yes		So-so		No
Comprehensiveness	1	2	3	4	5
Useful files can be downloaded?	1	2	3	4	5
Navigation around the website is "user-friendly"	1	2	3	4	5

15. In your opinion, does A = L + OE hold for NFP organizations?

16. Adopt the role of a member of the CICA's Accounting Standards Board, and prepare a rebuttal to Rosen's article (refer to this chapter's "Accounting, Organizations, and Society" section).

CASE: CICA and NFP Organizations

In May 1994, a university vice-president sent a letter to the Director, Accounting Standards, of the CICA. The letter set out the university's response to the CICA's re-exposure draft on NFP organizations. Excerpts from the letter follow:

We appreciate this opportunity to respond to the re-exposure draft, particularly since we are one of the largest of the organizations which will be affected by these recommendations ...

We continue to have serious concerns with the recommendations regarding the amortization of capital assets.

We disagree with the implicit assumption that all not-for-profit organizations are basically the same. Universities and most health care providers are quasi-government organizations in that their ability to charge fees for service is totally restricted by government whereas other not-for-profit organizations are not so controlled. This is a significant fundamental difference which has led the standard-setting body in the United States to exclude the quasi-government organizations from the requirement to amortize capital assets while retaining this requirement for other not-for-profit organizations. We urge the CICA to similarly take such significant differences into account. Further in this document we reproduced the reasons for our views previously expressed in our response to the exposure draft, that amortization of capital assets will not serve the needs of the users of our financial statements ...

Capital Assets held by Not-for-Profit Organizations:

Amortization of Capital Assets

The University has practically no control over its revenues since it is funded primarily by grants from the [provincial] government. In addition, fees for service, i.e. tuition fees charged to students, are substantially controlled by the government. The users of our financial statements need to understand how the University has operated within this constraint to deliver its programs. The important qualitative characteristics of relevance and representational faithfulness set out in section 1000 of the handbook, in our view, can only be satisfied by a matching of expenditures for capital assets with the funds received to purchase those assets. Amortization of capital assets as proposed, in combination with the requirement to recognize contributions in the period received, will not provide relevant information to our users.

If the above matching principle is not adhered to, the result will likely be misinterpretation of the financial health of the University by users of our financial statements. These users include government and other funding agencies, donors and potential donors, alumni, members of Governing Council and boards, faculty, staff and students.

We are concerned that users will be confused or misled by large increases in fund balances in years when contributions exceed the amortized amount and large decreases in fund balances when the reverse is true. If the Handbook is revised to reflect the proposals contained in the re-exposure draft, including amortization of capital assets, the University would be compelled to prepare two sets of financial statements: one for compliance with the Handbook to ensure an unqualified audit opinion, and another to satisfy the requirements of the users of our financial statements.

Alternatively, it would be appropriate to defer revenue used to purchase capital assets to the extent it exceeds the amount of amortization expense in the period. However, this would have the same net effect on the fund balance as the practice currently followed by the University of recognizing funds when received and expensing purchases. Accordingly, with little apparent benefit, the additional costs of implementing amortization of capital assets would be difficult to justify.

In addition to matching costs with revenues, the relevance of financial reporting may also be enhanced by matching costs to the appropriate period. This is the "cost of service" argument that has been put forward by the CICA in various presentations on this topic. In commercial enterprises and in not-for-profit enterprises which control their fees for service this argument has validity since the full cost of service is an important factor in setting fees. However, this is not the case with universities whose revenues are determined or regulated by government without direct regard to the cost of delivering programs. Therefore, amortization of capital assets by universities is not meaningful ...

The University will have to incur significant additional costs to comply with amortization of capital assets. Additional time would also be required to explain our financial statements to users who have generally not been exposed to amortization accounting.

Required:

(a) In what way is the letter writer using the term "matching"?

(b) Summarize and evaluate the letter writer's argument.

(c) Who are the users of a university's financial statements?

(d) Identify the additional costs of complying with amortization accounting.

CASE

A Large Urban Hospital

In a recent annual report, a large urban hospital published financial statements upon which the following two summarized financial statements are based:

Summarized Statement of Financial Position, as of March 31, 1992 ($millions)

	1991–92	1990–91
ASSETS		
Accounts and grants receivable	21.1	23.5
Inventories	2.3	2.2
Prepaid expenses	0.7	0.6
Current Assets	**24.1**	**26.3**
Long-term investments	17.1	17.1
Capital assets, net of amortization	164.2	158.9
Commercial operations assets	20.2	21.2
Restricted fund assets	10.0	7.8
Total assets	**235.6**	**231.3**

LIABILITIES AND FUND BALANCE		
Current liabilities	47.8	49.8
Obligations under capital leases	21.0	23.2
Deferred building and equipment grants	76.2	69.7
Commercial operations: current liabilities	2.1	2.0
Commercial operations: long-term debt	13.1	13.5
Restricted fund deferred revenue	1.4	1.9
Fund balance	74.0	71.2
Total liabilities and fund balance	**235.6**	**231.3**

Summarized Statement of Operating Revenue and Expense for the Year Ended March 31, 1992 ($millions)

	1991–92	1990–91
REVENUE		
Government hospital plan	188.5	168.2
Other operating revenues	60.1	45.6
Commercial operations	10.0	8.6
Total revenue	**258.6**	**222.4**
EXPENSE		
Salaries, wages and benefits	158.0	133.1
Drugs	8.7	7.5
Medical and surgical supplies	12.6	12.3
Other supplies and expenses	57.7	53.0
Depreciation	9.0	7.5
Commercial operations	12.0	8.7
Total expenses	**258.0**	**222.1**
EXCESS OF REVENUE OVER EXPENSE	**0.6**	**0.3**

A third financial statement, the Restricted Fund Statement of Revenue and Expense, indicated that there was an excess of research revenues over research expenses of $2.1 million in 1991–92, and $1.0 million in 1990–91.

Required:
Adopt the role of a potential donor of $2,000,000 for expansion of the hospital's community health clinic. Examine the summarized financial statements and develop a list of questions you will ask the hospital's senior administrators.

NFP and Collective Bargaining

The university balance sheet in Exhibit 11–2 shows an operating deficit of $16,173,000 in the operating fund as at April 30, 1994, and the operating statement shows that for the year ended April 31, 1994, the operating fund had an excess of revenues over expenses of $35,106,000. From information not provided in Exhibit 11–2, the operating fund's deficit as at April 30, 1993, was $3,646,000. A reconciliation between the operating deficit on the balance sheet and the excess of revenues over expenses on the operating statement is shown in the table below (in 000s).

Suppose that you are a member of the collective bargaining team representing university faculty in its negotiations with the university administration over salaries and benefits. The administration has indicated that, because there is a deficit in the operating fund's balance sheet, the university cannot afford to pay even a small salary increase this year. Prepare a response.

Excess of revenues over expenses	35,106
Transfer of equipment cost to capital fund	(25,750)
Net increase in reserve for expenditures	(21,883)
Net change in (deficit)	(12,527)
Deficit, beginning of year	(3,646)
Deficit, end of year	(16,173)

Inflation Accounting

This case is based on the appendix to this chapter. At a meeting of the board of directors of a hypothetical company that manufactures and distributes paper products, the following discussion ensued:

Jones: Even though the general inflation rate in the economy, measured by the Consumers' Price Index and other indexes, is in the 2% range, our suppliers are hitting us with price increases averaging about 5% per annum, and they expect this will continue for the next several years.

Hsei: And yet our financial statements, which we use to report to our shareholders, to help us decide how much of a dividend to pay out, to help determine managements' bonus, and a lot of other things, seem to ignore the very real impact of these price increases.

Indy: That's all too true, and we're recording record profits to boot! Our FIFO accounting policy has a lot to do with that, I'm sure. But our operating cash flow is just terrible!

Viola: Our audited financial statements seem hidebound ... they really act as a constraint on getting better information both inside and outside the company.

Finchola (company CEO): Now, let's not be too hard on our auditors — they have a tough job to do, and are we sure we want to make it tougher?

Required:

Adopt the role of a special accounting adviser to the company's board of directors, and prepare a report dealing with the above issues. The report is to be presented at the next board meeting.

Appendix
Accounting for Changing Prices

For several decades accounting writers, accounting professional bodies, managers, financial analysts, governments, and other users of accounting information have wrestled with the problem of developing accounting that recognizes in some fashion the fact that prices are changing. Historical cost accounting implicitly assumes that the monetary unit used to measure and report assets, liabilities, and all the other elements of financial statements has a constant value. Australian, British, American, and Canadian authoritative bodies, among others, have issued numerous exposure drafts and other documents that approach the "accounting for changing prices" issue from a variety of perspectives. But all of this activity has resulted in little change in the traditional historical cost financial accounting model that underlies much of GAAP.

Some companies did not wait for accounting professional groups to issue pronouncements on accounting for changing prices before they developed new ways to prepare financial statements. For example, in Canada a company by the name of Barbecon Inc. began publishing a complete set of "current cost" accounting financial statements in 1974. Barbecon manufactures envelopes, stationery, writing tablets, and similar products, and sells paper and printers' supplies at the wholesale level. In the early 1970s, Barbecon's management decided that the net income reported by the company's financial accounting system — which, of course, was a historical cost based system — was misleadingly high. Because of the severe inflation at the time, the prices Barbecon paid for its raw materials were increasing at unprecedented rates. Barbecon was accounting for its inventory using the average cost method, which worked as follows when prices increased:

Suppose Barbecon had no inventory of paper on hand at the start of January and purchased two batches of paper for the month of January, as follows:

Batch 1: 1,000 kg @ $1.00 per kg, received on January 10

Batch 2: 2,000 kg @ $1.50 per kg, received on January 20

Let us also assume that the company made one sale in January — 1,500 kg for $3.00 per kg on January 31 — and that all other expenses (other than cost of sales, that is) for January were $1,000. At January 31, Barbecon's supplier issued a new price list for the raw material of $1.75 per kg. An income statement under the historical cost model for January would look something like this:

Sales (1,500 kg @ $3.00)	$4,500
Cost of sales ([1,000 × 1.00] + [2,000 × 1.50]/3,000] × 1,500*	2,000
Gross margin	2,500
Other expenses	1,000
Net income	$1,500

*This calculation results in a "weighted-average" unit cost of inventory of $1.331/3.

Barbecon's management would have argued that the $1,500 net income was illusory, since the 1,500 kg sold would require an expenditure of 1,500 × 1.75, or $2,625, to replace at the current (January 31) replacement cost of $1.75 per kg. Thus, the difference between the "current" cost of sales of $2,625 and the historic cost of sales of $2,000 was — according to Barbecon's management — a type of "holding gain" that should not count as profit. But perhaps it's better to let Barbecon's management speak for itself:[9]

How we started

Barbecon is a medium-sized company ... We have a divisionalized organization and operate three basic businesses: the distribution of printing paper to the graphic arts industry; the manufacture of envelopes for printers and consumers; the manufacture and distribution of social stationery.

In 1974, our suppliers hit us with a series of significant paper price increases that created a perplexing situation. The most satisfying result was an unprecedented burst of profit: we were suddenly making money at almost twice the rate as at any time in the company's 100-year history. This, unfortunately, was the only good news. Although profits were extraordinary, we were pressing bank lines to the limit. The investment required to maintain physical inventory levels jumped with each price increase. Stockpiling in anticipation of further increases compounded the problem.

Cash was not the only concern. Each successive increase generated illusory, but fully taxable, inventory profits. Our directors asked whether we should distribute part of these profits as dividends. Our managers expected these windfall gains included in bonus calculations, even though they were not a reflection of operating performance. Earnings had never been better. But, instead of prosperity, capital erosion, cash flow problems and misleading financial results were the order of the day.

We needed a method of accounting that would both explain the effects of rapid paper price increases on our organization and be easily understood and practical in application. Current cost accounting satisfied these requirements.

The basic principle of current cost accounting is that you do not recognize profits until provision is made to replace physical operating capacity. In the case of inventory, for example, physical capital maintenance means splitting historical cost gross margins in two and distinguishing between trading and holding gains.

Let's use the simple example above to interpret what Barbecon's manager is saying in the excerpt just quoted. First of all, Clark seems to be indicating that the financial accounting information is used in several ways:

- To report to outside users, such as shareholders.
- To assist the company's directors in making important decisions, such as how much of a dividend to declare.
- To determine management bonuses.
- To determine the amount of corporate income tax the company must pay.

So, here we have one accounting information system serving many purposes (financial accounting, management accounting, and tax accounting). Several groups of people are thus affected very directly by the financial statements.

Second, Clark writes that the historic cost gross margin — which equals $2,500 in the example above — should be split in two as follows:

Sales	$4,500
Current cost of sales	2,625
Trading gain	**$1,875**
Current cost of sales	$2,625
Historic cost of sales	2,000
Holding gain	**$ 625**

Clark would then base Barbecon's income calculation on the current cost of sales; the result would be a lower gross margin and a lower net income number. The revised income statement would be as follows:

[9] From Richard S. Clark, "Current Cost Accounting: One Company's Case," *CAmagazine*, July 1980. Clark was a senior executive with Barbecon at the time, and was largely responsible for implementing the new accounting system.

Sales (as before)	$4,500
Cost of sales (as revised)	2,625
Gross margin (as revised)	1,875
Other expenses (as before)	1,000
Net income	$ 875

None of the "holding" gain would be permitted to be counted as income.

A journal entry to convert the transaction information to Barbecon's financial statements based on current costs would have to be similar to the following:

Dr Inventory	625	
Cr Revaluation account		625

The debit to "Inventory" simply increases the inventory to its higher current cost amount just before it is sold on January 31; thus, $2,625 (its current replacement cost) may be debited to "Cost of sales" by the following journal entry:

Dr (Current) cost of sales	2,625	
Cr Inventory		2,625

The credit of $625 to a "Revaluation" account may be explained as follows: This account is a special subdivision of shareholders' equity that is used to collect the credit side of journal entries that are used to convert things like inventory to their (presumably) higher current cost. Thus, Barbecon's shareholders' equity section of its balance sheet contained the following accounts:

Capital stock	XXX
Retained earnings	XXX
Revaluation account	XXX
Total shareholders' equity	XXX

The "Revaluation" account indicates that shareholders have more invested in the company than the "Capital stock" and "Retained earnings" accounts show.

At this point, we will leave the Barbecon example.[10] Partly because of the decline in inflation in the late 1980s and early 1990s, interest in developing financial accounting systems that provide for changing prices has trailed off significantly in many countries. In Canada, the CICA issued a *Handbook* section relating to this issue (section 4510, "Accounting for Changing Prices"), but compliance with it was never mandatory, and for that reason was always low. The section has since been removed from the *Handbook*. In the United States, FASB Statement No. 33, which required larger companies to disclose supplementary information on changing prices, was effectively undercut by the issuance of FASB Statement No. 89 in 1986, which encouraged the FASB No. 33 disclosures but also made them no longer mandatory. The fact that standards-setting bodies have backed off from an area of accounting does not necessarily make that area unimportant, and this is especially true for the topic of this appendix.

[10] Barbecon stopped publishing its unique current-cost financial statements in 1986, when it was taken over by another company.

Appendix

The Time Value of Money and an Application to Lease Accounting

Familiarity with the methods for performing time value of money calculations is useful in many areas of accounting, and also in related disciplines such as finance and economics. In the text, you saw that time value of money methods were useful in a variety of areas, including those in the following table:

Chapter	Use of time value of money
2	The net present value (or NPV) criterion for decision-making involving the choice among alternatives in the Ms. X example and also in the Gord and James case.
4	Introduction to accounting for capital leases.
11	Accounting for bonds and hybrid securities.

Interest and the Time Value of Money

"Interest" is defined in *Terminology for Accountants* as a "payment made at a specified rate for the use of borrowed money." So in order to calculate the amount of interest, we must multiply **P**, the amount of money borrowed or loaned, by the interest rate charged per period, **r**, and also by the number of periods for which the amount of money was loaned or borrowed, **n**. That is:

$$\text{Interest} = P \times r \times n$$

Notice that the interest rate charged per period, **r**, must correspond to the way the number of periods, **n**, is measured, so that if **n** is measured in years, **r** also must refer to an annual interest rate.

Interest can be simple or compound. *Simple* interest means that interest is calculated based only on the original principal amount; compound interest means that interest is calculated not only on the principal, but also on any unpaid interest. Let's illustrate the difference between the two with the following data: $10,000 is borrowed for five years at an annual interest rate of 8%. No payments are made until the end of the five years. Under a simple interest arrangement, at the end of the five years the total amount that must be repaid will consist of the original $10,000 loan plus interest of:

$$10{,}000 \times 0.08 \times 5 = \$4{,}000$$

or $14,000.

Under a compound interest arrangement, interest must be paid on unpaid interest as the unpaid interest accrues. If interest accrues at the end of each of the five years, the calculation of total interest over the five years will be as in the table on the left.

Year	Balance of Amount Owing Throughout the Year (A)	Interest at 8% [the amount in the column labelled "(A)" times 0.08]	Cumulative Amount of Interest
1	$10,000.00	$800.00	$800.00
2	$10,800.00	$864.00	$1,664.00
3	$11,664.00	$933.12	$2,597.12
4	$12,597.12	$1,007.77	$3,604.89
5	$13,604.89	$1,088.39	$4,693.28

Under compound interest, an extra \$693.28 in interest must be paid. This is because interest is not only being charged on the original principal of \$10,000, but also on the accumulating interest.

In the above compound-interest situation, a more convenient way of calculating the total interest of \$4,693.28 would be to use the following formula:

$$\text{Interest} = P\,(1 + r)^n - P$$

The calculation would then be:

$$\text{Interest} = 10{,}000\,(1 + 0.08)^5 - 10{,}000$$

or 10,000 (1.469328) – 10,000, or \$4,693.28.

Notice that the term $\mathbf{P(1+r)^r}$ by itself represents the total amount that would have to be repaid — principal of \$10,000 plus interest of \$4,693.28. In other words, it is the amount that \$10,000 would grow to, under a compound interest arrangement, at 8% per year over five years.

Suppose we change the situation slightly, so that the borrower must repay principal plus interest accrued each quarter-year instead of each year. The formula then changes to:

$$\text{Amount to be repaid} = P(1+r/4)^{4n}$$

and the amount then becomes 10,000 $(1.02)^{20}$, or 10,000 (1.4859466), or \$14,859.47. The interest has increased from \$4,693.28 to \$4,859.47. Thus, increasing the frequency of compounding results in higher interest charges. By the way, the general formula for compound interest, assuming that interest rates are quoted in annual terms but that there are **m** compoundings per year, is as follows:

$$\text{Amount to be repaid} = P(1+r/m)^{mn}$$

We'll now describe two general classes of time value of money situations: those involving a single sum of money, and those involving a stream of constant payments (called annuities).

Situations Involving a Single Sum of Money

In the above example under compound interest, \$14,693.28 was the amount that \$10,000 would grow to if the annual interest rate was 8% and interest accrued annually. The \$14,693.28 is referred to as the future amount or *future value*, and the \$10,000 is referred to as the *present value*.

Present value calculations

We know that \$10,000 invested at 8%, compounded annually, will grow to \$14,693.28 by the end of five years. The present value of \$10,000 is the current value of the future value of \$14,693.28, under the interest rate, compounding, and time interval conditions specified. Table A–1 on page 618 provides the present value of a single, or lump, sum under a wide variety of conditions. It is based on a slight rearrangement of this formula:

$$\text{Amount to be repaid} = P\,(1+r/m)^{mn}$$

where "amount to be repaid" is just the future value, FV. And we're replacing P with "PV," for present value.

$$FV = PV\,(1+r/m)^{mn}$$

Specifically, we are now interested in **PV**, the present value, so the formula becomes:

$$PV = FV/(1+r/m)^{mn} \qquad \text{FORMULA [A]}$$

Table A–1 gives **PV** *per dollar*.

Future value calculations

Table A–2 on page 620 provides the future value of a single, or lump, sum under a wide variety of conditions. As you might expect, each item in the body of Table A–2 is just the inverse (that is, "one divided by") of the corresponding item from Table A–1. This is because of the relationship between future and present value lump sums, as expressed by formula [A]. For example, look up the factor for 25 periods and 10% in Table A–2. You obtain 10.8347. Compute 1/10.8347 and you get 0.0923, the factor from Table A–1.

Solved Problems

A. How much money must Ms. Jones invest today if she plans on retiring 15 years from now and estimates that she will require $250,000 on the day she retires? Her financial adviser informs her that her investment can earn 7%, compounded annually.

Ms. Jones really wants to know the present value of $250,000 needed 15 years from today, if interest compounds annually and is 7% per annum. Thus:

$$\begin{aligned} PV &= 250{,}000/(1 + 0.07)^{15} \\ &= 250{,}000/(2.7590309) \\ &= 90{,}611.53 \end{aligned}$$

Therefore, Ms Jones must invest $90,611.53 today.

We could have used Table A–1 to solve this problem. The entry in Table A–1 for 15 periods and 7% is 0.3624. This amount multiplied by $250,000 gives $90,600, which is $11.53 out because of rounding error.

B. Mr. Sylvester wants to know how many years it will take for $5,000 to grow to $20,000, if the interest rate is 7% per annum, compounded annually.

We know that $PV = FV/(1+r/m)^{mn}$, and that $FV = PV(1+r/m)^{mn}$. So: $20{,}000 = 5{,}000 (1.07)^n$, where **n**, the number of periods, is the unknown quantity that Mr. Sylvester wishes to know.

We know that $(1.07)^n = 20{,}000/5{,}000 = 4.0$. From Table A–2, the factor 4.0 for 7% interest is between 20 and 21 periods, so Mr. Sylvester must wait between 20 and 21 years for $5,000 to grow to $20,000.

C. Ms. Linga has been offered the following two propositions, each costing $10,000:

- Receive $15,000 five years hence.
- Receive $30,000 ten years hence.

Interest compounds annually and is expected to always be 10%. Compute the net present value of each proposition. Which one should Ms. Linga accept? See the upper table on the left.

Proposition	Present Value of Benefits	Present Value of Costs	Net Present Value
Receive $15,000 five years hence	$15{,}000/(1.10)^5$ =15,000/1.6105 =9,313.88	10,000	– 686.12
Receive $30,000 ten years hence	$30{,}000/(1.10)^{10}$ =30,000/2.5937 =11,566.49	10,000	+1,566.49

We can compute the factors 1.6105 and 2.5937 in the second column of this table, or we can look them up in Table A–2.

Ms. Linga should accept the second proposition (all other things being equal), since it has the higher net present value (or NPV). In fact, the first proposition has a negative NPV.

D. Repeat Question C using a 15% interest rate.

The results are as shown in the table on the bottom left.

Proposition	Present Value of Benefits	Present Value of Costs	Net Present Value
Receive $15,000 five years hence	$15{,}000/(1.15)^5$ =15,000/2.0114 =7,457.49	10,000	– 2,542.51
Receive $30,000 ten years hence	$30{,}000/(1.15)^{10}$ =30,000/4.0456 =7,415.46	10,000	– 2,584.54

Ms. Linga should avoid both propositions if she can, since both have a negative NPV. But if she was compelled to choose one or the other, the first proposition is slightly better, since it has the less negative NPV.

E. We know this:

$$PV = FV/(1+r/m)^{mn} \qquad \text{FORMULA [A]}$$

Suppose that **PV** is $1, **r** is 12% (an annual interest rate), **n** = 3 years, and initially **m** = 1 (that is, compounding is once per year). Set up a table showing how **FV** changes as **m** increases from 1 to 4, in steps of one.

The required table is as follows:

m	Formula	FV (in dollars)
1	$1\ (1+0.12/1)^{1\times 3}$	1.404928
2	$1\ (1+0.12/2)^{2\times 3}$	1.418519
3	$1\ (1+0.12/3)^{3\times 3}$	1.423312
4	$1\ (1+0.12/4)^{4\times 3}$	1.425760

Situations Involving Annuities

Present value of annuities

An annuity is a series of cash flows (either inflows or outflows) that are fixed in amount and occur at constant time intervals. For example, if your great-uncle has provided for the following arrangement for you in his will, he has bequeathed you an annuity: "You are to receive $10,000 each January 1, beginning January 1, 1997, with the last payment being on January 1, 2001."

Payment Date	Present Value Factor at 10% (from Table A-1)	Present Value of This Payment
January 1, 1997	0.9091	10,000 × 0.9091= 9,091
January 1, 1998	0.8264	10,000 × 0.8264= 8,264
January 1, 1999	0.7513	10,000 × 0.7513= 7,513
January 1, 2000	0.6830	10,000 × 0.6830= 6,830
January 1, 2001	0.6209	10,000 × 0.6209= 6,209
TOTAL PRESENT VALUE OF THE ORDINARY ANNUITY		$37,907

Notice that each payment is constant (that is, $10,000), and that the payments occur at constant time intervals (that is, one year apart).

If *now*, the point in time at which the annuity bequest has been granted, is January 1, 1996, then the above annuity is called an ordinary annuity. In ordinary annuities, the first of the fixed amount cash flows occurs at the end of the first period. Alternatively, if *now* is January 1, 1997, the date on which the first cash flow occurs, then the annuity is called an annuity due. The same five equal cash flows are involved, but the timing is one period different. See the line art below.

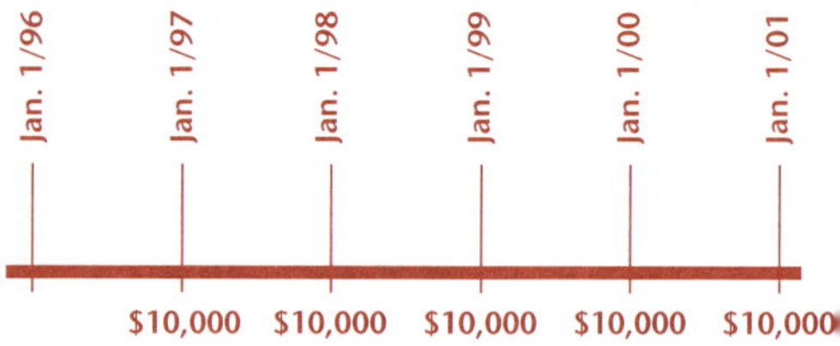

Let's illustrate how we can compute the present value of the above five-year, $10,000 annuity, in its ordinary annuity form, assuming that the interest rate is 10% (keep in mind that since this is an ordinary annuity, the present value is being computed as of January 1, 1996) See the table at the bottom left.

The present value of the ordinary annuity as of January 1, 1996, is $37,907.

If the annuity was an annuity due, then the calculation of its present value would be as shown in the table at the top of the following page.

The present value of the annuity due is greater than for the ordinary annuity since each payment for the annuity due is being present-valued for one period less than for the corresponding ordinary annuity.

Let's spend some time looking at ordinary annuities. Table A–3 on page 622 provides present value factors for ordinary annuities of $1, for a variety of periods and interest rates. We can compute the present value of the above $10,000, five-year ordinary annuity at 10% by selecting the appropriate factor from Table A–3 — that is, 3.7908 — and

Payment Date	Present Value Factor at 10% (from Table A-1)	Present Value of This Payment
January 1, 1997	[we know the factor here is 1.00]	10,000 × 1.0 = 10,000
January 1, 1998	0.9091	10,000 × 0.9091 = 9,091
January 1, 1999	0.8264	10,000 × 0.8264 = 8,264
January 1, 2000	0.7513	10,000 × 0.7513 = 7,513
January 1, 2001	0.6830	10,000 × 0.6830 = 6,830
TOTAL PRESENT VALUE OF THE ANNUITY DUE		$41,698

multiplying it by the $10,000 fixed payments, to get $37,908. The calculation for this amount gave us, remember, $37,907, so we have a $1 rounding error. We can also use Table A–3 to compute the present value of an annuity due. For the $10,000 example, just add the present value of a *four*-year annuity's present value to the $10,000 first payment. In doing so, we get 10,000 (3.1699) + 10,000, or $41,699 (again, a $1 rounding error as compared to our calculation), where the 3.1699 factor is the present value factor for an ordinary annuity of $1 for four years at 10%.

Future value of annuities

We could present tables showing the future value of both ordinary annuities and annuities due; instead, we'll compute the future value of annuities by first computing their present value (using Table A–3), and then computing their future value by using Table A–2. Now, Table A–2 is for computing the future value of single, or lump, sums, but that's all right, since by first deriving the annuity's present value, we have in effect turned it into a lump sum, and can very legitimately use Table A–2. Let's see how this works for the $10,000, five-year ordinary annuity, again using a 10% interest rate —

We already have computed that the present value of this annuity as of January 1, 1996, is $37,907. This is now a single sum. In order to compute its future value as of, say, January 1, 2001 (the date of the final $10,000 payment), we multiply it by the factor for five periods and 10% from Table A–2 — that is, 1.6105. The result is $37,907 × 1.6105, or $61,049.22. This means that if you don't touch any of the annual $10,000 payments that your great-uncle wills to you, and if interest is 10%, you will have $61,049.22 as of January 1, 2001.

Solved Problems

A. Set up a spreadsheet with the following interest rates along the horizontal axis: 5%, 6%, 7%, 8%, 9%, 10%, 20%, 50%, 100%, and 200%; and with the following numbers of periods along the vertical axis: 1, 2, 3, 4, 5, 6, 7, 8, 9, 10, 50, 100, 200, and 300. Fill in all of the cells in the spreadsheet with the present value of an ordinary annuity of $1 indicated by the various row and column headings. (See the chart on the following page.)

Notice that the present value of an ordinary annuity becomes a different constant amount for each different interest rate, as the number of payments and periods increases. For example, at 10% the constant amount is $10.00, and at 8% it is $12.50. This constant amount is really the present value of an ordinary annuity of an infinite, never-ending stream of $1 payments, and equals $1/r. In the case of 10%, this is $1/0.10, or $10.00, and in the case of 8%, it is $1/0.08, or $12.50. If the interest rate were 5%, this amount would be $1/0.05, or $20.00 — very close to the $19.99999 we obtain in the table for a 5% ordinary annuity for 300 periods.

B. A deferred annuity is an annuity in which the cash payments or receipts are deferred for two or more periods. For example, suppose a baseball player receives a signing bonus for a contract signed today (January 1, 1997), in the form of a deferred annuity with equal annual payments of $100,000 to be received for ten years beginning on December 31, 2010. What is the present

PRESENT VALUE OF AN ORDINARY ANNUITY											
				INTEREST RATE							
		0.05	0.06	0.07	0.08	0.09	0.1	0.2	0.5	1	2
	1	0.95238	0.94340	0.93458	0.92593	0.91743	0.90909	0.83333	0.66667	0.50000	0.33333
	2	1.85941	1.83339	1.80802	1.78326	1.75911	1.73554	1.52778	1.11111	0.75000	0.44444
PERIODS	3	2.72325	2.67301	2.62432	2.57710	2.53129	2.48685	2.10648	1.40741	0.87500	0.48148
	4	3.54595	3.46511	3.38721	3.31213	3.23972	3.16987	2.58873	1.60494	0.93750	0.49383
	5	4.32948	4.21236	4.10020	3.99271	3.88965	3.79079	2.99061	1.73663	0.96875	0.49794
	6	5.07569	4.91732	4.76654	4.62288	4.48592	4.35526	3.32551	1.82442	0.98438	0.49931
	7	5.78637	5.58238	5.38929	5.20637	5.03295	4.86842	3.60459	1.88294	0.99219	0.49977
	8	6.46321	6.20979	5.97130	5.74664	5.53482	5.33493	3.83716	1.92196	0.99609	0.49992
	9	7.10782	6.80169	6.51523	6.24689	5.99525	5.75902	4.03097	1.94798	0.99805	0.49997
	10	7.72173	7.36009	7.02358	6.71008	6.41766	6.14457	4.19247	1.96532	0.99902	0.49999
	50	18.25593	15.76186	13.80075	12.23348	10.96168	9.91481	4.99945	2.00000	1.00000	0.50000
	100	19.84791	16.61755	14.26925	12.49432	11.10910	9.99927	5.00000	2.00000	1.00000	0.50000
	200	19.99884	16.66652	14.28570	12.50000	11.11111	10.00000	5.00000	2.00000	1.00000	0.50000
	300	19.99999	16.66667	14.28571	12.50000	11.11111	10.00000	5.00000	2.00000	1.00000	0.50000

value today of the signing bonus, if the interest rate is 7%?

First, the present value of a ten-year ordinary annuity of \$100,000, at 7%, is computed, using the appropriate factor from Table A–3 — that is, \$100,000 × 7.0236, or \$702,360. But this is the present value as of January 1, 2010 (it's an ordinary annuity), which is 13 years from today, January 1, 1997. So, the \$702,360 single or lump sum must be present-valued through 13 periods at 7%, using the 0.4150 factor from Table A–1. From this, we find that the present value of the deferred annuity signing bonus as of January 1, 1997, is \$702,360 × 0.4150, or \$291,479.

C. Seymour Lang is a self-employed professional accountant. Having reached the age of 45, he has decided to begin planning for his retirement, which he expects will occur 20 years hence, when he reaches 65. After consulting with an actuary, he decides he should expect to live for 15 years after retirement. He feels that he will need \$100,000 per year during this time. He will withdraw the first payment from his retirement savings fund one year after he retires. He wishes to deposit an equal amount each year, beginning on his 46th birthday, so that he will have enough to fulfil his retirement financial requirements. Interest rates are expected to be 10%.

First, we compute the present value of a 15-year, 10% ordinary annuity of \$100,000. This is \$100,000 × 7.6061, or \$760,610. This is the present value of the amount Lang will need to fund his retirement cash needs, as of his retirement date on his 65th birthday. So this amount is also the future value of a 20-year ordinary annuity, at 10%, the fixed annual payments of which we as yet do not know. But we do know that the present value of the \$760,610 on Long's 45th birthday is also equal to the present value of the 20-year ordinary annuity, both at 10%. So, we can set up the following equation:

$$760{,}610 \times 0.1486 = L \times 8.5136$$

where **L** stands for the unknown annual fixed deposits that Lang must make for the next 20 years. The factor 0.1486 comes from Table A–1, and the factor 8.5136 comes from Table A–3. Solving for **L**, we obtain:

$$L = [760{,}610 \times 0.1486]/8.5136 = \$13{,}276.01$$

So if Lang deposits $13,276.01 at the end of each of the next 20 years, he will be able to withdraw $100,000 at the end of each of the subsequent 15 years. Of course, we have ignored other features of retirement planning, such as the impact of income taxes, in order to stress the impact of the time value of money.

D. Madame Zotique borrows $3,790.80 from a bank on December 31, 1997. The loan is to be repaid in five equal annual instalments, beginning one year from the borrowing date. Interest is 10%. Prepare an amortization table for the loan, and also prepare all journal entries from the point of view of the borrower, Madame Zotique.

We know that the present value of a five-year ordinary annuity at 10% must be $3,790.80. Letting the (as yet unknown) annual end-of-year payment be L, we have the following:

$$3{,}790.80 = L \times 3.7908$$

where the factor 3.7980 is from Table A–3.

Therefore, L = $1,000.00. Our madame must make five annual end-of-year payments of $1,000.00 in order to pay off the loan. An amortization table for this loan is as follows:

Year	Principal Outstanding During Year (A)	Payment at End of Year (B)	Interest at 10% [(A) x 0.10] (C)	Reduction of Principal [=(B)-(C)] (D)	Principal Outstanding Just After Year End Payment [=(A)-(D)] (E)
1998	3,790.80	1,000.00	379.08	620.92	3,169.88
1999	3,169.88	1,000.00	316.99	683.01	2,486.87
2000	2,486.87	1,000.00	248.69	751.31	1,735.56
2001	1,735.56	1,000.00	173.56	826.44	909.12
2002	909.12	1,000.00	90.88*	909.12	0

*A three-cent adjustment is needed because of rounding error.

The journal entries are as follows (from Madame Zotique's perspective):

December 31, 1997:

Dr	Cash	3,790.80	
	Cr Loan payable		3,790.80

December 31, 1998:

Dr	Interest expense	379.08	
Dr	Loan payable	620.92	
	Cr Cash		1,000.00

December 31, 1999:

Dr	Interest expense	316.99	
Dr	Loan payable	683.01	
	Cr Cash		1,000.00

December 31, 2000:

Dr	Interest expense	248.69	
Dr	Loan payable	751.31	
	Cr Cash		1,000.00

December 31, 2001:

Dr	Interest expense	173.56	
Dr	Loan payable	826.44	
	Cr Cash		1,000.00

December 31, 2002:

Dr	Interest expense	90.88	
Dr	Loan payable	909.12	
	Cr Cash		1,000.00

TABLE A–1
PRESENT VALUE OF A $1 SINGLE SUM

Number of Periods	1%	2%	3%	4%	5%	6%	7%	8%	9%	10%	N/R
1	0.9901	0.9804	0.9709	0.9615	0.9524	0.9434	0.9346	0.9259	0.9174	0.9091	1
2	0.9803	0.9612	0.9426	0.9246	0.9070	0.8900	0.8734	0.8573	0.8417	0.8264	2
3	0.9706	0.9423	0.9151	0.8890	0.8638	0.8396	0.8163	0.7938	0.7722	0.7513	3
4	0.9610	0.9238	0.8885	0.8548	0.8227	0.7921	0.7629	0.7350	0.7084	0.6830	4
5	0.9515	0.9057	0.8626	0.8219	0.7835	0.7473	0.7130	0.6806	0.6499	0.6209	5
6	0.9420	0.8880	0.8375	0.7903	0.7462	0.7050	0.6663	0.6302	0.5963	0.5645	6
7	0.9327	0.8706	0.8131	0.7599	0.7107	0.6651	0.6227	0.5835	0.5470	0.5132	7
8	0.9235	0.8535	0.7894	0.7307	0.6768	0.6274	0.5820	0.5403	0.5019	0.4665	8
9	0.9143	0.8368	0.7664	0.7026	0.6446	0.5919	0.5439	0.5002	0.4604	0.4241	9
10	0.9053	0.8203	0.7441	0.6756	0.6139	0.5584	0.5083	0.4632	0.4224	0.3855	10
11	0.8963	0.8043	0.7224	0.6496	0.5847	0.5268	0.4751	0.4289	0.3875	0.3505	11
12	0.8874	0.7885	0.7014	0.6246	0.5568	0.4970	0.4440	0.3971	0.3555	0.3186	12
13	0.8787	0.7730	0.6810	0.6006	0.5303	0.4688	0.4150	0.3677	0.3262	0.2897	13
14	0.8700	0.7579	0.6611	0.5775	0.5051	0.4423	0.3878	0.3405	0.2992	0.2633	14
15	0.8613	0.7430	0.6419	0.5553	0.4810	0.4173	0.3624	0.3152	0.2745	0.2394	15
16	0.8528	0.7284	0.6232	0.5339	0.4581	0.3936	0.3387	0.2919	0.2519	0.2176	16
17	0.8444	0.7142	0.6050	0.5134	0.4363	0.3714	0.3166	0.2703	0.2311	0.1978	17
18	0.8360	0.7002	0.5874	0.4936	0.4155	0.3503	0.2959	0.2502	0.2120	0.1799	18
19	0.8277	0.6864	0.5703	0.4746	0.3957	0.3305	0.2765	0.2317	0.1945	0.1635	19
20	0.8195	0.6730	0.5537	0.4564	0.3769	0.3148	0.2584	0.2145	0.1784	0.1486	20
21	0.8114	0.6598	0.5375	0.4388	0.3589	0.2942	0.2415	0.1987	0.1637	0.1351	21
22	0.8034	0.6468	0.5219	0.4220	0.3418	0.2775	0.2257	0.1839	0.1502	0.1228	22
23	0.7954	0.6342	0.5067	0.4057	0.3256	0.2618	0.2109	0.1703	0.1378	0.1117	23
24	0.7876	0.6217	0.4919	0.3901	0.3101	0.2470	0.1971	0.1577	0.1264	0.1015	24
25	0.7798	0.6095	0.4776	0.3751	0.2953	0.2330	0.1842	0.1460	0.1160	0.0923	25
26	0.7720	0.5976	0.4637	0.3607	0.2812	0.2198	0.1722	0.1352	0.1064	0.0839	26
27	0.7644	0.5859	0.4502	0.3468	0.2678	0.2074	0.1609	0.1252	0.0976	0.0763	27
28	0.7568	0.5744	0.4371	0.3335	0.2551	0.1956	0.1504	0.1189	0.0895	0.0693	28
29	0.7493	0.5631	0.4243	0.3207	0.2429	0.1846	0.1406	0.1023	0.0822	0.0630	29
30	0.7419	0.5521	0.4120	0.3083	0.2314	0.1741	0.1314	0.0994	0.0754	0.0573	30
31	0.7346	0.5412	0.4000	0.2965	0.2204	0.1643	0.1228	0.0920	0.0691	0.0521	31
32	0.7273	0.5306	0.3883	0.2851	0.2099	0.1550	0.1147	0.0852	0.0634	0.0474	32
33	0.7201	0.5202	0.3770	0.2741	0.1999	0.1462	0.1072	0.0789	0.0582	0.0431	33
34	0.7130	0.5100	0.3660	0.2636	0.1904	0.1379	0.1002	0.0730	0.0534	0.0391	34
35	0.7059	0.5000	0.3554	0.2534	0.1813	0.1301	0.0937	0.0676	0.0490	0.0356	35
36	0.6989	0.4902	0.3450	0.2437	0.1727	0.1227	0.0875	0.0626	0.0449	0.0323	36
37	0.6970	0.4806	0.3350	0.2343	0.1644	0.1158	0.0818	0.0580	0.0412	0.0294	37
38	0.6852	0.4712	0.3252	0.2253	0.1566	0.1092	0.0765	0.0537	0.0378	0.0267	38
39	0.6784	0.4619	0.3158	0.2166	0.1491	0.1031	0.0715	0.0497	0.0347	0.0243	39
40	0.6717	0.4529	0.3066	0.2083	0.1420	0.0972	0.0688	0.0460	0.0318	0.0221	40

Number of Periods	11%	12%	13%	14%	15%	16%	20%	22%	24%	25%	N/R
1	0.9009	0.8929	0.8850	0.8772	0.8696	0.8621	0.8333	0.8197	0.8065	0.8000	1
2	0.8116	0.7972	0.7831	0.7695	0.7561	0.7432	0.6944	0.6719	0.6504	.06400	2
3	0.7312	0.7118	0.6931	0.6750	0.6575	0.6407	0.5787	0.5507	0.5245	0.5120	3
4	0.6587	0.6355	0.6133	0.5921	0.5718	0.5523	0.4823	0.4514	0.4230	0.4096	4
5	0.5935	0.5674	0.5428	0.5194	0.4972	0.4761	0.4019	0.3700	0.3411	0.3277	5
6	0.5346	0.5066	0.4803	0.4556	0.4323	0.4104	0.3349	0.3033	0.2751	0.2621	6
7	0.4817	0.4523	0.4251	0.3996	0.3759	0.3538	0.2791	0.2486	0.2218	0.2097	7
8	0.4339	0.4039	0.3762	0.3506	0.3269	0.3050	0.2326	0.2038	0.1789	0.1678	8
9	0.3909	0.3606	0.3329	0.3075	0.2843	0.2630	0.1938	0.1670	0.1443	0.1342	9
10	0.3522	0.3220	0.2946	0.2697	0.2472	0.2267	0.1615	0.1369	0.1164	0.1074	10
11	0.3173	0.2875	0.2607	0.2366	0.2149	0.1954	0.1346	0.1122	0.0938	0.0859	11
12	0.2858	0.2567	0.2307	0.2076	0.1869	0.1685	0.1122	0.0920	0.0757	0.0687	12
13	0.2575	0.2292	0.2042	0.1821	0.1625	0.1452	0.0935	0.0754	0.0610	0.0550	13
14	0.2320	0.2046	0.1807	0.1597	0.1413	0.1252	0.0779	0.0618	0.0492	0.0440	14
15	0.2090	0.1827	0.1599	0.1401	0.1229	0.1079	0.0649	0.0507	0.0397	0.0352	15
16	0.1883	0.1631	0.1415	0.1229	0.1069	0.0930	0.0541	0.0415	0.0320	0.0281	16
17	0.1696	0.1456	0.1252	0.1078	0.0929	0.0802	0.0451	0.0340	0.0258	0.0225	17
18	0.1528	0.1300	0.1108	0.0946	0.0808	0.0691	0.0376	0.0279	0.0208	0.0180	18
19	0.1377	0.1161	0.0981	0.0829	0.0703	0.0596	0.0313	0.0229	0.0168	0.0144	19
20	0.1240	0.1037	0.0868	0.0728	0.0611	0.0514	0.0261	0.0187	0.0135	0.0115	20
21	0.1117	0.0926	0.0768	0.0638	0.0531	0.0443	0.0217	0.0154	0.0109	0.0092	21
22	0.1007	0.0826	0.0680	0.0560	0.0462	0.0382	0.0181	0.0126	0.0088	0.0074	22
23	0.0907	0.0738	0.0601	0.0491	0.0402	0.0329	0.0151	0.0103	0.0071	0.0059	23
24	0.0817	0.0659	0.0532	0.0431	0.0349	0.0284	0.0126	0.0085	0.0057	0.0047	24
25	0.0736	0.0588	0.0471	0.0378	0.0304	0.0245	0.0105	0.0069	0.0046	0.0038	25
26	0.0663	0.0525	0.0417	0.0331	0.0264	0.0211	0.0087	0.0057	0.0037	0.0030	26
27	0.0597	0.0469	0.0369	0.0291	0.0230	0.0182	0.0073	0.0047	0.0030	0.0024	27
28	0.0538	0.0419	0.0326	0.0255	0.0200	0.0157	0.0061	0.0038	0.0024	0.0019	28
29	0.0485	0.0374	0.0289	0.0224	0.0174	0.0135	0.0051	0.0031	0.0020	0.0015	29
30	0.0437	0.0334	0.0256	0.0196	0.0151	0.0116	0.0042	0.0026	0.0016	0.0012	30
31	0.0394	0.0298	0.0226	0.0172	0.0131	0.0100	0.0035	0.0021	0.0013	0.0010	31
32	0.0355	0.0266	0.0200	0.0151	0.0114	0.0087	0.0029	0.0017	0.0010	0.0008	32
33	0.0319	0.0238	0.0177	0.0132	0.0099	0.0075	0.0024	0.0014	0.0008	0.0006	33
34	0.0288	0.0212	0.0157	0.0116	0.0086	0.0064	0.0020	0.0012	0.0007	0.0005	34
35	0.0259	0.0189	0.0139	0.0102	0.0075	0.0055	0.0017	0.0009	0.0005	0.0004	35
36	0.0234	0.0169	0.0123	0.0089	0.0065	0.0048	0.0014	0.0008	0.0004	0.0003	36
37	0.0210	0.0151	0.0109	0.0078	0.0057	0.0041	0.0012	0.0006	0.0003	0.0003	37
38	0.0190	0.0135	0.0096	0.0069	0.0049	0.0036	0.0010	0.0005	0.0003	0.0002	38
39	0.0171	0.0120	0.0085	0.0060	0.0043	0.0031	0.0008	0.0004	0.0002	0.0002	39
40	0.0154	0.0107	0.0075	0.0053	0.0037	0.0026	0.0007	0.0004	0.0002	0.0001	40

TABLE A–2
FUTURE VALUE OF A $1 SINGLE SUM

N/R	1%	2%	3%	4%	5%	6%	7%	8%	9%	10%	N/R
1	1.0100	1.0200	1.0300	1.0400	1.0500	1.0600	1.0700	1.0800	1.0900	1.1000	1
2	1.0201	1.0404	1.0609	1.0816	1.1025	1.1236	1.1449	1.1664	1.1881	1.2100	2
3	1.0303	1.0612	1.0927	1.1249	1.1576	1.1910	1.2250	1.2597	1.2950	1.3310	3
4	1.0406	1.0824	1.1255	1.1699	1.2155	1.2625	1.3108	1.3605	1.4116	1.4641	4
5	1.0510	1.1041	1.1593	1.2167	1.2763	1.3382	1.4026	1.4693	0.5386	1.6105	5
6	1.0615	1.1262	1.1941	0.2653	1.3401	1.4185	1.5007	1.5869	1.6771	1.7716	6
7	1.0721	1.1487	1.2299	1.3159	1.4071	1.5036	1.6058	1.7138	1.8280	1.9487	7
8	1.0829	1.1717	1.2668	1.3686	1.4775	1.5938	1.7182	1.8509	1.9926	2.1436	8
9	1.0937	1.1951	1.3048	1.4233	1.5513	1.6895	1.8385	1.9990	2.1719	2.3579	9
10	1.1046	1.2190	1.3439	1.4802	1.6289	1.7908	1.9672	2.1589	2.3674	2.5937	10
11	1.1157	1.2434	1.3842	1.5395	1.7103	1.8983	2.1049	2.3316	2.5804	2.8531	11
12	1.1268	1.2682	1.4258	1.6010	1.7959	2.0122	2.2522	2.5182	2.8127	3.1384	12
13	1.1381	1.2936	1.4685	1.6651	1.8856	2.1329	2.4098	2.7196	3.0658	3.4523	13
14	1.1495	1.3195	1.5126	1.7317	1.9799	2.2609	2.5785	2.9372	3.3417	3.7975	14
15	1.1610	1.3459	1.5580	1.8009	2.0789	2.3966	2.7590	3.1722	3.6425	4.1772	15
16	1.1726	1.3728	1.6047	1.8730	2.1829	2.5404	2.9522	3.4259	3.9703	4.5950	16
17	1.1843	1.4002	1.6528	1.9479	2.2920	2.6928	3.1588	3.7000	4.3276	5.0545	17
18	1.1961	1.4282	1.7024	2.0258	2.4066	2.8543	3.3799	3.9960	4.7171	5.5599	18
19	1.2081	1.4568	1.7535	2.1068	2.5270	3.0256	3.6165	4.3157	5.1417	6.1159	19
20	1.2202	1.4859	1.8061	2.1911	2.6533	3.2071	3.8697	4.6610	5.6044	6.7275	20
21	1.2324	1.5157	1.8603	2.2788	2.7860	3.3996	4.1406	5.0338	6.1088	7.4002	21
22	1.2447	1.5460	1.9161	2.3699	2.9253	3.6035	4.4304	5.4365	6.6586	8.1403	22
23	1.2572	1.5769	1.9736	2.4647	3.0715	3.8197	4.7405	5.8715	7.2579	8.9543	23
24	1.2697	1.6084	2.0328	2.5633	3.2251	4.0489	5.0724	6.3412	7.9111	9.8497	24
25	1.2824	1.6406	2.0938	2.6658	3.3864	4.2919	5.4274	6.8485	8.6231	10.8347	25
26	1.2953	1.6734	2.1566	2.7725	3.5557	4.5494	5.8074	7.3964	9.3992	11.9182	26
27	1.3082	1.7069	2.2213	2.8834	3.7335	4.8223	6.2139	7.9881	10.2451	13.1100	27
28	1.3213	1.7410	2.2879	2.9987	3.9201	5.1117	6.6488	8.6271	11.1671	14.4210	28
29	1.3345	1.7758	2.3566	3.1187	4.1161	5.4184	7.1143	9.3173	12.1722	15.8631	29
30	1.3478	1.8114	2.4273	3.2434	4.3219	5.7435	7.6123	10.0627	13.2677	17.4494	30
31	1.3613	1.8476	2.5001	3.3731	4.5380	6.0881	8.1451	10.8677	14.4618	19.1943	31
32	1.3749	1.8845	2.5751	3.5081	4.7649	6.4534	8.7153	11.7371	15.7633	21.1138	32
33	1.3887	1.9222	2.6523	3.6484	5.0032	6.8406	9.3253	12.6760	17.1820	23.2252	33
34	1.4026	1.9607	2.7319	3.7943	5.2533	7.2510	9.9781	13.6901	18.7284	25.5477	34
35	1.4166	1.9999	2.8139	3.9461	5.5160	7.6861	10.6766	14.7853	20.4140	28.1024	35
36	1.4308	2.0399	2.8983	4.1039	5.7918	8.1473	11.4239	15.9682	22.2512	30.9127	36
37	1.4451	2.0807	2.9852	4.2681	6.0814	8.6361	12.2236	17.2456	24.2538	34.0039	37
38	1.4595	2.1223	3.0748	4.4388	6.3855	9.1543	13.0793	18.6253	26.4367	37.4043	38
39	1.4741	2.1647	3.1670	4.6164	6.7048	9.7035	13.9948	20.1153	28.8160	41.1448	39
40	1.4889	2.2080	3.2620	4.8010	7.0400	10.2857	14.9745	21.7245	31.4094	45.2593	40

N/R	11%	12%	13%	14%	15%	16%	20%	22%	24%	25%	
1	1.1100	1.1200	1.1300	1.1400	1.1500	1.1600	1.2000	1.2200	1.2400	1.2500	1
2	1.2321	1.2544	1.2769	1.2996	1.3225	1.3456	1.4400	1.4884	1.5376	1.5625	2
3	1.3676	1.4049	1.4429	1.4815	1.5209	1.5609	1.7280	1.8158	1.9066	1.9531	3
4	1.5181	1.5735	1.6305	1.6890	1.7490	1.8106	2.0736	2.2153	2.3642	2.4414	4
5	1.6851	1.7623	1.8424	1.9254	2.0114	2.1003	2.4883	2.7027	2.9316	3.0518	5
6	1.8704	1.9738	2.0820	2.1950	2.3131	2.4364	2.9860	3.2973	3.6352	3.8147	6
7	2.0762	2.2107	2.3526	2.5023	2.6600	2.8262	3.5832	4.0227	4.5077	4.7684	7
8	2.3045	2.4760	2.6584	2.8526	3.0590	3.2784	4.2998	4.9077	5.5895	5.9605	8
9	2.5580	2.7731	3.0040	3.2519	3.5179	3.8030	5.1598	5.9874	6.9310	7.4506	9
10	2.8394	3.1058	3.3946	3.7072	4.0456	4.4114	6.1917	7.3046	8.5944	9.3132	10
11	3.1518	3.4785	3.8359	4.2262	4.6524	5.1173	7.4301	8.9117	10.6571	11.6415	11
12	3.4985	3.8960	4.3345	4.8179	5.3503	5.9360	8.9161	10.8722	13.2148	14.5519	12
13	3.8833	4.3635	4.8980	5.4924	6.1528	6.8858	10.6993	13.2641	16.3863	18.1899	13
14	4.3104	4.8871	5.5348	6.2613	7.0757	7.9875	12.8392	16.1822	20.3191	22.7374	14
15	4.7846	5.4736	6.2543	7.1379	8.1371	9.2655	15.4070	19.7423	25.1956	28.4217	15
16	5.3109	6.1304	7.0673	8.1372	9.3576	10.7480	18.4884	24.0856	31.2426	35.5271	16
17	5.8951	6.8660	7.9861	9.2765	10.7613	12.4677	22.1861	29.3844	38.7408	44.4089	17
18	6.5436	7.6900	9.0243	10.5752	12.3755	14.4625	26.6233	35.8490	48.0386	55.5112	18
19	7.2633	8.6128	10.1974	12.0557	14.2318	16.7765	31.9480	43.7358	59.5679	69.3889	19
20	8.0623	9.6463	11.5231	13.7435	16.3665	19.4608	38.3376	53.3576	73.8641	86.7362	20
21	8.9492	10.8038	13.0211	15.6676	18.8215	22.5745	46.0051	65.0963	91.5915	108.4202	21
22	9.9336	12.1003	14.7138	17.8610	21.6447	26.1864	55.2061	79.4175	113.5735	135.5253	22
23	11.0263	13.5223	16.6266	20.3616	24.8915	30.3762	66.2474	96.8894	140.8312	169.4066	23
24	12.2392	15.1786	18.7881	23.2122	28.6252	35.2364	79.4968	118.2050	174.6306	211.7582	24
25	13.5855	17.0001	21.2305	26.4619	32.9190	40.8742	95.3962	144.2101	216.5420	264.6978	25
26	15.0799	19.0401	23.9905	30.1666	37.8568	47.4141	114.4755	175.9364	268.5121	330.8722	26
27	16.7386	21.3249	27.1093	34.3899	43.5353	55.0004	137.3706	214.6424	332.9550	413.5903	27
28	18.5799	23.8839	30.6335	39.2045	50.0656	63.8004	164.8447	261.8637	412.8642	516.9879	28
29	20.6237	26.7499	34.6158	44.6931	57.5755	74.0085	197.8136	319.4737	511.9516	646.2349	29
30	22.8923	29.9599	39.1159	50.9502	66.2118	85.8499	237.3763	389.7579	634.8199	807.7936	30
31	25.4104	33.5551	44.2010	58.0832	76.1435	99.5859	284.8516	475.5046	787.1767	1009.7420	31
32	28.2056	37.5817	49.9471	66.2148	87.5651	115.5196	341.8219	580.1156	976.0991	1262.1774	32
33	31.3082	42.0915	56.4402	75.4849	100.6998	134.0027	410.1863	707.7411	1210.3629	1577.7218	33
34	34.7521	47.1425	63.7774	86.0528	115.8048	155.4432	492.2235	863.4441	1500.8500	1972.1523	34
35	38.5749	52.7996	72.0685	98.1002	133.1755	180.3141	590.6682	1053.4018	1861.0540	2465.1903	35
36	42.8181	59.1356	81.4374	111.8342	153.1519	209.1643	708.8019	1285.1502	2307.7070	3081.4879	36
37	47.5281	66.2318	92.0243	127.4910	176.1246	242.6306	850.5622	1567.8833	2861.5567	3851.8599	37
38	52.7562	74.1797	103.9874	145.3397	202.5433	281.4515	1020.6747	1912.8176	3548.3303	4814.8249	38
39	58.5593	83.0812	117.5058	165.6873	232.9248	326.4838	1224.8096	2333.6375	4399.9295	6018.5311	39
40	65.0009	93.0510	132.7816	188.8835	267.8635	378.7212	1469.7716	2847.0378	5455.9126	7523.1638	40

TABLE A–3
PRESENT VALUE OF A $1 ORDINARY ANNUITY.

N/R	1%	2%	3%	4%	5%	6%	7%	8%	9%	10%	N/R
1	0.9901	0.9804	0.9709	0.9615	0.9524	0.9434	0.9346	0.9259	0.9174	0.9091	1
2	1.9704	1.9416	1.9135	1.8861	1.8594	1.8334	1.8080	1.7833	1.7591	1.7355	2
3	2.9410	2.8839	2.8286	2.7751	2.7232	2.6730	2.6243	2.5771	2.5313	2.4869	3
4	3.9020	3.8077	3.7171	3.6299	3.5460	3.4651	3.3872	3.3121	3.2397	3.1699	4
5	4.8534	4.7135	4.5797	4.4518	4.3295	4.2124	4.1002	3.9927	3.8897	3.7908	5
6	5.7955	5.6014	5.4172	5.2421	5.0757	4.9173	4.7665	4.6229	4.4859	4.3553	6
7	6.7282	6.4720	6.2303	6.0021	5.7864	5.5824	5.3893	5.2064	5.0330	4.8684	7
8	7.6517	7.3255	7.0197	6.7327	6.4632	6.2098	5.9713	5.7466	5.5348	5.3349	8
9	8.5660	8.1622	7.7861	7.4353	7.1078	6.8017	6.5152	6.2469	5.9952	5.7590	9
10	9.4713	8.9826	8.5302	8.1109	7.7217	7.3601	7.0236	6.7101	6.4177	6.1446	10
11	10.3676	9.7868	9.2526	8.7605	8.3064	7.8869	7.4987	7.1390	6.8052	6.4951	11
12	11.2551	10.5753	9.9540	9.3851	8.8633	8.3838	7.9427	7.5361	7.1607	6.8137	12
13	12.1337	11.3484	10.6350	9.9856	9.3936	8.8527	8.3577	7.9038	7.4869	7.1034	13
14	13.0037	12.1062	11.2961	10.5631	9.8986	9.2950	8.7455	8.2442	7.7862	7.3667	14
15	13.8651	12.8493	11.9379	11.1184	10.3797	9.7122	9.1079	8.5595	8.0607	7.6061	15
16	14.7179	13.5777	12.5611	11.6523	10.8378	10.1059	9.4466	8.8514	8.3126	7.8237	16
17	15.5623	14.2919	13.1661	12.1657	11.2741	10.4773	9.7632	9.1216	8.5436	8.0216	17
18	16.3983	14.9920	13.7535	12.6593	11.6896	10.8276	10.0591	9.3716	8.7556	8.2014	18
19	17.2260	15.6785	14.3238	12.1339	12.0853	11.1581	10.3356	9.6036	8.9501	8.3649	19
20	18.0456	16.3514	14.8775	13.5903	12.4622	11.4699	10.5940	9.8181	9.1285	8.5136	20
21	18.8570	17.0112	15.4150	14.0292	12.8212	11.7641	10.8355	10.0168	9.2922	8.6487	21
22	19.6604	17.6580	15.9369	14.4511	13.1630	12.0416	11.0612	10.2007	9.4424	8.7715	22
23	20.4558	18.2922	16.4436	14.8568	13.4886	12.3034	11.2722	10.3711	9.5802	8.8832	23
24	21.2434	18.9139	16.9355	15.2470	13.7986	12.5504	11.4693	10.5288	9.7066	8.9847	24
25	22.0232	19.5235	17.4131	15.6221	14.0939	12.7834	11.6536	10.6748	9.8226	9.0770	25
26	22.7952	10.1210	17.8768	15.9828	14.3752	13.0032	11.8258	10.8100	9.9290	9.1609	26
27	23.5596	20.7069	18.3270	16.3296	14.6430	13.2105	11.9867	10.9352	10.0266	9.2372	27
28	24.3164	21.2813	18.7641	16.6631	14.8981	13.4062	12.1371	11.0511	10.1161	9.3066	28
29	25.0658	21.8444	19.1885	16.9837	15.1411	13.5907	12.2777	11.1584	10.1983	9.3696	29
30	25.8077	22.3965	19.6004	17.2920	15.3725	13.7648	12.4090	11.2578	10.2737	9.4269	30
31	26.5423	22.9377	20.0004	17.5885	15.5928	13.9291	12.5318	11.3498	10.3428	9.4790	31
32	27.2696	23.4683	20.3888	17.8736	15.8027	14.0840	12.6466	11.4350	10.4062	9.5264	32
33	27.9897	23.9886	20.7658	18.1476	16.0025	14.2302	12.7538	11.5139	10.4644	9.5694	33
34	28.7027	24.4986	21.1318	18.4112	16.1929	14.3681	12.8540	11.5869	10.5178	9.6086	34
35	29.4086	24.9986	21.4872	18.6646	16.3742	14.4982	12.9477	11.6546	10.5668	9.6442	35
36	30.1075	25.4888	21.8323	18.9083	16.5469	14.6210	13.0352	11.7172	10.6118	9.6765	36
37	30.7995	25.9695	22.1672	19.1426	16.7113	14.7368	13.1170	11.7752	10.6530	9.7059	37
38	31.4847	26.4406	22.4925	19.3679	16.8679	14.8460	13.1935	11.8289	10.6908	9.7327	38
39	32.1630	26.9026	22.8082	19.5845	17.0170	14.9491	13.2649	11.8786	10.7255	9.7570	39
40	32.8347	27.3555	23.1148	19.7928	17.1591	15.0463	13.3317	11.9246	10.7574	9.7791	40

N/R	11%	12%	13%	14%	15%	16%	20%	22%	24%	25%	N/R
1	0.9009	0.8929	0.8550	0.8772	0.8696	0.8621	0.8333	0.8197	0.8065	0.8000	1
2	1.7125	1.6901	1.6681	1.6467	1.6257	1.6052	1.5278	1.4915	1.4568	1.4400	2
3	2.4437	2.4018	2.3612	2.3216	1.2832	2.2459	2.1065	2.0422	1.9813	1.9520	3
4	3.1024	3.0373	2.9745	2.9137	2.8550	2.7982	2.5887	2.4936	2.4043	2.3616	4
5	3.6959	3.6048	3.5172	3.4331	3.3522	3.2743	2.9906	2.8636	2.7454	2.6893	5
6	4.2305	4.1114	3.9975	3.8887	3.7845	3.6847	3.3255	3.1669	3.0205	2.9514	6
7	4.7122	4.5638	4.4226	4.2883	4.1604	4.0386	3.6046	3.4155	3.2423	3.1611	7
8	5.1461	4.9676	4.7988	4.6389	4.4873	4.3463	3.8372	3.6193	3.4212	3.3289	8
9	5.5370	5.3282	5.1317	4.9464	4.7716	4.6065	4.0310	3.7863	3.5655	3.4631	9
10	5.8892	5.6502	5.4262	5.2161	5.0188	4.8332	4.1925	3.9232	3.6819	3.5705	10
11	6.2065	5.9377	5.6869	5.4527	5.2337	5.0286	4.3271	4.0354	3.7757	3.6564	11
12	6.4924	6.1944	5.9176	5.6603	5.4206	5.1971	4.4392	4.1274	3.8514	3.7251	12
13	6.7499	6.4235	6.1218	5.8424	5.5831	5.3423	4.5327	4.2028	3.9124	3.7801	13
14	6.9819	6.6282	6.3025	6.0021	5.7245	5.4675	4.6106	4.2646	3.9616	3.8241	14
15	7.1909	6.8109	6.4624	6.1422	5.8474	5.5755	4.6755	4.3152	4.0013	3.8593	15
16	7.3792	6.9740	6.6039	6.2651	5.9542	5.6685	4.7296	4.3567	4.0333	3.8874	16
17	7.5488	7.1196	6.7291	6.3729	6.0472	5.7487	4.7746	4.3908	4.0591	3.9099	17
18	7.7016	7.2497	6.8399	6.4674	6.1280	5.8178	4.8122	4.4187	4.0799	3.9279	18
19	7.8393	7.3658	6.9380	6.5504	6.1982	5.8775	4.8435	4.4415	4.0967	3.9424	19
20	7.9633	7.4694	7.0248	6.6231	6.2593	5.9288	4.8696	4.4603	4.1103	3.9539	20
21	8.0751	7.5620	7.1016	6.6870	6.3125	5.9731	4.8913	4.4756	4.1212	3.9631	21
22	8.1757	7.6446	7.1695	6.7429	6.3587	6.0113	4.9094	4.4882	4.1300	3.9705	22
23	8.2664	7.7184	7.2297	6.7921	6.3988	6.0442	4.9245	4.4985	4.1371	3.9764	23
24	8.3481	7.7843	7.2829	6.8351	6.4338	6.0726	4.9371	4.5070	4.1428	3.9811	24
25	8.4217	7.8431	7.3300	6.8729	6.4641	6.0971	4.9476	4.5139	4.1474	3.9849	25
26	8.4881	7.8957	7.3717	6.9061	6.4906	6.1182	4.9563	4.5196	4.1511	3.9879	26
27	8.5478	7.9426	7.4086	6.9352	6.5135	6.1364	4.9636	4.5243	4.1542	3.9903	27
28	8.6016	7.9844	7.4412	6.9607	6.5335	6.1520	4.9697	4.5281	4.1566	3.9923	28
29	8.6501	8.0218	7.4701	6.9830	6.5509	6.1656	4.9747	4.5312	4.1585	3.9938	29
30	8.6938	8.0522	7.4957	7.0027	6.5660	6.1772	4.9789	4.5338	4.1601	3.9950	30
31	8.7331	8.0850	7.5183	7.0199	6.5791	6.1872	4.9824	4.5359	4.1614	3.9960	31
32	8.7686	8.1116	7.5383	7.0350	6.5905	6.1959	4.9854	4.5376	4.1624	3.9968	32
33	8.8005	8.1354	7.5560	7.0482	6.6005	6.2034	4.9878	4.5390	4.1632	3.9975	33
34	8.8293	8.1566	7.5717	7.0599	6.6091	6.2098	4.9898	4.5402	4.1639	3.9980	34
35	8.8552	8.1755	7.5856	7.0700	6.6166	6.2153	4.9915	5.5411	4.1644	3.9984	35
36	8.8786	8.1924	7.5979	7.0790	6.6231	6.2201	4.9929	4.5419	4.1649	3.9987	36
37	8.8996	8.2075	7.6087	7.0868	6.6288	6.2242	4.9941	4.5426	4.1652	3.9990	37
38	8.9186	8.2210	7.6183	7.0937	6.6338	6.2278	4.9951	4.5431	4.1655	3.9992	38
39	8.9357	8.2330	7.6268	7.0997	6.6380	6.2309	4.9959	4.5435	4.1657	3.9993	39
40	8.9511	8.2438	7.6344	7.1050	6.6418	6.2335	4.9966	4.5439	4.1659	3.9995	40

More Comprehensive Time Value of Money Example: Capital Leases

Recall that a lease agreement between a lessee accounting entity and a lessor accounting entity is as follows:

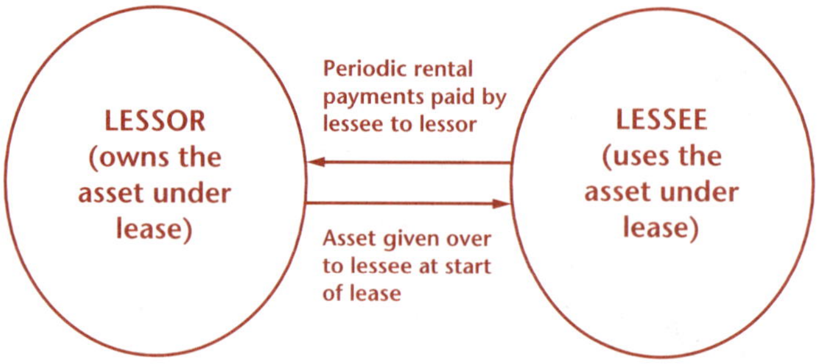

Once a lessee and lessor sign a lease contract, the existing GAAP for lease accounting in Canada, the United States, and many other jurisdictions is generally as follows:

1. The lessee determines whether the lease is a capital or an operating lease (that pervasive classification phenomenon again). The essential features of a lease agreement are shown in Exhibit A–4; the criteria for making this classification decision, which are set out in sections 3065.05 and 3065.06 of the *CICA Handbook*, are provided in Exhibit A–5.
2. If the lease is classified as an operating lease, the accounting is usually on the basis of debiting an expense account ("Operating lease rental expense," for example) at the time the monthly or other periodic payment is made to the lessor, and the lessee must disclose the information shown in Exhibit A–6 in its financial statements and footnotes. Of course, the other side of the entry is a credit to cash. No journal entry is made at the time the lease agreement is signed, unless the lessee is required to make a prepayment at that time.
3. If the lessee's management decides that the lease must be classified as a capital lease, then at the time the lease agreement is signed and becomes effective the lessee, under present GAAP, must record an asset and a liability. The debit to the asset account ("Assets under lease," for example) and the credit to the liability account ("Obligation under capital lease," for example) are generally equal to the present value of the lease payments as set out in the lease contract. Since lease agreements may be written in many ways (with contingent rental payments depending on the lessee's sales volume in the future, for example), there are almost always complexities in determining this amount. We ignore these complexities here.

EXHIBIT A–4
ESSENTIAL FEATURES OF A LEASE AGREEMENT

In section 3065, paragraph .03(n), the *CICA Handbook* defines a **lease** as "the conveyance, by a lessor to a lessee, of the right to use a tangible asset usually for a specified period of time in return for rent."

Essential features of a lease contract are:

- The parties to the lease agreement, lessee and lessor, are identified.
- The asset to be leased is precisely identified, including its value on the date the lease becomes effective.
- The obligations of each party are specified, including who is responsible for "executory costs" such as maintenance and insurance on the asset.
- The amount and timing of the rent is specified.
- The lease term is specified, including renewal or purchase options, if any.
- The conditions under which the lease is cancellable (including whether it is noncancellable) are set out, including any penalties for cancellation.
- What is to happen to the leased asset at the end of the lease is specified, as is the assumed value of the asset at that time (the "residual" value).

EXHIBIT A–5
CRITERIA FOR CLASSIFYING LEASES AS BETWEEN THE CAPITAL AND OPERATING LEASE CATEGORIES: CANADIAN GAAP

The *CICA Handbook* reads as follows (the following two paragraphs are intended by the Accounting Standards Board to be guidelines):

3065.05 The Recommendations in this section are derived from the view that property has benefits and risks associated with its ownership ... In the opinion of the [Accounting Standards Board], a lease that transfers substantially all of the benefits and risks of ownership to the lessee is in substance an acquisition of an asset and an incurrence of an obligation by the lessee and a sale or financing by the lessor.

3065.06 From the point of view of a lessee, a lease would normally transfer substantially all of the benefits and risks of ownership to the lessee when, at the inception of the lease, one or more of the following conditions are present:

(a) There is reasonable assurance that the lessee will obtain ownership of the leased property by the end of the lease term ...

(b) The lease term is of such a duration that the lessee will receive substantially all of the economic benefits expected to be derived from the use of the leased property over its life span ...

(c) The lessor would be assured of recovering the investment in the leased property and of earning a return on the investment as a result of the lease agreement ...

In view of the fact that land normally has an indefinite useful life, it is not possible for the lessee to receive substantially all the benefits and risks associated with its ownership, unless there is reasonable assurance that ownership will pass to the lessee by the end of the lease term.

EXHIBIT A–6
INFORMATION REQUIRED TO BE DISCLOSED IN THE FINANCIAL STATEMENTS AND FOOTNOTES FOR CAPITAL LEASES: CANADIAN GAAP

The following portions of the *CICA Handbook* that are written in italics are requirements, not guidelines. Non-italicized portions are nonmandatory:

3065.20 *In order to distinguish between assets that the enterprise owns and those that it only has the right to use, assets leased under capital leases would be disclosed separately. The related lease obligations would be separated from other long-term obligations.*

3065.21 *The gross amount of assets under capital leases and related accumulated amortization should be disclosed. Disclosure of leased property and accumulated amortization by major category, e.g., land, buildings, machinery, may be desirable.*

3065.22 *Obligations related to leased assets should be shown separately from other long-term obligations ... Significant restrictions imposed on the lessee as a result of the lease agreement should be disclosed ...*

3065.23 *Any portion of lease obligations payable within a year out of current funds should be included in current liabilities.*

3065.24 *Disclosure should be made of the future minimum lease payments in aggregate and for each of the five succeeding years. A separate deduction should be made from the aggregate figure for amounts included in the minimum lease payments representing executory costs and imputed interest. The resultant net amount would be the balance of the unpaid obligation.*

3065.25 *The amount of amortization of leased property included in the determination of net income should be disclosed separately or as part of depreciation and amortization expense for fixed assets. Disclosure should also be made of methods and rates of amortization.*

3065.26 *Interest expense related to lease obligations should be disclosed separately, or as part of interest on long-term indebtedness.*

For capital leases, at the end of each of the lessee's accounting periods over the term of the lease agreement, the lessee must prepare the following adjusting journal entries:

- An amortization entry, recording the amortization of the asset under lease. The number of periods over which the amortization is to be performed is the lesser of the expected service life of the leased asset or the lease term (which is defined by section 3065 of the *CICA Handbook* to include any renewals if such renewals are a foregone conclusion — say, because the lease payment under the renewal is so low).
- An accrual entry, recording the "implicit" interest expense in the lease agreement. In practice, this adjusting entry is usually combined with an entry to account for the cash payment by the lessee to the lessor.
- Also for capital leases, the lessee must provide the disclosure shown in Exhibit A-6 in its financial statement footnotes.

Let's illustrate this process for a capital lease with the following hypothetical data:

Simone Limited (SL) signs an agreement on January 1, 1996, with Apex Incorporated to lease a large boat to use in its sightseeing business. The lease agreement has the following features:

- The lease agreement runs for ten years and is not renewable.
- SL must make payments beginning on December 31, 1996, and every year thereafter until ten payments are made. The amount of each payment is $100,000.
- SL is responsible for all operating costs associated with the boat.
- If SL had wanted to purchase the boat on January 1, 1996, the cash purchase price would have been $565,000. Of course, SL signed the lease agreement instead. At the end of the lease term of ten years, both parties expect that the boat will be scrapped.
- At the time the lease agreement was signed, both the lessee and the lessor

agreed that the boat had a remaining expected service life of about 10 years.

- The contract is noncancellable by either party, and therefore the lessee is irrevocably committed to continue leasing the boat.

When we apply the criteria set out in Exhibit A–5 for determining whether a lease agreement should be classified as operating or capital, it is clear that this is a capital lease, since it runs for the remaining expected useful life of the asset and is noncancellable. In essence, SL has substantially acquired the risks and rewards of ownership of the boat, along with the obligation of the associated rental payments.

To do the accounting, we must first determine what the *interest rate implicit in the lease* is. To this end, we have prepared a table (see Exhibit A–7) that computes the present value of the stream of ten annual, end-of-year cash payments of $100,000 using interest rates ranging from 0% to 20% — we're going to use trial and error to see which interest rate causes the present value of the stream of future payments to be equal to the cash purchase price of the boat, namely, $565,000.

We're going to need this interest rate in order to calculate SL's interest expense for each year of the lease agreement.

EXHIBIT A–7
PRESENT VALUES OF THE TEN LEASE PAYMENTS USING VARIOUS INTEREST RATES

Interest Rate	Present Value of $100,000 10-year Annuity in Arrears*
0	$1,000,000.00
0.01	947,130.45
0.02	898,258.50
0.03	853,020.28
0.04	811,089.50
0.05	772,173.49
0.06	736,008.71
0.07	702,358.15
0.08	671,008.14
0.09	641,765.77
0.10	614,456.71
0.11	588,923.20
0.12	565,022.30
0.13	542,624.35
0.14	521,611.56
0.15	501,876.86
0.16	483,322.75
0.17	465,860.36
0.18	449,408.63
0.19	433,893.49
0.20	419,247.21

*Computed using the Present Value function in Microsoft Excel.

From the table, we can see that 12% is very close, with a present value of $565,022.30.

The journal entry that SL must record on January 1, 1996 (the date the lease agreement becomes effective and the boat is transferred to SL), is:

Dr	Asset under lease (B)	565,000	
	Cr Lease obligation (B)		565,000

This entry records on SL's books the asset and the liability arising from the signing of the lease agreement, and represents an extension of the traditional concept of a transaction, as we discussed back in Chapter 3.

On December 31, 1996, the first $100,000 payment must be made by SL. In order to account for this payment, we must construct an amortization table that shows how each payment is to be allocated between interest expense and reduction of the lease obligation liability. The amortization table is shown in Exhibit A–8. SL accounts for this first payment as follows:

Dr	Interest expense (I)	67,800	
Dr	Obligation under lease (B)	32,200	
	Cr Cash (B)		100,000

Also on December 31, 1996, SL must account for the amortization of the boat. Let's assume that straight-line amortization will be used; the amount to be amortized is the $565,000 (this assumes no residual value of the boat at the end of the lease). So, the annual amortization amount is $565,000/10 years, or $56,500:

Dr	Amortization expense (I)	56,500	
	Cr Asset under lease (B)		56,500

EXHIBIT A–8
AMORTIZATION TABLE FOR SL'S CAPITAL LEASE

[1] Date	[2] Balance of Obligation Under Lease	[3] Payment	[4] Interest @ 12% (0.12 × [2])	[5] Reduction of Obligation ([3] – [4])
Jan. 1, 1996	565,000.00			
Dec. 31, 1996	565,000.00	100,000.00	67,800.00	32,200.00
Dec. 31, 1997	532,800.00	100,000.00	63,936.00	36,064.00
Dec. 31, 1998	496,736.00	100,000.00	59,608.32	40,391.68
Dec. 31, 1999	456,344.32	100,000.00	54,761.32	45,238.69
Dec. 31, 2000	411,105.63	100,000.00	49,332.68	50,667.33
Dec. 31, 2001	360,438.30	100,000.00	43,252.60	56,747.41
Dec. 31, 2002	303,690.89	100,000.00	36,442.91	63,557.10
Dec. 31, 2003	240,133.79	100,000.00	28,816.05	71,183.95
Dec. 31, 2004	168,949.84	100,000.00	20,273.98	79,726.02
Dec. 31, 2005	89,223.82	100,000.00	10,706.89	89,293.15*

*Note the rounding error, since 12% is approximate.

Solved problems

A. Prepare SL's journal entries for the remaining nine years of the lease agreement.

The amortization entry each December 31 is the same as the entry December 31, 1996. The entry accounting for the debit side of the lease payment changes, however, to reflect the amortization schedule:

December 31, 1997

Dr	Interest expense (I)	63,936.00	
Dr	Obligation under lease (B)	36,064.00	
	Cr Cash (B)		100,000.00

December 31, 1998

Dr	Interest expense (I)	59,608.32	
Dr	Obligation under lease (B)	40,391.68	
	Cr Cash (B)		100,000.00

And so on.

B. Assume that the lease was an operating lease (that is, ignore the characteristics of the lease agreement that make it such an obvious capital lease). Prepare SL's journal entries for the 10-year period.

On December 31 of each year, assuming an operating lease:

Dr	Lease rental expense (I)	100,000.00	
	Cr Cash (B)		100,000.00

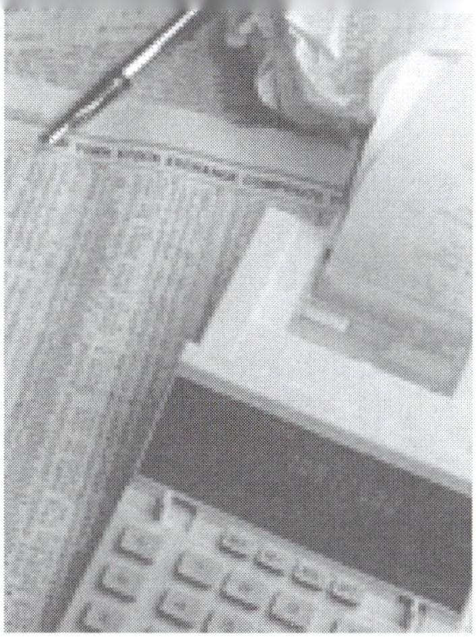

Index

cut here

STUDENT REPLY CARD

In order to improve future editions, we are seeking your comments on

FINANCIAL ACCOUNTING: Expanding Horizons

by Joel H. Amernic

After you have read this text, please answer the following questions and return this form via Business Reply Mail. *Your opinions matter. Thank you in advance for your feedback!*

Name of your college or university: ______________________________

Major program of study: ______________________________

Course title: ______________________________

Were you required to buy this book? yes _____ no _____

Did you buy this book new or used? new _____ used _____ ($_____)

Do you plan to keep or sell this book? keep _____ sell _____

Is the order of topic coverage consistent with what was taught in your course?

fold here

cut here

Are there chapters or sections of this text that were not assigned for your course? Please specify:

Were there topics covered in your course that are not included in this text? Please specify:

What did you like most about this text?

What did you like least?

If you would like to say more, we'd love to hear from you. Please write to us at the address shown on the reverse of this card.

cut here

fold here

cut here

Postage will be paid by

Mc Graw Hill

MAIL POSTE

Canada Post Corporation / Société canadienne des postes

Postage paid
If mailed in Canada

Port payé
si posté au Canada

Business Reply

Réponse d'affaires

0183560299 01

0183560299-L1N9B6-BR01

Attn.: Sponsoring Editor
College Division

MCGRAW-HILL RYERSON LIMITED
300 WATER ST
WHITBY ON L1N 9Z9